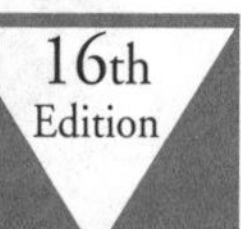

Frommer's

16th Edition

FRUGAL TRAVELER'S GUIDES

Ireland

FROM $45 A DAY

by Susan Poole

Macmillan • USA

About the Author

Raised in a Southern newspaper family, Susan Poole has written this guide to Ireland since the mid-1970s. Ms. Poole contributes feature articles to leading newspapers and travel magazines. Her poetic text to *Ireland,* an outstanding photographic book, exudes her love for the country. When not traveling, Ms. Poole divides her time between her homes in Ireland and New York. In 1985, this book won the Lowell Thomas Best Guide Book Award.

MACMILLAN TRAVEL

A Simon & Schuster Macmillan Company
1633 Broadway
New York, NY 10019

Find us online at **http://www.mcp.com/mgr/travel** or
on America Online at Keyword: **SuperLibrary.**

ISBN 0-02-860871-2
ISSN 0276-9026

Editor: Peter Katucki
Design by Michele Laseau
Digital Cartography by Ortelius Design
Maps copyright © by Simon & Schuster, Inc.

Special Sales

Bulk purchases (10 or more copies) of Frommer's Travel Guides are available to corporations at special discounts. The Special Sales Department can produce custom editions to be used as premiums and/or for sales promotion to suit individual needs. Existing editions can be produced with custom cover imprints such as corporate logos. For more information write to: Special Sales, Simon & Schuster, 1633 Broadway, New York, NY 10019.

Manufactured in the United States of America

To Dee, who has found her own special love for Ireland.

ACKNOWLEDGMENTS

First and foremost, my gratitude and personal thanks go to Peter Katucki, editor, who has worked long hours and weekends to help me make this book the very best it can be and, in turn, the most useful guide possible for our readers.

My heartfelt thanks to the people of Ireland, who have—from the moment I first set foot in their country—made me very welcome. Very special thanks to Bord Fáilté, whose marvelous staff should serve as a model for all other tourism organizations around the globe, and to Joe Lynam of the Dublin head office, in particular; to Aer Lingus, all that an Irish airline should be; to Mary McLoughlin and members of the Town & Country Homes Association; to Michael and Maryse O'Brien, who have made Ariel House my Dublin home away from home; to Frank and Siubhán Lewis and Kathleen Coffey, all of whom have given me a special insight into Killarney's splendors; and to scores of other good Irish friends who have joined in the researching of this book with typical Irish wit, good humor, and helpfulness.

Contents

19 County Donegal 441

20 The Midlands Region 469

21 Getting to Know Northern Ireland 485

22 Belfast 498

List of Maps

An Invitation to the Reader

In researching this book, I've discovered many wonderful places—hotels, restaurants, shops, and more. I'm sure you'll find others. Please tell me about them, so I can share the information with your fellow travelers in upcoming editions. If you were disappointed with a recommendation, I'd love to know that, too. Please write to:

Susan Poole
Frommer's Ireland from $45 a Day, 16th Edition
Macmillan Travel
1633 Broadway
New York, NY 10019

An Additional Note

Please be advised that travel information is subject to change at any time—and this is especially true of prices. We therefore suggest that you write or call ahead for confirmation when making your travel plans. The authors, editors, and publisher cannot be held responsible for the experiences of readers while traveling. Your safety is important to us, however, so we encourage you to stay alert and be aware of your surroundings. Keep a close eye on cameras, purses, and wallets, all favorite targets of thieves and pickpockets.

What the Symbols Mean

✪ Frommer's Favorites

Hotels, restaurants, attractions, and entertainment you should not miss.

The following abbreviations are used for credit cards:

ACC	Access	ER	enRoute
AE	American Express	EU	Eurocard
CB	Carte Blanche	JCB	Japan Credit Bank
DC	Diners Club	MC	MasterCard
DISC	Discover	V	Visa

1

The Best of Ireland for the Frugal Traveler

In Ireland, more than in any other country I've encountered in my travels, budgeting turns out to be fun. It's all a matter of knowing what you are looking for, what's available, and how to go about finding it. For several years now, I've done a *lot* of foot-slogging to ferret out every possible way of saving money in this lovely country, and now that I make my home here for most of every year, even more money-saving techniques seem to come my way. The things I've learned are outlined in this chapter, but the very *best* budget advice I can pass along is to keep your eyes open and observe just how the Irish themselves go about living here economically.

Just how expensive *is* Ireland for the visitor? Well, it certainly does not, these days, qualify as a "dirt cheap" destination—but, then, neither is it in the same class as many others that cost far more and often deliver far less. From a personal point of view, the Irish people are the country's most potent drawing card, and their warmth, wit, and friendliness won't cost you one red cent.

Prices here have, of course, steadily increased over the past few years, but our $45-a-day budget has been researched very carefully, and that daily expenditure (at exchange rates as we go to press) allows for a decent roof over your head each night and three more-than-adequate meals a day. At the current conversion rate of U.S. dollars into Irish punts, the $45-a-day budget allows for you to spend a maximum of $22.40 (IR£14) for a place to sleep and your breakfast, around $6 (IR£3.75) for a pub lunch, and no more than $16 (IR£10) for your evening meal. The following sections point the way to coming in at that figure.

Actually, it is possible to *lower* that daily cost if you choose the hostel or camping route. Whatever your choice, the following tips are signposts on the road to value for money—and that, after all, is the name of our game.

1 Sixty-Five Money-Saving Tips

SAVING MONEY ON ACCOMMODATIONS

1. If you're really counting pence, Ireland will put you up in **hostels** that in some cases are quite upmarket. If you're after real savings at the expense of a private room, you'll sleep in comfort

in dormitory-like space. What's more, many hostels now provide two- and three-bed rooms for much less than a B&B.

2. Book into the **An Oige hostel** in Killarney, the sort of magnificent old country mansion most travelers only glimpse from afar.
3. Ireland's biggest bargain is its goodly supply of **bed-and-breakfast homes** (in town and country) and **farmhouses.** I simply cannot sing their praises enough! So addicted to them have I become that even if they didn't provide attractive, comfortable sleeping accommodations, I'd suffer a less-than-perfect bed just to indulge in the friendly family life so graciously shared in all. That's a personal bias, and I know many travelers who couldn't care less about meeting and getting to know an Irish family and insist (in all too many cases) on hotel amenities at budget prices—*until,* that is, they experience firsthand a couple of B&B overnights, after which wild horses couldn't drag them back to the hotel route, amenities or no amenities.
4. If you are serious about budgeting, the cardinal rule is: Private baths are something you leave at home. **Forgoing that private bath** can save two, three, or five punts on each night's cost.
5. Most B&Bs, farmhouses, and guesthouses offer **reductions of 20% all the way up to 50% for children** under the age of 12 sharing a bedroom with their parents. Be sure to confirm the discount when booking. More and more of these accommodations are providing at least one family-size room.
6. If you book in for a solid week in or near, say, Waterford, using that as a base to explore the eastern and southeastern regions, then book for another week in the west, at the **discounted weekly rate,** you'll realize not only the traveling benefits I spoke of elsewhere, but a much healthier budget as well.
7. The Tourist Board publishes the illustrated booklet **Discover Ireland Holiday Breaks** for all ages, which catalogs discount packages and their substantial savings. Some apply to low-season months only and all have more-than-one-day-stay requirements.
8. **Golden Holidays,** for those over 55, details money-saving holidays for those in this age group. Available from Tourist Board offices.
9. Many hotels and guesthouses offer two- and/or three-day **midweek discounts** that bring the per-person rates down considerably.
10. Hotels, especially in the larger cities, offer discounts on **weekend rates,** many times including one dinner as well as breakfast.
11. In Cork, book into Forte Travelodge near the airport, or Jurys Inn in the city center, both of which have **per-room rates** for parties of three to four persons.
12. In Dublin, avail yourself of the **per-room rates** of Jurys Inn in the city center or Forte Travelodge on the outskirts.
13. Families or groups of friends traveling together can realize substantial savings by booking into **self-catering** accommodations. Per-person daily rates drop incredibly, and most units sleep four to eight people.
14. If at all possible, travel with a friend you won't mind sharing a room with, since single rates can cost from IR£2 to IR£5 more than what you'd pay if you shared the room. Those traveling on their own can **avoid the single supplement** by inquiring at local tourist offices for other single travelers in the locality who may be willing to share accommodations.
15. Bus Eireann and Irish Rail **package holidays** also offer substantial **discounts on accommodations.**

16. As you read through this book, look for the "Ask about possible **discounts to our readers** in accommodation listings. Reductions can range from 10% to 15%.
17. In Dublin, book into **Ariel House** at their **reader discount rate.**

SAVING MONEY ON MEALS

The next basic when traveling is eating three square meals a day. The first of those will be taken care of more than adequately in your B&B. An Irish breakfast is, simply put, overwhelming. As for the remaining two meals of the day, here are a few approaches.

18. Save by preparing **hostel meals**—you can buy dinner at the local grocer's and prepare it in a communal kitchen.
19. In Killarney, evening meals for residents of **Neptune's Killarney Town Hostel** are under IR£6 ($9.60).
20. **Self-catering meals** send costs plummeting. Quite aside from the savings, there's the fun of chatting with locals while grocery shopping—you may well go home clutching a few of their treasured recipes as unique souvenirs of your Irish stay.
21. In County Waterford, make the self-catering **Gold Coast Holiday Homes** in Dungarvan your base for exploring the Southeast and Cork city.
22. Traditionally, the Irish have always had their heartiest meal at midday. That's because as an agricultural nation, those working in the fields needed sustenance to see them through a long afternoon. The tradition still lingers, and for travelers, a hot **pub lunch** will provide as much to eat as most dinners, at several punts less in cost. Pub grub, in fact, generally means heaping plates of meat, vegetables, and at least one version of the potato—more than enough for anyone's main meal of the day. If that Irish breakfast did in your midday appetite, you should still head for the nearest pub and relish a light meal of homemade soup and brown bread, with a sandwich or a salad plate, all at a "peanuts" price.
23. **Make lunch the main meal** of the day, when prices are at least IR£5 ($8) less than evening meals, with much the same menu.
24. In Dublin, enjoy a "bust-out" meal in **Le Coq Hardi,** one of the city's finest restaurants, by opting for the IR£18 ($28.80) **set lunch** rather than the IR£30 ($48) set dinner.
25. Many restaurants now offer a three-course meal at an inexpensive price, under the heading **"Tourist Meals."** Menu choices are usually the same as for the four- or five-course dinners, and savings can run as much as IR£5 ($8).
26. In Waterford City, plan to eat at **Reginald's Bar and Restaurant,** where there's a good-value tourist menu.
27. Make your evening meal an early one to take advantage of **Early Bird Specials** offered by many restaurants between 5:30pm and 7pm.
28. In Tralee, opt for the Early Bird menu at **Larkins Restaurant** between 6pm and 7pm.
29. In Waterford, **Dwyer's of Mary Street** has an early-bird three-course, set-price dinner several punts cheaper than the later menu.
30. Moderately priced **hotel coffee shops** will feed you well at prices far below more expensive hotel dining rooms.
31. In Dublin, good meals are available at all hours of the day at the **Coffee Dock Grill** in Jurys Hotel for under IR£10 ($16).

32. In Limerick, the **Bridges Restaurant** in Jurys Hotel serves substantial meals for under IR£10 ($16).
33. Choose **high tea** instead of a dinner menu. Typically, high tea is a "mini-dinner" of only two courses—meat (often in a salad plate) and vegetables, but no soup or dessert. Nowadays, however, high tea is a rather ambiguous term. I have had a high tea (at about IR£5—$8) that was more nourishment than I could comfortably handle; and on the other side of the coin, I've had a high tea that consisted of one or two skimpy sandwiches, and maybe a sweet, that most certainly would *not* see me through the night. My best advice is, if your B&B or a local restaurant offers high tea, ask what it consists of. Having high tea rather than dinner can save you as much as 50%.
34. Take advantage of the **half-board rate** in B&Bs, guesthouses, and farmhouses, which includes bed, breakfast, and dinner each night at a good reduction.
35. Stop in a town or village, chat with the local grocer as you shop for **picnic** makings, then head for the country and lunch under the trees, on a mountainside, or at the shore and enjoy a picnic.

SAVING MONEY ON TRANSPORTATION

There are several money-saving ways to get to Ireland and, once here, to move around, all spelled out in detail in Chapter 3. Using one or a combination of the following methods will save pence that quickly add up to punts.

36. Budgeting for transportation begins with your flight over—be sure to take advantage of APEX and other **discounted airfares** that require advance booking.
37. **Charter flights** can lop off up to $100 from your transatlantic airfare.
38. Check with travel agents for **air/drive package** deals for two-prong transportation savings.
39. **Walking** is, without doubt, the cheapest way to see Ireland, and with such an extensive network of signposted walks around the country, it can be one of the most enjoyable—balm for the soul.
40. You need only be reasonably fit to enjoy a **cycling** tour of Ireland, with a small bike rental charge and physical stamina your only transportation costs.
41. Travel by rail or bus becomes a budget technique with the **Rambler Pass,** good for unlimited travel for 8 or 15 days throughout the Republic.
42. In Northern Ireland, the **Rail Runabout** is a money saver, good only in that province.
43. For itineraries that encompass both the Republic and Northern Ireland, there's the umbrella **Emerald Card,** good on both sides of the border.
44. Keep an eye out for Bus Eireann and Irish Rail limited-time **midweek, weekend, excursion, and promotion rates.**
45. Save on both transportation and accommodations by booking Bus Eireann **Breakaway** holiday packages.
46. Bus Eireann's **regional day trips** cost far less than driving, and few areas aren't covered.
47. In Dublin, ask bus drivers or at the Dublin Bus Office or Tourist Office about **city bus discounts** during certain hours of the day.
48. Holders of an International Student Identity Card travel at a **50% discount on Dublin buses and trains** with a Travelsave Stamp, obtained from the USIT Office, 19 Aston Quay, Dublin 2.

49. Avis Rent-a-Car/Johnson & Perrott offer readers of this book substantially **discounted auto rentals.** Book before leaving home, and be sure to ask for the discount.
50. Jet service stations cut **petrol** costs by about 15%.

SAVING MONEY ON SIGHTSEEING

51. Most sightseeing attractions have **family discounts** for parents traveling with two or more children. If they are not posted at the entrance, be sure to ask.
52. Substantial admission price **group discounts** are available at a wide range of attractions for parties of 10 or more. If you're traveling on your own, look around to see if you can join up with others to form a group.
53. **Student discounts** can cut admission prices as much as 50%.
54. In Dublin, **students** pay half the adult admission for Dublin Castle.
55. If you're in the 55 and older age bracket, never pay an admission fee without asking for the **senior discount** granted by almost all sightseeing highlights.
56. In Dublin, **seniors** pay only IR£1 ($1.60) for admission to Dublin Castle, rather than the adult price of IR£2 ($3.20).
57. Look for **combination tickets** to closely associated sightseeing attractions.
58. In Dublin, opt for the **combination ticket** to the Dublin Experience and Trinity College and Book of Kells, at a good discount.
59. In Blarney, County Cork, visit both Blarney Castle and Blarney House with the discounted **combination ticket.**

SAVING MONEY ON SHOPPING

60. **Dunnes' Stores** is a good chain to look for if you are in need of an extra shirt or blouse, skirt, trousers, etc. In most major cities and many of the larger towns, they carry a good line of clothing at excellent prices.
61. About the only **discount stores** you'll find in Ireland are the "£1 Shops" scattered around the country in cities and towns, both large and small. Well, they *do* have some items at that price, all right, but usually they also have a wide variety at higher prices—if it's **inexpensive souvenirs** you're after, go in and take a look.
62. **Seasonal sales** can be real moneysavers. Large department stores in Dublin, Cork, and Limerick run spring and fall sales with reductions of up to 50%. Sale items often include Waterford Glass, Royal Tara china, and the like.
63. Whenever possible, **use credit cards.** Aside from the obvious convenience of buying now and paying later—thus allowing you more cash for immediate needs and pleasures—you'll usually save a dollar or two when you use American Express or Visa credit cards (the two most widely accepted, along with Diners Club and ACC). Your billing will be at each company's exchange rate, which almost always averages several cents better per dollar than banks.
64. *Inside Ireland* (see "Visitor Information & Entry Requirements—Newsletters and Magazines" in Chapter 3) furnishes subscribers with an excellent Shopping and Touring Guide that also includes **cash vouchers** for many of the shops listed.
65. In Dublin, the House of Ireland gives you a **gift voucher** in the value of 10% of your purchases, and you select the gift.

2 Best Bets on a Budget

TOP ATTRACTIONS THAT ARE FREE—OR ALMOST

Ireland's most striking sightseeing attraction is her scenic beauty—and, of course, she imposes no charge at all to revel in it as you travel around the country! Furthermore, some of her most interesting historic and prehistoric ruins—castles, abbeys, monasteries, stone forts, etc.—sit quietly in lonely fields, with not a ticket seller in sight. Nor is there a charge for many top attractions in large cities, and if you're lucky enough to land in almost any city, town, or village when there's a festival in full swing, you'll have the time of your life without encountering even one outstretched palm.

The following are only 10 of my personal favorites, garnered over many years of traveling around and living in Ireland. These should give you some idea of what to look for, and you will find dozens more listed throughout the remaining chapters.

1. **National Museum of Ireland,** Kildare Street at Merrion Row, Dublin. A wonderful overview of Ireland's archeological, artistic, and historic past. (See Chapter 6.)
2. **Free open-air concerts.** Open-air concerts during summer months at St. Stephen's Green in Dublin and Fitzgerald Park in Cork. (See Chapters 6 and 11.)
3. **Walking tour of Waterford City.** IR£3 ($4.80) is a small price to pay for an informative guided tour that may send your imagination soaring back in time to the world of Vikings and Normans. (See Chapter 10.)
4. **The Vee.** A breathtaking scenic drive through the Knockmealdown Mountains. (See Chapter 10.)
5. **Cork City Tourist Trail.** A signposted, self-guided walking tour of the city, with a comprehensive guidebook available from the Tourist Office. (See Chapter 11.)
6. **Killarney Tourist Trail, Ring of Kerry, and Dingle Peninsula.** No charge at all for walking Killarney's tiny streets and sinking into the breathtaking beauty of this county's two most scenic peninsulas. (See Chapters 13 and 14.)
7. **Galway Town Self-Guided Walking Tours and Connemara.** Highlights of Galway Town and County are free for all to enjoy. (See Chapters 16 and 17).
8. **Sligo Tourist Trail, Yeats Country Drive, and Sligo Arts Festival.** Though long departed from this earth, the poet Yeats is still very much a vibrant presence in this part of the country. Much of the fun during Sligo's annual Arts Festival takes place on the streets. (See Chapter 18.)
9. **Inishowen 100 Scenic Drive.** A marvelous mix of wild mountain country, long sandy beaches, and traditional Irish music make up this fascinating route through Ireland's most northerly peninsula. (See Chapter 19.)
10. **Belfast City Walking Tours, Antrim Coast Drive, Walking Tours, Derry.** Northern Ireland's most historic and scenic attractions are free for the viewing. (See Chapters 22 and 23.)

SOME OF IRELAND'S BEST BUDGET ACCOMMODATIONS

Ireland's budget accommodations are so varied that it's virtually impossible to narrow the list to a mere 10. The following, however, are typical.

1. **Avalon House,** 55 Aungier Street, Dublin 2. Large Victorian-style hostel that offers private, double, and family rooms, some with private bath, as well as self-catering facilities. IR£8–IR£19 ($12.80–$30.40). (See Chapter 5.)

2. **Wavemount,** 264 Clontarf Road, Clontarf, Dublin 3. A small, intimate B&B overlooking Dublin Bay, within walking distance of Clontarf Castle, with a moderately priced restaurant next door—presided over by one of our most highly praised hostesses. IR£14–IR£17 ($22.40–$27.20). (See Chapter 5.)
3. **Foxmount Farm,** Dunmore East Road, Waterford. An elegant 1700s home on a working farm, an ideal base for exploring the entire Southeast. IR£20 ($32), with reductions for three or more days. (See Chapter 10).
4. **Kilmorna Farm Hostel,** Lismore, County Waterford. A beautifully appointed hostel that offers double and triple rooms and self-catering facilities. IR£7.50 ($12). (See Chapter 10.)
5. **St. Kilda,** Western Road, Cork, County Cork. In the University area, yet within walking distance of the city center, this B&B has friendly, helpful hosts. IR£16–IR£18 ($25.60–$28.80) per person without bath. (See Chapter 11.)
6. **Neptune's Killarney Town Hostel,** New Street, Killarney, County Kerry. A bright, modern hostel offering family rooms and self-catering facilities. Right in the heart of town, yet secluded from street noises. IR£6 ($9.60). (See Chapter 13.)
7. **Sailin,** Gentian Hill, Upper Salthill, Galway, County Galway. A lovely "no-smoking" B&B set in a secluded cul-de-sac overlooking a bird sanctuary. A good base for exploring Galway town and Connemara, with a terrific host family. IR£16 ($25.60). (See Chapter 16.)
8. **Barraicin,** Malin Head, County Donegal. This B&B in a modern bungalow is a friendly, comfortable place to stay when you've traveled as far north in Ireland as you can go. IR£13–IR£16.50 ($20.80–$26.40). (See Chapter 19.)
9. **Arradale House,** Kingscourt Road, Carrickmacross, County Monaghan. A peaceful, relaxing dairy farm with a warm, friendly hostess and excellent food. IR£15–IR£16 ($24–$25.60). (See Chapter 20.)
10. **Hilltop,** Delvin Road, Rathconnell, Mullingar, County Westmeath. A beautifully situated bungalow with outstanding host couple. Convenient for touring the midland counties. IR£16 ($25.60). (See Chapter 20.)

SOME OF IRELAND'S BEST BUDGET HOTELS

Again, the array of budget and good-value hotels is far from limited to those listed here, and it pays to do a little shopping around if you are traveling the hotel route. Bear in mind that budget hotels bear a higher price than other types of accommodations.

1. **Kelly's Hotel,** 36/37 Great George's Street, Dublin 2. Well-run city center hotel (no lift) with helpful owner/managers. IR£22–IR£28 ($35.20–$44.80). (See Chapter 5.)
2. **Jurys Inn,** Christchurch Place, Dublin 8. Located in a historic district of Dublin, this hotel has a money-saving per-room rate for up to four people. IR£49 ($78.40) per room. (See Chapter 5.)
3. **Forte Travelodge,** Swords By-Pass, N1 Dublin/Belfast Road, Swords, County Dublin. An excellent out-of-the-city base. Motel style, it has a per-room rate for up to three people. IR£33.50 ($53.60) per room. (See Chapter 5.)
4. **Jurys Cork Inn,** Anderson's Quay, Cork, County Cork. A bright, modern hotel just off Patrick Street in the city center. With a per-room rate for up to four people. IR£39 ($62.40). (See Chapter 11.)
5. **Forte Travelodge,** Kinsale Road, Roundabout, Blackash, Cork, County Cork. A modern, motel-type accommodation near the airport. With a good,

moderately priced restaurant and per-room rate for up to four people. IR£33.50 ($53.60). (See Chapter 11.)

6. **Aran View House Hotel,** Doolin, County Clare. A large country house hotel on a hilltop overlooking the Aran Islands. IR£25–IR£30 ($40–$48). (See Chapter 15.)
7. **Hyland's Hotel,** Ballyvaughan, County Clare. A small old-fashioned hotel loaded with charm. IR£20–IR£30 ($32–$48). (See Chapter 15.)
8. **Smyth Village Hotel,** Feakle, County Clare. A small family-run hotel, offering excellent dining and a pub that regularly draws local musicians. IR£17 ($27.20). (See Chapter 15.)
9. **Hyland Central Hotel,** The Diamond, Donegal, County Donegal. A lovely family-run hotel in the town center. The rear rooms have views overlooking the River Eske. IR£30–IR£40 ($48–$64). (See Chapter 19.)
10. **Dobbins Inn Hotel,** 6–8 High Street, Carrickfergus, County Antrim, Northern Ireland. An old historic inn, chockablock with artifacts and tall tales. A good base for touring Antrim Coast and Belfast. IR£32 ($51.20). (See Chapter 23.)

3 The Best in Shopping

The one shopping absolute for me in Ireland is to buy it when I see it. Never mind comparative shopping. There isn't really a big difference in prices around the country, as a rule, and I've found just the right woolly sweater in a little shop in Glengarriff, a beaten brass plaque depicting St. Brendan's epic voyage in a Donegal shop, and a few other items I might never have been able to call my own had I waited to find a better price elsewhere, since I've never come across them again.

ARAN SWEATERS

At the top of most visitors' shopping lists is one of Ireland's famed Aran knit sweaters. As much a part of the Irish landscape as stone walls and green fields, they're perfect to buy early in your trip to wear during chilly weather. They've been made in Ireland as far back as the 9th century, and originated with fishermen along the west coast (especially in the Aran Islands, hence the name), who valued their water resistance as well as their warmth. Today, most of the heavy natural oil has been removed from the wool and they're much softer than they used to be.

Designs, however, have changed not one whit and for good reason. Long ago, each stitch depicted a different part of Irish life: The cable stitch stood for the fisherman's strong rope (it's also supposed to bring good luck) and the trellis stitch represented stone walls. Using a combination of many such symbolic stitches, fishing villages designed patterns unique to each community, making it possible to return any drowning victim to his hometown for burial. Interestingly, in the beginning the sweaters were knit by men—women were relegated to the spinning of the wool.

A word of caution is in order about these sweaters (called "jerseys" in Ireland), since not all the creamy, off-white, cable-stitched sweaters you see are handmade. More and more machine-knits are appearing in shops, and if a lower price is your primary consideration or you prefer a lighter-weight garment, you may be just as happy with one of these. They will not, however, have anything like the longevity of the real thing. Hand-knits wear like iron, and I have one that I'm sure will be passed on for several generations. You should be able to tell the difference by the sheer weight of a hand-knit (or by that slip of paper in the pocket), but if you have any doubt, be sure to ask the salesperson.

You can expect to pay something like $60 to $95 for an adult's hand-knit pullover, slightly more for cardigans, and anywhere from one-half to one-third less for children's sizes. **Standun's,** in Galway, and **Macken of Ireland,** in Killarney, both have good stocks and prices.

WOOLENS AND TWEEDS

For centuries, Donegal homes came complete with looms from which poured the lovely tweeds and other woolens that are known all over the world. It is rare, however, to find a home loom today; most of the weaving is done in small factories concentrated in Donegal and in a few spotted around the country. You can watch a weaver at work if you call in on **Magee's of Donegal** in Donegal Town, or **Avoca Handweavers** in County Wicklow. All department stores carry woolens sold by the yard or made up into coats, suits, capes, and skirts, but some of the best buys are to be found at **Gillespi Brothers** in the little County Donegal town of Mountcharles; Magee's of Donegal; and **Padraic O Maille's** in Galway. The **House of Ireland,** in Dublin, has a stylish selection of woolen garments.

WATERFORD GLASS

Waterford "glass" is actually crystal, earning that distinction by the addition of 33% lead oxide to basic ingredients of silica sand and potash (crystal must contain no less than 22%, no more than 33½%). Around for two centuries (although actually produced for only one), Waterford is both beautiful and expensive.

You can tour the factory in Waterford (see Chapter 10) and browse through its shop. Waterford crystal is, of course, featured by many shops and department stores all around Ireland. Prices for Waterford virtually double when it's exported to the U.S. **Shannon Duty-Free Shops** carry a pretty good selection, and you'll find extensive stocks and good prices at **Joyce's** in Wexford, **Joseph Knox Ltd.** in Waterford City, and the **House of Ireland** in Dublin.

IRISH LACE

No purchase is more evocative of long-ago elegance and a more gracious age than Ireland's handmade lace from **Limerick** or **Carrickmacross.** Supplies are becoming more limited each year as a younger generation of women becomes less willing to spend days doing the exquisite but tedious and time-consuming handwork. You can, however, still purchase lace made in convents. Keeping the art alive, nuns supervise older women who practice the craft.

In Carrickmacross, County Monaghan (15 miles west of Dundalk, just off the road from Dublin to Belfast), it's **Carrickmacross Lace Co-op** (see Chapter 20), where a lovely collar and cuffs set will run about IR£40 ($64). In Limerick, a lace handkerchief will cost IR£50 ($80) and upward at the **Good Shepherd Convent** on Clare Street (see Chapter 15).

CRAFTS

Back in the 12th century, a traveler to Ireland wrote, "Fine craftsmanship is all around you. . . . Look carefully at it, and you will penetrate to the very shrine of art. You will make out intricacies so delicate and subtle, so exact and compact, with colors so fresh and vivid that you might say all this was the work of an angel, not of a man." Things haven't changed all that much over the intervening centuries. Today's statistics include more than 800 full-time craftsmen and more than 1,000 part-timers; more than 44 craft guilds, associations, and organizations affiliated with the Crafts Council of Ireland, which in turn is a member of the World Crafts Council and the Crafts Council of Europe, and a Minister for State responsible for crafts in the country.

Try to obtain a free copy of the *Crafthunter's Pocket Guide* from one of the Irish Tourist Board's U.S. offices, and failing that, plunk down the small charge for a copy at any Tourist Office within Ireland itself. It tells you exactly where to find which craftspeople, and it's indispensable in searching out particular crafts such as woodwork, leathers, pottery, and ceramics.

BOOKS

What better memento to carry home from Ireland than a book! After all, words have been pouring from those Irish minds to the printed page in a veritable flood since the beginning of recorded history. Any book lover is quite likely to go a bit mad at the sight of such a wealth of bookshops, and the bargain hunter will happily spend hours sifting through used-book stalls and bookstore basements with their tables of reduced-price volumes.

Dublin has lost a few of its oldest, most revered bookshops, which fell victim to increased taxes and rental costs. You'll still, however, find one or two family-run shops along the Liffey quays, and both **Greene's Bookshop** on Clare Street and **Parson's** on Baggot Street are havens to which I could repair for weeks on end. In addition to these traditional shops, there are bright, new, and large bookshops galore. In Galway, **Kenny's Bookshop** is virtually a national treasure, and a treat not to be missed. You'll find details on these and some others in the chapters that follow. Bookshops are tucked away in some of the most amazing places, and the Irish who run them are kindred spirits who'll wrap some memorable conversations along with the book you end up buying.

MISCELLANEOUS

Ireland has such an embarrassment of riches when it comes to **gifts and souvenirs** that I can only touch on a few in this book. Among those things to look for: **Connemara marble** in anything from bookends to letter openers to ashtrays to jewelry; **Owen Irish Turf Crafts,** pressed and molded turf that comes in inexpensive pendants and paperweights and pricier wall plaques, all adorned with Celtic designs; the **Claddagh ring,** with its traditional folk design of two hands clasping a heart that wears a crown (it was originally the Claddagh, County Galway, wedding ring) that comes in moderately priced silver versions as well as more costly gold; **recordings** of Irish traditional music groups; authentically dressed **character dolls** depicting such historical figures as the lady emigrant dressed in bonnet and shawl, or Molly Malone with her wheelbarrow of cockles and mussels (look for them at the House of Ireland in Dublin); the **Knockcroghery Dudeen,** an authentic replica of the clay pipes of Olde Ireland, now made by Anne Lally in her home, Mill House Pottery, Knockcroghery, County Roscommon, and sold in most good craft shops; and for a living souvenir that will spark Irish memories all summer long, look for **Irish Wildflowers** packets in gift shops and some tourist office shops, or stop in Irish Wildflowers, Ltd., Cooleen, Dingle, County Kerry (☎ 066/51000, fax 066/51991) to see their range of packagings (at prices of IR£1–IR£60 ($1.60–$96), with a mail order service available (see Chapter 14).

RECOVERING VAT

It has been true for many years that no items mailed or shipped out of the country are subject to the Value Added Tax (VAT), and in May of 1984 that relief was extended to those things you carry back home in your luggage. That is a big break and can make a difference—as much as 10% to 23%—in the cost of your Irish purchases.

When making your purchase, you must prove to the merchant that you are a nonresident of Ireland by presenting your passport or other documentation (U.S. driver's license, etc.). You'll be issued an invoice which must be stamped by Irish Customs to prove that you did, indeed, take the merchandise out of the country. That invoice must be returned to the vendor, whether he or she allows you the VAT exemption on the spot or sends you a refund upon receipt of the stamped invoice from Customs. One warning: It is possible—not probable, but possible—that the Customs officer may ask you to produce the items you've bought as you're outward bound. You can avoid having to search for them through all your luggage (as a friend of mine once did) by packing all purchases in one bag.

When you get the exemption is strictly up to the vendor (I know, you'd rather have those extra percents to spend in Ireland instead of after you're home—so would I, and the Irish government is probably missing out by not putting it in our hot-to-buy hands right then and there). Any shop is liable for the amount of the tax if it makes the deduction and you don't return that stamped invoice. So don't hassle your salesperson—just try to be as charming and as reliable-looking as you can to persuade them to give you the immediate deduction, then *be sure to return the invoice.* The whole refund procedure is simplified if you use credit cards instead of cash, of course, when it's a simple matter of issuing a credit to your account.

To collect your refund before leaving Ireland, at both Dublin and Shannon airports, you can present your receipts to the **Cashback** desk. This private company will hand over your refund in the currency of your choice for a sliding scale fee based on the amount of your purchases.

4 How This Guide Can Save You Money

The 65 money-saving tips and best bets, above in this chapter, will help you put together the itinerary that best suits your interests at the least possible cost. Below in this section, I've worked out a sample itinerary to illustrate how you can use this book to travel in Ireland from $45 a day. This is, of course, just one suggestion, and I'm sure you'll work out your own budget itineraries.

If You Have 3 Days (See Chapters 10, 11, 12)

With such a short stay, your best bet is to base yourself in one B&B and use day trips to explore a region; in this example, the Southeast. You can enjoy the long evening hours of daylight playing golf on nearby courses. Then head for the area's small town's lively pubs.

Day 1

Accommodation and Evening Meal: Book into the Toby Jug, Cappoquin (see Chapter 10), at partial-board (bed, breakfast, evening meal).

Cost: IR£22 ($35.20)

Day Trip: Clonmel, Waterford City, Dunmore East, Tramore, Dungarvan.

Lunch: The Munster, Waterford City.

Cost: IR£4 ($6.40)

Day 2

Accommodation and Evening Meal: As above.

Cost: IR£22 ($35.20)

Day Trip: Lismore, The Vee, Cahir, Cashel.

Lunch: The Galtee Inn, Cahir.

Cost: IR£3.50 ($5.60)

Day 3

Accommodation and Evening Meal: As above.

Cost: IR£22 ($35.20)

Day Trip: Ardmore, Youghal, Cork city, return to Cappoquin.

Lunch: Aherne's Pub and Seafood Restaurant, Youghal.

Cost: IR£6 ($9.60)

Total Costs for Three Days

Accommodation and Evening Meals: IR£66 ($105.60)

Lunches: IR£13.50 ($21.60)

Total: IR£79.50 ($127.20)

If You Have 7 Days (See Chapters 13, 14, 15)

A full week allows you to explore a good bit of the Southwest of Ireland and the Shannonside region. Again stay at a hostel or farmhouse for two or three days and make day trips. Begin in Killarney. In the interest of the budget, and keeping in mind that you will be touring most of each day, book into **Neptune's Killarney Town Hostel.** Located right in the heart of town, it has superior facilities as well as inexpensive meals for residents. The drive from Killarney to the Shannonside area is quite beautiful, and you have a choice of taking the time-saving ferry at Tarbert or following the Shannon all the way into Limerick. A Liscannor base is central to most major sightseeing.

Day 1

Accommodation: Neptune's Killarney Town Hostel, Killarney.

Cost (two-bed room): IR£9 ($14.40)

Sightseeing: Killarney town and environs.

Lunch: The Laurels Pub, Main Street.

Cost: IR£5 ($8)

Evening Meal: The King's Inn, Main Street.

Cost (Early-Bird Special): IR£10 ($16)

Day 2

Accommodation: As above.
Cost: IR£9 ($14.40)
Sightseeing: The Ring of Kerry.
Lunch: The Ring Lyne, Chapeltown, Valentia Island.
Cost: IR£5 ($8)
Evening Meal: Neptune's Killarney Town Hostel.
Cost: IR£6 ($9.60)

Day 3

Accommodation: As above.
Cost IR£9 ($14.40)
Sightseeing: The Dingle Peninsula.
Lunch: Tig an Tober, Ballyferriter.
Cost IR£6 ($9.60)
Evening Meal: Neptune's.
Cost: IR£6 ($9.60)

Day 4

Accommodation: Harbour Sunset Farmhouse, Liscannor, County Clare.
Cost: IR£13.50 ($21.60)
Sightseeing: Allow a full day for the drive from Killarney to Liscannor, with time out at Foynes and other points of interest along the way.
Lunch: This is an ideal day for a picnic; otherwise, stop in the Glin Castle Gate Shop, Glin, County Limerick (on the Shannon Estuary Drive).
Cost: IR£5 ($8)
Evening Meal: Harbour Sunset Farmhouse (Mrs. O'Gorman is noted for her cooking, and you'll be ready to settle in after the long drive).
Cost: IR£12 ($19.20)

Day 5

Accommodation: As above.
Cost: IR£13.50 ($21.60)
Sightseeing: Cliffs of Moher, Craggaunowen, Bunratty Folk Park.
Lunch: Durty Nelly's.
Cost: IR£5 ($8)
Evening Meal: Brogans Restaurant, Ennis.
Cost: IR£8 ($12.80)

Day 6

Accommodation: As above.
Cost: IR£13.50 ($21.60)
Sightseeing: Limerick City (King John's Castle, etc.).
Lunch: Nancy Blake's, 19 Denmark Street.
Cost: IR£4 ($6.40)

Evening Meal: Bunratty Medieval Banquet (I *know* it's a splurge, but you really should!).
Cost: IR£30 ($48)
Alternatively, eat at Durty Nelly's, Bunratty.
Cost: IR£10 ($16)

Day 7
Accommodation: As above.
Cost: IR£13.50 ($21.60)
Sightseeing: Kilkee and the Loop Head Peninsula, or Lisdoonvarna and Doolin.
Lunch: Bruach na Haille in Doolin, or Halpin's Hotel, in Kilkee.
Cost at either: IR£6 ($9.60)
Evening Meal: Harbour Sunset Farmhouse.
Cost: IR£12 ($19.20)

Total Cost for Seven Days
Accommodation: IR£81 ($129.60)
Meals: IR£100 ($160.00)
Totals: IR£181 ($289.60)
Note: Add IR£30 ($48) for Bunratty Banquet.

If You Have 10 Days (See Chapters 13, 14, 15, 20, 6, 7)

With three additional days, you have a choice: Head north to Galway and Connemara, or (as in the following itinerary) opt for the sights of Dublin and the Eastern Region.

Days 1–7
As above.
Total Costs IR£181 ($289.60)

Day 8
Accommodation: Avalon House, Dublin.
Cost (two-bed room with private bath): IR£19 ($30.40)
Sightseeing: Drive to Dublin via midland counties, choosing the sightseeing route that best suits your interests.
Lunch en route: Any of the pubs listed in the midland counties.
Cost: IR£4 ($6.40)
Evening Meal: Flanagan's, O'Connell Street.
Cost: IR£9 ($14.40)

Day 9
Accommodation (including continental breakfast): As above.
Cost: IR£19 ($30.40)
Sightseeing: Self-guided walking tour; National Museum, National Gallery, St. Stephen's Green, and other free attractions.
Lunch: The Stag's Head, pub lunch.
Cost: IR£5 ($8)
Evening Meal: The Coffee Dock Grill, Jurys Hotel.
Cost: IR£8 ($12.80)

Day 10

Accommodation: As above.

Cost:	IR£19 ($30.40)

Sightseeing: Choose a day trip by coach to the Eastern Region attraction of your choice (Hill of Tara, Newbridge, Glendalough, etc.). See Chapter 7.

Lunch: Pub lunch, depending on your choice of destination.

Cost:	IR£4 ($6.40)

Evening Meal: Gallagher's Boxty House, Temple Bar.

Cost:	IR£6 ($9.60)

Total Costs for Days 7–10

Accommodation:	IR£57 ($91.20)
Meals:	IR£36 ($57.60)

Total Costs for 10 Days

Accommodation:	IR£138 ($220.80)
Meals:	IR£136 ($217.60)
Totals:	IR£274 ($438.40)

2 Getting to Know Ireland

You know about Ireland, of course—it's that lovely isle that appeared when "a little bit of heaven dropped from out the sky one day." Skeptical? Well, look around for the most hard-nosed skeptic you know who's *been* to Ireland and then get set to listen to hours of rapturous memories!

Ireland has that effect on people. All people. For me, it began back in 1973, when I first encountered the incredible beauty of this small country's landscape and learned with amazement that the magnificent sum of $2.40 would make me an instant member of warm Irish families who were anxious to share their fireside, friends, favorite pub, innumerable cups of tea, and the most enormous breakfasts I'd ever seen.

I stayed three weeks that year, and haven't missed going back for a part of every year since. That's been possible for me—a confirmed budget traveler—because Ireland is still so *affordable.* Oh, prices have risen there quite as fast as they have everywhere else in the world, but Ireland remains one of the best travel buys I've come across.

But there's much, much more to it than that. There are some things that would be cheap at *any* price, and Ireland has more than its fair share of those priceless commodities. Each visit has brought fresh discoveries and new friends. There are always new tales to bring home, still more of the witty one-liners that spring so naturally to Irish lips to try to remember, more memories of nights of unplanned music and song that somehow just happened, still more miles of unbelievably beautiful coastline or mountains or rolling green fields suddenly unfolding around corners I'd not turned before, new Irish names to add to my Christmas list.

Perhaps even more important is the glow I bring back each year after spending a little time with people who have managed to hold on to basic values that in other parts of the world these days seem as elusive as a dream.

Blarney Stone blather? Not so. Just wait until you hear the ravings of your plane mates on the flight back home! I am just *one* of those Americans who every year head off to Ireland—a fan club hundreds of thousands strong. We're joined by thousands of enthusiastic English, French, Dutch, Germans, and a good number from countries as far away as Japan, New Zealand, and Australia, who send the total number of foreign visitors into the millions. Many

Europeans return year after year for superb fishing or golfing or biking or horseracing or theater or music—or simply to soak up the unique atmosphere of this little country and the extraordinary personality of its people. And each of us leaves Ireland filled with its special kind of magic, eager to spread the word to all and sundry. I'm willing to wager you'll do the same.

It's a formidable task to write about Ireland and the Irish. Back in 1842, William Makepeace Thackeray wrote an English friend: "I am beginning to find out now that a man ought to be forty years in this country instead of three months, and *then* he wouldn't be able to write about it!" Far be it from me even to attempt to beat Thackeray—I can only try to tell you about the Ireland *I* have discovered in several years of exhaustive research, pass along the finds of other travelers who have been kind enough to write, and tell you how *it is not only possible* to visit Ireland on our $45 a day—it's the *best* way to go!

WHAT YOU CAN EXPECT

Before diving into a detailed discussion of what you can expect to find in Ireland, let's talk about what you *won't* find. First of all, you won't find the stereotyped "stage Irish" of so many comedy skits. Nor will you find a land peopled entirely by saints and scholars (although, Lord knows, there's a plentiful supply of both). Or a land ravaged by violence, as the news media would sometimes lead you to believe—sure, it *does* exist, but it does *not* pervade the country. And as the Irish are the first to point out, you won't find a telephone system that works with anything like the efficiency you're used to at home (which can, I suppose, drive you a little dotty if you're in a hurry, but which can also, I *know,* lead to some pretty interesting telephone conversations with operators while you both wait to get your call through). One thing more: You won't find a populace out to take you for every cent in your holiday purse—in my experience, the phrase "what the traffic will bear" just doesn't exist in Ireland.

Today's Ireland is a land still covered with small farms in unspoiled countryside but moving away from an economy wholly dependent on agriculture, with more and more high-tech industries moving in and making scarcely a ripple on the smooth waters of the world's most relaxed way of life.

It's a land of cities whose antiquities live quite comfortably, elbow to elbow, with modern luxury hotels and an increasing number of sophisticated cabarets and nightclubs. A land filled with social centers that go by the name of pubs. Whose Tidy Towns competition each year rates even the tiniest hamlet on its success—or lack of it—in the ongoing battle against litter. Where there's never sweltering heat or bone-chilling cold, and a rainy day really *is* a soft day.

Ireland is where the word "friendly" probably originated. Where stopping to ask directions can land you in a family kitchen swapping tales over a "cuppa." Where the answer to every question is a short story. Where you may—as I once did—wind up as the Dublin house guest of an Irish lady you met quite casually over breakfast at a B&B in Kerry.

Today's Ireland will take over your heart the minute you land and send you away looking back over your shoulder with a head full of plans to come right back.

1 The Regions in Brief

The Lay of the Land To get the statistics out of the way: Ireland covers 32,524 square miles, stretched out 302 miles at its longest and 189 miles at its widest

Ireland

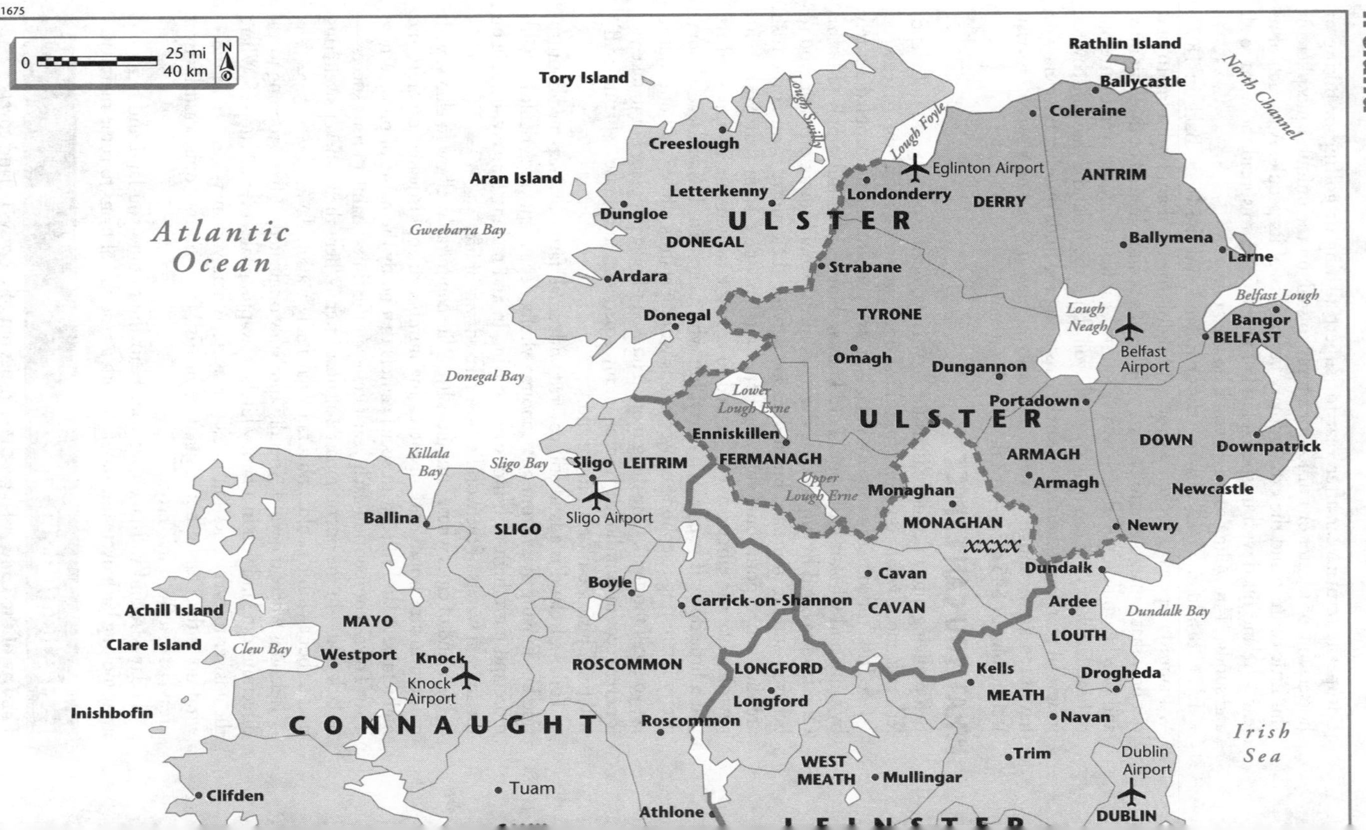

1675
0
25 mi
40 km
N
Tory Island
Rathlin Island
Ballycastle
North Channel
Coleraine
Lough Swilly
Lough Foyle
Creeslough
Eglinton Airport
ANTRIM
Aran Island
Letterkenny
Londonderry
DERRY
Dungloe
ULSTER
Atlantic Ocean
Gweebarra Bay
DONEGAL
Ballymena
Larne
Strabane
Ardara
Belfast Lough
Donegal
TYRONE
Lough Neagh
Bangor
BELFAST
Omagh
Dungannon
Belfast Airport
Donegal Bay
Lower Lough Erne
Portadown
ULSTER
Enniskillen
DOWN
Downpatrick
Killala Bay
Sligo Bay
Sligo
LEITRIM
FERMANAGH
ARMAGH
Upper Lough Erne
Monaghan
Armagh
Newcastle
Sligo Airport
Ballina
SLIGO
MONAGHAN
Newry
XXXX
Dundalk
Cavan
Boyle
Carrick-on-Shannon
CAVAN
Ardee
Achill Island
Dundalk Bay
MAYO
LOUTH
Clare Island
Clew Bay
Westport
Knock
Knock Airport
ROSCOMMON
LONGFORD
Kells
Drogheda
MEATH
Longford
Inishbofin
CONNAUGHT
Roscommon
Navan
Irish Sea
Trim
Dublin Airport
WEST MEATH
Mullingar
Tuam
Clifden
Athlone
DUBLIN

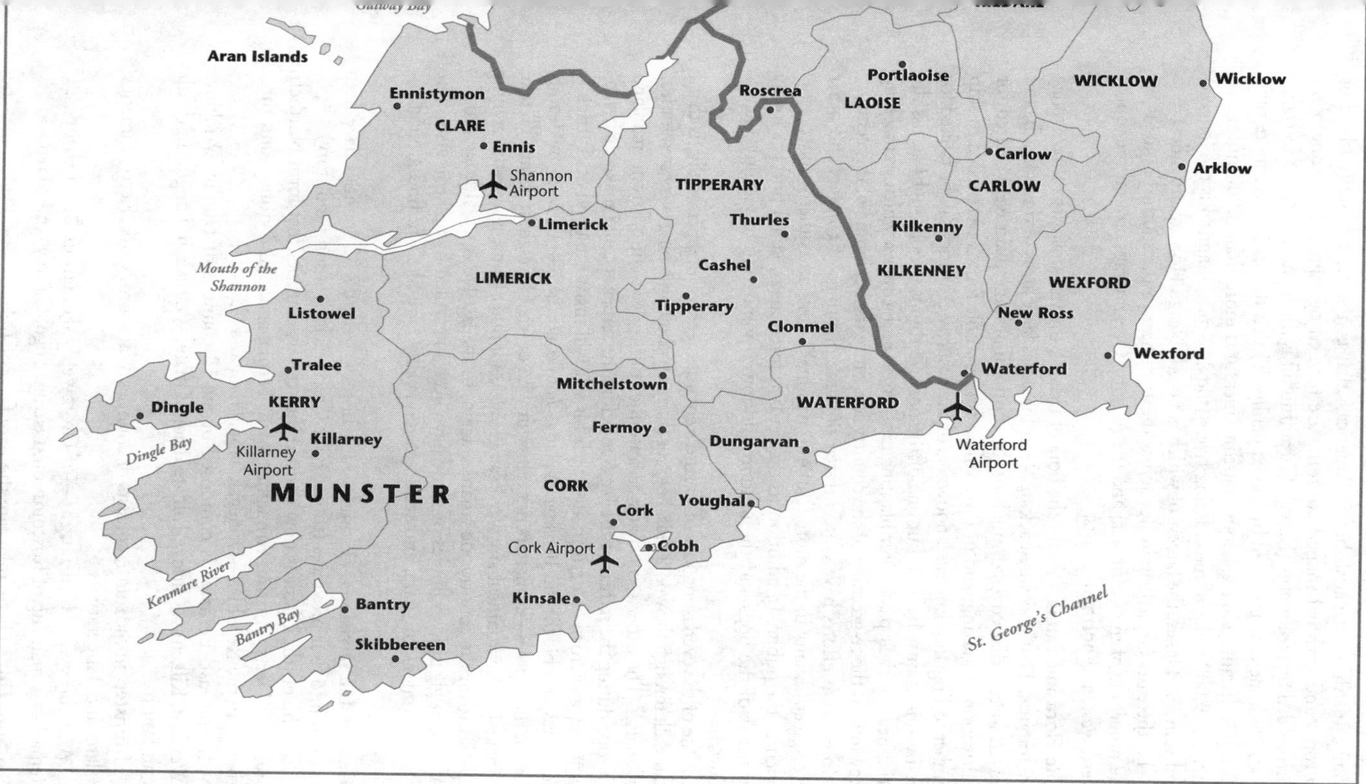
Aran Islands
Ennistymon
CLARE
Ennis
Shannon Airport
Limerick
Mouth of the Shannon
LIMERICK
Listowel
Tralee
Dingle
KERRY
Killarney
Killarney Airport
Dingle Bay
MUNSTER
Kenmare River
Bantry
Bantry Bay
Skibbereen
CORK
Cork
Cork Airport
Cobh
Kinsale
Youghal
Fermoy
Mitchelstown
Dungarvan
WATERFORD
Tipperary
Cashel
Thurles
TIPPERARY
Roscrea
Clonmel
LAOISE
Portlaoise
Kilkenny
KILKENNEY
Carlow
CARLOW
WICKLOW
Wicklow
Arklow
WEXFORD
New Ross
Wexford
Waterford
Waterford Airport
St. George's Channel

points. It's the "last parish before America," that is, the most westerly island of Europe, and its bowl-shaped contours are formed by a great limestone plain surrounded by mountains (Kerry's Carrantuohill is the highest at 3,414 feet).

Its coastline is so indented by jagged peninsulas that the sea is never more than 70 miles distant. That glorious coastline measures more than 3,000 miles and encircles 9,000 miles of meandering rivers (the 230-mile Shannon is the longest) and some 800 lakes, the largest of which is Lough Neagh (153 square miles).

To the east, Great Britain lies across the Irish Sea; to the south, France is on the other side of the Celtic Sea; and the Atlantic Ocean wraps around the southwest, west, and northern coasts.

The Flora and Fauna As for the flora of Ireland, the vast majority of trees today are imports. That's because back in Neolithic times large areas of the oak, ash, and rowan forests that covered much of the central limestone plain were cleared for cultivation or grazing; and in Elizabethan times, whole forests were felled to ship timber to England. English landowners of the past few centuries can be faulted for many sins against Ireland, but one of the positive things they brought across the Irish Sea was their passion for planting exotic trees and gardens, which went a long way toward the re-greening of the countryside. Since the beginning of this century, reforestation efforts have concentrated on large plantings of conifers and other ever-greens, many in the more than 400 national forests and other wooded areas open to the public. In addition to the verdant forest areas, you'll find the lovely heathers of the bogs and the unique wildflower population of County Clare's Burren.

One of the everlasting joys of Ireland's environment for me, personally, is that I can walk through the woodlands, bogs, or Burren without watching every step for fear of snakes. The experts say that's because the country was cut off from mainland Europe during the retreat of the Ice Age before the serpents could make their venomous way across; any Irishman worth his salt will insist the good St. Patrick is solely responsible for this blessing. As far as *I* am concerned—me, with my deathly fear of the reptiles—it matters not one whit who or what brought it about: I'll take a snake-free environment any way I can get it! As for other fauna, no life-threatening species roam the countryside (thanks, again, to the last Ice Age), although fossils of several gigantic examples of some have been unearthed by archeologists. The quite harmless fox, hare, and stoat are about all you're likely to find around today.

Geographic Divisions From its early history, Ireland's 32 counties have been divided into four provinces (those "Four Green Fields" of song and story).

To the north, **Ulster** is now divided into the six counties that form Northern Ireland—Derry, Antrim, Armagh, Down, Fermanagh, and Tyrone—and three that lie in the Republic—Donegal, Monaghan, and Cavan.

In the east, **Leinster** is composed of the 12 counties of Dublin, Wicklow, Wexford, Kilkenny, Carlow, Kildare, Laois, Offaly, Westmeath, Longford, Meath, and Louth.

Munster, in the south, consists of counties Waterford, Cork, Kerry, Limerick, Clare, and Tipperary.

And the west's **Connaught**—of Cromwell's slanderous "To hell or . . ." remark—is made up of Roscommon, Leitrim, Sligo, Galway, and Mayo.

To Sum Up There, then, are the bare facts of Ireland—and believe me, they are *bare.*

It's only when you see the delicate play of light and shade on the mountains while driving from Glengarriff in County Cork to Kenmare in County Kerry, or ride through the lush greenness of County Waterford byways, or stand and drink in the mystical moonscape of County Clare's Burren, or watch a grassy hillside fade from the brightest hue of green to silver-gray in the changing light, or gaze at a cloud-studded sky so enormous it makes infinity seem small, or stand on the rocky Dingle Peninsula shore at Ventry where legend says the King of the World went down to defeat at the hands of Fionn MacCumhaill ("Finn MacCool") and his Fianna warrior band—it's only then that the face of Ireland comes truly alive. Around every bend, that luminous, ever-changing landscape cries out for the poet, and many a poet has answered its call. Poor Thackeray—no *wonder* he was so frustrated!

George Bernard Shaw, however, put it quite simply:

There is no magic like that of Ireland.
There are no skies like Irish skies.
There is no air like Irish air . . .
The Irish climate will make the stiffest
and slowest mind flexible for life.

Amen!

2 Ireland Today

On the social front, the times they are a changing, indeed. Since St. Patrick introduced Christianity to the island, Ireland has been a predominately Catholic nation. Yet the past few years have seen an increasing alienation from the Catholic Church, especially among young members. As a result, lifestyles in Ireland are taking on a secular rather than a religious focus. Statistics reflect a drop in marriage and a rapid increase in couples living together without benefit of marriage. A constitutional referendum on divorce has been promised by the present government—a dramatic change in social mores. More than that—gasp!—condoms are now freely available, both over the counter and from vending machines.

Politically, it's now apparent that future governments will almost certainly be formed by a coalition of two or more political parties, replacing the old one-party format that's been a staple of the Irish scene for so many years. Another significant development came in January 1991 when Mary Robinson took office as the country's first woman president. Enormously popular at home, she has traveled widely, enhancing Ireland's worldwide standing tremendously.

Although the vast majority of the citizens use English as their first tongue, recently there's been an increase in adult students enrolled in Irish-language courses, run each summer in Donegal, Dingle, and Connemara. To throw in Irish expressions in everyday conversation is becoming rather trendy.

3 A Look at the Past

The landscape of Ireland is haunted by its history. Its ghosts lurk along every road, around every bend, behind every bush.

Stone Age Irish move eerily behind the mists of prehistory that cloak dolmens left in their wake.

Dateline

- **6000 B.C.** Stone Age settlers arrive.

continues

- **4000 B.C.** Neolithic farmers settle in Ireland.
- **2000 B.C.** Bronze Age metal workers come to seek copper and gold.
- **600 B.C.** The Celts arrive, with iron weapons and the Gaelic language.
- **A.D. 456** St. Patrick introduces Christianity to Ireland.
- **795** Vikings plunder monasteries and the coast, later founding the cities of Dublin, Wexford, Waterford, and Limerick.
- **1014** Battle of Clontarf: Brian Boru defeats the Vikings.
- **1169** Normans, led by Strongbow, begin England's long domination of Ireland.
- **1601** Decisive defeat of Irish forces and Spanish allies at Kinsale.
- **1608** The "Flight of the Earls."
- **1609** Plantations in Ulster begin, as English and Scottish Protestant settlers occupy Irish farms.
- **1649** Oliver Cromwell sweeps through Ireland to subdue the rebellious Irish.
- **1690** Catholic defeat at the Battle of the Boyne begins a century of Catholic oppression under the Penal Laws.
- **1791** United Irishmen founded by Wolfe Tone.
- **1798** Insurrection led by Tone, Robert Emmet, and others squelched by English forces.
- **1800** Act of Union hands direct rulership of Ireland to London Parliament.
- **1829** Daniel O'Connell achieves Catholic Emancipation.

continues

Visit the reconstructed crannog at Craggaunowen in County Clare, and Bronze Age men and women almost materialize before your eyes. Iron Age forts make a quiet day ring with the sounds, just beyond your ears, of those who sheltered there. Great monastic crosses and ruined abbeys accent the tremendous influence of early Christians, while some 60 round towers tell of the dangers they faced from Viking raiders. Listen carefully in Dublin and Waterford and you may hear the echoing footsteps of their Viking founders. Norman spirits inhabit ruined castles that squat along riverbanks, atop lofty cliffs, and in lonely fields.

The multifaceted history that shaped the fascinating Irish character we know today travels with you wherever you go in Ireland.

In the Beginning Ireland took on its present shape when the world's last Ice Age retreated and left the country with multitudes of scooped-out lakes and tumbled mountains plus a land bridge that connected it to Great Britain. Sometime around 6000 B.C., a race of Stone Age settlers crossed over that land bridge to Ireland, and others came by boat—we don't know where they originally came from, only that they clustered around the seashore and along inland riverbanks, fashioning crude flint tools and surviving by fishing and hunting.

Long after that land link to Britain had disappeared and Ireland had become an island—about 2000 B.C.—newcomers brought with them cows and other domesticated animals. They also brought the skill to clear the land and plant crops, thus beginning Ireland's long tradition of farming and cattle raising. It was this Neolithic race who cremated their dead and created communal burial chambers beneath stone cairns or inside earthen, tunnel-filled mounds. Newgrange, in County Meath, a full acre in size, is today the best known of the surviving tumuli and the one most of us visit to give a tip of the hat to those long-ago Irish.

The Metal Workers While the farmers in Ireland were tending their fields, European tribes were beginning to work with metals, which led to an ever-widening search for copper to be used in fashioning bronze weapons and tools, and gold for making exquisitely crafted ornaments and jewelry. The search eventually reached Ireland and its rich deposits of both metals. The Bronze Age had begun, an age that brought to this remote, primitive little island a whole slew of artisans, merchants, and peddlers who traveled all over western Europe, leaving examples of their arts and crafts scattered around the Continent.

Those who came to Ireland during this period were probably of Mediterranean origin. They were short, dark-haired, and swarthy-skinned and may have been Picts. The Romans knew them as the Iberni, but they were called the Uib-Ernai in Ireland, where they were believed to be descendants of the fertility goddess Eire, whose name means "noble." The island country was very soon known by that noble name, and today it is the oldest existing national name in the world (never mind that it's been corrupted by dropping the initial letter and tacking on "land"—*officially,* the country is still Eire).

As beautifully crafted as are the metal objects created by these early Irish settlers, they fade in significance when compared with the most important legacy they left us. A wealth of megalithic stone structures still stand in solid, silent testimony to incredible scientific knowledge and engineering skill. Great pillars and huge standing stones bear mute witness to feats of construction that must have required great organization, hundreds of workers, and a dedication that defies belief. The megaliths of Ireland are among its most valuable treasures, and to the traveler's delight, they stand in solitary splendor in the green fields and atop rocky hilltops with nary a neon sign or souvenir stand in sight!

And Then Came the Celts Tall, fair-skinned, and red-haired, the Celts were fierce, warlike people who roamed the face of Europe before migrating to Ireland in the 4th century B.C. They came with iron weapons and a military prowess that soon established them—and their language—as rulers of the land.

Some 100 tribes spread across the country, setting up small kingdoms under petty lords, or chieftains. Those smaller units, in turn, paid allegiance (at least in theory) to regional kings, and in time a High King of Ireland sat at Tara. The five regional kingdoms were known as Ulster, Munster, Leinster, Meath, and Connaught, which became the four provinces of Ireland as we know it when the Kingdom of Meath merged with Leinster.

- **1846** Potato famine causes widespread starvation; more than one million Irish emigrate.
- **1879** Land League founded by Michael Davitt to fight landlords and secure tenant landownership.
- **1905–08** Sinn Fein political party evolves with Irish independence its primary goal.
- **1912** Home Rule goes into effect, prompting formation of Ulster Volunteers by loyalists and the Irish Republican Army as a military adjunct of Sinn Fein.
- **1916** The Easter Sunday uprising, led by Patrick Pearse, James Connolly, and others; their execution unites Irish public opinion behind the cause for independence.
- **1921** Twenty-six counties of Ireland granted Dominion status as Irish Free State, sparking civil war that rages until 1923.
- **1937** New constitution put forth by Eamon De Valera.
- **1939–45** Ireland establishes policy of neutrality in World War II.
- **1948** The 26 counties become a republic with no constitutional ties to Great Britain.
- **1959** Ireland begins era of economic and industrial growth.
- **1968** Violence breaks out in Northern Ireland when Catholic civil rights advocates march in Derry.
- **1969** Great Britain stations military force in Northern Ireland to protect the peace.

continues

- **1970** Provisional IRA embarks on campaign of violence.
- **1973** The Republic of Ireland joins the European Economic Community.
- **1981** Republican prisoners in Northern Ireland stage hunger strikes; 10 die.
- **1986** Anglo-Irish Agreement gives the Republic limited input in Northern Ireland affairs.
- **1993** After months of discussions, the prime ministers of Ireland and Great Britain issue the Downing Street Proclamation.
- **1994** On August 31, the IRA declares an end to "military operations," followed three months later by a similar ceasefire by Loyalist paramilitaries.
- **1995** Early in the year the British and Irish governments jointly issue a Framework Document designed to move ahead talks between all parties in an attempt to reach a political solution to the Northern Ireland situation.

Hot-blooded Celts were not, however, about to let any of those titles and divisions go unchallenged. The countryside rang with the sounds of battle as petty king fought petty king, regional kings embarked on expansionary expeditions, and the High King of the moment never sat easy on his honorary throne. Peasants and bondsmen toiled for whichever chieftain was in power at the moment, and the free farmer anted up both tribute and loyalty, while craftily throwing up a sturdy earthen ring fort (also called a "rath" or "lis") as protection against roaming marauders. Those ring forts are still around, and many of today's town names reflect their locations. For example, Lismore, in County Waterford, takes its name from just such a large lis on its outskirts.

As for any sort of unity, it existed in the strong bonds of a common culture and traditions held together by the common language. Petty kingdoms might be at war, but all paid strict obedience to the traditional laws of the Brehons (lawyers), who traveled freely from one kingdom to another. Learned men in all professions were honored throughout the land and established schools that set intricately graded scales of achievement. Traveling bards who recited long epic poems of past heroic deeds were much revered and richly rewarded when they came up with new compositions that put a poetic purpose behind the latest exploits of whichever chieftain might be offering hospitality at the moment. Only slightly less homage was paid to the most skilled of the many artists and craftsmen who labored for each chieftain and often shared his table. Above everyone, the Druids were heralded as *all* tribes' wisest men and they conducted or prescribed the most sacred ceremonies.

It was this strange mixture of barbarous warring and a highly developed culture that greeted the arrival of Christianity in the 5th century A.D. And all the foregoing is the story of how it evolved—at least, that's the way archeologists and historians *think* it evolved, based on their best assumptions from carbon datings, artifacts, and educated guesses.

For another view of Ireland's early history, see "Myths, Legends, and Folklore" later in this chapter. Which version would *I* choose: Why, both, of course—with perhaps just the slightest leaning toward Finn MacCool and Cuchulainn.

Saints and Scholars The Romans, rampaging in southern Britain, never did get around to conquering Ireland, but in the mid–5th century A.D. a conquest of quite another nature took place. A pagan religion that had flourished for centuries surprisingly embraced quickly and with enthusiasm the doctrines and rites of Christianity that landed on Irish shores along with St. Patrick. A Roman by birth, in his youth the budding saint had tended swine in Ulster as a slave, escaped, and made his way back to the Continent, where he entered religious life. Even in those days, however, the magic of Ireland was at work, and he returned to his former captors as a missionary in 432 A.D.

Those early years among people who were to become his devout followers may well have given St. Patrick the insight to convert many pagan *practices* as well as pagan people, thus making it easier for them to make the switch than it might otherwise have been. Retaining just enough pagan roots to avoid hostile resistance, he managed to transplant rites and superstitions into Christian soil without a murmur—the healing powers of many Irish "holy wells," for example, are those attributed to them by ancient Celts long before St. Patrick arrived on the scene. His firsthand knowledge of Celtic love of the mystical—especially when applied to the natural world—perhaps inspired him to use the native shamrock to symbolize the Holy Trinity; it became Ireland's most enduring national symbol.

Irish king after Irish king listened to the missionary and led his subjects into the new religion, although none went so far as to abandon such distinctly Celtic pastimes as intra-kingdom warfare and riotous revelry within his own court. In homage to their new God (or maybe in penance for their more un-Christian practices), kings and other large landowners endowed His earthly representatives with lavish gifts of precious metals, land on which to build churches and monasteries, and other valuables that helped fund St. Patrick's work.

With the coming of Christianity, Celtic culture took a giant step forward. Already deeply respectful of learning in its higher forms, in the hundreds the Irish devoted themselves to a cloistered life within great monasteries that taught all the learning of their time, both Celtic and Roman. As Europe entered its culturally deprived Dark Ages, Ireland's monastic universities kept the lights of philosophy, theology, astronomy, literature, poetry, and most of the known sciences brightly burning, attracting thousands of students who fled the Continent during those centuries. Artistic achievement hit new heights inside their walls, as the exquisitely illustrated *Book of Kells* demonstrates. Until the end of the 8th century, Ireland's Golden Age was the brightest beacon in the Western world.

Away from these seats of learning, monks of a more mystical leaning moved out to more remote parts of the country and to rocky, misty islands just offshore. There they lived austere lives of meditation, building beehive-shaped stone dwellings still intact today and marvelously engineered little stone churches like Dingle's Gallarus Oratory, constructed entirely without mortar and watertight for the past 1,500 years. The impressive stone Celtic crosses that dot the landscape had their origins in the 7th century.

Eventually, Europe's age of darkness was forced into retreat, helped mightily by returning European scholars and Irish monks and scholars who left home to carry their teachings into cathedrals, royal courts, and the great universities they helped establish.

Viking Invaders The first invaders of Ireland's recorded history were terrifying Viking raiders who came by sea in A.D. 795 to launch fierce, lightning-fast strikes along the coastline, taking away plunder and captives and leaving behind only smoking ruins. Their superior mail battle dress and heavy arms made easy victims of even the most stouthearted, battle-loving Irish, and their raids moved farther and farther inland, with rich monastic settlements yielding the most valuable prizes. Churchmen found an answer to the danger in tall, round towers with their only entrance high above the ground (they stored their most precious treasures there, then pulled up long ladders to make access impossible). I have, incidentally, run across more than one seanachie (storytellers) whose story is that Finn MacCool built the first of these and the doorway was simply put at his natural entry-level—the monks just latched on to what turned out to be a perfect protective device. You'll find one of the best preserved at the Rock of Cashel, in County Tipperary.

As the years went by, raiders turned into settlers, establishing the first of a string of coastal cities at Dublin in 841, followed by Wexford, Waterford, Cork, and Limerick. Vestiges of city walls, gates, and fortifications remain to this day—Reginald's Tower in Waterford is one of the most perfect examples. Former raiders turned to peaceful trading and—in a pattern to be followed by subsequent "conquerors"—they were soon intermarrying with natives and becoming as Irish as the Irish themselves.

Not a few resident Irish chieftains, after disastrous defeats, began to take note of successful Viking battle methods and turn them back against the victors. But it wasn't until 1014 that Brian Boru—the High King of Ireland at the time—engaged his enemies at Clontarf, just outside Dublin, and won a decisive victory after a full day of battle. Interestingly, so intermixed had the two races become by that time that while a large part of the Viking forces consisted of "Irish" allies, Brian Boru's loyal "Norse" warriors were among the most valiant on the field! Boru was mortally wounded and ascended into the rarefied stratosphere of Ireland's most revered heroes.

The Normans Move In Brian Boru's death was followed by a century and a half of kingly tug-of-war to establish one central authority figure. It was one of those ambitious combatants who took the first step on Ireland's long path of involvement with the British. His name was Dermot MacMurrough, King of Leinster, and he made the fatal mistake of stealing the beautiful wife of O'Rourke, the King of Breffni, who promptly stirred up Leinster's minor chieftains and hounded MacMurrough out of Leinster.

MacMurrough crossed the Irish Sea to Britain, then under the rule of Norman conquerors from France for a little over a century, and followed King Henry II to France, finally persuading him to sponsor a volunteer army to help win back Dermot's lost throne. It arrived in 1169 and landed in Waterford under the command of the earl of Pembroke, popularly known as Strongbow. By marrying MacMurrough's daughter in Reginald's Tower, the wily Norman became King of Leinster when his father-in-law died the very next year.

Strongbow's military prowess quickly brought most of Leinster and Munster under his domination. He defeated Rory O'Connor (buried at Conmacnois, County Offaly), the last High King of Ireland, and appeared to be well on his way to achieving power to rival that of King Henry II. Needless to say, from Henry's point of view, something had to be done. Espousing a sudden interest in the religious eccentricities of Irish Catholics (who sometimes showed faint regard for the edicts of Rome—their Easter fell on a date different from that proclaimed by the pope, for instance), Henry rushed to Ireland clutching a document from the pope (Adrian IV, the only *English* pope in the church's history!) giving him feudal lordship over all of Ireland, Strongbow notwithstanding.

Under the guise of a religious reformer, Henry was able to win the support of most Irish bishops, and the papal authority gave him a potent lever to gain the submission of Irish kings, lords, and large landowners. Stating that he held absolute ownership of all lands, it granted him the undisputed right to rent it to such nobles as professed loyalty and withhold it from those who refused to do so. Many of the Irish kings, anxious to hold on to their territories even if it meant fealty to the English king, traveled to Dublin to make the required submission.

But that feudal lordship flew squarely in the face of long-established Irish law, which had insisted since the days of the Brehons that no king or lord had the right to take lands owned by individuals or groups and that any attempt to do so should be resisted, by force if necessary. That basic precept kept Anglo-Norman and Irish lords growling at each other across a legal chasm for the next 350 years. Although every English monarch who followed Henry laid claim to the lordship of Ireland, each was too busy with civil wars and foreign conquest to send armies to enforce that claim. Normans acquired title to more than half the country, building most of those sturdy castles in which you'll sightsee, banquet, or even spend the night during your visit.

All the while, however, the same thing that happened to the Vikings was happening to the Normans. Quickly adapting to their new homeland, they intermarried with the Irish and strayed so far from their sacred loyalty to the English throne and all things English that laws had to be passed in Parliament against their use of Irish dress, manners, and the native language—to my knowledge, the only time in the world's history that a *language* has been banished! Those laws turned out to be about as useless as the armed forces that never arrived—Norman families evolved into *Irish*-Norman families, with more loyalty to their own land holdings than to either Irish or English rulers.

As for those Irish chieftains and kings who refused to recognize English rights to their land, they just couldn't get their act together to oppose English claims with a united front. Instead, each Irish faction battled independently, with no central authority. Incessant warfare *did,* however, serve to concentrate the beleaguered English Crown forces in a heavily fortified area around Dublin known as "The Pale" and a few garrison towns around the country. Had not a pervasive religious dimension been thrown into the Irish stew, the Irish might have eventually managed to wrest control of their ancient land from British rulers. But King Henry VIII and the Reformation changed all that in the late 16th century.

An English "King of Ireland" and the Flight of the Earls Henry VIII brought to the throne of England a new approach to English rule in Ireland. Breaking with Rome, in 1541 he proclaimed himself King of Ireland by right of conquest rather than by papal decree. To convince those troublesome Irish and their Anglo-Irish cohorts of the legitimacy of his claim, he dubbed all opposition open rebellion against "their" king and set about driving rebel leaders from their lands, so that he might grant the properties to his loyal followers, be they English or Irish.

Enter religion on the scene in full battle array. By the time Elizabeth became queen, the Reformation was firmly entrenched in England and the staunchly Catholic Irish found themselves fighting for their religion with even more fervor than they had fought for their lands. The great chieftains led uprising after uprising and, when English forces proved too great, appealed to Spain for help in 1601 to make a decisive stand at Kinsale, in County Cork. The Spanish arrived and joined Irish forces to occupy the town, which was quickly surrounded by English troops. From up north, however, Irish chieftains O'Neill and O'Donnell mounted an epic winter march to come upon the British from behind. Hopes were high for an Irish victory, but it just wasn't in the cards.

As luck would have it, a drunken Irish soldier wandered into English hands and spilled the whole plan, enabling the English to win the day and send the brightest and best of the native chieftains into hiding, their lands in Ulster now confiscated *in toto* by the Crown and resettled by loyal—and Protestant—English and Scots. In 1608 the surviving Irish chieftains met in Rathmullen, County Donegal, and decided to set sail for the Continent as a body, vowing to return to fight another day—a vow never fulfilled. That "Flight of the Earls" marked the end of any effective organized resistance to English rule for generations.

Organized or not, the ornery Irish continued to harass the British with bloody attacks, always followed by even bloodier reprisals. Finally, in 1641, they mounted a long-planned offensive to retake the lands of Ulster, and thus brought down on the land one of the bloodiest episodes in Irish history, one mirrored across its landscape even today.

To Hell or Connaught By 1649 Irish incursions into Ulster and the massacre of hundreds of its Protestant settlers had so ravaged the land that Puritan general Oliver Cromwell arrived in force to squelch the rebellious Irish once and for all. Driven by religious fervor as well as political motives, Cromwell embarked on a campaign of devastation kicked off by the brutal slaying of more than 30,000 Irish men, women, and children at Drogheda.

From there, his trail of blood and destruction led to Wexford and thence across the country, leaving in its wake thousands dead, churches and castles and homes demolished, forests burned, and a degree of horror greater than any the Irish had known. Irish who escaped with their lives were shipped in the hundreds to work as slave labor on English plantations in the Sugar Islands—banishment to a virtual "hell"—or driven to the bleak, stone-strewn hills of Connaught.

To his loyal soldiers and their commanding officers, Cromwell awarded vast estates in the choice and fertile counties of the country. In the end, less than one-ninth of Irish soil remained in the hands of natives.

King Billy, the Treaty of Limerick, and the Penal Laws Irish spirits rose once more when a Catholic, James II, ascended to the English throne in 1688, and when he was deposed by supporters of William of Orange—King Billy—and fled to Ireland in 1689, they took up arms in his defense. In Ulster, Londonderry and Enniskillen became the major refuge for Protestants loyal to William, and the stout walls of Londonderry held against a 105-day siege by Jacobite forces. King Billy himself arrived in 1690 to lead his army to a resounding victory in the Battle of the Boyne, after which James once more took flight, leaving his Irish supporters to their own devices. Hoping to get the best possible terms of surrender, the Irish fought on under the leadership of Patrick Sarsfield until October of 1691, when they signed the Treaty of Limerick, which allegedly allowed them to retain both their religion and their land. Parliament, however, had no intention of sanctioning any sort of threat to the Protestant Ascendancy, and refused to ratify the treaty, instituting instead a series of measures so oppressive they became known as the Penal Laws.

Catholics, under the Penal Laws, were stripped of all civil and political rights—they could neither vote nor hold office; enter any of the professions, especially law; educate their children; own a horse valued at more than £5; bear arms; or (the origin of Ireland's tiny farmlands of today) will their land to only one son, being required instead to divide it into smaller plots for all male heirs. Forced to work the estates of absentee English landlords, Irish farmers paid enormous rents for the privilege of throwing up rude huts and using a small plot of ground to raise the potatoes that kept their families from starving.

It was a sorry state of affairs for the proud descendants of heroic kings and chieftains, and it was to last a full century.

United Irishmen, Union, Famine, and Emigration In the time-honored pattern of earlier Irish rulers, Anglo-Irish Protestants gradually came to feel a stronger allegiance to Ireland than to England, and in the late 1700s Henry Grattan led a Protestant Patriot party in demanding greater independence. What they got was a token Irish Parliament in 1782, which sat in Dublin but was controlled from London. Things seemed to be taking an upward turn as Penal Laws were gradually relaxed and trade began to flourish. Dublin's streets blossomed with the Georgian mansions and gracious squares that are still its most distinctive features.

Like a little learning, a little independence turned out to be a dangerous thing. With a newly independent France as a model, a group of Irishmen led by Protestant Wolfe Tone formed the Society of United Irishmen in 1791 to work for the establishment of a totally independent Irish republic. Enlisting military aid from France, Tone led a full-fledged insurrection in 1798 that ended in pure disaster on the battlefield and even greater disaster in the halls of the English Parliament.

British leaders now had the ammunition they needed to insist on ending any semblance of Irish parliamentary rule. Even so, it took considerable bribery, promises of seats in the London Parliament, and threats to get the Dublin MPs to vote the end of their supposed legislative power. But in 1800 the Act of Union passed and Ireland became an extension of British soil. That should have put Ireland in her proper place—again—but in 1803 the Irish were at it once more, and with Robert Emmet urging them on, they launched yet another uprising. It was the same old story, however, and ended with Emmet gallantly declaring from the gallows, "When my country takes her place among the nations of the earth, then, and not till then, let my epitaph be written."

In the 1820s a young Catholic named Daniel O'Connell started to make noises about Catholic Emancipation—a total repeal of the Penal Laws and the restoration of all Catholic civil rights. Elected to Parliament in 1828, he accomplished that goal the following year and embarked on a campaign for repeal of the Act of Union. About all he got for his efforts in that direction was the affectionate title of "The Liberator," and just as members of the Young Ireland movement were beginning to be heard on that score, tragedy struck and the Irish goal became one of simple survival.

It was in 1846 that a disastrous potato blight spread throughout the country, destroying the one food crop of most Irish families. Until 1849, crop after crop failed and a population of nearly nine million was reduced to a little over six million. Hundreds of thousands died of pure starvation—it became a common sight to see roadside ditches filled with bodies of famine victims who had nowhere else to die simply because they had been evicted from their wretched homes by landlords who continued to demand exorbitant rents from tenants who no longer had the means to pay them. Well over a million turned their backs on Ireland and set out for the United States and Canada on ships so overcrowded and filthy and disease-infested they were little more than floating coffins.

The Land League, Home Rule, and Sinn Fein By 1879 the Irish tenant farmers were so fed up with the oppressive rentals, which some had literally paid with their lives during the four years of famine, that they eagerly joined with Charles Stewart Parnell and Michael Davitt in forming a union known as the Land League.

They enlisted farmers around the country to strike back at any landlord who evicted tenants by the simple, but deadly effective, method of "boycott" (so called for the Captain Boycott against whom it was used for the first time). With their families shunned by an entire community and services of any kind cut off, landlords began to rethink their policies and to reduce rents to a fair level, grant some degree of guaranteed occupancy to tenants, and eventually to allow tenants to purchase their own acreage.

Far from being grateful for such small favors, the Irish continued to fan the flame of their inherited zeal for freedom from English rule. Parnell for years led an energetic campaign for Home Rule which would grant limited independence, but it wasn't until the eve of World War I that such a measure was adopted by the British. Even then, there was strong and vocal opposition by loyal Unionists in Ulster, Protestants all, who were determined to keep Ireland a part of the mother country. Outnumbered by Catholics, they feared Home Rule would become Rome Rule, and the Ulster Volunteers were formed to put up armed resistance against the equally determined Irish Republican Army, the military arm of Sinn Fein, a republican political party whose name is pronounced "Shin Fain" and means "ourselves alone." With the British army already firmly ensconced, the country fairly bristled with arms when everything was put on "hold" by the urgency of world conflict.

"A Terrible Beauty Is Born" To the astonishment of almost everyone—most of all, the Irish people—Easter Monday of 1916 put the whole question of Irish independence right back on a *very* hot front burner. Leading a scruffy, badly outfitted, and poorly armed little band of fewer than 200 patriots, Patrick Pearse and James Connolly marched up Dublin's O'Connell Street to the General Post Office and proceeded to occupy it in the name of a Provisional Government. Standing between the front pillars of the impressive building, Pearse read in stirring tones "The Proclamation of the Irish Republic to the People of Ireland." Behind him, his valiant little "army" prepared to dig in and hold their position as long as was humanly possible. Hopelessly small contingents were stationed at St. Stephen's Green and one or two other strategic points.

For six days following Pearse's proclamation, the post office stood embattled under the ancient symbol of Ireland (a golden harp on a pennant of brilliant green) and the Sinn Fein banner of green, white, and orange. The rebels numbered only about 1,000 all told, and their remarkable courage as they faced overwhelming British military might is the stuff of heroic legends—and, indeed, the very stuff of which Ireland's history is made!

It was a bloody, but unbowed, band that finally surrendered and was marched back down O'Connell Street to a future of prison or execution. Dubliners, many of them uncertain of where their loyalties lay, watched and waited to learn their fate. When Pearse, Connolly, and 14 others were executed by a firing squad and hundreds of others were imprisoned or exiled, Irish loyalties united behind their new Republic and world opinion stood solidly behind the ideal of Irish independence.

It was at that moment—as the executioners' gunsmoke cleared in Kilmainham Jail's yard—that Yeats was to proclaim "A terrible beauty is born."

In the years between 1916 and 1921 Britain tried every means at its disposal—including sending the ruthless Black and Tan mercenaries to terrorize the citizenry as well as rebels—to quell the rebellion, which continued to rumble even in defeat. In 1919, when Sinn Fein won a huge majority of parliamentary seats, they refused to go to London, but set up the National Parliament of Ireland in Dublin, which they christened the Dail (pronounced "Dawl" and meaning "meeting"). From then on, guerrilla warfare raged, replete with atrocities, ambush tactics, and assassinations. After two years of bitter bloodshed, a truce was finally called and negotiations began which ended in December of 1921 with the signing of the Anglo-Irish Treaty that named 26 counties as the Irish Free State. Still within the British Empire, it was to be self-governing in the same manner as Canada and other British dominions. Six counties in Ulster would remain—as they wished—an integral part of Great Britain and be ruled from London.

A Free State under the treaty terms was not, however, what many Irish believed they had been fighting for, and civil war raged until 1923. Eamon de Valera, at the head of the IRA, stood solidly against William Cosgrave's pro-treaty forces in the conviction that only a united Ireland which included all 32 counties was acceptable. Cosgrave and the newly formed government felt that the treaty terms were preferable to continued war with Britain and that in time the six counties of Northern Ireland would join the other 26 by constitutional means. That question still throws its divisive shadow over Ireland today.

Fighting between the two factions was made more bitter because it often pitted brother against brother and there was wholesale destruction of property. As it became clear that the Dublin government would endure, de Valera threw in the towel militarily and in three years' time had formed the Fianna Fail ("Feena Foil") party. When that party took office in 1932 the oath of allegiance to the British Crown was finally abolished, and in 1948 Great Britain formally declared Ireland outside the Commonwealth when a coalition government headed by John A. Costello declared that "the description of the State shall be the Republic of Ireland."

Onward and Upward Since the proud day it became truly independent, Ireland has set about catching up with the progress so long held at bay by her fight to become her own mistress. Efforts to develop Irish industry resulted in state companies such as Bord na Mona building a thriving business from one of the country's greatest natural resources, peat (or turf). Aer Lingus, the national airline, was established, and the Shannon Free Airport Development Company has developed one of the world's leading airports along with an industrial complex that attracts companies from all over the world. The Industrial Development Authority has assisted firms from the United States, Germany, Japan, Great Britain, and a score of other countries in setting up factories and processing plants (most of them remarkably *clean* industries) and providing employment opportunities for a new generation.

Along with all these developments, there have also been some interesting changes in demographics. In 1926, still feeling the decimation of its population by starvation and emigration that spanned a century following the famine of the 1840s, Ireland counted only 2.972 million inhabitants in its first official census. The vast majority lived in rural areas and looked to farming for a living.

A decline in population continued as recently as 1961, when the figures showed 2.818 million. Every census since then, however, showed a slight increase, with a 2.2% jump in the short period of 1979–1981. The 1981 report showed a population of 3.443 million and a shift in distribution. For example, Ireland now has one of Europe's youngest populations, with more than one-half under the age of 21, although the ranks of the young have been considerably thinned by emigration since 1986, as severe economic conditions have sent Irish youth abroad in search of jobs. More and more, the Irish are moving to towns and cities—or, to be more precise, to the metropolitan suburbs, since most Irish still cling to the notion of a private house with its own garden. Back in 1966, urban and rural populations were just about even, but in 1981 some 1.915 million lived in urban areas compared with 1.529 million in rural localities.

Luckily for you and me, along with industry, successive Irish governments have recognized the potential for tourism in this gloriously beautiful land. And why not, since they've been hosts to "visitors" in one form or another since the dawn of history! Bord Fáilté (the "board of welcomes") has worked closely with hoteliers, bed-and-breakfast ladies, restaurateurs, and entertainment facilities to see that we're well taken care of. And they've wisely insisted that the *character* of the country is as much an attraction for us as are the natural beauties and ancient relics we come to see.

Irish arts—theater, literature, painting, music—have seen a heartwarming revival, and people practicing ancient crafts are now producing works of beauty and utility to rival any in the world.

POLITICS

On the political front, Ireland steadfastly held on to its neutrality during World War II, even in the face of tremendous pressures from both Britain and the United States. Nevertheless, hundreds of Irishmen volunteered in the armed forces of both countries. Since 1955 Ireland has been a member of the United Nations and has sent peacekeeping forces to Cyprus, the Congo, the Sinai Desert, and Lebanon. As long as Northern Ireland remains under British rule, however, no Irish government has authorized NATO membership, since NATO is pledged to guarantee the territorial integrity of its members.

As a member of the European Union, Ireland shares in the joys and woes of the controversial alliance. With the rest of Europe, Ireland is busily gearing up for the integration of all 12 countries of the European Union into a single European market designed to simplify travel, trade, and—in due course—currency. (If you want to get a good "crack," or conversation, going almost anywhere in Ireland, just bring up the subject of EU membership—there are as many views on its results as there are Irish to discuss it!)

RELIGION

Religion has played an important role in Ireland from early times. Ireland has been a predominantly Catholic nation (see "A Look at the Past," above in this chapter). A little more than three million Irish in the Republic are members of the Roman Catholic Church, with an additional 700,000 Catholics living in Northern Ireland. There are four Catholic dioceses, with the archbishop of Armagh serving as Primate of all Ireland. Among Protestants, the Church of Ireland has some 375,000 members and Presbyterians number about 350,000, mostly in Northern Ireland. Methodists, Quakers, and Lutherans are represented in much smaller numbers. Most of the country's Jewish population (about 2,000) lives in Dublin or Belfast. A small Islamic community has its own mosque in Dublin.

4 The People

If it's hard to find words for Ireland itself, it's well nigh *impossible* to capture the personality of the people who live there. Flexible they most certainly are, to the point of a complexity that simply defies description. Warmhearted, witty, sometimes devious, filled with curiosity about visitors, deeply religious at Sunday's mass but the very devil in the pub on Saturday night, great talkers and even greater listeners, sometimes argumentative to the point of combativeness—and with it all, *friendly.* That's the Irish, all right. But it's the *style* in which they are all of the above that so delights when you visit them at home.

There's a certain panache about the Irish. Take, for example, the time I walked into a store in Cork and asked for a certain address, confessing that I was lost. With a smiling, sweeping bow, the owner allowed as how "You're lost no more, darlin', come with me." Whereupon he walked me to the building I was looking for several blocks away, chatting a steady stream and asking questions all the way. Now, *that's* panache!

Which is not to say, however, that you're going to be greeted at the airport by Irishmen rushing to bowl you over with all that chatter and charm. If there's anything they're not, it's intrusive—yours will have to be the first conversational move. But ask the first question, make the first comment, and you're off and running, your American accent an open invitation for the inevitable "And where in America would you be from?" followed up by the equally inevitable "Well, now, and didn't my own uncle Pat [or brother Joe or great-aunt Mary] go out to Chicago [or New York or Savannah or wherever it is you hail from]." And you're taken over by stories of the wandering relatives, more often than not over a pint or a cuppa with this perfect stranger who will, in his own good time, get around to what it was you wanted to know in the first place.

All the foregoing takes place, of course, in English. But it's the most melodic, lilting rendition of the language you'll ever hear. "Sure, the English gave us their language," say the Irish with a grin, "then we showed them how to use it." And they did, with writers like Jonathan Swift, Edmund Burke, Oscar Wilde, George Bernard Shaw, William Butler Yeats, James Joyce, and a host of others pouring out masterpieces of English prose as easily as most men tip the whisky jar. They're still at it today—I'll tell you about some of my favorite modern writers in Section 10 of this chapter. But your average Irishman—*or* woman—embellishes everyday conversation with all the eloquence of the greatest writers and with colorful, image-making phrases that would make any writer weep with envy. And they string them together in yarns that may be wildly fanciful but are never dull.

As for the celebrated Irish wit, Irish laughter creeps around words and phrases, then curls past curving lips to land in twinkling Irish eyes and a mischievous chuckle.

Tim Pat Coogan, in his excellent book *Ireland and the Arts,* suggests that the Irish have used their words and their wit as both a sly release from and effective weapon against cruel oppression suffered over long centuries of invasion and foreign rule. There's truth in that, for in today's Ireland—as another Irish writer in an *Inside Ireland* article stated categorically—"Exaggeration and lighthearted blasphemy are national pastimes."

There's more to the Irish, of course, than talk. There's the strong religious influence that passed from Celtic to Catholic rites without a hitch. And the fascinating mix of Celt, Viking, Norman, and Saxon blood that has melded into an "Irish" race of brunettes, blonds, and redheads. And the paradoxical nature that led Chesterton to write: "All their wars are merry, and all their songs are sad."

Mary Moran, up in Castlebar, County Mayo, passed along to me (and to other guests at her Lakeview House B&B) an unsigned poem that probably comes as close as anyone can to describing the Irish in these lines:

He's wild and he's gentle,
He's good and he's bad,
He's proud and he's humble,
He's happy and sad.
He's in love with the ocean,
  the earth and the skies,
He's enamored with beauty
  wherever it lies.
He's victor and victim, a star and a clod,
But mostly he's Irish,
In love with his God.

As I said, that's *close.* But it's a safe bet you'll go home thinking of "the Irish" in terms of John or Kitty or Siubhan or Michael—and you'll be as close as any poet can ever come!

5 Art, Architecture & Literature

ART

Visual art, in its many forms, has been nurtured and has flourished in Ireland from the very beginning. Indeed, even such utilitarian structures as the prehistoric burial chamber at Newgrange were embellished with artistic spirals and mystical designs. During the great metal-working age, exquisite chalices, pins, brooches, necklaces, and combs were designed with an eye to beauty as well as utility. In the 8th and 9th centuries in Ireland's great monastic seats of learning, Celtic designs were used to adorn the pages of important historical and literary works, such as the epic *Book of Kells.* That influence can still be traced in the work of many artists and craftspeople of the 20th century despite its virtual disappearance during the centuries when the country was overrun by Viking and Norman forces.

With the arrival of the 18th century there was a resurgence of the arts in Ireland, but painters and sculptors turned to landscape and other European painting styles. The introduction of a wealthy landowning class had a tremendous effect, since many of its members had both the means and the leisure to indulge their artistic talents and to encourage native-born artists. Irish painters traveled to London and continental capitals, many subsidized by wealthy patrons.

By the late 19th century, leading Irish painters such as John Lavery and Jack B. Yeats (brother of W. B. Yeats, the poet) had embraced the impressionist school of painting. Artists Sean O'Sullivan, Sean Keating, and Maurice MacGonigal led the flight from impressionism into realism during the 1930s, and they were, in turn, displaced by Anne Madden and Louis LeBrocquy when they, along with a few others, introduced modernism to Ireland in the 1940s. More recently, expressionist Michael Kane and one or two other painters have added yet another dimension.

Today, Ireland has a large body of artists working in a wide range of media, bringing a new vibrancy to the visual arts scene with the addition of video and film to the traditional art forms of painting and sculpture. Oisin Kelly, Connor Fallon, John Behan, and Jim Connolly in the Republic, as well as Carolyn Mulholland and

F. E. McWilliams in Northern Ireland, are leading contemporary sculptors. Among modern painters to look for are Pauline Bewick, James Scanlon, Camille Souter, Brian Burke, and Robert Ballagh in the Republic, and T. P. Flanagan, Gerard Dillon, and George Campbell in Northern Ireland.

Dublin's National Gallery and Municipal Gallery are important showcases, and Belfast has the Ulster Museum and Arts Council galleries. In both cities, there are a score of smaller private galleries. In Cork, there's the Crawford Gallery, and other major cities, such as Limerick and Waterford in the Republic and Derry in Northern Ireland, have frequent showings of contemporary and classical art. Be on the lookout, too, for the several excellent small private galleries like the Frank Lewis Gallery in Killarney and Raymond Klee's studio/gallery in Ballylickey, County Cork. Smaller towns often are venues for short-term exhibitions of Irish art, both contemporary and classic.

ARCHITECTURE

Ireland's earliest settlers probably lived in wooden huts, traces of which have disappeared into the mists of time. Excavations have revealed, however, that some lived in *crannogs,* or lake dwellings on artificially created islands. Although there are no remains of actual Iron Age dwellings, great circular earthworks known as *lisses* or *raths* and stone enclosures known as *cahers* have been found to be homesteads as well as fortified centers. Prehistoric Dun Beg on the Dingle Peninsula and Dun Aengus on the Aran Islands are survivors of this period, and the reconstructed crannog at Craggaunowen, in County Clare, presents a vivid picture of the daily life of lake dwellers.

It was during the early Christian age (700–1150) that enduring structures such as *clochans,* the small stone beehive cells of ecclesiastics, appeared. The most impressive surviving examples are to be found on Skellig Michael, County Kerry, and near Slea Head on the Dingle Peninsula. They were soon followed by churches, round towers, and oratories. Outstanding examples of this type of architecture (sometimes called Hiberno-Romanesque because of the barrel-vaulted ceilings that introduced the arch to Irish architecture) are Cormac's chapel on the Rock of Cashel, St. Kevin's church at Glendalough, and the Gallarus Oratory on the Dingle Peninsula. Most of Ireland's non-church-related residents lived in simple one-room cabins with walls of clay or stone, thatched roofs, dirt floors, and few (if any) windows.

During the Anglo-Norman period (1170–1700), the castles that are so much a part of Ireland's landscape cropped up all over the land. Most are fortified dwellings consisting of simple square towers with slit windows, though some have curtain walls with corner towers enclosing a central courtyard. Bunratty, Dublin, and Carrickfergus castles are well-preserved remnants of the castle-building era. Stout town walls of stone were also constructed during this period, and traces remain in Waterford, Wexford, Drogheda, Clonmel, Limerick, and Derry, where city walls are still intact. The humble mud or stone cabin was expanded to more than one room, and sometimes to an upper floor. Villages sported simple public houses and shops grouped around a square, or "green," and many were planned by wealthy landowners as a convenient source of labor for their vast estates. Kilkenny's Rothe House, which dates from 1594, is an excellent example of a well-to-do merchant's home.

Between 1680 and 1684, Ireland's first significant public building, the Royal Hospital at Kilmainham in Dublin, was constructed.

The 18th century saw a great wave of building and ornamentation. Castletown House is an outstanding example of the classical style that began to appear. Also of interest are many fine examples of the Palladian style, led by Dublin's Parliament House (now the Bank of Ireland) in 1729, the Custom House, and the Four Courts. This is also the period in which Dublin's renowned Georgian squares—St. Stephen's Green, Merrion Square, Fitzwilliam Square, Mountjoy Square, and Parnell Square—made their appearance. Cork (the Summerhill area, Camden Place, and the Ursuline Convent at Blackrock) and Limerick (the Custom House, the Town Hall, the crescent on O'Connell Street, Patrick Street, and St. John's Square) both have noteworthy examples of Georgian architecture. James Gandon (who designed the Custom House, Four Courts, and King's Inns) was one of Ireland's most prominent architects of this period. Others of importance were Francis Johnston (the General Post Office, St. George's Church, and the chapel in Dublin Castle), Richard Castle (Powerscourt, Leinster House, Russborough, and other fine private residences), and Francis Bindon, who collaborated with Castle on the design for Dublin's Rotunda Hospital.

By 1839 architecture had become so well established as a profession that the Royal Institute of Architects of Ireland was founded. The 1800s also saw a spate of church building, and for the first time, large-scale housing developments and industrial complexes were designed. In rural areas, improvements were made in the traditional cottage, as more windows made them brighter and slate or other materials created more durable roofs than thatch.

In Ireland, as in so many other parts of the world, 20th-century architecture has tended toward sameness, with modern bungalows springing up alongside the abandoned traditional cottage in the countryside, suburban housing estates built to standard specifications, and tall glass-and-steel structures dotting urban skylines. A distinctive modern Irish style has not yet crystallized, although architects such as Liam McCormick, in his church designs, have perhaps taken the first steps in that direction.

LITERATURE

Literature in Ireland has a long and rich history. The written word in literary form dates all the way back to the 6th century, but long before monks began their laborious transcribing in Ireland's monasteries, a bardic oral storytelling tradition reached back into prehistory, with glorious tales of fierce battles, passionate love affairs, and heroic deeds, related in both prose and poetry. It was, in fact, from that treasure trove of oral literature that the monks drew their first recorded stories. *Tain Bo Cuailgne* (The Cattle Raid of Cooley), *Lebor na Huidre* (The Dun Cow), and *Lebor Laigen* (The Book of Leinster) preserve the exploits, triumphs, and tragedies of such legendary figures as Finn MacCool and his Fiannan band, Cuchulainn, Oisin, and the beautiful Deirdre. These were written in Irish, which continued to be the dominant language of Irish literature until the 17th century and was widely used right up to the beginning of the 19th century.

In the early 7th century, the epic *Cuirt an Mhean Oiche* (Midnight Court) was a masterful satire by Brian Merriman on the strong aversion to marriage held by Irish men, while the *Annals of the Four Masters,* written by Franciscans under the direction of layman Michael O'Clery, and *Foras Feasa ar Eirinn* (History of Ireland), by Geoffrey Keating, both dealt with Irish history. Also notable during this period were the works of Padraigin Haicead, Daibhidh O'Bruadair, Egan O'Rahilly, Michael Comyn, and on a lighter note, the witty works of the blind poet Raftery and the roguish Owen Roe O'Sullivan.

By the end of the 17th century the Anglo-Irish literary movement was well launched, and during the 1700s such Irish writers as Oliver Goldsmith (*She Stoops to Conquer, The Vicar of Wakefield*) and Richard Brinsley Sheridan (*The School for Scandal, The Rivals*) penned English-style drawing-room comedies and English-manners novels. At the same time, Jonathan Swift—then dean of St. Patrick's Cathedral—was verbally flaying the English with his satires (*A Modest Proposal, A Tale of a Tub,* and *Gulliver's Travels*).

In the 1800s Maria Edgeworth (*Castle Rackrent*) joined the ranks of outstanding Anglo-Irish writers, as did Thomas Moore, Gerald Griffin, William Carleton, and James Clarence Mangan. The brilliant Oscar Wilde (*The Picture of Dorian Gray, The Importance of Being Earnest*), living and writing in London, suffered scandal, imprisonment, and poverty when his flamboyant lifestyle did him in. Toward the end of that century, dramatist George Bernard Shaw and novelist George Moore began brilliant careers that were to spill over into the next, as did poet William Butler Yeats and playwright John Millington Synge. On a smaller scale, two cousins living in West Cork, Edith Somerville and Violet Martin, were turning out comic sketches of Protestant life in rural Ireland and the notable "Big House" novel *The Real Charlotte.* Novelist Bram Stoker, on the other hand, loosed *Dracula* on the literary public.

The 20th century has brought with it a veritable explosion of literary talent in Ireland. Although three decades of the mid-1900s—1929 to 1959—were clouded by the oppressive Censorship Act that drove many Irish writers to foreign publishers, their vitality never flagged. Sean O'Casey's *Shadow of a Gunman, Juno and the Paycock,* and *The Plough and the Stars* put him in the forefront of Irish dramatists. Samuel Beckett, living in exile, was awarded the Nobel Prize, and Brendan Behan enjoyed an all-too-short burst of fame. James Joyce, who had to leave Dublin before he could write about it, is thought by many to be the greatest Irish writer of the 20th century.

As the last decade of this century begins, playwrights Hugh Leonard, Brian Friel, Bernard Farrell, Thomas Murphy, John B. Keane, and Frank McGuinness continue the tradition of dramatic excellence. Novelists and short story writers Ben Kiely, James Plunkett, Mary Lavin, John Banville, Francis Stuart, Edna O'Brien, John McGahern, Molly Keane, Dermot Bolger, and Maeve Binchy add their names to the list of such 20th-century greats as Frank O'Connor, Kate O'Brien, Sean O'Faolain, Brian O'Nolan (who used the pen names Myles na gCopaleen and Flann O'Brien), and Elizabeth Bowen. Christy Brown's brilliant autobiographical novels portraying life in the Dublin slums as seen through the eyes of a severely handicapped boy (*Down All the Days* and *My Left Foot*) stand in a literary class of their own. W. B. Yeats and Patrick Kavanagh head the list of distinguished 20th-century poets, with Thomas Kinsella, John Montague, and Seamus Heaney the most prominent of contemporary poets.

One last word: Your Irish reading should by no means be restricted to the authors listed here. There are scores of talented Irish writers hard at work—most to an extraordinarily high standard. So browse the bookshops, pick up any titles you find intriguing, and who knows—you may well discover the next "big name" on Ireland's literary scene.

6 Myths, Legends & Folklore

If you find yourself spellbound by that renowned Irish way with words, consider this: Every Irish child is born into and raised in an environment of storytelling—and it's been thus since man first walked the land. In the days of the great tribes, there were the *bards,* poets adept at singing the praises of each chieftain, often reciting from memory his lineage for generations on end. Later, every village had its resident *seanachai,* a storyteller who presided over long evenings around the hearth, telling and re-telling tales of larger-than-life heroes, gods and goddesses, and "little people." Every story was embellished with the most fantastic asides and details.

Of course, those ancient storytellers had some pretty great material. Beginning with the beginning, the early bards and seanachies told of three distinct racial groups involved in Ireland's early history: the "men of the quiver" (the Fir Bolg); the "men of the territory" (the Fir Domhnann), and the "men of Gaul" (the Fir Gaileoin). The legends of the seanachies are a delightful blend of fact, fancy, and mysticism. In a fit of revisionist history, they even came up with a quite satisfactory rationale for the shared traits of Irish and Scottish Celts. All were, these storytellers reckoned, descended from one man, Mileadh (Milesius), and they could look back in their lineage to one Gadelius and a lady know as Scota.

Some of the oldest legends tell of the coming of the Celts. Leinster was named for the iron-bladed spears *(laighens)* of the Celts, the bards explained. Other stories speak of the brave deeds of Conaire Mor, King of Ireland in the 2nd century B.C. The hero we know as Finn MacCool was born as Fionn MacCumhail in a blaze of glorified chivalry and courage as gigantic as the fictitious man himself. His faithful Fianna warrior band matched their leader in feats of bravery and daring.

There were tales of the Knights of the Red Branch in the north and of the Ulster hero, Cuchulainn. Queen Maeve, who ruled Connaught, and the tragic Deirdre of the Sorrows were chief among the heroines who figured in song and story. Every schoolchild in Ireland can tell you of the poor, tragic Children of Lir, who were turned into swans by a jealous stepmother and forced to wander the lakes and rivers of Ireland "until a noblewoman from the south would marry a nobleman from the north," for which event they had to wait nine hundred years to end their feathery exile. To this day, swans are a protected species in Ireland and are much beloved by all.

Then, of course, there are those "otherworld" tales. Like the mystical *Tuatha Dé Danann* (people of the goddess Dana), endowed with magical powers, who, in defeat at the hands of the Milesians, struck a bargain to divide Ireland between them, the Milesians residing above ground, and the Dé Dannans moving underground in *lios* (earthen hill forts), *cairns* (stone mounds), or even under hawthorn bushes. There, they inhabit grand palaces; indulge in fabulous feasts; and emerge at night for wild horseback rides, hunts, and football games, the story goes.

As Christianity gained a stronger and stronger foothold, the story of the *Tuatha Dé Danann* began to pale, and gradually they evolved into fairies (the people of the Sidhe)—those cunning little fellows we know as the wily *leprechauns* who hoard crocks of gold are believed to be their shoemakers. Fairies, it is said, move freely among humans, sometimes in human or animal form, other times garbed in their cloaks of invisibility. Disturb one of their dwelling places at your peril—great harm is certain to come to you and yours forevermore—no one in their right mind would risk disturbing a fairy field, bush, or mound!

Great tales, those, but do the Irish *really* believe them? I don't know. But I *can* tell you that to my Irish friends—even those who scoff the loudest—those legendary heroes are as alive and well in their minds and hearts today as when the bards of old spun their tales. You won't catch anyone *I* know taking a shortcut through a fairy field at night or hacking down a fairy bush!

7 The Irish Language

The lilting Irish language—complex and rhythmical—is rich in words and phrases that defy translation. From personal experience, I can tell you that this is one of the hardest languages on the face of the earth to get your tongue around—and one of the most rewarding when you master even a few words.

One of Western Europe's four original languages, Irish falls into the Gaelic branch of the Celtic tongue. Much like the Gaelic of Scotland, it's related to Welsh, to Breton, and to ancient Gaulish. Called "Irish" to distinguish it from other forms of Gaelic, it's the oldest written vernacular in Europe. Until the middle of the 19th century, it was the common spoken language in Ireland. Its decline, however, was rapid. By the beginning of the 20th century, it was largely confined to rather isolated areas in the south, west, and northwest. Academics such as Douglas Hyde (who eventually became the Republic's first president) and others of like mind founded the Gaelic League and managed to keep the language alive through those dark years. With the coming of independence, Irish became the country's official language, reclaiming an Irish identity nearly lost during long years of suppression; since 1922, Irish has been taught in all schools. State and semi-state agencies generally require a working knowledge of Irish for employment. The Irish-language radio station, Raidio na Gaeltachta, will be joined in late 1996 by an Irish-language television station. Irish takes first place on street signs, city and town name signs, and in governmental titles such as Taoiseach ("tee-shuck") for the prime minister or gardai ("guardee") for police or guards. Radio and television stations broadcast daily news reports ("Nuacht") and sign off in the native tongue.

Today, although the vast majority of the Irish use English as their first tongue, there are some 40,000 Irish speakers who use English only occasionally. Most live in closely knit communities called the Gaeltacht ("Gwale-tuct"), often in rural, rather isolated locations in the west. Donegal, Dingle, and Connemara form the largest part of the Gaeltacht, where natives will readily converse with you in English, with asides in Irish to their friends and neighbors.

8 Irish Cuisine: From Boiled Bacon to Guinness

For centuries, the Irish—sometimes by choice, sometimes from necessity—seemed to eat simply to exist, without much thought to anything beyond a basic diet of little more than tons of boiled potatoes and gallons of buttermilk. Before you begin to pity them *too* much, however, wait until you've tasted a real Irish potato—its mealy innards have a taste far superior to any grown on this side of the Atlantic, and when slathered with rich, golden butter, there just isn't much better eating. I must confess I could make a meal of them any day.

Be that as it may, however, while most of my Irish friends still make the potato a main part of their daily diet, these days the old spud comes to the table roasted, baked, mashed, or in the form of french fries. And far from being the main dish, it is strictly an accompaniment to local veal, beef, and lamb, or salmon (fresh and/or smoked), prawns, plaice, or trout from Ireland's abundant waters. Tender, sweet lettuce, tomatoes that taste of the sun, and cucumbers the size of our squash go into fresh salads, and vegetables both homegrown and from the gardens of Spain or Israel complete the heaping plates of "mains." Bread? It's that famous soda or brown bread, freshly baked and many times still warm, just waiting to be spread with pure, golden butter. Starters can be thick, tasty barley, beef, or vegetable soup or shrimp cocktail or homemade pâté or small portions of that wonderful smoked salmon. Desserts tend to be apple or rhubarb tart or sherry trifle, all topped with lashings of sweet, rich fresh cream. Tea, of course, comes in a bottomless pot to pour endless cups. All pretty plain foods, all wholesome, and all in *gigantic* portions.

That's in Irish homes. As for Irish restaurants, they've come a long way from the times when "chefs" were simply cooks who had moved from the home hearth into hotel dining rooms, small tea rooms, or the few fancy eateries concentrated mostly in Dublin. Today's chefs are likely to have been trained in leading culinary schools on the Continent or in one of Ireland's excellent hotel-training institutions. Menus are more varied than I ever thought I'd see in this land of plain-food eaters. International cuisine is available not only in Dublin, but in all the larger cities and many small villages tucked away beside the sea or in the basement of a mansion on the grounds of Bunratty Castle. French, Italian, Chinese, and even Russian restaurants are to be found, along with some very good ones that serve wonderfully prepared native dishes. More and more restaurants are offering vegetarian dishes. It is even possible nowadays to get a decent cup of coffee in many restaurants, although I find (even as a confirmed coffee hound at home) the tea in Ireland is so much better that I seldom long for coffee.

There are several native foods you should be sure not to miss while you're in Ireland. For me, dairy products top the list: never have I tasted butter or cream to compare with Ireland's. And if you're a cheese lover, you'll find some excellent cheddars made by creamery co-ops as well as commercial firms (I make it a practice to ask the locals about cheeses made in their locality, and I've struck real gold in Kerry's mountains as well as Waterford's fertile fields). Smoked salmon is not only a delicacy, it's *affordable* in Ireland, and you can gorge yourself to your heart's content. Dublin Bay prawns are a "don't miss," as is plaice, a freshwater fish served all over the country. Small-town bakeries often have soda bread for sale fresh from the oven, as well as some cream-filled pastries that are as light as a feather and as sweet as heaven itself.

But as pennypinchers, our main interest is in satisfying each day's hunger on the budget we've set for ourselves, and believe me, you'll do that and eat *well.* So well, in fact, that I'll wager you'll be able to treat yourself to at least one pricey meal in the Big Splurge restaurant of your choice. Remember, you're going to begin every day with a mammoth breakfast that will either carry you over all the way to dinner or at the very least call for only a light midday repast. Remember, too, that if you're staying in B&Bs, it is probable that you'll be served tea and scones or cake along about ten o'clock in the evening, and it won't cost you a cent!

Incidentally, the tea you'll be served all along your Irish travels is downright habit-forming, with a hearty, robust flavor that could make you foreswear coffee for all time. If you should find yourself addicted, you'll be glad to know that it can grace your own breakfast table (or midnight tray) when you get back home. Richard Bewley and his wife, Jo, members of the famed Bewley's tea and coffee shops family in Dublin, now live in the U.S. and have established a mail-order business for Bewley's tea and other Irish products. While they're primarily importers and wholesale distributors, they'll be happy to send you their mail-order catalog, as well as let you know if there's a shop in your area that carries their imports. Prices for the tea are quite reasonable, and there's no better memory-nudger than a steaming "cuppa" the Bewley's brew. Contact Bewley Irish Imports, 1130 Greenhill Rd., West Chester, PA 19380 (☎ 215/696-2682; fax 215/344-7618).

Ah, drink! The delight and the despair of the Irish! At least, that's the press they get. The truth of it is that they *do*, indeed, enjoy their drink, and Ireland surely has its fair share of dyed-in-the-wool alcoholics. On the other hand, it's tea you'll be offered as often as Guinness—and nonalcoholic drinks rank right up there with the hard stuff in homes as well as pubs.

In the past few years, several brands of bottled Irish spring water have appeared on the market. Ballygowan leads the pack; lightly carbonated, it comes plain and with a variety of flavors (my personal favorite is lime) and is a deliciously refreshing drink. Most pubs now stock Ballygowan, and it has proved to be very popular with locals, both young and old, as has Tipperary spring water.

Other nonalcoholic drinks include most sodas (call them "minerals") you know at home—Coca-Cola, etc.—plus a fizzy white lemonade or an orange drink that are both very popular.

Order a pint in an Irish pub and what you'll get—unless you specify otherwise—is Guinness, the rich, dark Irish stout served with a white, creamy head that—if it's a properly pulled pint—will last right down to the last drop.

The question of who pulls the best pint in Dublin, Killarney, Cork, etc., is a continually debated subject; and if your pint arrives just seconds after you order it, you may be very sure that *your* bartender is not among those in the running. There is a subtle, delicate art to drawing the stout, so be prepared to wait.

Guinness is Ireland's oldest brewery, dating back to 1759, and the stout is still brewed in its original location at St. James's Gate in Dublin and available on draft or bottled in every pub worthy of the name in Ireland.

Irish whisky was first distilled in 1609 at the Bushmill's plant in County Antrim, as it is even today. "Black Bush" is the affectionate name for 12-year-old Bushmill's, while that matured for only seven years goes by the name of the distillery. Other favorite brands are Jameson and Paddy. All are wonderfully smooth served on the rocks or neat, without ice. On a cold and/or rainy day nothing quite beats a hot whiskey (sugar, whiskey, hot water, lemon, and cloves). Unless, that is, it's the ever-popular Irish coffee. And because I knew you'd want to know, here are instructions for making it at home: Fill a large, stemmed glass with hot water, then empty when glass is warm. Pour in one full jigger of Irish whisky and add at least one teaspoon sugar (the more sugar, the more the cream rises to the top). Add hot black coffee (the hotter, the better) to about an inch from the top and stir. Top it off with lightly whipped cream (there's an art to doing that—pour the cream over the back of a spoon and just sort of float it off over the sides into the glass.

Lagers (beers) popular in Ireland are Harp, Budweiser, Carlsberg, and Murphy. Smithwick's is a popular ale. Dry cider has enjoyed an upsurge in popularity in recent years, with Stag topping the list. Among low-alcohol drinks, the one most called for is a fruity wine called West Coast Cooler.

Until the last ten years or so, sherry and port were about the only wines you were likely to encounter in Ireland. Not so these days. Most large supermarkets and all off-license shops now stock a respectable variety of wines from around the world. Spanish, Italian, and French wines are readily available, and show up regularly on Irish dinner tables. Most pubs also keep both red and white wine on hand.

9 Irish Pubs

A wise man once said that "a pub is the poor man's university." That it certainly is in Ireland! And it's an ongoing education as you encounter pubgoers from different regions and walks of life, each with an outlook on life, politics, religion, and any other subject as individual as his looks, and a highly developed personal way with words to expound on any of the above.

There's more to it than just that, however. Out in rural areas, the local pub is the social center around which everything revolves. What gossip and news isn't picked up at the creamery is dispensed as freely as a pint in the pub. Personal decisions that must be weighed and finally made are a topic of general conversation in which everyone present lights up the problem with his own particular perspective. I once spent the better part of an afternoon in a small County Waterford pub absolutely fascinated by the dilemma posed by the fact that a wedding and a funeral were both scheduled for the following day—after about two hours of wrestling with the problem of which to attend, my fellow imbibers *still* hadn't reached a conclusion when I reluctantly picked myself up and moved on. But I can tell you that there are aspects to that agonizing decision I'd never dreamed of before that afternoon!

Pubs are, by and large, also where you're most likely to find traditional music and song in the "singing pubs" that bring in leading musical groups or give performing space to the local lads aiming in that direction. It must be added that you're just as likely to find the familiar twang of country and western hits as the impassioned lyrics of Ireland's native music. Even if a pub is *not* known for music, however, the lyrical Irish spirit frequently bursts its bounds in the country's drinking places, especially toward the end of the evening, when a fiddle or tin whistle suddenly appears and song just sort of erupts—along with reams of poetry that can be from the classics or entirely spontaneous, depending on the clientele.

The pubs themselves range over a wide spectrum of décor. In cities like Dublin and Belfast you can have a jar in an ornate Victorian-style drinking establishment; a glitzed up chrome-and-mirrored abyss of pseudosophistication; an oldtime pub replete with time-worn wood, etched glass, and touches of brass; an elegant hotel bar that is considered a pub despite its fancy getup; or a bare-bones drinking place which depends on its colorful "regulars" for whatever décor might exist. Out in the country, a pub might well be one half of a grocery or hardware store; a traditional-style pub that's been dispensing drink and hospitality since the days of coaching inns; a cozy, wallpapered, and carpeted appendage to a guesthouse or small hotel; or a large barnlike room with linoleum on the floor and a telly behind the bar.

There are still pubs around with little blocked-off private rooms called "snugs" and lovely old etched-glass partitions along the bar to afford a bit of privacy. In some pubs, the dart board stays busy; in others, there's almost always a card game in progress; some keep the fireplace glowing. Most will have a main bar and an attached "lounge," which once was the only place you'd ever catch a female in what was exclusively a man's domain. Nowadays, the lounges are filled with couples of all ages, as well as singles (even males who, for one reason or another, prefer not to elbow it at the bar).

Pub etiquette is a delicate and complex matter, and your awareness of some of its intricacies can spell the difference between a night of unsurpassed conviviality and one of cool isolation that leaves you wondering where all that famed Irish pub joviality is to be found. Novelist and radio newscaster David Hanly once laid down the one vital ground rule that should see you safely through those first few minutes when you enter what many Irishmen consider their own personal club. He was writing about Dublin pubs, but the rule applies across the board: "If you are to be accompanied on this jaunt, choose a partner who is loud neither in dress nor in voice. Dubliners abominate strange noises in their pubs, and high, demanding voices—no matter what the accent—carry deadly imperial echoes." Need I comment that his reference to "partner" was a typically Irish, backdoor way of saying that *you* should tread softly?

So keeping your voice and manners suitably moderated, you take your place at the bar, order your brew (*never* a fancy mixed cocktail unless you're in one of those city hotel bars mentioned above) and gradually—oh, so gradually—drift into conversation by way of a question. You're on your own as far as the question is concerned; it doesn't really matter so long as you project a real need for assistance that only a local can provide. Inquiries about the best place to eat, the best traditional music group around, etc., will do just fine and open up a general conversation likely to run the length of the bar, with everyone in attendance anxious to lend a hand to a visiting Yank.

The times and economic pressures are slowly eroding one facet of Irish drinking etiquette that was once inviolate, that of "buying the round." That ritual consisted of each member in a drinking group picking up the tab for a round of drinks for everybody. It was (still *is* in many places) as deadly a breach of manners to leave *after* you'd paid for your round as before your turn rolled around. Everybody drank until everybody had bought his round. Keep that in mind should you run into drinking companions, however casual your acquaintance, who insist that you'll not be permitted to pay for your first drink at all; the round-buying tradition requires that you hang in there until your check-paying turn arrives and stay the course.

The only exception to the above routine concerns women. In all my years of visiting Ireland, I've only insisted on buying my round once, and my male drinking companions were so uncomfortable with the whole thing that I've resolved to relax and go with local custom without the slightest twinge of guilt. As I said, however, what with the high price of the pint these days, round-buying is disappearing from the Irish pub scene, with everyone buying his own more often than not.

One Last Word to the Women You'll be very welcome in Irish pubs, whether you're on your own, with a group of females, or with a male escort. You may, however, be more comfortable in the lounge than at the bar (that varies from pub to pub, so try to size up the place when you first come in). Even being a non-drinker is no reason for missing out on pub sociability: all Irish pubs stock soft drinks that go by the name of "minerals" (try the light, fizzy white lemonade) and nobody is going to look askance if you stick to those.

3

Planning a Trip to Ireland

This chapter may well contain the most important words between the book's covers. Not the most exciting, perhaps, but certainly careful reading of this part of your "homework" can make all the difference in whether you get back home bubbling over with happy memories unmarred by uninformed mistakes or slightly bewildered that you never *did* get to do and see the things you really wanted to.

1 Visitor Information & Entry Requirements

VISITOR INFORMATION

The native hospitality of the Irish begins long before you embark on your visit to their shores, and few countries send you off as well prepared as Ireland. The friendly folk at any branch of the Irish Tourist Board (Bord Fáilté, in Ireland) take their literal name, Board of Welcomes, quite seriously. They're an official government agency that somehow seems to escape the impersonal don't-care attitude that so often pervades bureaucratic institutions. My best advice (even if you're in the beginning stages of just *thinking* about an Irish holiday) is to hie yourself down to the ITB office (or contact them by mail or telephone) and plug in to one of the most helpful organizations in the ranks of international tourism.

On this side of the Atlantic, they'll supply you with literature to help with your initial planning, answer any questions that may come up, advise you on tracing your Irish ancestry, arrange for you to meet Irish families, and generally see to it that you're off to a good start.

TOURIST BOARD OFFICES

The **Irish Tourist Board** has offices in the following locations:

- **In New York** 345 Park Ave., New York, NY 10154 (☎ 800/223-6470 or 212/418-0800; fax 212/371-9052).
- **In Toronto** 160 Bloor St. East, Suite 1150, Toronto, ONT, M4W 1B9 (☎ 416/929-2777; fax 416/929-6783).
- **In London** 150 New Bond St., London W1Y OAQ (☎ 171/493-3201).
- **In Sydney** 36 Carrington St., 5th Level, Sydney, NSW 2000 (☎ 02/299-6177; fax 02/299-6323).

- **In Ireland** Baggot Street Bridge, Dublin 2, Ireland (☎ 01/676-5871; fax 01/676-4764). Send postal inquires to P.O. Box 273, Dublin 8.
- **In Northern Ireland** 53 Castle St., Belfast BT1 1GH (☎ 1232/327-888; fax 1232/240-201), and 8 Bishop St., Londonderry (☎ 1504/369-501).

Offices for the Northern Ireland Tourist Board are as follows:

- **In New York** 551 Fifth Ave., Suite 701, New York, NY 10176 (☎ 212/922-0101 or 800-NITB-1995; fax 212/922-0099).
- **In Toronto** 111 Avenue Rd., Suite 450, Toronto, Ontario M5R 3J8 (☎ 416/925-6368; fax 416/961-2175).
- **In London** All Ireland Desk, British Travel Centre, 12 Regent St., Picadilly Circus, London SW1 4PQ (☎ 171/824-8000).
- **In Ireland** 16 Nassau Street, Dublin 2 (☎ 01/679-1977 or 800/230-230).
- **In Northern Ireland** 59 North St., Belfast BT1 1NB (☎ 1232/246-609; fax 1232/240-960).

Tourist Board Publications and Information Sheets

The Irish Tourist Board's informative publications include booklets about trip planning covering accommodations (the Town & Country Association booklet has photos of individual homes); farm holidays (also illustrated with photos); self-catering accommodations (including photos); dining; special events; and historical sightseeing. And they can provide a good map showing scenic routes.

The board also issues information sheets that are concise, detailed reports on everything from sailing schools to hiking to museums to folk music.

Newsletters and Magazines

Inside Ireland is a quarterly newsletter written especially for the likes of you and me who want to keep up with what's going on in Ireland. Its publisher, Dubliner Brenda Weir, is an expert on many far-ranging subjects.

You get a sample copy by sending $3, or send $40 for a year's subscription, to *Inside Ireland,* P.O. Box 1886, Dublin 16 (☎ 01/493-1906; fax 01/493-4538).

Another publication that will keep your Irish memories fresh is *Ireland of the Welcomes,* a bimonthly magazine published by the Irish Tourist Board. Beautifully produced and illustrated, each issue has features by some of the country's leading writers, as well as those of other nationalities, but always on a subject intimately connected with Ireland. The cost is a mere $21 for a year's subscription, $37 for two years. Contact P.O. Box 2745, Boulder, Colorado 80322 (☎ 800/876-6336).

Irish Embassies & Consulates

- **Australia** The Irish Consulate is at 20 Arkana St., Yarralumla, Canberra, 2600 ACT (☎ 062/733-0222).
- **Canada** The Irish Consulate is at 170 Metcalfe St., Ottawa K2P 1P3, Ontario (☎ 613/745-8624).
- **Great Britain** 17 Grosvenor Pl., London SWIX 7HR (☎ 171/235-2171).
- **New Zealand** Contact the Irish Consulate in Canberra, Australia (see above).
- **The United States** The Embassy of Ireland is at 2234 Massachusetts Ave. NW, Washington, DC 20008 (☎ 202/462-3939). There are also Irish Consulates in Boston, Chicago, New York, and San Francisco.

ENTRY REQUIREMENTS

A valid passport is all that U.S. citizens need to travel for up to three months in Ireland or Northern Ireland. It is no longer necessary even to show proof of smallpox vaccination when returning to the U.S. If you're a British citizen born in Great Britain or Northern Ireland, you can travel freely in Ireland without a passport, but I'd strongly advise bringing it along if you have one, since on some occasions it may be the only acceptable form of identification (for picking up money orders sent from abroad, etc.). If you're a citizen of any other country, be sure to check with the Irish embassy in your area as to what additional documents you may need.

2 Money

The 1970s saw two significant changes in Irish currency. First, in 1971 the country went on the decimal system; that is, the Irish pound was divided into 100 pence. Since the Irish pound at that time maintained parity with the pound sterling, English notes and coins were interchangeable with Irish money.

In 1979, however, the second currency change occurred when, as a member of the European Monetary System, the Irish government linked its monetary values to those of major EC currencies and the Irish pound officially became the "punt." As a result, although English notes are now accepted on the same basis as any other foreign currency by many shops, restaurants, and hotels, life is simpler for the traveler if all transactions are in Irish punts (often still referred to as the "Irish pound").

The **Irish punt (IR£)** is divided into 100 **pence (p),** and coins come in denominations of 1, 2, 5, 10, 20, and 50 pence, and 1 punt. All banks make exchanges on the basis of daily quotations, and it is always wise to change your money at a bank or an American Express office. Some of the larger shops and hotels also work on daily quotations, but many more simply take a weekly average when figuring exchange rates, which can sometimes cost you more when changing notes.

At press time, IR£1 equals $1.60 U.S. ($1 U.S. = 63p), and that is the rate of exchange used in calculating the dollar values cited in this book. Fluctuations of the exchange rate, however, have been almost daily in recent months, so remember, these dollar values are given only as a guide and will likely be different when you arrive in Ireland.

The Irish Punt & the Dollar

IR£	U.S. $	IR£	U.S. $
.50	.80	22.50	36.00
1	1.60	25	40.00
2	3.20	27.50	44.00
2.50	4.00	30	48.00
3	4.80	35	56.00
5	8.00	40	64.00
8	12.80	50	80.00
10	16.00	75	120.00
15	24.00	100	160.00
20	32.00		

What Things Cost in County Kerry	U.S. $
Local telephone call	.30
Per person sharing at Killarney Park Hotel (deluxe)	92.80
Per person sharing, with bath, at Cleevaun (moderate)	29.00
Lunch for one at the Strawberry Tree (deluxe)	16.00
Lunch for one at the Armada Restaurant (moderate)	5.75
Lunch for one at the Laurels Pub (budget)	5.60
Dinner for one, without wine, at the Strawberry Tree (deluxe)	32.00
Dinner for one, without wine, at Linden House (moderate)	19.20
Pint of beer (draft lager)	2.90
Pot of tea with bread and butter	1.60
Roll of Kodacolor film, 36 exposures	7.25
Admission to Muckross House	4.80

What Things Cost in Dublin	U.S. $
Taxi from the airport to the city center	20.00
Tram (DART) discount day ticket inside the city	3.00
Local telephone call	.30
Per person sharing with bath, at Kilronan House (moderate)	56.00
Per person sharing, without bath, at Dublin I.Y.H. (budget)	24.00
Brunch at Davy Byrne's (moderate)	6.40
Lunch for one at Le Coq Hardi (deluxe)	28.80
Lunch for one at the Russell Room (moderate)	16.00
Lunch for one at Bewley's Cafe (budget)	6.40
Dinner for one, without wine, at the Lord Edward (deluxe)	35.20
Dinner for one, without wine, at the Russell Room (moderate)	24.00
Dinner for one, without wine, at Gallagher's (budget)	16.00
Pint of beer (draft Guinness)	3.05
Coca-Cola	.70
Cup of coffee	.70
Roll of Kodacolor film, 36 exposures	7.25
Admission to see the *Book of Kells*	4.80
Movie ticket	5.80
Theater ticket	16.00

A Note on Currency Exchange: In the last year or so, exchange rates of foreign currencies against the U.S. dollar have fluctuated more sharply than in the past; and you may want to consider this several months in advance of departure: Keep a sharp eye on U.S./Irish exchange rates and purchase punts when the rate is favorable. While it probably isn't advisable to convert more than one-third to one-half of your travel currency in advance, you can still realize a substantial increase in buying power if you take advantage of periods when the dollar is at its strongest.

Traveler's Checks For safety's sake, you'll want to carry most of your money in the form of traveler's checks, not in cash. Be sure to keep your traveler's checks separate from the record of their numbers so that any lost checks can be readily replaced.

Bear in mind, too, that you'll get a better exchange rate with traveler's checks than with cash.

3 When to Go

THE CLIMATE

The Atlantic brings along with it the Gulf Stream's warming currents to create a friendly climate that deals in moderation rather than extremes—seldom more than 65° Fahrenheit in July or August (occasionally "soaring" to 70°) or less than 40° in January or February.

Rave to the Irish about their glorious country and nine times out of ten the response will be, "Sure, it's nice enough, if it only weren't for the weather." It's no use trying to convince them that the weather really isn't *that* bad—they're apparently born with an apology complex about their climate, and that's that! However, that famous (or infamous) rainfall is heaviest and most frequent in the mountains of the west, and frequent enough in the rest of the country to keep at *least* 40 shades of green glowing. Showers come and go—sometimes several times in one day—but for the most part, they consist of a misty, almost ethereal sort of rain (nothing like the savage, slashing onslaught you might expect), one that adds an extra dimension to the landscape. If you want to see more sun than rain, you'll generally find it in May everywhere except in the midlands and southeast, where June is apt to be sunnier.

HOLIDAYS

In the Republic, national holidays fall on: January 1 (New Year's Day), March 17 (St. Patrick's Day), Good Friday and Easter Monday, the first Monday in June, the first Monday in August, the last Monday in October, December 25 (Christmas Day), and December 26 (St. Stephen's Day). The whole country shuts down for these days. Northern Ireland observes the same holiday schedule, with the exception that the August bank holiday is replaced by the first Monday in September and the Battle of the Boyne is celebrated on July 12.

Also, some towns observe an "Early Closing Day," with shops closing at 1pm; since the day of the week varies from community to community, be sure to inquire if you have shopping to do.

IRELAND CALENDAR OF EVENTS

Because publishing realities dictate that these dates are based on 1... contact the Irish Tourist Board for the current Calendar of Events during ... visit.

February

- **Ulster Harp National Steeplechase,** Downpatrick, Co. Down. Late February to early March.

March

- **International Marching Band Competitions.** Colorful (and tuneful!) one-day competitions held on successive days in Limerick and Galway. Mid-March.

✪ **St. Patrick's Week.** (His day is the 17th.) Celebrated throughout the country with parades, concerts, street performances, etc.

Where: Throughout the country. **When:** March 12–19. **How:** Public events.

April

- **World Irish Dancing Championship.** Cork. Irish dancers from around the globe congregate for a week of elimination performances. Second week in April.
- **Circuit of Ireland Car Rally.** Thrilling road race around the country, with fierce competition between drivers from year to year. Mid-April.
- **Pan Celtic Week,** Galway. Celts from all parts of Europe celebrate their ancient heritage in a variety of cultural events. Mid-April.

May

✪ **Fleadh Nua.** Festival featuring traditional Irish dance, music, and song. One of Ireland's most popular events, with music filling concert halls, hotel lounges, pubs, and the streets (be sure to book accommodations well in advance if you plan to attend this one).

Where: Ennis, Co. Clare. **When:** Last weekend of May. **How:** Contact Comhaltas Cheoiltoire Eireann, 32 Belgrave Sq., Monkstown, Co. Dublin (☎ 01/800-295) for information.

- **Cork International Choral and Folk Dance Festival,** Cork. Prestigious gathering of dancers and singers from Europe, North America, and other parts of the world. First or second week in May.
- **International Maytime Festival,** Dundalk, Co. Louth. A weeklong celebration of the coming of summer. Last week in May, sometimes stretching into the first week of June.
- **Writers' Week,** Listowel, Co. Kerry. Irish literature workshops, lectures, plays, etc., meant to inspire and assist beginning writers, but you don't have to be a writer to attend. Ireland's leading writers, playwrights, and poets are usually in attendance. Dates have varied from May to October in recent years.

June

- **Ballybunion International Bachelor Festival,** Ballybunion, Co. Kerry. Ireland's most eligible bachelors pay court to the swarms of maiden ladies who flock to West Kerry in search of a husband. Late June.
- **West Cork Festival,** Clonakilty, Co. Cork. Weeklong festivities featuring the rugged people of West Cork making music, singing, dancing, and competing in a variety of sports events. Late June.

July

- **Cobh International Folk Dance Festival,** Cobh, Co. Cork. Celebrated its 30th year in 1991. Second week in July.
- **Galway Race Week,** Galway. Seven days of gala parties, exciting horseracing, and revelry in the streets (book a year ahead if you want to stay in Galway—otherwise you'll be bunking in the hinterlands and driving in each day). Late July.
- **Mary from Dungloe Festival,** Dungloe, Co. Donegal. Festive events of all descriptions—Mary is to Dungloe and County Donegal what Molly Malone is to Dublin. Last days of July into the first week of August.

August

✪ **Puck Fair.** Much ado about goats, with one lucky ram reigning over one of the country's oldest festivals when the streets are filled with horses as traveling people and horse traders from all over Ireland deal and trade; two days of lively, sometimes riotous, fun.

Where: Killorglin, Co. Kerry. **When:** Mid-August. **How:** Book accommodations well in advance.

- **Rose of Tralee Festival,** Tralee (with some events in Killarney), Co. Kerry. Much revelry as beauties from around the world with Irish connections, no matter how tenuous, parade and perform in search of the Rose title. Last week in August (sometimes held in early September).
- **Fleadh Cheoll.** A three-day festival of traditional Irish music attracting an international crowd; there's no set venue, so check for the current location. Late August or early September.

September

✪ **Waterford Festival of International Light Opera.** Surprisingly professional performances, many times of little-known operas.

Where: Theatre Royal, Waterford. **When:** Mid-September. **How:** Call 051-74402 for tickets and information.

- **International Oyster Festival,** Galway. Unabashed tribute to gluttony, with all and sundry competing to see who can consume the most bivalves fresh from local waters—always washed down, of course, with many pints of Guinness. Last two days in September.

October

- **Guinness Jazz Festival,** Cork. One of Cork city's best, drawing leading jazz musicians from around the world—the streets, concert halls, recital halls, and pubs are literally alive with this American art form. Late October.

✪ **Wexford Opera Festival.** Eleven days of workshops, recitals, opera performances, and several "black tie" events.

Where: Theatre Royal, High Street, Wexford. **When:** End of October into first week of November. **How:** Call the box office (☎ 053-22144) for tickets and information.

DUBLIN CALENDAR OF EVENTS

February

- **International Rugby Championship.** Home matches played at Lansdowne Road stadium. Early February (matches sometimes held in late January).

- **Dublin Film Festival.** Films of all description—commercial, artistic, documentary, etc.—compete, and Dublin is filled with the greats, near-greats, and would-be-greats of the film world. Late February to early March.

March

- **Irish Motor Show,** Royal Dublin Society grounds, Ballsbridge. Early March.
- **Irish International Boat Show.** Draws an international crowd of seafarers. Late March.

✪ **St. Patrick's Day Parade.** Dubliners and international visitors line the streets of the capital; it's on a much smaller scale than New York City's miles-long parade, but there's something very special about honoring the saint in the country that he made his own. March 17.

May

- **Spring Show,** Royal Dublin Society grounds, Ballsbridge. Agricultural and industrial showcase with a "country fair" ambience; it's rather informal and lots of fun for youngsters as well as adults. Three days in late May.

June

- **Festival of Music in Great Houses.** Recitals by world-famous artists in lovely 18th-century mansions. Mid-June.

July

✪ **Kerrygold Dublin Horse Show.** Deemed by some to be the social event of the year; there are gala parties and balls all over the city resplendent with horse people from around the world dressed to the nines (requires booking far in advance for accommodations in Dublin—as much as a year ahead).

Where: The Royal Dublin Society, Ballsbridge. **When:** Mid-July. **How:** For a detailed program, contact the Royal Dublin Society, Merrion Road, Ballsbridge, Dublin 4 (☎ 01/668-0645).

September

- **All Ireland Hurling Finals,** Croke Park. One of Ireland's most popular sports events; tickets are next to impossible to obtain, but it's great fun to watch on the telly in a pub or with Irish friends at home. Early September.
- **All Ireland Football Finals.** Same as above, featuring football instead of hurling. Mid-September.

✪ **Dublin Theatre Festival.** Two weeks of superb theater featuring Irish and international troupes.

Where: Various venues. **When:** Late September to early October. **How:** Write to Dublin Theatre Festival, 47 Nassau St., Dublin 2, for information. Tickets are available at individual theaters.

4 Finding an Affordable Place to Stay

Ireland has several categories of budget accommodations. If your notion of budget travel is camping, there are good campgrounds located in just about every scenic section of the country, and backpackers will find a marvelous supply of hostels at dirt-cheap rates. Next up on the cost scale come those wonderful Irish family B&Bs, no two of which are alike. Then there are the farmhouses, which range from modern bungalows to great Georgian mansions, all on working farms. If you lean toward the "small inn" type of home-away-from-home, there are the guesthouses, a little higher up the price range. And for families or small groups traveling together, self-catering cottages may prove to be the most economical way of all to enjoy an Irish visit. There's even a countrywide holiday program that includes some very nice hotels with special midweek and weekend package rates that can only be called budget.

APPROVED ACCOMMODATIONS

The Shamrock (Approved) sign is your guarantee that you'll find clean premises that also meet other very high Department of Tourism standards. Ever-vigilant inspectors keep a sharp eye on every accommodation they approve, with annual, unannounced inspections. Hotels and guesthouses are graded under a star system: For hotels, five stars is the top rating; for guesthouses, it's four stars. Each approved accommodation is required to register its rate for the year and cannot charge more than that unless higher rates for holidays or special events are also registered and appear in Bord Failte listings. Certification also assures that you will get the exact accommodation you bargained for when you booked. If you run into what you think is a violation of these rules, you are expected to make your complaint known—first to the hostess, and failing satisfaction, to Bord Failte, Baggot Street Bridge, Dublin 2 (☎ 01/676-5871). If you think you've been overcharged, be sure to get a receipt to send on to Dublin. While there are some very good unapproved B&Bs in Ireland, it's a good rule of thumb to stick to approved places unless you have a recommendation from someone whose judgment you trust.

The Irish Tourist Board also offers a booking service, which frees you to move about as fancy dictates, secure in the knowledge that you have only to call the nearest ITB office when ready to move on. They'll happily telephone (you will be expected to pay telephone charges) ahead for your next night's lodgings. If you arrive in an Irish town with no place to lay your head that night, the local tourist office will perform the same service. However, during July and August some destinations may be booked almost solid, so if your trip falls in those months, it can pay to book ahead as far as possible.

One or two points will make your stay in any accommodation more enjoyable. First of all, when the Irish say "double room," they mean a room with a double bed; if a room has twin beds, it's called just that, a "twin-bedded" room. *Note:* In this book, I've used "double" to mean a room that will accommodate two people, so be sure to ask when you book.

Let me add here a word about central heating: Not all B&Bs have it, and you must remember that even where you do find it, Irish central heating is not as warm as that at home. Where it doesn't exist, there's almost always a small heater in your room to take the chill off. Your B&B hostess will gladly furnish a hot-water bottle to make your bed warm and toasty when you retire.

HOSTELS

Although they're called *youth* hostels, you'll be welcomed whether you're 6 or 60. The second thing to be said is that in order to use them, you must have a **Hostelling International Card,** which *must* be purchased before you leave home. They are available from **American Youth Hostels, Inc.,** P.O. Box 37613, Washington, DC 20013 (☎ 202/783-6161), and a 12-month membership costs $12 for those under 18, $17 for those 55 and over, and $27 for ages 18 to 54. For another $11.95 plus $3 postage and handling, you can purchase their *Guide to Budget Accommodation* in which Irish hostels are listed.

An Oige is the Irish Youth Hostel Association's official name. Hostels are situated in mountains, beside beaches, near lakes and rivers, etc., and there are also conveniently located hostels in major cities. They vary in shape and size, from a large mansion in Killarney to a Norman castle in Kilkenny. Each has self-catering facilities, dining room, common room, and separate sleeping and washing facilities for men and women. Many have resident house parents to help young hostelers during their stay.

Sheet bags (at a small charge), pillows, blankets, cooking utensils, and dishes are provided, and all you will need to bring is your own sleeping bag, cutlery, tea towel, and bath towel. Overnight charges are based on age, season, and location, and range from IR£5 to IR£10 ($8 to $16). At some locations, breakfast is included in the rate.

For full details, contact An Oige (Irish Youth Hostel Association), 61 Mountjoy St., Dublin 7 (☎ 01/830-4555; fax 01/830-5808). Any of their offices can furnish the *An Oige—Irish Youth Hostel Handbook* for a small charge, which includes a directory of hostels throughout the Republic and Northern Ireland, along with loads of information about international guest cards, advance bookings, and travel concessions available to hostel cardholders on certain ferry services. In Northern Ireland, contact the Youth Hostel Association of Northern Ireland, 56 Bradbury Place, Belfast BT7 1RU (☎ 01232/324733; fax 0234/439699).

If you arrive in Ireland without an International Youth Hostel Card but still want to go the hostel route, contact Paddy and Josephine Moloney, **Approved Irish Independent Hostels (Irish Budget Hostels),** Doolin, County Clare (☎ 065/74006; fax 065/74421). It's a link of privately owned hostels for which you need no registration card, and there's no age limit. Rates range from IR£6 ($9.60) upward.

BED-AND-BREAKFAST HOMES

B&Bs are absolutely the best travel buy in Ireland! It isn't only that the rates stretch your budget so far, it's also that they offer the best possible way to get to know the Irish as they live in their own homes.

No two B&Bs are alike. One night you may stay in a gorgeous city town house, the next in a seaside bungalow, the next in an idyllic country home. Many have only three or four rooms to rent, while others have added extensions to accommodate their guests. Nor are any two hostesses alike except in their friendliness.

If you'd like to have dinner at your B&B, many will accommodate you if you let them know by noon, and you'll be served a wholesome, well-prepared meal for about the same price as your room rate. Baby-sitters can usually be arranged at very modest fees, and almost all B&Bs offer reductions for children sharing a room with parents. Single travelers may have a problem finding a single room—there just aren't very many, and if you're given a double room, there may be a small supplementary charge.

You'll pay anywhere from IR£13 to IR£18 ($20.80 to $28.80) in the country and smaller towns, slightly more in cities. In Dublin, prices in the few B&Bs in the inner city are quite a bit higher, but there's a multitude of accommodations within easy suburban bus or train rides. Most B&Bs also offer a partial-board rate, a money-saving weekly charge for bed and breakfast plus the evening meal.

The **Town & Country Homes Association** publishes a *Guest Accommodation* booklet with pictures of all member homes. It's available for a small charge from any Irish Tourist Board office. The association is nationwide, and its members can book you ahead to your next destination with any other member. I find standards exceptionally high in these homes and have yet to find one I couldn't recommend, both for facilities and friendly hospitality.

FARMHOUSES

You'll find the very same sort of hospitality in Irish farmhouses. I can't imagine a more heavenly vacation for a child—or grown-up, for that matter—than one on an Irish farm. The one essential for a farmhouse holiday is a car, since almost all are off the beaten track and cannot be reached by public transportation.

Prices for farmhouse accommodations usually run one or two punts higher than town and country homes. They offer the budget-stretching partial-board weekly rates, and they're listed in the ITB *Accommodation Guide.* There's also an **Irish Farm Holidays Association (Failte Tuaithe)** publication (small charge) with pictures and a brief description of each member farmhouse. Standards are a little bit higher in association farmhouses, and they, too, will gladly book you with a fellow member along your itinerary. Many of the 600 members of the **Irish Organic Farmers and Growers Association** also have bed-and-breakfast accommodations. For an illustrated leaflet, contact IOFGA, 56 Blessington Street, Dublin 7 (☎ 01/830-7996). Reservations procedures for farmhouses are the same as in the town and country homes section above.

GUESTHOUSES

I don't know how to describe guesthouses accurately—it always seems to me they fit the pattern of a traditional small inn. Suffice it to say that they combine many of the services you expect in hotels (some, for instance, have telephones, hairdryers, etc., in guest rooms) with the personalized service and informality of a B&B. Some have been built for this specific purpose; others are in period residences; others have just sort of grown into being as a popular B&B that expanded to meet the demand.

Even though you'll be paying a higher rate than in the B&Bs, there are several advantages to staying in a guesthouse. For example, many have a restaurant right on the premises, which can be a real convenience. They are also allowed to sell wine (but not spirits) to guests. Rates are based on both single-person occupancy and per person sharing. In the disadvantage column, all guesthouse rates are subject to a small Value-Added Tax (VAT) for accommodation, food, drink, and other services. Still, their sheer attractiveness, convenience, and charm make the added tax seem a small price to pay. I can also assure you you'll find the same brand of hospitality as in B&Bs.

Guesthouse rates range, depending on facilities, location, and season, from IR£30 to IR£60 ($48 to $96) per person sharing. Not budget, but good value all the same. The Irish Tourist Board includes all approved guesthouses in their *Guest Accommodations* booklet, available for a small charge, and their *Be Our Guest* booklet includes pictures.

SELF-CATERING

One of the most effective money-saving devices is to rent your own "home" and eat in when it suits you. That doesn't necessarily mean that your travels are restricted, for it is quite possible to rent self-catering premises in a central location on Ireland's east coast for your first week, make easy day-trips from that home base, then shift to another on the west coast for your second week.

Self-catering accommodations come in all guises, from inner-city town houses and flats to freestanding houses in small towns, country and seaside bungalows, thatched cottages, and chalets. In off-season months, it is possible in some locations to rent for a few midweek days or weekends only, but most rental periods run from Saturday (beginning 4pm) to the following Saturday (ending before noon). There are three price periods: April, May, June, and September (mid-range prices); July and August (peak prices); and all other months (lowest price). Rates can range from about IR£95 to IR£275 ($152 to $440) in the high season for a cottage that accommodates seven. Rates drop sharply in low season. If you're traveling with a gaggle of children or friends, your per-person costs can be cut to the very bone by self-catering.

All the above applies to privately owned self-catering accommodations, but there is one very special scheme that has great appeal if you get dreamy-eyed at the thought of a traditional thatched cottage. The organization known as **Rent an Irish Cottage Plc.** has put together small villages of rental cottages in the west of Ireland that combine the traditional hearth, half-door, and raftered ceilings you've dreamed about with modern conveniences like central heating (when you really don't want to bother with a turf fire), electric kitchens (no wood to chop or heavy pots to hang over an open fire), and shiny bathrooms with showers.

For details and booking information, contact Rent an Irish Cottage Plc., 85 O'Connell St. Limerick, Co. Limerick (☎ 061/411-109; fax 061/314-821).

5 Health & Insurance

HEALTH

Medical facilities in Ireland are excellent! If you need a doctor, dentist, or hospital service, the first source of information should be your accommodations hostess or someone on the local scene. Failing that, the **Irish Medical Organization,** 10 Fitzwilliam Place, Dublin (☎ 01/676-7273), can put you in touch with local medical help.

If you take any form of medication, be sure to bring along prescriptions from your doctor in case you need refills. It's also a good idea to carry a copy of your prescription for glasses or contact lenses.

INSURANCE

Before leaving home, check to be sure that your property insurance is in good order, with premium payments up-to-date and full coverage for fire, theft, etc. If your present health and accident policy does not provide coverage when you're out of the country, check with your insurance carrier about temporary medical coverage for the duration of your trip. Most travel agents can arrange this, along with travel-delay or cancellation and lost-luggage insurance.

When renting a car in Ireland, the small premiums for both collision damage and personal accident insurance are a good investment. Although your credit-card company may offer such coverage when you use your card for car rentals, recently there have been a host of difficulties in settling claims through such companies—the premiums are a small price to pay for peace of mind.

6 Tips for Special Travelers

FOR TRAVELERS WITH DISABILITIES

Disabled should contact in advance the **National Rehabilitation Board,** 25 Clyde Rd., Ballsbridge, Dublin 4 (☎ 01/684181).

Bord Failte also publishes an information sheet entitled "Accommodations for the Disabled," which is a partial listing of premises that have been inspected and approved by the National Rehabilitation Board.

Avis Rent-A-Car (see "Getting Around" later in this chapter) can provide cars with hand controls.

The **Irish Wheelchair Association,** Blackheath Dr., Clontarf, Dublin (☎ 01/833-8241), with branches in Kilkenny, Cork, Limerick, and Galway, will lend wheelchairs without charge; book in advance.

In Northern Ireland, contact **Disability Action,** 2 Annandale Ave., Belfast (☎ 1232/491-011) for travel advice in Northern Ireland.

FOR SENIORS

Although relatively new to Ireland, accommodation discounts for those over 65 are becoming more and more frequent around the country. Tourist offices can supply the "Golden Holidays" booklet for those 55 and over. Most discounts apply to off-season or low-season rates at the moment. However, senior citizen discounts are the coming thing, so be sure to inquire when booking, and if you're booking through an agent, stress that the discount should be *requested* since it's seldom offered voluntarily.

You will also find some senior-citizen discounts identified for those hotels, guesthouses, and farmhouses listed in the illustrated "Discover Ireland" booklet, available from the Irish Tourist Board.

FOR STUDENTS

For students, Ireland has a lot going for it. First of all, with half its population age 25 and younger, Ireland is truly a haven for the young (*Tir na nog,* the ancient Celts called their version of heaven, and the Gaelic name translates to "Land of Youth"). Sports, music, dancing, and a host of other activities are geared for the young and available wherever you go in the country.

Not only are recreational and leisure pursuits at your fingertips in Ireland, but the ancient tradition of reverence for learning continues to this day, with all sorts of interesting educational experiences available (see "Educational Vacations" in Chapter 4).

For details of budget-priced hostel accommodations, see "Where to Stay," in Chapter 4.

ISIC (International Student Identity Card) This card opens doors to events and activities aimed only at students, as well as to substantial discounts on almost every facet of travel. You must, however, arm yourself with this valuable document before you leave home.

The 1995 price was $16, which may increase in 1996, and you can obtain your card through the **CIEE** (Council on International Educational Exchange), 205 E. 42nd St., New York, NY 10017 (☎ 212/661-1414), or at any of the 41 Council Travel offices or more than 450 campus issuing offices across the country. With the card in hand you'll be entitled to participate in all the listings below, as well as many, many more happenings you'll discover once you arrive on Irish soil.

USIT (Irish Student Travel Services) This is the student's best friend in Ireland. If you deplane at Shannon, your very first Irish stop should be the Limerick office at Central Buildings, O'Connell Street (☎ 061/415-064), open Monday through Friday from 10am to 2pm and 3:15 to 6pm, and from May to September also on Saturday from 10am to 1pm. The head office is in Dublin at 19 Aston Quay, Dublin 2 (☎ 01/679-8833), open Monday through Friday from 9:30am to 6pm and on Saturday from 11am to 4pm. In Waterford you'll find USIT at 33 O'Connell St. (☎ 051/72601).

USIT will arrange cut-rate travel between Ireland and other European destinations, help you plan itineraries both inside the country and beyond, and advise you about accommodations, camping, summer jobs, and student bargains in every area you can think of.

In Northern Ireland, you'll find USIT offices in the Sountain Centre, College St., Belfast BT1-6ET (☎ 1232/324-073) and at Queens University Travel, Student Union Bldg., University Rd., Belfast BT7-1PE (☎ 1232/241-830).

In the U.S., a USIT office at 895 Amsterdam Ave. (at West 103rd St.), New York, NY 10025 (☎ 212/663-5435), is open from June through September.

Transportation Savings One of USIT's most valuable services is the **Travel-save Stamp,** which when affixed to your International Student Identity Card entitles you to such benefits as a 50% discount on Dublin buses and trains, as well as 50% off all rail and bus travel throughout the country, and rail travel in Northern Ireland. In addition, students with a valid CIE stamp will be entitled to approximately one-third off round-trip weekend rail fares and 50% off the ferry service to the Aran Islands and B & I Ferry services.

With the International Student Identity Card in hand, you'll qualify for half-fare rates on all Bus Eireann routes around the country, an all-important money saver. In Dublin, you can purchase an **Educational Travel Concession Ticket** from Dublin Bus, 59 Upper O'Connell St. (☎ 720000), which permits unlimited travel on Dublin bus and train services at drastic discounts.

7 Getting There

BY PLANE FROM THE U.S.

Travel Time From New York to Shannon is a five-hour flight; from Shannon back to the States takes six hours; and there's a five-hour time difference, so you can count on having at least a touch of jet lag.

Seasons of Travel *When* you travel to Ireland is a very important money-saving factor. For example, travel from mid-September to mid-May eastbound, or mid-October to mid-June westbound, is considerably cheaper (it's called the "basic season" in airline jargon) than if you go during "peak season" (all other months). Specific dates for season changes can vary from one year to the next, so you should check with the airline before setting your departure date. You should be aware, too, of any restrictions concerning advance booking, stopovers, etc., that apply to some of the less expensive fares.

AIR CARRIERS

Aer Lingus is Ireland's national airline and offers by far the most frequent flights from New York to Shannon or Dublin in peak season and two flights daily during the basic season. It also has six weekly direct flights from Boston. During basic season, flights from New York and Boston are less frequent, so be sure to check before setting your dates. There are also connecting flights from over 100 U.S. cities to New York and Boston via major domestic carriers.

Contact Aer Lingus at 122 E. 42nd St., New York, NY 10168 (☎ 212/557-1110 or 800/223-6537).

If your itinerary includes the U.K. and the Continent and you are flying round-trip transatlantic via Aer Lingus, be sure to take advantage of their budget-stretching Euro Greensaver Pass, which in 1995 offered travel between Ireland and the U.K. at only $60 each way, $99 each way between Ireland and mainland Europe.

Aer Lingus also offers a frequent flyer program available to regular travelers on scheduled services. Ask about enrolling in the program when you make your booking.

If you really want to get a head start on your Irish visit, then let me offer a very personal recommendation. As far as I'm concerned, *my* Irish arrival begins at Kennedy Airport in New York the minute I walk up to the Aer Lingus check-in counter and am greeted by a smile and a lilt straight from the "auld sod."

Once inside the aircraft (which is named for a saint, adorned with a shamrock on its tail, and flies with the spiritual comfort of an annual blessing of the fleet), Irish accents mingle with those of Americans glowing with the contentment of being, if not yet in Ireland, at least surrounded by the Irish. Sentiment aside, Aer Lingus has consistently topped other airlines in punctuality for European and transatlantic schedules, and its warm, efficient, *friendly* service has won it no less than five prestigious awards in the last two years!

Delta flies to Ireland from Atlanta, a gateway that may be more convenient for those coming from the Southeast and Southwest. During peak season, flights are daily except Monday. In the basic season, there are three flights per week. Contact Delta Airlines, Hartsfield Airport, Atlanta, GA 30320 (☎ in the U.S. 800/241-4141, fax 404/765-2586; in Canada 800/843-9378).

BY PLANE FROM THE U.K.

TO IRELAND

Aer Lingus With the highest frequency of flights from Heathrow, Aer Lingus offers scheduled service from London to Dublin, Cork, and Shannon. Aer Lingus also has service between Dublin and Bristol, Birmingham, East Midlands, Edinburgh, Glasgow, Leeds/Bradford, Manchester, and Newcastle. Aer Lingus offers a variety of package holidays and weekend breaks in Ireland.

For details, contact Aer Lingus in the U.S. (☎ 800/223-6537); in London (☎ 181/899-4747); or in Ireland (☎ 01/377-777 in Dublin, 021/274-331 in Cork, 061/415-556 in Limerick).

Ryanair offers scheduled flights between London and Dublin, Cork, Shannon, and Knock. Ryanair can be contacted in London (☎ 171/435-7101)) or in Ireland (☎ 01/677-4422).

TO NORTHERN IRELAND

Scheduled service is also available to Northern Ireland from numerous points in Britain by the following carriers: **British Airways** (☎ 800/AIRWAYS in the U.S.; 1345/222-111 in the U.K.); **British Midland** (☎ 171/589-5599 in the U.K.); **Air U.K.** (☎ 800/249-2478 in the U.S., 416/485-8724 in Canada 1279/680-146 in the U.K.).

BY PLANE FROM THE CONTINENT

Aer Lingus has direct flights from Amsterdam, Brussels, Copenhagen, Düsseldorf, Frankfurt, Madrid, Milan, Paris, and Rome.

Other airlines serving Ireland from the Continent include KLM, Sabena, Air France, Lufthansa, Iberia, and Aeroflot.

BY SEA FROM THE U.K.

Ireland has excellent connections with the U.K. via the car-ferries listed below, and if you are not traveling by car, their offices can book your sea and overland transportation at the same time, at package rates. Ferry and overland transport can usually be arranged before you leave home through travel agents or the numbers listed for each line.

As we go to press, the one-way fares for foot passengers begin around $32, $140 for car and four passengers, and $95 for ferry/rail combination to London. Fares vary seasonally.

To Ireland

Stena Sealink operates daily car-ferry from Fishguard (Wales) to Rosslare and from Holyhead to Dun Laoghaire. Round-trip specials are offered from time to time, and they also have a selection of short break and holiday packages. In the U.S. and Canada, call 800/677-8585 or 212/575-2667; in Britain, Sealink British Ferries, Park Street, Charter House, Ashford, Kent TN24 8EX (☎ 1233/647-047; fax 0233/46024); in Ireland, 15 Westmoreland St., Dublin 2 (☎ 01/280-8844).

B&I Line provides daily Pembroke-Rosslare service and Holyhead-Dublin service. They have an attractive array of special offers and package holidays. In the U.S. and Canada, book through travel agents or B&I Line, c/o Lynott Tours, 350 Fifth Ave., Suite 2619, New York, NY 10118-2697 (☎ 212/760-0101, or 800/221-2474; fax 212/695-8347); in Britain, 150–151 New Bond St., London W1Y 0AQ (☎ 171/491-8682); in Liverpool, Reliance House, Water Street, Liverpool L28TP (☎ 11551/227-3131).

Swansea Cork Ferries operates ferry service between Ringaskiddy (a few miles outside Cork city) to Swansea, Wales. For schedules, fares, and bookings, contact them at 52 South Mall, Cork (☎ 021/271-166; fax 021/275-061).

To Northern Ireland

SeaCat. The quickest sea crossing is the 90-minute SeaCat service from Stranraer in Scotland to Belfast (☎ 01232/310910 to book).

Stena Sealink sails from Stranraer to Larne (see above for contact information).

P&O European Ferries has service from Cairnryan to Larne (contact Scots American Travel; ☎ 201/768-1187 in the U.S. and Canada or 01581/200-276 in the U.K.).

BY SEA FROM THE CONTINENT

You can extend your Irish holiday into Europe on Irish Ferries, with frequent sailings all year from Rosslare (near Wexford) to Le Havre; Rosslare to Cherbourg; and from June 20 to August 30, Cork to Le Havre and Cork to Cherbourg.

One-way fares in 1995 began at IR£85($136) for a foot passenger in a six-berth cabin (less with a Eurailpass), IR£260 ($416) for a car and four passengers. Sailing time is 21 hours to Le Havre and 17 hours to Cherbourg. The line also has some terrific holiday package plans that can mean real savings for a European holiday. Packages change from year to year, but they offer very good value and are well worth looking into. (Ask the Dublin office for their "Ferrytours" booklet, which describes all current plans.)

Most travel agents can make ferry bookings for you before you leave home through Irish Ferries, Lynott Tours, 350 Fifth Ave., New York, NY 10118-2697 (☎ 212/760-0101 or 800/221-2474); or Irish Ferries, 2–4 Merrion Row, Dublin 2 (☎ 01/610511).

BY BUS

There's good express coach service between London and several cities in Ireland, including Dublin, Cork, Waterford, Killarney, and Limerick. Round-trip tickets are good for 3 months and can have open return dates. "Superbus" bookings can be made at more than 3,000 National Express agents in the U.K. and at all National Coach stations. In Ireland, book through any Bus Eireann office.

PACKAGE TOURS

Dedicated budget watchers have long known that when it comes to travel, some of the best bargains going are chartered flights or tours (escorted or unescorted). Once upon a time that meant you were herded around with a group of other Americans, with little opportunity to break out on your own and freewheel it through a country. That is no longer true, and you can now realize enormous savings on airfare and accommodations and never see those other American faces except in the airplane going over and coming back. Not that I have anything against my countryfolk, you understand; it's just that I don't go to Ireland to be with Americans.

Aer Lingus (☎ 800/223-6537) offers a wide selection of such bargains. One of the most attractive for budgeteers is their "Discover Ireland B&B and Car," with 1995 prices (exclusive of airfare) ranging from $39 up per person per day, depending on car model and season.

Irish-owned **CIE Tours International Inc.,** 108 Ridgedale Ave., P.O. Box 2355, Morristown, N.J. 07962-2355 (☎ 201/292-3438 or 800/243-8687), can help you decide among the many package tours offered by CIE, both escorted and unescorted. Ask for their *The Best of Ireland & Britain* booklet for more details.

When it comes to escorted tours, it's hard to beat the dollar-for-value tours offered by Globus/Cosmos, a long-established tour company that operates excellent coach tours to Ireland from late April through October. Book tours through travel agents.

A package tour designed just for you? A fantasy no more. Contact Brian Mundy, of the **In Quest of the Classics** travel agency, P.O. Box 890745, Temecula, CA 92589-0745 (☎ 909/694-5866 or 800/221-5246—in California, 800/227-1393—fax 909/694-5873).

8 Getting Around

BY BUS/TRAIN

BUS EIREANN Bus Eireann's home office is at the Central Bus Station (Busaras), Store St., Dublin 1. The central number for schedule and fare information is 01/836-6111. Another Dublin office is at 59 Upper O'Connell St. (☎ 01/872-0000, ext. 3030). Timetables and other travel information are available in both, as well as at bus-ticket offices and train depots around the country.

In addition to regular commuter services, high-speed Expressway coaches operate between Dublin and all major points, with new coaches and up to three services a day each way.

Round-trip fares are only marginally more than one-way fares; children under 15 go for half fare. Also, Bus Eireann constantly offers special fares (weekends, midweek, etc.). Whenever you travel, be sure to ask about the cheapest fare available at the time.

One of Bus Eireann's most popular offerings is its **Breakaways program.** At time of press, prices range from IR£35 ($56) to IR£39 ($62.40) per person per night, including round-trip coach fare and bed and breakfast—a real bargain for those traveling on a strict budget. Some 25 hotels nationwide provide accommodation. Senior citizen discounts are offered.

In Northern Ireland, **Ulsterbus,** Europa Bus Centre, 10 Glengall St., Belfast (☎ 01232/333-000) serves all six counties and offers money-saving travel passes, as well as periodic special promotional fares (see Chapter 21).

IRISH RAIL Irish Rail's head office is at Dublin's Connolly Station, and the number to call for schedules and all passenger services is 01/836-6222. Night

Bus/Train Passes

The following passes are available from mainline railway stations and Bus Eireann ticket offices in Ireland, or you may purchase them through travel agents in the United States or CIE Tours International (☎ 201/292-0184 or 800/243-7687).

Eurailpass This single convenient card entitles you to unlimited rail travel throughout 17 European countries, including the Republic of Ireland (good on rail, Expressway coaches, and Irish Continental Lines ferries between Ireland and France), but not in the U.K. or Northern Ireland. It is available to any non-European resident, but must be purchased *before you leave home,* 21 days prior to departure. Eurailpasses are available through travel agents or by calling Rail Pass Express (☎ 800/722-7151).

Irish Explorer This money-saving pass allows unlimited travel within the Republic. In 1995, the five-day rail-only pass was $102; the eight-day combined bus and rail pass was $153.

Irish Rover Covering rail-only travel in both the Republic and Northern Ireland, this pass cost $128 for five days in 1995.

Emerald Card This card is valid on Irish Rail, Bus Eireann, Ulsterbus, and Northern Ireland Rail services and costs $168 for eight days, $288 for 15 days. Students are eligible for the Youth Student Pass at substantial discounts.

Rail Runabout Northern Ireland Railways has a Rail Runabout pass good for seven days of unlimited travel in Northern Ireland only, available at most railway stations in the province.

Brit/Ireland Pass This convenient, money-saving pass, *which must be purchased before you leave home,* covers rail travel throughout Great Britain, a round-trip Stella Sealink ferry crossing, and rail travel throughout Ireland. Available from Britrail Travel Int. (☎ 800/677-8585 or 212/575-2667) or CIE Tours International (☎ 800/243-7687 or 201/292-3438); in Canada, call 800/387-2667.

numbers operate from 5:30 to 10pm Monday through Friday (☎ 01/836-5420), Saturday from 7:30am to 10pm (☎ 01/836-5421), and Sunday from 5 to 10pm (☎ 01/836-5421).

Mainline passenger trains operate between Dublin and cities and towns throughout Ireland and to Belfast, and there are also commuter trains in the Dublin and Cork suburban areas. Services are fairly frequent and speedy (Galway, for instance, is just three hours from Dublin by train). Most long-distance trains have catering facilities, ranging from bar service and light refreshments to à la carte meals. Second-class travel is best for the budget, but you can go first class for a small supplement (best to book ahead for first class).

Irish Rail also operates many special trains: day-trips in the summer, pilgrimage trains, and special excursions to sporting and entertainment events, many offering discounts to groups and families. **Rail Breaks** holiday packages vary from luxury weekends in Cork, Dublin, Killarney, and Galway to three-day family breaks in several locations, with hotel or self-catering digs. For full details and current prices, contact any local station or the Irish Rail Travel Centre, 35 Lower Abbey St., Dublin 1 (☎ 01/836-6222), or the Travel Centre, 65 Patrick St., Cork (☎ 021/504-888).

There is excellent rail service between Dublin and Belfast. Within Northern Ireland, **Northern Ireland Railways,** Central Station, East Bridge St., Belfast (☎ 01232/230-310), connects Belfast to Derry, Coleraine, Bangor, and Newry. (See Chapter 21 for details of current fares and discounts for students and seniors.)

SIGHTSEEING TOURS Natives and visitors alike take Bus Eireann **day trips** to Ireland's most scenic spots at bargain prices, and for those addicted to escorted coach tours as a means of seeing a country with the least amount of personal planning, Bus Eireann provides some of the best. There are more than 60 day tours to more than 20 locations nationwide, and ticket offices, rail depots, and tourist offices can provide detailed brochures for each locality.

Bus Eireann also operates weeklong first-rate **escorted coach tours,** as well as self-drive, go-as-you-please tours using either hotel or B&B accommodations that represent exceptional value. Some tours feature two- and three-night stopovers, a real boon to those who hate packing and unpacking every day.

BY CAR

CAR RENTALS The first thing you must know about renting a car in Ireland is that it's absolutely necessary to book ahead. That's especially true from the first of July through the end of September, but in this small country, a run on the stock available can also develop suddenly if there's a special event of some kind that draws lots of visitors. You must be between the ages of 23 and 70 (top age with some companies is 65, while others add a surcharge for insurance for those over the age of 70, so be sure to inquire when you book).

The rates quoted will include third-party and passenger liability insurance, but unless you add on collision-damage insurance, you'll be responsible for the full cost of repairs should you be involved in an accident. I strongly advise you to take it—otherwise, you'll be required by most companies to make a refundable payment of as much as IR£150 ($217.50) or more if you are paying by cash. Some credit cards offer collision-damage insurance, but in recent years there have been serious difficulties in collecting on claims, and you'd be well advised to take the car-rental-company coverage. You may also be asked for a deposit at the time you

Irish Express Bus Routes

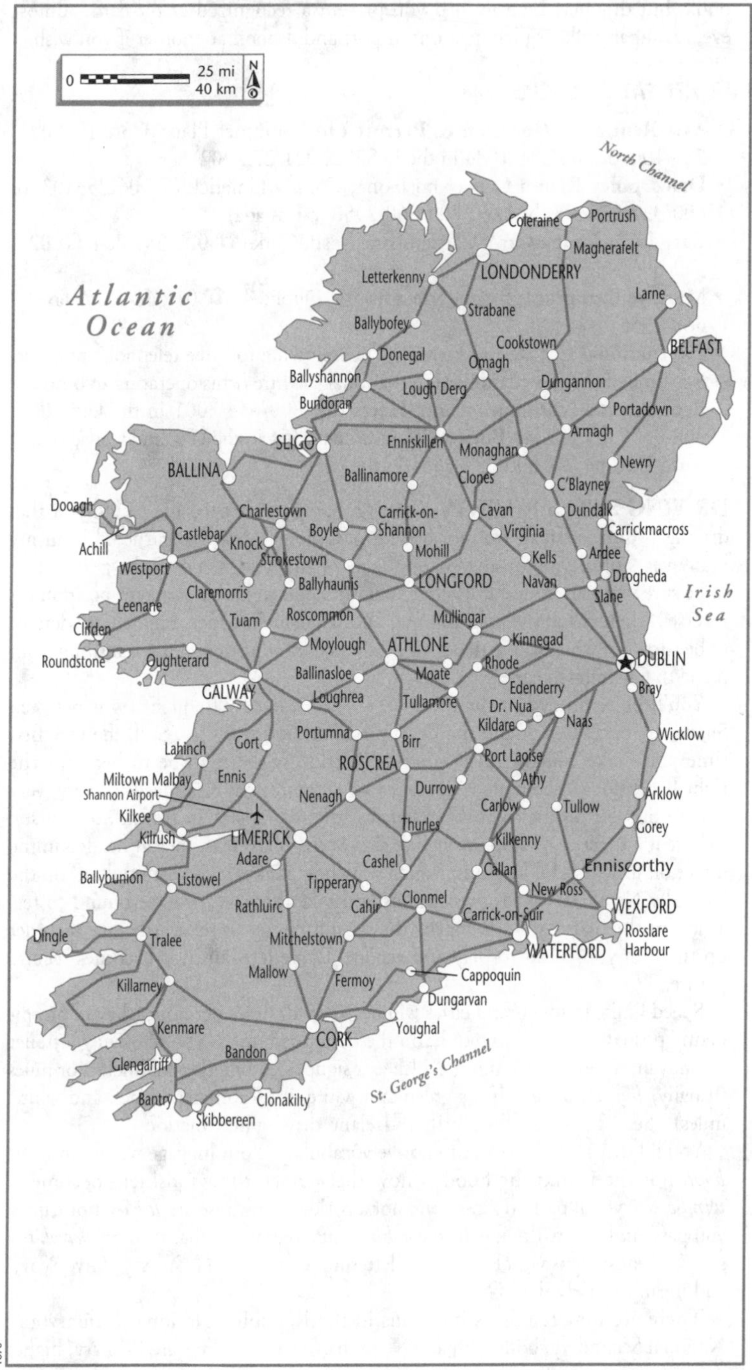

book, but this may be waived if you present a recognized credit card. Almost every company allows pickup at one airport and dropoff at another if you wish.

Car Rental Agencies

✪ **Avis Rent a Car/Johnson & Perrott Ltd.** Emmet Place, Cork (☎ 021/281-100, or 800/331-1084 in the U.S.; fax 021/272-202).

- **Dan Dooley Rent a Car** Knocklong, County Limerick (☎ 062/53103, or 800/331-9301 in the U.S., 800/668-2958 in Canada).
- **Eurodollar Rent a Car** Carrigrohane Road, Cork (☎ 021/344-884; fax 021/342-696).
- **Murrays Europcar** Baggot Street Bridge, Dublin 4 (☎ 01/668-1777; fax 01/660-2958).
- **International Car Rental Firms** The following toll-free telephone numbers list some of the more familiar international car-hire firms operating in both the Republic and Northern Ireland: **Hertz** (☎ 800/654-3001 in the U.S., 800/263-0600 in Canada); **Budget** (☎ 800/284-2354 in the U.S. and Canada); and **Auto Europe** (☎ 800/223-5555 in the U.S.)

DRIVING RULES & HINTS You probably don't need me to tell you that driving is on the left in Ireland, but I'll pass along a few tips garnered from my many years of driving on the "wrong" side of the road. Go over the gear system to be sure you understand it (every rental car seems to have a different position for reverse!), then check the light dimmer and windshield wiper. Elementary details, to be sure, but while you're doing all this, you'll be adjusting to the transition from plane to Customs to car.

You'll be reminded of the drive-on-the-left edict by frequent signs between Shannon and Limerick and the Dublin Airport and that city. Still, the very first time you make a sharp turn, your inclination is going to be to head for the right-hand side of the road. Also, when you stop for gas or a meal, it's very, very easy to pull off on the right side (which is the wrong side in Ireland, of course). I make it a practice to stop on the left side of the road, with the car headed in the direction in which I'll be going, which somehow makes it easier to pull off on the left side. No matter what precautions you take, however, you're bound to feel awkward the first day—and maybe the second. So try to set a little tape recorder up there in your head to play and replay "Drive left" until it becomes second nature.

Speed limits in towns and cities will be 30 or 40 miles per hour (they're prominently posted), and it's 60 m.p.h. on the open road unless you're towing a trailer or caravan, when it is 50 m.p.h. Mileage is signposted in either kilometers or miles (usually, *but not always,* if it's green and white, it's kilometers; black and white, miles). (See Chapter 21 for Northern Ireland driving information.)

You'll learn a whole new automotive vocabulary: Your luggage will go into the *boot,* not the trunk; the hood is now the *bonnet;* the windshield becomes a *windscreen;* you'll park in a *car park,* not a parking lot; those are *lorries,* not trucks, you pass; and you're driving a *car-for-hire,* not a rental car, that runs on *petrol,* not gas. And those signs with bold Gaelic lettering reading GEILL SL1 say "Give Way," and mean precisely that! Got it?

There are four road classifications in the Republic: National Primary and National Secondary, both with an "N" prefix (lower numbers are Primary; higher

Irish Rail Routes

than 50, they are usually Secondary); Regional, with an "R" prefix; and unclassified rural roads with no prefix.

One note of caution: U-turns can lead to disaster—no matter if you're driving on dual carriageways or country lanes. *One other caution:* In their rush toward efficiency and speeding up the flow of traffic, all those major highways (and, indeed, many rural roads) are simply broken out with something called "roundabouts" at what were once simply crossroads. Now, as accustomed as I am to American cloverleafs, multiple exits from major routes, and the like, somehow in the beginning these roundabouts gave me no end of trouble, and many American visitors seem to experience the same thing. The cardinal rule is to remember that *the driver on the right has right-of-way.* That means that if any other car is to your right in the circle, you must wait until the way is clear to enter. As you approach your exit, move into the left lane of the circle and signal a turn. If you miss it, just go around again.

There are some basic things you ought to know about those little roads. In early morning and evening you're sure to meet at least one farmer and his hard-working dog driving the cows to or from the fields—right down the middle of the road. Don't panic! Just stop like everybody else, relax, give the man a nod or a wave, and let the sea of cattle wash right around you.

Also, you're probably going to get lost at least once. That's because road signs sometimes mysteriously get turned around (leprechauns?), or you come to a junction with no signs. But let me tell you that getting lost in Ireland is a pleasant adventure. Stop at a pub to ask directions and you're in for some delightful conversation, especially if things are a little slow. The general discussion that erupts will enlighten you about all the alternative routes, and the advantages and disadvantages of each. When everyone has had his or her say (and not until then!), you'll be sent on your way with detailed instructions on where *not* to go as well as the right route. Many's the time a stern "You'll come to a crossroad with a church, but pay no mind to it and keep to the road straight ahead" has kept me from making a wrong turn.

GAS Gas (petrol) will cost anywhere from IR£3.25 ($5.20) a gallon up, and you'll find the cheapest prices at Jet stations. Those are imperial gallons—larger by volume than ours—and in a small car, you'll cover remarkable distances on a tankful of gas. Increasingly, gas is sold by the liter, and the conversion chart in the appendix will give you a quick comparison between liters, imperial gallons, and those we're accustomed to at home.

MAPS Your car-hire company will provide you with a map (not that it will keep you from getting lost), but many are not all that easy to follow. I highly recommend the **Holiday Maps** (regional, as well as for the entire country), which are much more detailed, have city maps (you'll need them), and give you a wealth of useful tourist information. They sell for about IR£3 ($4.80) and can be bought at most newsagents.

BY RV

In Ireland, RVs are known as *caravans,* and virtually all are drawn by a car. Rental rates at presstime ranged from IR£130 to IR£250 ($208 to $400) per week, depending on the size and season. In computing your costs, add the cost of a rental car (and you may have an additional cost for the fitting of a suitable hitch) and the IR£6 to IR£10 ($9.60 to $16) nightly site fee in caravan parks. The Irish Tourist Board publishes a comprehensive Caravan and Camping Holidays directory that includes Northern Ireland parks, available for a small fee.

BY AIR

Travel around the country by commuter plane can be a great convenience if your time in Ireland is extremely limited. **Aer Lingus** flies from Dublin to Cork, Farrenfore (County Kerry), Shannon, Galway, Knock, and Sligo. Thus in the course of one week you could spend a day or so in Yeats Country up Sligo way, another in Killarney, and add a day or so in Cork. It's not possible, however, to fly from one of these commuter airports directly to another—you must return to Dublin to connect to a flight to your next destination.

Aer Arann (☎ 091/55437) flies from Galway's Carnmore Airport to the Aran Islands from April through September. Call for current schedules and fares. (See Chapter 17.)

BY FERRY

With its many offshore islands, Ireland has a plethora of licensed boat services. The major ferries are listed here, and the tourist board's Information Sheet 50C, "Island Boat/Air Services," provides complete information. In County Clare, there's service from Doolin to two of the Aran Islands. County Cork has ferries from Baltimore and Schull to Cape Clear Island, and from Glengarriff to Garinish Island. Counties Kerry and Clare are linked by the Tarbert/Killimer Ferry that crosses the Shannon; in County Donegal there's a ferry between Burtonport and Arranmore Island; in County Galway, two ferry companies operate service from Rossaveal (near Galway town) to the Aran Islands; and Counties Waterford and Wexford are linked by Passage East/Ballyhack service.

HIKING, HITCHHIKING, & CYCLING

Hiking, hitchhiking, and cycling are all quite acceptable and very popular ways to get around Ireland. My only caution would be against hitchhiking alone. If you team up with a companion, however, there is little risk.

SUGGESTED ITINERARIES

Set itineraries present a very real danger in Ireland. They often get turned upside down! You see, a 15-minute pub break in an afternoon drive can easily turn into a two-day layover, all because your man behind the bar insists that you'll be very welcome at the evening's singsong with such conviction that it's suddenly very clear that the Blarney Stone can wait another day—which turns into yet another day when you fall in with such convivial company at the singsong that nothing will do but that you stay over for the next night! Now, don't misunderstand me: It's possible to "do" a very good, circular tour of Ireland in two weeks. But whether or not you get all the way around will depend entirely on how determined you are to stay on that schedule.

Right here, I'd like to make a suggestion based purely on my personal choice of how to travel. The first of my suggested itineraries is a circular tour, which anticipates that you will move from place to place almost every night. Well, I don't know about you, but I don't particularly enjoy packing and unpacking every single night. To avoid that, it is quite possible to select several major destinations along the route, settle in for a day or so and make longish day trips, returning to the

Ireland: Provinces & Counties

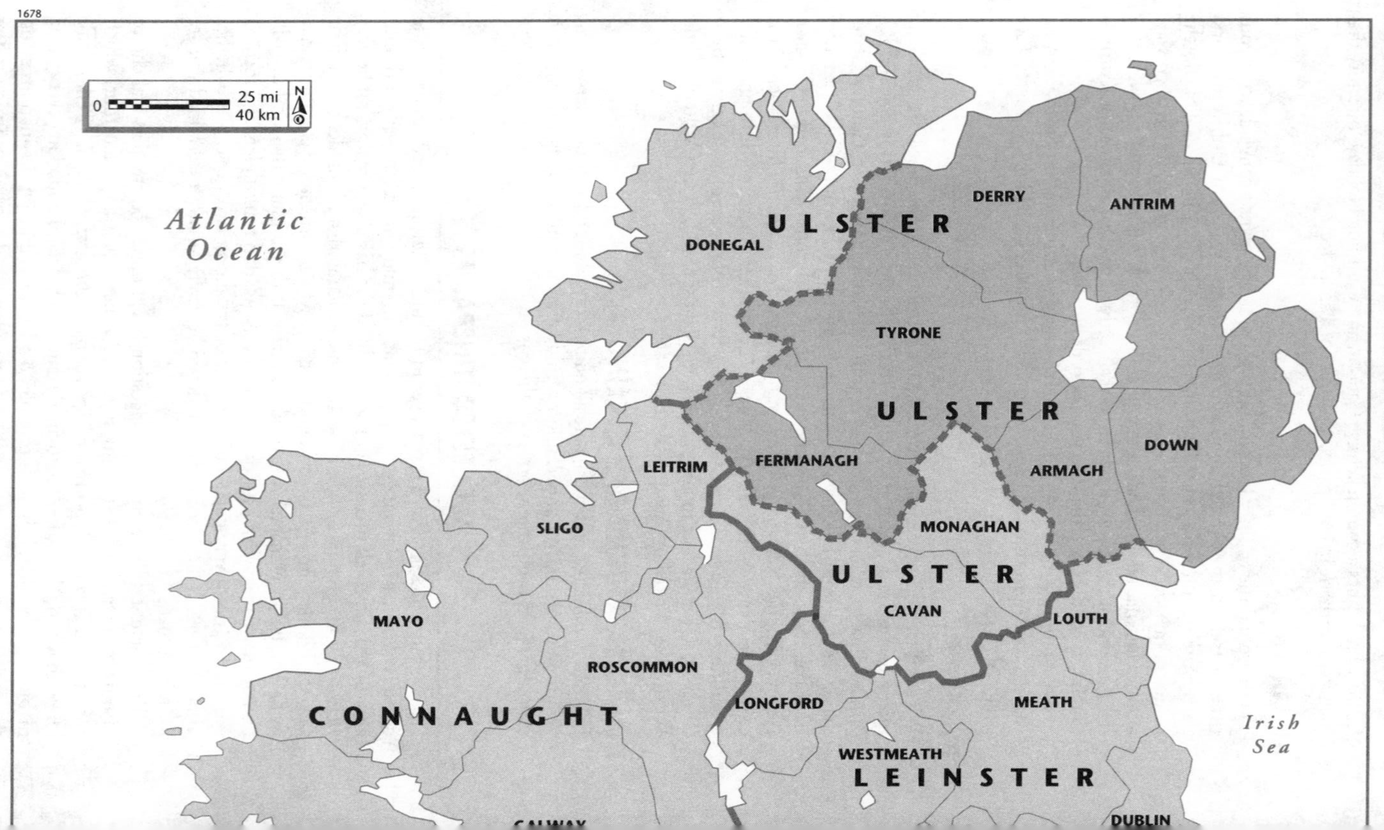

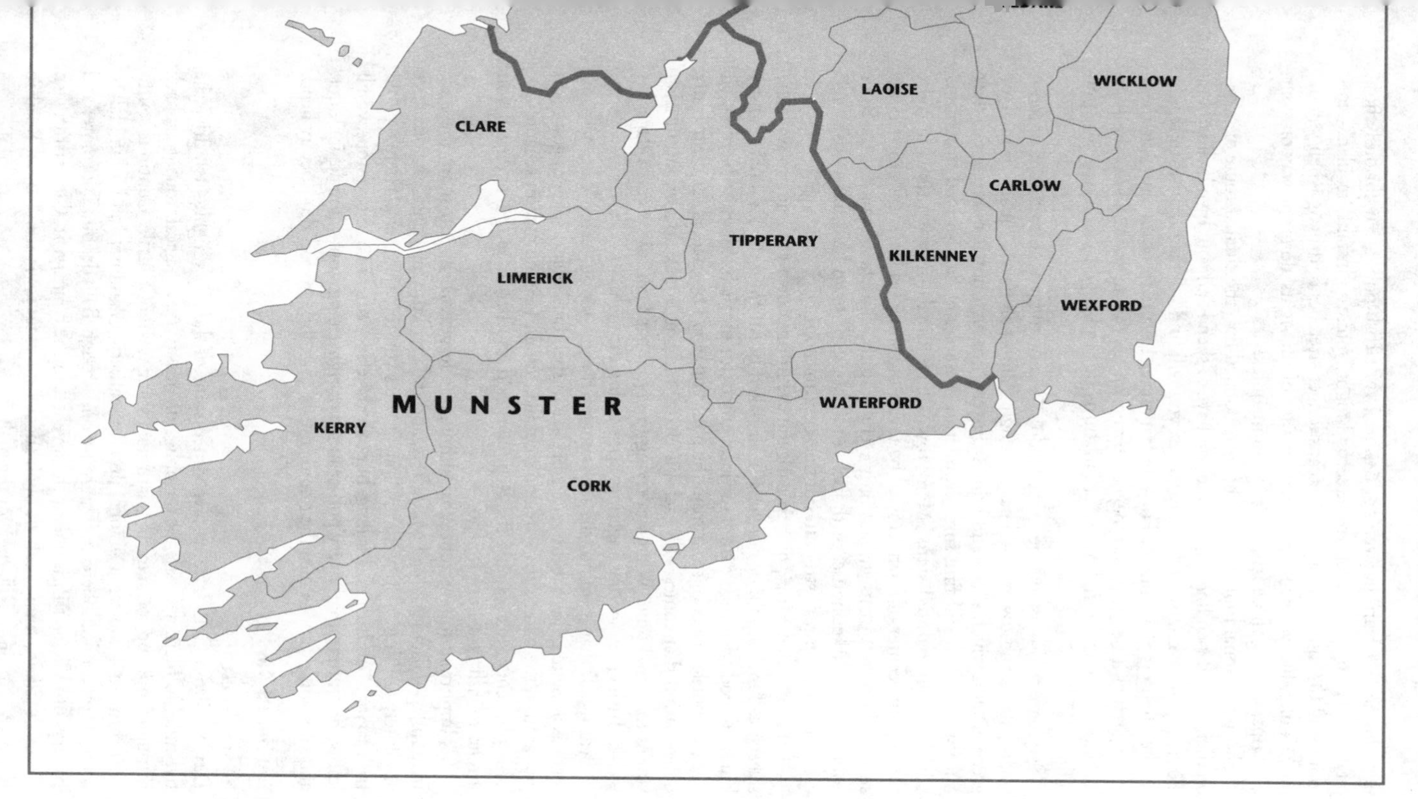
CLARE
LAOISE
WICKLOW
CARLOW
TIPPERARY
KILKENNEY
LIMERICK
WEXFORD
MUNSTER
WATERFORD
KERRY
CORK

same homey B&B in the evening. Besides, while Irish pubs are notoriously hospitable to visitors, if you return the second night, you're an instant "regular"—lots more fun! Of course, such a plan means longer stretches of driving when you do move along, but you will have taken in a lot of the sights along the way on your day trips, making those Irish miles go more quickly.

Shorter regional itineraries can be incorporated into the circular route or taken on their own, depending on the time you have to spend and your own inclinations. To help you make any such adjustments, you will find full details for each region in the chapters that follow. For one last time, I want to point out that these are suggested itineraries, and they are by no means cast in stone. Do as the Irish do and just "go with it," whatever "it" turns out to be, and you'll have a happy holiday.

No matter how you decide to travel, do take time to savor at least some of those small villages and towns you'll pass through. Almost all have a square, or mall, or green around which shops and homes cluster. Although not as numerous as they once were, you'll still find some wonderful examples of hand-carved storefronts with ornately painted signs. Many towns have canals or rivers flowing right through the center of town, crossed by lovely old stone bridges. Still others boast sturdy old towers or town halls or gracefully spired churches. Look for the local courthouse, market house, or tholsel (a toll house or town hall), many of which are early 19th-century structures of fine-cut limestone.

You might make it a point to park the car in one town each day to walk the streets; call into a pub; or purchase fresh-baked bread from the local baker and a hunk of good Irish cheese from the local grocer for picnic makings, to be rounded out by a bottled lager or stout from the pub. You won't be charged for the friendly conversation that comes with each purchase, and you'll pick up a wealth of Irish stories to carry home. What I'm trying to say is that Irish towns and villages, as well as Irish cities, are for lingering, not rushing through!

Bearing all that in mind, the recommended tours set out below can, perhaps, serve as a useful guide for the time you have to spend in Ireland. The longest takes you around the outer rim of Ireland's cuplike terrain (see the map in Chapter 2). This tour encompasses only the Republic: Add another three to five days if you intend to visit Northern Ireland.

It's important to remember that although mileages may appear short, these are Irish miles—distances, road conditions, and the usual driving considerations have absolutely nothing to do with how long it takes you to cover them. There's an old Irish saying: "An Irish mile is long, but easy traveled." After one or two stops, you'll know the truth in that! Every pub or lunch or sightseeing stop will make it clearer, and you won't want to miss the photo "musts" that lurk around almost every bend.

If You Have 3 Days

The Southwest

Day 1 From Cork (after you've visited some of the city's highlights), drive the five miles to Blarney Castle for the obligatory kiss of that magical stone, then back through Cork and south to the charming fishing town of Kinsale. Continue southwest through Timoleague, Clonakilty, Rosscarbery, Glandore, and Union Hall to the old town of Skibbereen. The route on through Ballydehob, Toormore, and Bantry into Glengarriff is one of the loveliest in the country. In Glengarriff, visit Garinish Island, then climb through rugged mountains via the Tunnel Road to Kenmare and on to Killarney for the night.

Day 2 Allow the entire day to drive the Ring of Kerry (110 miles), since you won't want to rush through some of Ireland's most spectacular sea and mountain landscape. From Killarney, head for Killorglin, Glenbeigh, Cahirciveen, Waterville, Derrynane, Castlecove, Sneem, and Kenmare before returning to Killarney for the night.
Day 3 See the Dingle Peninsula's very special charms. From Killarney, drive to Killorglin, then north to Castlemaine, west to Inch (where much of *Ryan's Daughter* was filmed). Annascaul, Dingle, Ventry, Slea Head, Dunquin, Ballyferriter, Murreagh, and back to Dingle. Cross Connor's Pass to the north side of the peninsula and Stradbally, Camp, and Tralee before heading back to Killarney. Alternatively, stay the night in one of the lovely B&Bs on the peninsula.

If You Have 1 Week

The West Coast

A good tour for those deplaning at Shannon.
Day 1 Stay in Limerick, visit Bunratty Folk Park, and take in a castle banquet in the evening (must be booked ahead).
Day 2 Drive to Ennis, then southwest to the picturesque seaside resort towns of Kilrush and Kilkee; head north to Lahinch and skirt Liscannor Bay to the mystical Cliffs of Moher; on to Lisdoonvarna, through the bleakly beautiful Burren to Black Head, Ballyvaughan, Kinvara, and Clarinbridge into Galway, where you'll spend the night.
Day 3 Head for Connemara by way of Spiddal, Costello, Screeb, Derryrush, Carna, Toombeola, Ballynahinch, and Clifden. Head northward to Letterfrack and Leenane, where a turn to the southeast will take you through Maam, Cong (setting of *The Quiet Man*), Ballinrobe, Ballintubber (stop to see the abbey), and into Castlebar. Visit Clonalis House, and make Castlebar your overnight stop.
Day 4 Drive to Westport and visit impressive Westport House with its magnificent mansion and zoo park. Take the road to Newport and travel through Mulrany to the Curraun Peninsula, Achill Sound, and on to the breathtaking views of Achill Island (reached by a causeway). Allow time to drive as far out as Keel and Dooagh. Stay overnight on Achill or return to Westport.
Day 5 Turn inland through a changing landscape to Castlebar, Claremorris (Knock and its celebrated shrine are a short detour away), Ballyhaunis, Castlerea, and Roscommon (visit its famous abbey) to Athlone for the night.
Day 6 Heading south from Athlone, drive to Birr and stop to visit the gardens at Birr Castle. Farther south, Nenagh's fine castle dates from about 1200. Turn due west for Portroe and drive along the shores of Lough Derg to Killaloe. From here, it's a short drive, via O'Brien's Bridge and Ardnacrusha, into Limerick.
Day 7 Departure for home.

The East Coast and Lakeland

Day 1 Arrival in Dublin, settle in, and perhaps take in a cabaret in the evening.
Day 2 Drive south through Dun Laoghaire, Dalkey, and Killiney along the Vico Road, with its spectacular views of Dublin Bay, into the seaside resort of Bray (leave the main road to detour along the seafront). Then head on to Enniskerry beneath Sugarloaf Mountain. Visit nearby Powerscourt Estate and Gardens. Glendalough and its timeless ruins are next along the scenic mountain drive, then on to Rathdrum, Avoca, and Woodenbridge into Arklow. Proceed to County Wexford's Gorey, Enniscorthy (stop in the museum), and into Wexford town,

where an overnight stop will give you time to walk its narrow streets and relive its gallant history.

Day 3 From Wexford, head southwest to Ballyhack to catch the ferry across Waterford Harbor to Passage East in County Waterford (if you're enamored of tiny seaside villages, make the short detour to Dunmore East). See Waterford's 1003 Reginald's Tower and remnants of its Viking-built city walls. Kilkenny is next, where you should stop to see Kilkenny Castle, Rothe House, and the Kilkenny Design Workshops. Then it's on through Tullamore (home of the famous Tullamore Dew) to Athlone, "capital" of the midlands. Make this your overnight stop.

Day 4 Drive northwest to Roscommon, look at Roscommon Abbey, then on to the market town of Longford, with its 19th-century cathedral. Head southeast to Edgeworthstown (where you may want to visit the museum dedicated to novelist Maria Edgeworth) and through the angling center of Castlepollard to see nearby Tullynally Castle. Lough Derravaragh, in the immediate vicinity, is the setting of the Irish legend of the Children of Lir. Detour to Fore to see its Benedictine abbey and ancient crosses, then back to Castlepollard and south to Mullingar to spend the night.

Day 5 From Mullingar, drive through Kinnegad to Trim, with its impressive Norman castle. Then head for Navan, where a short detour onto the Dublin road will bring you to the royal Hill of Tara before heading back to Navan and on to Donaghmore and Slane. Look for Bronze Age cemeteries at Brugh na Boinne and visit Mellifonte Abbey and Monasterboice; then go on north to Dunleer, Castlebellingham, and Dundalk. If there's time, drive a bit farther north to the rugged little Carlingford Peninsula, then back to Dundalk and along the coast through Clogher, Termonfeckin, Baltray, Drogheda, Balbriggan, Skerries, Rush, Swords, and Howth (where there are marvelous views of the bay) and on to Dublin by way of Sutton.

Day 6 Spend this day exploring Dublin.

Day 7 Departure for home.

If You Have 2 Weeks

A Circular Tour

The suggested starting point is Dublin. If you deplane at Shannon, however, you can simply begin with the Day 9 itinerary and follow the suggested route to the north or south, ending up again at Shannon for your flight home.

Days 1 and 2 *Dublin.* Allow your arrival day for settling into your Dublin digs and getting the feel of the city. Spend the second day exploring Dublin's fine historic buildings and Georgian squares, ending with a hotel cabaret or an evening's pub crawl.

Day 3 *Dublin to Waterford (or Tramore).* Get an early start and drive south to Enniskerry to visit the Powerscourt Estate and Gardens. Then on through Roundwood to Glendalough with its early-Christian ruins. Avoca is next, then south through Arklow to Enniscorthy, with time out to visit its small museum, and on straight through to Waterford—or detour over to historic Wexford before continuing on to Waterford. Stop for the night in the city itself, or drive on to the seaside resort of Tramore with its three miles of sandy beaches.

Day 4 *Waterford to Cork.* Drive south through the old market town of Dungarvan, then westward to Youghal. Stop at the clock tower in the middle of town to visit its interesting museum, allowing ample time for the walking tour described in a brochure available there, which will take you along some of Ireland's oldest surviving city walls. Then it's on to Cork, where you can play the famous Shandon Bells at St. Mary's, visit the city's many historic sites, enjoy an evening meal in one of its fine restaurants, and spend the night.

Day 5 *Cork to Killarney.* Stop by Blarney Castle to kiss the legendary stone, then head for Macroom, Ballingeary, and the Pass of Keimaneigh (you may want to make the short detour to Gougane Barra National Park). Go on to the lovely holiday resort of Glengarriff, then turn north through rugged mountain terrain to Kenmare and on to Killarney.

Days 6 and 7 *Killarney.* You'll want to spend one day visiting the famous lakes, islands, and ancient abbeys. The next day, Killarney is the ideal base from which to make either the 109-mile Ring of Kerry drive or a 93-mile circuit of the bewitching Dingle Peninsula.

Day 8 *Killarney to Limerick.* If you opted for the Ring of Kerry on Day 7, you can swing around Dingle en route to Limerick (but it makes for a long day of driving—Dingle is, in fact, a perfect place for one of those itinerary adjustments to allow for an overnight stop). Then back through Rathkeal, Newcastle West, and the beautiful village of Adare to Limerick (only 16 miles from Shannon Airport). Save this evening for the Bunratty or Knappogue Castle medieval banquet (which must be booked ahead).

Day 9 *Limerick to Galway.* Take time to explore Limerick's St. Mary's Cathedral before heading north; then add a few extra miles to take in the stunning Cliffs of Moher. Lisdoonvarna, the popular spa resort, is next, then the barren beauty of the Burren's limestone hills, Ballyvaughan, Clarinbridge, and Galway. Traditional music in a pub in Galway or nearby Salthill makes for a memorable evening.

Day 10 *Galway to Donegal.* A full day's drive will take you through Connemara to Moycullen, Oughterard, Recess, Clifden, Leenane, and along Clew Bay (with over 100 islands) into Westport. Not far away is Westport House, with its magnificent interior, beautiful gardens, and zoo park. Then head north through Castlebar, Pontoon, Ballina, and the seaside resort of Enniscrone. Then drive on to Sligo to see the 13th-century Franciscan friary and the county library museum or just walk the narrow old streets and soak up the atmosphere so dear to Yeats's heart. Finally, it's on to Bundoran, Ballyshannon, and Donegal.

Day 11 *Donegal.* Early in the day, explore Donegal town, with its Franciscan friary and castle. Then head off for a circular tour of County Donegal by driving west through Mountcharles, Killybegs, Ardara, Glenties, Maas, and Kincasslagh (Donegal tweed country). Push farther north through Annagry, Crolly, Bunbeg, Bloody Foreland, Gortahork, and into Dunfanaghy, nestled at the foot of steep cliffs along the shores of Sheephaven Bay. Drive south to Letterkenny (and if you've an extra day, I strongly recommend the 120-mile loop around the Inishowen Peninsula to Buncrana, Malin Head, and Moville—the scenery is truly spectacular and well worth the drive), then through the picturesque Finn Valley back to Donegal town.

Day 12 *Donegal to Carrick-on-Shannon.* Make this a leisurely driving day, south through Ballyshannon and Bundoran, then southeast to Manorhamilton (look for the ruins of a 1638 castle brooding over the town). Continue south through Drumkeeran and along the shores of lovely Lough Allen (a good place for a picnic lunch) to Drumshabo and Leitrim and into Carrick-on-Shannon, with its fleet of cruise boats bobbing at the wharves.

Day 13 *Carrick-on-Shannon to Dublin.* Drive through lake country to Cavan town by way of Mohill, Carrigallen, Killeshandra, and Crossdoney, and on through Bailieborough and Carrickmacross to Drogheda. From Drogheda, visit the prehistoric tomb at Newgrange, then drive on through Slane into Navan. A further six miles will bring you to the Hill of Tara, home of ancient Irish high kings. From there, it's back to Dublin via historic Trim, Black Bull, Clonee, Blanchardstown, and the Phoenix Park.

Day 14 *Dublin.* A day for odds and ends and departure.

FAST FACTS: Ireland

American Express The main office of American Express International, Inc., Travel Services, is at 116 Grafton St., Dublin 2 (☎ 01/677-2874; to report lost or stolen traveler's checks, toll free in Ireland 800/626-0000). Check with the Dublin office for addresses of travel agencies that represent American Express in Cork, Galway, and Limerick. Their services include currency exchange, selling traveler's checks, accepting mail for members, and full travel agency facilities.

The American Express representative in Northern Ireland is Hamilton Travel, 10 College St., Belfast BY1 6BT (☎ 01232/322-455).

Automobile Association In the Republic, the AA has main offices at 23 Rockhill, Blackrock, Dublin (☎ 01/283-3555), and 12 Emmet Place, Cork (☎021/276922).

Business Hours Banks close for the lunch hour all over the country, and are open Monday through Friday from 10am to 12:30pm and 1:30 to 3pm; they're closed Saturday, Sunday, and bank holidays. Some banks stay open until 5pm one day a week (in Dublin, it's Thursday, but days vary from location to location). Airport banks are open every day except Christmas from 7:30am to 11pm. Shops are open Monday through Saturday from 9am to 5:30pm (closed Sunday and holidays), and most large stores in Dublin have hours of 9am to 8pm one day a week (Thursday, as of this writing). Supermarkets and many small shops are open until 9pm on specified days of the week. Outside Dublin, some shops have a midweek early-closing day (usually 1pm), which varies from town to town.

Customs Citizens of non-EC countries may bring the following into Ireland: if you're over the age of seventeen, 200 cigarettes, 50 cigars, 9 ounces of tobacco, and 1 liter of distilled beverages and spirits exceeding 38.5 proof or 2 liters of other spirits; all ages may bring other dutiable goods valued at up to IR£32 ($51.20); and as much currency as you wish. (See "Drug and Firearms Laws," below, regarding those items.) On leaving, there are no restrictions on any Irish purchase you carry with you, but you may not take out of the country more than IR£100 ($160) in Irish currency (if you wind up with a surplus, be sure to have notes converted to traveler's checks—on which there is no restriction—at a bank prior to departure).

Upon reentering the U.S., you'll be allowed to bring back purchases valued up to $400 without paying Customs duties. Anything in excess of that amount will be assessed a flat 10%. Antiques that are more than 100 years old come in duty free, but you must have an authentication of age from the dealer from whom you bought them to present to U.S. Customs. The detailed booklet "Know Before You Go" (publication no. 512) is available without charge from the U.S. Customs Service, P.O. Box 7407, Washington, DC 20044.

Drug and Firearms Laws There are strict laws prohibiting the importation of drugs and/or illegal handguns or other firearms, with stiff prison sentences the penalty. If you have a legitimate reason to bring any kind of firearm into Ireland, *be sure* you check with your nearest Irish consulate for regulations and that you comply with them to the letter. There are consulates in New York, Boston, Chicago, San Francisco, and Ottawa.

Electricity Ireland's electricity is 220 volts AC, so if you must bring small appliances (like hairdryers), pack a voltage transformer and a variety of plug adapters. Electric shavers using 110 volts should present no problem, since there will be shaver points in virtually every accommodation.

Embassies and Consulates I hope you'll not need such services. But in case you lose your passport or have some other emergency, here's a list of addresses and phone numbers:

- **Australia** The embassy is at Fitzwilliam House, Wilton Terrace, Dublin 2 (☎ 01/676-1517).
- **Canada** The embassy is at 65 St. Stephen's Green, Dublin 2 (☎ 01/678-1988).
- **United States** The embassy is at 42 Elgin Road, Dublin 4 (☎ 01/668-8777).

Emergencies Dial **999** for fire, police, or an ambulance.

Etiquette You will find the Irish, on all social levels, still observing old-world courtesies and niceties (God forbid that a lady, especially a *visiting* lady, should carry a heavy package when there's an able-bodied Irishman around!), and they are extremely appreciative of others who follow their example. A demanding tone of voice, breaking into a queue, or any other form of "pushiness" is simply not acceptable. Such behavior may well go without comment (because of their own code of etiquette), but you may be very sure it does not go without notice. What is sure to bring beaming compliments is polite behavior on the part of American children, so a briefing to your young fry is definitely in order. Display old-fashioned good manners, and you won't go wrong. (See also Section 9, "Irish Pubs," in Chapter 2 for tips on pub etiquette.)

Liquor Laws You must be 18 years or over to be served alcoholic beverages in Ireland. That does not exclude under-18s from pubs and lounges, only from being served the hard stuff. During summer months, pubs are open Monday through Saturday from 10:30am to 11:30pm, and on Sunday from 12:30 to 2pm and 4 to 11pm. In winter, the closing hour is 11pm. Hotels and guesthouses can serve alcoholic beverages at any time of day or night to resident guests only.

Mail In the Republic, airmail postage to the U.S. for letters is 52p (83¢) for the first 20 grams, 22p (35¢) for each additional gram. The less expensive, post-paid air letters (called aerogrammes), available from all post offices, cost 45p (72¢) per letter, and you can save even more by asking for them in packs of five at IR£2.20 ($3.52). Postcards sent airmail to the U.S. require postage of 38p (61¢), and they may be purchased in packs of five for IR£1.20 ($1.92). Street mailboxes are painted green, and are either freestanding (usually at a street corner) or set into an outer wall.

General Delivery in Ireland is known as Poste Restante, and it is received at the General Post Office, O'Connell Street, Dublin, as well as local GPOs in other large cities around the country. Hours for pickup of mail in Dublin are Monday through Saturday from 10:30am to 8pm and on Sunday from 9am to 8pm; in other locations, it's Monday through Friday from 9am to 5:30pm, and some suboffices close at 1pm one day a week. Mail will be held a maximum of one month.

Newspapers and Magazines National daily newspapers are the *Irish Times, Irish Independent, Evening Herald, Irish Press, Evening Press, Cork Examiner,* and *Evening Echo.* National Sunday editions are the *Sunday Independent, Sunday Press, Sunday Tribune, Sunday World,* and the Irish-language *Anola.* There are many good regional newspapers published on a weekly basis—check newsagents in each locality.

Police Dial 999. Garda Siochana ("protector of the peace") is the Gaelic name for the Irish police force, and they're familiarly known as Garda (if there's just one) and Gardai ("*Gard-ee,*" collectively). Except for special detachments, they're unarmed, and they wear dark-blue uniforms.

Pub Hours In the Republic, pubs are open in the winter Monday through Saturday from 10:30am to 11pm, until 11:30pm in the summer months. On Sunday, they're open year-round from 12:30 to 2pm and 4 to 11pm.

Restrooms Even the smallest Irish town usually has public restrooms (which are usually clean and always safe to use), as do most hotels, department stores, pubs, restaurants, and theaters—gas (petrol) stations do not. A helpful tip: Some public toilets are not as well equipped as they might be, and it's a good idea to carry paper tissues in your handbag for emergencies. Restrooms are usually marked with the Gaelic *Mna* (women) and *Fir* (men).

Safety Your worst safety hazard in Ireland is likely to be on the roads—from driving on the left! Reread carefully the driving hints in Section 9 of this chapter.

Ireland enjoys a relatively low crime rate, and there is very little physical violence. I must, however, add a cautionary note about hitchhiking or wandering around city streets in the wee hours on your own. You are advised, in either case, to team up with someone. In larger cities, such as Dublin and Limerick, you should be careful to carry your wallet or handbag in a manner not conducive to pickpockets or purse snatchers. Whenever you are traveling in an unfamiliar city or country, it is your responsibility to stay alert and be aware of your immediate surroundings.

Dublin has been the victim of waves of car theft in recent years, so be sure you leave nothing in your parked car, even in guesthouse or hotel car parks.

Taxes VAT (Value-Added Tax) applies to virtually every phase of your Irish expenses, with the exception of B&B accommodations. The percentage varies with the category—hotels and guesthouses, restaurants, petrol, shop goods, etc.

Telephones Although they are fast being replaced by newer models, you may run into older coinboxes that operate on a Button A and Button B basis (you deposit your coins and dial, then push Button A when your party answers—Button B is for coin return). Newer pay phones, which accept 5p, 10p, 20p, and 50p coins, are simpler to use and have instructions printed right on the telephone. Local calls cost 20p (32¢), and you should have an ample supply of change if you're making a toll call.

To avoid a shortfall of change, you can purchase Phonecards in multiples of 20p (32¢) at post offices, newsagents, and some shops. Phonecard telephones are located at most public phone sites, and quite aside from the convenience, they are often the best way to avoid long lines waiting to use coin boxes. You pay less when calling from a private phone, and you can now dial international calls directly. The cheapest rates are on weekends and between 6pm and 8am on weekdays. Dial 1190 for telephone-number information.

To call Ireland, dial your international access code, then 353 (country code for Ireland), then Irish area code, *omitting the 0,* then the Irish telephone number. *Example:* From the U.S., 011-353-54-123-4567. To call the U.S. from Ireland, Ireland's international access code is 00—dial 00-1 (U.S. country code)-212-123-4567.

For collect calls, dial 1-800/550-000 for USA Direct service.

Time A good part of the charm of the Irish is their almost total disregard for time. Be that as it may, Ireland's official time is Greenwich mean time in winter and Greenwich summer time (daylight savings) from mid-March to October. There is a five-hour difference with U.S. eastern standard time. Summer days are brilliantly light (or mistily light, depending on the whimsical showers) until 10:30 or 11pm, while in winter darkness descends as early as 4pm.

Tipping There really is no hard-and-fast rule for tipping in Ireland—the tradition of no tipping at all still clings to some rural areas and in some social situations (such as pubs, where you never tip the man behind the stick), but in most cases the waitress, taxi driver, or anyone else rendering a service will accept your tip with courteous appreciation.

As a general rule, you'd want to tip porters carrying bags, waitresses, parking-lot attendants, hairdressers, and barbers. Many restaurants include a service charge on the bill, in which case it is usually printed on the menu and you need not tip additionally. If there is no service-charge information either on the menu or your bill, be sure to ask before you leave a tip. As for the amount you tip, observe the 10% to 15% rule, with one exception—your minimum tip should be 50p, whether or not a percentage of the bill amounts to that much. Actually, whether you tip or not, it's the sincere "thank you" that the Irish value most.

If you stay in a guesthouse or lodge, a small service tip will be welcomed. In B&Bs, tipping is not really called for unless someone has been especially helpful (but *never* your host).

Water No problems with Ireland's drinking water, and the beaches are remarkably pollution free—many were awarded the European Clean Water flag.

4 Outdoor & Special-Interest Vacations

Surrounded by water and stroked by Gulf Stream breezes, Ireland enjoys a temperate climate year-round—ideal for all types of outdoor activities. Irish waters are notably pollution-free—in the Dublin area alone, seven beaches can boast the European Blue Flag award. Those who don't demand summer temperatures much above 70 degrees Fahrenheit can swim at all those lovely beaches. Other water sports include surfing, waterskiing, and boardsailing (windsurfing). Personally, I find walking the sandy strands and deserted coves more fun than braving the waves—it's positively restorative to commune with sea and sun on long stretches when there's not another soul in sight. Yet for those who prefer more active vacations—biking, fishing, golfing, hiking, horseback riding—I offer the information below in this chapter. If you're unable to obtain any of the information sheets mentioned below, write to the **Irish Tourist Board, Distribution Centre,** P.O. Box 1083, Chancery Lane, Dublin 8, Ireland. They'll send you their "Publications Sales Order Form," which lists titles available and the small charges and postage costs for each.

The latter part of this chapter is devoted to special-interest vacations, such as Irish language programs, study programs at Trinity College and other schools, and tracing your Irish roots.

1 Biking

A favorite Irish sport as well as pastime, cycling can be done, of course, on your own or on an organized cycling holiday. Except for cows and sheep, the roads in rural Ireland and Northern Ireland are relatively traffic-free, so biking is quite leisurely. Contact the Federation of Irish Cyclists, 619 North Circular Road, Dublin 1 (☎ **01/855-1522; fax 01/855-1771).** Countrywide, the tourist board has information sheets that will be helpful in planning your tour; regional and countrywide itineraries are detailed.

For those who want to bike it on their own, rentals can be obtained through more than 100 **Rent-a-Bike** dealers around the country. Rates are IR£7 ($11.20) per day or IR£30 ($48) per week. A deposit of IR£40 ($64) is required. Advance booking is necessary for long bike trips during the months of July and August. Students can obtain a discount through USIT (see "Tips for Special Travelers," in Chapter 3). If you return your bike to a different office from the one you got it, a small extra fee is charged. In Dublin, Rent-a-Bike has an office at 58 Lower Gardiner St. (☎ 01/872-5399; fax 01/436-4763).

An excellent selection of one- and two-week tours are offered by **Celtic Cycling,** Lorum Old Rectory, Bagenalstown, Co. Carlow (☎ 0503/75282; fax 0503/75455). Join one of their standard tours or ask them to tailor one to your own special interests. Tours include a daily briefing of your itinerary and point-to-point transportation of your luggage; packed lunches are an additional small charge. Other companies that arrange guided biking vacations include **Backroads Bicycle Touring,** 1516 Fifth St., Berkeley, CA 94710 (☎ 800/245-3874 or 510/527-1555); **Classic Bicycle Tours & Treks,** P.O. Box 668, Clarkson, NY 14430 (☎ 800/777-8090 or 716/637-5930); **Destination Ireland,** 250 W. 57th St., Suite 2511, New York, NY 10019 (☎ 800/832-1848 or 212/977-9629); and **Gerhard's Bicycle Odysseys,** P.O. Box 757, Portland, OR 97207 (☎ 503/223-2402).

A bike tour from Dublin to Wicklow would take about one day. The terrain of this 27-mile trip varies from flat land to rolling hills. The route follows the coast road and crosses through pastureland. The best time to take this tour is May through July and during September. Another day trip is the 35-mile trip from Kilkenny to Cashel. Around the bustling Kilkenny area, the terrain is flat, but it becomes hilly halfway through the trip. This tour passes through the quiet villages; during the final miles, the Rock of Cashel comes in view.

2 Camping

If the great outdoors holds such appeal for you that tenting is the only way to go, then the very first item in your backpack should be the Irish Tourist Board's **"Accommodations" booklet,** which lists approved campgrounds, renters of camping equipment, and companies that rent vans, or RVs, known to the Irish as caravans. To be approved by the tourist board, campgrounds must provide good toilet facilities, water-supply points, rubbish-disposal facilities, and properly spaced sites for tents and caravans. Many offer far more than these minimum requirements, with laundry and recreational facilities, shops, and sometimes even a restaurant. Fees vary according to the location and season; they range from IR£5 to IR£10 ($8 to $16) per night for caravans or tents, with a small additional per-person charge.

Camping equipment can be rented from **O'Meara Camping Ireland Ltd.,** Ossory Business Park, off Strand Rd., Dublin 3 (☎ 01/836-3233). Advance reservations are necessary; a two-person tent runs from about IR£20 ($32) per week. For information on renting mobile homes, vans, and RVs, contact the **Irish Caravan Council,** P.O. Box 4443, Dublin 6 (☎ 061/377-118).

3 Cruise Boat & Barge Holidays

Boating on Ireland's hundreds of miles of inland waterways offers an ideal escape from the rigors of driving. Cruising along the magnificent Shannon, or from Belturbet to Belleek by way of Lower and Upper Lough Erne and its connecting river, or on the Grand Canal from Dublin all the way to the Shannon or Barrow invokes a tranquility that just doesn't exist behind the wheel of an automobile. Add to that the view of the countryside from the water and stopovers at riverside towns and villages.

A full list of companies renting cabin cruisers is available from the Irish Tourist Board. Costs range from IR£95 to IR£240 ($152 to $384) per person per week, depending on the size of the cruiser and the season. Cabin cruisers can be rented from **Carrick Craft,** Carrick-on-Shannon, County Leitrim (☎ 078/20236); **Emerald Star Line,** 47 Dawson St., Dublin 2 (☎ 01/679-8166); **Athlone Cruisers Ltd.,** Shancurragh, Athlone, County Westmeath (☎ 0902/72892).

4 Gaelic Football & Hurling

A century old in its present organized form, Gaelic football almost certainly has roots way back in the days of fierce tribal rivalries; encroaching civilizations undoubtedly shoved all that competitive spirit from battleground to football pitch. None of the fervor of either participants or spectators has been lost in the shift, however. An amateur sport, Gaelic football is played by two teams of 15. It's a field game similar to soccer and rugby, but it's played with the hands. Matches take place every weekend throughout the summer in all the 32 counties. For sheer excitement, nothing quite matches sharing the stands in early September at **Croke Park** in Dublin with more than 90,000 fans roaring support for their county teams in the **All Ireland finals,** the Irish "Super Bowl."

Unique to Ireland, hurling is one of the world's fastest field sports, and I sometimes think it takes the Irish to figure out its two-level scoring. An amateur sport, it's played by two teams of 15, using sticks and a little leather ball. Goals and points are earned depending on whether the ball is hit past the goaltender and over the goal line or over the goaltender's head between the upright goalposts—and there ends my personal comprehension of the scoring. My ignorance notwithstanding, I find a Sunday afternoon match irresistible—the skill and speed of agile athletes wielding hurleys (those wooden sticks not unlike our hockey sticks) are wondrous to behold.

5 Golf

Professional golfers and bumbling amateurs who just like to whack the ball around will be welcome guests at more than 200 golf courses around the country—about 50 of these are championship class. Teeing off is a sporting way to see some of Ireland's most appealing sights. Courses are as varied as the landscape. Lahinch, one of the Irish circuit's most challenging championship courses, is nestled near the Cliffs of Moher on the Atlantic. The seaside links at Salthill overlook Galway Bay. Killarney's twin courses rest amid a panorama of lake and mountain vistas. Royal County Down sits "where the Mountains of Mourne sweep down to the sea."

The booklets *Golf, Only the Best* and *Irish Golf Courses* are available from the Irish Tourist Board; these list all of Ireland's golf courses and detail their facilities and amenities. A calendar of golf events is published each year by the **Golfing Union of Ireland,** 81 Eglington Rd., Dublin 4 (☎ 01/269-4111; fax 01/269-5368).

Greens fees run from IR£8 to IR£20 ($12.80 to $32) per day. You're well advised to bring your own clubs, but some pro shops do rent clubs at about IR£4 ($6.40). At some of the larger courses, caddies can be booked ahead, but they're generally not available. Don't look for a golf mobile; the closest thing you'll find is a lightweight pull cart.

Golfing vacation packages can be arranged to include accommodations and golf clinics. Special golfing weekends for groups or societies can also be set up. For full particulars—or for help in making up an itinerary of your own—consult the Irish Tourist Board or travel agents. To reserve tee times—which can be a real problem during peak season—contact **Golfing Ireland,** 18 Parnell Square, Dublin 1 (☎ 353-1/872-6700, fax 353-1/872-6632, or toll free in Ireland 1850/423-423). No fee is charged for this reservation service. It's best to book as far in advance as possible.

More than three dozen tour operators offer golf vacation packages including **Aer Lingus Vacations,** 122 E. 42nd St., New York, NY 10168 (☎ 800/223-6537 or 212/557-1110); **Golf Getaways,** 30423 Canwood St., Suite 227, Agoura Hills, CA 91301 (☎ 800/991-9270 or 818/991-7015); **Golf International,** 275 Madison Ave., Suite 1819, New York, NY 10016 (☎ 800/833-1389 or 212/986-9176); **Ireland Golf Tours,** 251 E. 85th St., New York, NY 10028 (☎ 800/346-5388 or 212/772-8220); **Owenoak Tours,** 3 Parklands Dr., Darien, CT 06820 (☎ 800/426-4498 or 203/655-2531); and **Wide World of Golf,** Box 5217, Carmel, CA (☎ 408/624-6667).

6 Fishing

If there's such a thing as a fisherman's heaven, it must be located in Ireland. You can go angling for such freshwater fish (coarse fishing) as bream, dace, pike, and perch in all those rivers, streams, and lakes. You can stalk the famous Irish salmon in coastal rivers and their stillwaters and headwaters. Sea trout and brown trout are among the other challenging game fish. Sea anglers can shore-cast from rock piers, beaches, and promontories, and they'll find plentiful supplies of bass, whiting, mullet, flounder, plaice, pollack, and coalfish. All around the coast, deep-sea angling for shark, skate, dogfish, pollack, ling, and conger is yours for incredibly low costs.

For help in planning a fishing holiday, contact the Irish Tourist Board or the **Product & Promotions Department, Irish Tourist Board,** Baggot Street Bridge, Dublin 2 (☎ 01/676-5871). They can furnish helpful Information Sheets in three categories: Salmon, Sea Trout, and Brown Trout; Coarse and Pike Angling; and Sea Angling. They'll point you to the best fisheries and fishing festivals and will provide other useful contacts.

Many hotels and guesthouses near rivers or lakes offer private salmon and trout fishing privileges to guests. Otherwise, the cost of a salmon and sea trout license is IR£3 ($4.80) for one day, IR£10 ($16) for 21 days, IR£12 ($19.20) for a season (one district), or IR£25 ($40) for a season (all districts/all regions). A permit ticket for brown trout is IR£5 ($8) per day or less depending on the area. A complete day's fishing can be arranged for about IR£40 to IR£50 ($64 to $80) per day, with boats and ghillies (guides).

The seasons are as follows: salmon, January 1 to September 30; brown trout, February 15 to October 12; sea trout, June 1 to September 30; coarse fishing and sea angling, January to December.

The **Central Fisheries Board,** Balnagowan House, Mobhi Boreen, Dublin 9 (☎ 01/437-9206) will also provide information on seasons, license fees, and locations of inland and sea fisheries, and guidebooks published by the regional fisheries boards.

Fishing trips to the Republic and Northern Ireland can be arranged through **Adventure Safaris,** 8 S. Michigan Ave., Suite 2012, Chicago IL 60603 (☎ 312/782-4756); **Fishing International,** Hilltop Estate, 4010 Montecito Ave., Santa Rosa, CA 95405 (☎ 800/950-4242 or 707/542-4242); and **Owenoak Tours,** 3 Parklands Dr., Darien, CT 06820 (☎ 800/426-4498 or 203/655-2531).

7 Hiking, Hill Walking & Rock Climbing

The Irish countryside certainly lends itself to extended walks, especially on long summer days when the sun rises early in the morning and sets after 10pm. Trails can be followed though Ireland's scenic areas, its national parks, forest parks, and nature reserves. Contact the Irish Tourist Board for **Information Sheet No. 26A** on **"Hill Walking and Rock Climbing,"** which highlights spectacular climbs and off-the-main-thoroughfare spots of beauty. Other Information Sheets detail walks in Wicklow, Kerry, South Leinster, Kildare, Dingle, and Cavan. (Many of Ireland's cities and towns also offer guided walking tours for visitors.)

Five-day walking-tour packages in various regions of Ireland are offered by **Backroads,** 1516 5th St., Berkeley, CA 94710-1740 (☎ 510/527-1555; fax 510/527-1444). Meals in leading restaurants and overnights in top-class hotels are included.

Walking-tour vacations are also offered by **Brendan Tours,** 15137 Califa St., Van Nuys, CA 91411 (☎ 800/421-8446 or 818/785-9696); **Country Walks,** P.O. Box 180, Waterbury, VT 05676 (☎ 802/244-1387); **Destination Ireland,** 250 W. 57th St., Suite 2511, New York, NY 10019 (☎ 800/832-1848 or 212/977-9629); and **Irish Walking Trails/British Coastal Trails,** California Plaza Suite 302, 1001 B Ave., Coronado, CA 92118 (☎ 800/945-2438 or 619/437-1211).

8 Horseback Riding

Trail riding, hunting, guided point-to-point treks with overnight accommodations, and riding instruction for both children and adults—equestrian holidays can be had with all these themes. On a daily or hourly basis, more than 50 riding stables offer horses for hire. An hour's ride averages IR£10 ($15) in most locations.

A number of equestrian centers offer weeklong packages; you'll find these listed on **Information Sheet 16B,** available from the Irish Tourist Board. For more details on horsebacking riding in the Republic, contact the **Association of Irish Riding Establishments,** 11 Moore Park, Newbridge, County Kildare (☎ 045/31584). In Northern Ireland, contact the **Association of Riding Establishments,** Lessans Riding Stables, 126 Monlough Rd., Saintfield, County Antrim (☎ 1232/510-141).

Equestrian holiday packages are offered through **Cross Country International Equestrian Vacations,** P.O. Box 1170, Millbrook, NY 12545 (☎ 800/828-8768; fax 914/677-6077); **Destination Ireland,** 250 W. 57th St., Suite 2511, New York, NY 10019 (☎ 800/832-1848 or 212/977-9629); and **Keith Prowse USA,** 234 W. 44th St., New York, NY 10036 (☎ 800/669-7469 or 212/398-1430).

9 Horse-Drawn Caravans

Ireland is one of the few places left in the world where you can indulge the gypsy in your soul. (Breathes there a soul among us so dead it hasn't dreamed of gypsy caravans and campfires? I think not.) The gaily painted caravans are comfortably fitted out to accommodate up to four—in fact, you probably should have at least four in your party to travel this way—and your leisurely pace gives you many opportunities to drink in details of Ireland's gorgeous landscape that those traveling by car will never see.

The Tourist Board's **Information Sheet 16C** details the delights of traveling in a horse-drawn caravan. You can directly book trips with **Slattery's Travel Agency,** Attn. David Slattery, Slattery's Horse-Drawn Caravans, 1 Russel St., Tralee, County Kerry (☎ 066/26277; fax 066/25981). Slattery's offers caravans to the Dingle Peninsula, North Kerry, and Killarney. **Dieter Clissman Horse-Drawn Caravan Holidays,** Carrigmore, County Wicklow (☎ 0404/8188), offers caravans to the Wicklow mountains and coast. Reservations for these caravans should be made in advance.

10 Horseracing

As for spectator sports, Irish horseracing has got to be close to the top of the list. A day at a race meet is very like a day at a country fair, with bookmakers vying for punters (bettors) while shouting out odds that change momentarily, and punters shopping around to get their bets down when the odds are at their best. If your horse comes up a winner, you'll be paid from a big satchel at the bookmaker's stand at the odds in existence at the time you placed your bet (so timing can be important, and it pays to do a little shopping around). Irish horses, of course, are world famous, and it's a thrilling sight to see them round the last bend of a grass course against a backdrop of mountains or seashore or rolling green fields.

There are over 250 race meets each year, the Big Five being the **Irish Grand National** at Fairyhouse on Easter Monday, the **Leopardstown Steeplechase** in February, **Punchestown Steeplechases** in April, the **Budweiser Irish Derby** in the Curragh at the end of June or beginning of July, and (probably the most popular of all with the Irish) the **Galway Races** in July.

The tourist board offices can furnish exact dates, and if you should happen on a meet somewhere else in the course of your travels, there goes another itinerary change (one of the happiest Irish times in my personal memory was an evening race meet at Clonmel in County Tipperary when *my* itinerary called for me to be en route to Killarney!).

Ireland eagerly anticipates the World Equestrian Games to be staged for two weeks in August 1998. Show jumping, dressage, carriage driving, endurance riding, and vaulting, described as "gymnastics on horseback," will be part of the competitive events at the Royal Dublin Society in Dublin and the Punchestown Racecourse in Kildare. More than 50 teams from as many countries will participate. For more information, contact Bord Failte.

11 Hunting & Shooting

The hunting season runs from October to March. Horses, guns, and cartridges can be rented through local hunting clubs, to which you'll pay a membership fee. A list of all hunts allowing visitor participation is given on **Information Sheet 16D,** available from the tourist board. Hunts on horseback are recommended for experienced riders only. While fox hunting is the most popular, stag hunts and harrier packs are offered, too. Contact the **Irish Master of Foxhounds Association,** Thornton, Dunlavin, Co. Kildare (☎ 045/51294), or **Mount Juliet Estate,** Thomastown, Co. Kilkenny (☎ 056/24455; fax 056/24522).

Strictly controlled, shoots for woodcock, snipe, golden plover, pheasant, mallard, wigeon, teal, and other ducks is limited for visitors. Shooting without a guide is not condoned. Obtain **Information Sheet 24** for more details.

12 Sailing

With its coastline's many identations forming peaceful bays and harbors, Ireland has fostered generations of sailing folk. If skimming over the water under sails has great appeal to you, obtain the tourist board's **Information Sheet 28G;** it lists outstanding sailing schools with approved training programs. Also contact the **Irish Sailing Association,** 2 Park Rd., Dun Laoghaire, County Dublin (☎ 01/280-0239; fax 01/280-7558).

13 State Forests & Nature Preserves

Undeveloped, Ireland's parks are havens of nature trails, birdsong, and tranquility. With picnic sites and recreational facilities, such as boat slips and pony trekking, there are more than 300 of them. A few have self-catering chalets.

The comprehensive booklet ***Discovering Ireland's Woodlands: A Guide to Forest Parks, Picnic Sites, and Woodland Walks*** will help you do just that. It provides information on trails; main tree species and other flora; fauna; and some history notes. It's available from most tourist offices or from **Coillte Teoranta (The Irish Forestry Board),** Leeson Lane, Dublin 2 (☎ 01/661-5666).

OUTSTANDING PARKS IN THE REPUBLIC

NATIONAL PARKS

Connemara National Park (see Chapter 17), near Letterfrack in County Galway, covers nearly 4,000 acres, with an interesting visitors center, forest walks, and the beautiful Connemara ponies.

Glenveagh National Park (see Chapter 19), in the heart of the Donegal highlands, features 25,000 acres of spectacular woodlands, a castle, gardens, woodland walks, an audiovisual presentation, and a tea room.

Killarney National Park (see Chapter 13), in County Kerry, includes within its 25,000 acres the famous lakes, lake islands, waterfalls, riverside and woodland walks, and an Interpretative Centre with an audiovisual presentation on the park and a scale model of oak woodlands as habitat for birds and other wildlife.

FOREST PARKS

Gougane Barra Forest Park (see Chapter 12), in West Cork, consists of 350 acres, which include deeply wooded mountains, a small jewel of a lake, a small chapel on the island reputed to have been the site of St. Finbar's 6th-century monastery, and scenic walks and drives.

The John F. Kennedy Arboretum (see Chapter 8), near New Ross in County Wexford, includes a 622-acre arboretum devoted to trees and plants, 150 acres of forest, 163 acres of arboreal walks, picnic sites, and a visitors center.

Lough Key Forest Park (see Chapter 20), in County Roscommon, covers 865 acres of mixed woodlands surrounding Lough Key. It has a unique bog garden, lake islands, woodland walks, a full-service caravan park, and in summer a restaurant and shop.

NATURE PRESERVES

The Saltee Islands (see Chapter 8), just south of Wexford town, are a safe haven for scores of bird species, thousands of which either live here permanently or come seasonally.

Lough Hyne (see Chapter 12), southwest of Skibbereen, County Cork, is a highly respected marine nature reserve for several thousand marine and plant species, many of Mediterranean origin.

OUTSTANDING PARKS IN NORTHERN IRELAND

FOREST PARKS

Castlewellan Forest Park (see Chapter 24), in County Down, features a rhododendron wood, beds of dwarf conifers, a wood with brilliant autumn colors, and a spring garden, as well as a sculpture trail.

Tollymore Forest Park (see Chapter 24), near Newcastle, County Down, was Northern Ireland's first forest park (1955), and its walks amble through the foothills of the fabled Mourne Mountains, with an information center and cafe to begin or end your trek.

NATURE PRESERVES

Rathlin Island (see Chapter 23), across the sound from Ballycastle in County Antrim, is a natural drawing card for hundreds of species of sea birds, and its western end offers them a safe haven as a nature reserve.

Tollymore Forest Park (see Chapter 24), near Newcastle in County Down, is both a forestry and wildlife reserve, with sequoia and Himalayan cedars among its stars.

14 Educational Vacations

Published by the Irish Tourist Board, the booklet **"Live and Learn"** is a cornucopia of study possibilities in Ireland for all age groups. Many of these programs include accommodations in Irish homes, weekend travel, and cultural events. Study themes include literature, drama, music, archeology, crafts, and the Irish language. Registration for courses should be done as early as possible. Contact the **Youth and Education Department, Irish Tourist Board,** 345 Park Ave., New York, NY 10154 (☎ 800/223-6470 or 212/418-0800). The tourist board also publishes a **"Group Accommodations List"** of student residence halls, schools, and hotels that offer reduced rates to students.

Encounter Ireland is an Irish Studies summer course (late June to mid-August) given in association with **Trinity College,** Dublin. All full-time students at U.S. colleges and universities are welcomed. Students live with a Dublin family for four weeks; attend lectures, concerts, and art exhibits; and visit the sights in and around the city. A fifth week is left free for independent travel around the country. Contact **USIT,** Encounter Ireland Program, New York Student Center, 895 Amsterdam Ave., New York, NY 10025 (☎ 212/663-5435).

The Irish Way is an educational program for 9th through 12th graders, sponsored by the **Irish Cultural Institute.** During the five-week program (from early July to early August), students learn at both **Wesley College,** Dublin, and **St. Brendan's College** in Killarney, County Kerry. One full week is spent living in the home of an Irish family. Subjects include mythology, history and government, literature, folk music, and balladry. Field trips are arranged. A four-night tour, with hotel accommodations, is included. For details, contact the Irish Way, Irish American Cultural Institute, 433 Raymond Blvd., Newark, NJ 07105 (☎ 201/465-1513).

Summer study programs are also listed in the comprehensive **"Irish Summer Schools Directory,"** published as a supplement to ***Inside Ireland*** (see pg. 45). Details on credit and noncredit courses, accommodations, extracurricular activities, and prices are given.

15 Irish Language Programs

You can nurture your interest in and love of the ancient Irish language by enrolling in a one- or two-week conversation course (from mid-April through mid-September); these are conducted by **Cúrsai do Dhaoine Fásta, Oiddhreacht Chorca Dhuibhne,** Ballyferriter, County Kerry (☎ 066/56100; fax 066/56348). The program is directed at all levels from total beginners to those with a working knowledge to those who want to fine-tune their Irish. Conversation courses are given, as well as those devoted to archeology, folklore, botany, or the Irish language and heritage. Students stay in an Irish-speaking home in a Gaeltacht village. Locals are wonderfully helpful and supportive. Evening activities include Irish dancing, song, and pubbing.

16 Rural Living

One of the newest developments on the Irish tourism scene is Irish Country Holidays, a program that invites visitors to share everyday life with the Irish in communities usually off the tourist track. Visitors are put up in homes, farms, self-catering cottages, or hotels, and they're given the opportunity to take part in turf cutting, bread baking, cheese making, butter churning, salmon smoking, wood turning, and pottery making. Leisure activities—such as fishing, canoeing, rock climbing, hill walking, cycling, and horseback riding—are also part of the holiday. At night there's traditional Irish music, song, dance, and amateur drama productions. Each itinerary is custom-planned. For more information, contact Dervla O'Neill, **Irish Country Holidays,** Plunket House, 84 Merrion Sq., Dublin 2 (☎ 01/676-5790).

17 Tracing Your Irish Roots

If you're one of more than 40 million Americans whose forebears were Irish, it's a good bet you'll want to look up your family while in Ireland. Tracking down your Irish roots may not prove to be a simple matter. To find a particular branch of your family tree, you'll want to know all you possibly can about your family history before leaving home for Ireland. Search any and all records (letters, Bibles, relatives' memories, etc.). Try to get the names of the towns, villages, or counties where your folks lived and the year they emigrated. The more you know about what they did, who they married, and the like, the easier it will be to find your ancestral home or even a cousin once you arrive.

You could hire the services of a commercial agency to trace your ancestors. One of the best firms to contact is **Hibernian Research Co.,** P.O. Box 3097, Dublin 6 (☎ 01/496-6522; fax 01/497-3011). These researchers were trained by the Chief Herald of Ireland. If your ancestors were from the North, a similar service is operated by the **Irish Heritage Association,** The Old Engine House, Portview, 310 Newtownards Road, Belfast BT4 1HE (☎ 0203/455325). Minimum search fees average IR£50 ($80).

Interested in doing the research yourself? Dublin is the location for all the Republic of Ireland's centralized genealogical records, and Belfast is the place to go for Ulster ancestral searches.

You can receive a special consultation on how to trace your ancestry at **The Genealogical Office,** 2 Kildare St., Dublin (☎ 01/661-8811). This is the office of the Chief Herald. Minimum consultation fee is IR£20 ($32).

Present yourself and your records to the **Office of the Registrar General,** at Joyce House, 8/11 Lombard St. East, Dublin 2 (☎ 01/671-1000). Records of births, deaths, and marriages from 1864 to the present are kept here. A general search costs IR£12 ($19.20).

The **National Library,** Kildare St., Dublin 2 (☎ 01/661-9911), contains an extensive collection of pre-1880 Catholic records of baptisms, births, and marriages, as well as journals and directories relating to Irish families. The library has a comprehensive indexing system that will enable you to identify the material you need to consult.

A wealth of information can be looked up at the **National Archives,** Bishop St., Dublin 8 (☎ 01/478-3711). Formerly called the Public Record Office, this bureau holds genealogical and land-tenure records dating as far back as the 17th century. On microfilm are the Church of Ireland Parish Registers.

Land transactions back to 1708 are recorded with the **Registry of Deeds,** Henrietta St., Dublin 1 (☎ 01/873-2233). A fee of IR£2 ($3.20) per day is charged; this includes instruction on how to use the indexes.

For roots in Northern Ireland, consult the **Public Record Office of Northern Ireland,** 66 Balmoral Ave., Belfast BT9 6NY (☎ 0232/661621) and the **Presbyterian Historical Society,** Church House, Fisherwich Place, Belfast.

No matter how you plan to go about your "roots" search, my best and strongest advice is to subscribe to ***Inside Ireland*** (see pg. 45) and receive their **genealogical supplement** with your very first issue.

Once you have the basic data, it's off to the locality of your ancestors, where **parochial registers** often hold exactly what you're looking for. (You can also consult the various local genealogical centers and libraries throughout the Republic and Northern Ireland.) A talk with the parish priest may well send you off to shake the hand of a distant cousin or two still living in the neighborhood.

5 Settling into Dublin

Baile Atha Cliath ("Bolya-a-ha-cleea"—"the town of the ford of the hurdles") is its ancient Irish name (that ford was probably where the Father Matthew Bridge long ago replaced a frail wicker bridge—the "hurdles"—that once spanned the river); Norsemen called it Dubh-Linn ("black pool") when they founded the present city on the banks of the Liffey in 840; and a modern writer has called it "the most instantly talkative city in Europe."

Although Dublin was founded as a trading port by the Danes in 840, the *Irish Annals* relate that in 988 the Viking settlement was handed over to the High King of Ireland, and that's the date celebrated in 1988 when the city put on a yearlong festival to commemorate its millennium.

By any name, Dublin is one of Europe's loveliest capital cities, with proud old Georgian buildings, elegantly groomed squares of greenery (Fitzwilliam, Parnell, Merrion, etc.), and acres of shaded leisure space (St. Stephen's Green and the Phoenix Park).

Its heart beats to the rhythm of the Liffey, and its horizons extend to craggy Howth Head to the north, the softly curving shores of Dublin Bay to the east, and the slopes of the Dublin Mountains to the south.

This sheltered setting along a natural transportation route has been the focal point of a long, rich, and complex history that has left its mark on the face of its landscape as well as its people. Indeed, Dubliners are happily convinced their city is not only the centerpiece of Ireland's Eastern Region, but of Ireland and the *universe* as well (and they just as happily skip off to "the country" at the merest hint of an excuse!).

1 Orientation

ARRIVING

BY PLANE Just eight miles north of the city center, Dublin Airport is in Collinstown. There is an ample supply of luggage carts, so you won't need a porter. Should you land without a place to stay, help is at the Tourist Information Desk located in the Arrivals Terminal. It's open daily year-round. Hours are 8am to 6pm, January through April and late September through December; 8am to 8pm, May to mid-June; 8am to 10:30pm, mid-June to late September.

On the mezzanine there's an inexpensive cafeteria for hot or cold snacks, as well as a Grill Bar for more substantial fare: A light meal goes for under IR£5 ($8), and a four-course dinner for less than IR£10 ($16). You'll also find bars and snack bars in both the arrivals and departure halls.

The Bank of Ireland is on hand in both halls to change your money (closed only on Christmas Day). For those flying on to Britain or the Continent, there is a duty-free shop selling a full range of goods. Those headed to North America will be given a 45-minute shopping stopover at Shannon Airport to browse through its well-stocked duty-free shop. There is also an Aer Lingus booking office in the airport.

Getting Into Town Airport bus fares into the Central Bus Station will run IR£2.50 ($4) for adults, half that for children. A taxi into town will cost about IR£13 ($20.80).

BY TRAIN For rail information, call 01/836-6222 Monday through Saturday from 9am to 9pm and on Sunday from 10am to 6pm. The three major railway stations are Connolly Station, on Amiens Street near Busaras; Heuston Station, near the Guinness Brewery on St. John's Road; and Pearse Station, on Westland Row (serves suburban rail lines). Irish Rail trains meet all ferries arriving at Dun Laoghaire (pronounced "Dun Leary") and the seven-mile ride into Dublin can be included in the boat fare if it is specified on the boat ticket.

BY FERRY Bus Eireann supplies transport between Heuston Station and Dun Laoghaire Pier, the B&I ferryport and the Central Bus Station, and between Heuston Station and the B&I ferryport. There is also DART electrical rail service to the Dun Laoghaire Pier (fare determined by your destination).

VISITOR INFORMATION

The Dublin City and County Tourism Visitor Centre, 14 Upper O'Connell St. (☎ 01/284-4768), just across from the General Post Office, is open October to February, Monday through Friday from 9am to 5pm; and March to October, Monday through Saturday from 9am to 5pm; closed New Year's Day, St. Patrick's Day, Easter Monday, October Public Holiday, and St. Stephen's Day (December 26).

CITY LAYOUT

Today, as in its past, Dublin is delineated by the brown waters of the River Liffey, which flows from west to east, passing beneath some 10 bridges en route. O'Connell Bridge is probably the most important one for travelers, since it connects those sections of the mile-long city center north of the Liffey (to Parnell Square at the top of O'Connell Street) and south of the Liffey (to St. Stephen's Green at the end of Grafton Street). Keep that firmly in mind, since Dubliners locate everything by its relation to the river. "North of" and "south of" are a part of the city's vocabulary you'll soon adopt as part of your own.

The main thoroughfare north of the river is O'Connell Street, which extends from the bridge to Parnell Square at its northern end. This is where you'll find the historic General Post Office and statues of Parnell, Father Matthew, and Daniel O'Connell. At the base of O'Connell's statue, look for the heroic "Victories," representing Fidelity, Eloquence, Courage, and Patriotism. The Dublin City and County Tourism Visitor Centre is also on O'Connell Street, along with several good hotels, one large department store, and a jumble of smaller establishments, fast-food eateries, and a number of important office buildings.

Dublin at a Glance

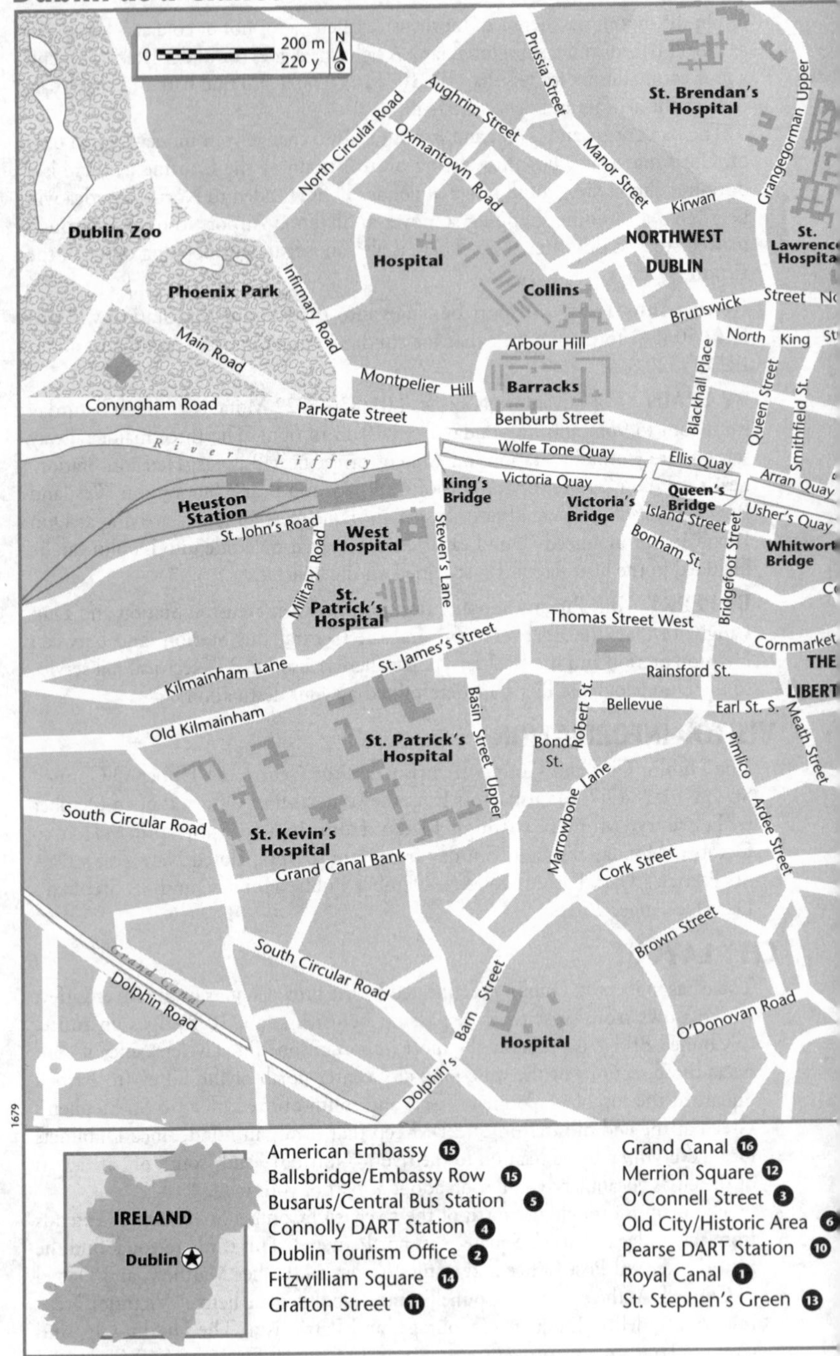

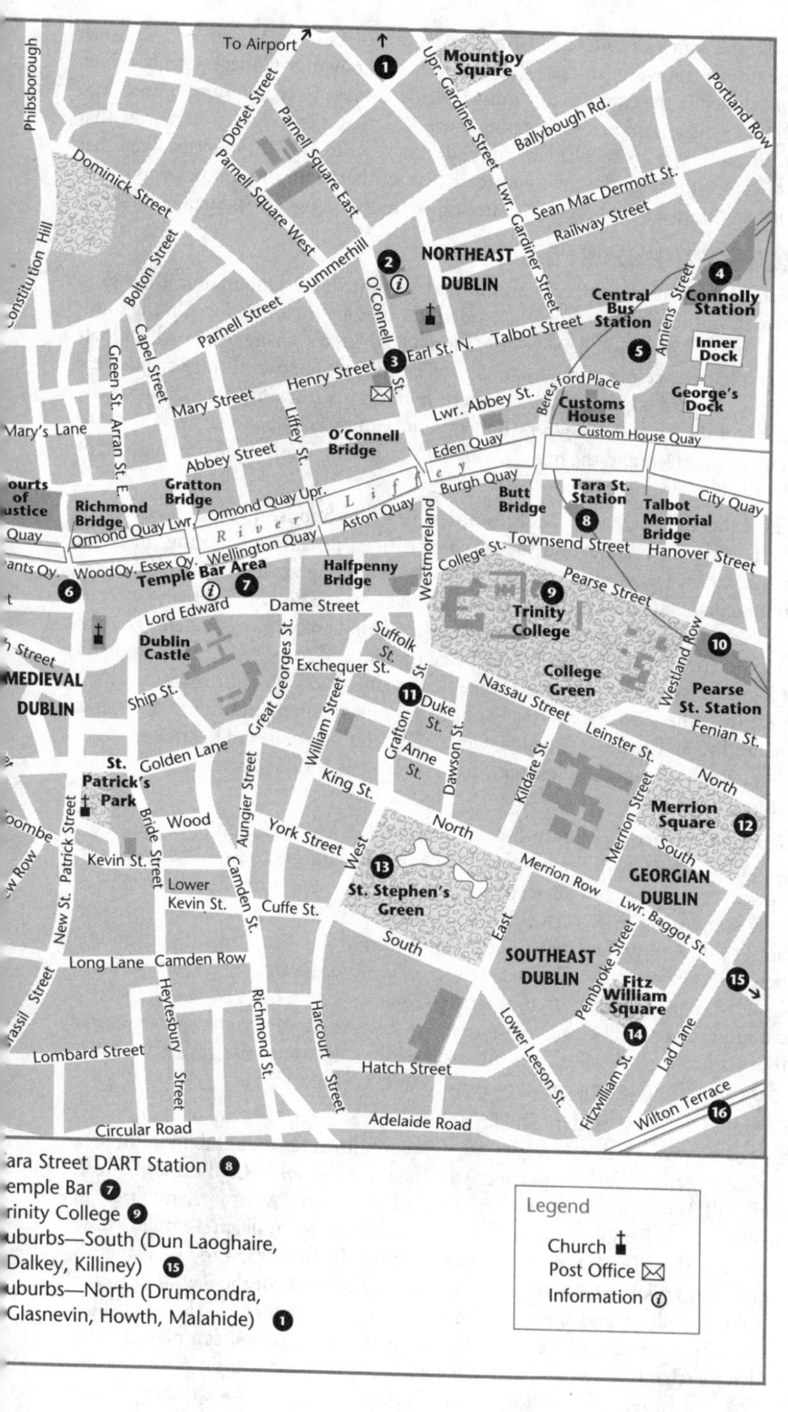

To Airport
Mountjoy Square
Phibsborough
Dorset Street
Parnell Square East
Parnell Square West
Upr. Gardiner Street
Lwr. Gardiner Street
Portland Row
Ballybough Rd.
Dominick Street
Sean Mac Dermott St.
Railway Street
Constitution Hill
Bolton Street
Summerhill
NORTHEAST DUBLIN
O'Connell St.
Amiens Street
Connolly Station
Central Bus Station
Parnell Street
Talbot Street
Earl St. N.
Inner Dock
Capel Street
Green St.
Arran St. E.
Henry Street
Mary Street
Beresford Place
George's Dock
Lwr. Abbey St.
Customs House
Custom House Quay
Mary's Lane
Liffey St.
O'Connell Bridge
Abbey Street
Eden Quay
Courts of Justice
Gratton Bridge
Richmond Bridge
Ormond Quay Upr.
Ormond Quay Lwr.
River Liffey
Burgh Quay
Butt Bridge
Tara St. Station
Talbot Memorial Bridge
City Quay
Aston Quay
Wellington Quay
Quay
Westmoreland
Townsend Street
Hanover Street
Wood Qy.
Essex Qy.
Temple Bar Area
Halfpenny Bridge
College St.
Pearse Street
Lord Edward
Dame Street
Trinity College
Westland Row
Pearse St. Station
Dublin Castle
Suffolk St.
Exchequer St.
College Green
MEDIEVAL DUBLIN
Ship St.
Great Georges St.
William Street
Duke St.
Nassau Street
Fenian St.
Leinster St.
Grafton St.
Anne St.
Dawson St.
Kildare St.
Golden Lane
St. Patrick's Park
Aungier Street
King St.
Merrion Street
North
Merrion Square
South
Wood
Bride Street
York Street
New St.
Patrick Street
Kevin St.
West
St. Stephen's Green
Merrion Row
GEORGIAN DUBLIN
Lower Kevin St.
Camden St.
Cuffe St.
Lwr. Baggot St.
East
South
SOUTHEAST DUBLIN
Pembroke Street
Long Lane
Camden Row
Fitz William Square
Heytesbury Street
Richmond St.
Harcourt Street
Lower Leeson St.
Lad Lane
Lombard Street
Hatch Street
Fitzwilliam St.
Wilton Terrace
Circular Road
Adelaide Road
Tara Street DART Station 8
Temple Bar 7
Trinity College 9
Suburbs—South (Dun Laoghaire, Dalkey, Killiney) 15
Suburbs—North (Drumcondra, Glasnevin, Howth, Malahide) 1
Legend
Church
Post Office
Information

To the south of O'Connell Bridge, the one-block-long Westmoreland Street gives onto the wide, statue-filled intersection known as College Green, which sprawls before the entrance to Trinity College. College Green, in turn, funnels into Dublin's most fashionable shopping thoroughfare, Grafton Street, so narrow that at certain hours it's blocked off for pedestrian traffic only. If you've walked that city-center mile, by the time you reach the southern end of Grafton, you'll sigh with gratitude for the beautifully landscaped, restful refuge of St. Stephen's Green.

NEIGHBORHOODS IN BRIEF

Medieval Dublin Little remains nowadays of medieval Dublin, but it is easy to trace its outlines and see how the modern city has grown around it. On the south bank of the Liffey, you'll see Christ Church Cathedral's square tower, which is almost the exact center of the original city. To the east, Grattan Bridge stands near the "black pool" that marked its eastern boundary. Little Ship Street follows the course of the River Poddle (now underground), once a city boundary on the south bank of the river, and the quays along the north bank marked another outpost of the ancient city.

The Liberties One of Dublin's oldest neighborhoods, its name stems from the fact that it was beyond the reach of official jurisdiction during medieval times. Located west of Upper Kevin Street, beginning at the Coombe (its main thoroughfare, named for the "coomb," or valley, of the Poddle River) and extending westward to rather indeterminate borders. Family roots of its residents go back for generations, and they have developed an accent and style all their own, instantly recognized by other Dubliners. Some of the city's most colorful characters have come from the Liberties, and many of the city's most important historic landmarks are nearby (St. Patrick's Cathedral, Christ Church Cathedral, and the Brazen Head public house, Dublin's oldest pub, scene of United Irishmen activity in the 18th century).

Georgian Dublin Eighteenth-century Dubliners left an elegant legacy of Georgian architecture, with the most notable examples clustered around Merrion and Fitzwilliam squares and adjacent streets. Wherever you walk, details delight. A silver street lamp inset with ornately wrought shamrocks glows softly against a rain-lit sky. A miniature white horse stands firm in the clear fanlight atop an unpretentious doorway while fluted Doric columns frame those who put on more airs. Cast- and wrought-iron foot scrapers, doorway lamp holders, door knockers, and railings are embellished with a remarkable variety of imaginative artisanry, from sea horses to clenched fists. Across the Liffey, 14 stone river gods glare down on the river from the magnificent facade of the Custom House.

Temple Bar Prompted by Dublin's 1991 term as European City of Culture, the city government set about creating an eventual cultural heart of Dublin in the area bounded by Essex, Wellington, and Aston quays to the north; Lord Edward Street, Cork Hill, Dame Street, and College Green to the south; Westmoreland Street to the east; and Fishamble Street to the west. Named for Sir William Temple, whose mansion and gardens occupied a large part of the site from 1554 to 1628, and his family river walkway (known as a "bar" in the vernacular of the day), the area is one of narrow lanes and alleys. A fashionable residential address in the late 1700s, it slowly became the habitat of bookbinders, tailors, drapers, cap makers, and woolen merchants, as well as tradesmen such as carpenters and tin-plate workers housed in a variety of building styles. During the 1800s, stockbrokers set up offices here to be close to the Stock Exchange opened in 1878 on (what else!) Exchange Street. In its latest transformation, the narrow lanes have been recobbled, and the ancient buildings, now restored, are home to an eclectic collection of boutiques, art galleries, atmospheric pubs, trendy restaurants, and some remarkable street art. This is Dublin's bohemia, set in an environment that reeks of the character and charm of yesteryear.

Southeast Dublin Running from Grafton Street east to Upper Fitzwilliam Street, and from Clare Street to Lower Hatch Street, this area encompasses what can rightly be called the heart of the city center, holding St. Stephen's Green, Leinster House (seat of Dáil Eireann, the national parliament), Trinity College, the Bank of Ireland, the Mansion House of the Lord Mayor of Dublin, the National Museum, and many other points of interest.

Northeast Dublin Extending roughly from the Custom House and Eden quays west to O'Connell Street and Parnell Square, then northeast along Denmark Street to Mountjoy Square, this area holds the General Post Office, the Abbey and Gate theaters, and the Municipal Gallery of Modern Art.

Northwest Dublin Running west from Ormond Quay to Wolfe Tone Quay, and north as far as Bolton Street, Northwest Dublin is where you'll find the Four Courts, St. Michan's Church, the Botanic Gardens, and the Phoenix Park.

Dublin's Southern Suburbs About 2½ miles southeast of the city center, Ballsbridge is a pleasant residential area and also the setting for Lansdowne Road's internationally famous football stadium, the American embassy, the Royal Dublin Society, and several posh hotels. Other suburban areas south of Dublin are Monkstown/Blackrock, Dun Laoghaire, Sandycove, Killiney, Dalkey, Stillorgan, Dundrum, Rathgar, and Templeogue.

Dublin's Northern Suburbs In the northern reaches of the city's suburbs you'll find Clontarf, Sutton, Howth, Raheny, Drumcondra, Glasnevin, and Finglas.

2 Getting Around

BY DART The suburban electric train service that runs from Howth to Bray stops at some 25 stations en route. Operated by Irish Rail and called the Dublin Area Rapid Transit (DART), the service is fast and silent. Departures are every five minutes during peak hours, every 15 minutes at other times. Service begins at 7am and ends at about 11:30pm. Easy access to the city by DART makes staying at a resort like Howth, Dalkey, or even as far south as Bray a feasible and money-saving option. Some 19 feeder bus lines link up with the rail system. Timetables can be obtained at most stations. Call 01/836-6222 for details.

BY BUS There is excellent bus service to all parts of Dublin and the outlying suburbs, making it easy to search out accommodations beyond the city center, where prices are considerably lower. Any bus marked "An Lar" ("the center") will be headed for the city center. Buses run from 7am (10am on Sunday) to 11:30pm sharp. If you're planning a late night in the city, better plan on taking a taxi to any outlying accommodation. Many buses depart from Eden Quay Bridge, but you can check on your particular bus line by picking up a copy of the Dublin District Bus and Rail Timetable from the Central Bus Station on Store Street or almost any newsagent. Fares are determined by distance traveled, and children under 16 travel for half fare.

BY CAR Just one word about driving in Dublin: *Don't!* Public transportation is efficient and frequent, traffic can be heavy (especially in early-morning and late-afternoon hours), and Dublin's one-way streets can be so confusing that I urge you to drive directly to your accommodation, park the car, and leave it there until you're headed out of town! Parking can also present a real problem, since most on-street spaces are metered for only two hours and car parks are often filled early in the day. All that is not to say, however, that it's impossible to drive around the city—but you'll come out better and save both time and nerves if you leave the driving to someone else.

Note: One bit of warning if you're driving in Dublin: Recently there has been a rash of rental-car break-ins, both on city streets and in guesthouse parking areas. The pattern has been for thieves to break the door lock to gain access. So you'd best leave all luggage, coats, cameras, purchases, etc., in your room and leave your locked car and trunk empty.

BY TAXI You should opt for at least one taxi ride just for the conversation—Dublin taxi drivers are both knowledgeable and entertaining. Taxis operate from ranks at all bus and rail stations, in the center of O'Connell Street, at College Green, at St. Stephen's Green, and at several leading hotels (listed in the telephone directory under "Taxi-cab Ranks"). Dublin is blessed with about 100 taxi companies, and you can call 478-3333 or 561111 for a taxi, but an extra service charge will be added to the fare. Minimum fare is IR£1.80 ($2.88) for the first mile (minimum charge of 75p/$1.20), plus 10p (16¢) for each additional $^{2}/_{15}$ of a mile or 1.2 minutes of waiting time. All taxis are metered, with a charge of 40p (64¢) for each additional passenger and each piece of luggage, and 80p ($1.28) on bank holidays. Between the hours of 8pm and 8am there's an additional charge of 40p (64¢) per trip. City Cabs (☎ 872-7272) has specialized taxis with easy wheelchair access.

BY BICYCLE Inner-city traffic conditions make cycling a hazardous undertaking, and narrow streets with both-side parking often reduce traffic lanes in both city-center and suburban streets to a *very* narrow lane. If you're an expert cycler and stout of heart, you'll pay about IR£30 ($48) per week for bike rental and be

Getting Around Dublin

1. Bus discounts are offered during certain hours on certain lines. One of the most useful is the shopping fare offered between 10am and 4:30pm. Ask about various discounts at Dublin Bus, 59 Upper O'Connell St. (☎ 873-4222).
2. Discounts on suburban rail travel are offered by DART; for details on commuter tickets and other discounts, call 836-6222.
3. Students can present their International Student Identity Card at the Irish Student Travel Service (USIT) and receive a Travel Stamp, which offers a 50% discount on Dublin buses and trains. USIT is located at 19 Aston Quay, Dublin 2 (☎ 01/677-8117 or 679-8833). It's open from Monday through Friday from 9:30am to 5:30pm and on Saturday from 10am to 4pm.
4. Big discounts also come with the Education Travel Concession Ticket, which covers unlimited travel on Dublin bus and train services; purchase it from Dublin Bus (see no. 1, above, for address and telephone number).

Dublin Area Rapid Transit (DART) Routes

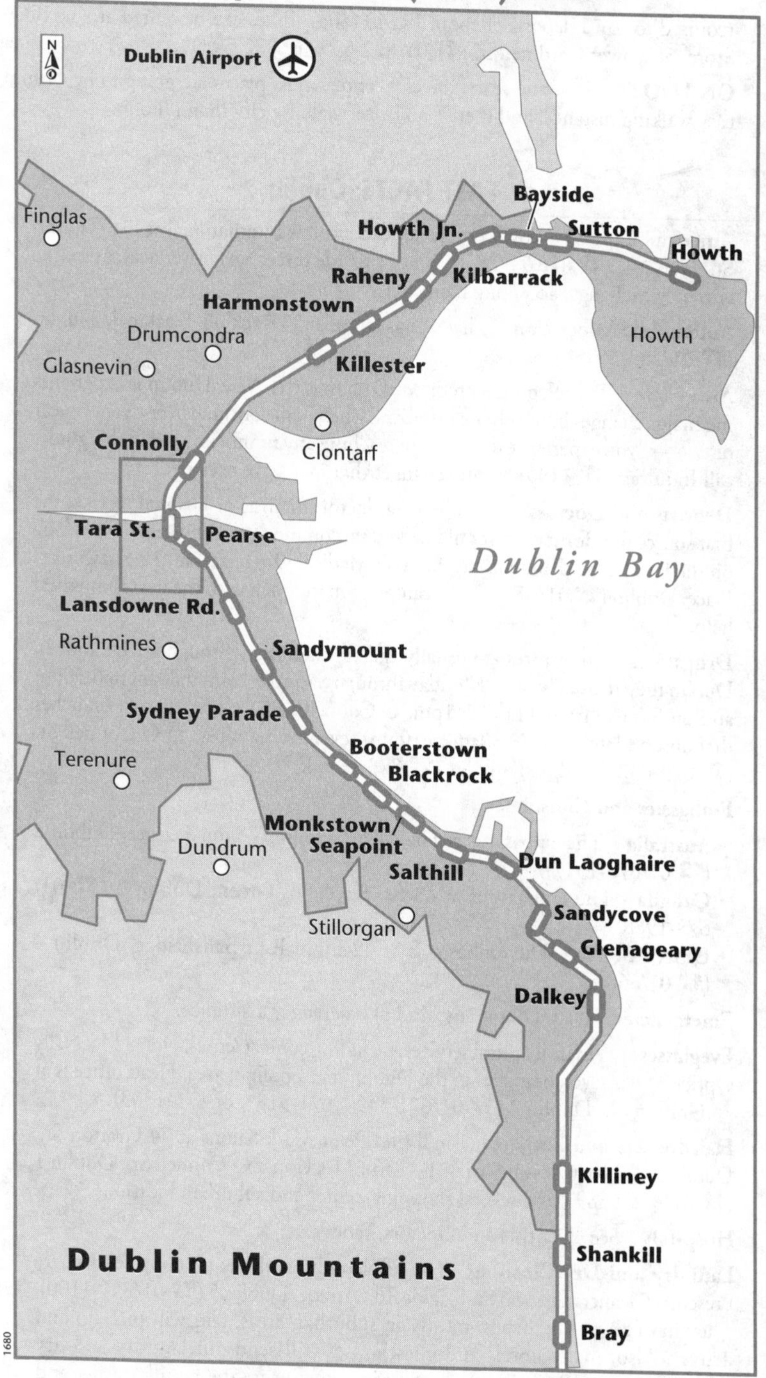

1680

required to pay a deposit of about IR£40 ($64). Bikes can be rented at The Bike Store, 58 Lower Gardiner St. (☎ 01/872-5399 or 872-5931).

ON FOOT Once you reach the city center, most places are going to be within easy walking distance, and there's no better walking city than Dublin.

FAST FACTS: Dublin

American Express You'll find American Express International at 116 Grafton St., Dublin 2 (☎ 01/677-2874). They provide travel-agency services, as well as currency exchange, accepting mail, etc.

Automobile Association The AA has offices at 23 Rockhill, Blackrock, Dublin (☎ 01/283-3555).

Area Code The telephone prefix for Dublin is 01. *Note:* Dublin is experiencing major changes in telephone numbers, which will continue over the next year or two—if you experience difficulty in reaching any numbers listed in this guide, call Inquiries (☎ 1190) for any changes that may have occurred.

Dentists and Doctors If you need a doctor, dentist, or hospital service, the first source of information should be your accommodations hostess or someone on the local scene. Failing that, the Irish Medical Organization, 10 Fitzwilliam Place, Dublin (☎ 01/676-7273), can put you in touch with the nearest medical help.

Drugstores Drugstores are usually called "chemists" throughout Ireland. In Dublin they're usually open Monday through Saturday from 9:30am to 6:30pm and on Sunday from 11am to 1pm. O'Connell's Pharmacy has two branches that observe late hours (8:30am to 10pm) seven days a week: 55 O'Connell St. (☎ 873-0427) and 6 Henry St. (☎ 873-1077).

Embassies and Consulates

- **Australia** The embassy is at Fitzwilliam House, Wilton Terrace, Dublin 2 (☎ 01/676-1517).
- **Canada** The embassy is at 65 St. Stephen's Green, Dublin 2 (☎ 01/678-1988).
- **United States** The embassy is at 42 Elgin Rd., Ballsbridge, Dublin 4 (☎ 01/668-8777).

Emergencies Dial 999 for any kind of emergency assistance.

Eyeglasses With full optical services, including contact lenses, Donal MacNally Opticians has seven branches in the Dublin metropolitan area. Head office is at 75 Grafton St., Dublin 2 (☎ 01/671-5499, 671-5181, or 873-1303).

Hairdressers and Barbers You'll find Peter Mark Salons at 74 Grafton St., Dublin 2 (☎ 01/671-4399 or 671-4136); 11A Upper O'Connell St., Dublin 1 (☎ 01/874-5589); and several shopping-center and suburban locations.

Hospitals See "Dentists and Doctors," above.

Laundry and Dry Cleaning For full laundry and dry-cleaning service, try Prescotts Cleaners Ltd., 56 St. Brigids Rd., Artane, Dublin 5 (☎ 01/831-1100). They have several branches, mostly in suburban areas, and will pick up and deliver. Also, many hotels and guesthouses will send out laundry and dry cleaning for you; B&B hostesses will sometimes share the family washer and dryer (but don't *depend* on that).

Lost Property Bus and rail stations have lost-and-found departments if you have suffered a loss in transit. For all other losses, contact the police.

Luggage Storage and Lockers There are luggage-storage facilities (called "Left Luggage" desks) at the Central Bus Station on Store Street, at Connolly Railway Station, and at Heuston Railway Station. Also, some hostels will store luggage during the day.

Photographic Needs For almost any photographic service, from new and used equipment to developing and jumbo-size printing, as well as good prices on film, try Dublin Camera Exchange, 98 Trinity St., Dublin 2 (☎ 01/679-3410), or Spectra Photo, 73 Grafton St. (☎ 01/679-6045).

Police Dial 999.

Post Office The General Post Office on O'Connell Street is located across from the Dublin tourist center and is open Monday through Saturday from 8am to 8pm (to 7pm only for mailing or receiving parcels) and on Sunday and bank holidays from 10am to 6:30pm. General Delivery mail can be picked up at the Post Restante desk until 8pm.

Religious Services The tourist board can furnish a list of Dublin churches and information telephone numbers for days and hours of services. Many of the world's religions—including Judaism, Islam, and Jehovah's Witnesses—are represented in Dublin, in addition to the dominant Catholic orders and the leading Protestant order, the Church of Ireland.

Restrooms The larger department stores and shopping centers all have public restrooms, as do city-center hotels and pubs.

Transit Information Phone 01/873-4222 for transit information.

3 Where to Stay

Of all of Ireland, you'll probably pay your highest accommodation rate in Dublin, which may not be as intimidating as it sounds, for "highest" can still keep you within the daily budget limit of this book with a little juggling of other costs. Dublin may well be where those convenient, albeit pricey, city-center accommodations will truly prove to be "Worth the Extra Money." You should know in advance, however, that as distance from the city center increases, prices decrease.

Accommodations in Dublin and its immediate environs are so numerous that it's possible to stay in almost any section you like and in almost any price range you prefer. There are good hostels, bed-and-breakfast homes, guesthouses, self-catering flats, small intimate hotels, and large luxury hotels. In the city center, however, you're going to have to pay more, and places in this area are often heavily booked.

An Oige and other hostels, as well as self-catering facilities, are Dublin's best budget-stretchers. Families will find a wide range of self-catering properties in Dublin at rates that—on a per-person basis—amount to an accommodations discount.

You might consider finding a room in one of the outlying suburbs such as Howth, Dalkey, Killiney, or Bray (in County Wicklow, but with rail service that makes it an easy commute). Then you can spend mornings on the beach and afternoons or evenings in town. On the other hand, if you want to be able to stay out later than those last buses and train departures, you'll find it good value to avoid the taxi fares and pay more to stay right in the city.

Keep in mind that prices in Dublin often soar during holidays and special events such as Easter, the Spring Show in May, the horse show in August, All-Ireland Finals in September, and international rugby matches. It's best to plan your visit to Dublin to avoid those events unless you have a special interest in them. If you do plan to come during one of these periods, be sure to reserve well in advance.

In the recommendations below, you'll find a smattering of all the accommodations categories mentioned above, including some higher-priced guesthouses in the city proper that give readers of this book a substantial discount, along with some accommodations that fall into the "Worth the Extra Money" category. For your convenience, they are listed by price and by location.

Reservations Dublin is one place I advocate arriving with a firm reservation. But if you should arrive without one, contact the Central Reservation Service, 1 Clarinda Park North, Dun Laoghaire, County Dublin (☎ 01/284-1765; fax 01/284-1751). Or pick up their publication "Guest Accommodations" and start telephoning around.

LESS THAN IR£20 ($32) PER PERSON

City Center

✪ Jurys Inn

Christchurch Place, Dublin 8. ☎ **01/475-0111** or in the U.S. 800/843-3311. Fax 01/475-0488. 172 rms, all with bath. A/C TV TEL. IR£49 ($78.40) *per room* (sleeps up to four). Breakfast extra. AE, CB, DC, MC, V. Bus: 21A, 50, 50A, 78, 78A, or 78B.

Situated smack-dab in the middle of Dublin's most historic area, Jurys Inn offers one of the city's best values for parties of three or four. Rooms are nicely appointed, with private bath, telephone, radio, and TV. There are also facilities for the handicapped, and the restaurant serves an inexpensive international grillroom-style menu (breakfast will cost about IR£5.50 [$8.90]). Each room will accommodate up to three adults or two adults and two children, bringing per-person rates down to IR£16 ($25.60).

Sinclair House

3 Hardwicke St., Dublin 1. ☎ **01/855-0792.** Fax 01/833-2377. 6 rms, none with bath. IR£16 ($25.60) per person double; IR£20 ($32) single. Reduction for children. (Rates include breakfast.) No credit cards.

Mrs. McMahon is hostess at this conveniently located B&B, off North Frederick Street. Guest rooms are comfortably furnished, and the house is centrally heated. Sinclair House is located north of the Liffey, very near Parnell Square, and is within easy walking distance of most major sightseeing attractions in the city center.

Clontarf

✪ Aisling

19/20 St. Lawrence Rd., Clontarf, Dublin 3. ☎ **01/833-9097** or 833-8400. Fax 01/833-8400. 9 rms, 7 with bath; 1 with shower. IR£17.50 ($28) per person sharing; IR£2.50 ($4) per person additional for private facilities. (Rates include breakfast.) No credit cards. Enclosed parking. Bus: 30 or 44A.

Joe and Mary Mooney are the hosts at Aisling. Their home, located on a quiet street just off the Clontarf-Howth road, is furnished with antiques such as the grandfather clock in the entrance hall and the Waterford glass chandelier that lights the dining room. Breakfast comes on china and linen tablecloths, with Galway crystal stemware and sterling flatware. The bedrooms are spacious and attractively decorated, and each has a phone, clock radio, hairdryer, and tea-making facilities. There's central heating and a private parking area.

Mrs. Bridget Geary

69 Hampton Court off Vernon Avenue, Clontarf, Dublin 3. ☎ **01/833-1199.** 3 rms, 1 with shower/bath and toilet. IR£14 ($22.40) per person sharing; IR£2.50 ($4) per person additional for private bath. 20% reduction for children. (Rates include breakfast.) No credit cards. Closed Oct–Mar. Bus: 44A. DART: 28, 29, 31.

Mrs. Geary's home is a modern bungalow convenient to the airport, car-ferry, and transport into town via either bus or train. Clontarf Castle, which serves good, moderately priced meals, is a mere 10-minute walk away. Mrs. Geary's hospitality and graciousness have earned her a loyal following with our readers—as one reader wrote, "It was just like being home and the meals were fantastic."

✪ Gresham House

384 Clontarf Rd., Clontarf, Dublin 3. ☎ **01/833-1794.** Fax 01/833-8595. 9 rms, 5 with bath; 4 with shower. IR£15 ($24) per person sharing with shower; IR£16 ($25.60) per person sharing with bath; IR£18 ($28.80) single with shower. (Rates include breakfast.) No credit cards. Private car park. Bus: 30.

Miriam McAllister is the gracious hostess of Gresham House, an attractive and comfortable three-story home overlooking the sea. Guest rooms are quite comfortable, some with complete bath and toilet, others with shower only. There's a welcoming TV lounge for guests, and Mrs. McAllister is happy to direct guests to attractions in the immediate area (St. Anne's Park, with its famed rose garden, is a short walk away; Howth Hill is visible from the house; and there's the beach, as well as a golf course). Good pub grub is a few steps away, and there are several very good restaurants in the area.

✪ Mrs. Eileen Kelly

17 Seacourt, St. Gabriel's Rd., Clontarf, Dublin 3. ☎ **01/833-2547.** 3 rms, 2 with bath. IR£15 ($24) per person sharing; IR£2.50 ($4) per person additional for private bath. (Rates include breakfast.) No credit cards. Closed Nov–Feb. Bus: 30 or 44A.

Mrs. Eileen Kelly is an outstanding hostess who welcomes guests into the family circle around a cozy open fire in the lounge. Her large bedrooms are tastefully furnished. All rooms have sinks, the house is centrally heated, and bus transportation to the city center is not far away.

✪ San Vista

237 Clontarf Rd., Clontarf, Dublin 3. ☎ **01/833-9582.** 3 rms, none with bath. IR£15 ($24) per person sharing; IR£18 ($28.80) single. (Rates include breakfast.) No credit cards. Bus: 30 or 44A.

Mrs. O'Connell is the lively hostess at this attractive house set on the seafront along Dublin Bay. She has been described by our readers as being "a good listener," and is always eager to share with her guests her extensive knowledge of places to go and things to see and do in Dublin.

✪ Springvale

69 Kincora Dr., Clontarf, Dublin 3. ☎ **01/833-3413.** 4rms, all with bath. IR£15 ($24) per person sharing; IR£20 ($32) single. 20% reduction for children under 12. (Rates include breakfast.) No credit cards. Closed Christmas. Bus: 30.

According to our readers, Moira Kavanagh serves "the best breakfast in Ireland." Add to that accolade her attractive home in a quiet residential area off Kincora Grove, with nicely appointed bedrooms, complete with tea/coffeemakers, central heating, and private parking, and it is easy to understand her popularity. Nearby

Dublin Accommodations

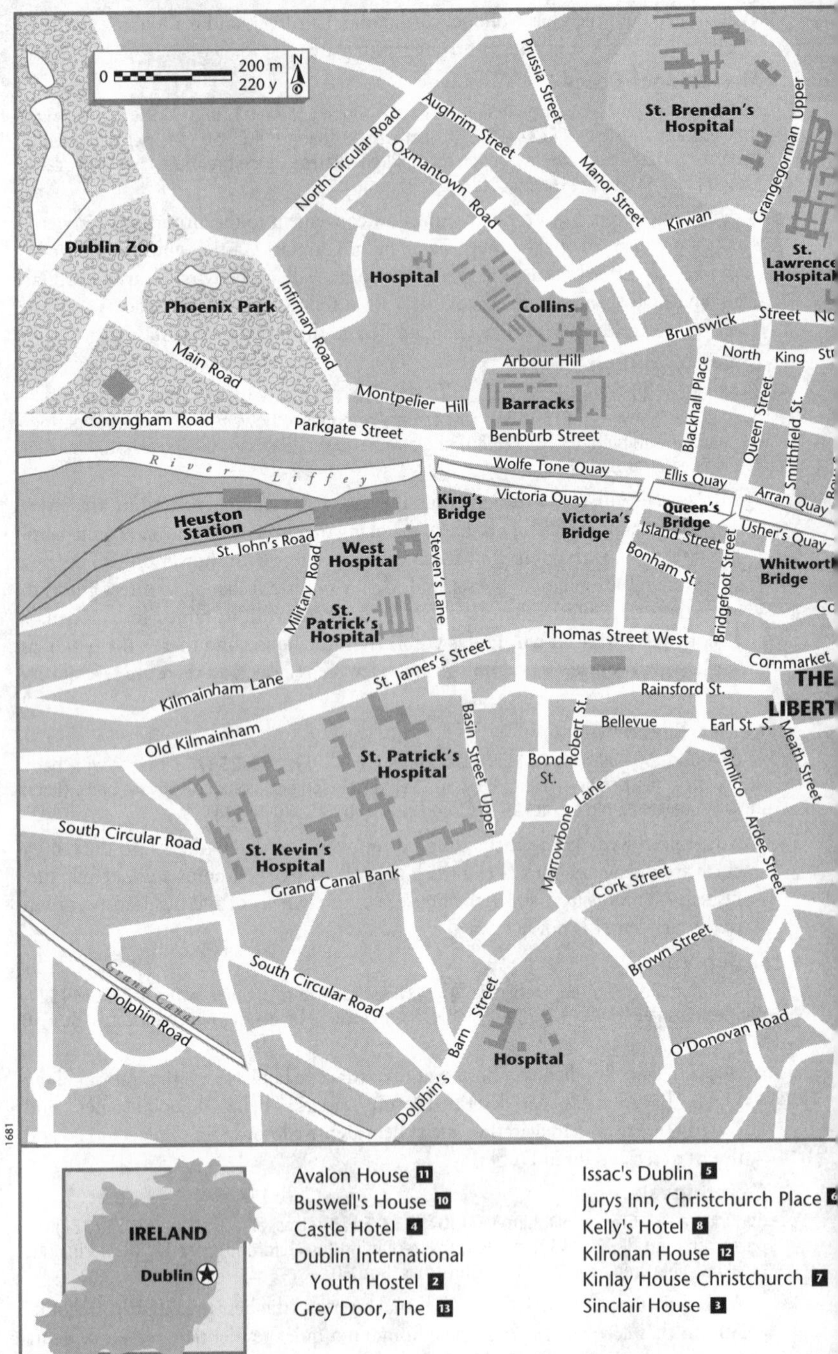

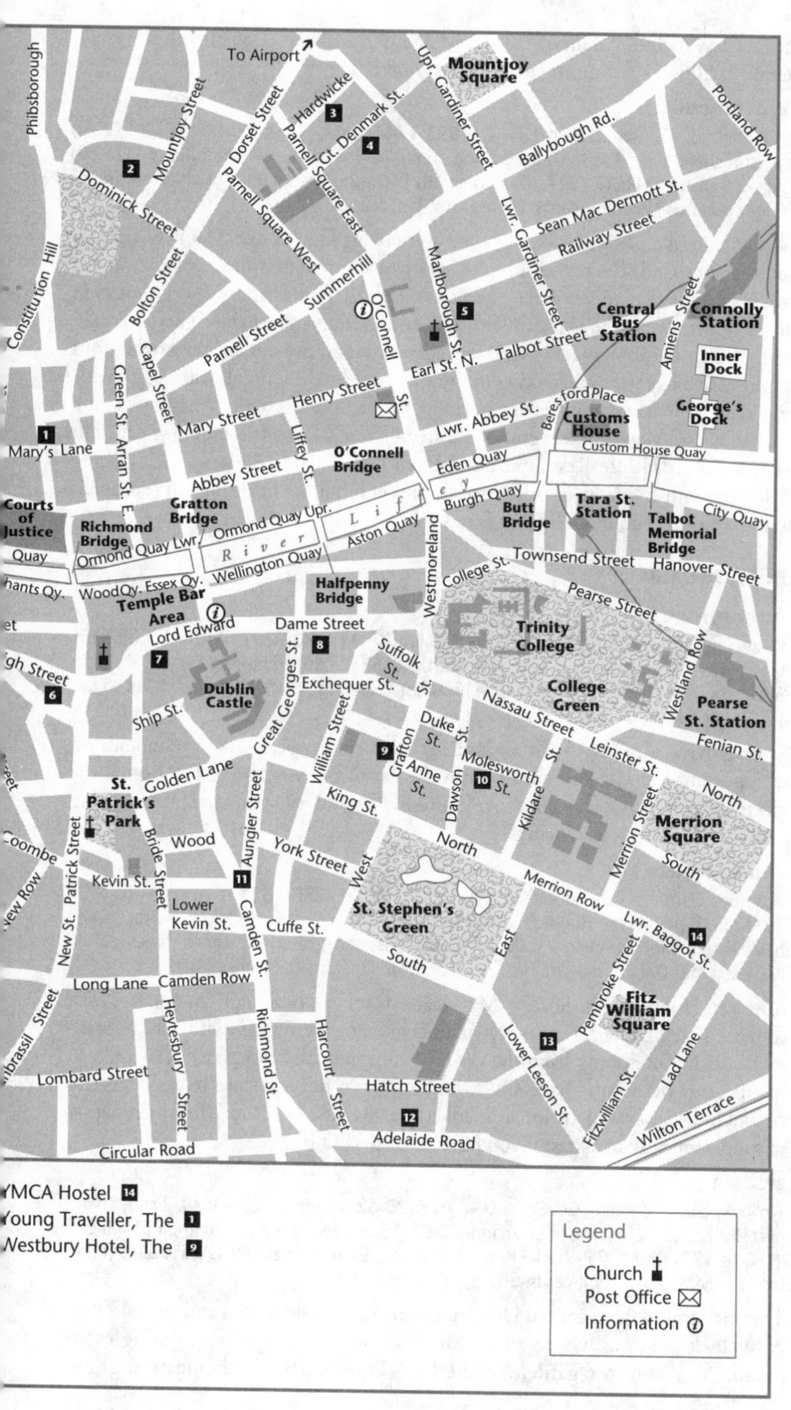
To Airport
Mountjoy Square
Phibsborough
Mountjoy Street
Dorset Street
Hardwicke
Gt. Denmark St.
Upr. Gardiner Street
Portland Row
Ballybough Rd.
Parnell Square East
Parnell Square West
Dominick Street
Sean Mac Dermott St.
Railway Street
Lwr. Gardiner Street
Constitution Hill
Bolton Street
Summerhill
O'Connell St.
Marlborough St.
Central Bus Station
Connolly Station
Amiens Street
Parnell Street
Talbot Street
Earl St. N.
Inner Dock
George's Dock
Capel Street
Green St.
Arran St. E.
Henry Street
Mary Street
Liffey St.
Lwr. Abbey St.
Beresford Place
Customs House
Custom House Quay
Mary's Lane
O'Connell Bridge
Eden Quay
Abbey Street
Courts of Justice
Gratton Bridge
Richmond Bridge
Ormond Quay Upr.
Ormond Quay Lwr.
River Liffey
Burgh Quay
Butt Bridge
Tara St. Station
Talbot Memorial Bridge
City Quay
Aston Quay
Wellington Quay
Westmoreland
Townsend Street
Hanover Street
Quay
Wood Qy.
Essex Qy.
Halfpenny Bridge
College St.
Pearse Street
Temple Bar Area
Lord Edward
Dame Street
Trinity College
College Green
Suffolk St.
Exchequer St.
Dublin Castle
Ship St.
Great Georges St.
William Street
Nassau Street
Westland Row
Pearse St. Station
Fenian St.
Leinster St.
Duke St.
Grafton St.
Anne St.
Dawson St.
Molesworth St.
Kildare St.
Golden Lane
St. Patrick's Park
Aungier Street
King St.
North
Merrion Street
Merrion Square
Wood
Bride Street
York Street
West
Coombe
New Row
New St.
Patrick Street
Kevin St.
Lower Kevin St.
Camden St.
Cuffe St.
St. Stephen's Green
Merrion Row
Lwr. Baggot St.
East
South
Long Lane
Camden Row
Heytesbury Street
Richmond St.
Harcourt Street
Pembroke Street
Fitz William Square
Lower Leeson St.
Lombard Street
Hatch Street
Fitzwilliam St.
Lad Lane
Wilton Terrace
Adelaide Road
Circular Road
YMCA Hostel 14
Young Traveller, The 1
Westbury Hotel, The 9
Legend
Church
Post Office
Information

attractions include Clontarf Castle, Malahide Castle, Hill of Howth, golf and tennis facilities, a swimming pool, and a good beach.

✪ Wavemount

264 Clontarf Rd., Clontarf, Dublin 3. ☎ **01/833-1744.** 3rms, 2 with shower. IR£14 ($22.40) per person sharing; IR£2 ($3.20) per person additional for private facilities; IR£16 ($25.60) single without bath, IR£17 ($27.20) single with bath. 25% reduction for children. (Rates include breakfast.) No credit cards. Closed Nov–Jan. Bus: 30.

Wavemount is a pretty, two-story home overlooking Dublin Bay. Maura O'Driscoll and her husband, Raymond, have earned glowing reports from readers over the years, and it's easy to see why. The house itself is spotless and shining, but even more impressive is the warmth with which this couple greet their guests. Breakfasts (featuring homemade bread) are generous, and presented in a bright front room with a bay window looking out to the sea. Mrs. O'Driscoll will also provide the evening meal with sufficient notice. One bedroom has a bay window and a marvelous sea view; all are centrally heated. There's a good restaurant next door (Dollymount House Restaurant and Bar); Clontarf Castle is within walking distance, with moderately priced meals and entertainment during the summer; and the Royal Dublin Golf Club is nearby.

Dun Laoghaire

✪ Annesgrove

28 Rosmeen Gardens, Dun Laoghaire, Co. Dublin. ☎ **01/280-9801.** 4 rms, 2 with bath. IR£18.50 ($29.60) per person sharing with bath, IR£16 ($25.60) without; IR£20 ($32) single. 25% reduction for children. (Rates include breakfast.) No credit cards. Closed Mid-Dec to Jan. Bus: 7, 7A, or 8 from O'Connell Bridge. DART: Dun Laoghaire.

Annesgrove is a pretty two-story home set in a cul-de-sac, close to train and bus transportation and a short walk from the car-ferry. Mrs. Anne D'Alton is the gracious hostess, and she will provide an early breakfast for those with a morning departure. All rooms have sinks.

Rosmeen House

13 Rosmeen Gardens, Dun Laoghaire, Co. Dublin. ☎ **01/280-7613.** 5 rms, 2 with bath. IR£16 ($25.60) per person sharing; IR£18 ($28.80) single; IR£4 ($6.40) additional for private bath. 20% reduction for children. (Rates include breakfast.) No credit cards. Parking available. Closed mid-Dec to mid-Jan. Bus: 7, 7A or 8. DART: Dun Laoghaire.

Rosmeen House and its hostess, Mrs. Joan Murphy, have long been popular with readers. This Mediterranean-style villa sits in its own grounds (with private parking), just minutes away from the car-ferry and train and bus transportation into town. Four bedrooms have sinks, but only two have private baths. There is central heating, as well as electric blankets on all beds, and Mrs. Murphy is happy to supply an early breakfast if you have an early sailing.

Scarsdale

4 Tivoli Rd., Dun Laoghaire, Co. Dublin. ☎ **01/280-6258.** Fax 01/284-3548. 3 rms, 1 with shower. IR£16 ($25.60) per person sharing; IR£2 ($3.20) additional with bath; IR£18–IR£20 ($28.80 to $32) single. 25% reduction for children. Evening meal IR£12 ($19.20). (Rates include breakfast.) No credit cards. Bus: 7, 7A, 8, or 46A.

This modern house in central Dun Laoghaire is nicely decorated and all bedrooms have clock-radios as well as sinks. Meals are served in a pleasant dining room looking out onto the garden, where Mrs. Doris Pittman, the hostess, grows flowers and vegetables. She'll furnish the evening meal with adequate notice, and give an early breakfast for ferry passengers.

RANELAGH

St. Dunstan's

25a Oakley Rd., Ranelagh, Dublin 6. ☎ **01/497-2286.** 3 rms, none with bath. IR£16.50 ($26.40) per person sharing. (Rates include breakfast.) No credit cards. Bus: 11, 11A, 13, 48A, 62, or 86.

Mrs. Bird's brick Edwardian home has been a favorite with readers for several years. Set in a lovely residential area near Rathgar, the house is also within walking distance of shopping and good restaurants. There's central heating, and the house is spotlessly clean. The attractive bedrooms all include sinks.

RATHFARNHAM

Mrs. Beatrice O'Connor

15 Butterfield Avenue, Rathfarnham, Dublin 14. ☎ **01/494-3660.** 3 rms, 2 with bath. IR£17 ($27.20) per person sharing with bath, IR£14.50 ($23.20) per person sharing without bath; IR£24 ($38.40) single with bath, IR£21.50 ($34.40) single without bath. 20% reduction for children under 12. (Rates include breakfast.) No credit cards. Private car park. Closed Nov–April. Bus: 15B to city center, 75 to Dun Laoghaire.

Only 5km from Dublin city center, this lovely modern home on a quiet residential street has nicely furnished guest rooms (one on the ground floor) and good bus transportation just outside the door. Mrs. O'Connor is most welcoming and enjoys helping her guests get the most from their Dublin stay.

SANDYMOUNT

✪ Dolores and Tony Murphy

14 Castle Park, Sandymount, Dublin 4. ☎ **01/269-8413.** 4 rms, 1 with bath. IR£15 ($24) per person sharing without bath, IR£17 ($27.20) with bath; IR£18 ($28.80) single. (Rates include breakfast.) No credit cards. Closed Oct–Apr. DART: Sandymount. Bus: 3.

Dolores and Tony Murphy are the delightful hosts of this bed and breakfast off Gilford Road. Their modern house is brightly decorated and guests are welcome to enjoy the sun in the small garden out back. Rooms have built-in wardrobes and sinks. The entire family seems dedicated to making guests feel at home, and Dolores will be glad to prepare the evening meal if you give her sufficient advance notice.

TEMPLEOGUE

Mrs. Noreen McBride

3 Rossmore Grove (off Wellington Lane), Templeogue, Dublin 6W. ☎ **01/490-2939.** Fax 01/492-9416. 4 rms, 2 with bath. IR£16.50 ($26.40) per person sharing with bath, IR£14.50 ($23.20) per person sharing without bath; IR£23.50 ($37.60) single with bath, IR£21 ($33.60) single without bath. (Rates include breakfast.) No credit cards. Private car park. Bus 150, 54A.

Mrs. McBride's modern suburban home is in a quiet, peaceful residential area, far removed from the hustle and bustle of the inner city, yet just one block from good public transportation into town. Guestrooms are comfortable and attractively furnished. Both Noreen and her husband, Dennis, are most helpful to guests in planning itineraries and sightseeing.

LESS THAN IR£35 ($56) PER PERSON

City Center

✪ Castle Hotel

Great Denmark St., Dublin 1. ☎ **01/874-6949.** Fax 01/872-7674. 26 rms, all with bath. TV TEL. IR£35 ($56) single; IR£29 ($46.40) per person sharing. AE, MC, V.

Moderately priced, comfortable accommodations north of the Liffey have been hard to come by in the recent past. With the reopening of the Castle Hotel at the top of O'Connell Street, you can now stay within easy walking distance of the central bus station, Connolly railway station, and such major attractions as the Municipal Art Gallery, the Abbey and Gate theaters, the Writers Museum, and the Garden of Remembrance. Recently refurbished to restore its traditional Georgian character, the Castle features lovely old staircases, open fires in marble fireplaces, and crystal chandeliers. The spacious guest rooms are nicely furnished, each with an individual decor, and tea/coffee-making facilities keep a welcome "cuppa" at hand whenever the fancy strikes you. A bonus for drivers is the private car park.

When booking, ask about possible discounts for holders of this book.

✪ Kelly's Hotel

36/37 S. Great George's St., Dublin 2. ☎ **01/677-9688.** Fax 01/671-3216. 24 rms, 18 with bath. IR£28 ($44.80) single without bath, IR£34 ($54.40) single with bath; IR£22 ($35.20) per person sharing without bath, IR£28 ($44.80) per person sharing with bath. (Rates include breakfast.) ACC, AE, BARC, MC, V.

Kelly's Hotel is in one of the city's most convenient locations, west of Grafton Street in the city center, within walking distance of many attractions. This rather old-fashioned, upstairs hostelry is presided over by the friendly owners/operators, Paula and Tom Lynam. There is also a delightful old-style pub/bar with tall windows and leather seating, offering TV and bar food.

Tips on Accommodations

1. Some Dublin guesthouses offer attractive weekend and three- or six-day package rates during the low season, with discounts for seniors, so be sure to ask when booking.
2. If your stay in Dublin is a week or longer, you'll save money by booking one of the city's many flats that are available on a self-catering basis. Minimum rental is usually one week, although some are available for three-day periods. Inquire about credit-card acceptance—many of these operators prefer to work on a cash basis, so don't depend on using that bit of plastic until you're sure it will be accepted.
3. From June 1 to September 30, Trinity College offers on-campus bed-and-breakfast accommodations to both individuals and organized groups for IR£30 ($48) per person. Guests have access to such facilities as laundry and dry cleaning. Good parking is provided. MasterCard and Visa are accepted. For reservations, contact Trinity College Accommodations Office, Dublin 2 (☎ 01/677-2941, ext. 1177; fax 01/671-1267).

Dublin Environs

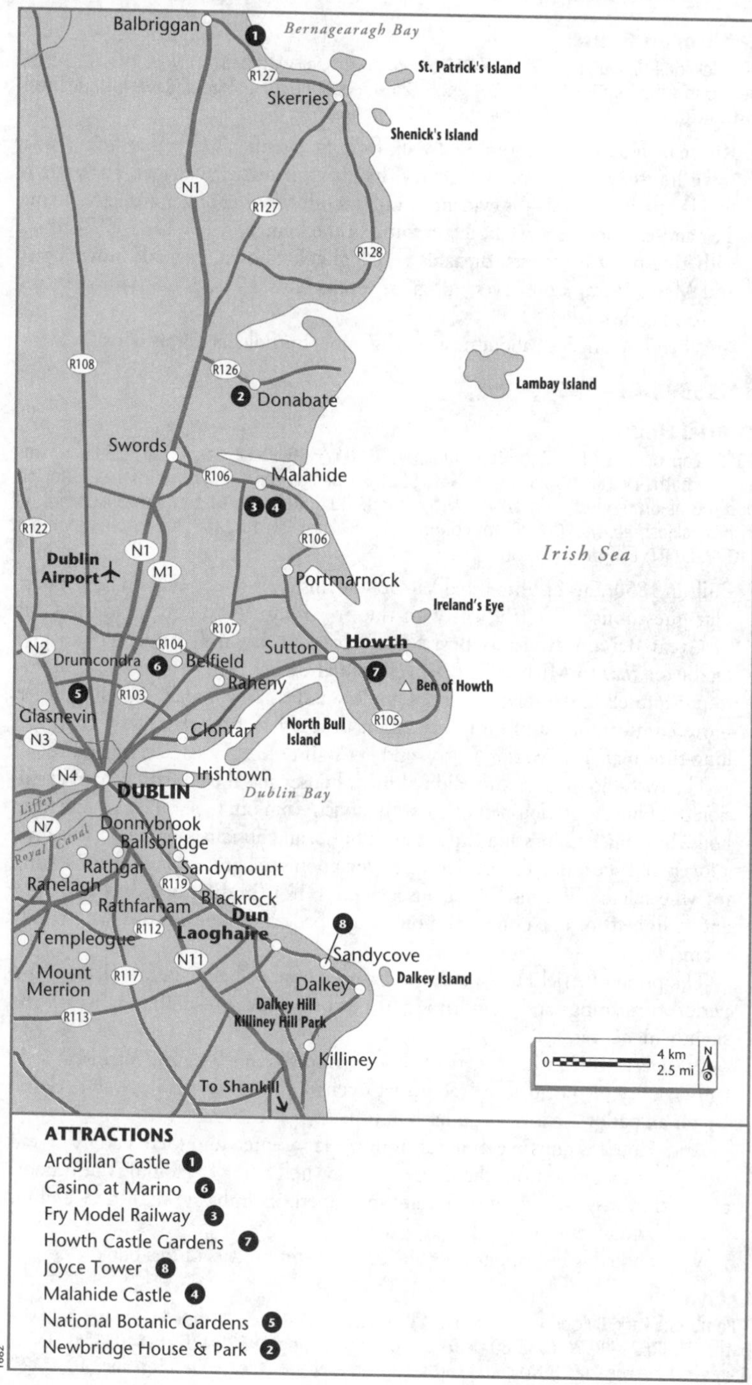

✪ Kilronan House

70 Adelaide Rd., Dublin 2. ☎ **01/475-5266.** 10 rms, all with bath/shower. TV. IR£35 ($56) per person sharing; IR£47 ($75.20) single. 25% reduction for children. (Rates include breakfast.) ACC, BARC, MC, V. Bus: 14, 15, 19, 20, or 46A.

Kilronan House, just a 5-minute walk from St. Stephen's Green, is a four-story town house. Mrs. Josephine Murray, its gracious owner/manager, has years of hotel experience, which is evident in the smooth running of her attractive home. Tea and cookies are served each evening in the lounge, which has a TV and is a gathering point for guests. Breakfasts are highlighted by homemade brown bread and Mrs. Murray's preserves. All guest rooms have a TV, radio, hairdryer, and tea- and coffeemaker.

When booking, ask about possible discounts for holders of this book.

BALLSBRIDGE

✪ Ariel House

50–52 Lansdowne Rd., Ballsbridge, Dublin 4. ☎ **01/668-5512.** Fax 01/668-5845. 30 rms, all with bath. TV TEL. IR£25–IR£35 ($40–$56) per person for standard rooms. Rates for period rooms on request. Add 10% service charge. IR£6.50 ($10.40) per person extra for full Irish breakfast, IR£4.50 ($7.20) for continental breakfast, IR£4.50 ($7.20) for afternoon tea. MC, V. DART: Lansdowne Road.

Built in 1850, this historic-listed Victorian mansion is one of Dublin's most popular guesthouses. In 1995, it won the prestigious Royal Automobile Club of Great Britain award as Best Small Hotel in Ireland. And you can give credit for *that* to Michael O'Brien, its genial owner, who has a unique ability to put himself in the traveler's shoes, understand what will make traveling easier, more comfortable, and more fun, then proceed to furnish exactly that! His long-time manager, Marion Garry, and her staff reflect the same caring attitude.

The two adjoining century-old red-brick houses and the modern garden extension combine the graciousness of age with modern comfort. Guest rooms in the main house have high ceilings and antique furnishings, and upstairs rooms are reached via a lovely old staircase. The garden-extension rooms are ground level, with a ramp for wheelchairs. Rooms have trouser presses, iron/ironing boards, hairdryers, and twin beds or one double and one single bed, and there are two large family rooms.

The pride of Ariel House are the elegant, spacious half-suites, with beautiful period furnishings and a multitude of personal touches—definitely worth the slightly higher rates.

Breakfast, with a wide variety of choices, is served in a beautiful Victorian-style conservatory or the adjacent room that opens into the conservatory. The classic Victorian parlor is a lovely trip back in time.

Ariel House is only five minutes from the city center, and there's a DART rail stop just a few steps from the house. Lansdowne Football Stadium is next door, and within easy walking distance are the American embassy, the Royal Dublin Society, and Chester Beatty Library.

When booking, ask about possible discounts for holders of this book.

✪ Elva

5 Pembroke Park, Ballsbridge, Dublin 4. ☎ **01/660-2931.** Fax 01/660-5417. 3 rms, all with bath. TV. IR£21–IR£25 ($33.60–$40) per person sharing; IR£25–IR£30 ($40–$48) single. (Rates include breakfast.) No credit cards. Parking available. Closed Dec–Feb. Bus: 10. DART: Lansdowne Road.

Convenient to the American embassy, Royal Dublin Society grounds, and the National Concert Hall, Elva is a lovely Victorian home presided over by Mrs. Sheila Matthews. All bedrooms have hairdryers, direct-dial phones, and TV. There is a private parking area and good transportation into the city center (only a short ride away). Restaurants are within easy walking distance.

✪ Montrose House

16 Pembroke Park, Ballsbridge, Dublin 4. ☎ **01/668-4286.** 4rms, none with bath. IR£19.50 ($31.20) per person. (Rates include breakfast.) No credit cards. Bus: 10, 46A, or 64A.

Just off Herbert Park, not far from the American embassy, Montrose House is a two-story, red-brick house fronted by a flower garden. Inside, you'll find lots of mahogany and antique furnishings, and the gracious hostess, Mrs. Catherine Ryan. The pretty white-walled dining room looks out onto the garden through a bay window. All four rooms are attractively done up and comfortable, with sinks, and there's central heating.

✪ Mount Herbert

7 Herbert Rd., Ballsbridge, Dublin 4. ☎ **01/668-4321.** Fax 01/660-7077. 135 rms, all with bath. TV TEL. IR£23.50–IR£28.50 ($37.60–$45.60) per person sharing, depending on season. Breakfast extra. ACC, AE, DC, MC, V. Enclosed private car park. DART: Landsdowne Road.

Once the residence of Lord Robinson, the central portion of Mount Herbert is a handsome three-story, slate-roofed white mansion with black trim. Today it is joined by extensions to form a guesthouse run by the Loughran family, set back from the road, with a walled parking lot protected by an excellent security system. The full Irish breakfast is served in a pleasant window-walled dining room overlooking the garden, and moderately priced lunches and dinners are available. In addition to the large lounge, there's a small, cozy sitting room that sports a fire in cool weather. Bedrooms are nicely furnished and come with color TVs with satellite channels, hairdryers, and trouser presses. Services include wheelchair access to both bedroom and shower in two ground-floor rooms, baby-sitting, and theater and car-rental bookings. Facilities include a solarium, sauna, badminton court, and gift shop.

Blackrock

✪ Chestnut Lodge

2 Vesey Place, Blackrock, Co. Dublin. ☎ **01/280-7860.** Fax 01/280-1466. 4 rms, all with bath. TEL. IR£35 ($56) single; IR£27.50 ($44) per person double. 50% reduction for children; IR£15 ($24) deposit required when booking. (Rates include breakfast.) ACC, MC, V. Bus: 7 or 8. DART: Monkstown.

Personable Nancy Malone has four bright, cheerful, and unusually spacious rooms in this 1840 Regency residence that has been refurbished to provide modern conveniences while retaining its 19th-century character. The house is just off the main Dublin–Dun Laoghaire road, about six miles from the city center and only a short stroll from the seafront and restaurants. The ferryport is also quite convenient. Facing a lovely little wooded park, it is a haven of subdued elegance and charm, and Nancy is the epitome of Irish hospitality, with an astounding knowledge of Dublin and a keen sense of what it takes to make your stay a happy one. Guest rooms overlook either the park or the landscaped back garden. A highlight of breakfast is the buffet of muesli, cereals, fresh-fruit compote, and yogurt that compliments your traditional breakfast. Chestnut Lodge is an ideal base for exploring Dublin, as well as Dalkey, Killiney, and County Wicklow.

Glasnevin

✪ Iona House

5 Iona Park, Glasnevin, Dublin 9. ☎ **01/830-6217.** Fax 01/830-6732. 11 rms, all with bath. TV TEL. IR£25–IR£29 ($40–$46.40) per person sharing. 50% reduction for children. ACC, AE, DC, V. Bus: 11, 13, 19, 19A, 34, or 34A.

Located in a charming Victorian section, Iona House is a lovely old red-brick house built around the turn of the century. Karen and Jack Shouldice provide such extras as perked coffee and American-style bacon to make visiting Yanks feel at home. There's a lounge and a private garden, plus central heating. Guest rooms (which tend to be on the small side) are attractive and comfortable, with hairdryers and radios. Both German and French are spoken here. There is also a restaurant offering meals at good value.

When booking, ask about possible discounts for holders of this book.

Swords (By Dublin Airport)

Forte Travelodge

Swords By Pass, N1 Dublin/Belfast Rd., Swords, Co. Dublin. ☎ **01/840-0255** or toll free 1/800/709-709 (daily 7am–10pm). No fax. 40 rms, all with bath. IR£33.50 ($53.60) per room (sleeps 3 adults, or 2 adults, a child, and an infant). AE, MC, V.

Located just 1½ miles north of Dublin airport (16 miles north of the city center) in the southbound carriageway of the Swords By Pass at the Swords roundabout, this new motel-type lodging is especially appealing to families and other groups. Rooms are quite spacious, with a double bed, single sofa bed, and a child's bed and/or baby cot if requested. Each has its own central-heating controls, as well as TV, radio/clock, and tea- and coffeemaking facilities. The adjacent Little Chef restaurant specializes in snacks, drinks, and a wide variety of moderately priced meals. Both the accommodations and the restaurant have facilities for the handicapped.

Templeogue

Arus Mhuire

8 Old Bridge Rd., Templeogue, Dublin 16. ☎ **01/494-4281** or 493-7022. 9 rms, 7 with bath. TV. IR£21 ($33.60) per person sharing with bath, IR£19 ($30.40) without bath; IR£28 ($44.80) single with bath, IR£26 ($41.60) without bath. (Rates include breakfast.) No credit cards. Parking available. Bus: 15B, 49, 65, or 65A.

Mrs. Colette O'Brien's modern home is four miles from the city center, but four bus routes are nearby. There's a laundry service for guests and a locked car park, very important in the Dublin area. Her bedrooms are comfortable and attractive, each with TV, clock radio, hairdryer, and tea/coffeemaker.

Hostels, YWCAs & Dorms

City Center

Avalon House

55 Aungier St., Dublin 2. ☎ **01/475-0001.** Fax 01/475-0303. 42 rms, 10 with shower, 3 dorms, 1- and 4-bedded rms. IR£8–IR£19 ($12.80–$30.40). (Rates include continental breakfast.) AE, MC, V. Bus: 16, 16A, 19, or 22.

Beginning life in 1879 as a medical school, this large red sandstone building sports all the embellishments of the Victorian era. Even though it saw service as an office building before its transformation into a top-notch hostel, such features as wide, high windows, large turf-burning fireplaces, and ornate wallpapers survived the invasion of modern business. All have been carefully retained to preserve the building's character, while hostel facilities are quite modern. In addition to facilities for the disabled, Avalon House offers shower facilities for all rooms, some rooms with private baths, coffee bar, restaurant, provisions for self-catering, a TV lounge, a reading room, bureau de change, personal security lockers, and luggage storage. Centrally located, it is next to Whitefriar's church (see "Attractions" Chapter 6), about a two-minute walk from St. Stephen's Green. *Note: Book as far in advance as possible during high season.*

✪ Dublin International Youth Hostel

61 Mountjoy St., Dublin 7. ☎ **01/830-4555.** Fax 01/830–5808. 400 beds. IR£8–IR£10 ($12.80–$16) per person. (Rates include breakfast.) MC, V. Bus: Most city center lines.

A warm welcome, comfort, and modern convenience set in a beautiful old building are features at An Oige's newest Dublin city hostel, only a five-minute walk from the city center, an excellent base for exploring the capital city. Facilities include hot showers, central heating, a restaurant in a converted chapel, weekend entertainment, bicycle rental, supervised car parks, and an information desk.

Isaac's Dublin

2–5 Frenchman's Lane, Dublin 1. ☎ **01/874-9321.** 214 dormitory beds, 32 family rms. IR£6 ($9.60) dormitory beds, IR£15–IR£18 ($24–$28.80) per person sharing double, twin, or triple rooms (some with private or semi-private baths). (Rates exclude breakfast.) No credit cards.

Just around the corner from Dublin's Central Bus Station (Busaras) and only minutes away from O'Connell Street, this superior hostel won an award for its restoration of the old wine warehouse it occupies. Dormitory and family rooms are comfortably furnished, and there is a self-catering kitchen. A moderately priced restaurant on the premises serves all three meals and snacks all day. Rental bikes are available for a small charge.

Kinlay House Christchurch

2–12 Lord Edward Street, Dublin 2. ☎ **01/679-6644.** 150 beds, 33 2-, 4-, and 6-bedded rms. IR£8–IR£14 ($12.80–$22.40). (Rates include breakfast.) No credit cards.

Open year-round and run by USIT, Kinlay House is located in one of Dublin's oldest neighborhoods, just steps away from Christchurch Catheral. Some semi-private rooms have private baths. A continental breakfast is included in the rates. Meeting/study rooms are available to guests.

The Young Traveller

St. Mary's Place, Dublin 7. ☎ **01/830-5000** or 830-5319. 15 rms, with toilet and shower. IR£8–IR£10 ($12.80–$16) per person. (Rates include breakfast.) MC, V.

This popular privately run hostel has a city-center location north of the Liffey, just a 5-minute walk from O'Connell Street. There are 13 four-bedded rooms with shower, one twin-bedded room with bath, and one room with kitchen facilities. Comforters, towels, and soap are provided, and there's hot water 24 hours a day. Amenities include an attractive lounge, TV lounge, and launderette.

YWCA Hostel

64 Lower Baggot St., Dublin 2. ☎ **01/660-8452.** 48 beds. IR£9 ($14.40) per person. Weekly rate available. (Rates include breakfast.) No credit cards. Open May–Sept, limited beds Sept–May. Bus: 10.

Located three blocks from St. Stephen's Green, the hostel is open most of the year to college students and working men and women, but tourists are welcomed during June, July, and August. Each room contains hot and cold water and accommodates from two to four people. Although the door is locked at midnight, a key will be provided if you must be out later.

Sandymount

YWCA Radcliff Hall

St. John's Rd., Sandymount, Dublin 4. ☎ **01/269-4521.** Fax 01/260-0584. 40 rms, none with bath; 20 chalets, all with bath. IR£12 ($19.20) per person, single or double without bath in the main house; IR£14 ($22.40) per person for twin-bedded chalet with bath. Weekly half-board (breakfast and dinner) rates available. Rates do not include 10% service charge. (Rates include breakfast.) No credit cards. Bus: 3, 6, 7A, 8, 18, or 52. DART: Sydney Parade.

Just two blocks from the sea, this YWCA was formerly a convent, and the chapel as well as the well-tended 2½ acres of flower gardens, lawn, and fruit trees have all been retained. The high-ceilinged rooms in the main building and chalets in the rear are attractive and comfortable, and all chalets have twin beds and private bath. The decor is simple and you're required to make your own bed in the morning. The modern dining room opens onto a patio, where meals are sometimes served in summer. Radcliff Hall is popular among both tourists and conference groups, and it caters mainly to students during winter months. Facilities include a library, laundry room with irons, and a TV and recreation room. Advance booking with a IR£10 ($16) deposit is an absolute must, especially if you'd like a room with a private bath.

Self-Catering

Ballsbridge and Sandymount

✪ Lansdowne Village

Ballsbridge, and **Sandymount Village,** Park Court Sandymount, c/o Mrs. Jacinta Stacey, Trident Holiday Homes, Unit 2, Sandymount Village Centre, Sandymount, Dublin 4. ☎ **01/668-3534.** Fax 01/660-6465. 28 units. IR£340–IR£510 ($544–$816) per unit per week, depending on season. Units sleep five to seven people. Holiday weekend rates available. AE, MC, V.

Trident Holiday Homes operates luxury self-catering facilities in many locations throughout the country, and both these Dublin properties offer superb two-story town house accommodations in private landscaped grounds. Although definitely in the luxury class, these town houses can run as low as IR£15 ($21.75) per person per day for parties of five to seven people. Two- and three-bedroom units are available, and each is outfitted with washer/dryer, TV, telephone, linen, towels, and central heat. Cots and high chairs can be requested, and there's a baby-sitting service. Each property is convenient to a DART station for convenient transportation into the city center.

Belfield

✪ Belgrove and Merville

UCD Village, Belfield, Dublin 4. ☎ **01/269-7111.** Fax 01/269-7704. 260 beds. Mid-June to mid-Sept, IR£350 ($560) per unit per week. Units sleep three to five people. MC, V.

Set in the landscaped grounds of University College, Dublin, these three-, four-, and five-bedroom apartments are just 3 miles from the city center, with frequent direct bus service. All linens are supplied; there is electric heating; and the sports complex has tennis courts, squash courts, a gym, and a running track. Shops, a coffee shop, restaurants, and a launderette in the village add to the convenience of these self-catering units.

DONNYBROOK

✪ Brookman Town Homes

Donnybrook Manor, Donnybrook, Dublin 4. ☎ **01/676-6784.** Fax 01/676-3166. 20 units. IR£395–IR£650 ($632–$1,040) per unit per week. Units sleep four to six. Electricity and telephone charges extra. IR£50 ($80.00) deposit when booking. MC, V.

These luxury two-, three-, and four-bedroom town houses are set in a secure off-street location and are quite convenient to the city center, with frequent bus service. Each is equipped with TV, telephone, and dishwasher, and there's also a washing machine in larger units. Breakfast pack on arrival.

MODERATELY PRICED LUXURY HOTELS OUTSIDE THE CITY CENTER

Although the rates for the following high-standard accommodations are above budget-level, they certainly represent value for the dollar. Lying outside Dublin, all are on the Dublin bus lines; they're ideal for those who prefer to avoid the hustle and bustle of inner-city accommodations. Three are a 10-minute drive from the city center, and the Green Isle is about 25 minutes away; all have good parking. They boast spacious, attractive rooms with baths, TVs, radios, telephones, and a bar, grillroom, and restaurant.

At time of press, rates were in the IR£76 to IR£99 ($121.60 to $158.40) range per room, single or double, yielding an attractive per-person rate for doubles. Credit cards (AE, MC, V) are accepted. Book through individual hotels, or in the U.S., the Doyle Hotel Group, Suite 115, 1900 Connecticut Ave. NW, Washington, DC 20009 (☎ 800/42-DOYLE or 202/986-7137).

Tara Tower Hotel, Merrion Rd., Dublin 4 (☎ 01/269-4666; fax 01/269-1027), overlooks Dublin Bay, just north of the city. Ask for a front room overlooking the sea. **The Skylon Hotel,** Upper Drumcondra Rd., Dublin 9 (☎ 01/837-9121; fax 01/837-2778), is also north of the central city on the main Dublin Airport/Northern Ireland road. **The Montrose,** Stillorgan Rd., Dublin 4 (☎ 01/269-3311; fax 01/269-1164) is a guest house located on the main road to the south of the country. It overlooks the grounds of University College Dublin campus. **The Green Isle Hotel,** Nass Rd., Dublin 12 (☎ 01/459-3406; fax 01/459-2178) is on the main motorway to the south and southwest, a bit farther out than the other three, but no more than a twenty-minute drive from the city center.

WORTH A SPLURGE

CITY CENTER

✪ Buswell's Hotel

25 Molesworth St., Dublin 2 ☎ **01/676-4013** or in the U.S. 800/473-9527. Fax 01/676-2090. 70 rms, with bath. TV TEL. IR£62 ($99.20) single, IR£51 ($81.60) per person double. Service charge of 13.33% and breakfast extra. Special winter weekend offers at considerable discounts. ACC, AE, DC, MC, V.

Buswell's is a Dublin institution. Over the years, it's hosted such Irish notables as Sir Roger Casement and Eamon De Valera. Located just across from the Dail, it offers center-city convenience, superb accommodations, and a dining room. The clientele in the restaurant and bar is liberally sprinkled with politicians, leading Dublin businesspeople, and colorful personalities.

Public rooms feature old prints, period furnishings, and ornate plasterwork. As for guest rooms, few are a "standard" size and shape, and each contemporary setting has touches of Victoriana. All come equipped with tea- and coffeemakers, trouser presses, hairdryers, and radio.

Dining/Entertainment: Georgian elegance surrounds you in the Emily Room Restaurant and the Georgian Bar. O'Callaghan's Cellar Bar offers conviviality along with excellent lunch and evening snack selections in a Tudor setting.

✪ The Grey Door

22/23 Upper Pembroke Street, Dublin 2. ☎ **01/676-3286.** Fax 01/676-3287. 6 rms, 1 studio suite, all with bath. TEL TV. IR£65 ($104) single; IR£42.50 ($68) per person sharing; IR£47.50 ($76) per person sharing double with sitting area; IR£50 ($80) per person for studio suite. Special weekend rate (two-night stay): IR£65 ($104) per night single or double, breakfast included. IR£7 ($11.20) full breakfast; IR£5 ($8) continental breakfast. Parking available nearby.

Its convenient city-center location is only one of the features that make The Grey Door worth a splurge. The decor, furnishings, and comfort of the bedrooms are all of the highest standards. Each has a trouser press (iron and ironing board are also available), hairdryer, coffee/tea facilities, complimentary daily newspaper, and a fax. One of Dublin's finest restaurants, also called The Grey Door, occupies the first floor (see "Where to Eat"), and there's an excellent, moderately priced basement bistro, Pier 32.

✪ The Westbury Hotel

Grafton Street, Dublin 2 ☎ **01/679-1122** or in the U.S. 800/223-6800 or 223-0833. Fax 01/679-7078. 203 rms, with bath. TV TEL. IR£126–IR£155 ($201.60–$248) single, IR£71–IR£78 ($113.60–$124.80) per person sharing. (Rates do not include breakfast.) 15% service charge. Some weekend rates available in low season. Valet parking.

In the heart of the city center, the Westbury is not only one of Dublin's poshest hotels, but it's without doubt one of the most beautiful. Its white marble entrance leads into a lower foyer carpeted in pale pink, and that same Navan/Youghal carpet extends up a sweeping staircase of cream-colored marble and brass to the upper foyer, lobby, and dining room. Walnut panels, peach-colored silk wall coverings, oil paintings, and wing-back Chinese Chippendale chairs are mixed companionably with modern furniture. Guest rooms and suites all are furnished in mahogany and brass, have canopies over beds, and marble bathrooms. They're among the most spacious I've encountered in Ireland. Some suites even have Jacuzzis.

Dining/Entertainment: The upper foyer Terrace provides soft music throughout the evening and for afternoon tea; the Russell Room's peach-and-mint-green decor is the setting for fine dining; the Seafood Restaurant Bar features shellfish from Dublin Bay; and the coffee shop serves inexpensive meals and snacks.

KILLINEY

Fitzpatrick's Castle Hotel

Killiney Hill Road, Co. Dublin. ☎ **01/284-0700.** Fax 01/285-0207. 90 rms; 7 suites, all with bath/shower. TV TEL. IR£75–IR£92 ($120–$147.20) single, IR£46–IR£62 ($73.60–$99.20) per person sharing. 15% service charge. ACC, AE, DC, MC, V. Drive: Hwy N11 south from Dublin to village of Killiney.

Having three-turreted towers and white battlements, this is one of Dublin's finest luxury hotels. It's about a 20-minute drive from the city center on the outskirts of an ancient and charming village, and the hotel runs a courtesy bus. On nine landscaped acres, it was built in 1740 as a manor house. A huge 15th-century stone fireplace, from a former house on the site, now dominates the Dungeon Bar (which has nightly entertainment). The castle is run by the Fitzpatrick family with graciousness and warmth.

Readers Recommend

Eileen and Jim McNamee, 15 Shangaugh Grove, Shanhill, Co. Dublin. ☎ 01/282-0370. *"This a superb place to stay, with outstanding hospitality and a big, beautiful breakfast."* —Marjorie Tannehill, Akron, OH

Mrs. Mary Monaghan, 46 Windsor Park, Blackrock, Co. Dublin. ☎ 01/284-3711. *"Dara, Mary, and their teenage sons Carl and Gary made me feel right at home. Their home is about a ten-minute walk from the Blackrock DART station and about a twenty-five-minute walk from downtown Dun Laoghaire. The rooms are immaculate, and Mary serves a hearty breakfast."* —Gary Eóghan Mead, US Air Force.

Latchford's, 99–100 Baggot Street, Dublin 2. ☎ 01/676-0784. *"A rare find for those looking for value and quality. Resting gently in the center of restored, picturesque Georgian Dublin, Latchford's is a short walking distance to Grafton Street shopping, four beautiful parks, and numerous museums and art galleries."*

—Marianne Begley, Portland, OR

Mrs. Kathleen Lee, 6 St. Ann St., South Circular Road, Dublin 8. ☎ 01/453-6615. *"Mrs. Lee is a very warm and helpful hostess. Her house is only 2 km from the city center, with a bus stop and a launderette nearby. Very nice single and double rooms."*

—M. R. Weate, Australia

The bedrooms facing the front have balconies with a table and chairs, and those at the back boast lovely canopied beds. Some luxury suites have magnificent views of Dublin Bay, others a Jacuzzi. Adjoining the castle is a block of modern, luxury time-sharing holiday homes that are often available for weekly rentals, providing self-catering facilities in addition to all the amenities of the hotel (contact the hotel for rates and availability if you're interested).

Dining/Entertainment: The already mentioned Dungeon Bar is a popular gathering place for Killiney locals. Truffles, the dining room, is a favorite of Dublin businesspeople for lunch and families in the evening.

Facilities: Indoor swimming pool, indoor squash courts, saunas, hairdressing salon, and gift shop.

4 Where to Eat

From picnics in St. Stephen's Green to pub grub, and from Tourist Menu meals to elegant splurges, Dublin offers wide variety in cuisine as well as price. Cuisine categories include "Traditional," which I have used instead of the usual "American" to mean a rather general menu selection of steaks, chops, poultry, fish, etc., that may be prepared in a slightly different manner than "American" as you know it. The "Irish" heading means *traditional* Irish.

Let me suggest that you read through listings for those restaurants that appear to be above your budget in price—lunch can quite often be very good value and well within budget limits. Look also for "Tourist Menu" listings, since they give you a limited selection from the pricey menu at a bargain price. Both these money-stretching strategies will broaden your Dublin dining experience considerably.

A final tip: Pick up a copy of the "Dining in Ireland" booklet published by the Irish Tourist Board and available for a small charge, and tuck it in your purse or pocket as a ready reference in every area of the city.

Dublin Dining

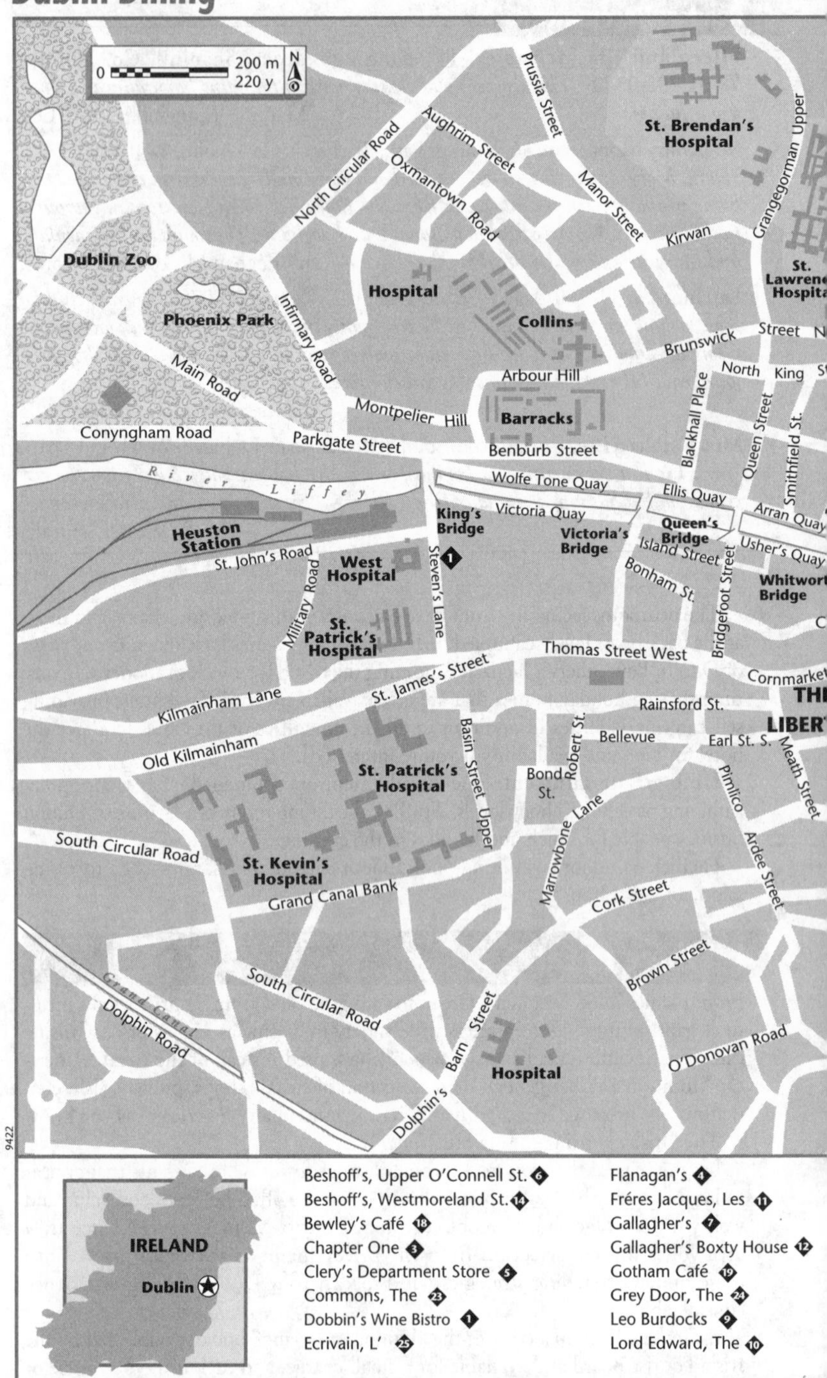

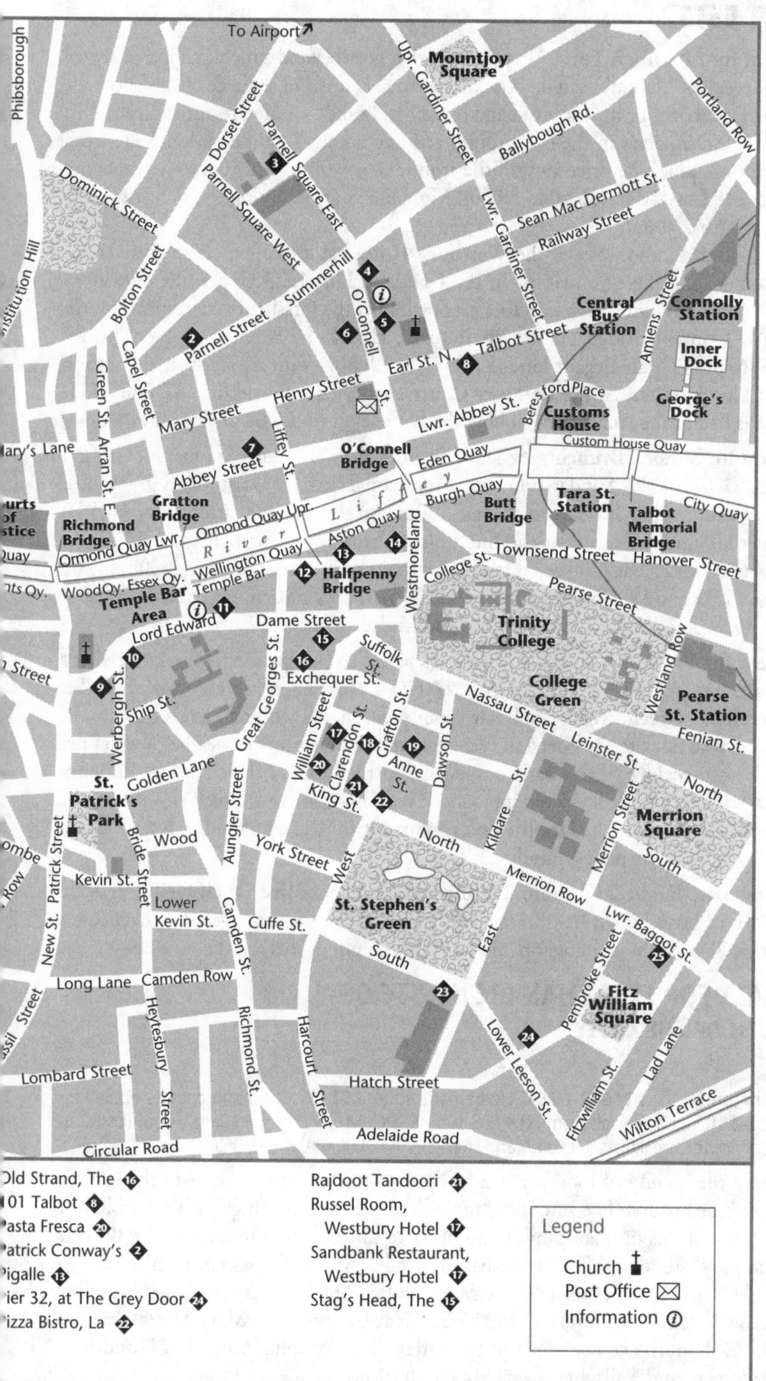

To Airport
Phibsborough
Mountjoy Square
Upr. Gardiner Street
Portland Row
Ballybough Rd.
Dorset Street
Parnell Square East
Parnell Square West
Dominick Street
Sean Mac Dermott St.
Railway Street
Lwr. Gardiner Street
Summerhill
Bolton Street
Parnell Street
O'Connell St.
Central Bus Station
Amiens Street
Connolly Station
Talbot Street
Earl St. N.
Inner Dock
George's Dock
Beresford Place
Customs House
Henry Street
Mary Street
Lwr. Abbey St.
Capel Street
Green St.
Arran St. E.
Liffey St.
Abbey Street
O'Connell Bridge
Eden Quay
Custom House Quay
Gratton Bridge
Richmond Bridge
Ormond Quay Upr.
Ormond Quay Lwr.
River Liffey
Burgh Quay
Butt Bridge
Tara St. Station
Talbot Memorial Bridge
City Quay
Aston Quay
Wellington Quay
Westmoreland
Townsend Street
Hanover Street
Wood Qy.
Essex Qy.
Temple Bar
Temple Bar Area
Halfpenny Bridge
College St.
Pearse Street
Trinity College
Lord Edward
Dame Street
Suffolk St.
Exchequer St.
Great Georges St.
Werbergh St.
Ship St.
College Green
Westland Row
Pearse St. Station
Nassau Street
Fenian St.
Leinster St.
William Street
Clarendon St.
Grafton St.
Anne St.
Dawson St.
Kildare St.
Merrion Street
Merrion Square
North
South
Golden Lane
King St.
St. Patrick's Park
Aungier Street
York Street
Wood
Bride Street
New St.
Patrick Street
Kevin St.
Lower Kevin St.
Cuffe St.
Camden St.
St. Stephen's Green
West
East
North
South
Merrion Row
Lwr. Baggot St.
Pembroke Street
Fitz William Square
Long Lane
Camden Row
Heytesbury Street
Richmond St.
Harcourt Street
Lower Leeson St.
Lombard Street
Hatch Street
Fitzwilliam St.
Lad Lane
Wilton Terrace
Adelaide Road
Circular Road
Old Strand, The 16
101 Talbot 8
Pasta Fresca 20
Patrick Conway's 2
Pigalle 13
Pier 32, at The Grey Door 24
Pizza Bistro, La 22
Rajdoot Tandoori 21
Russel Room, Westbury Hotel 17
Sandbank Restaurant, Westbury Hotel 17
Stag's Head, The 15
Legend
Church
Post Office
Information

BEST BETS

Best for Afternoon Tea Afternoon tea that goes beyond a mere "cuppa" is served in several of Dublin's leading hotels. The ritual consists of a choice of specialty teas, pastries, scones or brown bread and butter, and cake—all are presented nicely. Soft piano music plays in the background at some hotels. Traditional hours are from 3 to 4:30pm. The price varies little from one establishment to another, ranging from IR£4 to IR£6 ($6.40 to $9.60). More hotels are adopting this delightful custom, so ask about.

Just off Grafton Street, the **Westbury Hotel** has afternoon tea in the Terrace Lounge, and there's a pianist. At the **Gresham Hotel,** 23 Upper O'Connell St., ☎ 874-6881, tea is served in the relaxing lobby; the Gresham is four blocks north of O'Connell Bridge. At the **Shelbourne Hotel,** St. Stephen's Green North, ☎ 676-6471, an elegant lounge just off the lobby, with a pianist, is the setting for afternoon tea. At the **Berkeley Court Hotel,** Lansdowne Rd., ☎ 660-1711, tea is had in the comfortable lobby; the Berkeley is in the Ballsbridge area.

Best for Sunday Brunch At **Davy Byrne's Pub,** 21 Duke St., just off Grafton St., ☎ 677-5217, Sunday brunch is a traditional Irish breakfast for IR£4 ($6.40); drinks are extra. It's served from 12:30pm to 2pm. Reservations are essential for the Sunday Brunch at the **Shelbourne Hotel,** St. Stephen's Green North, ☎ 676-6471. The traditional Irish breakfast is served from noon to 2:30pm. The price is IR£16 ($25.60) for adults, IR£10 ($16) for children, plus a service charge of 15%. The setting is elegant, ditto the service and food.

Best for Picnic Fare One of the best places to buy picnic fixings is **Bewley's Cafe** (see below), 78 Grafton St., ☎ 677-6761. Then hie yourself off to **St. Stephen's Green,** where you'll have your picnic along with half of Dublin's work force, who flock to the Green in fine weather and sometimes in weather not so fine, such is their love of this oasis of greenery in the heart of the city. The **Phoenix Park** is another idyllic picnic spot, and if your hunger pangs attack and you aren't prepared, head for the **Dublin Zoo restaurant** to pick up a sandwich to be eaten elsewhere on the park grounds.

Best Late-Night/23½-hour Dining Both **The Coffee Dock Grill** (see page 118), in Jurys Hotel, Ballsbridge, and **The Old Stand** (see page 122), Exchequer St., will satisfy your hunger pangs late in the night or early in the morning.

MEALS FOR LESS THAN IR£10 ($16.00)

SOUTH OF THE LIFFEY

Bewley's Cafe

78 Grafton St. ☎ **01/677-6761.** Homemade soup IR£1 ($1.65); main courses IR£3–IR£5 ($4.80–$8); lunch specials from IR£4 ($6.40). AE, DC, MC, V. Daily 7:30am–10pm (continuous service for breakfast, hot food, and snacks). TRADITIONAL/PASTRIES.

Here the quality of food is never in doubt—nor has it ever been in the chain's 150-year history. The interior is much like old-time tea shops, with marble-top tables and lots of mahogany. In addition to lunch or a refreshing tea break, you can purchase teas, coffees, fresh-baked breads, and terrific pastries to take out.

This branch is between Nassau Street and St. Stephen's Green. Other locations are at 11/12 Westmoreland St., 13 S. Great George's St., Mary Street near the ILAC shopping center north of the Liffey, and shopping centers in Dundrum, Stillorgan, and Tallaght, as well as Dublin Airport.

Gallagher's Boxty House

20 Temple Bar. ☎ **01/677-2762.** A la carte IR£6–IR£10 ($9.60–$16); set menu Mon–Fri, noon to 5pm IR£5 ($8), weekends and evenings IR£10 ($16); sandwiches daily noon–5pm, IR£1.50–IR£5 ($2.40–$8). MC, V. Daily noon–11:30 pm. IRISH.

This truly traditional Irish restaurant one block south of the Liffey between Essex Street and Fleet Street grew out of brothers Padraig and Ronan Gallagher's fond memories of the boxty pancakes their mother always cooked on Friday nights when they were growing up. Now, with its menu featuring such specialties as boxty, bacon and cabbage, and bread-and-butter pudding, Dubliners are flocking to Gallagher's in homage to those very dishes—it seems the Gallagher boys are not the only ones nostalgic for them. This is definitely a place to bring the entire family, but be warned: No reservations are taken, and the place can be packed—in which case, you simply hie yourself across the road to the Auld Dubliner and wait to be called.

Gotham Café

8 South Anne St., Dublin 2. ☎ **01/679-5266.** IR£2–IR£8 ($3.20–$12.80). MC, V. Mon–Sat noon–midnight, Sun 12:30–10:30 pm. PASTA/GOURMET PIZZAS/FUNKY SALADS/GRILLS/SANDWICHES.

The menu at this smart, casual cafe can best be described as American-style/New Wave Italian. California influences show up in the avocado vegetarian salad, and New Yorkers will gravitate to the Bowery, Upper East Side, and Central Park gourmet pizzas. Pastas are variations on traditional Italian sauces, like ribbon noodle pasta in a creamy spinach sauce. Bright, breezy, and friendly. Good wine list. Just off Grafton Street.

✪ Leo Burdocks

2 Werburgh St. ☎ **01/454-0306.** IR£2.50–IR£3.50 ($4–$5.60). No credit cards. Mon–Fri 12:30–11pm, Sat 2–11pm. Closed holidays. FISH & CHIPS.

You really shouldn't leave Dublin without calling here at least once. For three generations, Brian Burdock's family has been serving up what is probably the best fish-and-chips to be found in the country. Cabinet ministers, university students, poets, Americans who've had the word passed by locals, and almost every other type in Ireland can be found in the queue, patiently waiting for fish bought fresh that morning and those good Irish potatoes, both cooked in "drippings" (none of that modern cooking oil!). Great people-watching while you wait, and all that good eating costs a pittance for the priciest choice—ray-and-chips (whiting-and-chips are at the bottom of the range). It's in the Liberties/Christ Church Cathedral vicinity.

Pasta Fresca

3–4 Chatham St. ☎ **01/679-2402.** Appetizers IR£2–IR£4 ($3.20–$6.40); main courses IR£5–IR£9 ($8–$14.40), MC, V. Mon–Sat 8am–11:30pm; Sun 12:30pm–8:30pm. ITALIAN.

This popular place, just off Grafton Street near St. Stephen's Green, in addition to serving such pasta staples as lasagna, spaghetti, and ravioli, offers a great variety of fillings (like beef and spinach, or cheese and walnut).

✪ La Pizza Bistro

1 St. Stephen's Green N. ☎ **01/671-7175.** Prices: IR£4–IR£8 ($6.40–$12.80); Tourist Menu. ACC, AE, MC, V. Daily 9:30am–11:30pm. Closed Good Friday, Christmas Eve, Christmas Day, and St. Stephen's Day. PIZZA/PASTA.

Both traditional and deep-pan pizzas are served in this attractive eatery at the bottom of Grafton Street, and there's a good selection of pasta dishes, as well as a salad bar and some vegetarian menu selections. They also serve a good breakfast for under IR£4 ($6.40), and it is fully licensed.

North of the Liffey, its duplicate is at 14/15 O'Connell Street (☎ **878-8010**); everything's the same.

✪ Sandbank Restaurant

In the Westbury Hotel, Clarendon St. ☎ **01/679-1122.** Appetizers IR£3–IR£5 ($4.80–$8); main courses IR£7–IR£12 ($11.20–$19.20); average dinner IR£9 ($13.05). Service charge 15%. ACC, AE, DC, MC, V. Mon–Sat 12:30–2:30pm and Mon–Sat 6:30–10:30pm. Closed public holidays, Good Friday, and Christmas Day. SEAFOOD/TRADITIONAL.

The Sandbank serves up terrific seafood in a cozy, pubby setting on the lower level of the Westbury Hotel, one block off Grafton Street. Lunch dishes might include fresh plaice on the bone with anchovy-and-garlic butter; oak-smoked salmon served with lemon, onion, and capers; or a fisherman's platter. For lighter eaters, there are soups, assorted hors d'oeuvres, and a delicious oak-smoked-salmon pâté.

BALLSBRIDGE

✪ The Coffee Dock Grill

In Jurys Hotel and Towers, Ballsbridge. ☎ **01/660-5000.** Appetizers IR£2–IR£4 ($3.20–$6.40); main courses IR£4–IR£10.50 ($6.40–$16.80). AE, MC, V. Daily 6am–5am. Bus: 7, 7A, 8, 45, or 84. TRADITIONAL/VEGETARIAN.

This is Dublin's only 23-hour restaurant—a handy place to know about at the end of a late evening or the early beginning of a day. It is also very much in the budget price range, with seafoods, salads, mixed grills, omelets, sandwiches, steaks, burgers, and spaghetti available, along with snacks and sweets. There is also a good wine list.

NORTH OF THE LIFFEY

Beshoff's

7 Upper O'Connell St. ☎ **01/872-4000.** Less than IR£5 ($8). No credit cards. Mon–Thurs 11:30am–midnight, Fri–Sat 11:30am–1am, Sun 12:30pm–midnight. FISH & CHIPS.

This attractive Edwardian-style eatery two blocks north of O'Connell Bridge is a far cry from your everyday fish-and-chips stand. The tables are topped with marble and nicely spaced. There's a bright, cheerful look to the large, bustling room. There are several varieties of fish on order, which come in various combinations, some including chicken, and there's a wine license. It's self-service, and there's a children's menu.

There's also a Beshoff's at 14 Westmoreland St. south of the Liffey, with similar decor and hours.

Clery's Department Store

O'Connell Street, Dublin 1. ☎ **01/878-6000.** IR£2–IR£7 ($3.20–$11.20). No credit cards. Mon–Sat lunch noon–2pm; tea rooms 9am–5pm; coffee shop 9am–5pm. CARVERY/SALADS/AFTERNOON TEA/SNACKS.

Clery's is one of Dublin's oldest department stores, and its sales are legendary. Shopping or not, any one of their three eateries represent good value, as well as convenience when you're on the Northside. The third-floor **Rooftop Restaurant** specializes in a good carvery lunch—beef, pork, lamb, etc. Salads and other light lunches are offered here, too, right on to 5pm. The first-floor **Tea Rooms** offer a full lunch menu and afternoon tea. A wide variety of hot and cold snacks are available all day from the basement **Coffee Shop.**

✪ Flanagan's

61 Upper O'Connell St. ☎ **01/873-1388** or 873-1804. Reservations not accepted. Appetizers IR£1.50–IR£3 ($2.40–$4.80); main courses IR£4.50–IR£10 ($7.20–$16); tourist menu (except Sat) IR£5.75 ($9.20). ACC, BARC, MC, V. Daily noon–midnight. Closed Good Friday, Dec 25–26. TRADITIONAL/VEGETARIAN/PASTA.

This large, popular eatery three blocks north of O'Connell Bridge is roomy and pleasant, with high backs on booths to afford privacy, and a staff that's as friendly and efficient (even when the place is packed) as any I've encountered. The extensive à la carte menu includes steaks (most run about IR£7.95/$12.72), fish, chicken, pasta, vegetarian dishes, curries, and a children's menu. The upstairs pizzeria maintains the same high standards. Wine is reasonably priced by the glass or bottle. Very good value for the dollar here—families with small children are welcomed.

✪ Gallagher's

83 Middle Abbey St. ☎ **01/872-9861.** Appetizers IR£1–IR£5 ($1.60–$8); main courses IR£4.25–IR£12.95 ($6.80–$20.72). MC, V. Sun–Thurs noon–midnight; Fri–Sat noon–1am. TRADITIONAL/VEGETARIAN.

There's soft lighting, lots of dark wood, and red velvet booths in this pleasant restaurant one block north of O'Connell Bridge just off busy O'Connell Street. The à la carte menu includes fish, steaks, pork, chicken, lasagna, pizza, salads, and hamburgers. Good for families.

101 Talbot

101 Talbot St. ☎ **01/874-5011.** Appetizers IR£1.50–IR£2.50 ($2.40–$4); main courses IR£3–IR£6 ($4.80–$9.60) at lunch, IR£6–IR£8 ($9.60–$12.80) at dinner. MC, V. Daily noon–3pm and 6:30–11pm; pasta menu all day. MEDITERRANEAN/VEGETARIAN.

There's a decidedly cheerful ambience in this bright, airy upstairs eatery that's just around the corner from the Abbey Theatre. The emphasis here is on wholesome food, with an excellent selection of vegetarian dishes. Broccoli and cheese parcels, Greek *spanikopita* (spinach and feta cheese pie), and parsnip stuffed with Brazil nuts and vegetables served with a red pepper sauce are outstanding, as are chicken breast with spinach mousse and médaillons of pork with a sauce of brandy and mustard sauce among the meat offerings.

MEALS FOR LESS THAN IR£15 ($24)

South of the Liffey

Pier 32

At The Grey Door, 22 Upper Pembroke St., Dublin 2. ☎ **01/676-3286.** Lunch IR£7–IR£10 ($11.20–$16), dinner IR£12–IR£19 ($30.40). AE, DC, MC, V. Mon–Fri 12:30pm–2:15pm; daily 6pm–11pm. SEAFOOD/IRISH/TRADITIONAL.

This downstairs old-style pub and restaurant recreates a rural west-of-Ireland setting right in the heart of Dublin. Specializing in native seafood, the blackboard menu changes regularly to feature dishes from each of Ireland's 32 counties. Regional treatments of lobster, scampi, oysters, and mussels make regular appearances, as well as traditional Irish dishes.

✪ Rajdoot Tandoori

26/28 Clarendon St. ☎ **01/679-4274** or 679-4280. Appetizers IR£2.75–IR£6.50 ($4.40–$10.40); main courses IR£8–IR£12.50 ($12.80–$20); fixed-price dinner IR£15–IR£20 ($24–$32) at dinner. Service charge 12½%. ACC, AE, MC, V. Mon–Sat noon–2:30pm and 6:30–11:30pm. Closed for lunch on all public holidays. INDIAN/VEGETARIAN.

Just off Grafton Street, between Wicklow Street and Chatham Street, in the Westbury Centre, this is one of Dublin's best Indian restaurants. Mr. Sarda, its owner, opened his first restaurant in London's Chelsea back in 1966. You enter the elegant restaurant beneath a glittering 200-year-old crystal chandelier from a maharajah's palace in India. Inside, subdued lighting, brass tables, statues, and Indian prints provide a proper setting for excellent northern Indian specialties. Tandoori dishes such as duck, venison, lamb, and fish appear along with curries and kebabs. Nan, roti/chapah, paratha, and other Indian breads are also delicious.

North of the Liffey

Chapter One

18/19 Parnell Square, Dublin 1. ☎ **01/873-2266** or 873-2281. Set lunch IR£10 ($16); dinner appetizers IR£3–IR£6 ($4.80–$9.60); dinner main courses IR£9.50–IR£13 ($15.20–$20.80). AE, DC, MC, V. Tue–Fri noon–2:30pm; Tue–Sun 6pm–11pm. TRADITIONAL.

In a setting of natural stonework, warm colors, and a network of small rooms, Chapter One serves an innovative menu based on simple, traditional ingredients. The poached rainbow trout is excellent, and lovely are the pan-fried lamb cutlets in a rosemary sauce. One of my favorites is the delicate quenelles of fish with cream and dill and fresh tomato sauces. Desserts include a nice selection of Irish farmhouse cheeses. The wine list is moderately priced, and the service is excellent.

Meals for Less than IR£25 ($40)

South of the Liffey

✪ Dobbin's Wine Bistro

15 Stephen's Lane. ☎ **01/676-4679.** Reservations recommended. Appetizers IR£3–IR£8 ($4.80–$12.80); main courses IR£10–IR£20 ($16–$32). ACC, AE, DC, MC, V. Mon–Fri 12:30–2:30pm; Tues–Sat 8–11:30pm. Closed holidays. INTERNATIONAL.

On a small lane off Lower Mount Street, this is one of those delightful, intimate spots so friendly that you begin enjoying a meal even before you're seated, and the food is superb. The cuisine is best described as international, since in addition to succulent Irish lamb roasted with fresh herbs, you'll find Szechuan boned duckling, paupiettes of sole stuffed with fresh salmon and scallops, a lovely croustade of fresh seafood in sauce aux crevettes, and dishes of veal, pork, chicken, and steak. The wine list is one of Dublin's best. There is a nice selection of hors d'oeuvres (baked mushrooms in garlic butter, smoked salmon, fresh Dublin Bay prawns, etc.) and salads that will do quite nicely for a less expensive lunch.

L'Ecrivain

112 Lower Baggot St. ☎ **01/661-1919** or 661-0617. Reservations recommended. Set lunch IR£14 ($22.40); set dinner IR£25 ($40); à la carte dinner average price IR£20 ($32); 10% service charge on food only. AE, DC, MC, V. Mon–Sat 12:30–2:30pm and 6:30–11pm. FRENCH/VEGETARIAN.

This elegant little downstairs restaurant serves an equally elegant menu, featuring such classic dishes as tagliatelle with oysters and baby vegetables, poached crab mousse on a bed of leeks, and baked teal farci en croûte with a sweet sherry sauce. A rack of Wicklow lamb is outstanding, and all vegetables are nicely prepared. There's an extensive wine list.

Les Freres Jacques

24 Dame Street, Dublin 2. ☎ **01/679-4555.** Reservations recommended. Appetizers IR£5–IR£8 ($8–$12.80); lunch main courses IR£7–IR£17 ($11.20–$27.20); dinner main courses IR£15–IR£20 ($24–$32). AE, MC, V. FRENCH/SEAFOOD/IRISH.

This gem of a French restaurant has a turn-of-the-century decor and specializes in fish, live lobsters, oysters, sole, turbot, and game. The freshest seasonal ingredients add an Irish dimension to French classics and a French dimension to Irish standards. Outstanding on the menu is lobster grilled and flamed with Irish whiskey. Weekend evening meals are accompanied by live piano music. Next door to the Olympia Theatre.

✪ Pigalle

14 Temple Bar. ☎ **01/671-9262** or 679-6602. Reservations recommended for dinner. Set lunch IR£12 ($19.20); set dinner IR£19.50 ($31.20); dinner appetizers IR£4.50 ($7.20); dinner main courses IR£11.50 ($18.40). 12½% service charge. MC, V. Mon–Fri 12:30–2:30pm; Mon–Sat 7–10:45pm. FRENCH.

Set in the bohemian Temple Bar area, this upstairs restaurant exudes an understated elegance, with exposed brick walls alternating with wood paneling, lots of hanging greenery, and formally set tables. There is nothing formal about the ambience, however, and staff are friendly, knowledgeable, and helpful. The menu is in French (half the fun of choosing is asking for translations from the staff), with specialties of duck, veal, chicken, fish, and filet mignon. Needless to say, there's a good wine list.

✪ The Russell Room

In the Westbury Hotel, Clarendon St., off Grafton St. ☎ **01/679-1122.** Reservations recommended. Appetizers IR£4–IR£6 ($6.40–$9.60); main courses IR£10–IR£18 ($16–$28.80); fixed-price meal IR£19 ($30.40) at lunch, 24 ($38.40) at dinner. Service charge 15%. ACC, AE, DC, MC, V. Daily 12:30–2:30pm and 7–10:30pm. Parking IR£1.50 ($2.40) 7:30pm–midnight. FRENCH/VEGETARIAN.

This hotel dining room is one of the most beautiful and relaxing restaurants in Dublin. Add to that the classic dishes that are superbly prepared from the finest seasonal ingredients, and friendly and attentive service, and you have a real winner. The spacious Westbury Terrace Lounge just outside is a perfect place for predinner cocktails accompanied by pleasant piano music, and in the restaurant, soft shades of pink, green, and cream set the mood. Among standard favorites here are the crisp roast duckling with lemon, lime, and coriander; fresh sea trout filet with hazelnut-and-honey sauce; sliced beef filet with brandy, black peppercorns, and cream; and Irish salmon flavored with lemon balm, white wine, and cream. The wine list is extensive and moderate to expensive in price, coffee is freshly ground (both decaffeinated and regular), and there's a nice selection of teas.

BALLSBRIDGE

Roly's Bistro

7 Ballsbridge Terrace, Dublin 4. ☎ **01/668-2611.** Reservations required. Appetizers IR£2.50–IR£4.75 ($4–$7.60); main courses IR£7–IR£15 ($11.20–$24); vegetables extra IR£1.50 ($2.40). AE, DC, MC, V. IRISH/CONTINENTAL.

Reservations are a must at this popular eatery, for both lunch and dinner. One of Ireland's best-known chefs, Colm O'Daly, presides over the busy kitchen, and his menu concentrates on traditional Irish cuisine, seasoned with a flair of his own. My favorites include roast rack of Wicklow lamb with Gruyere gougere and deep-fried fillet of plaice rolled in sesame seeds, with sorrel butter.

PORTOBELLO

✪ Locks Restaurant

1 Windsor Terrace, Portobello. ☎ **01/454-3391** or 453-8352. Reservations recommended. Appetizers IR£3–IR£7 ($4.80–$11.20); main courses IR£10–IR£18 ($16–$28.80); fixed-price

meals IR£14 ($22.40) at lunch, IR£22 ($35.20) at dinner. Service charge 12½%. ACC, AE, DC, V. Mon–Fri 12:30–2pm; Mon–Sat 7:15–11pm. Closed bank holidays, one week at Christmas. Bus: 10, 23, 25, 26, 51, or 51B. FRENCH.

Sitting on the banks of the Grand Canal not far from the city center is this delightful French provincial–style restaurant whose menu includes classic dishes as well as simpler choices. Only the freshest seasonal ingredients are used, and they come to table reflecting the touch of a master chef, both in taste (exquisite) and presentation (picture perfect). Among the fish dishes, you might choose filets of brill with a Noilly Prat and lettuce sauce, escalopes of wild salmon with a mint sauce, or the daily recommendation from the fish market. There's a lovely escalope of chicken with a tarragon-and-butter sauce, and grilled lamb cutlets are superb. Service is top-notch and friendly, and the informal decor and ambience add to the enjoyment of a meal here. Dress is informal. Highly recommended.

PUB GRUB

The listings below barely scratch the surface of Dublin's pubs serving excellent and inexpensive meals during the lunch hours. You can pop into virtually any one of the scores of pubs offering pub grub and be assured of good quality *and* quantity. In fact, if you've foregone that gigantic Irish breakfast in your B&B, this could well be your main meal of the day at a tiny fraction of the cost of a full restaurant meal.

SOUTH OF THE LIFFEY

✪ The Lord Edward

23 Christchurch Place. ☎ **01/454-2420.** IR£4–IR£10 ($6.40–$16). ACC, AE, MC, V. Mon–Fri noon–3pm. TRADITIONAL.

The Lord Edward, in the Liberties, near Christ Church Cathedral, has a genuine old-world atmosphere, complete with stone fireplaces, beamed ceiling, and white stucco walls in the ground-floor pub. Upstairs is one of the city's finest seafood restaurants (see "Worth a Splurge," below), but the same high-quality food and excellent service come at modest prices in the pub during lunch hours. Choose from heaping plates of hot dishes (roasts, fish, chicken) or a nice selection of salad plates.

The Old Stand

Exchequer St. ☎ **01/298-7123.** Lunch IR£6 ($9.60); dinner IR£6–IR£10 ($9.60–$16). No credit cards. Mon–Fri 12:30–3:30pm and Mon–Fri 5–9:30pm. TRADITIONAL.

A Dublin tradition, especially among sports figures. A century and a half ago this was a forge, but today you'll find outstanding figures of the sporting world gathered to enjoy "the crack" (talk) and exceptionally good pub grub. There's a daily special of soup, meat, vegetables, and tea or coffee, as well as omelets or salad plates, and hot platters of chicken, steak, or fish.

Note: This is one of the very few pubs serving meals during evening hours—a terrific budget-stretcher. It's just off Great George's Street.

✪ The Stag's Head

1 Dame Court. ☎ **01/679-3701.** IR£3–IR£6 ($4.80–$9.60). No credit cards. Mon–Fri 12:15–2:15pm. TRADITIONAL.

Built in 1770, the Stag's Head had its last "modernization" in 1895. There are wrought-iron chandeliers, stained-glass skylights, huge mirrors, gleaming wood, and of course, mounted stags' heads. Choose a light lunch of soup and toasted sandwiches or heaping hot platters of bacon, beef, or chicken plus two vegetables.

The pub is just off Exchequer Street (from Great George Street); or look for the mosaic depicting a stag's head imbedded in the sidewalk of Dame Street in the middle of the second block on the left side coming from College Green, then turn onto the small lane that leads to Dame Court—complicated, but worth the effort.

NORTH OF THE LIFFEY

✪ Patrick Conway's

70 Parnell St. ☎ **01/873-2474.** IR£4–IR£6 ($6.40–$9.60). No credit cards. Mon–Fri 12:30–2:30pm. TRADITIONAL.

Dating from 1754, Patrick Conway's is just off O'Connell Street, opposite Rotunda Hospital and the Gate Theatre. You'll often find theater people bending an elbow here before and after a show in the evening. At lunchtime, however, there's very good pub grub on offer (they are especially known for their hot apple tart). It's a large, rambling place, but do take notice of the huge circular bar just inside the entrance which encloses a carved wooden structure of Gothic proportions. For those visitors who need to know more about Dublin, just ask Lorcan, your host, who is a wealth of information.

DUN LAOGHAIRE

The Purty Kitchen

Old Dunleary Rd., Dun Laoghaire. ☎ **01/284-3576.** IR£4–IR£10 ($6.40–$16). MC, V. Mon–Fri 12:30–2:20pm. TRADITIONAL.

This popular bar (see "Dublin Nights" in Chapter 6) specializes in seafood dishes, with a menu that ranges from snacks to full hot and/or cold plates.

WORTH A SPLURGE

SOUTH OF THE LIFFEY

The Commons Restaurant

Newman House, 85–86 St. Stephen's Green, Dublin 2. ☎ **01/478-0530** or 478-0539. Reservations required. Set lunch IR£18 ($28.80); set dinner IR£30 ($48); à la carte at dinner, appetizers IR£5–IR£12 ($8–$19.20), main courses IR£17–IR£22 ($27.20–$35.20). 15% service charge. AE, DC, MC, V. EUROPEAN.

Two of Dublin's most elegant 18th-century town houses are the setting for this tastefully appointed restaurant, which looks out over lovely private gardens. The striking art on the walls is by some of Ireland's leading contemporary artists. Gourmet specialities include grilled tournedos of beef with wild mushroom sauce and lamb served with oregano jus.

✪ The Grey Door

23 Upper Pembroke St., ☎ **01/676-3286.** Reservations recommended. Appetizers IR£7 ($11.20); main courses IR£13–IR£15 ($20.80–$24); fixed price meal IR£23 ($36.80) at dinner; average à la carte dinner IR£22 ($35.20). Service charge 12.5% ACC, AE, DC, V. Mon–Fri 12:30–2:15pm; Mon–Sat 7–11pm. Closed bank holidays. Bus: 7, 7a, 8, 45, or 84. SCANDINAVIAN/RUSSIAN/CONTINENTAL.

This elegant restaurant is in the upstairs drawing room of a town house, three blocks east of St. Stephen's Green, off Baggot Street. The splendid dishes such as blinis, borscht, Kotlet Kiev, steak Rasputin, and salmon Severnaya are served with aplomb. Be assured that once you've tried the extraordinary array of European and Russian dishes, you'll be back.

✪ The Lord Edward

23 Christchurch Place. ☎ **01/454-2420.** Reservations required. Bar lunch IR£4–IR£10 ($6.40–$16), average à la carte dinner IR£22 ($35.20). ACC, AE, DC, MC, V. Mon–Fri noon–3pm; Mon–Sat 5:30–10:45pm. SEAFOOD.

The Lord Edward, in the Liberties, near Christ Church Cathedral, has already been recommended as an exceptionally good pub-grub source. For a memorable seafood lunch or dinner, make your way to the small upstairs restaurant. The cozy, bay-windowed dining room is intimate, with velvet chairs and soft lighting. The menu offers as many as eight prawn dishes and the freshest of seafood—the owners make two daily shopping forays, one for lunch, another for dinner. The service is expert. A wide variety of specialty coffees is offered, from Cossack (with vodka) to Calypso (with Tia Maria). The Irish coffees are some of Dublin's best. Before your meal, you could make a stop at the middle-floor bar, with a beamed ceiling, and imbibe a premeal refresher before the glowing fireplace.

Ballsbridge

✪ Le Coq Hardi

35 Pembroke Rd., Ballsbridge. ☎ **01/668-9070.** Reservations required. Fixed-price lunch IR£18 ($28.80); fixed-price dinner IR£30 ($48). Service charge 12.5%. ACC, AE, DC, V. Mon–Fri 12:30–2:30pm; Mon–Sat 7:30–10:45pm. Closed bank holidays, one week at Christmas, two weeks in Aug. Bus: 7, 7A, 8, 45, or 84. FRENCH.

Dublin's finest French cuisine is served here; it's a blend of haute, bourgeois, and nouvelle. In a Georgian house, with a warm decor of rosewood and brass, you can order such specialties as filet of spring lamb with fresh tomato and tarragon or milk-fed veal with sauce of wild mushrooms, apple brandy, and cream. The star of the menu is undoubtedly the Coq Hardi (it means the brave cock); it's breast of chicken stuffed with mashed potatoes, mushrooms, and secret seasonings; wrapped in bacon; baked, and then flamed with Irish whiskey at your table.

Howth

The King Sitric Fish Restaurant

East Pier, Howth Harbour. ☎ **01/832-5235** or 832-6729. Reservations recommended. Appetizers IR£3–IR£10 ($4.80–$16); main courses IR£15–IR£20 ($24–$32); fixed-price dinner IR£23 ($36.80). ACC, AE, DC, V. Mon–Sat 6:30–11pm. Closed 10 days at Christmas, Easter. DART: Howth. SEAFOOD.

Out in Howth, set right on the edge of Dublin Bay in the old Georgian-style harbormaster's house, this is one of the best seafood restaurants in the country. As for the menu, it all depends on the season. Your best bet is to ask the waiter about the day's catch. From time to time, you can expect to see dishes featuring salmon, bass, plaice, turbot, brill, scallops, prawns, and lobster (with more exotic fish depending on just what the trawlers have snared that day). Upstairs, you'll find a cozy seafood/oyster bar.

What to See & Do in Dublin

6

Dublin's face today mirrors the lines and wrinkles, blemishes and beauty spots left by a long, rich, and colorful history.

There were people living near the Liffey's hurdle bridge long before the Vikings arrived to found a proper town in 840. They came first as raiders, but gradually intermarried with the Irish and settled down to become traders and craftsmen.

When St. Patrick passed this way in 448, it is a fact that there were already several small churches, and possibly there was a monastery. But it was not until Viking King Olaf was baptized shortly before his death in 979 that Christianity gained any sort of foothold. His son, Sitric, founded Christ Church Cathedral in 1038, one of three medieval buildings that have survived through the centuries. St. Patrick's Cathedral, the second medieval structure to survive, dates back to 1191, and in 1204 King John authorized the building of Dublin Castle, the last of city's medieval relics still standing.

There were few substantial changes in Dublin after that until the 17th century, when Dublin's first notable public buildings were constructed. Those magnificent Georgian buildings began to appear in the 18th century, with many examples of the Palladian style as well as Dublin's famous Georgian squares. The Victorian age in the mid 1800s left traces in railway stations, banks, pubs, markets, and hospitals, as well as some commercial buildings in the College Green vicinity. From 1916 to 1922 Dublin's face was scarred by the ravages of uprising, although careful rebuilding and restoration have erased most of the scars.

The 1960s brought the "office revolution" and the advent of characterless glass-and-concrete boxes to hail Ireland's new progressive era. Indeed, in a fit of "progressive" zeal, the grand old city came close to demolishing many of its finest legacies. Fortunately, concerned citizens halted the destruction at an early stage so that today's visitor may happily browse through the architectural treasures of the past along with the modern monstrosities.

In 1991, Dublin was the officially designated European City of Culture. The occasion was marked by the opening of a Writers Museum in Parnell Square; the reopening of the Customs House after an extensive facelift; the launch of the *Book of Clashganna,* a 20th-century version of the *Book of Kells* that includes the work of leading contemporary Irish writers and artists; and a Festival of Literature in recognition of the 50th anniversary of James Joyce's death.

VISITOR INFORMATION

Your very first order of business should be a stop at the main tourist office, 14 Upper O'Connell Street, Dublin 1 (☎ 01/284-4768). They can furnish literature and/or details on Dublin attractions, from the best known right through to some not so well known. Be *sure* to pick up their excellent inner-city street map. A gift shop here stocks Irish crafts, souvenirs, books, and unique items. The O'Connell Street office is one of the best tourist bureaus in the country, but other Dublin offices at the following locations are worth a stop-in when you're in the vicinity:

18 Eustace Street, Temple Bar, Dublin 2 (☎ 01/671-5717, ask for the excellent street map and guidebook of this area); Baggot Street Bridge, Dublin 2 (☎ 01-676-5871); Arrivals Hall, Dublin Airport (☎ 01/844-5387); St. Michael's Wharf, Dun Laoghaire (☎ 01/280-6984).

SIGHTSEEING DISCOUNT A good investment available at the tourist office is "Dublin Alive Alive O, Your Passport to Dublin's Heritage." It costs a mere IR£2 ($3.20) and gives you a 10% discount on top attractions in the city such as the Writers Museum, Guinness Hop Store, Museum of Modern Art, the National Museum, and many others.

SUGGESTED ITINERARIES

Time constraints and your own special interests will determine just *how* you spend the time you've allotted for the capital city. There are, however, sightseeing techniques that can help you cover the most territory in any time frame. Herewith, a few suggestions.

If You Have 1 Day

Let Dublin Bus get you around hassle free via the "Dublin Heritage Trail" tour (see "Organized Tours," below, for details). Take the first departure (10am) and explore in depth those sightseeing attractions that appeal to you most; have lunch in one of the city's lively pubs; spend the afternoon in further exploration or call it a day in midafternoon and do a bit of browsing through Dublin's shops. Evening hours can be devoted to theater, cabaret, a traditional music session, or pub-hopping.

If You Have 2 Days

On your first day visit Dublin's outstanding attractions (see "What's Special About Dublin" above). On your second day, reach back in time to Ireland's past and/or the scenic spots surrounding Dublin. Bus Eireann has a nice variety of all-day tours to points of interest within a short distance of the city. Each tour runs on specified days of the week, so your itinerary will be decided by just which day you can travel. Choose from the Boyne Valley tour, which includes such prehistoric relics as the Hill of Tara and Newgrange; the Avondale, Glendalough, and Wicklow Hills tour; or take one of the several half-day tours to outlying areas and spend the afternoon exploring city streets on foot. Use evening hours each day to enjoy theater, cabaret, traditional music sessions, or pub-hopping.

If You Have 3 Days

See the above suggestions for the first two days. On your third day, spend the morning in the Phoenix Park, with lunch at the zoo. In the afternoon, take in *The*

Dublin Experience or *Dublinia* (see below for details)—both, if you're energetic and ambitious enough. Choose among the evening activities suggested above.

If You Have 5 Days or More

With five days at your disposal, you can spread the suggestions above over a more leisurely time frame, adding to them more of Bus Eireann's half-day tours beyond city limits, the Dublin Literary Pub Crawl, or another of the organized walking tours of the city. You'll have time, too, for at least one lunchtime picnic on St. Stephen's Green, and a visit to the Guinness Hop Store. If you're staying in Dublin for *all* of your Irish visit, use one day for a Bus Eireann all-day excursion to Waterford and New Ross, Kilkenny, or the Carlingford Peninsula. Or invest in their money-saving "Days Away" round-trip ticket that can give you a day on your own to any of the above-named cities, as well as Wexford, Cahir, and Cashel, and even points as far away as Cork and Limerick.

Be sure to save one evening for the Abbey Tavern out in Howth to take in their terrific Irish music show.

1 Attractions

THE TOP ATTRACTIONS

✪ Christ Church Cathedral

Christ Church Place (off Lord Edward St.). ☎ **01/677-8099.** Admission IR£1 ($1.60). Daily 10am–5pm. Bus: 21A, 50, 50A, 78, 78A, or 78B.

Christ Church is one of the oldest and most beautiful of Dublin's buildings. Founded by King Sitric in 1038, it was originally a wooden structure, but was rebuilt in stone after the Norman invasion in 1169. Strongbow, the Anglo-Norman leader who was instrumental in the rebuilding, lies here, and this is also where four Irish kings were knighted by Richard II in 1394 when they pledged allegiance to that monarch. In 1689 James II prayed here for divine protection before marching off to the Battle of the Boyne, and a victorious King William came back to offer thanks after that battle. There are lovely architectural details and stonework in the nave, transepts, choir, and chancel, and the crypt (the oldest section) is said to be one of the best of its kind in Europe. Tours are available on Sunday at 12:15 and 4:30pm.

Dublinia

Christ Church, St. Michael's Hill, Winetavern St. at High St. ☎ **01/679-4611.** Admission IR£4 ($6.40) adults; IR£3 ($4.80) children, students, and seniors; IR£10 ($16) family ticket. Daily 10am–5pm. Bus: From Fleet Street, 21A, 78, or 78B; from Aston Quay, 50 or 50A.

Cross the elegant bridge from Christ Church Cathedral to this lovely old building, and you walk straight into medieval Dublin as it was between 1170, when the Anglo-Normans arrived, and 1540, when its monasteries were closed. Pick up your personal audio headset, then enter the Medieval Maze, where lifelike exhibits depict dramatic, sometimes mystical, episodes in this period. Everyday life in the city is portrayed in full-scale reconstructions of the 13th-century Wood Quay and a 15th-century merchant's residence; while a scale model of this long-ago Dublin sets out the streets and public buildings. By the time you reach the Great Hall, you will feel very much at home as the sights and sounds of the medieval city envelop you via a dramatic cyclorama and audiovisual production. Great appeal for all ages.

Dublin Sights & Attractions

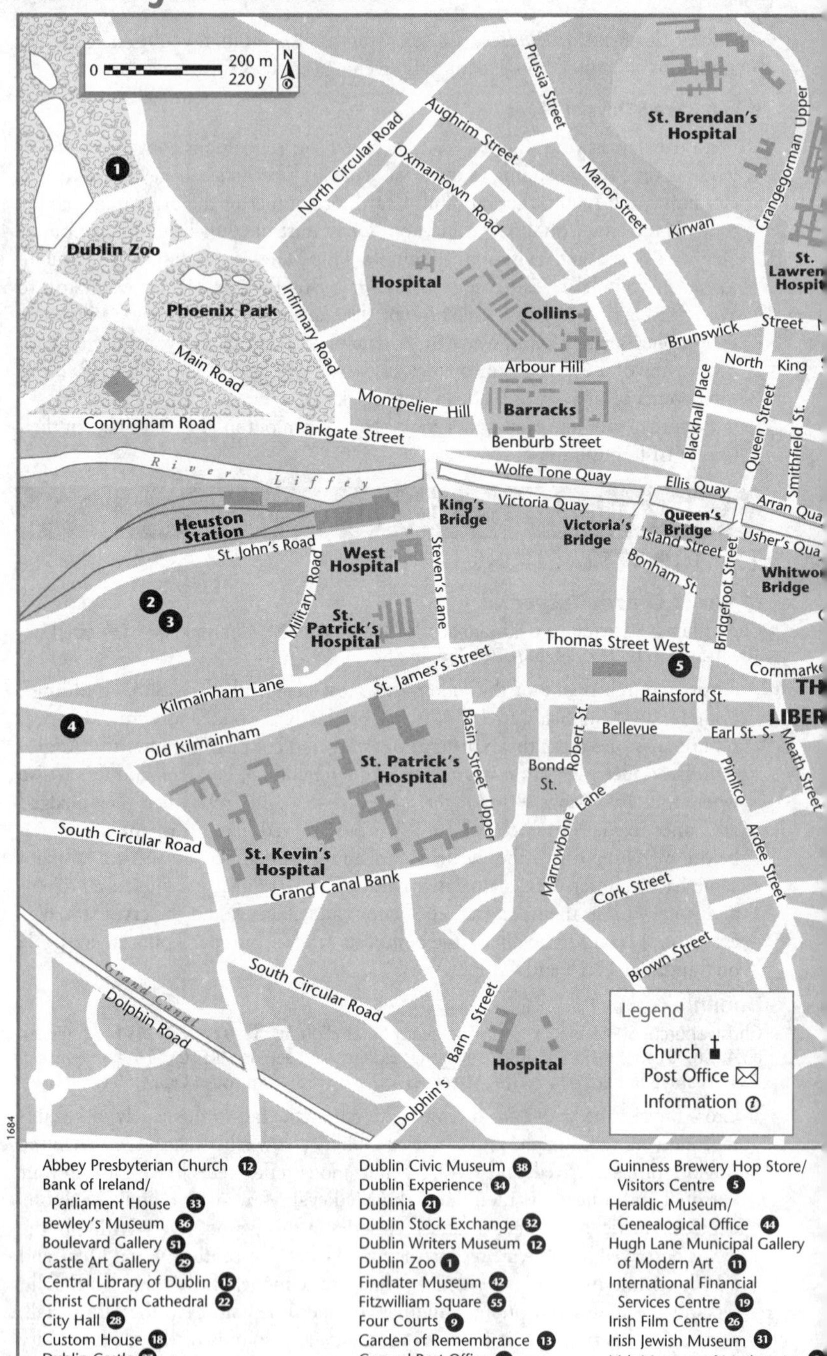

- Abbey Presbyterian Church 12
- Bank of Ireland/ Parliament House 33
- Bewley's Museum 36
- Boulevard Gallery 51
- Castle Art Gallery 29
- Central Library of Dublin 15
- Christ Church Cathedral 22
- City Hall 28
- Custom House 18
- Dublin Castle 27
- Dublin Civic Museum 38
- Dublin Experience 34
- Dublinia 21
- Dublin Stock Exchange 32
- Dublin Writers Museum 12
- Dublin Zoo 1
- Findlater Museum 42
- Fitzwilliam Square 55
- Four Courts 9
- Garden of Remembrance 13
- General Post Office 17
- Guinness Brewery Hop Store/ Visitors Centre 5
- Heraldic Museum/ Genealogical Office 44
- Hugh Lane Municipal Gallery of Modern Art 11
- International Financial Services Centre 19
- Irish Film Centre 26
- Irish Jewish Museum 31
- Irish Museum of Modern Art 2

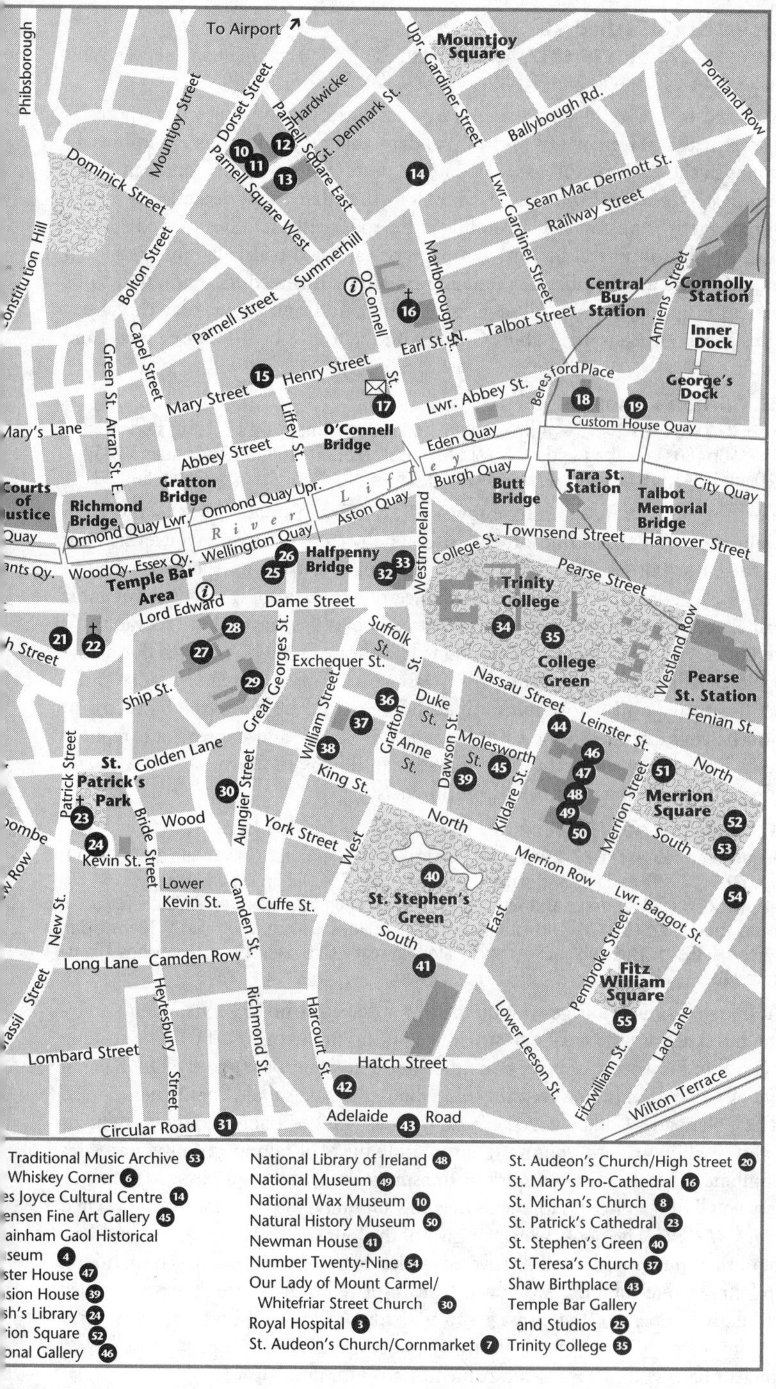
To Airport
Mountjoy Square
Phibsborough
Mountjoy Street
Dorset Street
Hardwicke
Parnell Square East
Gt. Denmark St.
Upr. Gardiner Street
Portland Row
Ballybough Rd.
Dominick Street
Parnell Square West
Sean Mac Dermott St.
Railway Street
Lwr. Gardiner Street
Constitution Hill
Bolton Street
Summerhill
O'Connell St.
Marlborough St.
Central Bus Station
Connolly Station
Amiens Street
Inner Dock
Parnell Street
Talbot Street
Earl St. N.
Capel Street
Green St.
Henry Street
Mary Street
Beresford Place
George's Dock
Lwr. Abbey St.
Mary's Lane
Arran St. E.
Liffey St.
O'Connell Bridge
Custom House Quay
Abbey Street
Eden Quay
Courts of Justice
Gratton Bridge
Burgh Quay
Butt Bridge
Tara St. Station
Talbot Memorial Bridge
City Quay
Richmond Bridge
Ormond Quay Upr.
River Liffey
Aston Quay
Ormond Quay Lwr.
Wellington Quay
Westmoreland
Townsend Street
Hanover Street
Quay
Wood Qy.
Essex Qy.
Halfpenny Bridge
College St.
Pearse Street
Temple Bar Area
Trinity College
Dame Street
Lord Edward
Suffolk St.
Westland Row
Exchequer St.
College Green
Pearse St. Station
Ship St.
Great Georges St.
William Street
Nassau Street
Duke St.
Fenian St.
Grafton St.
Leinster St.
Golden Lane
Anne St.
Dawson St.
Molesworth St.
Patrick Street
St. Patrick's Park
Aungier Street
King St.
Kildare St.
Merrion Street
Merrion Square North
Merrion Square South
Bride Street
Wood
York Street
North
Kevin St.
St. Stephen's Green West
Merrion Row
Lower Kevin St.
Camden St.
Cuffe St.
St. Stephen's Green
St. Stephen's Green East
Lwr. Baggot St.
New St.
St. Stephen's Green South
Pembroke Street
Long Lane
Camden Row
Fitz William Square
Heytesbury Street
Richmond St.
Harcourt St.
Lower Leeson St.
Lad Lane
Lombard Street
Hatch Street
Fitzwilliam St.
Wilton Terrace
Adelaide Road
Circular Road
Traditional Music Archive 53
Whiskey Corner 6
es Joyce Cultural Centre 14
ensen Fine Art Gallery 45
ainham Gaol Historical
useum 4
ster House 47
sion House 39
sh's Library 24
rion Square 52
onal Gallery 46
National Library of Ireland 48
National Museum 49
National Wax Museum 10
Natural History Museum 50
Newman House 41
Number Twenty-Nine 54
Our Lady of Mount Carmel/
Whitefriar Street Church 30
Royal Hospital 3
St. Audeon's Church/Cornmarket 7
St. Audeon's Church/High Street 20
St. Mary's Pro-Cathedral 16
St. Michan's Church 8
St. Patrick's Cathedral 23
St. Stephen's Green 40
St. Teresa's Church 37
Shaw Birthplace 43
Temple Bar Gallery
and Studios 25
Trinity College 35

✪ St. Patrick's Cathedral

Patrick's Close. ☎ **01/475-4817.** Admission IR£1.50 ($2.40) contribution. Mon–Fri 9am–6pm, Sat 9am–5pm, Sun 10am–4:30pm. Bus: 50, 50A, 54, 54A, or 56A.

Founded in 1190, St. Patrick's has, over its varied history, served purposes as disparate as a university (1320–1465) and a stable for the mounts of Cromwell's troops in the 17th century. Its best-known dean (1713–45) was Jonathan Swift, author of *Gulliver's Travels* and a host of other sharp-tongued attacks on the humbuggery of his times. His tomb is in the south aisle, and his beloved "Stella" (Esther Johnson in real life) lies nearby. The cathedral had fallen into near ruin by 1860, when a member of the Guinness family financed its restoration to its present magnificent state. All services are ecumenical, and all weekday choral services are also open to the public. Check with the tourist board for exact days and hours.

✪ St. Michan's Church

Church St. ☎ **01/872-4154.** Admission IR£1.50 ($2.40) adults, IR£1 ($1.60) students and seniors, 50p (80¢) children under 12. Mid-Mar–Oct, Mon–Fri 10am–12:45pm and 2–5pm, Sat 10am–12:45pm; Nov–mid-Mar, Mon–Fri 12:30–3:30pm. Vaults closed Sun. Bus: 34.

North of the Liffey, the square tower of St. Michan's dates back to the 1096 Danish church that stood on this site. The present structure, however, is of 17th-century origin. Handel is said to have played its organ (perhaps when in Dublin to conduct the first performance of his *Messiah* in 1742). But most visitors are drawn by the perfectly preserved bodies that have lain in its vaults for centuries with no sign of decomposition. The Sheare brothers, executed during the 1798 rebellion, rest here, and on my last visit it was a young Crusader and a 15th-century nun whose mummified bodies could be viewed. The rector of St. Michan's attended Robert Emmet in his last hours, and the patriot is reputed to be buried in the churchyard (the guide can fill you in on the story). A souvenir shop sells reasonably priced Irish products.

✪ Trinity College, *The Book of Kells,* and The Dublin Experience

College Green. ☎ **01/677-2941.** Old Library and Colonnades Gallery, IR£3.50 ($5.60) adults, IR£3 ($4.80) students and seniors, under 12 free. The Dublin Experience, IR£3 ($4.80) adults, IR£2.50 ($4) students and seniors. Combination and group rates available for both. Walking tours IR£4 ($6.40). Old Library and Colonnades Gallery, Mon–Sat 9:30am–5pm, Sun noon-4:30pm. The Dublin Experience, late May–early Oct, daily, hourly showings 10am–5pm including Sun.

Although Trinity College was founded by Elizabeth I in 1592, its oldest surviving buildings are the red-brick structures put up in the early 1700s. The striking West Front is worthy of note, as are the 1740 Printing House and the Dining Hall dating to 1760. It is, however, the Old Library that you should be sure not to miss. The Colonnades Gallery, together with the lofty, vaulted Long Room (which holds over 200,000 ancient volumes), and marble busts of famous Trinity graduates combine to create an awe-inspiring atmosphere you'll not soon forget. In the gallery you'll find a priceless link with Ireland's antiquity, the magnificently illustrated ***Book of Kells.*** The book, which consists of the four Gospels laboriously handwritten in Latin by monks and discovered in the monastery at Kells, has been bound in four separate volumes, two of which are displayed in glass cases. Pages are turned regularly to open a different page spread, and you may well find yourself returning for a second look. Other illustrated manuscripts are on display, as well as an ancient harp said to have accompanied Brian Boru into battle.

Trinity College

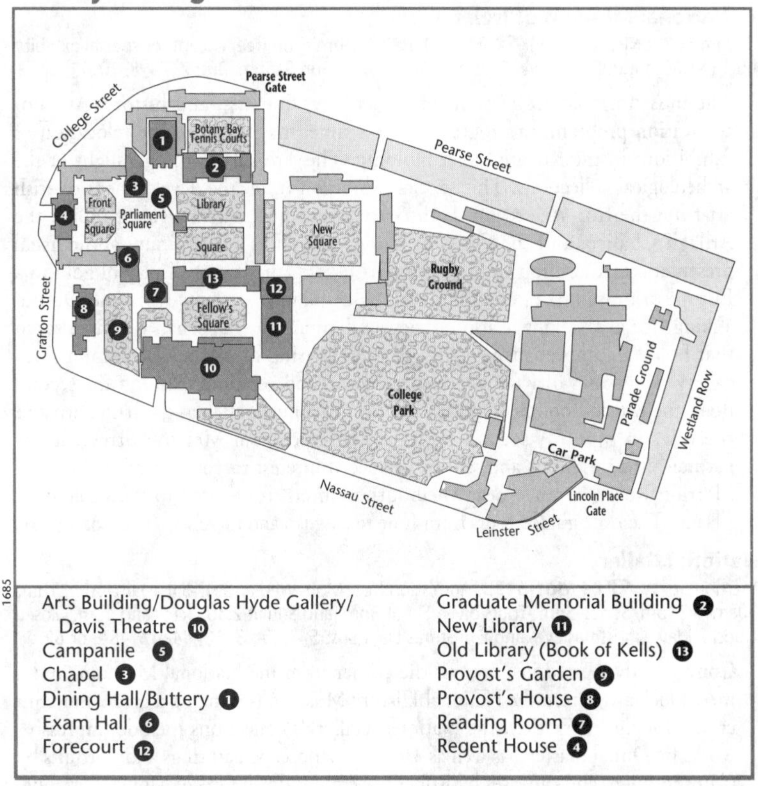

The Dublin Experience, located in the Davis Theatre in the Arts Building on campus, is a dramatic multimedia show that traces the history of the city from its earliest days and introduces visitors to the modern city and its people. Really a great way to begin your stay in Dublin, and one that will make each day you're there more meaningful.

From early June to late September, there are student-guided tours of the college. Meet them just inside the main entrance to the college.

Bank of Ireland

College Green. ☎ **01/677-6801.** Admission free. Mon–Fri 10am–4pm. Guided tours Tues at 10:30am, 11:30am, and 1:45pm. Closed holidays.

Just across College Green from Trinity, the Bank of Ireland building was once the seat of the Irish Parliament. This is where the hated Act of Union was passed in 1800. An ailing Henry Grattan, whose statue now stands across the way, donned his worn Volunteer uniform and rose in these halls to bid an eloquent farewell to the independent Parliament. Today you can visit the House of Lords simply by asking directions from any of the bank's uniformed attendants. Not so the House of Commons, however, for when the building was acquired by the bank, it was on the condition that the lower house be demolished to avoid any possible coup d'état.

✪ National Museum of Ireland

Kildare St. (at Merrion Row). ☎ **01/661-8811.** Admission free, except for special exhibits; IR£1 ($1.60) for guided tours. Tues–Sat 10am–5pm, Sun 2–5pm. Bus: 7, 7A, 8, 10, 11, or 13.

The museum holds collections of archeology, fine arts, and history. A major renovation program, in progress at press time, may result in the relocation of exhibitions in the Kildare Street building. The Treasury is the highlight of the archeological collections. This special exhibition traces the development of Irish art from the Iron Age to the 15th century and includes the Tara Brooch, the Ardagh Chalice, and the Cross of Cong, as well as a 20-minute audiovisual presentation. An exhibit of prehistoric Irish gold (the largest display of gold in a European museum) opened in 1991. A display of artifacts from the Dublin Viking Age excavations is also on view. Adjoining the main hall is a large room that holds a comprehensive study of the Uprising of 1916. The second-floor gallery holds cases of Irish silver, coins, glass, and ceramics. Also on the second floor, the Music Room features traditional instruments such as the Irish harp and the uileann pipes. A second building, entered from Merrion Street, holds natural-history exhibits and will be of special interest to youngsters. A third, on Merrion Row (entrance near Shelbourne Hotel), is devoted to the geology of Ireland. There are guided tours from June to August, and there's an inexpensive cafe.

National Gallery

Merrion Sq. W. ☎ **01/661-5133.** Admission free. Mon–Wed and Fri–Sat 10am–6pm, Thurs 10am–8:30pm, Sun 2–5pm. Tours given Sat at 3pm, and Sun at 2:30, 3:15, and 4pm. Closed Good Friday, Christmas Eve, and Christmas Day. Bus: 5, 7, 7A, 8, 10, 44, 47, 48A, or 62.

Conveniently located just around the corner from the National Museum, and a mere block away from the National History Museum (setting up a great "museum crawl" for the energetic!), the National Gallery's collections include impressive works by Dutch masters, as well as 10 major landscape paintings and portraits by Gainsborough, and canvases by Rubens, Rembrandt, El Greco, Monet, Cézanne, and Degas. John Butler Yeats, perhaps Ireland's greatest modern portrait painter, is well represented, as are leading 18th- and 19th-century Irish artists. Portraits of Irish historical figures over the past three centuries are hung in the National Portrait Gallery. The collection includes 2,500 paintings, pieces of sculpture, and objets d'art. The young George Bernard Shaw spent much time browsing through the National Gallery and felt such a debt of gratitude for the education it afforded him that he bequeathed it a substantial monetary sum. There is also a souvenir bookshop. The gallery has a self-service restaurant that offers traditional Irish cuisine. As many as five fish courses are offered, along with six meat or poultry selections and a couple of vegetarian dishes. Classical music plays in the background. Appetizers IR£1.50–IR£3 ($2.40–$4.80); main courses IR£2–IR£5 ($3.20–$8).

✪ Kilmainham Gaol Historical Museum

Kilmainham. ☎ **01/535984.** Admission IR£1.50 ($2.40) adults, IR£1 ($1.65) seniors, 60p (96¢) students and children, IR£4 ($6.40) family rate. Tours given June–Sept, Wed and Sun 11am–6pm; to arrange a tour on other days, phone 535984. Bus: 21, 78, 78A, 78B, or 79 at O'Connell Bridge.

Within these walls political prisoners languished, and were tortured and killed, from 1796 until 1924, when the late President Eamon De Valera left as its final prisoner. Its rolls held such names as the Sheares brothers; Robert Emmet, who went from here to his death, proclaiming, "When my country takes her place among the nations of the earth, then, and not till then, let my epitaph be written!";

Charles Parnell, who directed Land League boycott strategy from within Kilmainham's walls; the Invincibles of 1883, five of whom lie buried here where they were hanged; scores of Volunteers who rose up in rebellion during Easter Week of 1916; and Eamon De Valera, who was imprisoned twice—once in 1916 and again in 1921 when he opposed the Treaty of Union. It was, however, James Connolly and the 14 who were executed with him at Kilmainham Gaol in May 1916 whose sacrifice for Irish independence so fired their countrymen that the national will was united and, in the words of Yeats, "a terrible beauty" was born. The old gaol lay abandoned from the time of De Valera's exit until 1960, when a group of dedicated volunteers determined to restore it as a national shrine to Ireland's fight for freedom. Fittingly, it was President De Valera who opened the museum at Easter 1966. To walk along its corridors, through the exercise yard, or into the Main Compound is a moving experience that lingers hauntingly in the memory.

✪ Dublin Castle

Castle St. ☎ **01/777129.** Admission IR£2 ($3.20) adults; IR£1 ($1.60) children, students, and seniors. Tours given Mon–Fri 10am–12:15pm and 2–5pm, Sat–Sun and holidays 2–5pm. Because the castle is sometimes closed to the public for official state functions, be sure to check with the Tourist Office before going, to avoid disappointment.

West of Dame Street, just off Lord Edward Street (behind City Hall), Dublin Castle occupies the site of an earlier Danish fortress. The only remaining portions of the castle built between 1208 and 1220 are a bit of a curtain wall and two towers. You can get a pretty good idea of the original outline, however, from the **Upper Castle Yard.** The **Record (or Wardrobe) Tower,** with its 16-foot-thick walls, is the most outstanding relic of the 13th-century Anglo-Norman fortress. Dating from the 15th century, **Bermingham Tower** was the state prison when Red Hugh O'Donnell was kept there in the 16th century. The **Church of the Most Holy Trinity** was formerly the Chapel Royal. British viceroys resided in the opulent **State Apartments,** which were converted into a Red Cross hospital during World War I. It was from these apartments that the prisoner James Connolly, patriot leader of the 1916 Uprising, was taken by stretcher to Kilmainham Gaol to be executed, thus arousing international outrage and hastening the goal for which he gave his life. They have now been restored to their former elegance, and today every president of Ireland is inaugurated in these splendid quarters.

Start your visit at the Visitors Centre, and be sure to stop a moment at the **memorial** outside the main gate honoring those Irish killed here during Easter Week of 1916—it stands on the spot where heads of Irish kings once were displayed publicly on high spikes.

General Post Office

O'Connell St. Admission free. Mon–Sat 8am–8pm, Sun and bank holidays 10:30am–6:30pm.

To touch more recent Irish history, take a look around the imposing General Post Office, built in 1818. The massive granite building with its six fluted columns is where Padraic Pearse in 1916 gathered his Volunteers, hoisted the Irish Tricolour, and from its portico proclaimed to the Irish people and the world that Ireland would henceforth be an independent Republic. From the nearby Liffey, an English gunboat shelled the building, starting a fire that gutted its interior, now completely restored. In a front window position facing O'Connell Street, look for a statue of Ireland's ancient mythical warrior hero Cuchulain, who tied himself upright to a stake in order to fight a superior force to the death. A memorial to the men who fought here, its marble base is inscribed with the words of Pearse's Proclamation.

Dublin Castle

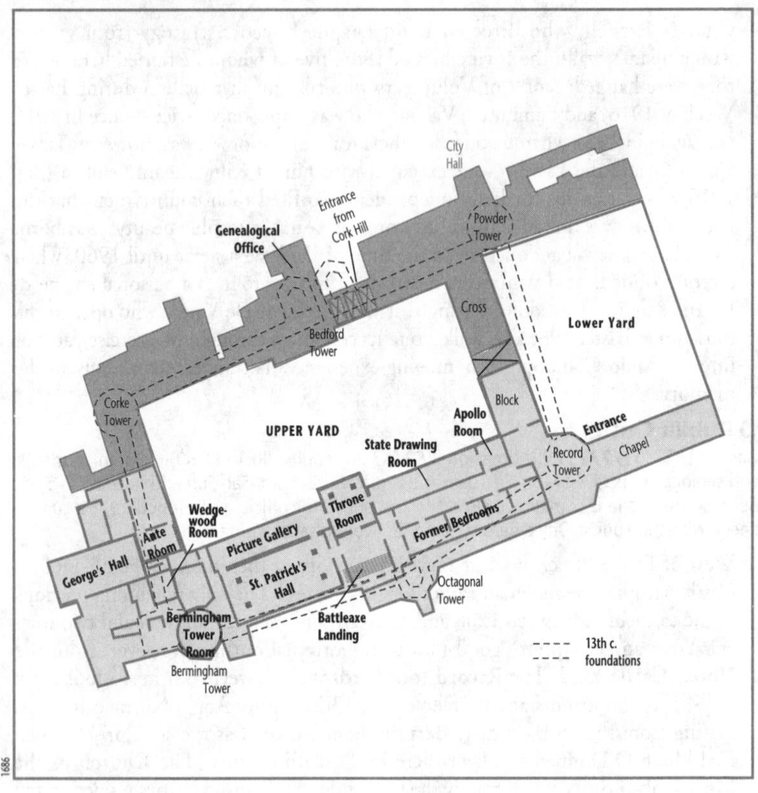

MORE ATTRACTIONS

✪ St. Stephen's Green

Grafton St. Admission free. Mon–Sat 8am–dark, Sun 10am–dark.

St. Stephen's Green has been preserved as an open space for Dubliners since 1690. Over the years it has evolved into the beautifully planted park that today finds city residents and visitors alike strolling along its paths, enjoying a lunch break picnic-style, or simply soaking up its rustic charm as the city's traffic swirls around the edges. Formal flowerbeds, the arched stone bridge crossing one end of the artificial lake, shaded pathways, and statuary placed in pockets of shrubbery make this a very special place.

Leinster House

Kildare St. Admission free. You'll have to be introduced by a member to gain admittance when the Dail is in session. Check with the tourist board for hours when the Dail is not meeting. Bus: Any city-center bus.

Leinster House, in the city center south of the Liffey, is the home of the Parliament (Dail Eireann, pronounced "Doil") that came into being when Ireland's long struggle finally brought liberty. If you can wangle an invitation to a session of the Dail, don't miss the chance to see Ireland's governing body in action. Otherwise, the chambers are somewhat impressive, and well worth a visit for those interested in government.

Dublin Civic Museum

58 S. William St. ☎ **01/679-4260.** Admission free. Tues–Sat 10am–6pm, Sun 11am–2pm. Bus: 10, 11, or 13.

There's a treasure trove of Dublin detail housed in the city's own museum—streets and buildings, traders, industry, transport, political history, and scores of maps and views of Dublin provide great browsing. Exhibits also include artifacts from the Viking Age, and there's a model of the Howth tram. Every few months, other exhibits are mounted on a temporary basis. Located next to the Powerscourt Town House Centre.

✪ Natural History Museum

Merrion St. ☎ **01/661-8811.** Admission free. Tues–Sat 10am–5pm, Sun 2–5pm. Bus: 7, 7A, or 8.

This marvelous zoological museum is a delight for young and old alike. Its ground-floor Irish Room collections illustrate the country's wildlife, both vertebrate and invertebrate. Mammals (red deer, badger, fox, etc.) occupy the center of the room; a magnificent basking shark is suspended from the ceiling; there's a terrific display of Irish birds that features sea birds and kingfishers; and butterflies and other insects are on view at the rear of the room. On upper floors you'll find their World Collection, which includes impressive displays of Asian and African wildlife (the Indian elephant, giant panda, pygmy hippopotamus, etc.). Look for two whale skeletons (salvaged when the giants of the deep were stranded on the Irish coast).

Hugh Lane Municipal Gallery of Modern Art

Parnell Sq. ☎ **01/874-1903.** Admission free. Tues–Fri 9:30am–6pm, Sat 9:30am–5pm, Sun 11am–5pm. Bus: 11, 12, 13, 16, 16A, 22, or 22A.

North of the Liffey, near the top of O'Connell Street, this gallery occupies a fine Georgian mansion that was once the residence of Lord Charlemont. Among the art you're likely to find in residence are paintings by Manet, Corot, Monet, Daumier, and contemporary Irish artists. Before his death by drowning on the *Lusitania* in 1915, Sir Hugh Lane had lent his collection to the National Gallery in London. A codicil to his will, however, left the pictures to Dublin's Municipal Gallery, but the codicil lacked the two essential witnesses to his signature. After a long legal dispute between the two museums, an agreement has been reached to divide the 39 pictures into two groups, one to be housed in London, the other in Dublin, with exchanges to be made every 14 years.

Just across the way from the Hugh Lane is the beautiful **Garden of Remembrance,** dedicated in 1966 to those who died in the 1916 fight for liberty.

A restaurant on the gallery's lower floor offers traditional cuisine. Choose from curries with rice, beef, chicken, lamb, pork; a selection of salad plates; and desserts that include chocolate roulade, apple pie, and ice cream. Wine is served by the glass. Appetizers IR£1.50–IR£2 ($2.40–$3.20); main courses under IR£5 ($8).

The Irish Museum of Modern Art

Royal Hospital, Kilmainham, Dublin 8. ☎ **01/671-8666.** Fax 01/671-8695. Admission free except for special exhibitions. Tues–Sat 10am–5:30pm, Sun noon–5:30pm. Bus: 68A, 69, 78A, 123, and 90. DART: Feeder bus from Connolly and Tara Street stations to Heuston. Unlimited parking.

Through its permanent collection and temporary exhibitions, this museum-cum-art gallery, criss-crosses a spectrum of 20th-century Irish and international art. In the historic Royal Hospital are a bookshop and a coffee shop. Entrance is on Military Road, beside Heuston Station.

✪ Chester Beatty Library and Gallery of Oriental Art

20 Shewsbury Rd. ☎ **01/269-2386** or 269-5187. Admission free. Tues–Fri 10am–5pm, Sat 2–5pm. Guided tours given Wed and Sat at 2:30pm. Closed Tues following public holidays. Bus: 5, 6, 7, 7A, 8, or 10. DART: Sandymount station.

Sir Alfred Chester Beatty, an American mining millionaire who made his home in Dublin, bequeathed his extensive collections to the city. Highlights are the biblical papyri, Persian and Turkish paintings, Qur'ans, Japanese wood-block prints, and Chinese jade books.

✪ Marsh's Library

St. Patrick's Close. ☎ **01/454-3511.** Admission free, but a voluntary contribution of IR£1 ($1.60) is expected. Mon and Wed–Fri 10am–12:45pm and 2–5pm, Sat 10:30am–12:45pm. Anyone involved in research can make application for other hours.

This impressive library was built by Archbishop Narcissus Marsh in 1701, and was the very first public library in Ireland. It houses four main book collections of more than 25,000 volumes, and the archbishop's wide-ranging interests extended to theology (of course), medicine, ancient history, Syriac, Greek, and Latin and French literature. The scholarly notes he scribbled in many of the volumes are still legible, and there are some 250 volumes in manuscript. Since these priceless books cannot be checked out to the public, Marsh's Library really qualifies as a literary museum. In fact, to peruse any book, you'll be ushered into an elegant wired alcove not too unlike an upmarket cage.

Dublin Writers Museum

18/19 Parnell Sq. ☎ **01/872-2077.** Admission IR£2.75 ($4.40) adults, IR£2 ($3.20) students and seniors, IR£1.25 ($2) ages 3–11, IR£7.50 ($12) family (two adults and up to four children). Oct–Mar, Fri–Sat 10am–5pm, Sun 1–5pm; June–Aug, Mon–Sat 10am–5pm, Sun 1–5pm; Apr–May and Sept, Tues–Sat 10am–5pm, Sun 1–5pm. Bus: 11, 12, 13, 16, 16A, 22, or 22A.

Dublin celebrates its rich literary heritage in two splendid 18th-century Georgian mansions. Permanent displays are replete with mementos of such greats as George Bernard Shaw, Sean O'Casey, W. B. Yeats, James Joyce, Brendan Behan, and a host of other writers who have enriched the fabric of Dublin's past with the brilliant colors of genius. Special-interest exhibitions are mounted on a regular basis. Contemporary writers are nurtured through the Irish Writers' Centre, which provides workrooms, offices, and meeting rooms for their use. The fully licensed restaurant, Chapter One, is much favored by Dubliners as well as visitors (see "Where to Eat" in Chapter 5), and there's also a coffee shop. The superb bookshop, with mail-order service and specialized book lists, stocks a wide range of Irish titles, and also provides a unique out-of-print and antiquarian search service.

Number Twenty-Nine

29 Lower Fitzwilliam St. ☎ **01/702-6165.** Admission free. Tues–Sat 10am–5pm, Sun 2–5pm. Bus: 6, 7, 8, 10, or 45. DART: Pearse.

If you've wondered just what it would be like to live in one of Dublin's fashionable Georgian town houses, do plan a visit to this restored four-story residence. Meticulous attention has been devoted to re-creating the home environment of a middle-class Dublin family in the 1790–1820 period. Furnishings, carpets and

A Dublin Taxi Experience

At least once during your visit, hop into a Dublin taxi for a Dublin experience to be treasured. It's as though Dublin cabbies feel an obligation to ask about your holiday, then fill you in on their city's charms, with entertaining stories liberally sprinkled with Irish wit, couched in phrases you'll not soon forget.

draperies, decorative accessories, and artwork reflect the lifestyle of that long-ago time. Especially appealing is the nursery, which holds toys and dolls.

The Irish Film Centre

6 Eustace S, Dublin 2. ☎ **01/679-5744;** Box Office 679-3477. Institute free; movie theaters IR£2–IR£4 ($3.20–$6.40); *Flashback* IR£2.50 ($4) adult, IR£2 ($3.20) seniors and students. Institute daily 10am–11:30pm; theaters daily 2–11:30pm; *Flashback* June–Sept, Wed–Sun showings 11am, noon, and 1pm. Bus: 21A, 78A, 78B.

Dublin's historic Friends Meeting House has been incorporated into this complex, which includes the Irish Film Archive, two movie theaters, a library, a bookshop, a bar/restaurant, and offices of several film-industry organizations. The audio-visual presentation *Flashback* traces the development of the film industry in Ireland since 1896.

Irish Architectural Archive

93 Merrion Sq. ☎ **01/676-3430.** Admission free. Tues–Fri 10am–1pm, Sat 2:30–5pm. Closed Aug.

While neither a museum nor an art gallery, this archive will certainly intrigue anyone interested in Ireland's past. Since its establishment in 1976, the archive has become the central source of information on architecturally and historically significant Irish buildings from 1600 to the present. In addition to more than 200,000 photographs and 50,000 architectural drawings, the reference library holds a vast number of publications such as pamphlets, press cuttings, historical manuscripts, and engravings. While the emphasis is on architecture, as you would expect, all sorts of extraneous information can be gleaned from browsing through the box files of photos, many of which are fascinating shots of landscapes, period village street scenes, craftsmen such as thatchers and masons at work, a hunt meet at a country mansion, etc. Who knows, the cottage from which your ancestors left for America, long since demolished, may show up in one of these old pictures! Pamphlets from the past also make good reading, while giving unique insights into Ireland's social history.

Customs House and the Four Courts

Admission free. Four Courts, Mon–Fri 9:30am–5pm (closed Aug–Sept and public holidays); court sittings, Mon–Fri 11am–1pm and 2–4:45pm. Bus: Any city-center bus to O'Connell Street.

Two of Dublin's more impressive sights are on the north bank of the Liffey, especially at night when floodlights illuminate the noble outlines of the 1791 Customs House on Customs House Quay and the dignified domed Four Courts building on Inns Quay. Both were burned-out shells after the 1921 Troubles but have been totally restored and are now in use for their original functions.

Whitefriar Street Carmelite Church

56 Aungier St. ☎ **01/475-8821.** Admission free. Mon, Wed–Thurs, and Sat 8am–6:30pm; Tues and Fri 8am–9pm; Sun 8am–7:30pm. Bus: 16, 16A, 19, 19A, 22, or 22A.

Readers Recommend

The Irish Jewish Museum, Walworth Road. (☎ 01/453-1797). *"This interesting museum depicts the history of the Jewish community in Ireland over more than 300 years. It's open Sunday, Tuesday, and Thursday from 11am to 3:30pm in summer, on Sunday only from 10:30am to 2:30pm in winter, and it is well worth a visit."*
—J. Forer, Fair Lawn, NJ

The State Heraldic Museum, Kildare Street, Dublin 2 (☎ 01/661-1626). *"This is great browsing country for anyone interested in Irish history. Worth the trip alone are the magnificent robes worn by the Knights of St. Patrick and the uniform of the Principal Herald during the reign of George II. One exhibit displays the arms of Irish counties, towns, and cities, as well as those of all the presidents of Ireland. All sorts of other artifacts make this a fascinating place—it's open Monday through Friday from 10am to 4pm."* —S. Murchoch, Norfolk, VA

If you've a romantic bone in your body, you may well want to drop in to pay your respects to that saint most revered by lovers around the globe, St. Valentine. The saint was beheaded about A.D. 269, but his remains were moved here from Rome in 1835, presented as a gift from Pope Gregory XVI to Father Spratt, prior of this church, in recognition of his holy work. February 14, the saint's feast day, was once believed to be the day on which birds mated and the day on which an unmarried girl should choose her sweetheart (the origin, of course, of the Valentine card custom). As for the church itself, it stands on the site of a 1539 Carmelite priory, although this structure dates back only to 1825. Look for the impressive life-size oak figure of Our Lady of Dublin and ask about her rather checkered history.

✪ National Botanic Gardens

Botanic Rd., Glasnevin. ☎ **01/837-4388.** Admission free. Summer, Mon–Fri 9am–5:15pm, Sat 9am–5:45pm, Sun 2–5:45pm; winter, Mon–Sat 10am–4:15pm, Sun 2–4:15pm. Bus: 13, 19, 34, 34A.

The gardens were founded in 1795 by the Royal Dublin Society to "increase and foster taste for practical and scientific botany." Spread over 50 acres of an estate that once was the home of the poet Thomas Tickell, they are now under the direction of the Department of Agriculture and Fisheries. In addition to exotic trees, shrubbery, and tropical plants, there is an economic garden (for economic and poisonous plants), a vegetable garden, and a lawn garden. Just inside the gates you'll find Thomas Moore's famous "Last Rose of Summer."

St. Anne's Park Rose Garden

Mount Prospect Ave., Clontarf. Admission free. Daily dawn–dusk. Bus: 44A or 30.

This is one of the prettiest in the city, with climbers, floribunda, hybrid tea, and old garden roses in profusion. In April and May, daffodils are in full bloom.

Especially for Kids

The younger set will find many engaging attractions in Dublin. Children take special delight in the Natural History Museum, St. Stephen's Green, and the natural history exhibits in the National Museum (Merrion Street building). The attractions listed below will also keep kids quite happy during their Dublin stay.

✪ The Phoenix Park and Dublin Zoo

Entrances from Parkgate St. N. Circular Rd. ☎ **01/677-1425.** Park, free; zoo, IR£5.50 ($8.80) adults, IR£2.90 ($4.64) children under 12 and seniors. Family rates available. Park, daily 24 hours; zoo, Mon–Sat 9:30am–6pm, Sun 11am–6pm. Bus: 10, 25, or 26.

Northwest of the city center, with its main entrance on Parkgate Street, this is one of the world's most beautiful parks. Dubliners always refer to it as "The" Phoenix Park. Within its nearly 2,000 acres are the residence of Ireland's president, that of the American ambassador, the lovely People's Gardens, the Zoological Gardens, and Dublin Zoo. As a small boy, Winston Churchill lived here in the 1870s with his grandfather, then the Lord Lieutenant of Ireland. Today, the park's lofty trees shade all manner of humans during daylight hours and a free-roaming herd of deer after dark.

The zoo is especially noted for breeding lions and other large cats, having bred the first lion cubs in captivity in 1857. Its fame also rests on the picturesque landscaping and gardens surrounding two natural lakes (alive with pelicans, flamingos, and scores of ducks and geese) and the spacious outdoor enclosures that house all manner of animals and birds. Youngsters will delight in the small **Children's Zoo,** where they can take a pony ride, pet tame animals, and wish on the Wishing Seat.

The Visitor Centre, in the park's Ashtown Castle, houses all kinds of displays, models, and an audiovisual theater, as well as fascinating information on such topics as the Phoenix Park Murders, the Wellington Testimonial (about a servant who allegedly was walled up in the castle's base in error), and wildlife. Youngsters will love the "crawlway," and there's an inviting tearoom.

National Wax Museum

Granby Row, Parnell Sq. ☎ **01/872-6340.** Admission IR£2.50 ($4) adults, IR£1.50 ($2.40) children. Mon–Sat 10am–5:30pm, Sun 1–5:30pm. Bus: 11, 13, 16, 22, or 22A.

Grown-ups as well as children will be enchanted by the exhibits centered around the heroes and legends from Ireland's past. Life-size figures include Robert Emmet, Wolfe Tone, Parnell, the leaders of the heroic 1916 Uprising, and such literary luminaries as Joyce, Yeats, and their contemporaries. The crowning touch is an excellent educational narrative for each, activated by the push of a button.

As for the young fry, they'll want to head straight for the **Children's World of Fairytale and Fantasy,** a wonderland that will set their imaginations flying. There's even a **Kingdom of Fairytales,** where they'll set off on their own magical journey in search of the genie and his wondrous lamp. You may, however, want to think twice before letting their little feet wander into the **Chamber of Horrors,** where horrible screams and the clanking of chains can send the imagination veering off the happy track of fairytales and fantasy.

SPECIAL-INTEREST SIGHTSEEING

For the Literary Enthusiast

Ireland's greatest gift to the rest of the world may well be its writers, whose keen, sharp-witted, and uniquely phrased insights into the foibles of those who walk this earth are timeless and universal. From this sparsely populated little island have sprung some of civilization's greatest wordsmiths; and of them, a good many were born, lived, or died in Dublin. While some of the landmarks they left behind have disappeared and others have changed since they figured in their lives, the following will surely bring you closer to those whose legacy of such a wealth of words has prodded the minds and hearts of the rest of us.

The house at 7 Hoey's Court where **Jonathan Swift** was born is now gone, but it stood very near St. Patrick's Cathedral, where he was its most famous dean, serving 32 years, and where he was laid to rest. Listen for his footsteps, too, at Trinity College, where he was a student.

Thomas Moore also studied at Trinity, and you'll find his birthplace at 12 Aungier St.

Oscar Wilde began his tumultuous life in Dublin in the year 1854 at 21 Westland Row.

The Nobel prize–winning playwright and essayist **George Bernard Shaw** was born at 33 Synge St., also in 1854. The house is now restored as a museum; there's a small admission fee.

W. B. Yeats was born at 5 Sandymount Ave., and 42 Fitzwilliam Square was his residence from 1928 to 1932.

James Joyce was born in Rathgar at 42 Brighton Square West, and from his self-imposed exile mapped the face of his native city in unremitting detail. The Martello Tower he occupied with Oliver St. John Gogarty in 1904 is now a Joyce museum (see "County Dublin" in Chapter 7). Devoted Joyce followers can trace the Dublin meanderings of his Leopold Bloom as unerringly as if Joyce had written a guidebook rather than his *Ulysses* masterpiece. This is such an intriguing pastime for visitors that the tourist board offers a *Ulysses Map of Dublin* of the book's 18 episodes for a small charge, and if you should be in Dublin on June 16, there are scores of events commemorating "Bloomsday." A James Joyce Cultural Centre is, at time of press, being organized in North Great George's Street.

Sean O'Casey was born in the Dublin slums in 1884. He became the Abbey Theatre's leading dramatist until he broke with them in 1928. His experiences are detailed in his four-volume autobiography, which is a vivid and realistic chronicle of Dublin and Ireland in the first part of the century.

Brendan Behan captured the heart and soul of modern Dublin in words that his countryfolk sometimes agonized over but never denied. He was born in Dublin in 1921 and remained its irreverent, wayward son until the early end of his life in 1964, when the president of Ireland led a huge crowd to Glasnevin Cemetery for the interment. His spirit no doubt still roams the city streets and lingers in numerous pubs, reveling in the things that have changed and those that have remained the same.

Novelist **Elizabeth Bowen** was born at 15 Herbert Place, off Lower Baggot Street, in 1899.

Cornelius Ryan, author of outstanding World War II novels, first saw the light of day in 1920 at 33 Heytesburn Street, off the South Circular Road.

Bram Stoker, whose *Dracula* lives after him, was born at 15 Marino Crescent, Clontarf, in 1847.

A Literary Pub Crawl One terrific way to see this "writers' city" as its writers have seen it is to join the Dublin Literary Pub Crawl. This, you understand, is no heavy academic exercise. It's an evening of the sort of conviviality that sustained the likes of Beckett, Joyce, Behan, and Kavanagh, in pubs that sometimes figured in their written works. The spirit and the characters that inspired them are still very much in evidence, and you'll finish the evening with a new insight to your favorite Irish author's Dublin life after dark.

The tour begins at the Bailey pub on Duke Street every night during the summer; at 7:30pm call for afternoon and winter schedules. It costs a mere IR£6 ($9.60), and you pay for your own drinks. You can book at the tourist office on O'Connell Street, or call **454-0228.**

FOR THE ARCHITECTURE ENTHUSIAST

Dublin is a fascinating mixture of architectural styles, and the following are a few buildings that are of particular interest. Most are described in detail above.

- **St. Patrick's Cathedral,** Patrick's Close, built between 1220 and 1254.
- **St. Michan's Church,** Church Street, dating from 1095, rebuilt in 1685.
- **The General Post Office,** O'Connell Street, designed by Francis Johnston and completed in 1818.
- **The Customs House,** Customs House Quay, designed by James Gandon in 1781.
- **Dublin Castle,** Castle Street, parts of which date to 1204, others from the 1400s.
- **Trinity College,** College Green, founded in 1592, present buildings dating from 1755–59, with a cruciform complex centered around quadrangles and gardens, and a 300-foot Palladian facade designed by Henry Keene and John Sanderford.
- **Leinster House,** Kildare Street, a 1745 mansion designed by Richard Castle for the Earl of Kildare.
- **The Bank of Ireland,** College Green, designed by Sir Edward Lovett Pearce in 1729 as the Parliament House.
- **Four Courts,** Inn Quay, designed by James Gandon in 1785, destroyed by fire in 1922, and rebuilt as a square central block with a circular hall and a shallow dome.
- **Mansion House,** Dawson Street, the official residence of the Lord Mayor of Dublin, built in 1705.
- **Powerscourt House,** South William Street, a classic mansion of 1771, designed by Robert Mack, now housing a shopping center, but with many fine architectural details preserved.
- **Merrion Square,** with its elegant Georgian mansions.

BREWERY TOURS

✪ Guinness Hop Store

James's Gate. ☎ **01/453-6700,** ext. 5155. Admission IR£2 ($3.20) adults, IR£1.50 ($2.40) seniors and students, 50p (80¢) children. Mon–Fri 10am–4pm. Closed weekends and holidays. Bus: 68A, 78A, 123.

A sightseeing attraction in a class by itself is the sprawling Guinness Brewery, set on 60 acres south of the Liffey. The largest brewery in Europe, Guinness exports more beer than any other company in the world. The rich, dark stout it has produced since 1759 is truly the "wine of Ireland," and you'll no doubt be a devout convert after your second pint (it's sometimes an acquired taste!). Because of an extensive modernization and reconstruction program, there are no tours of the plant at present, but you are invited to call by the Guinness Hop Store (it's clearly signposted and just around the corner from the brewery front gate). The historic four-story building—which, as its name suggests, was once the storehouse for the hops used in brewing Guinness—has been carefully refurbished and restored, and you'll see a film about the brewing process, sample a glass or two of the dark stuff in a traditional-style bar, and browse through the Brewery Museum, which includes interesting sections on coopering and transport. If you'd like a souvenir of your visit, there's a very good shop on the premises.

✪ The Irish Whiskey Corner

Bow St. ☎ **01/872-5566.** Admission IR£3 ($4.80). Tours, Mon–Fri 11am and 3:30pm. Bus: 34, 70, or 80.

The unique blend of barley, yeast, and water that is Irish whiskey was first (back in the 6th century) called *uisce beatha* ("*ish*-ke *ba*-ha"), which translates as "the water of life." When King Henry II's soldiers spread its fame to England, the name took on an anglicized sound, *fuisce,* before eventually evolving into "whiskey." From the beginning, nothing about this blend was usual, and today it is still unique, even in the spelling of its name. It is the only European whisk(e)y that is spelled with an "e"!

The Irish Whiskey Corner has been established by the Irish Distillers Group (which includes all seven of the great whiskey houses in Ireland) to present an all-encompassing picture of the history of Irish whiskey, as well as a demonstration of how it's made. The old warehouse that was once used to mature whiskey has been converted into an exhibition center where you can view a short film on whiskey's history, see a copper-pot still and distillery model and other implements of the trade, view the lifelike figure of a cooper fashioning the oak casks that are so important in its aging, and perhaps be chosen as one of four tasters to try various brands. To top things off, everyone gets a sample in the Ball of Malt bar. Group tours can be booked by appointment, with a small charge.

WALKING TOUR
Old Dublin

Start: Capel Street Bridge.
Finish: River Liffey Quays.
Time: About three to four hours.
Best Times: Weekdays.
Worst Times: Sundays during church services or bank holidays.

If you'd like to wander Dublin's streets on your own, begin south of the Liffey at the Capel Street Bridge and walk east toward Dame Street. On your right is the Palace Street gate of:

1. **Dublin Castle.** Continuing east, turn right from Dame Street onto South Great George's Street, a broad and colorful shopping street. Look for the Victorian shopping arcade on the left, which has all the vigor and color of an old-time bazaar. At the end of the arcade is South William Street, where you will find the:
2. **Dublin Civic Museum.** Continue on Aungier Street (an extension of South Great George's Street) to Whitefriar Street, location of the:
3. **Whitefriar Street Carmelite Church.** Poet and songwriter Tom Moore was born at no. 12 on this street.

   Aungier Street now becomes Wexford Street. Turn right onto Lower Kevin Street, and cross Heytesbury Street onto Upper Kevin Street, where you will pass the Garda barracks before coming to:
4. **Marsh's Library.** Walk west to the intersection at The Coombe, which marks the beginning of the Liberties.

   Turn right into Patrick Street to reach:
5. **St. Patrick's Cathedral.** Continue uphill to Christchurch Place and:

Walking Tour — Old Dublin

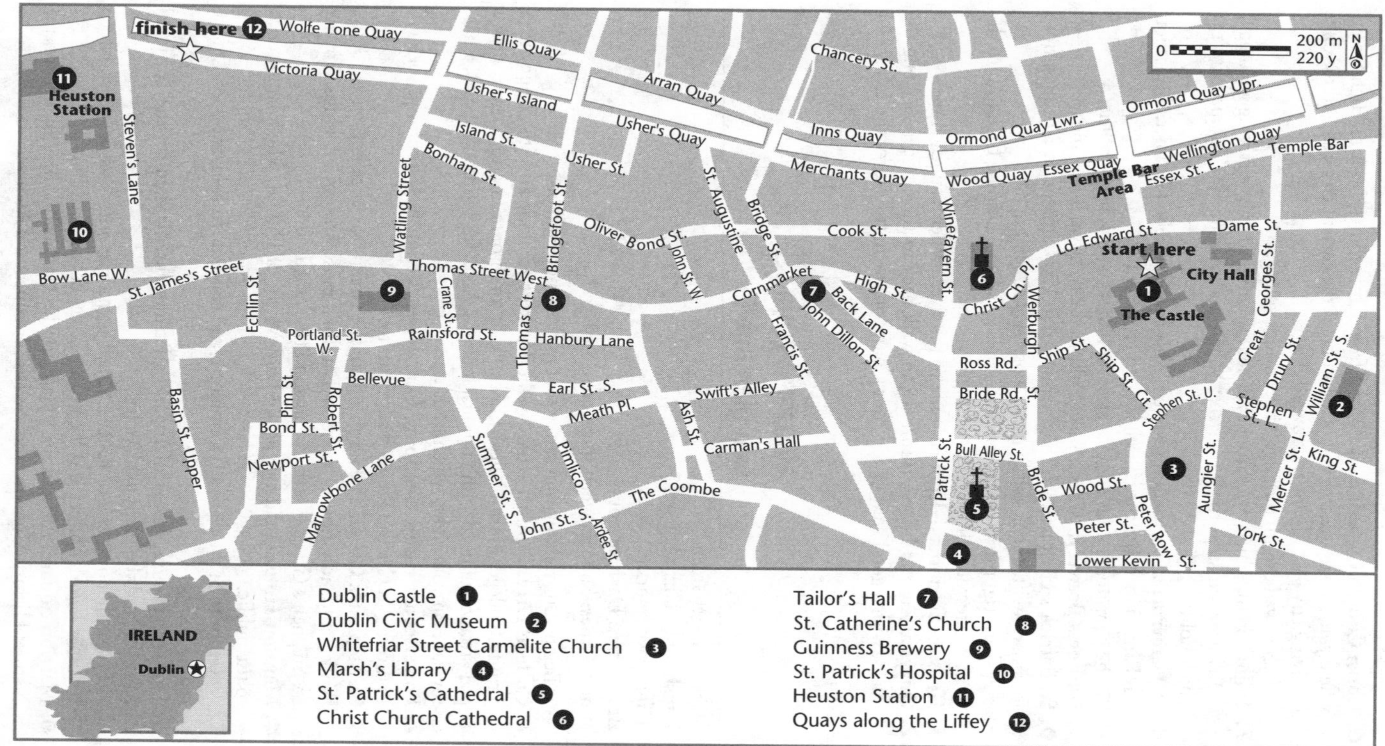

6. **Christ Church Cathedral.** Walk west from Christchurch Place to High Street, where you can see a restoration of a portion of the ancient city wall and the only surviving city gate (down and toward the river).

   A short walk south on High Street brings you to:

7. **Tailor's Hall,** which dates from 1796 and is Dublin's only surviving guild hall.

   Retrace your steps to Cornmarket Square and continue on Thomas Street, which holds:

8. **St. Catherine's Church,** on your left. This is where Robert Emmet, the patriot, was hanged in 1803; the church is open to the public.

   The continuation of Thomas Street is James's Street, home of the:

9. **Guinness Brewery.** James's Street forks to the right via Bow Lane to:
10. **St. Patrick's Hospital,** which was founded in 1764, funded by a bequest from Jonathan Swift, and is still in use as a psychiatric center.

    A sharp right turn brings you onto Steeven's Lane, heading back toward the river, where you will pass the striking:

11. **Heuston Station** rail depot en route to the river. When you reach the:
12. **Quays along the Liffey,** turn right to walk back to the city center along the quays, with a good view of the Four Courts on the north side of the Liffey.

WALKING TOUR
Georgian Dublin

Start: College Green.
Finish: Fitzwilliam Square.
Time: Two hours.
Best Times: Daylight hours.
Worst Times: Sunday, when shops are closed.

Begin your walking tour at the foot of Westmoreland Street at:

1. **College Green.** On the right is the Bank of Ireland, and just opposite is Trinity College. From College Green, walk south onto Grafton Street, now a pedestrian mall lined with fashionable shops. Look for Johnson's Court, a narrow lane on your right, which leads to:
2. **Powerscourt House Shopping Centre** (see Section 5, "Shopping," below). Returning to Grafton Street, walk south to:
3. **St. Stephen's Green.** The north side of the Green was once known as "Beaux Walk," and now houses some of Dublin's most prestigious clubs. Follow St. Stephen's Green North to Dawson Street, site of the:
4. **Mansion House,** residence of the Lord Mayor of Dublin, which is not open to the public.

   Return to St. Stephen's Green North and continue to Kildare Street. On the right is:

5. **Leinster House,** home of Ireland's Parliament, flanked by the National Museum and the National Library.

   From the north end of Kildare Street, turn right onto Nassau Street, which becomes Leinster Street and then Clare Street before reaching:

6. **Merrion Square.** Around the square are the National Gallery of Ireland, the Natural History Museum, and the Irish Architectural Archive.

Walking Tour — Georgian Dublin

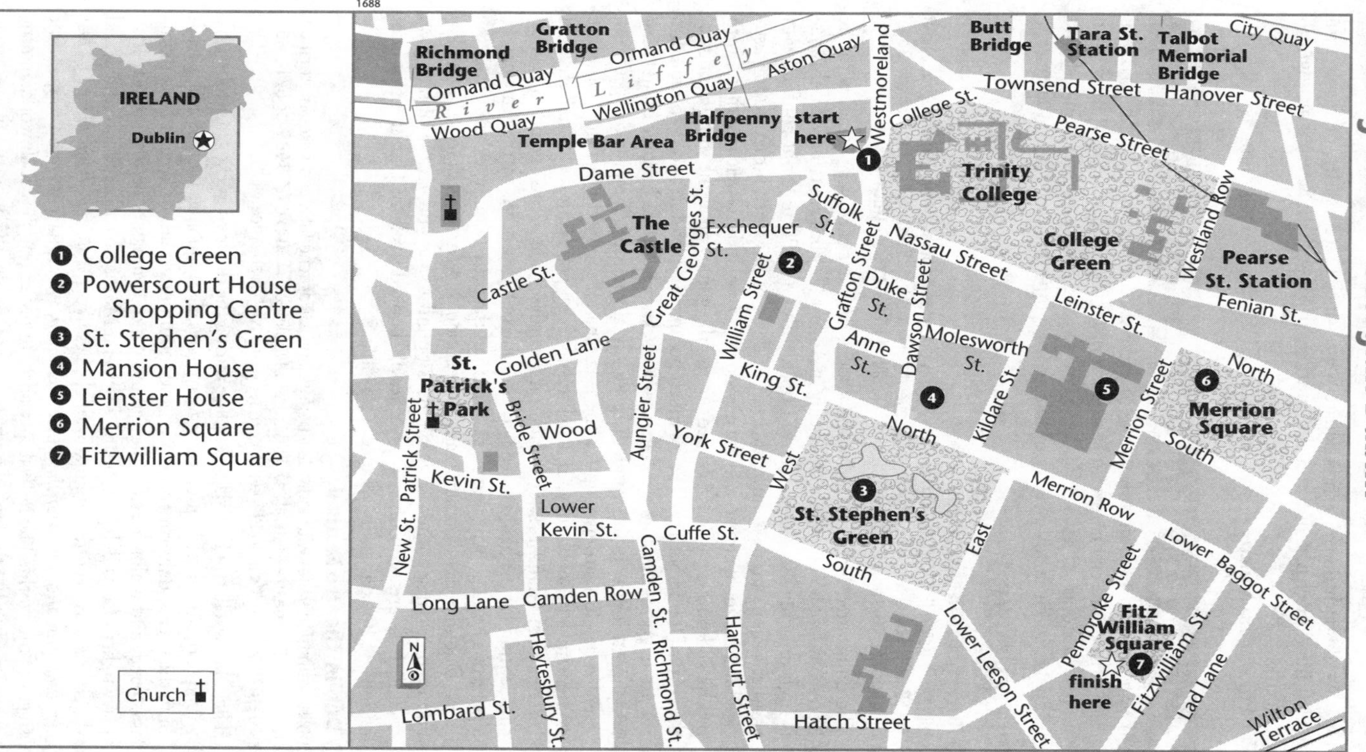

Walk south along Merrion Square West, which becomes Merrion Street, turn left into Lower Baggot Street and continue to Fitzwilliam Street. Turn right to reach:

7. **Fitzwilliam Square,** surrounded by elegant Georgian mansions.

2 Special & Free Events

If you arrive in Dublin during one of these special events, you're in for a real treat—the entire city enters into the spirit of the occasion. Check with the Irish Tourist Board about specific dates the year of your visit; accommodations should be booked as far in advance as possible and will probably cost you a little more.

SPECIAL EVENTS

✪ Kerrygold Dublin Horse Show

Dublin. Admission IR£25 ($40) for all events, or a one-day general admission ticket for about IR£6 ($9.60). For a detailed program of events and ticket information, contact the Royal Dublin Society, Merrion Road, Ballsbridge, Dublin 4 (☎ **01/668-0866**).

The undisputed highlight of Ireland's social calendar each year comes with the Kerrygold Dublin Horse Show, usually in August (but be sure to check if this one is high on your list—it was moved up to July in 1990 to avoid conflict with another major European horse show). For one glorious week it draws a sophisticated international crowd, and the city dons its best duds to welcome them, with private and public parties scheduled around the goings-on at the showgrounds of the Royal Dublin Society. There's much pomp and splendor, and even more fun and frolic. As for the show itself, in what are acknowledged to be some of the finest jumping enclosures in the world, there are virtually nonstop jumping competitions. The Kerrygold Nations Cup for the Aga Khan Trophy competition raises the excitement level on Friday, and the whole thing winds up with the Kerrygold International Grand Prix of Ireland on Saturday. Side events include a fashion competition for the best-dressed lady on Ladies Day, concerts by the army bands, a gorgeous floral display, and an exhibition of the prize-winning exhibits from the Royal Dublin Society's annual crafts competition. It's a great week to be in Dublin, and even one day at the showgrounds is bound to net you a score of new Irish friends. It is also probably the most heavily booked week for Dublin accommodations, so book as far in advance as possible.

✪ Dublin Theatre Festival

Dublin. Admission varies with individual performances. For schedules and ticket information, contact Dublin Theatre Festival, 47 Nassau St., Dublin 2 (☎ **01/677-8439** or 671-2860, Fax 01/679-7709). It's a good idea to contact them well in advance.

The Dublin Theatre Festival takes place during the first two weeks of October. It's a unique theatrical celebration that incorporates all of Dublin's theaters and spreads onto the streets, university campuses, and community halls. Innovative Irish drama is offered, and major overseas theater and dance companies perform. Great Irish playwrights such as Behan, Leonard, Friel, and Murphy have been represented, and the festival has been the originator of classics like *Da, Philadelphia Here I Come!, Translations,* and *The Morning After Optimism,* which have gone on to grace the stages of the world. The festival specializes in presenting new Irish work, and the central weekend of the festival offers visitors to Dublin the opportunity to see nine new Irish plays over a period of three days. Other highlights are international theater and dance of the highest standards from countries such as Sweden, South Africa, the United States, Britain, France, Germany, and many others, representing all types of theater, from comedy to classics, experimental theater, mime, and musicals. A Festival Club, where the theatergoers mingle with actors, directors, and members of the international press, as well as workshops, exhibitions, and an international theater conference, all make this a very special celebration.

3 Sports

SPECTATOR SPORTS

Pick your sport, and Dublin probably can come up with an event. The following are highlights of spectator sports in Dublin, but if you have a special interest in a sport not listed (bowling, cricket, etc.), consult the tourist board's current "Calendar of Events in Ireland" to see if a tournament or match is on in the Dublin area during your visit.

✪ **GAELIC FOOTBALL** Matches are regularly held in Croke Park, but the biggie of the year is the All Ireland Football Finals played in mid-September. As with the hurling finals, tickets are scarcer than hen's teeth unless you buy them months and months ahead. Still, it's great fun to share the entire city's excitement even if you can't make it into the park. For details, contact the Gaelic Athletic Association (☎ 01/836-3222).

HORSERACING There are four racecourses in the Dublin area, and meets are scheduled in at least one (sometimes more) during every month of the year. All can be reached by public transportation from the city, and if you insist on driving, be prepared for traffic congestion and a long hike from your parking space to the stands. Horseracing events for the entire year are listed in the back of the "Calendar of Events in Ireland."

- The Curragh (☎ 045/41205), 30 miles west of Dublin in County Kildare, is the home of Ireland's classic races, such as the Kerrygold International Grand Prix. Special buses and trains run from Busaras and Heuston Station on race days. Call for ticket information and race schedules.
- Leopardstown (☎ 01/289-3607) is on the outskirts of the city and can be reached via Bus no. 86. Phone for schedules and ticket information.
- Punchestown (☎ 045/97704) is 23 miles southwest of Dublin in County Kildare, and special buses run from Busaras on race days.
- Fairyhouse (☎ 01/825-6167) is some 16 miles to the north of the city in County Meath, and there are special race-day buses from Busaras.

HURLING The All Ireland Hurling Finals are held in Croke Park the first week in September. Tickets are sold out months in advance, but that doesn't dampen the enthusiasm of fans gathered around the telly in pubs all over the city. For details of this and all other hurling, soccer, and Gaelic football matches, call the Gaelic Athletic Association (GAA) (☎ 01/836-3222).

RUGBY Ireland is regularly represented in international rugby finals, and all home matches for the International Rugby Championship are played at Lansdowne Road stadium, usually in late January or early February. Contact the tourist board or call the GAA (see above) for details.

OUTDOOR ACTIVITIES

If you'd rather participate than spectate, Dublin is a good venue for most forms of active recreation.

BEACHES The following afford safe swimming and sandy beaches, and all can be reached by city buses:

- Dollymount, 3½ miles from Dublin.
- Claremount, 9 miles from the city.
- Sutton, 7 miles out.
- Portmarnock (one of the best), 9 miles from Dublin.
- Donabate, 13 miles away.
- Malahide, 9 miles from Dublin.

BICYCLING Cyclists should head first for the tourist office for a copy of Information Sheet no. 14B, "Cycling—Dublin and the Eastern Seaboard." It outlines cycling tours from Dublin, Dun Laoghaire, and Bray.

Bikes can be rented from the Bike Store, 58 Lower Gardiner Street (☎ 872-5399 or 872-5931), which has a good selection of sports and mountain bikes in stock. Raleigh Rent-A-Bike is represented by McDonald's Cycles Ltd., 38 Wexford Street (☎ 475-2586).

GOLF There are some 35 golf courses in the Dublin area. Most are private, but nearly all will grant temporary membership to visitors. Those listed below are just a sampling of 18-hole courses; for a complete list contact the tourist office:

- Clontarf Golf Club, 2½ miles from Dublin (☎ 311305).
- Dun Laoghaire Golf Club, 7 miles from Dublin (☎ 801055 or 805166).
- Howth Golf Club, 9 miles from the city (☎ 323055).
- The Royal Dublin Golf Club, Dollymount, 3 miles from Dublin (☎ 337153).

HIKING/WALKING As I've said before, Dublin is truly a walker's city. Follow a specified route through its streets, on the lookout for sightseeing attractions, or simply pick a neighborhood and walk with no purpose other than pure enjoyment.

A lovely three-mile walk along coastal roads is that **from Baldoyle to Portmarnock.** There are good Dublin Bay views all along the way, and you'll wind up at one of the Dublin area's best beaches. Take DART to Baldoyle and return to the city from Portmarnock via bus no. 32.

Another bracing coastal walk is out in **Dalkey,** beginning at Bulloch harbor, continuing through the village and up Coliemore Road, past Coliemore harbor, stopping in a small seaside park for a breather, and then on to Vico Road, which is a marvelous vantage point for viewing Killiney Bay and Bray Head. It's about a two-mile walk, and you can get to Bulloch harbor via bus no. 8 from the city center.

Dedicated hikers can tread in the footsteps of the ancient Irish if they walk **The Wicklow Way,** part of which traverses the same route as one of the five great roads radiating from the Hill of Tara. The Wicklow Way begins in Marlay Park, County Dublin, and extends about 132km (80 miles) to Clonegal, County Carlow. It can be done in shorter stages, however, and even one stage will be a memorable experience as you follow sheep trails and old bog roads. The route is set out in detail in the tourist board's Information Sheet no. 26B, and it is recommended also that you arm yourself with the Ordinance Survey Map, *Wicklow Way.*

HORSEBACK RIDING Equestrians who yearn to ride a horse in the Dublin area can contact the following:

- Ashtown Equestrian Centre, Castleknock (☎ 838-3236).
- Black Horse Riding School, Castleknock (☎ 838-6021).
- Castleknock Equestrian Centre, Dublin 15 (☎ 820-1104).

TENNIS You'll find public tennis courts at the following locations:

- Bushy Park, Terenure (☎ 490-0320).
- Herbert Park, Ballsbridge (☎ 668-4364).
- St. Anne's Estate, Dollymount (☎ 831-3697).

4 Organized Tours

Organized tours can be terrific budget and time stretchers, as well as a great way to save shoe leather and the mental effort of advance planning. Dublin is blessed with an array of tours that can get you to virtually any attraction you fancy. If your time in Dublin is short, this is one of the best ways to make the most of it.

One thing to remember, however: On Saturday and Sunday, many of the leading attractions are closed, so be sure to check when choosing your tour.

BUS TOURS

BOOKING You can pick up brochures for the following bus-tours companies from the tourist office. You can usually join a tour on the day of travel, but there's always the possibility that the tour will be fully booked; my advice: book ahead if possible.

Bus Eireann Sightseeing Tours

Central Bus Station (Busaras), Store St. ☎ **836-6111.**

Even if you're driving, Bus Eireann's **full- and half-day excursions** can save you time, money, and wear and tear on the nervous system in exploring those attractions outside Dublin. You'll find full descriptions of most in Chapter 7, and in making your tour selections, *be sure to check that they run on the day you want to book.* Some of the most appealing tours are: the Boyne Valley, which visits Tara, Slane, and Newgrange; Avondale, Glendalough, and the Wicklow Hills; Powerscourt Gardens and Pine Forest; and Russborough House and Blessington Lakes. Days and hours of departure vary, and fares range from IR£10 ($16) to IR£20 ($32), half-price for children.

Dublin Bus Tours

59 Upper O'Connell St. ☎ **01/873-4222.**

Half-day city tours are a wonder of organization, giving you a glimpse of no fewer than 55 city landmarks, historic buildings, and other points of interest, with background information on every one. To add to the fun, if the day is fine, you'll travel in an double-deck, open-air bus (top deck enclosed in inclement weather). Departures are from 59 Upper O'Connell St., April to October, daily at 10:15am and 2:15pm, and fares are IR£9 ($14.40) for adults, IR£4.50 ($7.20) for children.

The **Dublin Bus Heritage Trail Tour** is a sort of *semi*-organized tour. You can stay on the bus right around its entire itinerary, accompanied by an excellent commentary all the way, or you can opt to hop off at any of eight top attractions for a more in-depth exploration, then catch the next bus to continue the tour. The

10 tour stops include such landmarks as Trinity College, St. Patrick's Cathedral, and Christ Church Cathedral. Departures from 59 Upper O'Connell St. are frequent from 10am to 4pm, and you can join the tour at any one of the stops. Purchase tickets at the address above, the tourist office, or directly from the bus driver. Adults pay IR£5 ($8); children under 16, IR£2.50 ($4); family ticket, IR£12.50 ($20)—and your ticket is valid all day.

Gray Line Tours Ireland

3 Clanwilliam Terrace, Grand Canal Quay. ☎ **01/661-9666.** Fax 661-9652.

Gray Line Tours offer a full range of tours in and around Dublin City. Half-day tours of the city are priced from IR£8 ($12.80) and full-day-or-more countryside and historic tours range upwards from IR£26 ($41.60), with destinations that include extended tours (two days) on the Ring of Kerry, as well as two-week jaunts. Book through the above address or their desk in Dublin Tourism, 14 O'Connell St. (☎ 01/874-4466, 878-7981, or 661-9666).

GUIDED WALKING TOURS

As an alternative or supplement to your own wanderings, excellent guided walking tours are available in the city.

Old Dublin Tours

90 Meath St., Dublin 8. ☎ **01/453-2407.**

Conducted by knowledgeable Dubliners, these two-hour tours concentrate on medieval and Viking relics in the city. You join the group at the Christ Church Cathedral. From May through September, tours leave daily at 10:30am and 2pm; from October through April, they are offered Friday and Saturday only at 10:30am and Sunday at 2pm. The price is IR£4.50 ($7.20) per person.

PERSONALLY TAILORED TOURS

Tour Guides

For those who prefer a one-on-one guided tour of Dublin, it is possible to engage a personal tour guide, one who can tailor a tour to your own special interests and share a firsthand knowledge of Dublin's rich heritage. The tourist board publishes a "Directory of Approved Guides," all of whom have passed a written and practical examination given by the Council for the Education, Recruitment, and Training of personnel in tourism industries. Some are multilingual (languages include French, German, Italian, Spanish, and Dutch). For the directory and full details, contact the **Tourism Services and Facilities Department, Bord Failte Eireann,** Baggot Street Bridge, Dublin 2 (☎ 676-5871).

Cab Tours

If the mere thought of slogging through city streets makes you groan, City Cabs (☎ 872-7272) offers excellent personally conducted tours of the city tailored to meet your own interests. They have cabs with specialized wheelchair access, as well as limo service. Two of the best drivers I've encountered are Alan Brabazon (ask for driver 400) and Chris Kearns. Both know Dublin inside and out and enjoy letting you in on a Dub's-eye view of the city. Prices depend on just how long you want to engage them.

Horse-Drawn Carriage Tours

Finally, the *ultimate* in a Dublin tour must surely be by way of a horse-drawn carriage. A ride in one of the handsome carriages is an experience in itself, but it is really the "pure-Dub" narrative from your driver that makes the tour. You can engage a carriage for a short drive around St. Stephen's Green, the half-hour tour of Georgian Dublin, or a full-hour tour of the Old City. At prices of IR£5 to IR£30 ($8–$48) for two to five passengers, it's a treat not to be missed. Just take yourself down to the Grafton Street side of St. Stephen's Green and negotiate with the drivers at the carriage stand there. You can also book by ringing 01/453-8888 or 821-6463.

5 Shopping

THE SHOPPING SCENE

The tourist board issues an excellent free booklet called "Shopping in Dublin" to help you find anything you could possibly want to purchase in the city. It contains a very good center-city map, as well as a guide to sizes (many of which differ from those in America) and Customs regulations.

Gifts of any value can be mailed duty free to addresses outside Ireland.

Main Shopping Areas Principal city-center shopping areas south of the Liffey are Grafton Street, Nassau Street, and Wicklow Street; north of the river, shopping is best on O'Connell Street and Henry Street.

Shopping Hours Unless otherwise stated, the shops listed below are open Monday through Saturday from 9am to 5pm; closed on Sunday.

VAT Return Be sure to save your receipts for the Value-Added Tax refund for all purchases you are taking out of the country.

SHOPPING CENTERS & DEPARTMENT STORES

SOUTH OF THE LIFFEY

✪ Powerscourt Town House Centre
Clarendon St.

If you just can't get excited about shopping centers, wait till you see this one! It's set in a 1774 mansion built by Lord Powerscourt, and the house and courtyard have been expertly renovated to accommodate small shops, wine bars, and restaurants. Among the shops, there's an antiques gallery, high-fashion clothing shops, designer shoes and bags, and a hairdresser. Several restaurants, moderately priced, and a resident pianist in the central courtyard help make this a good place to begin your shopping, or just your browsing, for that matter. Look for the sign on Grafton Street at Johnson's Court between Chatham and Wicklow streets. Open Monday through Saturday from 9am to 6pm and Thursday until 7pm.

St. Stephen's Green Centre
Grafton St. and St. Stephen's Green.

This huge, striking, and very modern structure is Dublin's largest shopping center. There are more than 100 shops within its walls, encompassing just about every category in existence.

Switzers
92 Grafton St.

Considered by some to be Dublin's leading department store, Switzers carries very upmarket goods in a wide variety of clothing, housewares, furnishings, personal toiletries and cosmetics, linens, jewelry, gifts, etc.

Readers Recommend

Patrick Flood, Gold and Silversmith, in the Powerscourt Town House Centre in downtown Dublin. *"Patrick Flood does his own designing and crafting, and has reasonable prices on silver Claddagh rings and other fine jewelry."*

—N. Rounsefell and S. Gilmore, Baton Rouge, LA

Brown Thomas & Co. Ltd.
15–20 Grafton St.

One of the city's most prestigious department stores, with both upmarket and moderate goods and prices.

Royal Hibernian Way
Dawson St.

On the site of the old Royal Hibernian Hotel, this shopping arcade holds some 30 shops, including high fashion, and a number of small restaurants.

North of the Liffey

Ilac Centre
Talbot St.

Good concentration of moderately priced shops, offering a wide variety of goods. Restaurants are in the moderate price range.

Irish Life Centre
Moore St.

Another cluster of shops and restaurants offering goods and food in the moderate price range.

Clery's
O'Connell St.

A Dublin tradition, Clery's is the oldest and largest department store on the north side of the river. It's a complete department store, stocking everything from upmarket fashion, jewelry, and gifts to housewares and hardware. There are three good inexpensive restaurants on the premises.

Roches Stores Ltd.
54/62 Henry St.

This is the Dublin branch of a department-store chain with good, middle-of-the-road merchandise and moderate prices. It's a good place to shop for fashionable clothing at sensible prices.

Dunne's Stores
Ilac Centre, Talbot St.

Crowded, busy, and not much charm, but Dunne's is a terrific place to pick up good buys in clothing, as well as the little necessities of life (toothpaste, hose, etc.).

BEST BUYS & WHERE TO FIND THEM

Books

Inquire at the tourist office about the **Book Barrow Fair** held monthly in the Mansion House. About 30 booksellers come from around the country to set up stalls for one day only, many selling old and rare volumes for bargain prices.

Cathach Books

10 Duke St. ☎ **01/671-8676.** Fax 01/671-8676.

This centrally located shop has a large stock of Irish literature, local history and genealogy publications, maps, and fine prints. Ask for their catalog.

✪ Greene & Co.

16 Clare St. ☎ **01/676-2554.** Fax 01/678-9091.

Book lovers can browse for hours through two floors of new and secondhand books, or the rows of trays out front on the sidewalk. The staff is both friendly and helpful, and they'll hunt down scarce or out-of-print books at no charge. They'll send a free mail-order catalog, and they accept most major credit cards.

✪ Fred Hanna Ltd.

27/29 Nassau St. ☎ **01/677-1255** or 677-1936.

They have good stocks of books of Irish interest here, as well as extensive stocks of the newest publications and children's, secondhand, and antiquarian books. They'll mail overseas.

✪ Waterstones Bookshop

7 Dawson St. ☎ **01/679-1415.**

A branch of the English chain, its stocks are extensive, and there are special reading areas. They have a good book-search service, as well as mail- and telephone-order departments. Late hours accommodate office workers and weary travelers: Monday through Friday from 9am to 8:30pm, on Saturday from 9am to 7pm, and on Sunday from noon to 7pm.

CRAFTS

Ida Tower Design Craft Centre

Pearse St. at Grand Canal Quay.

This is where you'll find all manner of craftspeople in more than 30 workshops. Good buys in traditional crafts: gold and silver jewelry, handmade pottery, designer handknits for ladies and children, pewter, and heraldic art. There's also a restaurant with lunch and snacks available every day except Saturday and Sunday.

FASHION/FABRICS

Blarney Woollen Mills

21/23 Nassau St. ☎ **01/671-0068.**

This shop specializes in Irish sweaters, Pallas linen womenswear, and Donegal tweed suits and coats styled by leading Irish designers. They have a good selection of Waterford crystal and Belleek china, and will mail anywhere in the world.

Cleo

18 Kildare St. ☎ **01/676-1421.**

Around the corner from the Shelbourne Hotel, this shop specializes in designer woolens, as well as linens. Smashing designs follow both classic and contemporary styles, all executed in top-quality fabrics. One of Dublin's top shops.

Dublin Woollen Mills

41 Lower Ormond Quay. ☎ **01/677-5014** or 677-0301.

A Dublin institution, this shop at the foot of the Ha'penny Bridge was founded by the Roche family in 1888 and four succeeding generations have carried on the high standards set in the beginning. As its name suggests, woollen goods are featured, with a wide selection of traditional and designer-style knitwear, as well as shawls, scarves, blankets, and interesting craft items.

Kevin and Howlin

31 Nassau St. ☎ **01/677-0257.**

Tweed tailor-made jackets and suits for men are good value here, and last so long they're an investment rather than just a purchase. There's also a large range of ready-made men's clothing and moderately priced Donegal tweed hats and caps (walking hats, town hats, *Quiet Man* hats, etc.). It's located at the bottom of Dawson Street, facing Trinity College.

✪ Monaghan's

Grafton Arcade. ☎ **01/677-0823.**

Monaghan's has my highest recommendation for Aran sweaters to fit all members of the family, as well as lambswool, cashmere, other sweaters, and a good stock of menswear. They ship worldwide and offer a mail-order catalog. There's another branch at 4/5 Royal Hibernian Way.

Jenny Vander

20–22 Market Arcade, George's St. ☎ **01/677-0406.**

This interesting shop stocks antique clothes, shoes, and jewelry, as well as Irish linen and lace sheets, curtains, and tablecloths. Lots of bric-a-brac and men's clothes. Great fun, and prices are quite reasonable.

GIFT/SPECIALTY STORES

Fergus O'Farrell

62 Dawson St. ☎ **01/677-0862.**

Some of the most unusual replicas of antique Irish jewelry, copper and wood handcrafts, and other top-quality items with historical emphasis can be found here.

✪ House of Ireland

37/38 Nassau St. and Dublin Airport Departures Hall. ☎ **01/677-7949** or 671-4543. Fax 679-1023.

This shop is a standout for finding anything from Waterford crystal to Belleek, Wedgwood, Irish Dresden, and Royal Tara china to fine tweeds, special cashmeres, knitcrafts, linens, Celtic jewelry, pottery, blackthorn walking sticks, and a wide range of quality souvenir items. Of particular interest to Americans are the lovely Irish porcelain dolls dressed in traditional handcrafted clothes. Chosen by owner Eileen Galligan, who delighted in their quaint view of an Ireland not altogether past, they are a perfect gift for the collector. Outstanding service from a friendly staff. They will mail or ship overseas. Be sure to ask about their 10% discount on purchases.

McConnell and Nelson

38 Grafton St. ☎ **01/677-4344.**

This is the best place to buy smoked Irish salmon to take home. Sean Nelson and his staff will seal it for travel, and prices are considerably below those at the airport duty-free shops.

Patricia's Irish Crafts

Grafton Arcade.

Run by Patricia York, a noted authority on heraldry, the shop has a good stock of heraldic items as well as craft items and souvenirs.

Trinity Fair

1 Nassau St. ☎ **01/671-1554.**

Owner John Leader's small shop holds an amazing array of unusual brass items, many small enough to carry home tucked away in a corner of your case. Other giftware, ornaments, and souvenirs are also outstanding.

PIPES

Kapp & Peterson Ltd.

117 Grafton St. ☎ **01/671-4652.**

Dedicated pipe smokers will know Peterson pipes, which has been making superior pipes in Dublin since the 1860s. They are justly famed for their classic designs, and feature such unusual models as the Sherlock Holmes and the Mark Twain pipes.

RECORDINGS

Claddagh Records

2 Cecilia St., Temple Bar. ☎ **01/677-0262.**

Claddagh has one of the most comprehensive stocks of traditional Irish records, tapes, and compact discs, as well as blues, Cajun, country, Asian, European, and African. There's a mail-order service, and their catalog includes a full listing of all Irish recordings.

Virgin Megastore Ltd.

14–18 Aston Quay. ☎ **01/677-7361.**

This huge multistoried store on the south side of the Liffey is bound to have whatever you fancy in the line of recorded music, videos, entertainment magazines, books, posters, and games. Music selections range from traditional Irish to country-and-western to rock.

Waltons Musical Gallery

2/5 N. Frederick St. ☎ **01/674-7805.**

The best all-around music store in Dublin is at the top of O'Connell Street. The stock of Irish traditional records and sheet music is tremendous, and they also sell a complete line of musical instruments.

6 Dublin Nights

Check the "Entertainment" listings of Dublin newspapers during your stay. Pick up a copy of the "Dublin Event Guide" from newsagents and other shops, too. It's published every other Wednesday and includes listings for the next two weeks.

THEATER

Tickets for all theaters can be purchased at box offices or through the department stores Brown Thomas (☎ 677-6861) and Switzer's (☎ 677-682) on Grafton Street.

✪ Abbey Theatre

Lower Abbey St. ☎ **01/878-7222.** Fax 01/872-9177. Matinées and previews IR£8 ($12.80); evening performances IR£10–IR£12.50 ($16–$20).

This is the national repertory company, born in 1898 when Augusta Lady Gregory, W. B. Yeats, and Edward Martyn determined to perform Irish plays with Irish casts. It provided a voice for such passionate writers as Sean O'Casey and J. M. Synge, even when conservative Irish audiences rioted at the showing of Synge's *Playboy of the Western World.* Siobhan McKenna, Cyril Cusack, Sara Allgood, and Barry Fitzgerald are just a few of the stage talents who blossomed to stardom through their training at the Abbey. The original Abbey was quite small, and when it burned in 1951, members were pleased that the government would have to provide them with more spacious quarters. They did gain a modern, functional theater with the best in stage equipment—but it took 15 years for the government to get the job done. All the while the company performed in a variety theater to stay alive. The theater's emphasis is still on Irish playwrights (contemporary and classic) and Irish actors, with an occasional import. The Abbey stays booked year-round, and to avoid disappointment you should contact them directly a minimum of three weeks in advance to book the performances you want to see.

Andrews Lane Theatre

12/16 Andrews Lane. ☎ **01/679-5720.** Tickets IR£6–IR£12 ($9.60–$19.20).

Contemporary theater is featured in this small theater near Trinity College, and experimental productions are staged in a studio-theater.

✪ Eblana Theatre

Store St. ☎ **01/679-8404.** Tickets IR£6–IR£12 ($9.60–$19.20).

This intimate little theater is downstairs in Busaras (the Central Bus Station), and has made quite a name for itself in recent years for outstanding productions of contemporary plays.

The Gaiety Theatre

S. King St. ☎ **01/677-1717.** Prices vary with the production, but tickets average about IR£16 ($25.60).

The Gaiety presents popular Irish drama, musicals, and a spectacular pantomime at Christmas each year.

The Gate Theatre

Parnell Sq. ☎ **01/874-4045.** Tickets IR£10–IR£12 ($16–$19.20). Half-price student tickets on a standby basis and special group rates available (for details, call 874-4368).

Housed in a beautifully restored 18th-century European-style theater, its resident company stages established and modern classics, with a bias toward Irish plays and plays with a strong visual appeal. It's a small, intimate place, with only 370 seats and a cozy bar.

Olympia Theatre

Dame St. ☎ **01/677-7744.** Prices vary with the production.

This grand old ornate theater is very much in the music-hall style, and its program through the year can vary widely, from contemporary plays to musicals to opera.

Peacock Theatre

Lower Abbey St. ☎ **01/878-7222.** Tickets IR£6–IR£8 ($9.60–$12.80).

Downstairs at the Abbey, this small theater hosts literary and poetry readings, experimental contemporary drama, and sometimes a retrospective of the classics.

✪ The Project Arts Centre

39 E. Essex St. ☎ **01/671-2321.** Tickets IR£6–IR£10 ($9.60–$16).

Located in an interesting old Dublin neighborhood that was once known as "Smock Alley," this is an artists' cooperative where anything might happen, from poetry readings to rock music to the best of new Irish writing and productions of European theater classics. For the past three years the Project has won most of the principal Harveys (the Irish equivalent of the Tonys), including best actor, best music, best set design, and best costume design. Late-night Friday and Saturday shows in summer feature Irish and European left-wing cabaret artists. There is free admission to the gallery and other events such as contemporary music (most Saturday afternoons at 2:30pm).

MUSICAL CONCERTS

✪ National Concert Hall

Earlsfort Terrace. ☎ **01/671-1533.** Fax 01/478-3797. Tickets IR£5–IR£12 ($8–$19.20).

A splendid auditorium that features first-rate musical events. The prestigious National Symphony Orchestra and the Irish Chamber Orchestra perform here regularly, and visiting artists run the gamut from harpists to jazz stars. During just one month, the productions here included a performance of *The Merry Widow,* a series of jazz concerts, the Dresden Philharmonic Orchestra, a Folk Aid Concert for Ireland, the Johann Strauss Orchestra of Vienna, a recital by an international opera singer, and about a dozen others! This is superb entertainment at bargain-basement prices. Check with the concert hall or the tourist office to see what's on during your visit. Bus: 14A, 46A, 46B, or 86.

The Point Depot

East Link Bridge, North Wall Quay. ☎ **01/836-3633.** Tickets IR£10–IR£50 ($16–$80).

One of the largest performance halls in Ireland, the Point seats 3,000. Concerts feature international entertainers, and first-rate musicals are often staged here. Bus: 5A. DART: Connolly Station.

TRADITIONAL IRISH MUSIC & DANCE

To hear Irish music as it pours from the Irish heart in Ireland is something you almost always have to stumble onto when the music and song are totally unplanned. In Dublin, however, that same joyous or melancholy or rebellious spirit is yours to share out at Monkstown. **Comhaltas Ceoltoiri Eireann,** the organization dedicated to preserving Irish culture in all its forms, sponsors the functions listed below in its own headquarters building there, as well as some remarkable performing troupes of dancers, singers, and musicians who tour around the country during summer months. Keep an eye out for them as you travel, or inquire at local tourist offices. Admissions average about IR£5 ($8).

✪ Culturlann Na Heireann

32 Belgrave Sq., Monkstown. ☎ **01/280-0295.** Admission IR£2 ($3.20).

Some kind of traditional entertainment is on every night of the week, but to hear some of the best musicians in the country, go along on Friday, Saturday, or Sunday. Fiddlers fiddle, pipers pipe, whistle players whistle, dancers take to the floor, and singers lift their fine Irish voices in informal sessions that bear little resemblance to the staged performances mentioned above. Things get under way about 9pm and carry on until 12:30am.

✪ The Piper's Club

32 Belgrave Sq., Monkstown. ☎ **01/800295.** Admission IR£4 ($6.40).

The Piper's Club makes Saturday night special, when the members of this popular Dublin institution hold forth during those same hours. Other nights, there's ceili dancing that will get you out on the floor and stage shows featuring step dancers and traditional music. Call to find out what's on when you're there, then hightail it out to Monkstown. If you call, you can book an inexpensive dinner of traditional, home-cooked Irish food in their kitchen/restaurant.

A Musical Pub Crawl

The absolute best way to enjoy Irish traditional music in its natural habitat is to join the **Traditional Irish Musical Pub Crawl,** operated by Discover Dublin, Inc., 82 Aungier Street, Dublin 2 (☎ 01/478-0191). You'll hit some of Dublin's most outstanding pubs, in the company of a professional musician who will share his knowledge of Irish music and discuss its impact on contemporary world music. Just so you won't turn into a mere audience—strictly not allowed when a sing-song breaks out!—you'll receive a copy of the book "Discover Dublin Song and Poetry." The evening ends with a traditional session in O'Donoghues, one of the great music pubs.

Admission is IR£5 ($8). Tickets are available at the Tourist Office, or at Gogarty's on the night.

Hours are 7:30pm every night except Friday. Meet at Oliver St. John Gogarty's pub, 52 Fleet Street, in Temple Bar.

CABARET

Cabaret in Dublin is served up with distinctly Irish seasonings: "Danny Boy" and "The Rose of Tralee" are favorites; there's an Irish comic telling Irish jokes; pretty, fresh-faced colleens dancing, singing, playing the harp, etc.; at least one Irish tenor or baritone; and usually one or more of those captivating Irish youngsters in traditional dress to step a lively jig or reel or hornpipe. They're loads of fun and the performances are usually well above average. Audiences are mostly visitors, but with more than a few Irish families in from the country. Most shows are held in hotels, and you can opt for dinner (featuring typical Irish specialties) and the show or the show alone. Prices vary slightly between venues and are shown in the listings below.

The most popular cabarets are those at **Jurys Hotel and Towers,** Ballsbridge (☎ 01/660-5000), IR£34 ($54.40) for dinner and show, IR£22 ($35.20) for show and two drinks; the ✪ **Burlington Hotel,** Upper Leeson Street (☎ 660-5222), IR£33 ($52.80) and IR£19 ($30.40). You must book ahead, which can be done directly with the hotels or through the tourist office.

GrayLine Tours Ireland, 3 Clanwilliam Terrace, Grand Canal Quay, Dublin 2, offers a **Nightlife Tour** that's a handy way to take in cabaret. Book through their desk at the tourist office, 14 O'Connell St. (☎ 874-4466, 878-7981, 661-2325, or 661-9666). They'll pick you up and deliver you back to your hotel. Prices run IR£15 to IR£30.90 ($24–$49.44).

DANCE VENUES

Dancing is the national pastime among Ireland's youth. Although Dublin's discos and nightspots are constantly changing, you'll always find a cluster along Lower Leeson Street (sometimes called "The Strip"), with admission charges of about IR£5 ($8) weeknights and IR£10 ($16) weekends. Some are fully licensed, others sell wine only.

Probably the best jazz in Dublin can be found Sunday evenings, when Paddy Cole and his All Stars are in session at the **Harcourt Hotel,** 60 Harcourt St. (☎ 478-3677); **Bad Bob's Backstage Bar,** 35–37 East Essex St. (☎ 677-5482) features country music every night of the week; and it's rock at the **Rock Garden,** Crown Alley (☎ 679-9773).

THE PUB SCENE

Dublin pubs are their own special kind of entertainment. It makes no difference if you wander into one known for its conversation (craic), its music, or its pint (actually, there probably isn't a pub in Dublin that won't tell you they "pull the best pint in the city"). My Irish friends agree that the best possible beginning and/or end to any Dublin evening is in one or more of the city's pubs.

If you're planning on one of the famous "pub crawls," however, better gear up your strongest will to move from one to another. Chances are very slim that you'll be able to walk out of the first one you enter, and very good that you'll settle in with the first pint as a newly appointed "regular," if only for that night.

With more than 1,000 pubs to choose from, every Dubliner you ask will come up with a different favorite (or list of favorites), and there probably won't be a clunker in the lot. The problem is to be selective, and in the section below I'll share with you the ones I've found most interesting. Whatever you do, however, don't confine yourself to my list. Pop into the nearest establishment anywhere in the city when you're overcome with a terrible thirst, and you'll likely come home raving about your own list of favorites.

And for nondrinkers, one last word: Irish pubs are centers of sociability, where you can chat the night away just as happily with nothing stronger than soda.

Pub hours are daily from 10:30am to 11:30pm in summer, to 11pm in winter.

SOUTH OF THE LIFFEY

✪ The Brazen Head

20 Lower Bridge St. ☎ **01/677-9549.**

Licensed by Charles II in 1666, this is the oldest drinking place in Ireland. It is said to have got its name in memory of a curious redheaded beauty who stuck her head out a window during one of Dublin's public disturbances and promptly lost it to an English sword. Be that as it may, this ancient pub sits at what used to be the only place you could cross the Liffey by bridge. It's tucked away at the back of a courtyard down an arched alleyway on the west side of Bridge Street, and the entrance is easily overlooked. Low ceilings, brass lanterns, and ancient, uneven wooden floors are the same as when patriots like Wolfe Tone and Daniel O'Connell came in to drink and when Robert Emmet lodged here while plotting his ill-fated uprising (his writing desk is pointed to with pride).

Davy Byrnes

21 Duke St. ☎ **01/671-1296.**

James Joyce fans may want to look up the "moral pub" of *Ulysses* hero Leopold Bloom. It's been modernized into a tastefully sophisticated sort of cocktail lounge that one writer has called the closest thing Dublin has to a singles' bar. The 1890s wall murals are still here, and you can still get a very good pint, but there are now likely to be more orders for mixed drinks than for the old stuff. Specializes in seafood pub lunches.

✪ Doheny & Nesbitt

5 Lower Baggot St. ☎ **01/676-2945.**

This old pub looks exactly like a Dublin pub *should*—a great old wooden front with polished brass proclaiming TEA AND WINE MERCHANT, high ceilings, mirrored partitions along the bar, iron-and-marble tables, and a snug. It has been here for more than 130 years, and no doubt has always enjoyed the popularity it does today, with Dubliners of every age and inclination claiming it as their "local," including the likes of journalists, politicians, artists, architects, etc. A great place for conversation and people-watching, equally good at the front bar or in the back room.

McDaids

3 Harry St. ☎ **01/678-4395.**

If you're a Brendan Behan devotee, you'll know about this dark, high-ceilinged pub in which he claimed a corner for himself, his pint, and his typewriter. Patrick Kavanagh and Flann O'Brien are other literary lights who drank here, and the clientele is still very much concerned with the written word and those doing the writing.

✪ Mulligan's

Poolbeg St. ☎ **01/739-1249.**

Known to Dubliners as "Mulligan's in Poolbeg Street," this Dublin institution is located next door to the *Irish Press* offices ("within an ass's roar of the Liffey and the Port of Dublin," according to Dublin writer David Hanly). Since 1782 it has pulled pints for the likes of dockers, journalists, and in recent years, scores of students from nearby Trinity. Its front bar and four rooms still retain many of their original trappings, including 19th-century gas lights. As in the past, when the likes of James Joyce and other Dublin notables were regulars, there's the ring of clubby conversation, especially around 5 in the afternoon; then it settles down a bit as the evening progresses. Lots of newspaper types can be found hanging out among the students.

Neary's

1 Chatham St. ☎ **01/677-8596.**

Neary's backs up to the Gaiety Theatre's stage door, and both patrons and the crack often center around things theatrical. You'll recognize Neary's by the two black sculptured bronze arms holding light globes at its entrance. Inside, the decor is neo-Edwardian, with a pink marble bar, brass gas lamps, mirrored walls, and lots of mahogany.

✪ The Old Stand

37 Exchequer St. ☎ **01/677-0821.**

Named for the "old stand" at Lansdowne Road rugby ground, it sometimes seems that half the rugby players (past and present) have congregated in this popular pub. Celebrated athletes like Moss Kene, Phil Orr, and Ollie Campbell are familiar faces here, and the talk centers around sports 90% of the time. The clientele is made up of all ages and occupations, and at around 5 in the afternoon you'll find some of Dublin's most attractive younger set relaxing after a day of toiling in an inner-city office. It's also popular for its excellent pub grub (see Section 4, "Where to Eat," in Chapter 5).

✪ Palace Bar

21 Fleet St. ☎ **01/677-9290.**

Just off Westmoreland Street, near Trinity College and not far from the river, the Palace is a bit of Old Dublin much loved by present-day Dubs. Cartoons, old prints, and paintings depict the history of the city and the bar. Lots of journalists hang out here, and the *craic* (conversation and ambience) is always good.

✪ The Stag's Head

Dame Court. ☎ **01/679-3701.**

This is one much favored by natives. Getting there is a bit complicated, but easy if you leave College Green on the left side of Dame Street and in the middle of the second block keep your eyes glued to the sidewalk, where you'll find a stag's head set in mosaic right in the pavement. It fronts a small alleyway on the left and at its end you emerge right at this beautiful old pub that has been here since 1770. Coming from Great George's Street, turn onto Exchequer Street and keep your eyes peeled for Dame Court. An interesting mix of ages, occupations, and character types drink here in the evening; young executive types, tourists, etc., come for the excellent pub lunch (see "Where to Eat," in Chapter 5).

Toner's

139 Lower Baggot St. ☎ **01/676-3090.**

This venerable pub has been around more than a century and a half and is the hangout of art students and other cultural types. The long mahogany bar is set with partitions to provide a bit of privacy at the bar. W. B. Yeats drank here.

North of Liffey

Barry Fitzgerald's and Sean O'Casey's

90–92 Marlborough St.; 105 Marlborough St.

Frank Quinn, owner of the venerable Toner's, south of the Liffey, also has these two atmospheric pubs on the north side. Both are close to O'Connell Street and the Abbey Theatre, and both serve pub lunches and pretheater meals.

✪ Kavanagh's

1 Prospect Sq., Glasnevin.

Next to what was once the main gate to Glasnevin Cemetery, this pub has been in existence for a century and a half, and proprietor John Kavanagh is the eighth generation of his family to run the business. His fund of stories is endless, many of which concern the gravediggers who worked next door and who popped over to bang stones against the pub's wall, whereupon drinks were passed through an opening and placed on the poor man's shovel so he could get on with his work in a livelier state. (You can still see marks from those bangings on the wall outside.) This is, as it has always been, a workingman's pub—sawdust on the floor, worn wooden booths and cubbyholes, a dart game or two, and the relaxed chatter of men who have finished an honest day's work.

✪ Patrick Conway's

70 Parnell St. ☎ **01/873-2687.**

This pub is just across from the Gate Theatre and the Rotunda Maternity Hospital. You'll usually find a good mix of theater types and obstetricians welcoming friendly tourists, along with a good many Dublin regulars. Some of my best pub conversations have been at Conway's, and the pub lunches are terrific (see Section 4, "Where to Eat," in Chapter 5). This claims to be Dublin's second-oldest pub, dating from 1745, and while it has been modernized into comfort, there's still much of the traditional wood, brass, and convivial atmosphere. Take note of the back bar, a marvel of carved mahogany. For visitors who need more information, just ask Lorcan, your jovial host, or any of his friendly staff, all of whom know Dublin inside out.

✪ Ryan's

28 Parkgate St. ☎ **01/677-6097.**

This is one of Dublin's very special pubs over in the Phoenix Park area. It has been in the Ryan family since 1920 and is largely undiscovered by tourists. I've heard Dubliners claim that it's the finest pub in town, and they'll get no argument from me! It's a traditional place, with a marvelous old oak-and-mahogany central bar fixture that holds a double-faced mechanical clock. There is a superb collection of antique wall mirrors, and four antique brass lamp fittings are mounted on the bar counter. The bar, incidentally, is partitioned with ornate dividers with beveled mirrors. Many heads of state and celebrities from the movie and theater worlds regularly pass through its doors. Great atmosphere, great staff, and a good place for a pub lunch or evening meal in the fine upstairs restaurant.

Pubs with Music

Many Dublin pubs have sing-along nights from time to time, so check newspapers and "What's On in Dublin" (available from the tourist office) when you're there. Here are just a few:

✪ The Abbey Tavern

Howth. ☎ **01/839-0307.** Admission IR£32 ($51.20) for dinner and show, IR£12 ($19.20) for show and two drinks.

This is probably the best ballad club in all of Ireland, some nine miles north of Dublin on the peninsula that curves around to form the northern end of Dublin Bay. The village itself is a beauty, with cliff walks, narrow winding streets and pathways, gorgeous sea views, Howth Castle gardens with a collection of over 2,000 rhododendrons, and some very good seafood restaurants. Spend a day exploring this place—perhaps with a boat trip out to Ireland's Eye (an uninhabited island just offshore) thrown in—topped off with dinner and music at the Abbey. The cozy bar/restaurant is low-ceilinged and candlelit, and has a fireplace glowing on cool nights. Every night of the week The Barn out back is filled with music-loving souls coming to hear the Abbey Singers (instrumentalists as well as vocalists) and their host of ballads. The show is so popular that you must reserve at least a day ahead, more than that in summer months. There's good bus and train service out to Howth—just be sure you leave the Abbey in time to catch the last one back to town. Show time is 8:30pm daily.

O'Donoghue's

15 Merrion Row. ☎ **01/661-4303.**

Not strictly a "singing pub," O'Donoghue's is seldom without music of one sort or another, provided on a spontaneous basis by the bearded, bejeaned, and instrument-wielding horde who crowd in here to play traditional Irish music, bluegrass, and country-and-western on guitars, uilleann pipes, bones, spoons, etc. It's a lively, fun-filled gathering spot if you don't mind the crush. Or you could take the advice of readers Ann and Brian O'Connell, who wrote me that they found Sunday after church (12:45 to 2pm) to be less crowded and they could relax and enjoy the conversation and music without someone's elbow in their faces.

The Purty Kitchen

Old Dunleary Rd., Dun Laoghaire. ☎ **01/284-3576.**

This large, popular pub features traditional, blues, jazz, Cajun, country-and-western, folk, and rock music on varying nights of the week in the upstairs Purty Loft. Call ahead to see what type of music is on offer when you want to go.

Slattery's

Capel St. ☎ **01/872-7971.** No charge for entertainment in the bar; small charge for upstairs music lounge.

North of the Liffey, in the city proper, Slattery's features traditional Irish music nightly during the summer and on Sunday from 12:30 to 2pm. It's a session that's been going on for 25 years, and one of the city's best.

✪ The Wexford Inn

26 Wexford St. ☎ **01/751588.**

Presided over by congenial host Oliver Barden, the Wexford Inn showcases the very best in popular Irish ballads, with the Wolfe Tones, the Furey Brothers, the Dubliners, Dublin City Ramblers, and Paddy Reilly all performing there regularly.

7

The Eastern Region: Excursions from Dublin

The five counties of Dublin, Louth, Meath, Kildare, and Wicklow make up the Eastern Region. Rich in antiquities and blessed with a plethora of scenic beauty, these five counties are a sightseer's dream come true. This region, in fact, has been at the center of so much Irish history and is literally so strewn with relics that it's hard to venture far without tripping over at least one.

To the north of Dublin, the Boyne Valley runs through northern County Dublin and Counties Louth and Meath, holding the Royal Hill of Tara, the ancient burial mound at Newgrange, and monastic ruins at Mellifont and Monasterboise, as well as memories of the Battle of the Boyne, which changed the course of Irish history. For lovers of the elegant, Malahide Castle, Newbridge House, and Trim Castle will be the drawing card. South of the city, for the literary-minded there are memories of James Joyce in southern County Dublin, the awesome beauty and mystery of Glendalough, the gardens at Powerscourt and Mount Usher, and the idyllic beauty of the Meeting of the Waters near Avoca. The great mansions of Russborough in County Wicklow and Castletown in County Kildare evoke the elegance of a bygone era.

In the sections that follow, we'll take an in-depth look at each county in the region, and I can only add a word of warning: You're likely to be so beguiled by this part of Ireland that you may forget there's a mother lode of treasures just as beguiling beyond its borders—it's easy to linger too long around here, so read on before you even begin to draft an itinerary.

SEEING THE DUBLIN REGION

Whether you elect to make your base right in Dublin or opt for accommodations in a more relaxed country atmosphere, you'll be no more than an hour's drive from most of the sightseeing highlights of Counties Dublin, Wicklow, Louth, Kildare, and Meath.

INFORMATION For detailed information on sightseeing, accommodations, and any other subjects, contact the Dublin and Dublin Regional Tourist Organization, Tourist Office, St. Michael's Wharf, Dun Laoghaire (☎ 01/280-6984 or 280-6985).

GETTING THERE BY BUS & DART The following attractions can be easily reached by bus or DART from Dublin (see individual listings for details): Malahide Castle, James Joyce Museum, Glendalough, Russborough House, Castletown House, and Mount Usher.

ORGANIZED TOURS Many of the Eastern Region's attractions are reached via narrow and winding country roads, which can be a strain on drivers new to the country or this region. My best recommendation is to avail yourself of Bus Eireann's coach tours that get you there and back in comfort and provide informative narrative all along the way. See "Organized Tours" in Chapter 6 for details.

DRIVING ITINERARIES Each of these suggested itineraries can be covered in a full day of driving. However, be warned that for the first two, it will be a *long* day, and you may well want to take two days for each route.

North of Dublin Leave Dublin on the main Navan road (N3) and watch for the unclassified road signposted Tara (about 24 miles from Dublin); leaving Tara, look for the small, unclassified road signposted Trim (four miles), good for a lunch break and a tour of the castle. From Trim, head north on T26, continue through Navan on N51 (the main Navan-Drogheda road), and shortly after passing through Slane, watch for the unclassified road signposted Newgrange a few miles east of Slane. Rejoin T26 (N51) to Drogheda (nine miles), passing the obelisk marking the site of the Battle of the Boyne. From Drogheda, drive north on N1 and watch for the signposted unclassified road to Monasterboice Abbey (six miles northwest of Drogheda). From Monasterboice, follow the unclassified road to reach T25 and another unclassified road signposted Mellifont. From Mellifont, rejoin T25 to reach Drogheda. From Drogheda, take N1 south past Balbriggan to L91A and turn left to Donabate and Newbridge House. Rejoin N1 to Swords, then turn left onto L143 to Malahide. Rejoin N1 back to Dublin (nine miles).

South of Dublin The James Joyce Museum at Sandycove is best reached by DART from Dublin (see below).

From Dublin, take N11 to Bray and a few miles outside town turn right to Enniskerry; then take R755 to Roundwood and turn left on R764 to Mount Usher. Return to R755 via R763 and drive south to Laragh, turning left on R756 to Glendalough. From Glendalough, rejoin R755 and drive south to Rathdrum; Avondale is one mile south of Rathdrum. Return to Rathdrum and take R752 to Rathnew, then N11 back to Dublin (11 miles).

To visit Castletown House and Russborough House, leave Dublin via N6 to Lucan, then R403 to Celbridge (about nine miles from Dublin) and look for the Castletown House signpost. From Celbridge, return to Lucan, then take L200 to Newcastle and turn east, cross over N7 to join N81, turn south and drive to Blessington. Russborough House is two miles from Blessington (signposted). Return to Dublin via N81.

1 County Dublin

The county of Dublin is blessed with a coastline sometimes soft and gentle, sometimes wild and rugged. The majestic crescent of Dublin Bay curves from Howth on its rocky perch in the north to Dalkey and its island at the southern tip. Its scenic fishing villages and pleasure-ridden seashore resorts north and south of the bay beckon invitingly to the visitor. Then there are the mountains that form a verdant, dramatic backdrop for bustling city, sleepy villages, and that enchanting seascape.

WHAT TO SEE & DO

Shades of James Joyce, King Billy, the High Kings of ancient Ireland, saints, and monks—they all roamed the hills and valleys of the North County Dublin, and their haunts are there for you to visit.

NORTH OF DUBLIN

Malahide Castle

Malahide. ☎ **01/846-2184** or 846-2516. Castle, IR£3 ($4.80) adults, IR£2.25 ($3.60) seniors and students, IR£1.50 ($2.40) children, IR£8 ($12.80) family ticket. Railway, IR£2.50 ($4) adults, IR£2 ($3.20) seniors and students, IR£1.50 ($2.40) children, IR£7 ($11.20) family ticket. Combination ticket, castle and railway, IR£4.50 ($7.20) adults, IR£3.50 ($5.60) senior citizens and students, IR£2.50 ($4) children, IR£11 ($17.60) family ticket. Castle, Jan–Dec Mon–Fri 10am–5pm; Nov–Mar Sat, Sun, and public holidays 2–5pm; Apr–Oct Sat 11am–6pm, Sun and public holidays, 11:30am–6pm. Railway, Apr–Sept Mon–Thurs 10am–6pm, Sat 11am–6pm, Sun and public holidays 2–6pm. Open Fridays Jun, July, and Aug only. Bus: 42 from Talbot Street. Train: From Connolly Station, then a half-mile walk to the castle.

This stately castellated residence was occupied until 1976 by the descendants of Lord Talbot de Malahide, its founder in 1185. One of the many historic happenings within its walls occurred on the morning in 1690 when some 14 Talbot cousins sat down to breakfast together before leaving to fight for King James in the Battle of the Boyne, a battle in which all lost their lives. Patrick Sarsfield and Oliver Plunkett were cousins of the Talbot family and visited the castle. Set in a 268-acre demesne whose formal gardens alone are worth a visit, the castle still retains traces of the original moat, and holds a rich collection of portraits of historical Irish figures as well as many fine examples of Irish period furniture.

A separate building holds the **Fry Model Railway Museum,** the first of its kind in Ireland. On display are model trains, trams, and railroad artifacts left by the late Cyril Fry.

Newbridge House

Donabate. ☎ **01/843-6534.** IR£2.50 ($4) adults, IR£2 ($3.20) seniors and students, IR£1.50 ($2.40) children. Combination tickets available for house and farm. Apr–Oct Tues–Fri 10am–1pm and 2–5pm, Sat 11am–1pm and 2–6pm, Sun and holidays 2–6pm; Nov–Mar Sat–Sun 2–5pm. Bus: 33B from Eden Quay. Train: From Connolly Station, then a half-hour walk.

Set in a magnificent desmesne of some 120 acres, Newbridge House dates from the 1700s. Its great Red Drawing Room is just as it was when the Cobbe family was in residence here, giving you a perfect picture of how wealthy families entertained in this kind of Georgian home. To see how the "downstairs" staff kept the wheels turning, visit the kitchen and laundry, as well as the coach house and various workshops.

There's a coffee shop that remains open during lunch hours, and the Traditional Farm is open for a slight charge.

SOUTH OF DUBLIN

James Joyce Tower Museum

Sandycove. ☎ **01/280-9265** or 872-2077. IR£2 ($3.20) adults, IR£1.60 ($2.56) seniors, students, and children. IR£6 ($9.60) family ticket. Apr–Oct Mon–Sat 10am–1pm and 2–5pm; Sun and holidays 2–6pm. Other months by appointment. Bus: 8 from Eden Quay. DART: Sandycove Station.

Built during the Napoleonic Wars in the early 19th century, the Martello Tower that was home, briefly in 1904, for James Joyce and Oliver St. John Gogarty is now a museum holding such Joyce memorabilia as first editions, personal letters, and manuscripts, his walking stick and waistcoat, books, photographs, and other personal possessions. The first-floor livingroom has been reconstructed, and there are marvelous sea views from the parapet.

A Historic Pub

No matter what your itinerary, it's worth planning a visit to ✪ **Fox's Pub,** in the little village of Glencullen, County Dublin (☎ 01/295-5647). A little more than a scenic fifteen-mile drive from Dublin up into the Dublin mountains, it bills itself as the highest pub in Ireland. Fox's is steeped in tradition; Daniel O'Connell was a regular when he lived in the village. With a beamed ceiling and log fires, the rustic interior is a step back in time. Owners Tony and Geraldine McMahon have retained the sawdust on the floor and horse tack on the walls. Most of all, they keep alive an ambience that draws locals, Dubs, and visitors like yourself. The *craic,* as they say, is mighty. While I'm not here to *guarantee* you'll hear some pretty wild Irish tales, it's a pretty good bet you'll leave with stories to tell at home. There's first-rate evening entertainment (this is where Luke Kelly, of the Dubliners, recorded his famous "Raglan Road") seven days a week. In the summer, Fox's Summer Hooley nights are legendary. In truth, you could hardly plan a more perfect evening any time of year than dinner in their terrific seafood restaurant (see "Where to Eat" below) followed by a night of rousing Irish music and good fun. If you can't make it after dark, a lunch stop is only minus the crowds and the music.

WHERE TO STAY

For accommodations in Dun Laoghaire, see "Where to Stay" in Chapter 5.

Bed-and-Breakfast Accommodations North of Dublin

✪ Mrs. Margaret Farrelly

Lynfar, Kinsealy Lane, Kinsealy, Malahide, Co. Dublin. ☎ **01/846-3897.** 4 rms, 1 with bath. IR£20 ($32) single; IR£14 ($22.40) per person double; IR£2 ($3.20) extra for private bath. 25% reduction for children. (Rates include breakfast.) No credit cards. Closed Nov–Jan. Bus: 42, 32A, or 102 from the DART station.

In a location beside Malahide Castle, this is a comfortable, attractive house that's only 10 minutes from Dublin Airport and a short drive from Portmarnock's famed Velvet Strand. The house is centrally heated, guest rooms have sinks, and there is a lovely lounge for guests. There are good moderately priced restaurants in nearby Malahide village. Mrs. Farrelly is a gracious hostess and most helpful to guests.

✪ Mrs. Marie Tonkin

29 Martello Court, Portmarnock, Co. Dublin. ☎ **01/846-1500.** 3 rms, none with bath. IR£15 ($24) single; IR£14 ($22.40) per person double. No credit cards. Closed Nov–mid-Jan. Bus: 32, 32A, or 102 from the DART station.

Mrs. Tonkin has won accolades from our readers. Her warm, comfortable, and attractive home is convenient to nearby sightseeing, as well as a good base for exploring the Eastern Region north of Dublin. Dublin Airport is only 15 minutes away.

A Guesthouse North of Dublin

Sea-View Guesthouse

Strand Rd., Portmarnock, Co. Dublin. ☎ **01/846-2242.** 10 rms, all with shower. IR£22 ($35.20) single; IR£18 ($28.20) per person double. 25% reduction for children. (Rates include a full Irish breakfast.) No credit cards. Private car park. Bus: 32, 32A, or 102 from the DART station.

Maura and James Grogan's large, comfortable home is convenient to Dublin Airport and the B&I Ferry. The ten pretty bedrooms all have sinks and showers. The house is centrally heated.

SOUTH OF DUBLIN

✪ Kingswood Country House and Restaurant

Kingswood, Naas Road, Clondalkin, Dublin. ☎ **01/459-2428.** 7rms, all with bath. Mid-week IR£50 ($80) single, IR£70 ($112) per person sharing; weekends IR£40 ($64) single, IR£55 ($88) per person sharing; weekend special (2 nights B&B plus 1 dinner) IR£76 ($121.60) per person sharing. Service charge 12.5% extra. (All rates include breakfast.) ACC, AE, DC, MC, V. 20 minutes drive from Dublin, on Naas road (N7), 1.5 miles past Newlands Cross, signposted on left coming from Dublin.

A sprawling pink farmhouse, Kingswood sits behind high stone walls. Although the O'Byrne family have transformed the former home of famed Irish tenor Josef Locke into an acclaimed restaurant (see "Where to Eat") and accommodation that draws leading figures from Dublin, the ambience here is anything *but* stuffy and formal. The staff's friendliness is a hallmark of the place. The ground floor is occupied by connected dining rooms and lounges. The upstairs guest rooms are spacious and individually decorated in country house style. Surprisingly for a house of this size, there's 24-hour room service.

WHERE TO EAT

MALAHIDE, NORTH OF DUBLIN

Eastern Tandoori

1 New Street, Malahide, Co. Dublin. ☎ **01/845-4154.** Average lunch IR£10 ($16); average 3-course dinner IR£20 ($32); set meals IR£15–IR£19 ($24–$30.40). AE, MC, DC, V.

It would be hard to be more authentically Indian—in decor, staff, and cuisine—than this upstairs restaurant overlooking the marina. You can choose from no fewer than four set-price selections, as well as an extensive à la carte menu. The degree of spiciness is up to you—from mild to burn-your-mouth. The wine list is good but expensive; opt for their Cobra Indian beer, a perfect accompaniment and less pricey.

✪ Mullach Cottage

4 Church Rd., Malahide, Co. Dublin. ☎ **01/845-1346.** Main courses IR£4–IR£10 ($6.40–$16); set dinner IR£15 ($24); sandwiches and snacks IR£2–IR£5 ($3.20–$8). MC, V. Daily 9am–11pm. Bus: 42 from Talbot St. Train: From Connolly Station. SEAFOOD/STEAK/VEGETARIAN/SANDWICHES.

Set in a traditional two-story house, this is one of Malahide's oldest eateries and has won several prestigious awards. The home cooking here is superb, and readers have especially praised their traditional Irish stew and seafood Mornay. Service is both friendly and professional.

✪ Roches Bistro

12 New St., Malahide, Co. Dublin. ☎ **01/845-2777.** Lunch main courses IR£5–IR£12 ($8–$19.20); set lunch IR£11 ($17.60); dinner main courses IR£10.50–IR£15 ($16.80–$24); set dinner IR£20 ($32). ACC, AE, MC, V. Tues–Sat noon–2:30pm; Thurs–Sat 7–10:30pm. Closed 2 weeks after Christmas, and public holidays. Bus: 32, 32A, or 102. FRENCH.

Excursions from Dublin: The East Coast

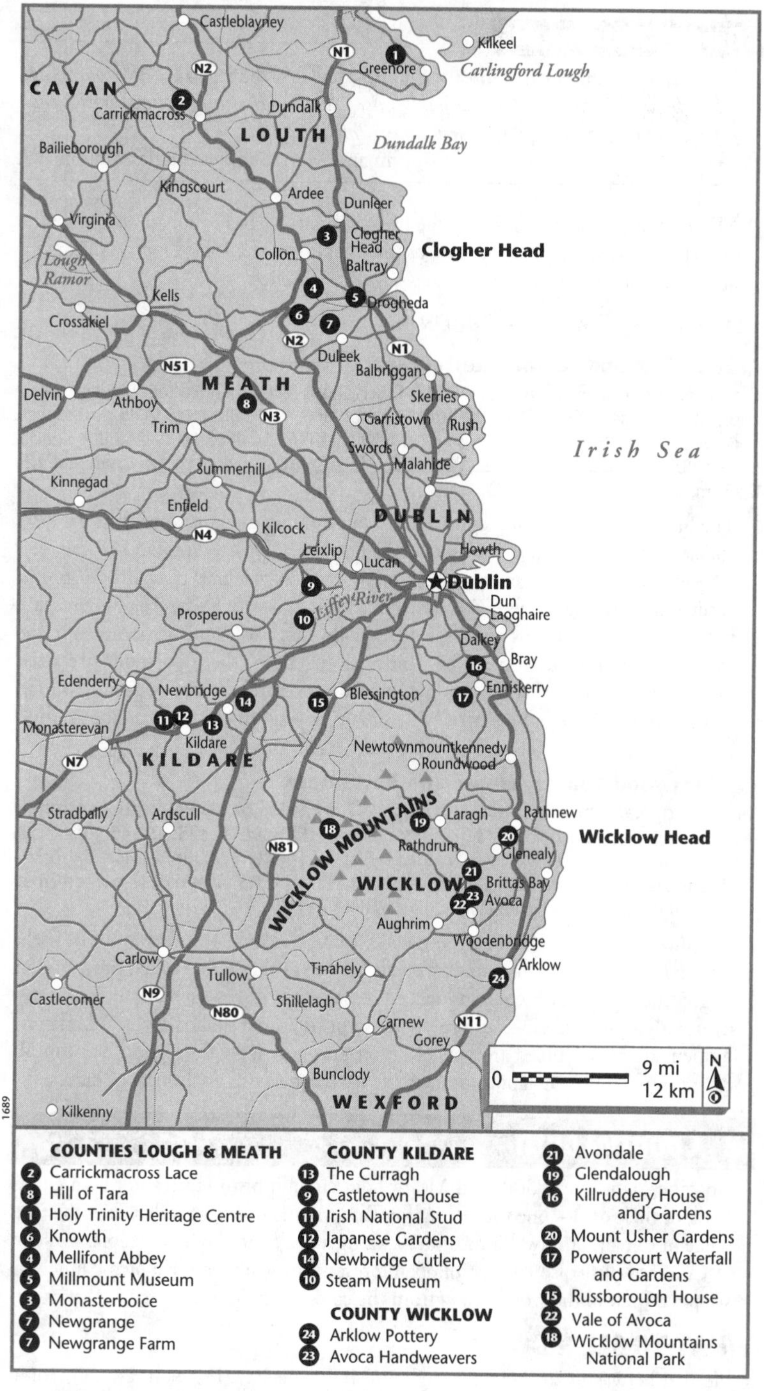

Readers Recommend

Liscara, Malahide Road, Kinsealy, Dublin 17. ☎ 01/848-3751. *"After our weary, all-night flight from New York, we found Liscara with its charming hostess Jane Kiernan a haven of rest and comfort while we overcame jet lag."*

—John and Mary Sumner, Fairfax Station, VA

This cozy little bistro serves only the freshest produce, beautifully prepared by the owner and his sister. Seafood stars on the menu (try the John Dory with tomato and chive sauce), which also includes vegetarian dishes.

GLENCULLEN, SOUTH OF DUBLIN

✪ Fox's Pub and Seafood Restaurant

Glencullen, Co. Dublin. ☎ **01/295-5647.** Reservations recommended for dinner on weekends. Main courses IR£9–IR£15 ($14.40–$24); set dinner IR£18–IR£25 ($28.80–$40); lunch selections under IR£6 ($9.60); soups and sandwiches IR£2.50–IR£5.50 ($4–$8.80); special coffees IR£2.75–IR£3.30 ($4.40–$5.28). ACC, AE, DC, MC, V. Mon–Fri 12–10pm, Sat 12–8:45pm, Sun 4–10pm. SEAFOOD.

The highest accolade I can bestow on this outstanding eatery is to say that the food and service are as outstanding as its ambience (see "What to See and Do," above). The menu is extensive and varied. For my money, the crab claws tossed in hot garlic butter and garnished with salad, washed down with a glass of Guinness, are the kind of lunch dreams are made of. Equally good, wild mussels steamed in the shell are a house specialty. When indecision sets in, there's a moderate-sized Hungry Fisherman's Platter. For a whopping appetite, the eye-popping Seafood Lovers Shellfish Delight platter will satisfy. Come to think of it, for seafood lovers, there simply *isn't* a bad choice in the lot.

✪ Kingswood Country House and Restaurant

Kingswood, Naas Road, Clondalkin, Dublin. ☎ **01/459-2428.** Reservations strongly recommended. Set lunch IR£13 ($20.80); set dinner IR£21–IR£29 ($33.60–$46.40). 12.5% service charge. ACC, AE, DC, MC, V. Mon–Fri and Sun 12:30–2:30pm, Mon–Sat 6:30–10:30pm. 20 minute drive from Dublin, on Naas road (N7), 1.5 miles past Newlands Cross, signposted on left coming from Dublin. IRISH/FRENCH/FISH.

Elegance in this lovely country house (see "Where to Stay") extends from its firelit dining rooms to the polished yet friendly service to the sophisticated presentation of gourmet dishes. A French influence is reflected in dishes such as sautéed lamb's liver with a madeira sauce and roast sirloin of beef on a shallot sauce. A basket of homemade brown bread and lots of butter grace the table throughout your meal. Save room for their delicious homemade ice creams with a selection of sauces.

2 County Louth

Together, Counties Louth and Meath hold enough historic sites to fill an entire book of their own—one the setting for Tara's home of Irish royalty, the other the scene of one of Cromwell's most devastating assaults on the Irish people.

County Louth also has restful open forest areas, which invite a picnic lunch or simply a walk in the woods away from the cares of civilization.

WHAT TO SEE & DO

Nestled between Carlingford Lough and Dundalk Bay, the picturesque **Cooley Peninsula** is the scenic setting for many of Ireland's myths and legends. Well known to Cuchulainn, Queen Maeve, and the great giant Finn McCool, its mountains, rivers, and woodlands cast a spell on today's visitors as potent as in those long-ago days. This area of County Louth is well worth a day or two of just poking around. Wander through the little medieval town of **Carlingford,** with its narrow streets and the brooding castle ruins overlooking the water from its lofty perch. Come in May and take part in the **Great Leprechaun Hunt,** when forty leprechauns are concealed on Carlingford Mountain, with prizes for the finder of each one. If you land here in July, join in the fun-filled **Medieval Festival,** when those tiny streets are filled with all sorts of goings-on, and locals break out in colorful period costumes. For an outstanding **walking tour,** call Harry Jordan (☎ 73223), whose narration will bring this quaint old town to vivid life.

In **Dundalk,** before heading off on foot, go by the **Heritage Centre** on Jocelyn Street and pick up information on **St. Patrick's Cathedral,** the striking **Church of the Redeemer,** and (to cater to your vices) tours of the **P. J. Carroll cigarette factory** (☎ 042/36501) and **Harp Lager Brewery** (☎ 042/34793). Then rest your weary feet with a soul-restoring stop at the Old World–style **Windsor Pub** on Dublin Street (where you can also get a terrific pub lunch).

It was near the ancient town of **Ardee,** on the banks of the River Dee, that Cuchulainn and Ferdiad fought hand-to-hand for four days in the Cattle Raid of Cooley, subject of one of Ireland's best-known epics. Look for the main street's two medieval castles, **Kings Castle** and **Hatch Castle,** as well as the majestically rebuilt (in 1693) St. **Mary's Abbey,** which was burned in 1315 by Edward Bruce, while sheltering the men, women, and children of the town.

✪ Mellifont Abbey ("The Big Monastery")

IR£1 ($1.60) for adults; 75p ($1.20) for seniors; 50p (80¢) for children. Daily 10am–5pm. Drive six miles west of Drogheda on a signposted unclassified road off T25.

To walk in the footsteps of monks who founded Ireland's first Cistercian monastery here on the banks of the Mattock River back in 1142 is to drink in the peacefulness of a setting that invites meditation. The Chapter House and ruins of the cloister still remain from the structures built in the 13th century, but the foundations alone are left of the original building.

✪ Muiredach's Cross

Monasterboice. Admission free. Drive six miles northwest of Drogheda on a signposted unclassified road off N1.

Standing a majestic 17 feet above this site, which once held a large monastic community and now consists of a small churchyard and round tower, this 10th-century cross is universally recognized as the finest example of the sculptured high crosses. The unknown master carver who created its many figures and ornamental designs used one piece of stone for this memorial to Muiredach, about whom we know only that he ordered the inscription on the shaft that asks for prayers on his behalf. Those dents in the base were left by immigrants who took chips of the cross with them as they crossed the seas to new homes.

Townley Hall (Halla de Túinlé)

Open Forest. Admission free. Drive 3½ miles northwest of Drogheda on N51 (T26) and turn right at the signpost for 1 mile.

There are forest walks, nature trails, and picnic sites in this open forest, which lies just off the Boyne Valley Road to Navan and encompasses the Battle of the Boyne site. A lovely respite from the road.

WHERE TO STAY

Aisling House

Baltray, Drogheda, Co. Louth. ☎ **041/22376.** 4 rms, 3 with bath. TV. IR£14 ($22.40) per person without bath; IR£16 ($25.60) per person with bath. 20% reduction for children under 10. High tea, IR£11 ($15.95). No credit cards.

Convenient to Dublin (it's 2 1/2 miles from Drogheda on the Bus Eireann Dublin-Drogheda route) and overlooking the Boyne River, this nice modern bungalow is the home of Mrs. Josephine McGinley. The house is centrally heated and just 100 yards from a good golf course and restaurant. There are five attractive bedrooms, three of which have private shower, and they all have sinks and color TVs.

Carraig Mor

Blakestown, Ardee, Co. Louth. ☎ **041/53513.** 5 rms, 3 with bath. IR£19 ($30.40) single; IR£14 ($22.40) per person sharing without bath, IR£15 ($24) per person sharing with bath. 50% reduction for children under 12. (Rates include breakfast.) No credit cards. Closed Christmas.

The guestrooms in Mrs. Sheila Magennis' attractive modern bungalow have large, multi-paned windows that overlook fields and gardens. The dining room is especially light and airy. The house is nicely decorated, and there's central heating. Mrs. Magennis is not only charming but especially helpful to guests who are touring the area. It's 1 mile from Ardee on N2, the Dublin/Donegal/Derry road. Ample parking.

Delamare

Ballyoonan, Omeath, Co. Louth. ☎ **042/75101.** 3 rms, all with bath. IR£15 ($24) per person. 50% reduction for children under 10. (Rates include breakfast.) No credit cards. Private car park. Closed Nov–Mar.

Mrs. Eileen McGeown is the charming hostess in this modern bungalow overlooking Carlingford Lough and the Mourne mountains in a lovely rural area. The house is set in beautiful surroundings and is very peaceful, and—a blessing for those who travel on their own—Mrs. McGeown warmly welcomes singles. It's three miles from Carlingford and half a mile from Omeath on the Carlingford-Omeath road, opposite Calvary Shrine.

✪ Harbour Villa

Mornington Rd., Drogheda, Co. Louth. ☎ **041/37441.** 4 rms, none with bath. IR£19 ($30.40) single; IR£15 ($24) per person sharing. (Rates include breakfast.) No credit cards. Private parking.

An ideal base for exploring the Eastern Region north of Dublin and convenient to Dublin Airport, Harbour Villa is a beautiful two-story home in its own grounds right on the River Boyne one mile from Drogheda, off the main Dublin road. There's a pretty sun lounge and private tennis courts. One reader heaped laurels on the Dwyers and their home, saying they were "among the most interesting and helpful people that we met in a country full of exceptionally interesting and helpful people. They were available and concerned but our privacy was never endangered for one moment. Mrs. Dwyer's food (at breakfast and especially at high tea) was the best we were served in Ireland. The house is attractively furnished, immaculately clean, set in beautifully landscaped grounds on the tidal estuary of the Boyne." I couldn't have said it better!

✪ Jordan's Town House

Newry Street, Carlingford, Co. Louth. ☎/Fax **042/73223.** 4 rms, all with bath. TV TEL. IR£30 ($48) per person sharing; IR£5 ($8) single supplement. (Rates include breakfast.) ACC, AE, MC, V.

Harry and Marian Jordan have converted this lovely 1800s stone building from its former life as a warehouse into a warm, luxurious town house. Each of the beautifully furnished (antique pine, pastel colors) guestrooms looks out to Carlingford Harbour. (See the listing for its restaurant in "Where to Eat," below.)

Krakow

190 Ard Easmulnn, Dundalk, Co. Louth. ☎ **042/37535.** 4 rms, all with bath. IR£19–IR£20 ($30.40–$32) single; IR£14–IR£15.50 ($22.40–$24.80) per person sharing. Dinner IR£11 ($17.60). 25% reduction for children under 12. (Rates include breakfast.) No credit cards.

This modern, conveniently located town house is the home of Marian and Larry Witherow, who love to share their knowledge of the area with guests. Guestrooms, all on the ground floor, include two single rooms, which can be a rarity and a real find for those traveling alone. The house has central heating, and there's parking.

✪ Lynolan

Mullaharlin Road, Heynestown, Dundalk, Co. Louth. ☎ **042/36553.** 6 rms, 5 with bath. IR£19–IR£20 ($30.40–$32) single; IR£14–IR£15.50 ($22.40–$24.80) per person sharing. Dinner IR£11 ($17.60). 50% reduction for children. (Rates include breakfast.) No credit cards. Closed Christmas.

If you have a problem with stairs, you'll be glad to know that Mrs. Evelyn Carolan's lovely two-story house has two guestrooms on the ground floor. An additional four are upstairs. Set back from the road, with a stone fountain and terrace out front, the house looks out onto surrounding green fields. Flower beds border large back garden. The peaceful rural setting is a bonus for travelers, yet Dundalk is only 2 miles away. Central heating and plenty of parking space. Located on the Dublin/Belfast road (N1)—turn at Dundalk Garden Centre, south of Dundalk, and drive one mile.

✪ Rosemount

Dublin Road, Dundalk, Co. Louth. ☎ **042/35878.** 6 rms, 4 with bath. IR£16.50–IR£18.50 ($26.40–$29.60) single; IR£14.50–IR£16.50 ($22.40–$26.40) per person sharing. 50% reduction for children under 12. (Rates include breakfast.) No credit cards.

Maisie and John Meehan are the gracious hosts in this modern house on the outskirts of town. Maisie is the very soul of Irish hospitality, and John is a fount of information on this part of Ireland. The pleasant guestrooms are attractively furnished, and the breakfast room looks out to a back garden. There's central heating and a car park, and a golf course nearby.

WHERE TO EAT

✪ The Brake

Main Street on Seafront, Blackrock, Co. Louth. ☎ **042/21393.** Main courses IR£6–IR£12 ($9.60–$19.20); salads IR£4.50–IR£7 ($7.20–$11.20); sandwiches IR£2 ($3.20). ACC, MC, V. Mon–Sat 6:30–10:30pm; Sun 6:30–9:30pm. SEAFOOD/STEAKS/CHICKEN/SALADS/SANDWICHES.

This appealing, rustic-style restaurant has been run by the Smyth family for nearly 25 years. Directly on the seafront, its stone-walled interior is a delightful blend of old prints, lamps, jugs, old posters, and artifacts like the bellows that the Irish call a "wind machine." Service is as warm as the glowing open fireplace. The menu offers something for all tastes and budgets. Two of my personal favorites are the deep-fried scampi and the chicken Kiev.

The Gables House and Restaurant

Dundalk Rd., Ardee, Co. Louth. ☎ **041/53789.** Average dinner IR£20 ($32). 10% service charge. AE, MC, V. Tues–Sat 7–10pm. Closed first two weeks in June, Christmas, and public holidays. SEAFOOD/GAME/TRADITIONAL.

Located north of Drogheda, just off the N2, the Gables is a fully licensed restaurant much beloved in these parts. There's a friendly, relaxed air about the place, and the menu features only the freshest ingredients, whether it be fish from nearby waters or game in season. Soups and desserts are outstanding, and portions are more than ample.

✪ Jordans Town House Restaurant

Newry Street, Carlingford, Co. Louth. ☎ **042/73223.** Set lunch IR£13 ($20.80); Sun lunch IR£15 ($24); set dinner IR£22 ($35.20); à la carte menu from IR£10 ($16). ACC, AE, MC, V. Daily 12:30–2pm and 6:30–10pm. SEAFOOD/LAMB/BEEF/CHICKEN.

In the heart of this medieval village, midway between Dublin and Belfast, this outstanding restaurant (winner of many national awards) adjoins Jordan's Town House (see "Where to Stay," above in this chapter). Harry and Marian Jordan insist on the freshest ingredients and feature organically grown vegetables. Oven-roasted loin of Carlingford lamb coated in herbs and served in a port sauce and the traditional crubeen (boned pigs' trotter) stuffed with bacon and served with a rich sauce are typical of the menu.

✪ McKevitt's Village Hotel

Market Square, Darlingford, Co. Louth. ☎ **042/73116.** Lunch IR£3.50–IR£5.50 ($5.60–$8.80); set dinner IR£18 ($28.80); Sun lunch IR£11 ($17.60). ACC, MC, V. Daily 12:30–2:15pm and 5:30–9pm. SEAFOOD/TRADITIONAL.

Oysters and other shellfish star on the menu of this bright, cheerful eatery—I especially like the oysters in Guinness. Other locally produced ingredients assure freshness in all the menu items. The service is both friendly and efficient.

3 County Meath

For centuries there was a Royal Meath province, which included Westmeath, ruled by pagan and early Christian kings. Traces of those ancient rulers, as well as the prehistoric Bronze Age, are scattered over the face of modern-day County Meath.

WHAT TO SEE & DO

✪ Hill of Tara

☎ **046/25903.** IR£1 ($1.60) adults, 70p ($1.12) seniors, 40p (64¢) students and children. Summer, daily 9:30am–6:30pm; winter, daily 9:30am–5pm. Bus: 20, 40, or 43 from Dublin or Navan; it's six miles South of Navan, off N3.

From the time that pagans worshipped here, the Hill of Tara has figured in Irish history and legend. It was here that the High Kings were seated, and there's a rock that legend says roared when a new king was found to be acceptable—its silence spelled a candidate's doom. Burial mounds here go back some 4,000 years, and there are earthworks and low walls of earth left from a fortification of the Bronze Age. All else of Tara's regal trappings must be left to your imagination as you view this low hillside with the mind's eye and feel the mystical presence of pagan priests and ancient royalty. It's a magical place—the setting for many of Finn McCool's exploits, the home of Grainne when she deserted Finn and fled with Diarmaid, and the very center of religious and political power until the coming of Christianity—and your imagination is bound to take wings as you walk the grassy hills and see the gentle mounds that outline once-majestic palaces and banqueting halls. Don't miss the audio-visual show in the Visitor Centre.

✪ Newgrange, or Brugh Na Boinne (Palace of the Boyne)

☎ **041/24488.** IR£2 ($3.20) adults, IR£1 ($1.60) students and children, IR£1.50 ($2.40) seniors, IR£ 5 ($8) family ticket. May–Sept daily 10am–7pm; Oct–Apr daily 10am–dusk. Drive 7 miles west of Drogheda, just off N51.

Newgrange and the burial mounds of Knowth and Dowth are the most striking of some 30 passage graves in this vicinity. Of those three, Newgrange is easily the most impressive. Even older than the burial mounds at Tara, Newgrange was probably built by the first farmers who came to Ireland from the Continent some 5,000 years ago. We know almost nothing about them, or what the ornamental spirals and other decorations at this impressive burial mound symbolized. We don't even know for whom the structure was built, whether holy men, chieftains, or kings. What we do know is that they were skilled builders, for the corbeled roof above the burial chamber has kept out the dampness of 50 centuries, and the 62-foot-long passage still serves quite well as an entry to the chamber, the stone at its entrance an enduring testament to prehistoric craftsmanship. Archeologists are constantly carrying out research at Newgrange in an effort to unravel such mysteries as the reason an opening above the doorway is so placed that the sun's rays reach the burial chamber only on the shortest day of the year, December 21, and then for exactly 17 minutes!

✪ Newgrange Farm

Slane. ☎ **041/24119.** IR£2 ($3.20) per person, IR£8 ($12.80) family ticket. Apr–Sept, daily tours as requested.

Just 100 yards from the Tourist Offices and entrance to Newgrange, this traditional 333-acre working farm grows barley, wheat, and other grains. But it is the farmyard, bustling with beef cows, bulls, heifers, goats, pigs, ponies, a horse, Hampshire Downs sheep (they're the ones that have a "teddy-bear" coat—children love them), rabbits, dogs, and poultry that are the main attraction for visitors. One of the farmers will lead you through this thriving menagerie, with a running commentary on just how the farm works. The coffee shop serves home baking. Owned and operated by the Redhouse family, the farm is a delightful experience for all ages.

Trim Castle

Trim. Admission free. Daily 10am–6pm. Bus: 44 or 45 from Dublin; it's nine miles southwest of Navan on T26.

Ireland's largest Anglo-Irish castle, built by Hugh de Lacy in 1172, is in this pretty little town. From its tall, gray central tower you can see across the river to ruins of town walls dating from the 14th century. The site of an abbey, which once held a statue of the Virgin credited with miracles, is marked by what is called locally the Yellow Steeple. The castle's drawbridge tower once hosted England's Prince Hal, and its grounds have yielded up a mass grave of skeletons minus their heads who may have been the unfortunate (and unsuccessful) defenders of the stronghold against the forces of Cromwell.

WHERE TO STAY

Close enough to Dublin for frequent trips into the city, and centrally located for exploring the northern part of the Eastern Region, County Meath is an ideal base for those who prefer accommodations outside the city.

BED-AND-BREAKFASTS

Aisling

Baltrasna, Ashbourne, Co. Meath. ☎ **01/835-0359** or 835-1135. 9 rms, 6 with bath. IR£19–IR£22 ($30.40–$35.20) single; IR£15–IR£18 ($24–$28.80) per person sharing. (Rates include breakfast.) No credit cards.

Evelyn and Seamus Daly preside over this modern bungalow just 9 miles north of Dublin. It's on the Dublin/Derry road, N2 (about 15 minutes from Dublin airport). In addition to the nicely appointed guestrooms, there's an inviting TV lounge, central heating, and a private car park.

Taraside House

Growtown, Dunshaughlin, Co. Meath. ☎ **01/825-9721.** 4 rms, 2 with shower. IR£15 ($24) per person. 50% reduction for children. (Rates include breakfast.) No credit cards.

Mrs. Bridie McGowan's modern bungalow is located on N3, the main Dublin-Navan road, set on two acres of landscaped gardens. There is a good restaurant nearby and the house is centrally heated. There are five bedrooms, two of which have showers, and they all have sinks.

White Lodge

Lackanash, New Road Trim, Co. Meath. ☎ **046/36549.** 4 rms, 2 with bath. TV. IR£19–IR£21 ($30.40–$33.60) single; IR£14–IR£15.50 ($22.40–$24.80) per person sharing. 20% reduction for children under 12. (Rates include breakfast.) ACC, MC, V. Closed Christmas.

The gracious hostess in this modern bungalow is Elizabeth (call her "Libby") O'Loughlin. Her guest rooms are attractive. Just 600 meters from town in a peaceful setting, the house sits back from the road, with a garden out front. Central heat and private car park.

Woodville

Enfield, Co. Meath. ☎ **0405/41113.** 4 rms, 2 with bath. IR£18–IR£20 ($28.80–$32) single; IR£15–IR£16.50 ($24–$26.40) per person sharing. 25% reduction for children under 12. (Rates include breakfast.) Dinner IR£12 ($19.20). No credit cards. Closed Christmas.

Just off the N4 motorway, Woodville is a pleasant bungalow with comfortable guest rooms and a warm, hospitable hostess. Teresa Prendergast takes pride in helping guests tour the area. In addition to the abundant sightseeing in this county, she can point you to good golf and fishing nearby. Central heating and good parking.

A FARMHOUSE

Pauline Mullan

Lennoxbrook Farm House, Kells, Co. Meath. ☎ **046/45902.** 5 rms, none with bath. IR£15 ($24) per person sharing; IR£5 ($8) single supplement. 20% reduction for children. No credit cards.

This rambling beef-and-sheep farm home 40 miles north of Dublin, three miles north of Kells on N3, has been the Mullan family home for five generations, and there's an inviting, homey air about the place. Two of the five comfortable guest rooms have bay windows, and a real showplace is the upstairs bathroom that Pauline has given a quaint country look. Dinner, of homegrown meats, is available if you book before 3pm. Lennoxbrook is an ideal "home away from home" when touring this historic area.

WHERE TO EAT

Monaghan's Lounge

Kells, Co. Meath. ☎ **046/40100.** Main courses IR£3–IR£12 ($4.80–$19.20); average lunch IR£6 ($9.60). Tourist Menu. ACC, MC, V. Daily 10:30am–2:30pm and 5–11:30pm. TRADITIONAL.

You can get just about anything from take-aways to steaks at this pub-cum-health-club in the town center. There's music on weekend nights during the summer. In addition to beef, pork, chicken, and seafood dishes, there are always vegetarian dishes on offer. The friendly, efficient staff include speakers of French, Spanish, and German. *Note:* There's also a 65-bed approved hostel here with rates of IR£5 ($8) to IR£8 ($12.80).

✪ Wellington Court Hotel

Trim, Co. Meath. ☎ **046/31516.** Main courses IR£8–IR£18 ($12.80–$28.80); fixed-price meal IR£10–IR£18 ($16–$28.80); bar lunch under IR£5 ($8). MC,V. Daily 12:30–2:30pm and 6:30–9:30pm. Closed Good Friday, Christmas Day. TRADITIONAL/IRISH.

In this charming, small hotel dining room, beef, pork, chicken, and fish are standards, and dishes such as pork en croûte are excellent, as is the roast lamb. Traditional Irish dishes, such as Irish stew or boiled ham, are also on offer. Portions are *huge,* but if you can save room, try the apple tart. The Tourist Menu is available May through September. Children are welcomed here, good news for harried parents.

4 County Kildare

Kildare's flat fields and bogs have seen historic figures come and go, and today hold not only stables that have bred racehorses of international fame but also the world-famous Curragh racecourse, where modern-day sports-world history is written by homegrown champions of the sport.

WHAT TO SEE & DO

While a visit to most of Kildare's great stud farms can only be arranged by invitation, racing fans can see the stables' proud offspring in action when there's a scheduled meet. Sightseers will delight in Ireland's largest country house.

A delightful and relaxing break from holiday rushing around is a **barge trip** along the Grand Canal. Contact **Robertstown Barge Trips,** Robertstown Canal Hotel, Robertstown, Co. Kildare; ☎ 045/70005 for schedules between May and September. Take 15 minutes to climb to the summit of the legendary **Hill of Allen** (near Allenwood) for fantastic views over the flat **Bog of Allen,** which begins just outside Newbridge and extends for miles. Finn McCool and the Fianna often roamed these parts and climbed the Hill of Allen. Go by **Kes Print Ltd.,** Whitechurch, Straffan, Co. Kildare (☎ 01/627-2256) to pick up reasonably priced gifts that range from Celtic tweed hangings to tweed scarves to other Celtic design items.

Stop by the **Kildare Tourist Office,** Market House, Kildare Town (☎ 0507/31859) for information on a host of other activities and attractions in the county.

Castletown House

Celbridge. ☎ **628-8252** for information. IR£2.50 ($4) adults, IR£2 ($3.20) seniors and students, IR£1 ($1.60) children, IR£6 ($9.60) family ticket. Apr–Sept Mon–Fri

10am–6pm, Sat 11am–6pm, Sun and holidays 2–6pm; Oct Mon–Fri 10am–5pm, Sun and holidays 2–5pm; Nov–Mar Sun and holidays 2–5pm.

About 13 miles from Dublin on N4, the Galway road (gates at end of main street in Celbridge), this is Ireland's largest classical country home, and was designed in the Palladian style by the celebrated Italian architect Alessandro Galilei for the Speaker of the Irish House of Commons, William Conolly; construction began in 1722. It's an imposing structure from the outside, approached via a long, tree-lined avenue. The interior, however, holds truly magnificent plasterwork, and there's a splendid Long Gallery painted in the Pompeian manner and lighted by Venetian chandeliers. Also of note are the Red Drawing Room and Print Room. Frequent social and cultural functions in this elegant setting draw large numbers from Dublin.

Irish National Stud & Japanese Gardens

Tully, Kildare, Co. Kildare. ☎ **045/21617.** IR£4 ($6.40) adults; IR£3 ($4.80) seniors and students; IR£2 ($3.20) children; IR£10 ($16) family rate. Open mid-Feb–Oct, daily 9:30am–6pm.

Stroll around Ireland's most famous breeding grounds off N7 (Dublin/Limerick road), and you'll understand why Irish horses are so prized around the world. You're welcome to visit the stalls (some 288 of them) and watch the horses being groomed and exercised. The Horse Museum traces the history of the horse from prehistoric times to the present day.

The Japanese garden, whose design symbolizes the lifespan of man, took four years to lay out (1906–1910). Today, it's considered Europe's finest Oriental garden. The Orient also stars in the Japanese-style visitor center, which houses a restaurant and a craft shop.

Sports and Recreation

✪ The Curragh Racecourse

☎ **045/41205.** Admission varies with the race; IR£6–IR£12 ($9.60–$19.20). On scheduled dates throughout the year. Bus and Train: Special buses depart Busaras and there are trains from Heuston Station on race days; it's seven miles northwest of Naas, one mile from Newbridge, just off N7.

The headquarters of Irish horseracing today is on that vast County Kildare plain known as The Curragh. Since ancient times, this has been a leading venue for the sport, and nearly all of Ireland's classic races are held here. If a meet is on during your visit, and if you're a fancier of horseflesh par excellence, you won't want to miss a visit to The Curragh. The Budweiser Irish Derby in late June is Ireland's top sporting (and social) event.

Curragh Golf Course

☎ **045/41238.**

Just east of the celebrated racecourse, this is an excellent 18-hole golf course, very popular with the locals and Dubliners. If you want to get in a game, reserve your tee-off time well in advance.

WHERE TO STAY

Bed-and-Breakfast

Hillview House

Prosperous, Naas, Co. Kildare. ☎ **045/68252.** 10 rms, 8 with bath. IR£19–IR£21 ($30.40–$33.60) single; IR£14.50–IR£16.50 ($23.20–$26.40) per person sharing; 25% reduction for children under 10. (Rates include breakfast.) High tea IR£8.50 ($13.60) extra; dinner, IR£12 ($19.20). No credit cards. Large private car park.

Joe and Sheila O'Brien are the friendly hosts in this large, modern house 22 miles south of Dublin, a 10-minute drive from N7. There's a comfortable lounge and a relaxed atmosphere, and a fixed-price dinner is available for guests at 6 o'clock. The O'Briens can provide baby-sitting, and the house is centrally heated.

A FARMHOUSE

Barberstown House

Straffan, Co. Kildare. ☎ **01/627-4007.** 4 rms, all with bath. IR£20 ($32) per person sharing; IR£5 ($8) single supplement. 50% reduction for children under 12. (Rates include breakfast.) ACC, MC, V. Closed Christmas.

John and Marie Ryan are as gracious as their 18th-century stone farmhouse itself. Their spacious guest rooms are furnished with antiques and look out onto lawns, gardens, and old stone farm outbuildings. Elegance without pretension reigns here. The Ryans are happy to help their guests with sightseeing information and activities such as horseracing, golfing, and horseback riding.

WHERE TO EAT

✪ O'Brien's Hillview House

Prosperous, Naas. ☎ **045/68252.** Reservations recommended. High tea IR£8 ($12.80); fixed-price dinner IR£12 ($19.20); à la carte IR£11 ($17.60). No credit cards. Daily 5:30–6:30pm. Large car park. TRADITIONAL.

Good traditional dishes of beef, lamb, pork, chicken, and fish appear on the menu at this family-run eatery 22 miles south of Dublin, a 10-minute drive from N7. For a fuller description, see "Where to Stay," above.

✪ Curryhills House

Prosperous, Naas. ☎ **045/68150.** Reservations recommended. Lunch IR£10.50–IR£12 ($16–$19.20); set dinner IR£19 ($30.40); Tourist Menu (7–11pm). ACC, AE, MC, V. Mon–Sat 12:30–2pm and 7–11pm. Closed Good Friday, Dec 24–31. TRADITIONAL/IRISH.

Set in a Georgian-style country house 21 miles from Dublin on N7, the dining room at Curryhills is the pride and joy of owner/managers Bridie and Bill Travers. Decor is Tudor, and the cuisine features gourmet dishes prepared from local, fresh ingredients. On Friday there's traditional Irish music, and on Saturday you're invited to an old-fashioned sing-along. The Traverses also have luxury guest rooms.

Manor Inn

Main Street, Naas, Co. Kildare. ☎ **045/97471.** Average meal IR£13–IR£15 ($20.80–$24). AE, DC, MC, V. Daily 12:30–2:30pm and 6–10pm. FISH/STEAKS/PASTA/GRILLS.

Right in the center of Naas, this pub-style eatery is convenient to the Curragh Racecourse. Along with fish and steaks, there's a good selection of pastas (including a vegetarian pasta bake) and grills. House specials range from tiger steak (with cajun spices) to chicken cordon bleu to rack of lamb. Children's menu and lunchtime snack menu.

✪ Moyglare Manor Country House and Restaurant

Maynooth. ☎ **01/628-6351.** Reservations required. Fixed-price meal IR£24 ($38.40). Service charge 12½%. ACC, AE, DC, V. Mon–Fri 12:30–2:15pm; daily 7–9:30pm. Closed Good Friday, Dec 23–26. INTERNATIONAL.

The dining room is the epitome of elegance, with tall, draped windows, oil paintings, and the sheen of well-polished antique furniture. As for the menu, you might try the roast quail in burgundy sauce, pan-fried brill St. Germain, or simply a very good steak. Whatever your choice, the accompanying vegetables are sure to be fresh from the garden. Exceptionally good wine list.

✪ Silken Thomas

The Square, Kildare Town, Co. Kildare. ☎ **045/22232.** Average lunch IR£7 ($11.20); average dinner IR£12 ($19.20). AE, MC, V. Daily 12:30–2:30pm and 6–10pm. BEEF/LAMB/FISH.

If you're traveling the Dublin/Cork motorway, you can't miss this large, pink restaurant in the town center of Kildare. Set on the grounds of a Norman castle keep, Silken Thomas has a Victorian look to it, with lots of wood and leaded glass. Monkfish Provençale, Gaelic steak, and supreme of chicken are among the house specialties.

✪ Tonlegee House

Athy. ☎ **0507/31473.** Reservations recommended. Five-course fixed-price dinner IR£20–IR£23 ($32–$36.80). MC, V. Mon–Sat 7:30–10:30pm. INTERNATIONAL.

Marjorie and Mark Molloy fell in love with this lovely old country house 13 miles southwest of Naas on N78, and in 1990, after extensive renovations, they opened a restaurant that has garnered accolades. The relaxing dining room, with its chocolate-colored walls, chintz curtains, and soft lighting is the perfect setting for a cuisine that can only be described as gourmet. Mark, in fact, has broad experience as a chef in London and in one of Dublin's most prestigious restaurants, and that experience and expertise show up on the menu. Worthy of note are the roast rack of lamb with a crépinette of vegetables and a shallot sauce, the escalope of salmon with mussels and tarragon sauce, and the breast of Barbarie duck with a brandade of duck leg. Desserts include thin apple tart with cinnamon cream and chocolate-and-almond Marjolaine (a creamy blend of chocolate, cream, and almonds). Highly recommended. *Note:* This is also an elegant guest house, with rates of IR£35 to IR£55 ($56–$88).

5 County Wicklow

Wicklow glows with the greens and blues of a landscape often dubbed the "Garden of Ireland." Midlands East Tourism provides a year-round Tourist Information Office in the **Wicklow Gaol Visitor Centre,** Kilmantan Hill, Wicklow town (☎ 0404/69117; fax 0404/69118). Here you can obtain detailed information on the region's many attractions, activities, evening entertainment, restaurants, and accommodations.

WHAT TO SEE & DO

Powerscourt Estate and Gardens

Enniskerry. ☎ **01/286-7676.** IR£3 ($4.80) adults, IR£1.75 ($2.80) children, with a small additional charge for the waterfall. Mar–Oct, gardens daily 9:30am–5:30pm. Waterfall (reached by its own gate, four miles from Enniskerry) summer, daily 9:30am–7pm; winter, daily 10:30am–dusk.

The O'Tooles, Lords of Glencullen, once occupied a castle on the site of Powerscourt House, an impressive 18th-century mansion of hewn granite that was gutted by fire in 1974 and is no longer open to the public. From its perch on high ground with a view of Great Sugarloaf Mountain, magnificent Japanese and Italian gardens slope downward, dotted with statuary and ornamental lakes. The 1,000 acre demesne, which includes the River Dargle, holds rare shrubs, massive rhododendrons, and a deer park. Its most noted feature, however, is the Powerscourt Waterfall, which tumbles nearly 400 feet from a clifftop and is the highest waterfall in Ireland—it's at its most magnificent after a rainy spell. Outside the fortified tower stand two cannon from the Spanish Armada. A tearoom and a giftshop featuring Irish goods are housed in a modern building at the entrance.

✪ Glendalough

☎ **0404/45325.** Admission free. Mid-Apr to mid-June Mon–Sat 10am–5pm; mid-June to mid-Sept daily 10am–7pm; mid-Sept to mid-Oct daily noon–5pm; Nov–Mar Tues–Sat 10am–1pm, Sun 2–5pm. Bus: Two buses daily from Dublin year-round, departing College of Surgeons, St. Stephen's Green, Dublin; it's seven miles east of Wicklow on T7 via Rathdrum.

"Valley of Two Lakes" is the literal translation of its name, and when St. Kevin came to this place of exquisite natural beauty, he found the solitude and spiritual atmosphere he was seeking. No visitor today can leave unaffected by that same peaceful atmosphere, which seems to cling to the hills and lakes and woods. For many years St. Kevin lived here as a hermit, sleeping sometimes in a tree, sometimes in a small cleft in the rocks. When his sanctity and wisdom began to draw disciples to his side, a great school grew up that attracted thousands of students from all over Ireland, Great Britain, and the Continent. By the time of his death in 617 at an advanced age, the school had already become recognized as a great institution of learning.

Scattered around the shores of Glendalough's Upper and Lower Lake are ruins that trace the history of this mystical glen. There are relics of its great European influx, the Danish plunderers, the skirmishes between Wicklow chieftains, and Anglo-Norman invaders. On the south shore of the Upper Lake (and reached only by boat) stands the Church of the Rock (Tempall na Skellig), with St. Kevin's Bed (a tiny hollowed-out hole) to the east of the oratory and about 30 feet above the lake. The main group of ruins are just east of the Lower Lake and those farther east are near the mouth of the valley, where the monastic city developed long after St. Kevin's death.

"Meeting of the Waters"

The spot at which the Avonmore River and Avonbeg River come together in an idyllic setting inspired Thomas Moore's tribute:

There is not in the wide world a valley so sweet
As the vale in whose bosom the bright waters meet.

There's a flagstone path from the road down to the riverbanks, leading to a clearing which holds a bust of the poet, and the tree stump on which he sat while composing his famous lines is marked with a plaque. It's about four miles south of Rathdrum.

Avondale House and Forest Park

☎ **0404/46111.** Admission Forest Park, IR£2.50 ($4) per car; house, IR£3 ($4.80) adults, IR£2 ($3.20) seniors and children under 16, IR£5 ($7.25) family ticket. Daily 11am–6pm. Closed Christmas.

Avondale House, one mile south of Rathdrum, dates from 1777 and is an integral part of Ireland's history. It witnessed the triumph and tragedy of Charles

Stewart Parnell, one of the nation's greatest leaders. Now restored to its original glory, it is a museum honoring the great man. There's a nice restaurant on the premises, as well as a gift shop.

Mount Usher Gardens

Ashford. ☎ **0404/40205** or 40116. IR£3 ($4.80) adults, IR£1.80 ($2.88) seniors, students, and children. Mid-Mar to Oct daily 11am–6pm.

This privately owned garden ranks among the leading—and loveliest—horticultural centers in Ireland. Its 20 acres of flowers, trees, shrubs, and lawns lie in the sheltered Vartry River Valley, and although it's not a true botanical garden, its plants come from many parts of the globe. Spindle trees from China, North American sweet gum and swamp cypress, the New Zealand ti tree, African broom, and Burmese juniper are among those represented in a harmony of color in a magnificent setting of superb landscaping. There's also a tea room at the entrance (serving coffee, sandwiches, snacks, and afternoon tea), as well as a shopping courtyard.

✪ Avoca Handweavers

Avoca. ☎ **0402/35105.** Admission free. Mon–Fri 9:30am–5:30pm; Sat–Sun 10am–6pm.

Not far from the junction of the two rivers, the little town of Avoca is where you'll find the oldest hand-weaving mill in Ireland. Save some time to stop by, where second- and third-generation weavers staff the mill that sits across a little bridge from the sales shop. The history of the mill is fascinating, as it went from near closing to its current humming state of good health. The patterns and weaves from this mill are marketed all over the world, and in the shop you'll find marvelous buys in bedspreads, cloaks, scarves, and a wide variety of other items, many fashioned by home workers from all over the country.

There's also another Avoca Handweavers shop on the Dublin road in Kilmacanogue, where tweeds are transformed into finished products right on the premises, and there's a very good shop at Bunratty in County Clare. But for my money, the original mill is a very special place to visit.

Noritake Arklow Pottery

South Quay, Arklow. ☎ **0402/32401** or 31101. Admission free. Mon–Fri 9:30am–5pm; Sat–Sun 10am–5pm. Call to book a guided factory tour June–Aug to watch the craftspeople at their trade.

Beautifully situated overlooking the sea, Arklow is a seaside resort town, a fishing village, and home to these makers of fine earthenware, porcelain and bone-china tableware, tea sets, dinner sets, combination sets, and giftware, incorporating both modern and traditional designs. The retail shop attached to the factory carries a great selection of shapes and patterns.

SHOPPING

✪ Clare Salley

Ashford. ☎ **0404/46480.**

The exquisite Carrickmacross lace of Ireland is fast disappearing, since few young women are willing to take up the painstaking skill. Clare, however, is a true artist, devoted to this particular form of art, specializing in the leaf, floral, shamrock, and harp designs. Her prices are remarkably low: about IR£65 ($104) for a shoulder bridal veil, IR£35 ($56) for a first communion veil, and much less for handkerchiefs, collars, cuffs, and mats. She does all the work herself, and will quote on special orders and look after mail orders promptly.

Bushy Park Ironworks

The Forge, Enniskerry, Co. Wicklow. ☎ **01/286-9077.**

Located in the picturesque little village of Enniskerry, about 12 miles from Dublin (near Powerscourt), this company turns out some of the most beautiful ironwork in the country. You can watch them craft such items as entrance gates, spiral staircases, and handwrought garden seats. Their smaller items like a single-stemmed candlestick at IR£18 ($28.80) or a more expensive floor-standing 5-branch candlebrum are wonderfully different souvenirs.

Traditional Irish Music

In the town of Wicklow, there are traditional Irish music sessions one night a week during the summer months at the **Boathouse.** Inquire at the tourist office for schedules.

Outdoor Activities

By far the most popular outdoor activity in this beautiful county is **walking the Wicklow Way** to explore its mountains and coastline. The tourist office can furnish details that will let you pick and choose bits and pieces of the scenic walk if time constraints prevent your tramping the entire way. Or look for a copy of J. B. Malone's excellent guidebook ***The Complete Wicklow Way Walks,*** published by O'Brien Press.

While in the Blessington area, leave time for the one-hour **Waterbus Cruise** on Blessington Lakes. They depart at regular intervals from Blessington Lakes Leisure Pursuits Centre (☎ 045/91111), and the live commentary relates the history and folklore of the lake. You must book ahead, and fares are IR£5 ($8) for adults, IR£2.50 ($4) for children, and IR£15 ($24) for families.

WHERE TO STAY

Bed-and-Breakfasts

See Section 3, "Where to Stay," in Chapter 5 for an outstanding bed-and-breakfast choice in Bray.

Abhainn Mor House

Corballis, Rathdrum, Co. Wicklow. ☎ **0404/46330.** 6 rms, all with bath. IR£14–IR£16 ($22.40–$25.60) per person sharing. 25% reduction for children under 10. (Rates include breakfast.) Dinner IR£12 ($19.20) extra. ACC, MC, V. Private parking. Closed Dec–Jan.

This very attractive Georgian-style house on the Rathdrum-Avoca road is run by Mrs. Thérèse Murphy-Kyriacou and is convenient to Glendalough and a forest park. The house is centrally heated and there is a garden for guests to use. The six pretty bedrooms all have private facilities and tea/coffee makings.

✪ The Arbours

Avoca, Co. Wicklow. ☎ **0402/35294.** 4 rms, none with bath. IR£14 ($22.40) per person. (Rates include breakfast.) Dinner IR£11 ($17.60) extra. No credit cards. Closed Nov–Feb.

Mrs. Maisie Caswell is the lovely and hospitable hostess of this modern bungalow set in a forest six miles from Arklow, with a beautiful view of the Avoca valley and river. Mrs. Caswell is well known for her good cooking, and dinner is available with advance notice. She also has golf clubs and a golf cart for use by guests.

Ashdene

Knockantree Lower, Avoca, Co. Wicklow. ☎ **0402/35327.** 5 rms, 4 with bath. IR£14 ($22.40) single without bath, IR£19 ($30.40) single with bath; IR£14 ($22.40) per person

Readers Recommend

Rathsallagh House, Dunlavin, Co. Wicklow. ☎ 045/53112. Fax 045/53343. *"We found a pricey, but worth it, very special place not far from Dublin and close to many interesting sightseeing places. Joe and Kay O'Flynn are warm, welcoming hosts, and the house itself is beautiful. In short, the rooms, the food, and the service are simply superb. But one needs to reserve a long time ahead."* —Dr. Helga Winkler, Austria

sharing without bath, IR£16 ($25.60) with bath. 25% reduction for children under 10. Special weekend and midweek package rates available off-season. (Rates include breakfast.) ACC, MC, V. Private car park. Closed Nov–Easter.

This modern, tastefully appointed house sits in a beautiful setting near the Avoca Handweavers, and not far from Glendalough. Mrs. Jackie Burns has elicited many letters of praise from readers for her friendly and thoughtful manner with guests. The guest rooms are attractive as well as comfortable, there's a grass tennis court, and the house has central heating.

Escombe Cottage

Lockstown, Valleymount, Blessington, Co. Wicklow. ☎ **045/67157.** Fax 045/67450. 6 rms, 4 with bath. IR£16.50 ($26.40) per person sharing. (Rates include breakfast.) Five-course dinner IR£14.50 ($23.20) extra. No credit cards. Closed Nov–Feb.

Mrs. Maura Byrne is the charming hostess of this modern bungalow overlooking Blessington lakes (ask for directions when booking). The house is centrally heated and dinner is available. The six bedrooms all have sinks.

✪ Silver Sands

Dunbur Rd., Wicklow, Co. Wicklow. ☎ **0404/68243.** 5 rms, 3 with bath. IR£14 ($22.40) per person without bath; IR£2 ($3.20) per person additional with bath. 20% reduction for children. IR£1 ($1.60) discount to our readers. (Rates include breakfast.) Dinner IR£13.50 ($21.60). No credit cards. Private car park.

Mrs. Lyla Doyle's lovely bungalow looks out to the Irish Sea and the Sugarloaf mountains, with magnificent views and bracing cliff walks. Her home is nicely decorated, and guest rooms are quite attractive, some with TV and tea/coffee makings. There are sandy beaches, fishing, and golf nearby. Mrs. Doyle is very helpful to all her guests and extends a warm welcome to our readers. Driving through Wicklow town, take the Coast Road; the house is on the right about 500 yards from the monument.

✪ Thomond House

St. Patrick's Rd., Upper Wicklow, Co. Wicklow. ☎ **0404/67940.** 5 rms, 3 with bath. IR£14 ($22.40) per person sharing without bath; IR£16 ($25.60) per person sharing with bath. 20% reduction for children. (Rates include breakfast.) No credit cards. Private car park. Closed Nov–Feb.

Mrs. Helen Gorman is the charming owner of Thomond House, which has splendid views of both the sea and the Wicklow Mountains. There's central heating and private parking. Wicklow is just half a mile away (St. Patrick's Road is just off the main street, about half a mile past the Catholic church). It's located 30 minutes from Glendalough and 45 minutes from Dublin, and Mrs. Gorman is very knowledgeable when it comes to exploring the area. She will also meet you at the bus or train station if you call ahead.

Worth a Splurge

✪ The Old Rectory Country House

Wicklow, Co. Wicklow. ☎ **0404/67048** or 800/223-6510 in the U.S. 6 rms, all with bath. TV TEL. IR£46 ($73.60) per person. (Rates include breakfast.) Fixed-price dinner IR£27 ($43.20) extra. ACC, AE, DC, V. Private parking. Closed Nov–Mar.

Linda and Paul Saunders welcome guests to their lovely 1870s Greek Revival–style rectory with a complimentary coffee tray with chocolates, tourist information, fresh flowers, and a welcome card. Set in landscaped grounds and gardens a mile off N11 on the Dublin side of Wicklow town, the Old Rectory features Victorian wood paneling, high ceilings, log fires in marble fireplaces, and individually decorated guest rooms with tea and coffee trays, radios, stationery, hairdryers, and assorted toiletries. Your full breakfast can be of the Irish, Scottish, or Swiss variety, and is accompanied by *The Irish Times*—it's even possible to have breakfast served in bed! Evening meals here have gained the Saunders an enviable reputation (see "Where to Eat," below). Dublin is only an hour's drive away, and County Wicklow's many sightseeing attractions are right at hand, including riding and golf.

WHERE TO EAT

✪ Chester Beatty's

Ashford. ☎ **0404/40206.** Main courses IR£6–IR£10 ($9.60–$16); bar food IR£4–IR£6 ($6.40–$9.60). No credit cards. Mon–Sat 12:45–2:45pm and 6–9:30pm, Sun 4:30–9:30pm. TRADITIONAL/IRISH.

The sign outside says HOME COOKING, but after a few meals here, I think it should be amended to read SUPERB HOME COOKING. This cozy bar/restaurant just north of Wicklow on N11 (the main Dublin road), in what was once a wayside inn, dishes up some of the best meals I've encountered in Ireland, and the decor is as inviting as the food if you're drawn to open fires, etched glass, and beamed ceilings. Very Irish, as is the clientele of locals mingling with passersby. Credit for the success of this popular place must go to the two Caprani brothers, Bobby and Paul, and their charming wives, Carol and Kitty. As for the food, chef Myles Moody uses only the freshest local produce to turn out traditional Irish dishes (such as Irish stew—not always easy to find) and mouthwatering fish, beef, chicken, and pork items. Plates come to table heaped high with huge portions, and homemade scones arrive piping hot and with plenty of butter, all served by a cheerful, friendly staff. This is a terrific meal break en route from Wicklow to Dublin, and if you happen by on a Friday or Saturday, you may be tempted to stop overnight for dinner and dancing in their adjacent nightclub. Very good value.

Grand Hotel

Wicklow. ☎ **0404/67337.** Main courses IR£10–IR£15 ($16–$24); fixed-price meal IR£11 ($17.60) at lunch, IR£19 ($30.40) at dinner. Service charge 13%. ACC, MC, V. Daily 12:30–2:30pm and 5:30–9:30pm (to 8pm in Aug). TRADITIONAL.

This lovely, moderately priced restaurant in the town center has glass walls that overlook the gardens. All three meals are served daily, good to know if you've missed your B&B morning meal because of an early start. The lower-priced Tourist Menu is also served year-round, and there's a bar food menu.

✪ The Old Rectory Country House

Wicklow. ☎ **0404/67048.** Reservations required. Fixed-price dinner IR£27 ($43.20). ACC, AE, MC, V. Sun–Thurs one seating at 8pm, Fri–Sat 7:30–9pm. Closed Nov–Mar. SEAFOOD/TRADITIONAL/VEGETARIAN.

This 1870s Georgian-style rectory a mile off N11 on the Dublin end of Wicklow town has blossomed as one of County Wicklow's premier eateries under the loving guidance of Paul and Linda Saunders. Set in its own gardens, the house exudes tranquil elegance, with spacious public rooms, high ceilings, and cheerful log fires. Dinner is served by candlelight, with Linda in the kitchen and Paul attending to the very personal service in the lovely dining room. Fresh seafoods and local produce and meats are the basis of the gourmet menu, and there's a good wine list. Advance booking is absolutely essential.

✪ Hunter's Hotel

Rathnew. ☎ **0404/40106.** Reservations strongly recommended. Fixed-price meal IR£14 ($22.40) at lunch, IR£20 ($32) at dinner. AE, MC, V. Private car park. Daily 1–3pm and 7:30–9:30pm. Closed Christmas Day. TRADITIONAL.

This charming country inn 28 miles south of Dublin on the Coast Road (south of Greystones) is a terrific place to stop in for lunch or afternoon tea if you're traveling (be sure to call ahead, however). It's an even better overnight stop for regional sightseeing (see "Where to Stay," above) and one of their marvelous dinners. Vegetables come straight from the hotel's own garden, seafood is freshly caught, and roasts, steaks, and other meats are locally produced. Service is the pampering kind.

8

County Wexford

The "Sunny Southeast," they call it—there are more sunny days along this part of Ireland's coast than anywhere else in the country—and it encompasses Counties Wexford, Carlow, Kilkenny, Waterford, and South Tipperary. The Southeast is one of Ireland's most scenic regions, with lush greenery, good beaches, seascapes from cliff drives, wild mountain country, and some of the country's best fishing in rivers and coastal waters. Two American presidents, John F. Kennedy (County Wexford) and Ronald Reagan (South Tipperary), had family roots in this beautiful region. Since you'll encounter County Wexford first if you're coming from Dublin along the coast, we'll start there and move on to the other Southeast counties in following chapters.

Father Murphy, of legend and song, led a valiant band of rebels to Vinegar Hill near Enniscorthy in 1798, where for nearly a month the ill-fed and ill-armed patriots held out against the English king's forces. For Americans, there is a strong tie to their own history in the John F. Kennedy Arboretum out by New Ross, not far from the birthplace of his ancestors. Down on the Hook Peninsula, a light to guide sailing ships has burned continuously for more than 1,500 years, winking across the water to Crook Castle on the Waterford side and giving rise to Cromwell's declaration that he would sail up the river "by Hook or by Crook." Today's invaders are tourists such as you and I, who find the now-peaceful countryside a haven for sightseeing, sailing, fishing, and swimming.

Either Wexford or Waterford, a mere 40 miles apart, will serve as a base from which to explore this part of the southeast region in easy day trips. Your decision may well rest on whether you prefer Wexford's small-town informality or Waterford's slightly more sophisticated big-town ambience (by no means, however, a big-city "bustle"). Whichever you choose, be sure not to neglect the other.

1 Wexford

90 miles S of Dublin, 39 miles NE of Waterford

Wexford is a small, prosperous town with industry, agriculture, and tourism happily blending into a relaxed atmosphere that makes it virtually impossible for the visitor to hurry through. Its annual opera festival draws international artists and draws thousands of visitors.

Because of its shallowness, the harbor was named *Waesfjord* (The Harbor of the Mud Flats) by the Vikings, but it was the legendary Fir Bolgs who christened the River Slaney after their leader Slaigne. Vikings came to build a town at the edge of the harbor to use as a base for plundering excursions on land and at sea. And there they stayed until the first Norman forces to land in Ireland arrived on Wexford's coast in 1169 and settled in. And *they* stayed, in spite of uprisings followed by bloody massacres and a liberty-loving native populace that gave them little peace.

Today, although very much in touch with the modern world, the town also displays with pride the many marks of its colorful past. Westgate and the wall at Rowe Street Church are relics of the Danish town wall later reinforced by the Normans. The sturdy bronze pikeman in the Bull Ring commemorates the bravery of those freedom-loving natives who stood—and fell—against tyranny in 1798.

GETTING THERE Car and passenger ferries from Fishguard, Wales, and Le Havre, France, dock at Rosslare Harbour, 13 miles to the southeast of Wexford town; there's good bus and train service between Wexford and the port. Wexford can be reached by train from Dublin and by bus from most cities and towns around the country. For train information, call 01/836-5420. For bus information, call Bus Eireann at 01/836-6111 or inquire at local bus stations around the country.

CITY LAYOUT You can walk most of Wexford's streets in a half hour or so, which means it has never seen fit to install a public transportation system. The railway station is at the northern end of town on Redmond Place.

Main Street—so narrow you can very nearly stand in the middle and touch shops on either side with outstretched arms—is ideal for strolling, people watching, and shopping. One block from the water, Main Street runs parallel to the line of quays.

The Bull Ring is a wide intersection at the northern end of Main Street, where the Norman aristocracy once practiced bull baiting.

The quay runs for six blocks along the water's edge with an inset semicircular Crescent Quay near the center facing a statue of Commodore John Barry.

VISITOR INFORMATION The Tourist Information Office is at Crescent Quay (☎ 053/23111). It's open Monday through Saturday from 9am to 6pm (later in summer months). Current activities and a town map are available in the free booklet "Welcome to Wexford," published by the Junior Chamber of Commerce from June to October and distributed by the tourist board, shops, and hotels.

SPECIAL EVENTS I can't wish anything happier for you than that you should arrive in town in October for the ✪ **Wexford Opera Festival.** It's 18 days of music and revelry, with international and home-grown companies presenting both standard favorites and lesser-known operas, all with casts and orchestral support of the National Symphony Orchestra. Three are performed throughout each week, along with recitals, workshops, and a host of other related activities. The festival celebrated its 40th anniversary in 1991. For detailed information on scheduled performances and recitals, ticket prices, and booking, contact: Wexford Festival of Opera, Theatre Royal, Wexford, County Wexford (☎ 053/22144). Tickets vary from year to year, but run around IR£42 ($67.20) for Gala Night and weekends, less for midweek performances.

GETTING AROUND **By Taxi** Private for-hire cars are available in lieu of taxis. They meet most trains and buses, and can be called to pick up fares at hotels and guesthouses. There's no standard rate and no meter, so you should agree on

Wexford Town

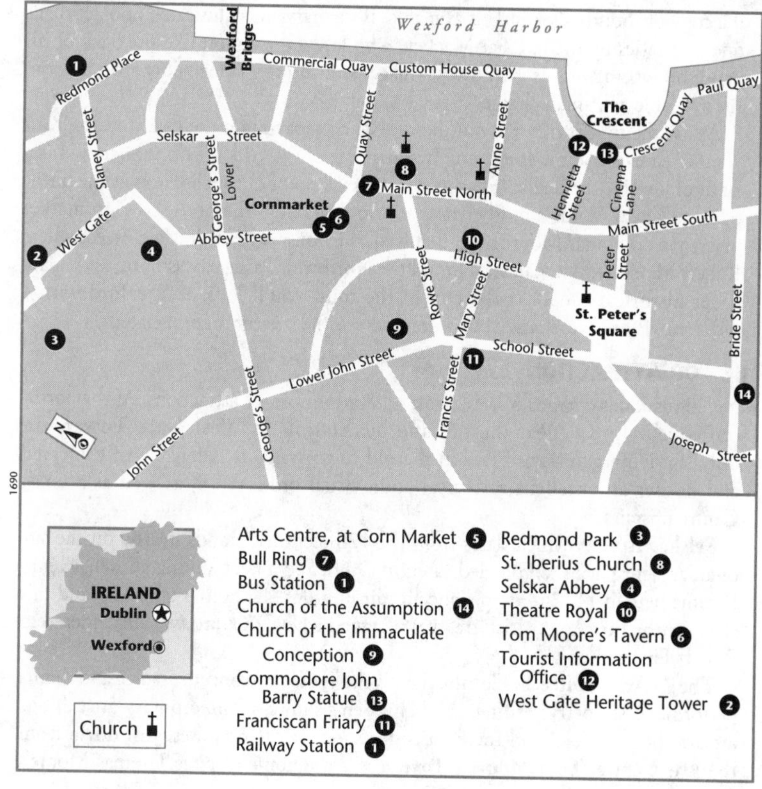

a fare when you engage a car. The tourist board can furnish local telephone numbers.

By Car My best advice is to park the car and walk. Wexford's narrow streets can be tough going for most drivers, but there are public parking lots on the quay and just back of Main Street. All are prominently marked and charge a very small hourly fee.

Fast Facts: County Wexford

Area Code The telephone area code is 053.

Emergencies Dial 999 and tell the operator which service you need to contact (police, ambulance, fire).

Mail/Telegraph/Telex The General Post Office is on Anne Street, and is open Monday through Saturday from 9am to 5:30pm. Telegraph service is available by dialing 196 (if you are dialing from a coin-box telephone with A and B buttons, dial 10 and tell the operator what you want). Most hotels in Wexford can provide telex facilities. Wexford's only Bureau de Change is located in the G.P.O.

WHAT TO SEE & DO

The very first thing you should do is stop in at the tourist office and browse through their selection of helpful maps and brochures of the town and county. Ask if a copy of "South Wexford" is available. It's a marvelous illustrated booklet that's one of a series by the late Pat Mackey, who knew the region like the back of his hand; his writing brings each town, village, and country lane vividly alive for you. It's available at a small charge.

Ask at the tourist office about the time and place to join the free **walking tour** conducted every summer evening by members of the Old Wexford Society. It's a labor of love for the dedicated group, and they'll point out such places as the birthplace of Oscar Wilde's mother next to the Bull Ring, the house in Cornmarket where poet Thomas Moore's mother lived, the house on North Main Street where Robert McClure, the man who found the Northwest Passage, was born, and many other historical spots. At the end of the tour, you'll look at Wexford with a different vision. No charge, but a donation to the society is appreciated.

The Top Attractions

No admission is charged to view most of Wexford town's attractions. At the northern edge of town, near the rail and bus station, is **West Gate Tower,** the only surviving gateway of five in the old town walls. It is fairly well preserved and houses an excellent historical audiovisual production, as well as a Craft Centre upstairs.

Selskar Abbey, which dates from the 12th century, stands nearby on the site of an ancient pagan temple dedicated to Odin, and a later Viking church. Henry II came here in 1172 to do penance for his murder of Thomas à Becket, and this is where the first Anglo-Irish treaty was signed when Wexford was surrendered to Robert Fitzstephen.

The ✪ **Arts Centre,** at Cornmarket, is the venue for concerts, dance and drama performances, poetry readings, and children's shows. Contemporary art exhibits are also housed here, and there's a coffee shop on the premises. Just down from the Arts Centre, **Tom Moore's Tavern** was the home of poet Thomas Moore's mother, a Wexford native.

Go by the **Bull Ring,** in the wide intersection at the north end of Main Street, and spend a few minutes reflecting on the bravery of the pikemen of the 1798 rebellion who are commemorated by the bronze statue there. It was here that Cromwell visited his wrath on the town in 1649, leaving only 200 survivors of the 2,000 residents. A great high cross stood here, and the valiant Irish knelt in prayer before it as Cromwell dealt out wholesale death.

Visit the **Commodore John Barry statue,** on Crescent Quay, presented to the people of Wexford by the American government to honor this native son who became the "Father of the American Navy." If you pass through Ballysampson, Tagoat (some 10 miles from Wexford), tip your hat to his birthplace. He is credited with founding the American navy after being appointed by George Washington in 1797.

An attraction unto itself, narrow little ✪ **Main Street** is always alive with the buzz of friendly commerce. It's pedestrianized, with an intriguing mix of traditional storefronts, boutiques, pubs, and gift shops. The house in which Cromwell stayed during his Wexford rampage stood on the present-day site of Woolworth & Co., 29 S. Main St.

The **Franciscan Friary,** on John Street, is built on the site of an earlier friary founded in 1230. It's noteworthy for its fine stucco work on the ceiling and for the reliquary of St. Adjutor, a young boy who was martyred in ancient Rome and whose remains are encased in a wax figure.

Nearby Attractions

✪ Irish National Heritage Park

Ferrycarrig. ☎ **053/41733,** 22211, or 23111. Admission IR£3.50 ($5.60) adults, IR£2 ($3.20) students and seniors, IR£9 ($14.40) family ticket. Apr–Oct, daily 9am–7pm. Bus: During summer months, special buses from Wexford town make regular trips to and from the park; check with the Tourist Board for fares and schedules; it's three miles northwest of Wexford town, just off N11 (well signposted).

Don't leave Wexford without a visit to this unique heritage park. Just three miles outside town, the park holds reconstructions of a campsite, farmstead, and portal dolmen from the Stone Age (7000–2000 B.C.); a cist burial and stone circle from the Bronze Age (2000–500 B.C.); an ogham stone, ring fort and souterrain, early Christian monastery, corn-drying kiln, horizontal water mill, Viking boathouse, and an artificial island habitat known as a crannog, all from the Celtic and early Christian ages (500 B.C.–A.D. 1169); and a Norman motte and bailey, the first Norman fortification in Ireland, and a round tower, from the Early Norman Period (A.D. 1169–1280). There's also a nature walk of real beauty. Work is still continuing on this fascinating look back into Ireland's past, and there may well be many other reconstructions by the time you visit.

Irish Agricultural Museum

Johnstown Castle. ☎ **053/42888.** Admission IR£2 ($3.20) adults, IR£1 ($1.60) children and students. June–Aug, Mon–Fri 9am–5pm, Sat–Sun 2–5pm; Apr–May and Sept, Mon–Fri 9am–12:30pm and 2–5pm, Sat–Sun 2–5pm; Nov–Mar, Mon–Fri 9am–12:30pm and 1:30–5pm.

Four miles southwest of Wexford town on the road to Murrintown, this interesting museum is in early 19th-century farm buildings on the grounds of Johnstown Castle. This major museum of agriculture and Irish rural life features displays on farming methods, life in the farmyard and the rural household (with a major collection of country furniture), and rural transport. There are also reconstructions of workshops of rural craftsmen. There's a tearoom, as well as a bookshop and an Irish-made-souvenir shop (open June through August).

Sports & Outdoor Activities

Check with the tourist office for dates of race meets at the Wexford Racecourse. This is a horse-mad town, and meets here are attended by hours and hours of debate and sociability in Wexford pubs. Great fun!

Also see the tourist office staff for information on how you can participate in local hunting, fishing, boating, and golfing. There's a good beach at Rosslare, although the Irish Sea is not the warmest water you'll run across.

Shopping

Barker's

36 S. Main St. ☎ **053/23159.** Fax 053/23738.

Good gift selections, and they ship overseas. Stocks include a large selection of Waterford crystal, Royal Tara china, Belleek, Irish linen, bronze, and pottery. Open Monday through Saturday from 9am to 5:30pm.

✪ The Book Centre

7 N. Main St. ☎ **053/23543.**

Extensive stock of books on Irish topics, as well as a wide range of other fiction and nonfiction publications. It's open Monday through Saturday from 9am to 5:30pm.

Faller's Sweater Shop

North Main Street. ☎ **053/24659.**

Treat yourself to a browse at Faller's, with its wide variety of sweaters, ranging from hand-knit jumpers to cardigans to cotton or linen crewnecks. They also carry accessories that include linen, woolen, and mohair scarves, stoles, tweed caps, capes, and gloves. Open Monday through Saturday from 9am to 6pm.

✪ Joyces China Shop

1 S. Main St. ☎ **053/42744.**

An excellent place to shop for Waterford crystal, Belleek china, and high-quality Irish souvenirs. Murt Joyce, who has visited the States and has a special fondness for Yanks, has a large stock of such items, competitive prices, and frequent specials on even the pricier merchandise. Open Monday through Saturday from 9am to 5:30pm.

WEXFORD AFTER DARK

Some say that it was shipwrecked Cornish sailors who first brought ✪ **mumming** to Wexford. No matter how it arrived, however, it has survived, albeit with a decidedly Irish accent, down through the centuries, and it is unique to this county. The medieval folk-dance with sword play was based on the miracle-play triumph of good over evil. Today's mummers portray Irish patriots like Wolfe Tone and Robert Emmet. The three or four groups are composed of Wexford natives who have inherited their place in the ritualistic performances from family members going back several generations. They don't follow a regular schedule, but the tourist office will usually be able to tell you when the next appearance is likely to occur in one of the local pubs. If you can track one down, don't miss it.

For other evening entertainment, check what's on at the Arts Centre.

THE PUB SCENE

Pubs and lounges are open Monday through Saturday from 10:30am to 11:30pm (to 11pm during the winter) and on Sunday from noon to 2pm and 4 to 10pm. Highlights of Wexford's lively pub scene are the **Cape of Good Hope,** N. Main St. (☎ 053/22949); the ✪ **Crown Bar,** Monck St.; and **Tim's Tavern,** 51 S. Main St. (☎ 053/23861).

WHERE TO STAY

In addition to the following listings, many B&Bs and farmhouses are within easy driving distance of the town.

Note: Prices are usually higher during the opera festival in October.

IN TOWN

Glenfarne

5 Richmond Terrace, Spawell Road, Wexford. ☎ **053/45290.** 3 rms, all with bath. IR£20 ($32) single; IR£15 ($24) per person sharing. (Rates include breakfast.) No credit cards. Closed Mid-Dec–Jan.

Niall and Florrie O'Flaherty's large Georgian house is only steps away from downtown Wexford. From it, you have a lovely view across the river. Guest rooms are spacious, with tea/coffee makings in each. O'Flaherty's warm hospitality has drawn high praise from Frommer readers.

Westgate House Guest House

Westgate, Wexford, Co. Wexford. ☎ **053/24428** or 22167. 12 rms, 7 with bath. TV. IR£17 ($27.20) single without bath; add IR£3 ($4.80) for private bath; IR£15 ($24) per person sharing without bath, IR£18 ($28.80) per person sharing with bath. (Rates include breakfast.) MC, V. Private car park.

Mr. and Mrs. Allen have won high praise from readers for their warm hospitality. The comfortable guesthouse at the north end of town is within easy walking distance of the town center and is especially convenient to the rail and bus depot.

Nearby Accommodations

Clonard House

Clonard Great, Wexford, Co. Wexford. ☎ **053/23141.** 10 rms, all with bath. IR£17–IR£20 ($27.20–$32) per person. 50% reduction for children. Five-course dinner IR£14 ($22.40) extra. (Rates include breakfast.) No credit cards. Closed Nov–Mar.

This lovely 1783 Georgian house two miles from Wexford, an eighth of a mile off the N25/R733 roundabout (signposted at the roundabout) was John Hayes's family home. Its 120 acres are still operated as a dairy farm, and his wife, Kathleen, and their four children now offer warm Irish hospitality. The bedrooms are unusually spacious, attractively decorated (some with four-poster beds), with bucolic farm views from every window (my favorite is the top-floor room under the eaves, overlooking the century-old farmyard with its interesting outbuildings). Log fires and a piano make the lounge a friendly gathering place, and Kathleen's evening meals are fast gaining a faithful following. Wine is available at the dinner hour.

Rockcliffe

Coolballow, Wexford, Co. Wexford. ☎ **053/43130.** 4 rms, 2 with bath. IR£14 ($22.40) per person without bath; IR£2 ($3.20) per person extra for private bath. 20% reduction for children. (Rates include breakfast.) No credit cards. Private parking. Closed Nov–Easter.

Just two miles from town and about a half mile down the Johnstown Castle road (off the Wexford-Rosslare road), Mrs. Sarah Lee's attractive, modern home is set high on an acre of beautifully landscaped grounds. The bedrooms are nicely furnished and attractively decorated, and the house is centrally heated. The Rosslare ferry is 6 miles away, and Mrs. Lee is happy to fix an early breakfast for departing guests. From Rosslare Harbour, take N25 and at the roundabout take the Wexford exit; it's signposted at the next left turn (just after Farmer's Kitchen Bar/Restaurant).

Worth a Splurge

Wexford Lodge Hotel

The Bridge, Wexford, Co. Wexford. ☎ **053/23611.** Fax 053/23342. 18 rms, all with bath. IR£25–IR£35 ($40–$56) per person. (Rates include breakfast.) ACC, AE, MC, V. Enclosed car park.

This small, two-story hotel directly across the bridge from Wexford town quays on R741 overlooks Wexford harbor, with good views of Wexford town across the water. Owned and operated by the Igoe family, its public rooms are attractive and inviting, and guest rooms are nicely done up, with glassed-in balconies for year-round comfort. Adjacent to the hotel is a heated swimming pool and sauna. The restaurant here has, in a very short time, established a name for excellent seafood at moderate prices.

WHERE TO EAT

The Bohemian Girl

N. Main St., at Quay St. ☎ **053/24419.** Lunch IR£5 ($8); dinner IR£10 ($16); Tourist Menu (available Mon–Sat). ACC, MC, V. Daily 10:30am–11:30pm. PUB GRUB/TRADITIONAL/ VEGETARIAN.

This Tudor-style pub is a homey place, supervised by owner-chefs Eugene and Lorraine Gillen, with a loyal local following and Bar Catering Competition Awards proudly displayed. Soups and brown bread are homemade, and on hand are pâté and smoked salmon and other seafood.

The Granary Restaurant

West Gate. ☎ **053/23935.** Main courses IR£7–IR£15 ($11.20–$24). ACC, V. Mon–Sat 5:30–10:30pm. Closed several days at Christmas. SEAFOOD/TRADITIONAL.

This cozy, old-world-style restaurant has a warm, inviting ambience, with individual booths in the dining room and wooden beams in the cellar bar. Paddy and Mary Hatton feature local seafood, with such specialties as Wexford mussels, Kilmore scallops, monkfish and prawn provençal, and sole on the bone. Steaks, duckling, venison (in season), lamb, and chicken are also featured, and there is always at least one vegetarian selection. The Granary is on the north end of town past the rail and bus depot, on N25, opposite the West Gate (a five-minute walk from Main Street).

✪ Tim's Tavern

51 S. Main St. at the corner of Upper King St. ☎ **053/23861.** Lunch IR£6 ($9.60); dinner IR£11 ($17.60). No credit cards. Year-round, Mon–Sat noon–2:30pm; July–Oct, Mon–Sat 6–8pm. PUB GRUB.

This Tudor-style pub features exposed beams, whitewashed walls, and a thatch-roofed bar. All soups, meats, vegetables, and desserts are home-cooked, with portions more than ample. You can choose from a varied menu with everything from toasted sandwiches to open sandwiches of prawns, smoked or fresh salmon, or chicken, to delicious salad plates of fresh or smoked salmon, prawns, or chicken. Evening meals include a 12-ounce sirloin steak, french fries, and vegetables, plus a good selection of salad plates. The food is exceptional, but even better is the clientele, many of whom lead off a singsong at the slightest provocation, and others who are only too eager to share their expertise at betting the horses at Wexford race meets or others around the country. This is a place you well could come to dinner and wind up staying until, "Time, gentlemen, please."

✪ Wren's Nest

Custom House Quay. ☎ **053/22359.** Prices IR£1–IR£5 ($1.60–$8). No credit cards. Hot foods daily noon–3pm; snacks daily noon–7pm. PUB GRUB.

Readers Recommend

Healthfield Manor, Killurin, Co. Wexford. ☎ 053/28253. *"This huge manor house, run by Loretto Colloton, is just five miles from Wexford and two miles from the Heritage Park. It's beautifully furnished with antiques and has huge suites for one or two people. The rates are surprisingly low and very good value for money."*

—Rich and Ginny Hutton, Sayville, NY

This is one of the best places in Wexford for a good, inexpensive lunch. It's a good-looking—and award-winning—bar whose backroom lounge features an attractive stone fireplace. The menu includes a hot-plate special, salads, the house pâté and brown bread (excellent), and sandwiches. It sits facing the harbor, a little north of the Crescent.

✪ The Conservatory Restaurant

In the Ferrycarrig Hotel, Ferrycarrig Bridge. ☎ **053/22999.** Prix-fixe five-course dinner IR£22.50 ($36); lunch about IR£12 ($19.20). ACC, AE, MC, V. Mon–Sat 12:30–2:15pm, Sun 12:45–2pm; daily 7–9pm. SEAFOOD/TRADITIONAL.

The pretty, greenery-filled Conservatory is a leading restaurant in the Wexford region. With marvelous views of the River Slaney just across the lawn, the room exudes a warm, inviting glow, and the menu is as inviting as the setting. There is a comfortable and spacious lounge in which to have a before-dinner drink and place your order from selections such as poached Atlantic sea-fresh filet of pink salmon with Dutch-Gewurtz hollandaise garni, sautéed suprême of chicken with orange and lakeshore whole-grain-whiskey mustard, and escalope of succulent veal au Cinzano bianco with saffron risotto. Desserts might include home-baked apple pie with that good fresh Irish cream, a crispy almond basket of assorted ice creams, or a selection of Irish farmhouse cheeses. The hotel is two miles north of Wexford on N11, just over the Ferrycarrig Bridge.

2 Around County Wexford

County Wexford entices you to ramble along a coast dotted with fine, sandy strands, or to wander from one historically significant point to the next. County Wexford is pure charm, from the solid stone ruins of Norman castles to whitewashed farmhouses overlooking rolling fields and wooded pastures to thatched cottages and fishing villages.

SEEING COUNTY WEXFORD While a car is essential to see many of County Wexford's attractions, those without wheels can, with careful planning, make day trips that rely solely on public transportation.

By Bus Bus service is available to the following: Enniscorthy, from Wexford, Ferns, and Dublin; Ferns, from Wexford, Enniscorthy, and Dublin; Courtown Harbour, from Gorey and Wexford; New Ross, from Wexford, Waterford, and Dublin; Rosslare and Rosslare Harbour, from Wexford; and Kilmore Quay, from Wexford on specified days of the week. *Remember, however, that bus schedules must be carefully studied if you want to go and return in a single day—service can be infrequent to some points.*

By Train Trains reach Enniscorthy and Rosslare and Rosslare Harbour from Wexford and Dublin.

By Car With a Wexford town base, all of County Wexford can easily be explored by car. The tourist board in Wexford town has an excellent (and free) magazine, entitled *Skylines,* that outlines 10 touring routes throughout the entire Southeast. Unless you wish to return to Wexford town each night, you can combine any or all of these excursions to make a circular tour of the county.

ENNISCORTHY

Using Wexford town as a base, drive 11 miles north on N11 to Enniscorthy, with its strong links to this region's history.

WHAT TO SEE & DO

Historic relics are displayed in the ✪ **Enniscorthy County Museum,** town center, Enniscorthy (☎ 054/35926), housed in a remarkably intact Norman castle built in the early 13th century. It is said that Spenser wrote some of his epic *Faerie Queen* while living here. Cromwell gave it a battering, and it was on its way to becoming just another ruin until it was reconstructed in 1900. Today its rooms hold items that figured in the lives of Irish country people in years past, as well as mementos of the tragic 1798 uprising and the 1916 rebellion, which had a happier outcome. There's a still in such good condition it could be put to work today turning out Ireland's brand of moonshine, poteen ("pot-*sheen*"). Other interesting items include the collection of rush lights that were the first torches in the country. There's a small admission charge, and it's open April to September, daily from 10am to 6pm; all other months, Sundays only from 2 to 5:30pm.

At the eastern edge of town, **Vinegar Hill** provides superb views from its 390-foot summit, and you'll share them with the ghosts of valiant Wexford pikemen who made their last stand here in June 1798, led by the indomitable Father Murphy. There's a convenient car park, and no admission fee.

WHERE TO STAY

✪ Ivella

Rectory Rd., Enniscorthy, Co. Wexford. ☎ **054/33475.** 3 rms, none with bath. IR£16 ($25.60) single; IR£13 ($20.80) per person sharing. (Rates include breakfast.) No credit cards.

This modern house sits on a hillside abloom with colorful garden flowers. There are three attractive guest rooms, two with double and single beds to accommodate families, and one double room. Breakfast comes with homemade brown bread and jam, and Miss Ann Heffernan, who is as bright and sparkling as her home, also serves guests fresh strawberries from her own garden, topped with generous dollops of fresh cream.

Ballyorley House

Boolavogue, Co. Wexford. ☎ **054/66287.** 4 rms, 1 with bath. IR£23–IR£50 ($36.80–$80) single; IR£20 ($32) per person sharing; IR£1 ($1.45) per person extra for private bath. 50% reduction for children. (Rates include breakfast.) No credit cards. Closed Jan–Feb.

Mrs. Mary Gough presides over this lovely Georgian house three miles off the main Wexford-Dublin road (N11). Her four bedrooms are nicely decorated and very comfortable. With advance notice, she will also provide the evening meal.

Oakville Lodge

Ballycarney, Rosslare-Carlow Road (N80), Enniscorthy, Co. Wexford. ☎ **054/88626.** 5 rms, 2 with bath. IR£19–IR£22 ($30.40–$35.20) single; IR£14–IR£16 ($22.40–$25.60) per person sharing. (Rates include breakfast.) V. Apr–Oct. Closed Nov–Mar.

Mrs. Attracta Doyle's attractive two-story home overlooks the River Slaney in a tranquil, wooded setting. Her comfortable, nicely appointed guest rooms make an ideal base not only for this county's top sightseeing attractions, but also for a host of outdoor activities, including golf, horseback riding, mountain walks, and salmon and/or sea trout fishing.

Where to Eat

✪ The Antique Tavern

Enniscorthy. ☎ **054/33428.** Under IR£5 ($8) inclusive. No credit cards. Daily 12:30–2:30pm. BAR FOOD.

Proprietor Vincent Heffernan is proud of the fact that the Antique Tavern has won "best pub" awards for both County Wexford and the entire Leinster province. It certainly serves some of the best bar lunches I've had in Ireland—homemade soups with homemade brown bread and a vast and varied selection of sandwiches, washed down with either tea or coffee. On the northern outskirts of town on N11 (Gorey road), it's a cozy, friendly place, with all the atmosphere of an old Irish pub.

FERNS

Some eight miles farther north on N11 is Ferns (21 miles north of Wexford town) and its impressive historical ruins. The little village of Ferns was once the capital of all Leinster, and relics of its long history invite a ramble. Look for impressive **Ferns Castle,** which dates from the 13th century, the 12th-century **Augustinian abbey** (now in ruins), and on a hill just outside the village, the 16th-century **St. Peter's Church.**

Where to Stay & Eat

Clone House

Ferns, Co. Wexford. ☎ **054/66113.** 8 rms, 3 with bath. IR£15 ($24) per person sharing without bath; IR£18 ($28.80) per person sharing with bath; IR£5 ($8) single supplement. 25% reduction for children. (Rates include breakfast.) High tea IR£11 ($17.60) extra; dinner IR£14 ($22.40). No credit cards. Closed Nov–Feb.

Built in 1640, this delightful farmhouse is set in some 300 acres of farmland, and its pretty garden has won several National Garden awards, while the house has received the Best Farm House award. Mrs. Betty Breen and her whole family have been very popular with readers. The house is centrally heated, and electric blankets are supplied if needed. It's a working farm and excellent home-produced cuisine is guaranteed. A real convenience is the laundry facilities, available to any guest who may need them. The River Bann runs through the farm, providing good trout fishing. It's two miles off N11 at Ferns Village, five miles from Enniscorthy, and 21 miles from Wexford.

GOREY

It was on Gorey Hill, at the western edge of Gorey, that those 1798 rebels pitched camp on their way to march on Arklow, and a granite Celtic cross near the hill commemorates their brave, albeit ill-fated, effort. In July and August, the **Funge Arts Centre,** on Rafter Street, hosts an arts festival that attracts participants from around the world.

Where to Stay & Eat

Woodlands House

Killinierin, Gorey, Co. Wexford. ☎ **0402/37125** or 37133. 5 rms, all with bath. TV. IR£19 ($30.40) per person sharing. 25% reduction for children. (Rates include breakfast.) Five-course dinner IR£16 ($25.60) extra. Family and 2-, 3-, or 7-night stay rates available in low season. Closed Dec–Feb.

Mrs. Phyllis O'Sullivan is the hostess of this large farmhouse, whose amenities include a playroom, pool table, and amusements. There are spacious, pleasant lawns and gardens surrounded by a forest which has beautiful walks. It is centrally heated, but there's also a log fire in the TV lounge. Some bedrooms are traditionally furnished, as befits this 140-year-old Georgian house. Meals include fresh, homegrown ingredients and home baking, and there's a good wine list. It's a mile off the Gorey-Arklow road (N11) near the Wexford-Wicklow border, 28 miles north of Wexford.

Worth a Splurge

✪ Marlfield Country House

Gorey, Co. Wexford. ☎ **055/21124.** Fax 055/21572. 19 rms, all with bath. IR£50–IR£95 ($80–$152) per person sharing, depending on season. (Rates include full Irish breakfast.) ACC, AE, MC, V. Closed two weeks in Jan.

Surrounded by some 35 acres of wooded countryside and landscaped gardens, 1¼ miles from Gorey on the Courtown road (R742), this stately Regency house was once the home of the earl of Courtown, and is filled with antiques, gilt-framed mirrors, and crystal chandeliers. Log fires in the public rooms add a gracious note of warmth, and a lovely curved staircase sweeps up to elegantly furnished guest rooms. With warm friendship, Mary and Ray Bowe, the owners who have brought the old home back to its former glory, as well as daughter Margaret, go out of their way to see that guests are catered to.

Dining: Even if you are not staying at the hotel, you may want to have a memorable meal at the excellent restaurant. Mary Bowe is known for her expertise with seafoods, although any choice from the menu will consist of homegrown or locally produced ingredients prepared with a gourmet cook's touch. A personal tip: Try the baked salmon stuffed with asparagus and a lemon butter sauce. The restaurant is set in a Victorian-style conservatory, with sweeping views of the lawns and gardens. It's altogether charming and the epitome of luxury dining. A fixed-price lunch costs IR£18.50 ($29.60); a fixed-price dinner, IR£30 ($48). It's open for lunch daily from 1 to 2:30pm, and for dinner daily from 7:30 to 9:30pm.

ROSSLARE & ROSSLARE HARBOUR

To reach Rosslare, 11 miles southeast of Wexford, a popular seaside resort with good beaches, or Rosslare Harbour, five miles farther south, ferry port for the U.K. and France, follow N25 south from Wexford town. The **Tourist Information Office** (☎ 053/33623) is set back from N25 (on your right coming from Wexford) between Rosslare and Rosslare Harbour, open April to September. An Information Office in the ferry building is open year-round.

Main attractions here are the six-mile-long beach that arcs along the coast at Rosslare and, of course, the ferry port at Rosslare Harbour.

To reach the Hook Peninsula from Rosslare Harbour, turn onto R736 from N25. For Kilmore Quay and the Saltees, continue on R736 and turn south on R739. From Kilmore Quay, you can travel to New Ross by following R736 north until it joins N25.

Where to Stay

Kilrane House

Kilrane, Rosslare Harbour, Co. Wexford. ☎ **053/33135.** 6 rms, all with bath. Rates IR£20 ($32) single; IR£15 ($24) per person sharing. 33% reduction for children. ACC, AE, MC, V.

This 19th-century house on the Wexford–Rosslare Harbour road (N25), half a mile from Rosslare Harbour, has one of the most elegant lounges I've come across in a B&B, with beautiful plasterwork and a decor of shades of rose. Siobhán Whitehead extends a special welcome to families. She has one large family room that sleeps 5, and is happy to supply cots for the little ones. All rooms have tea/coffeemakers.

✪ Marianella

Kilrane, Rosslare Harbour, Co. Wexford. ☎ **053/33139.** 5 rms, 2 with bath. Rates IR£14 ($22.40) per person sharing without bath, IR£15 ($24) with bath. 30% reduction for children under 10. ACC, EU, MC.

Margaret Roche welcomes guests to her pretty bungalow on the main Wexford-Rosslare road (N25), half a mile from Rosslare Harbour, which is screened from the busy highway by a high hedge. With flowers, a pond, and a fountain, the grounds are rather like a small private park. Guest rooms are nicely done up, all with tea/coffeemakers; there's a pine-paneled dining room and a TV lounge.

A Farmhouse

O'Leary's Farm

Killilane, Kilrane, Co. Wexford. ☎ **053/33134.** 10 rms, 7 with bath. IR£14 ($22.40) single without bath; IR£13 ($20.80) per person sharing without bath; IR£15 ($24) per person sharing with bath. 25% reduction for children. (Rates include breakfast.) High tea IR£7 ($11.20) extra; dinner IR£12 ($19.20). No credit cards.

Mrs. Kathleen O'Leary and her engaging offspring (along with a grandchild or two) make you feel part of the family. Their farmhouse, three miles from Rosslare Harbour, prominently signposted on N25, looks out to the sea across flatlands that focus the eye on ferry comings and goings at Rosslare Harbour. The farmhouse, which provides large family rooms as well as the usual doubles, features a glassed-in front porch that takes advantage of the seascape, while an open fire warms the lounge (there is also central heating). One of the O'Learys is always on hand to pick up and deliver guests to the ferry port with advance notice.

Where to Eat

✪ Tuskar House Hotel

Rosslare Harbour. ☎ and fax **053/33363.** Main courses IR£6–IR£12 ($9.60–$19.20); fixed-price dinner IR£18 ($28.80). Service charge 10%. ACC, AE, MC, V. Daily 12:30–3pm and 6:30–10:30pm. SEAFOOD/TRADITIONAL.

The pleasant dining room in this seafront hotel in the town center, with a window-wall overlooking the sea, takes pride in the freshness of the seafood that comes to table. Menus are extensive and varied, and I'm especially fond of the way they do mussels in garlic sauce. Nonlovers of seafood will find a host of meat and fowl dishes, and service is especially friendly and accommodating.

NEW ROSS & FOULKSMILLS

Some 15 miles west of Wexford town (on L160, off N25), the farming area around Foulksmills is fertile ground for farmhouse devotees who long for a landscape of rolling pastures, tilled fields, and wooded countryside.

From Wexford town, take N25 to New Ross (21 miles northwest of Wexford) and watch for the signpost on your left just before you reach the town for the turn to the John F. Kennedy Arboretum. From New Ross, you can reach Kilmore

Quay, the Saltees, and the Hook Peninsula by taking N25 east (toward Wexford), then turning southeast toward the coast on R736.

What to See & Do

In 1848, when Patrick Kennedy left Dunganstown (near New Ross) for America, it was to escape the ravages of a devastating famine. He left behind a five-room thatched home set among stone farm buildings. A little more than a century later, his great-grandson, John Fitzgerald Kennedy, held the high office of president of the United States and returned to his ancestral home. The little thatched cottage had been replaced, but the outbuildings remained as they had been in his great-grandfather's time. Mrs. Ryan, a Kennedy by birth, and her daughter greeted the president and showed him around the place. Today the Kennedy homestead, on a pleasant river road, is marked by a small plaque on an outside wall, and if you'd like to take a look (from the road, please—Mrs. Ryan does not open the house to the public), make the short detour en route from Wexford to New Ross.

John F. Kennedy Arboretum

New Ross. ☎ **051/388-171.** Admission IR£2 ($3.20) adults, IR£1.50 ($2.40) seniors, IR£1 ($1.60) children and students, IR£5 ($8) family groups. May–Aug, daily 10am–8pm; Apr and Sept, daily 10am–6:30pm; Oct–Mar, 10am–5pm.

A little over seven miles from New Ross, this outstanding plant collection is the tribute paid to the young slain American president by the Irish government and United States citizens of Irish origin. It was officially opened by the late President Eamon De Valera in 1968 and covers some 623 acres, of which more than 300 are set aside for the plant collection. Already there are more than 4,500 species of shrubs, and the number is expected to reach 6,000. In the forest plots, there are trees from five continents. There are lovely shaded walks throughout, with shelters and convenient resting spots. If you follow the signposts to the top of Slieve Coillte, you'll be rewarded by a marvelous panorama of southern Wexford and the splendid estuary of the Rivers Barrow, Nore, and Suir. Be sure to stop by the reception center and see the explanatory display fashioned in beaten copper.

✪ The *New Ross Galley*

The Quay, New Ross. ☎ **051/21723.**

Skipper Dick Fletcher conceived the idea of this cruising restaurant some 25 years ago, and now the *Galley* sets sail for lunches (two hours), afternoon teas (two hours), and dinners (three hours). Whichever you select, you'll spend two to three relaxing hours in the comfortable, heated cruiser as you slide between the scenic banks of the Rivers Barrow, Nore, or Suir. No canned music, no commentary—just the blissful comfort of good food, drink (the *Galley* is fully licensed), and conversation, and if you're curious about the ancient stately homes, castles, abbeys, and wildlife you glimpse along the shore, read the menu pages that give details of the

Readers Recommend

Saunders Court, Crossabeg, Co. Wexford. ☎ 053/41833. *"Val and Theresa O'Connor's B&B overlooks Slaney Estuary, and the view is terrific. Our room was huge, with a private bath, and breakfast was great."*

—Harlie and Barbara Cooley, Rancho Mirage, CA

area. That menu features delicious specialties created from locally grown produce, meats, and fish. There's seating for just 70, and the skipper is usually aboard in the role of gracious host. This is definitely a don't-miss!

Fares: IR£12 ($19.20) for the lunch cruise, IR£5 ($8) for the afternoon-tea cruise, IR£17–IR£20 ($27.20–$32) for the dinner cruise; IR£4–IR£9 ($6.40–$14.40) for the cruise only. Reservations essential. Book through Wexford or Waterford tourist offices or the above telephone. No credit cards accepted.

Hours: From New Ross quays: Lunch and tea, June–Aug, daily at 12:30 and 3pm; Apr–May and Sept–Oct on demand. Dinner, Apr–Aug at 7pm, Sept at 6pm. From Waterford quays: June–Aug, daily at 3pm (frequency and departure times flexible, check locally).

WHERE TO STAY

Inishross House

96 Mary St., New Ross, Co. Wexford. ☎ **051/21335.** 6 rms, none with bath. IR£14 ($22.40) per person. 10% reduction for children. (Rates include breakfast.) Dinner IR£12 ($19.20) extra. No credit cards.

Mrs. Mary Doyle's six pretty bedrooms are nicely decorated and furnished, all with sinks. There's a TV lounge, private parking, and central heat. One reader had this to say: "The hosts were friendly and helpful, the rooms were very nice, and breakfasts were superb." Inishross House is in the town center, 200 yards from the bridge on N25.

Killarney House

The Maudlins, New Ross, Co. Wexford. ☎ **051/21062.** 3 rms, 2 with bath. IR£14.50–IR£15.50 ($23.20–$24.80) per person per night. 50% reduction for children under 10. (Rates include breakfast.) No credit cards. Closed Oct–Apr.

Mrs. Noreen Fallon's home has two things to make it highly recommendable: Guest rooms on the ground floor (a boon for those troubled by stairs), and a breakfast menu with several selections. Then there's the peaceful country setting, 1 1/4 miles from New Ross. All four bedrooms in this modern bungalow are equipped with sinks and electric blankets; there's a TV lounge for guests, central heating, and ample parking.

Riversdale House

Lower William St., New Ross, Co. Wexford. ☎ **051/22515.** 4 rms, all with bath. TV. IR£20 ($32) single; IR£16 ($25.60) per person sharing. 20% reduction for children. (Rates include breakfast.) No credit cards.

This lovely split-level home is the domain of Mrs. Ann Foley, whose hospitality is legendary, as attested to by her "National Housewife of the Year" award. The house is set in spacious grounds overlooking the town park and the river, and all the attractive bedrooms have tea/coffeemakers. Mrs. Foley is generous with her knowledge of the locality and her willingness to provide an early breakfast for those departing Rosslare Harbour, some 45 minutes away.

A Farmhouse

Farm House

Foulksmills, Co. Wexford. ☎ **051/63616.** 10 rms, none with bath. IR£14 ($22.40) per person sharing; extra IR£5 ($8) single. 20% reduction for children. High tea IR£7 ($11.20) extra; dinner IR£12 ($19.20). (Rates include breakfast.) No credit cards. Closed Dec–Feb.

Mrs. Joan Crosbie's homey, rambling farmhouse, 14 miles west of Wexford (N25/L160), 18 miles northwest of Rosslare, and seven miles west of the seaside, is of 17th-century vintage; the "newer" wing only goes back to the 18th century. This is the wing that houses the 10 comfortable guest rooms. There's central heating, but wood fires add a warmth of their own in both lounge and dining room.

Where to Eat

The Old Rectory

Rosbercon, New Ross. ☎ **051/21719.** Lunch IR£7.50–IR£8.50 ($12–$13.60); dinner IR£15–IR£16 ($24–$25.60); snacks less than IR£5 ($8). ACC, DC, V. Daily 12:30–2:30pm and 6:30–9:45pm. Closed four days at Christmas. SEAFOOD/TRADITIONAL/CONTINENTAL/SNACKS.

Set in scenic grounds overlooking the River Barrow just over the bridge from the town center, this old country house is tastefully decorated with antiques. Fish and other seafoods are fresh each day from local sources, meats are locally produced, and the garden furnishes all the herbs used in the kitchen. Roast lamb with homemade mint sauce is especially good here, as is grilled Dover sole when available. Homemade bread and pastries are also outstanding. There's wheelchair access, and they cater to children (up to 8pm) and nonsmokers.

KILMORE QUAY & THE SALTEES

From Wexford town, drive south on N25 (the Rosslare road) and turn right onto R739, running southwest and well signposted, which will take you into Kilmore Quay. From New Ross, head toward the coast on R736, pass through Wellington bridge and Bridgetown to R739, where a right turn will lead you to the picturesque village of Kilmore Quay. To return to Wexford, take R739 to N25 and turn north; to reach Rosslare (11 miles southeast of Wexford), a popular seaside resort with good beaches, or Rosslare Harbour (5 miles farther south), ferry port for the U.K. and France, turn south on N25.

What to See & Do

County Wexford has a very special sightseeing attraction in the **Saltee Islands,** four miles offshore from the pretty little fishing village of Kilmore Quay, 14 miles south of Wexford town. Local boatmen will take you out to the island after you've negotiated a fee (fishing trawlers will sometimes drop you off as they leave for the day's fishing and pick you up on the way home). A day on the Saltees can be soul-restoring even if you're not a birdwatcher, but if you qualify as the latter, you'll be treated to the sight of razorbills, kittiwakes, puffins, and thousands of gulls, along with hosts of seagoing species. It was in one of the Great Saltee's sea caves that the rebel leader of 1798, Begenal Havey, was captured and taken back to Wexford, where he was tortured and finally beheaded.

On your way to Kilmore Quay, you'll pass through **Kilmore Village,** a quaint little place with many traditional cottages crowned with roofs of thatch. Between the village and the quay, look for **Brandy Cross,** where you'll see a mound of little wooden crosses beside a certain bush. They've been put there by mourners on their way to the graveyard to bury a loved one—no one knows exactly why, but it's an ancient custom.

On the waterfront, have a look at the ✪ **Maritime Museum,** Kilmore Quay (☎ 053/29655). This is the former lightship *Guillemot,* which has been converted into a maritime museum. It's well worth a visit to view the many seafaring items, pictures, and models of famous ships and items of local history. If you'd like to visit this community-run project outside normal hours, contact Ann Kelly (secretary) or Reg Jarvis (curator and chairman), Kilmore Quay Maritime Society, at the above telephone number. There's a small admission fee, and it's open June to October, daily from noon to 6pm; other months by appointment.

THE HOOK PENINSULA

To drive down the Hook Peninsula, take R733 at the roundabout just outside Wexford town on N25 (the exit is well signposted for Arthurstown, Duncannon, and Ballyhack). From Rosslare Harbour, take N25, then R736; it will get you to Arthurstown and Duncannon, and signposts will direct you to such points as Fethard, Churchtown, and Ballyhack. (For directions from New Ross, see above.) If your ongoing route lies through Waterford, this is an off-the-beaten-track approach via the Ballyhack–Passage East ferry (see below).

WHAT TO SEE & DO

The ruins of the Knights Templars foundation still stand at **Templetown. Hook lighthouse** is the oldest in Europe, built over seven centuries ago. Near **Fethard-on-Sea,** at the now-buried town of Bannow, the Normans first landed in Ireland.

Ballyhack Castle, which began life in 1150 as home to the Knights Hospitallers of St. John, has been reincarnated as a **Heritage Information Centre.** Fascinating are the models that recreate the living quarters of the Crusader knights, medieval monks, and Normans of noble birth. On a grimmer note, one depicts prisoners' cells. A small admission fee is charged. It's open daily in July and August from 10am to 6pm; from April to June and in September, hours are noon to 6pm from Wednesday to Sunday.

From Ballyhack, catch the car-ferry over to Passage East on the County Waterford side to see these shores from the water as they were seen by Viking and Norman invaders. The ferry runs continuously April to September, Monday through Saturday from 7:20am to 10pm and on Sunday from 9:30am to 10pm (the last departure is at 8pm during other months). One-way fare is IR£4 ($6.40); round-trip, IR£6 ($9.60).

WHERE TO EAT

✪ The Neptune Restaurant

Ballyhack Harbour. ☎ **051/389-284.** Reservations recommended. Fixed-price meal IR£8 ($12.80) at lunch, IR£15 ($24) at dinner; Tourist Menu (includes glass of wine) in evenings only. ACC, AE, MC, V. Tues–Sat 12:30–3pm and 6–9:30pm. Closed Oct 1–16 and Dec 23–Mar 17. SEAFOOD.

This attractive little restaurant sits next to Ballyhack Castle just across from the harbor, and the seafood comes right out of local waters. Most other meats come from local sources, and everything is prepared by the owner himself. Service is friendly, and prices are only a little higher than moderate. It only seats 30, so best call ahead to reserve. For a small corkage fee, you can bring your own wine.

9 Counties Kilkenny & Carlow

If you're pressed for time, you may want to head straight for Waterford, Cork, and points west, but Counties Kilkenny and Carlow are an enticing swing inland from the usual around-the-rim tour of Ireland, and each holds attractions well worth the detour.

1 County Kilkenny

County Kilkenny's lovely pastoral landscape is dotted with Norman castles and keeps. It is in Kilkenny city, whose streets are haunted by vivid memories of medieval merchants and witches, that you will find the most splendid castle of all. In this castle's stables is the Kilkenny Design Centre, displaying the work of some of Ireland's leading designers and artisans.

SEEING COUNTY KILKENNY

By Bus Bus Eireann reaches Kilkenny city, as well as most small towns and villages throughout the county, from all major Irish cities. Bus schedules to smaller towns, however, tend to be sporadic and will require some careful study.

By Train There's train service from Dublin to Kilkenny city, but not to other destinations in the county.

By Car Kilkenny city is 73 miles southwest of Dublin, 27 miles northwest of New Ross, and 30 miles north of Waterford city. From a Kilkenny city base, follow R700 southeast to Bennetsbridge and Thomastown, then take N9 to nearby Jerpoint Abbey. If your next destination is Waterford city, follow N10 south until it becomes N9, which goes on into the city.

KILKENNY CITY

The city of Kilkenny is virtually a sightseeing destination in itself—its narrow, winding streets and well-preserved structures make it perhaps the most perfect example in Ireland today of a medieval town.

Sometimes called the "Marble City" because of the fine limestone quarried hereabouts, its Irish name is *Cill Chainnigh,* or St. Canice's Church, after a little monastery established here by the good saint in the sixth century on the grounds of the present St. Canice's Cathedral (the round tower dates back to the original settlement).

But it was the Normans, and later the Anglo-Normans, who built up the dignified town as a trading center that enjoyed the protection of royalty up until the mid-14th century. In 1366 the infamous Statutes of Kilkenny forbade any mingling of the Anglo-Normans with the native Irish.

By the time Oliver Cromwell arrived in 1649, the city's population was pretty well demoralized, making it an easy matter for him to seize the town, stable horses in the cathedral and smash its beautiful stained-glass windows, and slaughter many residents. Others he banished to Connaught so he could confiscate their property.

Despite its turbulent history, Kilkenny has held on to a cultural tradition that makes it a natural site for one of the most respected craft centers in Ireland today, the Kilkenny Design Centre, housed in the one-time stables of Kilkenny Castle (more about that later).

WHAT TO SEE & DO

VISITOR INFORMATION The Tourist Information Office is in Shee's Alms House, on Rose Inn Street, Kilkenny city (☎ **056/51500**). It's open daily from May to September, with varying hours other months. Their outstanding City Scope exhibition is a "don't miss" (small charge).

For a personalized special-interest, sports- and/or family-holiday or weekend break, contact **Tynan Heritage Services,** 2 Castle Yard, Kilkenny (☎ 056/52066; fax 056/52062). They also tailor-make sightseeing tours.

✪ Kilkenny Castle

The Parade. ☎ **056/21450.** Admission IR£3 ($4.80) adults, IR£2 ($3.20) seniors, IR£1.25 ($2) students and children, IR£7.50 ($12) family. Apr–May, daily 10:30am 5pm; June–Sept, daily 10am–7pm; other months by appointment for guided tour only.

Built in the late 1100s by the earl of Pembroke, impressive Kilkenny Castle dominates the city. The Butler family purchased it for a mere IR£800 in 1391 for King Richard II's first visit to Ireland. Cromwell made a right mess of it during his stopover in 1650, and in 1660, the first duke of Ormond set about restoring it to be used as a residence—which it remained until 1935. Given to the state in 1967, the castle has undergone extensive restoration to bring it back to its former glory. Visitors are welcomed with an audiovisual presentation, after which a knowledgeable, friendly, and enthusiastic staff takes them through the principal rooms—drawing room, library, dining room, and bedrooms—with their elegant furnishings and meticulously authentic wall coverings. The castle is rich in artworks, and there are miles of oil portraits and tapestries in the grand Long Gallery, as well as modern art in the Butler Gallery. Guides are well versed in stories of the people who have lived here—ask about Black Tom; then get set to hear some rather outrageous tales.

Rothe House

Parliament St. ☎ **056/22893.** Admission IR£2 ($3.20) adults, IR£1 ($1.60) students and seniors, 75p ($1.20) children. Apr–Oct, Mon–Sat 10:30am–5pm, Sun 3–5pm; winter, Sat–Sun 3–5pm.

This home of a prosperous Tudor merchant, built in 1594 and now a museum and library, has been meticulously restored. You'll come away keenly aware of life in medieval Ireland's merchant class. Take time to examine the old pikes and other relics of local historical and cultural significance.

The Tholsel

High St. Admission free. Inquire at the tourist office, about 100 yards away.

This 1761 toll house (exchange market) features a rather curious clock tower, and a front arcade that extends over the pavement. Inside are old records, charters, and the mayor's sword of 1609.

Shee's Alms House

Rose Inn St. ☎ **056/51500.** Admission free. Hours vary seasonally.

This interesting old building dates from 1594, so take time to look around when you drop in to the Tourist Information Office, which is housed here.

✪ Kyteler's Inn

St. Kieran's St. ☎ **056/21064** or 21888. You pay only for food and drink. Daily 10:30am–11:30pm. Closed Good Friday, Christmas Day.

This historic building was once the home of Dame Alice Kyteler, a beautiful woman who grew rich by the successive deaths of her four husbands. When the Lord Justiciar of Ireland condemned her to death on charges of witchcraft, Dame Alice skipped town (nothing was ever heard of her again) and left her convicted accessories to go to the stake alone. Within the walls of this solid stone house had been found a vast array of herbs, ointments, and other makings of magic spells.

There are no magic potions in the food now, however—it's a pub/restaurant that is really a "don't miss" in Kilkenny city. Even if you don't make it for a meal, stop in for a drink and cast a leery eye at the "witchy" courtyard with its two wells that supplied Dame Alice with water to mix her deadly potions.

St. Canice's Cathedral

Off Dean St. Admission free. Daily 9am–1pm and 2–6pm.

This Church of Ireland cathedral, dating from the 13th century and thought to be on the site of a sixth-century church, is easily one of the most beautiful ecclesiastical buildings in Ireland. Cromwell's troops left it a roofless ruin in 1649, but careful repair and restoration has been carried out over the centuries, and it is notable today for its outstanding Early English windows, several stone tomb effigies, and many fine medieval monuments. There's also a 100-foot-high round tower, whose conical cap has been replaced by a domed roof.

SHOPPING

✪ The Book Centre

10 High St. ☎ **056/62117.**

This is one of three excellent bookshops (in Waterford and Wexford) that carry extensive stocks of books on Irish and general interest topics. Open Monday through Saturday from 9am to 5pm; late-night and Sunday opening during summer season.

✪ Kilkenny Design Centre

Castle Yard. ☎ **056/22118.**

Created for the sole purpose of fostering good design in Irish industry, the center is just across the street from the castle and occupies its former stables and coach houses. Its horseshoe archways and carriage-wheel windows are in quaint contrast to the highly contemporary display inside. The workshops, originally government sponsored, are now operated as a private company. First-rate designers and craftspeople are provided with equipment and work space to develop new designs for textiles, ceramics, glassware, jewelry, metals, and clothing for both sexes. The showroom where these designs are for sale is a good place to do at least part of your shopping. There's also an excellent self-service restaurant overlooking the courtyard. Open Monday through Saturday from 9am to 6pm, Sunday from 10am to 6pm.

Kilkenny City

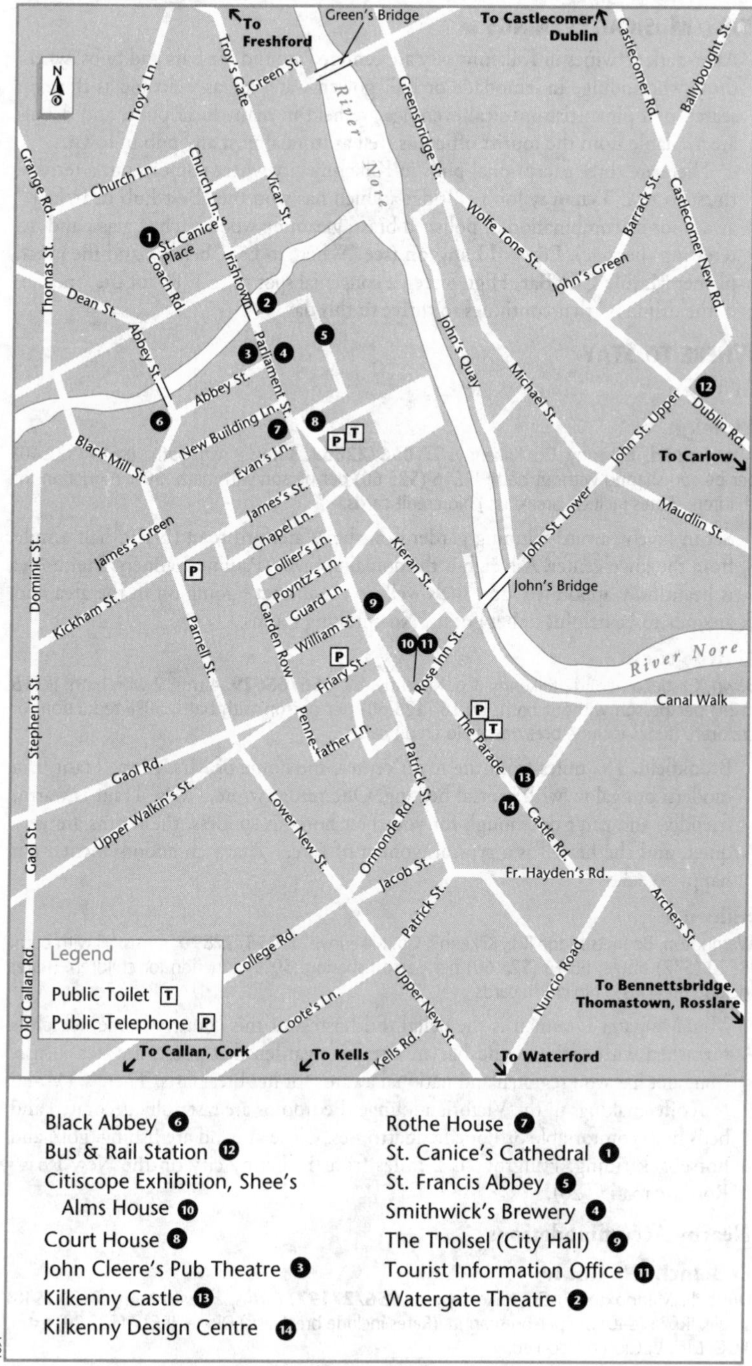

Pubs/Musical Evenings

After-dark activities in Kilkenny city are centered around the bars and pubs, where those who indulge in lemonade or Ballygowan water are as welcome as those in search of a pint. Irish musical evenings are held in many local pubs, and details are available from the tourist office, as well as from almost any pub in town.

There are three exceptional pubs in Kilkenny city where you can put a terrible thirst to rest: **Tynan's,** John's Bridge (which has won the "Best Pub in Ireland" award for its combination of polished brass, gleaming wood, etched glass, and interesting clientele); **Edward Langton** (see "Where to Eat," below); and the much plainer **Marble City Bar,** High Street, a congenial spot since 1789 for the "meetin' o' the drinkers" that continues to thrive to this day.

Where to Stay

In Town

Ashleigh

Waterford Rd., Kilkenny, Co. Kilkenny. ☎ **056/22809.** 3 rms, 2 with bath. IR£14 ($22.40) per person sharing without bath; IR£16 ($25.60) per person with bath. 50% reduction for children. (Rates include breakfast.) No credit cards.

Set in lovely, award-winning gardens on the Waterford road (N10), half a mile from the town center, Ashleigh is the domain of Mrs. Pauline Flannery. Her home is beautifully appointed, and she's well up on all that's going on in the area and anxious to be helpful to her guests. No-smoking rooms.

✪ Brookfield

Bawn, Castlecomer Rd., Kilkenny, Co. Kilkenny. ☎ **056/65629.** 4 rms, 2 with bath. IR£15 ($24) per person without bath; IR£16 ($25.60) per person with bath. 50% reduction for children. (Rates include breakfast.) No credit cards.

Brookfield, 1¼ miles from the town center, the home of Mrs. Mary Trant, is a modern bungalow with central heating. One reader wrote, "Mrs. Trant is warm, friendly, and can't do enough for you. Her home is spotless, the rooms are very quiet, and she herself is a typical woman of Eire." That's an endorsement I am happy to echo!

Hillgrove

Warrington, Bennetsbridge Rd., Kilkenny, Co. Kilkenny. ☎ **056/22890.** 4 rms, all with bath. IR£20 ($32) single; IR£16 ($25.60) per person sharing. 50% reduction for children. (Rates include breakfast.) No credit cards.

Mrs. Margaret Drennan is the delightful hostess of this country home, which is furnished with antiques and has an attractive garden that guests are free to use. Margaret has won regional and national awards for her breakfasts. There's TV and tea/coffeemakings in the Victorian lounge. Bedrooms are tastefully decorated and beds have comfortable orthopedic mattresses. Close at hand are fishing, golf, and horseback riding. Hillgrove is 2 miles from Kilkenny city on the New Ross–Rosslare road (T20).

Nearby Accommodations

✪ Blanchville House

Dunbell, Maddoxtown, Co. Kilkenny. ☎ **056/27197.** 6 rms, all with bath. IR£30 ($48) single; IR£25 ($40) per person sharing. (Rates include breakfast.) Dinner IR£17 ($27.20) extra. ACC, MC, V. Closed Dec–Feb.

Monica Phelan's warm hospitality has won raves from our readers, as has her elegant Georgian-style home, just a 10-minute drive from Kilkenny city. The early-19th-century home is the heart of a working farm and retains many of its original features such as the drawing room, with many original furnishings and an open fire. Bedrooms are tastefully furnished and have tea/coffeemakers. Meals feature homegrown produce translated into traditional dishes (dinner must be booked before noon). There's central heating and private parking.

WHERE TO EAT

✪ Edward Langton Restaurant and Bar

69 John St. ☎ **056/65133** or 21728. Main courses IR£5–IR£10 ($8–$16); bar food under IR£5 ($8). ACC, AE, MC, V. Mon–Sat 10:30am–11pm, Sun 12:30–11pm. Closed Good Friday, Dec 25–26. IRISH/TRADITIONAL/VEGETARIAN/BAR FOOD.

It's no wonder that this bar and eatery has won national awards for several years running—the food here is not only superb but it's also great value for money. This restaurant is just the right place for vegetarians, although it offers all of the traditional choices as well. The old-style setting of the restaurant is perfectly delightful. Even if you don't plan to eat a meal here, at least nip in and have a pint—it's worth the trip.

Kilkenny Design Centre Restaurant

Castle Yard, Kilkenny, Co. Kilkenny. ☎ **056/22118.** Average meal under IR£10 ($16); snacks IR£5–IR£8 ($8–$12.80). AE, DC, MC, V. Apr–Sept, Mon–Sat 9am–6pm, Sun 10am–6pm, other months 9am–5pm. TRADITIONAL/IRISH/SNACKS.

Overlooking Kilkenny Castle's cobbled courtyard, this attractive self-service restaurant features a wide range of hot dishes, along with a large selection of salads based on seasonal produce, quiches, soups, and pâté. Layered terrines and fresh salmon are outstanding, as are fruit pies served with cream. The Irish cheeseboard is excellent.

Kyteler's Inn

Kieran St. ☎ **056/21064.** Main courses IR£5–IR£12 ($8–$19.20); fixed-priced Sun lunch IR£10 ($16); bar food under IR£6 ($9.60). ACC, MC, V. Daily 10:30am–11:30pm. Closed Good Friday, Christmas Day. IRISH/TRADITIONAL/VEGETARIAN.

Kyteler's Inn is a sightseeing attraction as well as a pleasant bar-cum-restaurant. The menu features dishes based on local meats and vegetables, with a nice selection for seafood and meat lovers, as well as vegetarian dishes prepared from fresh local produce.

Readers Recommend

Bregagh, Dean Street, Kilkenny, Co. Kilkenny. ☎ 056/22315. *"Located just a block or two from the city center, Bregagh is within easy walking distance of St. Canice's Cathedral, the Black Abbey, and the Catholic cathedral. Mrs. Brennan and her husband's amazing friendliness, service, and attention made this place most memorable. When my wife was confined to bed for two days, Mrs. Brennan brought her meals in bed and gave her great care."* —Francis Greene, Spokane, WA

Tir Na Nog, Greenshill, Kilkenny, Co. Kilkenny. ☎ 056/65250. *"Proprietors Mary and Eamonn offer guests a private sitting room with books and materials on local events and historical points of interest. Their five bedrooms all have private bathrooms and other little comforts usually not found in B&Bs. This is a very charming and comfortable place to stay, less than five minutes' walk from Kilkenny town center."*
—Geraldine and Mark Bulwicz, Doylestown, PA

BENNETSBRIDGE, GRAIGUENAMANAGH & THOMASTOWN

The area around Bennetsbridge has attracted a host of craftspeople, and the Tourist Information Office in Kilkenny can furnish helpful lists and pamphlets to help you find them. One of the most interesting (and most popular with our readers over the years) is the ✪ **Nicholas Mosse Pottery,** Bennetsbridge (☎ 056/27126). About 4½ miles south of Kilkenny on R700, on the banks of the Nore, Nicholas Mosse has set up a workshop for his award-winning pottery. His mother runs the shop and a tiny museum of old Irish cottage pottery. She's so friendly that, to quote Nicholas, "Many's the visitor who gets a tour of the house and a cuppa." They're open year-round Monday to Saturday from 10am to 6pm, and during July and August on Sunday as well, from 2 to 6pm. Well signposted on R700. **The Millstone Restaurant,** across the road from the pottery, is an excellent lunch stop—good food, friendly service, and prices that won't break the budget (open Tuesday to Sunday, May to September, from 10:30am to 7:30pm).

About 1½ miles southwest of Thomastown, look for ✪ **Jerpoint Abbey,** Thomastown. One of the finest monastic ruins in Ireland, this Cistercian abbey dates from 1158, and in 1540 it suffered the fate of many such institutions when the order was suppressed and its lands handed over to the Ormond family. There are interesting sculptures in the partially restored 15th-century cloisters. Other features of interest are the 15th- and 16th-century tombs of the Walsh and Butler families, and the square central tower with its distinctively Irish stepped battlements. The ruins are open for visitors June to September, daily from 10am to 1pm and 2 to 7pm; the rest of the year, by obtaining the key from the caretaker, Mrs. Wallace, in the adjoining house.

Stop by **Jerpoint Glass Studio,** Stoneyford, Co. Kilkenny (☎ 056/24350), where Keith and Kathleen Leadbetter sell factory seconds at reduced prices. Open Monday through Friday from 9am to 6pm, Saturday from 11am to 6pm.

In Graiguenamanagh, you can visit the showrooms of the **Duiske Handcut Glass factory** (☎ 053/24174), open Monday through Friday from 9am to 5pm (closed one week at Christmas).

WHERE TO STAY

The Nore Valley Villa

Inistioge, Co. Kilkenny. ☎ **056/58418.** 5 rms, 3 with bath. IR£14 ($22.40) per person sharing without bath; IR£2 ($3.20) per person additional with bath. 20% reduction for children. (Rates include breakfast.) ACC, MC, V. Private parking. Closed Dec–Feb.

Overlooking the River Nore outside Inistioge, five miles from Thomastown, on the Rosslare to Kilkenny-Athlone road, this Georgian villa is close to Woodstock Forest and makes an ideal base for day trips to historical sites nearby. In addition to sightseeing, you'll find golf, fishing, and hill-walking within easy reach, and not the least of its location charms is a local pub where "the crack is mighty." Leslie and Lucy Rothwell can steer you to all these attractions and more. The house is centrally heated.

✪ Stablecroft

Mooneen, Graiguenamanagh, Co. Kilkenny. ☎ **0503/24714.** 4 rms, 3 with bath. IR£17 ($27.20) per person sharing; IR£3 ($4.80) single supplement. (Rates include breakfast.) Dinner IR£14 ($22.40). No credit cards.

Sheila and Alan Forrest were called by one reader "the perfect hosts," a compliment I heartily endorse. Their stone house fits naturally into its wooded farmland setting. Views of Mount Leinster and the Blackstairs Mountains rooms are large, beautifully decorated, and comfortable. The ho and a conservatory. Even though there's full central heating, and one lounge have cheerful log-burning stoves. Alan, a knowledg operates a power boat for fishing expeditions. Both the Forrests del helping guests plan sightseeing and outdoor activities.

Farmhouses

Brandon View House

Ballyogan, Graiguenamanagh, Co. Kilkenny. ☎ **0503/24191.** Fax 0503/24451. 4 rms, 1 with bath. IR£18 ($28.80) per person. 20% reduction for children. (Rates include breakfast.) Dinner IR£16 ($25.60) extra. No credit cards. Private parking.

Mrs. Alice McCabe and her family will welcome you to their 18th-century farmhouse, set in scenic surroundings eight miles from New Ross and eight miles from Thomastown, well signposted on R705. In addition to the comfortable guest rooms, there's a restful sitting room with a log fire and a piano that has sparked many a singsong session. The large garden overlooks Brandon Lake, at the foot of Brandon Hill. Scenic walks on the farm are signposted. Dinner is available and is made with fresh, organically grown fruits and vegetables from the kitchen garden. The house is centrally heated. There's also a stone self-catering cottage; details on request.

✪ Cullintra House

The Rower, Inistioge, Co. Kilkenny. ☎ **051/23614.** 5 rms, 1 with bath; family suite, with shower. IR£20–IR£23 ($32–$36.80) per person sharing. Dinner IR£16 ($25.60) extra. Special rate for weekly B&B plus dinner. 10% reduction for children. Minimum stay two nights. (Rates include breakfast.) No credit cards. Private parking.

Miss Patricia Cantlon is the gracious hostess at this 200-year-old farmhouse (six miles from New Ross, five miles from Thomastown, on the Kilkenny road, R700) which is a member of the Hidden Ireland Country Homes Association. Actually, "gracious" aptly describes the overall ambience at Cullintra House, and it's not at all unusual for a house-party atmosphere to break out, complete with singsongs and storytelling. The house is centrally heated, the food is delicious, and dinner is by candlelight before a log fire. There's also a large art studio/conservatory with free tea- and coffeemaking facilities for guest use. There are four comfortable bedrooms, all with handbasins and hairdryers, and one three-room suite with private shower. Highly recommended.

Where to Eat

✪ The Loft

Mount Juliet, Thomastown. ☎ **056/24455.** Reservations recommended. Main courses IR£10–IR£14 ($16–$22.40). Sunday brunch IR£14 ($22.40). ACC, AE, MC, V. IRISH/TRADITIONAL/SEAFOOD.

This delightful restaurant is located in the Hunter's Yard sporting center of the luxurious Mount Juliet Estate just outside Thomastown (see above). It's a bright, cheerful place, with informality the keynote, and it's open to nonresidents at both lunch and dinner.

The menu features the freshest ingredients, many from local sources, and among the starters from the á la carte menu you'll find the likes of lamb kidneys in an Irish whiskey and mustard sauce or local Irish smoked salmon. Main dishes might

Southeast

Nenagh
N7
Rathdowney
LAOIS
N77
Templemore
Templetouchy
Ballyragget
Silvermines
Johnstown
Borrisoleigh
Freshford
Urlingford
N8
Thurles
Milestone
Holycross
Cappamore
Ballingarry
Cappawhite
Killenaule
Caherconlish
Rock of Cashel
N24
TIPPERARY
N76
Herbertstown
Cashel
Callan
N74
Fethard
Windgap
Tipperary Town
Slievenaman Mountain
R697
R688
Ahenny
Knocklong
Glen of Aherlow
Cahir
Kilfinane
Galty Mountains
Clonmel
Ballylanders
N8
Carrick-on-Suir
Burncourt
LIMERICK
R678
Portlaw
Clogheen
R671
R665
R676
Mitchelstown
Ballyporeen
R677
N73
WATERFORD
Kildorrery
R626
Kilmacthomas
N8
Knockmealdown Mountains
N25
Lemybrien
R672
Ballyduff
Bunmahon
N72
Cappoquin
R666
Fermoy
N72
Dungarvan
Clonea Strand
Lismore
N72
Rathcormac
R628
Tallow
R671
Ring
Ballyknock
R614
R634
Watergrasshill
N25
R626
N8
R627
Ardmore
N20
Youghal
Cork
Midleton
N25
N22
Cobh
N71
CORK
Ballycotton
1692

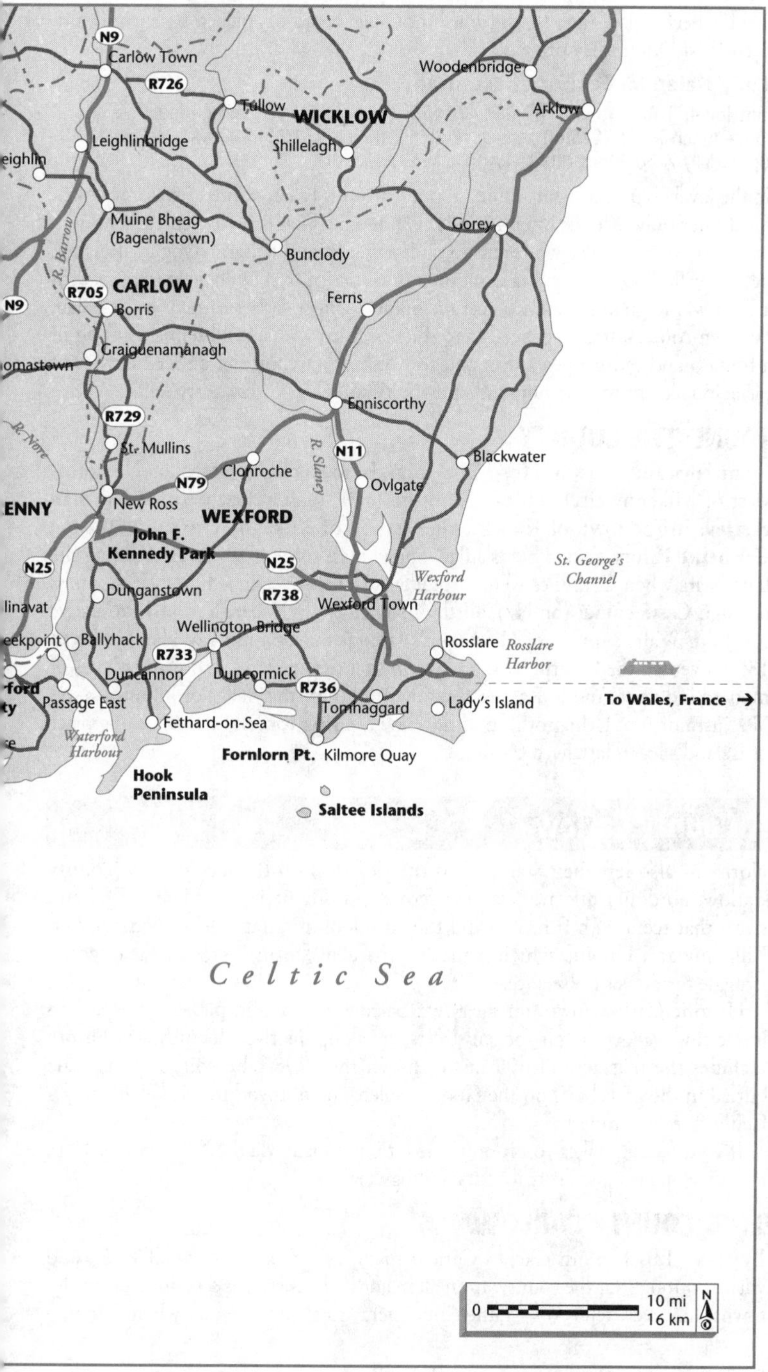

N9
Carlow Town
R726
Woodenbridge
Tullow
WICKLOW
Arklow
Leighlinbridge
eighlin
Shillelagh
Muine Bheag
(Bagenalstown)
Gorey
R. Barrow
Bunclody
R705
CARLOW
Ferns
N9
Borris
Graiguenamanagh
omastown
Enniscorthy
R729
R. Nore
St. Mullins
N11
Blackwater
Clonroche
R. Slaney
N79
Ovlgate
New Ross
ENNY
WEXFORD
John F.
Kennedy Park
N25
N25
St. George's
Channel
Wexford
Harbour
Dunganstown
R738
Wexford Town
linavat
Wellington Bridge
eekpoint
Ballyhack
Rosslare
Rosslare
Harbor
R733
Duncannon
Duncormick
R736
rford
ty
Passage East
Tomhaggard
Lady's Island
To Wales, France →
Fethard-on-Sea
Waterford
Harbour
Fornlorn Pt.
Kilmore Quay
Hook
Peninsula
Saltee Islands

Celtic Sea

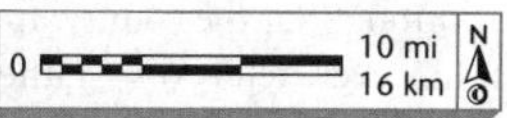

include beefsteak, Guinness-and-mushroom pie, breast of chicken with garlic, and deep-fried Dublin Bay prawns.

✪ Lady Helen McCalmont Restaurant

Mount Juliet, Thomastown. ☎ **056/24455.** Reservations recommended. Five-course set-price lunch IR£16 ($25.60); set-price dinner IR£33 ($52.80). AE, MC, V. Sun 12:30–2:30pm; daily 7–10:30pm. IRISH/TRADITIONAL/SEAFOOD.

In the lovely blue-and-white dining room at Mount Juliet, nonresidents are booked for dinner only. Menus often include such items as oak-smoked cured ham on a bed of marinated baby white turnip with a cumin and balsamic-yogurt dressing; lightly grilled ocean prawn tails set on a thin slice of fresh wild river salmon with a light whole-grain mustard sauce; melon-and-ginger sorbet to refresh the palate between courses; breast of free-range chicken filled with a mild fennel stuffing in a tomato and red-pepper sauce; and to finish off, a choice of an iced dessert of pistachio ice cream or lemon-and-strawberry sorbet in a strawberry sauce.

AROUND THE COUNTY

From Tinacashel crossroad (two miles from the town of Urlingford, on N8 northwest of Kilkenny city) you can count no fewer than a dozen **Anglo-Norman castles.** In the town of Knocktopher (south of Kilkenny city on N10), the **Carmelite Priory** garden holds a flat-topped mass stone that was used during the long years when Catholics were forbidden to practice their religion. If you pass through **Castlecomer** (on N77 north of Kilkenny city), spare a thought to native son John Walker (uncle of New York's famous mayor Jimmy Walker), who in 1899 invented the Caterpillar track system that revolutionized so many phases of modern industry. And in Rathosheen townland (near the village of Johnstown, on N8, just north of Urlingford), tradition says the **ring fort** is the final resting place of Ireland's legendary hero Oisin.

2 County Carlow

Normans also left their stamp (and their castles) on the face of tiny County Carlow, no doubt drawn by land as fertile and productive as it is beautiful and rivers that teem with fish. Nor did they overlook its strategic location between Kilkenny and Dublin, which made it a frequent storm center in the ongoing struggle for power in Ireland.

Historic Carlow town, on the River Barrow, is a bright, pleasant place, with interesting walks through ancient streets and along the river. Its turbulent history includes the massacre of 600 insurgents in the 1798 rebellion (some 400 lie buried in the gravel pits on the Graiguecullen side of town, the site marked by a Celtic cross memorial).

If your touring takes you from Carlow to Stradbally via the N80, Windy Gap, the drive opens up some truly outstanding views.

SEEING COUNTY CARLOW

By Bus Bus Eireann reaches Carlow town, as well as most small towns and villages throughout the county, from all major Irish cities. Bus schedules to smaller towns, however, tend to be rather infrequent, so check carefully when planning day trips.

By Train There's train service from Dublin to Carlow town.

By Car Carlow town is some 52 miles southwest of Dublin on N9, and 36 miles directly north of New Ross, County Wexford, on R705 and N9. A short drive east of town on R726 will take you to the Brown's Hill Dolmen. Return to town, then take N9 south to the picturesque village of Leighlinbridge on the River Barrow. Still heading south, take R705 to Bagenalstown, and stay on R705 south to Borris. Still farther south on R705 is Graiguenamanagh. If you're going on to County Kilkenny, turn west on R703 to reach Thomastown and nearby Jerpoint Abbey on N9. Return to Thomastown and follow R700 through Bennetsbridge to Kilkenny city.

CARLOW TOWN

In July and August, there's a **Tourist Information Office** (☎ **0503/31554**) in the Town Hall in Carlow town, with varying hours.

WHAT TO SEE & DO

Near the Barrow bridge, in the grounds of the Corcoran's Mineral Water Factory, you'll find the ruins of imposing **Carlow Castle.** This was one of Cromwell's victims in 1650, but survived to be returned to the earls of Thomond in the 1800s. Its final demise came about when a local doctor, who wanted to use it as a lunatic asylum, tried to thin its walls with explosives, rendering it so unsafe that it finally had to be demolished. The ruins are open Monday through Friday from 9am to 5pm, with permission of the factory staff; no admission charge.

The 1833 cruciform, Gothic-style **Cathedral of the Assumption,** off Tullow Street, holds a marble monument by the celebrated Irish sculptor Hogan to a Bishop Doyle, who wrote extensively about 19th-century politics, using a pen name to stay out of trouble. Its lantern tower is some 151 feet high, and there are magnificent stained-glass windows, designed by Harry Clarke. Open daily from 10am to 6pm, with no admission fee.

Housed in an old theater, the **Haymarket Museum,** adjacent to Town Hall (☎ 0503/31532), is an interesting little museum that features a reconstructed forge and kitchen, as well as tools and military and religious relics. There's no charge, and it's open in summer daily from 9am to 1pm and 2 to 5pm (closed the rest of the year).

Two miles east of Carlow on L7, **Browne's Hill** demesne holds an impressive dolmen—its capstone weighs 100 tons, the largest in Europe.

Cyclists can explore the lovely Barrow and Nore valleys on a seven- or fourteen-day tour available through **Celtic Cycling,** Lorum Old Rectory, Bagenalstown, Co. Carlow (☎ 0503/75282, fax 0503/75455). Included are the bike rental, safety equipment, rain gear, maps, insurance, and B&B accommodations. The suggested itineraries can be modified to fit your own skill and stamina.

WHERE TO STAY

Meeltrane House

Link Rd., Brownshill, Carlow, Co. Carlow. ☎ **0503/42473.** 4 rms, 2 with bath. IR£18 ($28.80) single; IR£14 ($22.40) per person sharing; IR£1 ($1.60) per person extra for private bath. (Rates include breakfast.) No credit cards. Closed Sept–May.

In the Brownshill section of Carlow town, 1¼ miles from the town center on Link Road, Mrs. Mary Ruane's modern, two-story home features guest rooms that are spacious, and Mrs. Ruane is a helpful and accommodating hostess.

The Squires

Link Rd., Brownshill, Carlow, Co. Carlow, ☎ **0503/43771.** 5 rms, 1 with bath. IR£13.50 ($21.60) per person without bath, IR£14.50 ($23.20) per person with bath. (Rates include breakfast.) ACC, MC, V.

This is the bright, modern home of Eva and Mike Byrne (he's Irish, she's English). There is little I can add to the testimonial of one of our readers, who wrote: "Eva is an animal lover and a marvelously friendly person who puts her guests at ease and will go out of her way to accommodate them. We found their home very attractive, and our breakfast was excellent." The Squires is 1 1/2 miles from the town center.

Where to Eat

✪ The Beams Restaurant

59 Dublin St. ☎ **0503/31824.** Reservations recommended. Five-course fixed-price dinner IR£18.50 ($29.60). DC, V. Tues–Sat 7–9:30pm. SEAFOOD/CONTINENTAL.

This lovely old coaching inn (with original old beams retained, hence the name) has been lovingly restored and now houses an excellent eatery presided over by Betty and Peter O'Gorman. It's an intimate sort of place, seating only 40, and the menu features a wide variety of fish and seafood dishes—oysters, scallops, wild salmon and trout, John Dory, and other unusual fish as they are available. There's also a very good selection of beef, veal, lamb, pork, and chicken dishes, and an extensive award-winning wine list.

LEIGHLINBRIDGE, BAGENALSTOWN & BORRIS

In Leighlinbridge, look for the ruins of 12th-century **Black Castle.** Bagenalstown is a lovely little canalside town with many fine public buildings, and Borris is a charming village in a wooded setting adjoining **Borris Castle.** Cyclists can explore the lovely Barrow and Nore valleys in detail by booking a seven- or fourteen-day tour with **Celtic Cycling,** Lorum Old Rectory, Bagenalstown, Co. Carlow (☎ 0503/75282, fax 0503/75455). Included are the bike hire, safety equipment, rain gear, maps, insurance, and B&B accommodations, and suggested itineraries can be modified to fit your own skill and stamina.

Where to Stay

✪ Kilgraney Country House

Bagenalstown, Co. Carlow. ☎/Fax **0503/75283.** 5 rms, 4 with bath. IR£20–IR£30 ($32–$48) per person sharing, IR£8 ($12.80) single supplement. (Rates include breakfast.) Dinner IR£18 ($28.80). ACC, MC, V. Closed Nov–Jan. Enclosed car park.

Partners Brian Leech and Martin Marley have taken in hand this fine 1800s house, giving it the respect its high ceilings and beautiful mouldings deserve. They've created an attractive, eclectic decor. Furnishings include interesting items picked up on their travels abroad, and guest rooms are downright charming. Brian stars in the kitchen, and his meals are outstanding—one reader calls them "gourmet." The house is just off the R705 (L18), 3.5 miles from Bagenalstown on the Borris road; turn right at Kilgraney crossroad, and the house is the first entrance on the left.

✪ Lorum Old Rectory

Kilgreaney, Bagenalstown, Co. Carlow. ☎ **0503/75282.** 5 rms, 4 with bath. IR£25 ($40) single; IR£20–IR£25 ($32–$40) per person sharing. 20% reduction for children. (Rates include breakfast.) Dinner IR£16 ($25.60) extra. ACC, MC, V. Closed Christmas.

I can't imagine a more scenic place to stay than Bobbie and Don Smith's 150-year-old stone farmhouse, right in the middle of County Carlow's rich countryside, at the foot of the Blackstairs Mountains, a mere 15 miles from Kilkenny and midway between Bagenalstown and Borris on R704/L18. It's a good base for local sightseeing or crafts shopping, and croquet, tennis, and lawn games will help while away your leisure hours, with golf, swimming, tennis, and horseracing nearby. Furnishings include many antiques, homegrown fruits and vegetables grace the table, and there's central heating as well as electric blankets and open fires.

Where to Eat

✪ Danette's Feast

Urglin Glebe, Bennekerry, Carlow, Co. Carlow. ☎ **0503/40817.** Set dinner IR£20 ($32). Reservations essential. Wed–Sat 7–10pm, Sun 7–9pm. INTERNATIONAL.

Should you arrive in Carlow on Monday or Tuesday, it's well worth changing your itinerary to stay over for at least one meal between Wednesday and Sunday in this superb little restaurant. *Be sure, however, to book ahead*—it only seats 30, and it is very popular with locals as well as visitors. The restaurant is in the main Georgian section of the very large house, and an 18th-century two-story cottage is now the kitchen. Bright, strong colors are used throughout: Drinks and "nibbles" or dips are served in the Red Room (which Danette likens to the color of Rioja wine). From there, you proceed to one of the two dining rooms. Partners Danette O'Connell and David Milne are both musicians (he's Head of Music at Kilkenny College), and if things are quiet enough, you may find him at the piano. The kitchen is Danette's domain, and her creations often combine ethnic flavors (like her chili rellenos with goat cheese, Parma ham, and a puree of sun-dried tomatoes—Mexican and Italian—or Mediterranean minced lamb with a red pepper sauce). The menu selection is quite varied and always includes a vegetarian dish, as well as organically grown vegetables whenever possible. Two things not to be missed: her tomato and fennel bread and, to finish off the meal, her caramelized lemon tart made from the eggs of their free-range hens. The restaurant is just three miles from Carlow town, immediately off the Hacketstown Road, in a wooded site with a 150-yard drive up to the house.

Lord Bagenal Inn

Leighlinbridge. ☎ **0503/21668.** Appetizers IR£3–IR£5 ($4.35–$7.25); main courses IR£10–IR£12 ($14.50–$17.40); fixed-price dinner IR£18 ($26.10). DC, V. Mon–Sat 12:30–10:30pm, Sun 12:30–9pm. Closed Christmas Day. CONTINENTAL/SEAFOOD.

Set on the banks of the River Barrow in the village of Leighlinbridge just off the Dublin-Carlow-Kilkenny road (it's signposted), the Lord Bagenal has a warm, inviting, old-world air. Locally grown vegetables and meats are used, and shellfish are kept in a tank to ensure freshness with each order. Roast duck, tournedos steak, escalopes of pork, and a wide variety of seafood and fish are menu stars.

10 County Waterford & South Tipperary

Say "Waterford" to most Americans and they'll promptly reply "crystal." And certainly a visit to the Waterford Crystal Factory is a highlight of any visit. But save time for a ramble through the rest of this beautiful and picturesque county. County Waterford is one of the most scenic counties in the Southeast, with a landscape that shades from a coastline of rugged headland cliffs and deep-cut bays ringed by sandy beaches, to the Comeragh mountains in the north and center and the Knockmealdown range farther south, to gentle hills and fertile valleys that separate the sea and mountains. Prehistoric dolmens, promontory forts, and passage graves in the area speak of the earliest settlers. Legends of valor and beautiful early Iron Age metalwork mirror the two sides of the battle-loving and artistic Celtic clan of the Deise.

Sharing County Waterford's mountain ranges is the southernmost portion of County Tipperary, making it impossible to consider one without including the other (North Tipperary can best be explored from the Shannonside region, as discussed in Chapter 15). Tipperary is Ireland's largest inland county, straddling the country from east to west. Along with that vast territory, South Tipperary holds a wealth of antiquities that also straddle much of Ireland's past.

1 Waterford

103 miles SW of Dublin, 40 miles W of Wexford, 40 miles NE of Cork City

Just 40 miles from Wexford, Waterford is Ireland's fourth-largest city. Every phase of Irish history has left its traces here, and the harbor today is as alive with freighters along the broad River Suir (as wide here as the Thames at Westminster Bridge) as in the days when Viking longships plied its waters.

The most extensive remains of Viking walls in the country and massive Reginald's Tower (which has stood intact for 1,000 years) remind us of those fierce sea raiders. They came in 853 for a safe haven from which to launch their plundering forays, and stayed to become settlers and traders for more than 300 years. The Normans, who claimed the city in 1170, left a legacy of dozens of towers like the "Half-Moon" on Stephen Street. And the modern Waterford Crystal Factory, one of the city's most persistent claims to fame, is a descendant of the 1783 enterprise begun at the west end of the Quay by George and William Penrose.

The Irish call it Port Lairge ("Lairge's Landing Place"), and to the Vikings it was Vadrefjord. Always this city on the Suir has been the main seaport of the Southeast. Today it maintains a thriving shipping trade with the Continent and England. In 1210 King John of England dubbed it "a pearl of great price." Its walls withstood a siege by Oliver Cromwell in 1649, then fell to one of his generals the next year. James II was loyally received when he stopped in Waterford in 1690, en route to Kinsale after a crushing defeat at the Battle of the Boyne. Hot on his heels came the victorious King William III to receive the city's surrender on honorable terms.

The people of Waterford are an amiable blend of all those who came over the centuries as settlers, conquerors, and/or artisans, and they are especially warm in their welcome to those of us who only come to visit. As far back as 1586 it was written by one Richard Stanihurst, "The people are cheerful in their entertainment of strangers." And so you will find them today!

GETTING THERE There is bus service from most major points in Ireland; train service from Dublin and Cork; and air service from London. For bus and train information, call 051/73401; for flight information, call 051/71701.

ESSENTIALS Orientation As cities go, Waterford is small, easy to find your way around in, with shank's mare the only vehicle you'll need for a good day's sightseeing. Its focal point is the broad quay that runs along the Suir's south bank and is named simply The Quay. Distinctive Reginald Tower is at one end, the Clock Tower is at near center (an important landmark), and a bridge crossing the Suir is at the other. Narrow streets and lanes, as well as somewhat wide Barronstrad Street, lead off The Quay to the half-dozen or so streets on which are concentrated a great many of Waterford's sightseeing attractions, restaurants, pubs, and a few first-rate accommodations. The tourist office can supply an excellent and easily followed street map.

Information The Irish Tourist Office is at 41 The Quay (☎ 051/75788; fax 051/77388), open from 9am to 6am Mon–Sat during summer, and Mon–Fri Oct–Mar. This is an especially friendly office with a very helpful staff and with facilities for booking accommodations, transportation, sightseeing—in short, as they say with pride, "anything that's bookable in Ireland."

Pick up their excellent street map.

The tourist board also has the helpful ***Waterford County Guide*** (for a small charge) as well as an excellent selection of maps and Irish publications. They will book you for a tour of the Waterford Crystal Factory (see below) and bring you up-to-date on what's going on in town during your stay and advise you on Bus Eireann day trips around the area.

There are two weekly Waterford newspapers: the *Munster Express* and the *Waterford News & Star.*

Walking Tours From May to October, the Waterford Tourist Service conducts guided walking tours daily. The one-hour walk takes you to the most important historic buildings in the city and fills you in on the city's development since the Middle Ages. Tours leave from the reception desk of the Granville Hotel, The Quay, 12pm and 2pm, and cost IR£3 ($4.80) per person. No need to book in advance—just show up at the appointed times.

Bus Tours Ask at the tourist office about all-day coach tours of the area that are offered from time to time.

SPECIAL EVENTS Wexford has its opera festival, but Waterford has the ✪ **International Festival of Light Opera,** a lighthearted gathering of amateur companies that converge on the city in September from Europe, the U.S., Great Britain, and all parts of Ireland. During each of the festival's 16 nights there are performances of such musicals as *Brigadoon* and *Showboat,* all of amazingly high standard, and things wind up with the presentation of a beautiful Waterford Glass trophy. Light opera, however, is not the only thing going on during this time. There are singing pub competitions (with all pubs granted an extension of hours up to 1am) and a host of auxiliary activities, with a special Festival Office set up to see that you get to the event of your choice.

Individual performances range from IR£3–IR£8 ($4.80–$12.80). For reservations, write: Booking Office, International Festival of Light Opera, Waterford, County Waterford.

GETTING AROUND By Bus and Train The bus and rail depot is at the northern end of the Suir Bridge. Bus Eireann has a good variety of day trips around the region. For bus and rail information, call 051/79000 Monday through Saturday from 9am to 5:30pm, 051/73408 at other times. There is city bus service, but routes are limited and service can be infrequent. City buses are not numbered, and most depart from the Clock Tower on the Quay—inquire of drivers for specific routes.

By Taxi There is a taxi stand at the rail and bus station, and you can telephone 53333 for a cab to pick you up anywhere in the city.

On Foot As noted above, Waterford is a walking town, and you'll seldom need to resort to other forms of transportation within the city.

By Car It's fairly easy to drive around Waterford if you stick to the broad streets. Good parking is provided along the Quay for a small hourly charge, and at the top of Barronstrand Street (usually quite congested).

FAST FACTS: WATERFORD

Car Service The Automobile Association is on The Quay (☎ 051/73765).
Emergencies In an emergency (police, medical, fire), dial 999.
Mail The General Post Office is on The Quay a few blocks from Reginald's Tower, open Monday through Friday from 9am to 5:30pm, and on Saturday from 9am to 1pm (closed Sunday).

WHAT TO SEE & DO

THE TOP ATTRACTIONS

✪ Reginald's Tower Museum

The Quay. Small fee for adults, free for children when accompanied by an adult. Combination ticket including Heritage Centre, IR£1 ($1.60). Open Mid-Apr to Oct, Mon–Fri 10am–7pm, Sat 10am–6pm; ask at the City Hall (on the Mall) about winter hours.

At the end of the Quay, which turns into the Mall, Reginald's Tower stands sentinel as it has for 1,000 years, though today, as a museum, it guards gems from Waterford's historical treasures. When Reginald McIvor, the Danish ruler, built this stronghold, its 12-foot-thick walls stood right at the river's edge, and it was constructed so that entrance could only be gained from inside the city walls. In the centuries since, the tower has proved its worth as the strongest fortification on the River Suir, having resisted attack from all sides (even Cromwell failed to conquer it, although the bitterly cold winter may have had something to do with his unsuccessful siege). And it has witnessed events of major significance in Ireland's

Waterford City

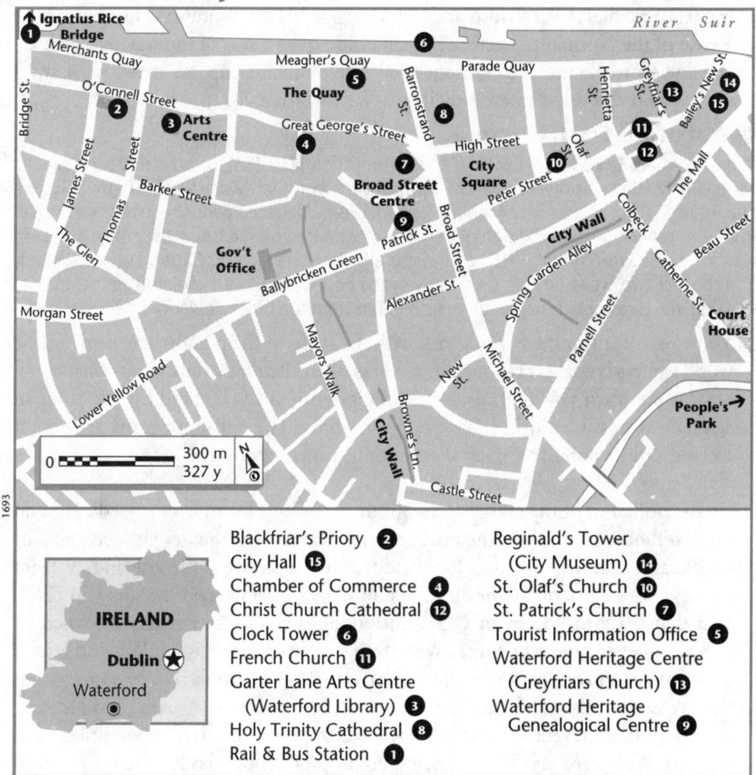

history, such as the marriage in 1170 of Strongbow to Eva, Irish King MacMurrough's daughter, which marked the beginning of England's entanglement with Irish affairs.

Today you enter the fascinating museum through what was once the tower's dungeon (wherein the Sitrics met their end and Reginald and O'Faolain were imprisoned). On the upper floors you'll find King John's mace and sword, along with many of the city's 30 royal charters. Interesting to Americans is the display on Timbertoes, the wooden bridge across the Suir (now replaced by a modern structure) that was the work of Boston architect Lemuel Cox in 1797. The following year, rebels who participated in the uprising of 1798 were hanged from its beams. There's also a bronze plate over which currency changed hands back in the 18th century—it's called simply the "Nail," and has entered our vocabulary through the expression "paying on the nail."

Waterford Heritage Centre

Greyfriars St. ☎ **051/71227.** Small admission fee, children free with an adult; combination ticket including Reginald's Tower, IR£1 ($1.60). Open Apr–May Mon–Fri 10am–1pm and 2–6pm, Sat 10am–1pm; June–Sept Mon–Fri 10am–7pm, Sat 10am–1pm and 2–5pm.

Just down the Quay from Reginald's Tower on Greyfriars side street, the Heritage Centre focuses on the wealth of archeology in Waterford, with particular emphasis on the period A.D. 1000 to 1500. Among the more interesting exhibits are a model of medieval Waterford and a drawing of Viking Waterford just before the arrival of the Normans. There are fascinating explanations of the way in which archeologists work and the methods they employ to "dig up" Waterford's past, as well as a host of other interesting items. Well worth a visit.

✪ Waterford Crystal Factory

Kilbarry. ☎ **051/73311.** Fax 051/78539. Admission IR£2 ($3.20) adults. Open Apr–Oct Mon–Sat 8:30am–5pm, Sun 10am–5pm. Tours Apr–Oct Mon–Sat 8:30am–3:15pm, Sun 10am–3:15pm; Nov–Mar Mon–Fri 9am–3:15pm. No reservations required. Because of insurance regulations, no children under 10 are permitted on the tours; they may, however, wait in the showroom and watch a 20-minute film on the factory. Closed last week in July and the first two weeks in Aug (this can vary, so best check), but a skeleton staff continues working and a restricted tour is still available. Bus from the Clock Tower on the Quay.

You won't want to leave Waterford without a trip to the plant where some of the world's finest crystal is fashioned into works of art. Before we talk about what you'll see, let me warn you that, to avoid disappointment, you should book as far in advance as possible during the summer months. The half-hour tours are one of Ireland's most popular attractions and only a small group is allowed through at a time.

The brilliance of the crystal comes from the unique formula of ingredients, and the fastidious approach to the mixing of the "batch" (raw materials) accounts for its fire and sparkle, as well as for the difficulty in blowing. George and William Penrose began production of the crystal in modest premises on the Quay in 1783. Less than a century later, in 1851, horrendous taxes on raw materials closed its doors, but even after its demise, Waterford's reputation persisted. When the Irish government moved to revive the industry in 1947, it took five years to gather the necessary artisans and build a proper facility. Some 30 master glass blowers, cutters, and engravers were brought from Europe to train Irish apprentices, and in 1951 Waterford crystal was once more in production. Today there's a staff of hundreds, turning out 90,000 finished pieces of the beautiful crystal every week, of which about 60% is shipped to the U.S.

The tour begins in the blowing department, where teams of four to six work swiftly and expertly with molten glass as it emerges from the kiln, since in the space of three minutes it will become too hard to work. Once blown, the piece moves past checkers whose sole purpose is to spot even the slightest flaw—only two-thirds of the pieces make it through this minute inspection and go on to the cutting department, where cutters work in teams of six (four qualified cutters and two apprentices). Some 15% of the pieces fall by the wayside at this stage. The still-dull cut surfaces are dipped into a mixture of acids, followed by a bath in soapy water and a final rinse in white vinegar, by which time the characteristic fire and sparkle of Waterford crystal shine forth in all their glory.

For years, Waterford crystal was not available at its source. However, the factory has opened a sales showroom. Don't expect any discounts, however—prices will be about the same as you find them around the country. The cafeteria serves tea, coffee, soft drinks, and light snacks.

Garter Lane Arts Centre and Theatre

5 and 22a O'Connell Street. ☎ **051/55038.** Admission free. Gallery Mon–Sat 10am–6pm.

The work of contemporary Irish artists, many of them local, is showcased at 5 O'Connell Street, at what was once the old Waterford Library. The former Friends Meeting House at 22a is home to the innovative Garter Lane Theatre and an art gallery. Artists from around the country gather here in July and August for a crafts fair.

✪ The New Ross Galley
The Quay. ☎ **051/21723.**

Reservations are essential for the afternoon tea cruise, which leaves from the Quay—book through the tourist office. From June to August the cruise departs daily at 3pm from the Quay (frequency and departure times are flexible, so check with the tourist office. (See "What to See and Do—Around County Wexford" in Chapter 8 for details.)

THE RUINS Some of Waterford's most interesting sightseeing attractions are its extensive ruins, relics of its long, turbulent history. Look for traces of the old Viking-built city walls at the railway station, Mayor's Walk, and Castle Street. On Greyfriars Street, the ruins of the French church are all that remain of the Franciscan foundation built in 1240 that once housed Huguenot refugees. And all along the Quay, shopfronts reflect the city's beginnings and evolution over the centuries.

GOLFING Visiting golfers are welcomed on the Championship course at Waterford Castle (☎ 051/71605 to book).

NEARBY ATTRACTIONS

Before leaving the city, pick up the detailed "Discover East Waterford" brochure from the tourist office.

The nine miles from Waterford city to ✪ **Dunmore East** via R683/684 are picturesque; and when you reach the little town perched above its historic harbor (mail ships used to put in here, as did smugglers, pirates, and a variety of other characters), fine beaches, and sheltered coves, you'll be tempted to stay a day or two for the fishing, swimming, sailing, and/or the good crack with some of the friendliest Irish in the country.

If you're traveling to Dunmore East around lunchtime—or should a terrible thirst attack—my best advice is to take a short detour on the Cheekpoint road (about four miles from Waterford city) to **Jack Meade's Pub.** Nestled beside the old stone bridge at Halfway House, the pub has been here since 1705, and it's been owned by the same family for well over a century. Proprietors Carmel and Willie Hartley continue the tradition of a warm welcome in a setting made cozy by open fires, antiques, and fascinating pictures that depict local history. Outside, there's an attractive beer garden, as well as wooded walkways. From May through September, sandwiches and light meals are available from 1 to 9pm daily; an outdoor barbecue on Sunday evenings in fine weather; and you'll usually find a singsong or other musical activity Wednesday, Friday, Saturday, and Sunday nights.

A little farther along, you'll pass through the quaint little village of **Passage East,** with its narrow, winding streets and whitewashed cottages. This is where Henry II and his 4,000 armed forces landed back in 1171 on his visit to elicit loyalty oaths from Irish chieftains. These days, it's the landing place of the car-ferry across to Ballyhack on the Wexford side of the river (see "The Hook Peninsula" in Chapter 8). Down the road a bit, only the signposted Crooke church marks the landmark village of Cromwell's "By Hook or by Crooke" remark. If time permits, stop at Woodstown to walk the mile-long sandy strand (it's a good place for a sea dip if the tide is in).

As you enter Dunmore East, steep hills along the way are crowned by neat thatched cottages and the picturesque harbor is filled with fishing vessels and pleasure boats. From 1813, when this tiny village became Waterford's mail-packet station, its basic fishing industry has been matched by an influx of summer visitors who make this one of Ireland's most popular east coast seaside resorts. Clifftop walks and strolls to the busy harbor, alive with craft of all description as well as swirling flocks of seabirds, are highlights of any visit to Dunmore East. Excellent bar food and restaurant meals at the Ocean Hotel, Candlelight Inn, and Strand Inn feature seafood fresh from these waters, and prices are quite moderate. ✪ **Power's Bar,** set in an old butcher shop on the main street, pulls a good pint and is a well-loved meeting place for locals and visitors alike.

When you're ready to get on with your journey, head for the coast drive to Tramore (R685) that winds along the clifftops with glimpses of the sea.

SHOPPING

✪ The Book Centre

Barronstrand St. ☎ **051/73823.** Fax 051/70769.

If you're looking for publications on subjects of Irish interest, history, contemporary fiction and nonfiction, poetry, travel—or just about anything else—chances are you'll find it in this bright, modern bookshop. Open Monday through Saturday from 9am to 5:30pm, Fri until 9pm.

Faller's Sweater Shop

20/21 Broad Street. ☎ **051/54576.**

A terrific selection of sweaters—wool, cotton, and linen in a variety of styles. Offered, too, are a wide range of stylish accessories—linen, wool, and mohair scarves; stoles; tweed caps; and lovely cashmere capes. Open Mon–Sat 9am–6pm, late opening Fri.

✪ Joseph Knox Ltd.

3/4 Barronstrand St. ☎ **051/75307.** Fax 051/79058.

This has long been one of Ireland's leading outlets for Waterford glass, fine bone china, and porcelain. They'll mail (a superb mail-order catalog is available on request), and they accept major credit cards. Open Monday through Saturday from 9:30am to 5:30pm.

✪ Thomas Phelan

14 George's St. ☎ **051/74288.**

Pipe smokers will love this shop. It's a relic of the days when gentlemen smokers were catered to by other gentlemen who loved the trade, and those behind the counter at Phelan's continue that tradition (catering just as happily to the odd lady pipe smoker like myself!). There's a good selection of pipes, as well as cigars, cigarettes, lighters, and tobacco. Open Monday through Saturday from 9:30am to 5:30pm.

✪ Wool Craft

11 Michael St. ☎ **051/74082.**

One of Ireland's leading suppliers of hand-knits and hand-loomed knitwear, this shop is loaded with Aran sweaters, along with a whole range of woolens. Best of all, prices average about 30% less than most other sweater shops, woolen mills, or department stores. Open Monday through Saturday from 9:30am to 5:30pm.

PUBS & EVENING ENTERTAINMENT

THE PERFORMING ARTS

Garter Lane Theatre

22-A O'Connell St. ☎ **051/77153.** Fax 051/71570. Admission IR£3–IR£10 ($4.80–$16).

New plays, old standbys, and musical performances appear at the Garter Lane, with local and imported acting ensembles. The box office or the tourist office can tell you what's doing when you're in Waterford.

✪ Theatre Royal

The Mall. ☎ **051/74402.**

This beautiful old theater is the venue of musicals and amateur drama productions these days, and it comes back into its past glory during the Light Opera Festival.

Red Kettle Theatre Company

☎ **051/79688.** Admission IR£3–IR£7 ($4.80–$11.20).

This exciting, award-winning theater company is currently based in the Garter Lane Art Centre (see above) and sometimes performs in Dublin's Abbey Theatre. Plans are afoot, however, for a theater of their own in Waterford. In the meantime, check at the tourist office or call the number above for any production during your visit and just where it will be performed.

The Forum

The Glen, Waterford, Co. Waterford. ☎ **051/71111.** Off Bridge Street.

This large hall is the venue for national and international stars in the entertainment firmament. Advance booking is usually necessary, and the box office hours are Mon–Sat 11am–1pm and 2–4pm. Tickets are in the IR£8–IR£15 ($12.80–$24) range for most events.

TRADITIONAL MUSIC SESSIONS On Saturday and Sunday nights there's traditional Irish music (and a good time!) at the ✪ **Munster Bar** behind Reginald's Tower on Bailey's New Street (☎ 051/74656). Call in around 9:30 or 10pm, when things should be just getting lively. Music is sometimes to be found in **Meade's Bar,** Ballycanvan, Halfway House (☎ 051/73187); ✪ **Mullane's,** 15 Newgate St. (☎ 051/73854); and **T&H Doolans,** 32 George's St. (☎ 051/72764); as well as other Waterford pubs, but seldom on a regular basis, so check with the tourist office and in local papers.

THE PUBS

✪ The Munster Bar

Bailey's New St. ☎ **051/74656.**

This cozy, wood-paneled, etched-glass haven of conviviality began life as a coaching inn 200 years ago. In 1950 it was taken over by Pete Fitzgerald, and the small room known as Peter's Bar is a gathering place for some of Waterford's liveliest conversationalists. On cool evenings a coal fire reflects off wall sconces and chandeliers of "old" (pre-1851) Waterford glass. Peter's sons—Peter, Michael, and Tom—carry on their father's traditions of hospitality, and will see to it that you're not long a stranger. On Saturday and Sunday nights the large upstairs room rings to the strains of traditional music, and singsongs erupt spontaneously.

What was probably the stables for the old Munster Inn has been converted into an extension of the original Munster. It can be mobbed at lunchtime (see "Where to Eat," below), and evening finds it filled again with convivial Waterford imbibers.

✪ Henry Downes & Co., Ltd.

10 Thomas St. ☎ **051/74118.**

Step into the marvelous maze of rooms that make up Downes, and you step back into a world long gone. Dating from the 1700s, the pub's spacious seating areas are made cozy by lots of old wood, and on one wall, a spotlighted glass wall highlights an ancient spring-fed well that has been left open. Lots of locals, good crack (conversation), and a superb "No. 9" Irish whiskey that Downes has produced since 1797 (ask about the origin of its name) make this one a personal favorite.

✪ Jordan's American Bar

The Quay. ☎ **051/75024.**

Don't be fooled by this pub's name—it is *not* an American-style bar! The name comes from sailing-ship days in the early 1800s, when passengers heading for America bought their tickets here. The original etched-glass door panels, lots of dark wood, and a unique spindle-edge back bar help retain the character of that era, and there's no lack of distinctly Irish friendliness and hospitality from the staff. Bar lunches are served weekdays from 12:30 to 2:30pm.

The Reginald Bar

The Mall. ☎ **051/55087.**

The Reginald Bar, directly behind Reginald's Tower, has its antiquity attested to by a plaque on the left-hand wall as you enter which bears the inscription BUILT CIRCA A.D. 850 BY SITRIC THE DANE. One of the original city walls, its arched stone alcoves once served the Vikings as "sally ports," through which small boats were launched to "sally forth" along the river that back then was just outside. For the most part, the Reginald is a pub for congenial mingling, but there's music from time to time, and on most Sunday afternoons between 12:30 and 2pm there are jazz sessions by very good local musicians. Visiting instrumentalists are welcome to join the local group.

T. & H. Doolan's

32 George's St. ☎ **051/72764.**

You'll know T. & H. Doolan's by its Tudor-style front and frosted-glass door. Inside, there's a wonderfully eclectic collection of old farm implements, whiskey jars, stone crocks, mugs, copper jugs, and anything else the late Thomas Doolan took a fancy to hang from rough wooden beams or the whitewashed walls. He was, of course, the "T" of the proprietorship, and if anything went amiss, blame promptly fell on the "H" of that partnership—and thereby hangs a tale. H. Doolan, it turns out, was purely a figment of T. Doolan's imagination, who came into being when "Thomas" was too long, "T." and "Tom" too short, for the establishment's sign. The spirited characters of T. & H. still linger in this 150-year-old pub that was for many years a stagecoach stop.

✪ Thomas Maher's

O'Connell St.

Gentlemen, leave your ladies behind when you head for this pub. This one-of-a-kind old pub that dates back to 1886 is presided over by Thomas Maher, a small, white-haired, blue-eyed man who has been behind the bar some 64 years and knows his own mind when it comes to running his pub. "I don't want to see anyone too early, too late, or too long," he declares. He brooks no swearing, no singing—and no ladies (except for his charming wife, Mary, who sometimes joins him behind the bar). With those rules in force, you may well ask, who comes? Crowds of devoted "regulars," that's who comes, for behind a traditional storefront that has won many an award for its design there's an interior that has changed little, if at all, over the years. You may drink your pint in a glass stamped with a '20s or '30s date (since 1928, all pint glasses must bear a date stamp), and if there's no date at all, chances are it's one left from as far back as 1916. If you like, you can purchase spirits bottled by Mr. Maher himself. He and his pub are a Waterford institution. You'll find Thomas behind the bar Monday through Friday from noon to 2pm, 5 to 7pm, and 8:30 to 10pm.

WHERE TO STAY IN TOWN

✪ Annvill House

The Orchard, Kingsmeadow, Waterford, Co. Waterford. ☎ **051/73617.** 5 rms, 4 with bath. IR£15 ($24) per person sharing. 10% reduction for children. (Rates include breakfast.) Dinner IR£11 ($17.60) extra. No credit cards. Bus from the Clock Tower.

Phyllis O'Reilly is the hostess of this attractive, modern two-story home and is happy to arrange tours and to help with any other holiday plans. The guest rooms are bright, attractive, and comfortable, with built-in wardrobes and tea/coffee facilities. There's central heat and off-the-street parking. This is 100 yards off the Waterford-Cork road (N25), on the right-hand side of the roundabout, opposite the Waterford Crystal Factory entrance.

Derrynane House

19 The Mall, Waterford, Co. Waterford. ☎ **051/75179.** 7 rms, 1 with bath. IR£14 ($22.40) per person. (Rates include breakfast.) No credit cards. Closed Dec–Feb.

Americans with a historic bent of mind will be drawn to this house. It was here that Thomas Francis Meagher was arrested by the British in 1848 and sent off to Tasmania. After escaping and making his way to America, he eventually rose to the rank of brigadier general in the Union's Fighting 69th Brigade during the Civil War. The four-story house is of Georgian style, with a wide, gracious entry hall. There's a large family room with its own bathroom, and six others have sinks and are served by two shower rooms and two bathrooms. Eilish O'Sullivan presides, and maintains a homey TV lounge for her guests.

Mayors Walk House

12 Mayors Walk, Waterford, Co. Waterford. ☎ **051/55427.** 4 rms, none with bath. IR£13 ($20.80) per person. (Rates include breakfast.) No credit cards. Closed Nov–Mar.

Kay and John Ryder welcome you to their immaculate three-story home, and provide copious information on local attractions, restaurants, and shopping. There's a bath and shower on each floor, and rooms are pleasant, attractive, and comfortable. The location is ideal—a short walk from the town center and convenient to bus transportation to the Waterford Crystal Factory. The rail and bus depot are also not too far away.

✪ Prendiville's Restaurant and Guesthouse

Cork Rd., Waterford, Co. Waterford. ☎ **051/78851.** 9 rms, all with bath. IR£19–IR£25 ($30.40–$40) per person. (Rates include breakfast.) MC, V.

Paula and Peter Prendiville have transformed this beautifully restored Gothic lodge into one of Waterford's loveliest guesthouses and an outstanding restaurant. All guest rooms have telephones and TVs, and there's private parking. As attractive and appealing as this place is, its owners are even more so, and the combination makes for a charming and memorable Waterford visit. See "Where to Eat," below, for details of their superb restaurant.

Roselda

Cork Rd. (N25), Waterford, Co. Waterford. ☎ **051/73922.** 7 rms. 6 with bath and shower. IR£13.50 ($21.60) per person without bath, IR£15 ($24) with bath. 10% reduction for children. (Rates include breakfast.) No credit cards. Bus: From the Clock Tower.

Mrs. Ann Walsh is an extremely helpful hostess. Husband Tommy worked as a cutter at Waterford Crystal for some 28 years and has a beautiful private collection, with many pieces of his own design. Rooms are attractive and comfortable, all with sinks, and the house is centrally heated. The Waterford Crystal factory is just three minutes away.

Talginn

Ballynaneashagh, Cork Rd. (N25), Waterford, Co. Waterford. ☎ **051/73798.** 4 rms, all with bath. IR£20 ($32) single; IR£15 ($24) per person sharing. (Rates include breakfast.) No credit cards. Closed Nov–Mar. Bus: From the Clock Tower.

Mrs. Margaret Power is a warm hostess, and her immaculate dormer bungalow, set in landscaped gardens, is 1¼ miles from the town center and a mere three minutes from the Waterford Crystal Factory (she's happy to book tours for guests). Guest rooms are attractive in decor and very comfortable, with ample bathrooms for those without private facilities. She also presents a breakfast menu that offers choices other than the traditional Irish spread.

Worth a Splurge

✪ Dooley's Hotel

30 The Quay, Waterford, Co. Waterford. ☎ **051/73531.** Fax 051/70262. 40 rms, all with bath. TV TEL. IR£38–IR£42 ($60.80–$67.20) single; IR£29–IR£39 ($46.40–$62.40) per person sharing. Children under 10 stay free in parents' room. AE, MC, V.

Dooley's central location, friendly staff, and general character may well tempt you to go over budget bounds. This was a leading 19th-century coaching inn, and the grandniece of the Dooley family still books in whenever she's in Waterford, even though for more than 40 years the hotel has been owned and managed by Mrs. June Darrer and her family. The staff are longtimers who cater to guests as if the hotel were their own. The lobby and lounge bar (see "Where to Eat," below) are warm with rich reds and greens, stained glass, oil paintings, and leather circular booths. Guest rooms vary, according to whether they're in the older section, with its odd-shaped rooms (some small and cozy, others large and full of interesting nooks), or the newer wing, where rooms are more standard, although still furnished in the hotel's traditional style.

✪ Waterford Castle

The Island, Ballinakill, Waterford, Co. Waterford. ☎ **051/78203** or 80332. Fax 051/79316. 31 rms, all with bath. TV TEL. IR£75–IR£100 ($120–$160) per person sharing; IR£275 ($440) suite. ACC, AE, MC, V.

I can't think of a better place to spend extra dollars than in this castle, whose setting and history push romance right to the brink of fantasy—it sits on its own wooded 311-acre island, which divides the River Suir at a point leading to Waterford city's deep-water port 1½ miles upstream. Its strategic location accounts for a long and colorful history, but it's the sheer beauty of that location that overwhelms when you board the small chain-link-driven car-ferry to cross some

300 yards of the Suir. The fine stone castle, a FitzGerald family stronghold from 1160 to 1958, is modest in size. The Great Hall, although a bit on the small side, is impressive, with a large stone fireplace at one end. At the opposite end of the hall is one of the castle's original tapestries, depicting a hunting scene that looks as if it could have taken place right on the island.

Bedrooms are in the two Elizabethan-style wings (added in the 1800s) and all have views onto the Suir, woodlands, or the landscaped lawn out front. There's a magnificent oak-paneled dining room (once the ballroom), where superb meals are served with Waterford crystal glassware and Wedgwood dinnerware bearing the FitzGerald crest on the table. On the castle grounds are a championship golf course, all-weather tennis courts, lovely wooded walks, horseback riding, fishing, and hunting.

NEARBY ACCOMMODATIONS

Dunmore East

Ashgrove

Coxtown, Dunmore East, Co. Waterford. ☎ **051/83195.** 4 rms, 3 with bath. IR£18.50 ($29.60) single; IR£13.50 ($21.60) per person sharing without bath, IR£15 ($24) per person sharing with bath. 25% reduction for children. (Rates include breakfast.) No credit cards. Closed Nov–Feb.

About half a mile from Dunmore East, Mrs. Breda Battles' pretty, modern bungalow sits back off the road on a slight rise. Guests often take evening walks along nearby clifftops to reach secluded coves or sandy beaches. Guest rooms are attractive and comfortable; they have tea/coffeemakers. Mrs. Battles is eager to share her knowledge of the area with her guests.

✪ Beechmount

R683/4, Dunmore East, Co. Waterford. ☎ **051/83293.** 3 rms, none with bath. IR£13 ($18.85) per person. 20% reduction for children. Dinner IR£12 ($17.40) extra. (Rates include breakfast.) No credit cards. Parking available.

On the outskirts of Dunmore East (seven miles from Waterford city), Beechmount is a pretty country bungalow set on a hill overlooking the village and harbor, with a well-kept acre of lawn and garden. Mrs. Rita Power's bright and sparkling home is furnished with interesting antiques (you may want to take your impressive bedroom pieces home!); each guest room has a sink. The stone fireplace is a focal point in the lounge, which has windows overlooking the garden. The two Power teenagers, William and Victoria, are great sailing and windsurfing fans and love to talk to guests about their favorite sports. There's central heating and a graveled car park.

✪ Copper Beech

Dunmore East, Co. Waterford. ☎ **051/383-187.** 4rms, all with bath. IR£19 ($30.40) single, IR£15 ($24) per person sharing. 25% reduction for children under 12. (Rates include breakfast.) No credit cards. Private parking. Closed Christmas.

Maureen and Sean Quinn are among Ireland's most welcoming hosts. Their modern dormer bungalow is located in the heart of this lovely seaside village. Tastefully decorated throughout, its guest rooms are nicely furnished. Two rooms have views of the sea and Hook lighthouse. The extensive breakfast menu can be a bonus if you are getting a little tired of the traditional meal. Central heat.

Creaden View

Dunmore East, Co. Waterford. ☎ **051/383-339.** 4 rms, all with bath. IR£20 ($32) single, IR£15 ($24) per person sharing. 25% reduction for children under 12. (Rates include breakfast.) No credit cards. Closed Christmas.

Mrs. Kathleen Martin's charming home, right in the center of Dunmore East, has lovely views of nearby cliffs and the sea. Bedrooms are quite spacious and comfortably furnished; they're a restful retreat when the spirit begins to flag. Kathleen is always delighted to share her knowledge of this beautiful area with her guests.

✪ Dunmore Lodge

Dunmore East, Co. Waterford. ☎ **051/383-454.** 4 rms, 3 with bath. IR£20–IR£24 ($32–$38.40) single without bath, IR£23 ($36.80) single with bath; IR£15–IR£17 ($24–$27.20) per person sharing without bath, IR£16–IR£19 ($25.60–$30.40) per person sharing with bath. Off-season discounts. (Rates include breakfast.) V. Open mid-Mar–Nov.

Set back from the street in its own grounds and tree-lined gardens, Dunmore Lodge is a lovely country lodge that dates from the early 1800s. Overlooking the Suir Estuary, it retains the Old World atmosphere of its early years, and Mrs. Zoe Coffee has skillfully combined antique furnishings with modern facilities. Mrs. Coffee will pack a picnic lunch for you to take on your sightseeing, by request. It has central heating.

✪ Foxmount Farm

Dunmore East Rd., Waterford, Co. Waterford. ☎ **051/74308.** 6 rms, none with bath. IR£20 ($32) per person. Special three-, five-, and seven-day rates. 25% reduction for children. (Rates include breakfast.) Dinner IR£15 ($20) extra. No credit cards. Closed Dec–Feb. Parking available.

This is perennial favorite with readers. The 230-acre working farm is four miles out of town just off the Dunmore East road (at Maxol Garage turn left on Passage East road; keep right at next junction, where it's signposted, then right at the bridge. The elegant old home, dating from 1700, sits on a slight rise overlooking a verdant lawn edged with flowering shrubs, pastures, and tilled acres. Margaret and David Kent are always eager to accommodate their guests, whether by booking a glass-factory tour, explaining the history of the region, or simply showing them around the farm. Children delight in riding Planet, the obliging resident donkey (there are also a horse and pony) and exploring the farmyard. Other amenities include table tennis and a tennis court.

The house is furnished with lovely antiques, and evening tea around a glowing fire in the drawing room is a special event. Meals are superb, featuring all fresh ingredients and home baking, and you're welcome to bring your own wine. Let Margaret know by noon if you want the evening meal. Central heat.

✪ The Ocean Hotel

Main St., Dunmore East, Co. Waterford. ☎ **051/83136.** Fax 051/83576. 12 rms, all with bath. IR£25–IR£30 ($40–$48) per person; weekend rate (two nights, one dinner) available; also, special three-, five-, and seven-day rates available. (Rates include breakfast.) AE, MC, V.

Brendan Gallagher, owner/operator of this charming small hotel set in the upper village, is the epitome of Irish hospitality. Guest rooms, most of which have both a double and a single bed, are nicely furnished, with telephone and TV. The small, old-style bar/lounge is a cozy haven of dark wood and comfortable seating. It opens into a larger back lounge with an open fire, where there's entertainment nightly during summer months, and on weekends in the off-season. The bar food menu (served continuously from noon to closing) is one of the most extensive I've run across, and there's a crab and seafood plate (for under IR£5, $8) that I find positively habit-forming. Full evening meals, also moderately priced, are served in the pleasant dining room. The busy harbor is just a short stroll away, as are safe, sandy beaches.

Slieverue

Ashbourne House

Milepost, Slieverue, Waterford, Co. Waterford. ☎ **051/32037.** 7 rms, all with bath. IR£15 ($24) per person; 25% reduction for children. (Rates include breakfast.) High tea IR£7 ($11.20) extra; dinner, IR£11 ($17.60). MC, V. Closed Nov–Mar.

Mrs. Agnes Forrest is the gracious hostess of this lovely two-story, renovated farmhouse on 20 acres of mixed farming two miles northeast of Waterford just off N25, the Waterford-New Ross road (well signposted). One ground-level room (with bath) has its own entrance. The scenic setting can be enjoyed from the garden, and both river and sea angling are close by, as is horseback riding.

✪ Diamond Hill

Slieverue, Waterford. ☎ **051/332-855** or 332-254. Fax 051/332-254. 10 rms, all with bath. IR£16.50–IR£17.50 ($26.40–$28) per person sharing. (Rates include breakfast.) MC, V. Private car park.

This pretty, modern house is set in lawns and gardens that have won the National Garden Award for guesthouses no fewer than four times. Its interior is as attractive as the exterior, with a nice lounge, beautifully decorated bedrooms featuring many built-ins and central heating. Mary and John Malone have won many devoted fans among our readers. The hospitable Malones take a real interest in their guests, and in good weather set out chairs in the sunny gardens for a bit of outdoor relaxation. There is also a delightful craft shop displaying the best of Irish handcrafts at very reasonable prices. Diamond Hill is just off the Waterford-Rosslare road (N25) signposted at Slieverue Junction, about two miles outside Waterford.

Kilmeaden

Glencree

The Sweep, Kilmeaden, Co. Waterford. ☎ **051/384-240.** 5 rms, 3 with bath. IR£18.50 ($29.60) single without bath; IR£13.50 ($21.60) per person sharing without bath, IR£15 ($24) per period sharing with bath. 20% reduction for children. (Rates include breakfast.) High tea IR£6 ($9.60) extra; dinner IR£10 ($16). No credit cards. Parking available.

Readers have been lavish in their praise of Mrs. Rena Power and her family; typical comments are, "More than anything else, I was impressed by their hospitality," and "Of the many B&Bs in which we stayed, hers was the best." The attractive Power bungalow, in its scenic setting, is as warm as their welcome to guests, and guest rooms are bright, cheerful, and comfortable. They are happy to advise on local attractions and happenings, and there's ample private parking. Glencree is 5½ miles from Waterford, just off the Cork road (N25); it's signposted from the highway.

WHERE TO EAT

✪ Dooley's Hotel

The Quay. ☎ **051/73531.** Main courses IR£6–IR£14 ($9.60–$22.40); bar snacks under IR£5 ($8); children's menu IR£4 ($6.40). ACC, AE, MC, V. Daily 12:30–2:30pm and 5:30–9:30pm. BAR FOOD/TRADITIONAL.

There's good bar food in Dooley's cozy bar/lounge, as well as a three-course Business Person's Luncheon Special in the main dining room May through October. Excellent four-course lunches are featured on the regular menu (seafood, beef, chicken, pork, lamb) and served in the pretty dining room.

✪ Dwyer's of Mary Street

8 Mary Street (on a back street near the bridge). ☎ **051/77478.** Reservations strongly recommended. Main à la carte courses IR£11–IR£20 ($17.60–$32); early evening set dinner IR£14 ($22.40). ACC, DC, MC, V. Mon–Sat 6–10pm, early evening set dinner 6–7:30pm. Closed 1 week Christmas, Good Friday, 2 weeks July. TRADITIONAL.

From Waterford's old R.I.C. barracks, Martin and Sile Dwyer have carved out a small (it only seats 30), intimate restaurant. The decor is semiformal, and the friendly service pampers diners but on an unpretentious footing. It is the food here, however, that has won Dwyer's a warm spot in the city's affections. Martin is the chef, and while he uses largely fresh local products in traditional dishes, he brings a touch of the adventurous that never goes over the top. Just one example is the medallions of fillet steak with onion and thyme sauce—safe enough for the conservative diner, but with that little bit of difference from the usual. The early evening set dinner is especially good value.

Granville Hotel

The Quay. ☎ **051/55111.** IR£2.50–IR£6 ($4–$9.60). ACC, AE, MC, V. Daily 12:30–2:30pm. BAR FOOD.

Such specialties as smoked salmon and brown bread, along with several tasty hot dishes, salad plates, and snacks are available in the attractive ground-floor bar of the Granville.

✪ The Munster

The Mall. ☎ **051/74656.** IR£2.50–IR£6 ($4–$9.60). No credit cards.Mon–Sat 12:30–2:30pm. PUB GRUB/TRADITIONAL.

The Munster serves a wide selection of budget-priced plates and half of Waterford's young working crowd at lunch. More than just pub grub, the heaping plates of roast beef, ham, or chicken with potato and two vegetables are ample enough to be the main meal of the day. If you're not that hungry, there's soup and sandwiches, cold salad plates, and something called a "blaa" (lettuce, meat, onion, and tomato on a small roll), found only in Waterford, that goes for about IR£1 ($1.60). With an entrance on the Mall, this is the "back room" of the Munster Bar on Bailey's New Street (see "The Pubs" in "What to See and Do," above).

✪ The Olde Stand

45 Michael St. ☎ **051/79488.** Bar food IR£1.50–IR£6 ($2.40–$9.60); main courses IR£6.95–IR£10.95 ($11.12–$17.52); fixed-price five-course dinner IR£15 ($24). Tea-Time Special and Early Bird Menu about IR£5 ($8); carvery lunch under IR£5 ($8). ACC, EU, MC, V. Mon–Sat 10:30am–10:30pm; Sun 12:30–7pm. SEAFOOD/STEAKS/CARVERY/BAR FOOD.

This lovely authentic-looking Victorian-style pub and restaurant is the creation of Eamon Reid, who has combined lots of mahogany (the back bar came from an old church in England), deep shades of green, and a liberal dose of charm to come up with an ambience chock-full of character. The downstairs bar is a cozy, intimate space, and the upstairs restaurant has two pleasant, relaxing rooms, with candles on the tables and a fireplace adding a cheery glow. As for the food, the lunchtime carvery features a roast joint (beef, lamb, pork) of the day, as well as homemade soups, salad plates, and a salad bar. From teatime on, the menu lists seafood (fresh from local waters), steaks from Ireland's Golden Vale, chicken, lamb, duck, and other local specialties. An excellent Irish cheese board puts a perfect finish to your meal. As a crowning touch, the staff here is both friendly and efficient.

✪ Prendiville's Restaurant and Guesthouse

Cork Rd. ☎ **051/78851.** Business lunch IR£7.25 ($11.60); set lunch IR£10 ($16); main courses IR£8–IR£14 ($12.80–$22.40). MC, V. Mon–Fri 12:15–2:15pm; Mon–Sat 6:15–9:45pm. IRISH/SEAFOOD/BAR FOOD.

Set in a Gothic-style gate lodge (see "Where to Stay," above), Prendiville's is one of Waterford's finest restaurants. Owner/chef Paula Prendiville, a member of the prestigious Euro Toque Chefs Society, specializes in creative dishes based on traditional Irish cuisine. My personal favorites include a lovely escalope of poached wild salmon with a peach-cream-and-mint sauce and roast lamb sliced and served on an herb jus. Actually, I could make a meal of the old-fashioned crab-fish cakes with butter sauce on the appetizer menu. Paula also includes at least one vegetarian dish.

The Reginald Bar and Restaurant

The Mall. ☎ 051/55087. Pub grub IR£2–IR£6 ($3.20–$9.60); main courses IR£5–IR£8 ($8–$12.80); set dinner IR£17 ($27.20); Tourist Menu in the restaurant IR£8.50 ($13.60). ACC, AE, MC, V. Bar, lunch daily 12:30–2:30pm; restaurant, Mon–Sat 10:30am–10:30pm, Sun noon–9:30pm; Tourist Menu daily 5:30–7:30pm. Closed Good Friday, Christmas Day. PUB GRUB/TRADITIONAL.

There's a choice at the Reginald—soup and sandwiches, salad plates, and hot dishes (meat plus two vegetables) in the bar, or full four- or five-course meals in the restaurant, with beef, lamb, chicken, fish, and some vegetarian dishes offering a wide variety.

✪ Waterford Castle

The Island, Ballinskill. ☎ **051/78203.** Reservations recommended for dinner. Fixed-price meal IR£14–IR£16 ($22.40–$25.60) at lunch, IR£25–IR£30 ($40–$48) at dinner. Daily 12:30–2:30pm and 6–9:30pm. SEAFOOD/TRADITIONAL.

Even if your plans don't include a stay at this lovely small castle set on its own wooded island (see "Where to Stay," above), a meal here will be a luxurious treat. The setting is idyllic, the dining room decor reflects the elegance of a bygone era, and chef Paul McCluskey's menu makes extensive use of fresh garden herbs and vegetables from the castle gardens and local suppliers. Vegetarians will usually find a savory vegetable terrine on offer, and other dishes might include veal with calvados, duck with honey-and-ginger sauce, and fresh fish and shellfish from nearby waters.

2 Around County Waterford & South Tipperary

The delights of this part of the Southeast are legion and are too often overlooked by visitors rushing from Waterford city to Cork and Blarney. The coastal drive from Waterford to Dungarvan dips from clifftops to secluded bathing coves; Lismore's castle looms over a site once occupied by a great monastic community; the River Blackwater (Ireland's Rhine) at Cappoquin is a salmon fisherman's dream; Ardmore is a pleasant mixture of historic ruins and modern resort comforts; and South Tipperary contributes the great medieval leftovers of Cahir Castle and the Rock of Cashel.

In the sections that follow, you will find accommodations listed under the nearest town, but it's important to remember that wherever you base yourself, easy day trips will let you explore the entire region. I suggest that you select an accommodation that appeals to you, regardless of its proximity to any one sightseeing attraction, and return each night to the same bed, breakfast, local pubs, and host family.

SEEING COUNTY WATERFORD AND SOUTH TIPPERARY

By Bus/Train Bus Eireann serves most towns in County Waterford and South Tipperary, and there are several excellent sightseeing day trips by coach departing from Waterford (check with the bus depot or the tourist office for destinations and schedules). There's train service only to Waterford from Cork and Dublin. For bus and rail information, call 051/79000 Monday through Saturday from 9am to 5:30pm, 051/73408 at other times.

By Car The shortest route from Waterford to almost any of the destinations listed below is along Highway N25, which will carry you straight into Cork city, some 78 miles to the southwest, or N72, signposted a few miles north of Dungarvan, which goes through Cappoquin and Lismore before heading off to Killarney. Scenic driving routes are listed under each heading below as a basic guide that can be as flexible as you wish.

A SUGGESTED ITINERARY FROM TRAMORE TO CASHEL VIA CAPPOQUIN

Tramore is eight miles south of Waterford (via the Cork road, N25, to the well-marked turnoff onto R682) and 10 miles from Dunmore East on the coast road, R685. Dungarvan, 26 miles southwest of Tramore, is best reached via the breathtakingly scenic coastal drive, R675, which passes through the small resort of Annestown and tiny Bunmahon, once a busy copper-mining center. Rugged cliffs, tall rock "stacks" rising from the sea offshore, and small coves line the route all the way to Clonea, where the landscape flattens out. A short, well-marked detour three miles northeast of Dungarvan will bring you to Clonea Strand and its broad, sandy, pollution-free beach. From Dungarvan, you can join the Cork road, N25, to reach Ardmore via a signposted turnoff 15 miles southwest of Dungarvan, or you can turn onto N72 for Cappoquin, 10 miles northwest of Dungarvan, saving Ardmore for a day trip. To reach Cappoquin from Ardmore, take R671 (signposted "Clashmore") through lush farmlands and wooded hills to its junction with N72 four miles outside Cappoquin.

From Cappoquin, follow N72 to Lismore. On the eastern edge of town, look for "The Vee" signpost and turn right onto R668 for the scenic drive over the beautiful mountain pass (see "A Scenic Drive Over the Vee," below in this chapter). At Clogheen, on the western end of the pass, turn right and follow signposts for Cahir (R668), then take N8 on to Cashel.

TRAMORE

Just eight miles south of Waterford city, Tramore is a popular seaside resort with a three-mile-long beach and a 50-acre amusement park that includes Splashworld, an enclosed swimming complex (the kids will love it!). For the older generation, there's an 18-hole golf course; call the Tramore Golf Club (☎ 051/386-170). That giant of a statue you'll notice looking down on the bay from Great Newtown Head is known hereabouts as the Metal Man, and legend has it that any unmarried female who hops three times around its base on one foot will hop down the aisle within the next 12 months. It's open (last admissions one hour before closing) Apr–May, Mon–Fri 10am–5pm, Sat–Sun 11am–6pm; June, daily 10am–8pm;

July–Aug, daily 10am–10pm; Sept, daily 10am–6pm; rest of year by appointment only.

From Tramore, the coast road continues climbing and dipping among spectacular views through picturesque little towns until you reach Dungarvan. En route, take the short detour over to **Stradbally,** a seaside village that has won several awards for its sheer beauty (floral, best-thatched cottage, Tidy Towns, etc.). This is where you'll find **Carrigahilla Gardens** (☎ 051/93127), a complex of some ten interlocking gardens (Victorian, rose, cottage, woodland, etc.) designed and planted by Margaret Morrissey. They're open daily during daylight hours.

Where to Stay

Glenorney

Newtown, Tramore, Co. Waterford. ☎ **051/381-056.** Fax 051/381-103. 4 rms, 3 with bath. IR£19–IR£22 ($30.40–$35.20) single; IR£13.50–IR£16 ($21.60–$25.60) per person sharing. 20% reduction for children. (Rates include breakfast.) No credit cards. Off-street parking. Open Mar–Oct. Opposite Tramore Golf Club.

Marie Murphy welcomes guests with a cuppa (tea or coffee) in this modern dormer bungalow overlooking Tramore Bay. Guest rooms are spacious and well appointed, and several can be combined into family suites.

✪ Rushmere House

Tramore, Co. Waterford. ☎ **051/381-041.** 6 rms, 4 with bath. IR£14 ($22.40) single without bath; IR£14 ($22.40) per person sharing without bath; IR£4 ($6.40) per person additional with bath. 25% reduction for children. (Rates include breakfast.) ACC, MC, V. Closed Dec–Jan. Large public car park directly opposite.

Mrs. Rita McGivney is the friendly hostess of this century-old, three-story Georgian house, which is flanked by wide chimneys at each end and sits on a rise looking across Tramore Bay to Brownstown Head. It's eight miles from Waterford on the main Waterford-Tramore road as you enter town. The six guest rooms (three are family-size, with a double and a single with bath) are spacious, with high ceilings and tall windows, and the house is centrally heated.

✪ Seaview Lodge

Seaview Park, Tramore, Co. Waterford. ☎/Fax **051/381-122.** 5 rms, all with bath. TV. Rates IR£23 ($36.80) single; IR£16 ($25.60) per person sharing. Dinner IR£12 ($19.20) extra. MC, V.

Frances Darcy has won high praise from our readers, with comments that she "gives that little extra effort to guests that separates the great from the merely good." Her spacious bungalow, with its private car park, has a beautiful sea view, and the attractive guest rooms have TVs and tea/coffeemakings. There's also a breakfast menu, just in case you want a change from the traditional fare. Mrs. Darcy is one of Ireland's most obliging hostesses, always ready to help with itinerary plans and local sightseeing.

Where to Eat

Pine Rooms

Turkey Rd., Tramore. ☎ **051/381-683.** Main courses IR£8–IR£12 ($12.80–$19.20). MC, V. Lunch summer months only, daily 12:30–2:30pm; dinner year-round, daily 5:30–10:30pm. Closed Sun–Tues in Jan, Feb, Christmas week. SEAFOOD/TRADITIONAL.

This attractive restaurant is set in a former residence, with pine furniture and sanded floors. Try their "Molly Malone" cockles and mussels starter, then opt for a seafood dish or one of their excellent steaks (peppered, with garlic butter, is a good choice). Vegetables are especially nicely done. Service is both friendly and efficient. The restaurant is in the town center on the main Waterford-Tramore road, near the car park, promenade, and tourist office.

DUNGARVAN

The bustling market town of Dungarvan straddles the safe, secure harbor formed by the River Colligan as it empties into Dungarvan Bay. Named for a 13th-century saint who founded a monastery here, the town's importance as a port made it a military center during the Norman invasions. After withstanding several sieges during the wars of 1641, the town surrendered to Cromwell in 1649, and the church and castle were destroyed—the remains of the castle, built by King John in 1185, are down along the quays a short way from the bridge crossing the Colligan. All that remains of the 13th-century Augustinian priory in Abbeyside (across the river from the town center) is a square tower resting on groined arches, which now serves as a belfry for the adjacent church.

There's an excellent small ✪ **museum** in the restored 1649 Market Building at the top of North Main Street, and the **Tourist Information Office** is located in the square (ask about the small walking-tour booklet). **Golfers** can arrange to play the nine-hole course nearby by calling the West Waterford Golf Club (☎ 058/43216). For a day of **deep-sea fishing** in the Irish Sea, contact Dungarvan Charter Angling, Paddy O'Riordan, Kilossera (☎ 058/43286). And from November through February, Clonea Strand Hotel can arrange for visitors to join one of the four **fox-hunting** packs in this locality. A visit to the nearby Gaelic-speaking community of **Ring** (six miles from Dungarvan) is worthwhile to visit Eamonn Terry, master craftsman whose **Criostal no Rinne** workshop (☎ 058/46174) produces beautiful hand-cut crystal giftware at reasonable prices.

WHERE TO STAY

✪ Ballyguiry Farm

Dungarvan, Co. Waterford. ☎ **058/41194.** 6 rms, 3 with bath. Rates IR£15($24) per person daily (including breakfast); IR£175 ($280) per person per week (including breakfast and dinner). 50% reduction for children. Dinner IR£12 ($19.20). No credit cards. Closed Nov–Mar.

This lovely Georgian house in the foothills of the Drum Hills 2½ miles south of Dungarvan, just off N25, the main Dungarvan-Youghal road (signposted), dates from the 1830s. Kathleen and Sean Kiely make guests feel right at home, as do their four charming children. They will even map out sightseeing itineraries on an ordnance survey map for your use on day trips. There's central heating, and the guest rooms are exceptionally pretty, with floral wallpaper, pastel bedspreads, and electric blankets for added comfort. Three family suites with private baths are suitable for parents and up to three children. There's a playground, hard tennis court, and a pony for children to pet and ride. Dinner comes with farm-fresh ingredients.

Bayside

Gold Coast Road, Dungarvan, Co. Waterford. ☎ **058/44318.** 3 rms, all with bath. TV. IR£16–IR£18 ($25.60–$28.80) single, IR£14.50–IR£15.50 ($23.20–$24.80) per person sharing. (Rates include breakfast.) No credit cards. Private parking. 1 mile south of R675.

Overlooking Dungarvan Bay, Mrs. Sheila Norris' spacious modern home is adjacent to the Gold Coast Golf & Leisure complex. The Dungarvan Golf Range is right on the premises (for duffers who want a little practice before heading off to the links)—with two free vouchers for each guest. All guest rooms are attractive as well as comfortable. A hair dryer and trouser press is available for guests' use.

Fialaan

Clonea Strand, Dungarvan, Co. Waterford. ☎ **058/42564** or 43260. Fax 058/42880. 3 rms (all with bath). TV. IR£17.50–IR£20 ($28–$32) single; IR£15–IR£17.50 ($24–$28) per person sharing. (Rates include breakfast.) No credit cards. Private parking. Open Mar–Sept.

The attractive young couple Helen and Sean McGrath share their modern brick home—just steps away from Clonea Strand's wide, curving beach—with guests. Guest rooms are especially appealing, all have tea/coffeemakers, and one will accommodate three people.

Rosebank House

Coast Road (R675), Dungarvan, Co. Waterford. ☎ **058/41561.** 4 rms (3 with bath). IR£18.50–IR£20 ($29.60–$32) single, IR£13.50–IR£15 ($21.60–$24) per person sharing. ACC, DC, MC, V. Closed Christmas. Near Clonea Strand, 2 miles from Dungarvan.

Mrs. Margo Sleator makes her guests feel right at home by welcoming them with a cup of tea or coffee. The attractive guest rooms all feature orthopedic beds and electric blankets. Her varied breakfast menu includes French toast, freshly percolated coffee, and home-baked Irish soda bread—the speciality of the house. That glorious Clonea strand is only one mile away, as is a good golf course.

Self-Catering

✪ Gold Coast Cottages

Ballinacourty, Dungarvan, Co. Waterford. ☎ **058/42416.** Fax 058/42880. 16 cottages. TV. IR£200–IR£500 ($320–$800) per week per cottage, depending on season. Cottages sleep six. Oct–May, attractive midweek and weekend rates are available. Rates include bed linens, with an extra charge for electricity. ACC, AE, MC, V.

Set in a semicircle right at the edge of Dungarvan Bay, two miles outside Dungarvan, just off R675, the Dungarvan-Tramore coast road (signposted), each superior-grade semidetached cottage has its own garden area, and there's a seasonal restaurant and lounge bar on the premises. The cottages are two-storied, are carpeted throughout, and have living/dining rooms with fireplaces, fully equipped kitchens (microwave oven, dishwasher, and fridge/freezer), two bedrooms on the ground floor and one upstairs, and two baths. Bedrooms have built-in wardrobes and dressing tables, and there's one double bed and four twins in each cottage. Six people can be accommodated comfortably, and there's plenty of room to install an extra cot in the spacious upstairs bedroom. Rates include use of the indoor leisure center at the Gold Coast Golf Hotel & Leisure Centre (see below).

Worth a Splurge

✪ Clonea Strand Hotel Leisure Centre

Clonea Strand, Dungarvan, Co. Waterford. ☎ **058/42416.** Fax 058/42880. 40 rms (all with bath). TV TEL. IR£31–IR£39 ($49.60–$62.40) per person sharing; IR£10 ($16) single supplement. Midweek and weekend special rates available. 50% discount for children under 12. (Rates include breakfast.) ACC, AE, MC, V.

Clonea Strand is one of County Waterford's widest beaches, as well as one of its cleanest, having earned both the EC Blue Flag symbol of a pollution-free beach and the Starfish award signifying that it has never been polluted. This hotel, which has recently completed a multimillion-pound renovation, sits right at the edge of the beach nine miles north of Dungarvan, just off R675, the Dungarvan-Tramore coast road (well signposted), and the transformation brought about by its owners, Ann and John McGrath, moves it far up the ranks of Ireland's seafront resorts. They and their children are all involved in the day-to-day operation of the hotel, adding personal attention to its other attractions.

The three-story-high, skylighted atrium foyer features teak and soft rose-colored, velvet-covered seating, a decor repeated in the pretty, window-walled Ocean Lounge overlooking the sea. All guest rooms have magnificent sea views and are exceptionally spacious, with hairdryer, tea/coffee facilities, solid oak built-ins, and one double and one single bed.

There's good sightseeing—Waterford, Tramore, Cork, Blarney, The Vee, Cahir, and Cashel are all an easy drive away. The hotel can also arrange golf, deep-sea fishing, and fox hunting.

Dining/Entertainment: The restaurant has gained an enviable reputation locally. There is a resident pianist in the Ocean Lounge in the evening, and separate facilities for disco.

Facilities: The leisure center features a 20-meter indoor swimming pool housed in a soaring, timber-lined hall made light and airy by the skylight roof, a fully equipped gymnasium, games rooms, saunas, a Jacuzzi pool, sunbed room, ten-pin bowling alley, and beauty salon, all under the direction of gymnast and nurse Claire Morrissey.

Gold Coast Golf Hotel & Leisure Centre

Ballinacourty, Dungarvan, Co. Waterford. ☎ **058/42416.** Fax 058/43378. 36 rms (all with bath). TEL TV. Rates, including breakfast, same as for Clonea Strand Hotel & Leisure Centre, above.

Sister to the Clonea Strand Hotel & Leisure Centre, the Gold Coast Golf Hotel faces Dungarvan Bay, overlooking the Golf Club's 9-hole, 72-par, beautifully tended course. The links border the water, with a backdrop of cliff heads across the bay. Greens fees start at IR£10 ($16), the course is open from sunrise to sunset, and lessons can be booked. Hotel guest rooms are bright and spacious, with a cozy seating area, hairdryer, and tea/coffeemaker. Dining, entertainment, and leisure center facilities are on a par with the Clonea Strand.

WHERE TO EAT

✪ An Bialann

Grattan Sq. ☎ **058/42825.** Snacks, salads, savories, and hot dinners IR£1.50–IR£8 ($2.40–$12.80). No credit cards. Mon–Sat 9:30am–7pm (8:30pm in summer), Sun 11am–7pm in summer. BREAKFAST/TRADITIONAL/SALADS/SAVORIES/SANDWICHES.

This cozy little restaurant has an attractive traditional front and high-backed booths inside. Everything on the menu is fresh and home-cooked, and selections range from soup and sandwiches to salad plates, hot savories (try the curried chicken and savoury rice), spaghetti bolognese, pizza, quiche, and five-course complete meals. There's a children's menu, a full à la carte menu, and beer, wine, and specialty coffees. Since service is continuous, this is a handy, relaxing stop any time of day, and any full meal here usually runs under IR£5 ($8).

✪ Merry's Restaurant and Bar

Lower Main St. ☎ **058/41974** or 42818. Reservations recommended for dinner, especially on weekends. Main courses IR£9–IR£12 ($14.40–$19.20); fixed-price dinner IR£13 ($20.80); Sun lunch IR£8 ($12.80); bar food IR£2–IR£4 ($3.20–$6.40). ACC, DC, MC, V. Daily 12:30–3pm and 6–10pm. Closed Good Friday, Christmas Day. SEAFOOD/TRADITIONAL/BAR FOOD/GAME.

Mrs. Carmel Feeney has transformed a centuries-old wine merchant's premises into a warm, cozy bar with adjacent restaurant. There's bar food available for lunch and during the afternoon. The dinner menu of this relaxed, intimate place is extensive and innovative, including scallops cooked in Noilly Prat, with leek, tomato, and basil; monkfish with a sweet-and-sour sauce; grilled sole on the bone; baked salmon in puff pastry and anchovy sauce; roast duckling with orange sauce; and pork steak marinated in whiskey and coriander and served in a whole-grain-mustard sauce. In season, there are also game dishes. Desserts include homemade cakes and pastries and a selection of Irish and continental cheeses.

✪ The Seanachie Restaurant and Pub

Pulla, Ring. ☎ **058/46285.** Main courses IR£6–IR£15 ($9.60–$24); bar food IR£2–IR£4 ($2.90–$5.80). ACC, MC, V. Bar food daily 10:30am–midnight; dinner daily 7:30–11pm. SEAFOOD/TRADITIONAL/IRISH/BAR FOOD.

If it's tradition you're looking for as well as good food, keep a lookout for this thatched bar and restaurant a few miles outside Dungarvan just off N25, the main Dungarvan-Ardmore-Youghal road (well signposted). It began life as a public house back in 1847, at the peak of the Great Famine, and a mass grave from those pitiful times is just next to the parking lot. These—happier—days, however, there's pub food in the rustic bar (with soup and brown bread hearty enough to be a full meal), and a restaurant that features such delicacies as Helvick Head turbot, lobster, and Blackwater salmon. The Seanachie has won numerous national awards for its food and restoration of the premises. In peak season, traditional music and dancing in the courtyard on Sunday afternoons reminds us that this was once the scene of crossroads dancing, when rural Irish gathered to dance away the shadows of oppression.

✪ The Shamrock Restaurant

O'Connell St. ☎ **058/42242.** Complete dinners IR£4–IR£10 ($6.40–$16); light meals IR£2–IR£5 ($3.20–$8); dessert and tea IR£1.50 ($2.40). ACC, MC, V. Mon–Sat 9am–9pm. TRADITIONAL.

The Shamrock is a cozy, attractive restaurant upstairs (past the square on the Cappoquin route) that serves all three meals at prices that can only be called "bargain." The extensive menu ranges from a T-bone steak with salad or vegetable or buttered trout with two vegetables to burgers, quiche Lorraine, and a variety of other light meals. There's a full wine license, and there's continuous service, making this a good place for an afternoon snack or one of the delicious and inexpensive desserts and tea.

ARDMORE

Set on Ardmore Bay, with a long, sandy beach, Ardmore is a very pretty little seaside village, the descendant of a 7th-century settlement founded by St. Declan. It has won Ireland's Tidy Town Award seven times, and has a fine group of ecclesiastical remains, including **St. Declan's Oratory** is a tiny early church, with a grave in one corner that tradition says is the final resting place of the good saint himself. The cathedral remains show traces of architectural designs ranging from the 10th to the 14th centuries, and its west gable is adorned on the outside with a remarkable group of round-headed panels filled with sculptured figures. The **round tower** soars 97 feet into the air, with its four stories clearly delineated by rings of projecting stones. Overlooking the sea, this cluster of ancient ruins is bound to set your imagination roaming.

WHERE TO STAY

✪ Byron Lodge

Ardmore, Co. Waterford. ☎ **024/94157.** 6 rms, 3 with bath. IR£18.50 ($29.6) single without bath; IR£13.50 ($21.60) per person sharing without bath; IR£2 (3.20) per person additional with bath. 20% reduction for children. (Rates include breakfast.) Dinner IR£11.50 ($18.40) extra. No credit cards. Closed Nov–Mar.

More than a century and a half old, Byron Lodge is a Georgian home with lovely views of Ardmore's beach and monastic ruins (it's signposted on Main Street in the town center). Guest rooms are exceptionally spacious, and both Kathleen Casey and Mary Byran Casey are steeped in the area's history and sightseeing attractions, as well as being very active in Ardmore's Tidy Towns Committee. They will gladly arrange tours of the Blackwater and Youghal areas. Dinners, which must be booked in advance, feature seafood specialties.

CAPPOQUIN

Ten miles from Dungarvan, the small town of Cappoquin sits in a sharp bend of the Blackwater River, a superior fishing river, whose waters yield up vast quantities of roach, dace, sea and brown trout, and salmon. Fishermen descend on Cappoquin in droves, year after year, to try their luck. If you'd like to try your hand in these waters, helpful John Noonan, proprietor of **The Toby Jug** (☎ 058/54317) can arrange a license, fishing gear, tackle, and advice on the best fishing spots (John also pulls a good pint!).

However, even if you're not a fisherman, I'd like to tempt you to stop a while in this quiet spot and learn something of the inner workings of all those "typical" Irish towns you've been passing through—not, mind you, a picture-postcard-pretty village with thatched cottages and "quaint" natives, just an average Irish small town that will give you an insight into everyday life in Ireland. This is a town I know well, and I'll share with you some of its daily life and some of the people who enrich it so.

Let me suggest that you take time to meander (that's slower than stroll!) down the short Main Street, taking in some of the traditional shopfronts that have not, as yet, been gussied up. Stop in the Toby Jug for a pint and a chat with handsome young redhead John Noonan and locals who happen to be in residence at the time. And for a unique Irish experience, drive (or walk) out to the **West Waterford Vineyards** (☎ 058/54283), 1½ miles from Cappoquin, just off the Dungarvan road, open daily from 10:30am to 8pm. Personable Patricia and David McGrath have set some 2,000 vines to create a small winery, from which they produce two marvelous white wines, as well as country wines such as apple and strawberry. Prices are a mere IR£3.50 to IR£6 ($5.60 to $9.60) per bottle. The McGraths insist you taste the wines and buy only if they appeal to your own tastes (*Fionghort,* their table wine, is a personal favorite).

If, by then, you've begun to sink into the rhythm of this Irish town, it's time for a picnic. Still farther down Main Street, you'll come to **Maurice Kellerher's Supermarket,** which resembles the ones you left at home—until, that is, one of the pretty Irish lassies behind the counter smiles and inquires if you're having a good holiday. Pick up a bit of Irish cheese (cheddar from the West Waterford creamery or one of the locally made farmhouse cheeses—Knockanore smoked cheddar or Bay-Lough reduced-fat farmhouse cheese), fruit, etc. Then head back up Main Street and around the Allied Irish Bank corner (that's Cook Street, but nobody ever calls it that). Halfway down, you'll find **Mrs. Barron's bakery,** where you can pick up fresh-baked loaves of brown, soda, or white bread and mouthwatering pastries. There's been a member of the family baking here for over 200 years, and believe me, they've learned all the secrets of the trade. Then stop by the **Lonergan brothers' tailor shop** (they may be the only tailors who still sit in the window on a platform to do their work) and buy a small jar of the honey they gather from hives they keep in local fields. Now take all your goodies out to **Glenshelane Park,** about a quarter mile outside town (signposted as "**Glenshelane River Walk**" on the Mount Mellary road). Known locally as "The Glen," it's a shaded spot on the banks of a tumbling stream that flows beneath a charming old stone bridge, and there are picnic tables where you can spread out your lunch. Now, if the peace of the ages doesn't descend on your head, there's no hope for you a'tall!

Special note: Cappoquin is home to one of Ireland's foremost painters. English by birth, but Irish "by inclination," artist **Arthur Maderson** (Derriheen House, ☎ 058/54861) has chosen to bring his family to this scenic region of Ireland, the source of endless inspiration for his oil paintings. His passion for the fleeting effects of light flows through his brush and brings a shimmering magic to his romantic, impressionistic canvases. Although tagged a "contemporary impressionist" by those in the know in the art world, one look at his work convinces me that his talent goes far beyond that, bringing the misty realism of Ireland itself to stretched linen. Winner of several prestigious awards and the subject of one-man exhibitions in major galleries in the U.K. and Ireland, this fine artist is delighted to show visitors examples of his recent work *by appointment only.* The cost of a painting ranges from IR£300 to IR£3,000 ($480–$4,800). I consider one a value-for-the-money investment.

Mount Mellary

Four miles east of Cappoquin, in the foothills of the Knockmealdown Mountains, you'll find Mount Mellary. A monastic center for the Cistercian Order of the Strict Observance, it was built over a century ago when the monks were banished from France. There's an impressive stone church and a cluster of other large stone buildings. The monks have transformed a bare mountainside into productive fields and pastures, rising at 2am to do all their own work and retiring at 8pm each evening. Until recently they observed a strict rule of silence, with only the guestmaster permitted to speak. Visitors are welcome here, and many Irish Catholics come to stay for several days in the peaceful retreat.

The Nire Valley Drive and Clonmel

The Nire Valley Drive winds through the heart of the Comeragh Mountains among mountain peaks and pastures dotted with sheep and cattle. Turn off the Dungarvan-Cappoquin road onto the signposted Clonmel route (R671), which is well paved all the way. About halfway along the Nire Valley Drive you'll find **Melody's Nire Valley Riding Stables,** Ballymacarbry, County Waterford (☎ 052/36147). Experienced rider or novice, you can explore this beautiful mountain country from horseback. Guides Ann McCarthy and Niamh Melody will see that you are seated correctly (even children are safe in their care); the horses are gentle and sure-footed; and there's a choice of paths from 5 to 12 miles, through wooded mountainsides and alongside rushing river waters and sparkling lakes. For those who absolutely refuse to sit a horse, there are jaunting cars. Several three- and four-day riding holidays are available. Especially in July and August, it's advisable to phone ahead and book for these popular trails.

Anyone at Melody's can direct you to a mountainside shrine to Irish patriots and leaders who met in March of 1923 in what is now known as the **Knockanaffrin Republican Cottage** ("The Cottage in the Glen of the Secrets") to talk in well-guarded secrecy of plans to bring an end to the bloody Civil War. In the simple whitewashed cottage, the ghosts of De Valera, Liam Lynch, and others rise up unbidden to remind you that it was in secluded locales such as this that so much of Irish history was forged.

From Ballymacarbry, the Nire Valley Drive continues to **Clonmel,** the South Tipperary county town (in Irish, Cluain Meala, "Meadow of Honey") on the banks of the River Suir. Its rich history reaches back to the 1100s, and its town walls and fortifications withstood a three-week siege by Cromwell in 1650. In later years, it was a garrison town and the home of Charles Bianconi, a poor Italian who founded the first public transport system in Ireland with a coaching service based here.

Today a thriving market town, Clonmel retains traces of the original town walls (you can't miss the impressive West Gate in the very center of the town), as well as several impressive public buildings. The Old St. Mary's Church of Ireland was built in the 13th century and is dedicated to Our Lady of Clonmel. Other buildings of note are the Town Hall, the Court House, and the Franciscan Friary. Just outside the West Gate, call in to John and Carol Kinsella's Pub, an atmospheric spot for refreshment (sandwiches and soup as well as beverages).

Note: Cahir is only 10 miles to the west, and Cashel 15 miles northwest, and you can include either or both of these on a circular tour that will take you back to Cappoquin via the Vee and Lismore (see below).

WHERE TO STAY

✪ Coolhilla

Ballyhane, Cappoquin, Co. Waterford. ☎ **058/54054.** 3 rms, all with bath. IR£18.50 ($29.60) single; IR£14.50 ($23.20) per person sharing. (Rates include breakfast.) Dinner IR£12 ($19.20) extra. 50% reduction for children. No credit cards. Closed Christmas.

Mrs. Catherine Mary Scanlan greets arriving guests with a complimentary cuppa as a warm welcome to her attractive country home. She is also quite helpful in planning regional sightseeing, and in addition to the bright, comfortable guest rooms, there's a cozy open fire in the TV lounge and a play area in the spacious grounds. Coolhilla is three miles east of Cappoquin on the Dungarvan road (N72).

Hill Crest

Powerstown Rd., Clonmel, Co. Tipperary. ☎ **052/21798.** 5 rms, 1 with bath. IR£13 ($20.80) per person. IR£1 ($1.60) extra for private bath. 33% reduction for children. (Rates include breakfast.) No credit cards.

Mrs. O'Reilly and her husband will welcome you warmly to their comfortable modern home which is convenient to town and the bus and railway station. Located in a nice quiet area just off the Waterford road (N24), the house is centrally heated and there is a garden which guests can use. The four pretty bedrooms share two bathrooms and three toilets; all have sinks.

✪ River View House

Cook St., Cappoquin, Co. Waterford. ☎ **058/54073.** 21 rms, 1 with bath. IR£16 ($25.60) per person. (Rates include breakfast.) Dinner IR£8 ($12.80) extra. 33% reduction for children. No credit cards. Enclosed car park. Book as far in advance as possible.

This three-story rambling house built by the Sisters of Mercy as an orphanage in the late 19th century has blossomed as one of the most unusual lodgings in the country under the loving direction of Evelyn and John Flynn. On N72 as you enter town from Dungarvan, the house is fascinating, with multiple stairways and corridors, a private dining room in what was once the chapel, two lounges (color TV in one), and a games room with pool tables, table tennis, darts, and board games. My favorite rooms are the four on the top floor under the eaves, whose swing-out windows open up views of the town and the Blackwater River. Outside is a play area with swings, swing balls, pitch-'n-putt, croquet, and a merry-go-round. Children are very welcome here, and the Flynn family makes certain that no River View guest, young or old, is neglected. The house is centrally heated.

Evelyn is always up-to-date on what's going on—the best fishing holes (the Blackwater is one of Ireland's best fishing rivers), where entertainment may be found locally—and if you're planning a day trip, she'll gladly pack a lunch. John will see that you have bait and fishing equipment if you decide on the spur of the moment to test your skill. Evening meals are very good, and tea and homemade scones (no charge) are a regular feature in the evening.

✪ The Toby Jug

Main St., Cappoquin, Co. Waterford. ☎ **058/54317;** fax 058/54532. 8 rms, 2 with bath. IR£15 ($24) single; IR£13 ($20.80) per person sharing; IR£2 ($3.20) per person extra with bath. (Rates include breakfast.) Dinner IR£11 ($15.95). No credit cards. Closed Nov–Jan.

The Toby Jug is a favorite with anglers who come to fish the Blackwater River, as well as with overseas visitors. Denise (everyone calls her "Dee") and John Noonan are the attractive young couple who have taken over its management from John's parents, who ran things for more than 30 years. Both know the area well and are happy to point visitors to scenic drives and sightseeing attractions nearby. John can organize fishing on the Blackwater, and Denise is a graduate of the celebrated Ballymaloe Cookery School and turns out superb evening meals (see "Where to Eat," below). There are eight comfortably furnished upstairs bedrooms, six with handbasins and two with private baths, as well as a cozy TV lounge for guests. The pretty dining room and the popular public bar occupy the ground floor. Dinner must be booked by noon, and Dee will fix a luncheon basket for a small charge if requested the night before.

FARMHOUSES

✪ Aglish House

Aglish, Cappoquin, Co. Waterford. ☎ **024/96191.** 3 rms, 2 with bath. TV. IR£20 ($32) per person. 50% reduction for children. (Rates include breakfast.) Dinner IR£18 ($28.80), wine extra. No credit cards.

Even the approach to Aglish House is scenic—down winding country roads lined with lush farmlands, handsome estate mansions, and wooded hills. (Take the Clashmore-Youghal exit from the roundabout on N25 in Dungarvan; Aglish House is signposted on the Clonmel-Youghal portion of this road.) From the 200-year-old farmhouse, views are of green fields and distant hills, and the large guest rooms (two will hold family groups of up to six people), with their floor-length windows, look out onto rural serenity. This is the working dairy farm of Tom and Terry Moore and their six children, and there's no warmer welcome in Ireland than you'll get from this lively, hospitable family. Lovely antique pieces are scattered among the furnishings, and Terry is happy to furnish a cot for young children. Terry is flexible about breakfast and dinner hours.

Clonanav Farm Guest House

Nire Valley, Ballymacarbry, Co. Waterford. ☎ **052/36141.** 10 rms, all with shower. TEL. IR£20–IR£22 ($32–$35.20) per person sharing. 50% reduction for children. (Rates include breakfast.) Dinner IR£14–IR£15 ($22.40–$24) extra. Package angling and walking, holiday rates available. ACC, AE, MC, V.

Eileen and Larry Ryan's deluxe farmhouse, well signposted 1½ miles from Ballymacarbry on the Clonmel-Dungarvan road (T27), has one of the most peaceful, scenic settings around, with landscaped gardens and beautiful Nire Valley views. The house itself has nicely furnished, comfortable guest rooms, a cozy family room with a glowing fire, a conservatory with a free tea/coffee bar, central heating, and an electric blanket on every bed. Meals are a delight in the spacious dining room, with prime Irish meats, fish, fruit, and vegetables and herbs fresh from their garden. It is, however, the Ryans themselves, and their eight children, who have won the most accolades. As one reader wrote, "Guests from England, Holland, Belgium, the U.S., and Ireland gathered around the fireplace each evening for conversation and refreshments, and Eileen was glad to help research genealogical records in the Waterford area. We loved staying here and hated to leave."

✪ Hanora's Cottage Guesthouse

Ballymacarbry, Nire Valley via Clonmel, Co. Waterford. ☎ **052/36134.** Fax 052/25145. 6 rms, all with bath. IR£32–IR£35 ($51.20–$56) single; IR£22.50–IR£25 ($36–$40) per person sharing. (Rates include breakfast.) Dinner IR£17.50 ($28) extra. Special midweek and weekend rates available. MC, V. Closed last two weeks in Dec.

Mary and Seamus Wall have built up a loyal following among our readers, many of whom tell me they look forward to return visits. Small wonder, really, when you consider the idyllic setting of Hanora's at the foot of the Comeragh Mountains, its pleasant Nire River garden, and the sense of peace and tranquillity that seems to envelop the place. Named for Seamus's great-grandmother, the ancestral cottage has undergone a conversion that includes tastefully furnished guest rooms and a dining room presided over by their son, whose gourmet meals are the result of Ballymaloe Cookery School training. Seamus is a past captain of the Clonmel Golf Club and is happy to arrange for guests to play the course.

Hotel Minella

Coleville Rd., Clonmel, Co. Tipperary. ☎ **052/22388.** Fax 052/24381. 70 rms, all with bath. IR£40–IR£100 ($64–$160) single; IR£35–IR£80 ($56–$128) per person sharing. (Rates include breakfast.) Suites with private Jacuzzis available. Dinner IR£20 ($29) extra. AE, DC, MC, V.

The Minella, a beautiful former Quaker mansion, has been transformed into a lovely country hotel set beside the River Suir, just a mile outside Clonmel. The tastefully furnished guest rooms have telephones, radios, TVs with cable, hairdryers, and tea/coffeemakers. Most also enjoy superb river or mountain views. Public rooms reflect the elegance of their past, and the oak-paneled dining room overlooks the garden. Elizabeth and John Nallen, the owner/managers, represent the family that has owned the hotel for some 35 years.

✪ Richmond House

Cappoquin, Co. Waterford. ☎ **058/54278.** Fax 058/54988. 10 rms, all with bath. TEL. IR£27–IR£31 ($43.20–$49.60) single; IR£25–IR£30 ($40–$48) per person sharing. (Rates include breakfast.) Dinner IR£22 ($35.20). AE, DC, MC, V. Closed Jan.

Mrs. Jean Deevy is the gracious owner of this 18th-century Georgian country home just outside Cappoquin, which once belonged to the estate of the earl of

Cork and Burlington. Restored to their original elegance, the public rooms escape the stiff formality of many such houses and exude a warm friendliness, aided and abetted by glowing log fires. Guest rooms are nicely furnished. The restaurant, run by chef Paul Deevy, draws diners from the entire area, as well as being very popular with locals (See "Where to Eat").

Where to Eat

✪ The Paddock

In the Clonmel Arms Hotel, Sarsfield St., Clonmel. ☎ **052/21233.** Hot plates IR£4–IR£5 ($6.40–$8); salad plates IR£3 ($4.80); sandwiches and snacks IR£1–IR£4 ($1.60–$6.40). MC, V. Lunch (hot plates) daily 12:30–3:30pm; salad plates, sandwiches, and snacks daily 12:30–8pm. HOT PLATES/SALADS/SANDWICHES/SNACKS.

The Paddock is one of those eateries with continuous food service that are such a godsend to the traveler, since a lunch stop is not always possible during normal serving hours. Nicely appointed, it offers a fish plate, roast plate, and hotpot plate during lunch hours, and such niceties as prawn cocktail and marinated mussels, both with brown bread, and cold salad plates after 2:30pm.

✪ Richmond House

Cappoquin, Co. Waterford. ☎ **058/54278.** Fax 058/54988. Reservations recommended. Set dinner IR£22 ($35.20). Daily 6–9pm. MC, V. IRISH/FRENCH

This restaurant in a beautifully decorated 18th-century country home features locally caught salmon and trout in dishes such as baked delice of Blackwater salmon with an herb-butter sauce. A strong French influence is evident in specialties like Cappoquin lamb au jus, with a touch of garlic and oregano, and confit of duck breast on a pillow of spiced cabbage.

Fast Food

Kearney's Takeaway

Main Street, Cappoquin. Blackboard menu under IR£4 ($6.40). Daily noon–2:30pm, 5:30pm–1am. FISH & CHIPS/BURGERS/SNACKS.

For pickup lunches and late-night snacks, Cappoquin's "chipper" is a godsend. Very popular with locals after pub closings.

The Saddler's Tea Shop

The Square, Cappoquin. ☎ **058/54045.** IR£1.25–IR£4 ($2–$6.40). No credit cards. Daily 9am–6pm. SALADS/SANDWICHES/HOT PLATES/PASTRIES.

This bright, cozy place is very popular with locals, who drop in all during the day for tea and snacks. Its specialties are home-cooked meats and home baking. Hot plates and cold salads are superb, as are the delicious scones and pastries (which are fresh from Barron's Bakery next door).

✪ The Toby Jug Guesthouse

Main St., Cappoquin. ☎ **058/54317.** Set dinner (must be booked by noon) IR£11 ($17.60). No credit cards. Open Feb–Oct, hours by appointment. TRADITIONAL.

Denise Noonan, who took her culinary training at the Ballymaloe Cookery School, will serve dinner if notified by noon of the same day. She offers a choice of three main courses, depending on what's available at the market, since she prides herself on using fresh native meats embellished with her special sauces. Among her specialties are tarragon chicken, lovely lamb marinated with herbs, and steak with pepper sauce. Desserts include a luscious chocolate mousse, a tart gooseberry fool, and apples with Irish Mist (my personal favorite). When you book, just let her know the hour you'd like to dine.

LISMORE

Four miles west of Cappoquin on N72, the town of Lismore on the south bank of the Blackwater has been designated a Heritage Town, not surprising in light of its long, rich history. To appreciate just how dramatic that history has been, make your first stop the Heritage Centre (☎ 058/54975; open 9:30am to 5:30pm Monday to Saturday, noon to 5:30pm Sunday) in the Old Courthouse on the main street to view the excellent **"Lismore Experience,"** an exceptionally beautiful and informative multimedia presentation that chronicles the story since St. Carthage arrived in 636. Take time to browse through the small museum, where one exhibit reconstructs the motte and bailey that crowned the original **Lios Moir** from which the town draws its name. The *lios,* a great earthen ring fort, is about a mile east of town on the "back road" to Cappoquin—not really a sightseeing attraction, but a pretty impressive high conical mound.

On Main Street, look for **Eleanor Howard's pottery shop**—her high-fired earthenware for the table includes teapots, jugs, and other pieces, many with decorative handles. Prices run IR£5 ($8) to IR£45 ($72), and she's open Mon–Sat, 9am–5pm.

The majestic lines of picture-perfect ✪ **Lismore Castle** loom over town and river, and the castle is clearly the dominant feature of Lismore's landscape—absolutely spectacular when floodlit at night! King John had it built in 1185 on the site of St. Carthage's monastery of the 7th century. It was, for centuries, one of the most world-renowned of Ireland's distinguished learning institutions, and its many famous students include King Alfred the Great. In time, it became the target for Viking raids, as well as Norman and English conquests. It was here that Henry II came to accept homage from Irish chieftains, but the monastic community was finally destroyed by Raymond le Gros in 1173.

Sir Walter Raleigh is listed among the castle's former owners, as is Richard Boyle, the earl of Cork. Since 1753, however, it has been the Irish seat of the dukes of Devonshire, one of whom married Lady Charlotte Boyle and thus acquired the property. Today it is certainly among the most impressive still-lived-in castles in the country, and along with its mass of square towers, crenellated walls, and great halls, there are comfortably furnished apartments. The people of Lismore recall with a special fondness the years that Fred Astaire's sister, Adele, lived here as a duchess of Devonshire and was well loved in the town.

The public is not admitted to the castle, but the beautifully tended **gardens** are open from 1:45 to 4:45pm from early May to early September, for a small admission charge. One note of caution, however: There are those in Lismore who will tell you that the shades of murdered monks still roam the castle grounds in the dark of night—so, just don't go wandering about in the dark of night! There are, however, no ghostly figures (at least, as far as I know) wandering the lovely riverside ✪ **Lady Louisa's Walk** and the interesting **Town Walk,** both of which are signposted.

Another Lismore link with history is the **Cathedral of St. Carthage,** also floodlit. Although it was rebuilt in 1633, there are 9th- and 11th-century grave slabs with inscriptions in Irish in the west wall of the nave. An altar tomb is dated 1557.

For a quiet drink in an old-fashioned pub, stop in ✪ **Michael and Eileen O'Donnell's pub** on Bridge Street in Lismore. In the old tradition, there is a hardware shop on one side, a pub on the other—not too many left like that these days, and the friendly locals who inhabit the place always welcome a chat with visitors.

Golfers can arrange a round or two at the **Lismore Golf Club** (☎ 058/54026).

If you're in this part of Ireland on a Wednesday between the last week in June and the last week in August, don't miss a performance of **The Booley House** in St. Michael's Hall, Ballyduff, Co. Waterford (book through Lismore Heritage Centre, ☎ 058/54975 or 60287); admission is around IR£5 ($8). Staged by talented locals, it's an authentic—and delightful—look into Ireland's rural past, when farm families moved cattle and sheep to the hills for summer grazing. Many of the small stone cottages you see today on high lands once served as homes for farm families during the more carefree months, and they were the scene of many a gathering of an evening for homegrown entertainment of music, song, dance, and storytelling. Tea, scones, and cake were always on hand then, and the Booley House carries on that tradition. Lightfooted dancers float through the old step and set dances; the fiddles, whistles, and bodhrans swing into jigs and reels of long ago, and a storyteller brings on fits of laughter.

WHERE TO STAY

Lismore's limited accommodations are often booked out in summer months, in which case, any one of those listed in the section above would make a convenient base for the area.

Beechcroft

Deerpark Rd., Lismore, Co. Waterford. ☎ **058/54273.** 3 rms, all with bath. IR£16 ($25.60) single, IR£14 ($22.40) per person sharing. (Rates include breakfast.) Closed Nov–Mar.

June Powers is the hostess in this bright, modern bungalow on the edge of town. Guest rooms are nicely done up, with built-in wardrobes and comfortable furnishings. She also has a four-bedroom self-catering bungalow next door.

Ballyrafter House Hotel

Lismore, Co. Waterford. ☎ **058/54002.** 11 rms, all with bath. IR£30–IR£34 ($48–$54.40) single IR£26–IR£30 ($41.60–$48) per person sharing. (Rates include breakfast.) DC, MC, V. Closed Nov–Mar.

Set on a small rise at the outskirts of town, set back from the Cappoquin road, Ballyrafter House looks out over the Blackwater to Lismore Castle. Fine Irish horses gambol in the field out front that separates the hotel from the roadway, and the wooded and landscaped grounds fairly exude peace and tranquility. Guest rooms are rather plain, but quite comfortable, and there's a pleasant guest lounge, a friendly bar, and a pretty dining room overlooking the grounds. It's owned and operated by the Willoughby family, whose tradition of friendly hospitality is reflected in every member of the staff.

A Very Special Hostel

Kilmorna Farm Hostel

Lismore, Co. Waterford. ☎ **058/54315.** 12 triple bunk beds. 3 private rooms, double and triple. IR£7.50 ($12) per person. Family rates available. IR£3 ($4.80) breakfast (on request). No credit cards. 3 miles east of Lismore.

About a fifteen-minute walk from Lismore along a scenic country road, Kilmorna is a working farm centered around a Georgian-style farmhouse. If you thought "hostel" meant only "backpacking," this place could well change forever your perception of the word. For families traveling the B&B route, I heartily recommend an overnight here to give the children a very special farm experience. Horses, cows, sheep, geese, hens, dogs, and cats roam the fields. Tara and Julia, daughters of the house, delight in showing their guests around the farm. Owner Sibylle Knobel has transformed old stone outbuildings centered around a cobblestone courtyard into attractive accommodations with central heating and just loaded with character. Whitewashed one-story buildings hold double and triple rooms, a laundry, showers, and toilets. Lots of natural wood and puffy duvet coverlets create a warm, inviting decor. Light-toned wood paneling is used in the bright communal kitchen and adjoining lounge that overlooks the farmyard. Although you are requested to bring your own towels, there's no need to bring linens or cooking utensils, which are furnished at no extra charge.

Where to Eat

✪ Bride View Pub and Guesthouse

Tallow Bridge, Tallow, Co. Waterford. ☎ **058/56522.** Hot meals IR£3.45–IR£4.75 ($5.52–$7.60), light meals IR£1.50–IR£3.25 ($2.40–$5.20), steaks IR£9.95 ($15.92). No credit cards. Daily noon–9pm. On outskirts of Tallow, about 5 miles west of Lismore via N72. STEAK/TRADITIONAL/SNACKS.

Alan and Gina Sivyer preside over this attractive pub on the banks of the River Bride. Eat inside the cozy pub or in fine weather outside at the picnic tables set along a riverside walk under shady trees. The hot meals here (chicken Kiev, savory chicken or ham vol-au-vents, etc.) are terrific. Even the burgers and other light meals reflect Gina's expertise in the kitchen. A bonus for travelers are the long hours of continuous service. If you fall for this idyllic location, inquire about their guest rooms and self-catering cottage on the grounds.

✪ Eammon's Place

Main St., Lismore, Co. Waterford. Lunch IR£3.50–IR£5 ($5.10–$7.25); dinner IR£5–IR£8 ($7.25–$11.60). No credit cards. Mon–Fri noon–9pm. BAR FOOD.

This attractive little pub is a cozy place, with a corner fireplace and three-legged iron pot for turf and wood. Try Eammon Walsh's chicken-liver pâté on Joan's homemade brown bread—scrumptious! And if local Blackwater salmon is available, I guarantee you'll get portions so ample you'll be hard-pressed to finish the plate. There's a fixed-price meal which varies from roast beef to bacon and cabbage. You'll be missing some of the best home cooking in Ireland if you don't stop in at least once.

Kearney's Golden Grill and Take Away

Main Street, Tallow, Co. Waterford. ☎ **058/56663.** Main courses IR£3.95–IR£7.95 ($6.32–$12.72), take-aways under IR£5 ($8). No credit cards. Daily 9:30am–1:30am, Take-away daily noon–1am. TRADITIONAL.

Kearney's meals are excellent value for money—good home cooking and overflowing portions. The extensive menu lists dishes such as grilled or poached salmon steak Hollandaise, chicken Maryland, and sirloin steak garni, along with lighter fare of pizza, omelettes, and salad plates.

A Scenic Drive Over the Vee

As you can see from the above, there are several scenic drives around the Cappoquin/Lismore area. One of the most breathtaking is that through a gap in the Knockmealdown Mountains known as the Vee (R668). It's signposted from the outskirts of Lismore and climbs to a height of 1,114 feet, through mountainsides covered with heather to the V-shaped pass, with lay-bys that o look sweeping views of Tipperary's Golden Vale, before descending to the littl town of ✪ **Clogheen,** County Tipperary. Between the gap and Clogheen, keep a watch on the high side of the road for one of the most curious graves in the world, that of one **Samuel Grubb,** onetime owner of Castle Grace, who so loved his lands that he decreed he should be buried upright on the mountain slopes overlooking them. There's a small pathway leading up to the stone cairn that is his final resting place. About halfway over the Vee, you pass into South Tipperary.

CAHIR

✪ **Cahir Castle** (☎ 052/41011) stands on a rocky islet in the River Suir that has been the natural site of fortifications as far back as the 3rd century. Brian Boru maintained a residence here as High King of Ireland. The castle you see today on this ancient site was built by the Norman de Berminghams, in the 13th century, and was held by the Anglo-Norman Butlers until 1599, when the earl of Essex captured it after a short siege. In 1650 it was surrendered to Cromwell without a single shot, and within its walls the articles ending the long Cromwellian wars were signed in 1652. Butler descendants held the castle title until the last of them died in 1961. After years of neglect, the state took over in 1964 and opened the castle to the public in 1971. Restored to near-original condition, Cahir Castle has figured in a number of films. With its residential apartments refurnished in authentic reproductions, it brings alive the life and times of all its centuries-old history.

Admission is IR£2 ($3.20) for adults, IR£1.50 ($2.40) for senior citizens, IR£1 ($1.60) for children and students, IR£5 ($8) for family ticket. It's open April to mid-June, daily from 10am to 6pm; mid-June to mid-September, daily from 9am to 7:30pm; mid-September to March daily, with varying hours.

Guided tours are conducted by request during summer months, when there's a resident tourist office; in winter there's an informative caretaker on hand.

Just across from the castle, the **Crock of Gold** craft and tea shop has an excellent selection of crafts and books of Irish interest, and tea comes in Royal Tara cups.

Swiss Cottage

Cahir (off N8-Cork/Dublin Road), Co. Tipperary. ☎ **052/41144.** Admission IR£2 ($3.20) adult, IR£1.50 ($2.40) seniors, IR£1 ($1.60) children and students, IR£5 ($8) family ticket. Mid-Mar–Apr and Oct–Nov, Tues–Sun 10am–1pm and 2–4:30pm; May–Sept, daily 10am–6pm. Access by guided tour only.

Odd to find a *Swiss* cottage in Ireland? Maybe nowadays, but back in the early 1800s, Irish romantics held the notion that this picturesque rustic style was just right for hunting and fishing lodges. Designed by the famous Regency architect John Nash and built on the estate of the Earls of Glengall, the two-story thatched cottage is fairly broken out with timberwork more akin to architecture in Switzerland and/or England than in Ireland. Rustic it may be, but no expense was spared—some of the wallpaper was, in fact, produced in Paris!

WHERE TO STAY

Bansha House

Bansha, Tipperary, Co. Tipperary. ☎ **062/54194.** 6 rms, 4 with bath. MC, V. IR£20–IR£23 ($32–$36.80) single; IR£17–IR£20 ($27.20–$32) per person sharing without bath, IR£16 ($23.20) per person sharing with bath. 25% reduction for children. (Rates include breakfast.) Dinner IR£10 ($14.50) extra. Closed Dec–Feb.

arnane is hostess of this lovely Georgian house with beautiful views f Aherlow and the Galtee mountains, just 3½ miles from Tipperary use is centrally heated and the food is delicious, cooked in traditional ding holidays are available with full use of their Equestrian Centre.

✪ Castle

Cork Rd., Cahir, Co. Tipperary. ☎ **052/41370.** 5 rms, 2 with bath. IR£14.50 ($23.20) per person without bath. IR£17 ($27.20) per person with bath. (Rates include breakfast.) ACC, MC, V.

Peg and Sean Butler have turned Sean's ancestral home into a fitting representative of castle hospitality of old. The 1600 castle on the edge of town has a colorful past, having twice been used as a prison for rebellious Irish, but since Sean's father regained possession in 1919, it has taken back its function as family home. Bedrooms have been fashioned from the original upstairs rooms—this may be the only B&B in Ireland in which you enter your bedroom through a centuries-old stone doorway.

Peg is a thoughtful hostess, always ready with the extra cup of tea, as well as good advice about sightseeing in the area. Her son, David, takes a special interest in greeting and assisting guests. The house is centrally heated, and there's a fire in the lounge on cool evenings.

Clonmore

Cork-Galbally Rd., Tipperary, Co. Tipperary. ☎ **062/51637.** 6 rms, all with bath. IR£18 ($28.80) single; IR£15 ($24) per person sharing. 20% reduction for children. (Rates include breakfast.) No credit cards. Closed Nov–Mar. Private parking.

Mrs. Mary Quinn's pretty bungalow sits in its own grounds, within sight of the Galtee mountains and a five-minute walk from town. The house is centrally heated, and guest rooms are both attractive and comfortable, with electric blankets to ward off the chill. There's also a sun lounge.

Where to Eat

✪ The Galtee Inn

The Square. Cahir. ☎ **052/41247.** Main courses IR£5.95–IR£10.45 ($9.52–$16.72); bar food IR£2–IR£5 ($3.20–$8). Morning coffee Mon–Sat 10am–noon; bar lunches Mon–Sat 12:30–2:30pm; full à la carte menu Mon–Sat 12:30–10:30pm. TRADITIONAL/BAR FOOD.

The Malone family (John, Alan, and Rosealeen) have created a bright, cheerful eatery as an adjunct for this popular pub. A skylight makes the place light and airy, and there's lots of brass and wood. In addition to full meals, morning coffee is served, and sandwiches are available all day, making this a good place to drop in for a snack, coffee, tea, Irish coffee, or a relaxing drink from the bar. Bar lunches include a full range of salad plates and hot dishes. There's also an à la carte menu available until 10:30pm, with a good selection of starters (featuring smoked salmon, homemade pâté, etc.) and main dishes that include steak in several guises, lamb cutlets, pork cutlets, chicken, and a homemade steakburger in thick mushroom sauce.

CASHEL

Soaring above the South Tipperary town of Cashel (Caiseal, or "Stone Fort") is Ireland's most majestic historical landmark, the lofty ✪ **Rock of Cashel** (☎ 062/61437). It stands 300 feet above the surrounding plains, and is an awe-inspiring presence. Its summit encompasses a full two acres; its view is measured in miles. Ancient Celts worshipped here, and Irish kings built palaces

Readers Recommend

Tir-na-nOg, Dualla, Cashel, Co. Tipperary. ☎/Fax 062/61350. *"I really want to share with others this place and its hostess Eileen Creed. One of the most special things about the Creeds were their gourmet-quality evening meals—super suppers!"*

—Geri Dawson, Riverside, CA

on the sacred site. In the 5th century the King of Munster erected a cashel, or stone fort, and it was there that St. Patrick came in the year 450 to preach to the King of Munster, Aengus, using the humble shamrock as a symbol of the Christian trinity. Aengus (Angus) saw the light and with his family accepted baptism. Murtough O'Brien presented the Cashel of the Kings to the church in 1101, and in 1127 Cormac MacCarthaigh (McCarthy), King of Desmond, built the little chapel that is his namesake, a miniature gem of Romanesque style. In the years that followed, construction was begun on a massive cathedral; King Henry II came to receive homage from such Irish princes as Donal O'Brien, King of Thomond; Edward the Bruce (Robert the Bruce's brother, who attempted to make himself king of all Ireland in 1315) held a Parliament here; the first Protestant service was held in the cathedral; it was burned in 1495, restored, and damaged again by Cromwell's ruthless troops; and in 1748 the archbishop of the day left it abandoned and unroofed because—or so the Irish say—his coach and four could not make it up the steep incline to its great west door.

The Rock's mystical sense of ages past and ages yet to come can only be experienced as you watch the audio-visual presentation, then follow the guided tour, then leave it to wander on your own among the ancient stones and ruins, and gaze at the stone Cross of Cashel whose base may once have been a pre-Christian sacrificial altar.

Admission is IR£2.50 ($4) for adults, IR£1.75 ($2.80) for senior citizens, IR£1 ($1.60) for children and students, IR£6 ($9.60) for family ticket. June to September, tours are conducted daily from 9am to 7:30pm; other months, daily from 9:30am to 4:30pm.

At the foot of the Rock of Cashel, you'll find the ✪ **Brú Ború Heritage Centre** (☎ 062/61122). Set around a village green, the center is devoted to the preservation of native Irish song, music, dance, storytelling, theater, and Celtic studies. There's a Folk Theatre, with daily performances (admission IR£5, $8); Teach Ceoil, where informal music sessions erupt spontaneously, and storytellers are usually on hand; an International Heritage School; a Genealogy Centre; an exhibition hall with multidimensional displays; a craft shop, and a restaurant. Stay for the evening dinner and show, followed by a céili.

Nearby Attractions

Holycross Abbey is four miles south of Thurles (pronounced "*Thur*-less" or, native style, "*Tur*-less") on the west bank of the River Suir, some 13 miles north of Cashel on R660. It was founded in 1168 and was a revered place of pilgrimage because it held a particle of the True Cross, preserved in a golden shrine set with precious stones, that had been presented to King Murtagh O'Brien, grandson of Brian Boru, in 1110. The shrine is now in the Ursuline Convent in Blackrock, Cork, but the abbey still contains many interesting and religiously significant ruins, and Sunday pilgrimages still take place from May to September.

From Cashel, take R688 southeast, then turn onto R692 for a 20-minute drive to the little village of **Fethard,** where you'll find the **Fethard Folk and Transport Museum,** Cashel Road, Fethard (☎ 052/31516). It's in the Old Railway Goods Store and holds a wonderful collection of rural antiques relating to farming, family life, and transport. Kids will love the Victorian china dolls and prams, mom will get a kick out of the 1880 sewing machine, and dad will smile at the old-time bicycles. The proprietors, Christopher and Margaret Mullins, live on the site and will open it at any time by request, but regular summer hours are Monday through Saturday from 10am to 6pm and on Sunday from 1:30 to 6pm; there's a small admission fee.

If you come along on Sunday from March through December, there's good browsing at the "car boot" sale and the collectors' market.

WHERE TO STAY

Thornbrook House

Dualla Rd., Cashel, Co. Tipperary. ☎ **062/62388.** 5 rms, 3 with bath. IR£20 ($32) single without bath; IR£14 ($22.40) per person sharing without bath; IR£2.50 ($4) per person additional with bath. 20% reduction for children. (Rates include breakfast.) MC, V. Private car park. Closed Nov–Mar.

Mary and Willie Kennedy will welcome you warmly to their modern bungalow half a mile from Cashel on the Dualla-Kilkenny road. The house features antique furniture, open fires, and a large lawn overlooking the Rock of Cashel. They'll help you plan sightseeing, golf, fishing, or horseback riding.

Farmhouses

✪ The Chestnuts

Dualla-Kilkenny Rd. (R691), Cashel, Co. Tipperary. ☎ **062/61469.** 5 rms, 2 with shower. IR£18 ($28.80) single without bath, IR£20 ($32) with bath; IR£15 ($24) per person sharing without bath, IR£17 ($27.20) per person with bath. 20% reduction for children. (Rates include breakfast.) Dinner IR£13 ($20.80) extra. No credit cards. Closed Christmas.

Phyllis and John O'Halloran extend what one reader described as "the warmest welcome we received in Ireland." Their modern bungalow is set in mature gardens and 100 acres of farmland in a beautiful rural landscape. Just 2$^1/_2$ miles from Cashel, the Chestnuts is an ideal touring base, with nicely appointed guest rooms, a "relaxation room" with TV and an open fire, and meals that feature home baking. In the village just down the road, traditional music is usually on tap.

Rahard Lodge

Kilkenny Rd. (R691), Cashel, Co. Tipperary. ☎ **062/61052.** 6 rms, 4 with bath. IR£13.50 ($21.60) per person without bath; IR£15.50 ($24.80) per person with bath and breakfast. 20% reduction for children. Dinner IR£12 ($19.20) extra. V. Closed Dec–Jan.

Mrs. Moira Foley runs this pretty, modern farmhouse overlooking the Rock of Cashel, on the outskirts of town. It's in a nice quiet area and has lovely gardens and lawns. The house is centrally heated as well as having an open fire, and electric blankets are available. Dinner can be arranged with advance notice.

WHERE TO EAT

The Bishop's Buttery

In the Cashel Palace Hotel, Main St., Cashel. ☎ **062/61411.** Main courses IR£8–IR£15 ($12.80–$24); fixed-price dinner IR£18 ($28.80); snacks IR£1.50–IR£4 ($2.40–$6.40). ACC, AE, MC, V. Daily 10am–10pm. IRISH/TRADITIONAL/SALADS/SNACKS.

Readers Recommend

The Spearman Restaurant, 97 Main St., Cashel, Co. Tipperary. ☎ 062/61143. *"We were amazed at the sophistication of Spearman's menu. Somehow, we didn't expect to find chicken baked with Gruyère cheese and Dijon mustard or steak with red pepper and mushroom sauce in this small Irish town. Prices were more than reasonable, and we would heartily recommend it to others."*

—Mary and Susan Farley, Austin, TX

Not for budgeteers is the Four Seasons Restaurant, the Cashel Palace's main dining room. This elegant first-class hotel was erected in 1730 as a palace for the archbishop of Cashel. The drawing room overlooks gardens and a breathtaking view of the Rock of Cashel. Down stone stairs, the flagstone cellar holds the Derby Bar and the Bishop's Buttery, where you can hoist a pint or order salad plates and hot dishes or a simple snack of homemade soup and hot scones before a gigantic stone fireplace.

✪ Chez Hans

Rockside, Cashel, Co. Tipperary. ☎ **062-61177.** Reservations strongly recommended. Main courses IR£14.50–IR£19.50 ($23.20–$31.20). MC, V. Tues–Sat 6:30–10pm. Closed bank holidays and three weeks in January. At the foot of the Rock of Cashel.

Chez Hans, set in a former Wesleyan chapel, is undoubtedly one of Ireland's finest restaurants. Owner/chef Hans-Peter Matthia consistently presents diners with such innovative versions of traditional cooking as his breast of free-range chicken with Cashel blue cheese and leek Sabayonne and escalope of turbot or brill with Dublin Bay prawns in a champagne sauce.

CARRICK-ON-SUIR

Elsewhere in South Tipperary, visit Carrick-on-Suir, where the **Ormond Manor House** is believed to be the birthplace of Anne Boleyn, and the town is, for sure, that of the Clancy Brothers and cyclist Sean Kelly. **Tipperary Crystal,** Ballynoran (☎ 051/41188), is headquartered three miles from town on N24, where skilled master craftsmen with Waterford Crystal training create the lovely pieces you'll find in their factory shop, located in a traditional thatch-roofed cottage.

11 Cork City

This grand old city that native son and actor Niall Tobin has described as "an intimate higgledy-piggledy assemblage of steps, slopes, steeples, and bridges" is, to quote one visitor, "strewn like a bouquet along the valley."

Limerick was, Dublin is, and Cork shall be
The finest city of the three.

So says "The Old Prophecy" as quoted by Dean Hole in 1859. Well, never mind about "shall be," any Corkman worth his salt will tell you that Cork is, and always has been, the finest city in Ireland! And with more than a little justification, I might add.

Suffice it to say that Cork is friendly, cosmopolitan without the pseudo-sophistication of some large cities, and fun to visit. Its great age (its charter was conferred in 1185) imbues Cork with enormous pride. As a native once assured me with a perfectly straight face, "Sure, it's only an accident of geography that Dublin is the capital of Ireland." Not that anyone really cares if it is the capital: To be Cork is quite enough.

Its ancient Irish name is Corcaigh, or "Marshy Place." In this place of marshes, Druids once held their religious rites in the dense woods of the southern hills that rose above it. Celtic tribes built forts and fought battles over territorial rights in the hills to the north. And in the 7th century, St. Finbar came to establish a monastery on a small island in the swamp, asserting that there would be "an abundance of wisdom continually in Cork."

Attracted by the religious foundation's riches, the Vikings arrived in the 9th century to plunder, and then to settle in. Normans took over in the 12th century, fortified the city, and proceeded to build great churches and abbeys. But it was the advent of Oliver Cromwell, who captured Cork in December 1649, that settled the hash of natives in the district.

Unlike the Danes and Normans, who had assimilated happily with the resident populace, those who came after Cromwell held in contempt everything that was Irish and imposed harsh penalties on any who attempted to live with them amicably. No doubt it is from the strangling repression of this period that present-day Corkmen date their fierce sense of independence and abhorrence of injustice. Nor did being on the losing side ever lessen their fighting spirit. For a few centuries, in fact, they consistently allied themselves with defeat, standing behind the pretender to the throne Perkin Warbeck, Charles I, and James II.

That the blood has never stopped flowing hot in their veins at any hint of injustice is clear from the fact that when their lord mayor, Terence MacSwiney, died after a 74-day hunger strike, his comrades-in-arms locked the door of St. George's where the requiem mass was to be held, opened his coffin, clothed his body in his I.R.A. commandant uniform, and inscribed on his coffin "Murdered by the Foreigners in Brixton Prison, London, England, on October 25th, 1920, the Fourth Year of the Republic." Blissful in his ignorance, the archbishop conducted the mass, never knowing the message of the Irish inscription.

For centuries all that history slogged through acres of marshland, right up until the end of the 1700s. Vessels sailed up Patrick Street as late as 1760 (it was paved in 1791), and in 1780 there was a canal down the center of the Grand Parade and a bridge where the Berwick Fountain now stands between Tuckey Street and Oliver Plunkett Street.

Today the citizens of Cork are reckoned to be among the ablest merchants and traders in Ireland. They are a lively, cultural bunch, much attuned to the arts, and quick to welcome strangers. Theater, traditional music, and one of Europe's best jazz festivals are highlights of each year, while street musicians carry on the tradition of ballad singers down through the ages and the old piper who once trod Winthrop Street wheezing out "An' de Vallee Lay Smilin' Afore Me."

1 Orientation

ARRIVING **By Plane** There are regularly scheduled direct flights to Cork city from Dublin, England, and the Continent. From Cork city, there are connecting flights to other Irish destinations. For flight information, phone 021/313131.

By Bus There is direct bus service to Cork city from Dublin and other major cities, with connecting service from virtually any point in the country. The bus station is on Parnell Place, one block down from St. Patrick's Bridge. For bus information, phone 021/506-066.

By Train Cork city has direct rail service from Dublin and Limerick. The railway station is on Lower Glamire Road. For information, phone 021/506-766.

By Ferry Service to and from the Continent is provided by Brittany Ferries, 42 Grand Parade (☎ 021/277801), and Irish Ferries, 2–4 Merrion Row, Dublin 4 (☎ 01/610714). Ferry service from Cork city to Great Britain is provided by Swansea Cork Ferries, 1A South Mall (☎ 021/276000).

VISITOR INFORMATION The Tourist Office is centrally located at Tourist House, Grand Parade (☎ 021/273251). It's open in July and August, Monday through Saturday from 9am to 7pm and on Sunday from 3 to 5pm; other months, Monday through Friday from 9:15am to 1pm and 2:15 to 5:30pm and on Saturday from 9:30am to 1pm.

CITY LAYOUT Cork's city center is on an island in the River Lee, which can be confusing when you suddenly encounter the river you thought you'd just left behind. Some 16 bridges cross the Lee, and the city center's maze of one-way streets and narrow lanes can confound the best drivers in the world. My best advice to drivers is to get to your accommodation, park the car, and leave it there. Public transportation (via lovely double-decker buses and a good taxi service) is excellent and can take you virtually anywhere you wish to go. Besides, Cork is a great town for walking. Another bit of advice is to go by the Tourist Office and pick up one of their free city maps. It will save you a lot of grief in getting around Cork.

The River Lee cuts across the city from east to west, and the hills bound it on the north and south. Major points of reference are St. Patrick's Street (called simply Patrick Street) and the Grand Parade. Other main arteries are Washington Street (which becomes Western Road as it runs past University College and heads out toward Killarney); South Mall, from which you turn onto Anglesea Street en route to both Kinsale (and the airport) and Douglas Road; and Glanmire Road, leading out to Fota Park, Cobh, and the main Youghal-Waterford road, with a turn-off to the Dublin road. Just across St. Patrick's Bridge at the foot of Patrick Street, a hill so steep you'll swear your car is going front over back leads to the Montenotte section, where the cream of Cork's merchant crop built great Georgian houses on the hillside overlooking the river.

GETTING AROUND **By Bus** Double-decker buses travel 14 routes crossing the city from north to south. Service is frequent, and most buses can be boarded on Patrick Street. From the Parnell Place bus station, there's local bus service to Blarney and Crosshaven. For detailed route information, call 021/506066.

By Taxi Taxis are stationed at the rank in the center of Patrick Street as well as at bus and railway stations and the airport, or you can telephone 961311 or 502211. They're metered, with a minimum fare of IR£1.80 ($2.88).

On Foot While Cork is a large, spread-out city, it's still a delightful walking town. The trick is to take it by neighborhoods (the city center, Shandon, etc.), using city bus transportation or taxi to get you from one area to the other.

By Car As I said above, my best advice is to leave the car at your accommodation. One-way streets, sometimes quite narrow, can be a real problem. If you *must* drive, however, you should know that a disc parking system operates in the city center every day but Sunday, and you must find a newsagent, shop, or office that sells the discs (they're long, printed slips of paper to be affixed to your window), which cost 20p (32¢) per hour. There are several good parking lots, and two multistory car parks, which are marked on the city map provided by the Tourist Office (where you can also pick up the useful "Parking in Cork" pamphlet).

FAST FACTS: Cork City

Area Code The telephone prefix for Cork is 021.

Automobile Association There's an AA office at 12 Emmet Place (☎ 021/276922).

Car Rentals The head office of Avis Rent-a-Car Johnson & Perrott is on Emmet Place (☎ 273295) (see "Getting Around" in Chapter 3); Great Island Car Rentals, 47 MacCurtain St. (☎ 503536), is a reliable local car-rental firm; and most major car-rental companies have desks at Cork Airport.

Emergencies For police, fire, or an ambulance, dial 999.

Hospitals General medical services are offered at the Cork Regional Hospital, Wilton (☎ 546400), and specialized service at the Cork Eye, Ear, and Throat Hospital, Western Road (☎ 274162).

Police Dial 999.

Post Office The General Post Office is on Oliver Plunkett St. (☎ 272000), open Monday through Saturday from 9am to 5:30pm.

2 Where to Stay

Prices in Cork are often higher during holiday and special-events periods.

CITY CENTER

Jurys Cork Inn

Anderson's Quay, Cork, Co. Cork. ☎ **021/276-444.** Fax 021/276-144. 133 rms, all with bath. TV TEL. IR£39 ($62.40) *per room* (rooms sleep up to two adults and two children). ACC, AE, DC, MC, V. Beside the River Lee, next to bus station.

In the heart of the city, this five-story hotel is only a short walk from Patrick Street. A very good value, its guest rooms are furnished with light woods. The moderately priced restaurant is good, and the pub is lively.

WORTH A SPLURGE

Morrison's Island Hotel

Morrison's Quay, Cork, Co. Cork. ☎ **021/275-858.** Fax 021/275-833. 40 suites, all with bath. TV TEL. IR£375 ($120) single, IR£55 ($88) per person sharing. ACC, AE, MC, V. Just off the South Mall.

Cork's first all-suite hotel overlooks the River Lee. Every room boasts city and/or river views. Furnishings are modern; contemporary paintings are prominent parts of the decor. Each suite consists of living room, dining area, kitchen, one or two bedrooms, and bath. The excellent River Bank restaurant is a favorite with local businessmen. Best of all, it is just steps away from Patrick Street.

WESTERN ROAD AREA (INCLUDING UNIVERSITY AREA)

As its name implies, this area lies west of the city center. University College Cork is located here, and some parts of the area are also called Wilton. There's heavy truck traffic along this road, but those accommodations listed below are either on quiet side streets just off the Western Road or are set back from the street in their own grounds. This area is within walking distance of the city center (a rather long walk), and there's frequent bus service.

Antoine House

Western Rd., Cork, Co. Cork. ☎ **021/273494.** Fax: 021/273-092. 5 rms, all with bath. TV. IR£25 ($40) single, IR£20 ($32) per person sharing. (Rates include breakfast.) ACC, AE, DC, MC, V. Parking available. Bus: 5 or 8.

This is an exceptionally nice accommodation, with well done up guest rooms equipped with tea/coffeemakers, central heating, and private parking. Mrs. Joan Cross is helpful to guests in planning their time in and around Cork city.

Garnish House

1 Aldergrove, Western Rd., Cork, Co. Cork. ☎ **021/275111.** Fax 021/273872. 6 rms, all with bath. TV. IR£18–IR£22 ($28.80–$35.20) per person. (Rates include breakfast.) ACC, AE, DC, MC, V. Private car park. Bus: 8.

Hinse and Conor Luasa have won great praise for their beautiful Georgian home. Elegantly decorated, it's only about a five-minute walk from the city center, and has a private parking area. Hinse has won compliments for her excellent breakfasts.

This is a relaxing accommodation in a homey atmosphere, and fishing, golf, tennis, cricket, and swimming are all nearby.

Killarney House

Western Rd., Cork, Co. Cork. ☎ **021/270179.** 17 rms, all with bath. TEL TV. IR£25–IR£30 ($40–$48) per person sharing. (Rates include breakfast.) AE, MC, V. Parking available. Bus: 5 or 8.

Mrs. Margaret O'Leary, a nurse for many years, now devotes her time and energies to the comfort of her guests. Home cooking is a specialty, and coffee and biscuits appear every evening. She'll also furnish sandwiches upon request, and she can organize Irish language courses. It is centrally heated and has a large car park.

✪ Mrs. Rita O'Herlihy

55 Wilton Gardens, Wilton, Cork, Co. Cork. ☎ **021/541705.** 3 rms, 2 with bath. IR£13.50 ($21.60) per person without bath; IR£14.50 ($23.20) per person with bath. (Rates include breakfast.) No credit cards. Bus: 5 or 8.

Just off the Killarney road, near the university, this modern two-story home has a warm, welcoming air. There is central heating, and good parking is available, as well as a garden for relaxing in nice weather.

Roserie Villa

Mardyke Walk, Cork, Co. Cork. ☎ **021/272958.** Fax 021/274087. 16 rms, all with shower. TEL TV. IR£30 ($48) single; IR£25 ($40) per person sharing. (Rates include breakfast.) AE, DC, MC, V. Bus: 8.

Mrs. Nora Murray is hostess here, and her guest rooms are both attractive and comfortable, with central heating. Rooms have tea/coffeemakers, ironing facilities, and hairdryers, and there's private parking. The villa is only a short stretch of the legs into the city center, and away from Western Road traffic, opposite the university.

St. Kilda

Western Road, Cork, Co. Cork. ☎ **021/273095.** Fax 021/275015. 14 rms, 12 with bath. IR£16–IR£18 ($25.60–$28.80) per person without bath; IR£18–IR£20 ($28.80–$32) per person with bath. ACC, MC, V. TEL TV. Opposite University College Cork. Bus: 8.

This is the three-story old-style home of the Hickey family. Painted a striking blue and set behind a low wall, it has been recently refurbished by hosts Pauline and Pat Hickey. Most of the cozy double, twin, and family bedrooms have a private bath, as well as hairdryers. A guest lounge is complete with hospitality trolley, and many guests appreciate the breakfast menu.

MONTENOTTE (SUMMERHILL, ST. LUKE'S) AREA

The hilly section of Montenotte and Summerhill is located across from the railway station on the northeastern banks of the River Lee. For most locations, turn left up the hill at St. Luke's Church (also called St. Luke's cross, for crossroad).

Gabriel House

Summerhill, Cork, Co. Cork. ☎ **021/500333.** Fax 021/500178. 22 rms, all with bath. TV TEL. IR£13–IR£18 ($20.80–$28.80) per person, depending on season. (Rates include breakfast.) Dinner IR£12 ($19.20). MC. V. Private car park. Bus: 12.

Only a few minutes' walk from the city center, Gabriel House is in a quiet location near the railway station and St. Luke's Church. Mrs. Monica King is the hospitable hostess. There are large gardens, a private parking area, and magnificent views of the harbor. Mrs. King also welcomes pets.

Cork City Accommodations and Dining

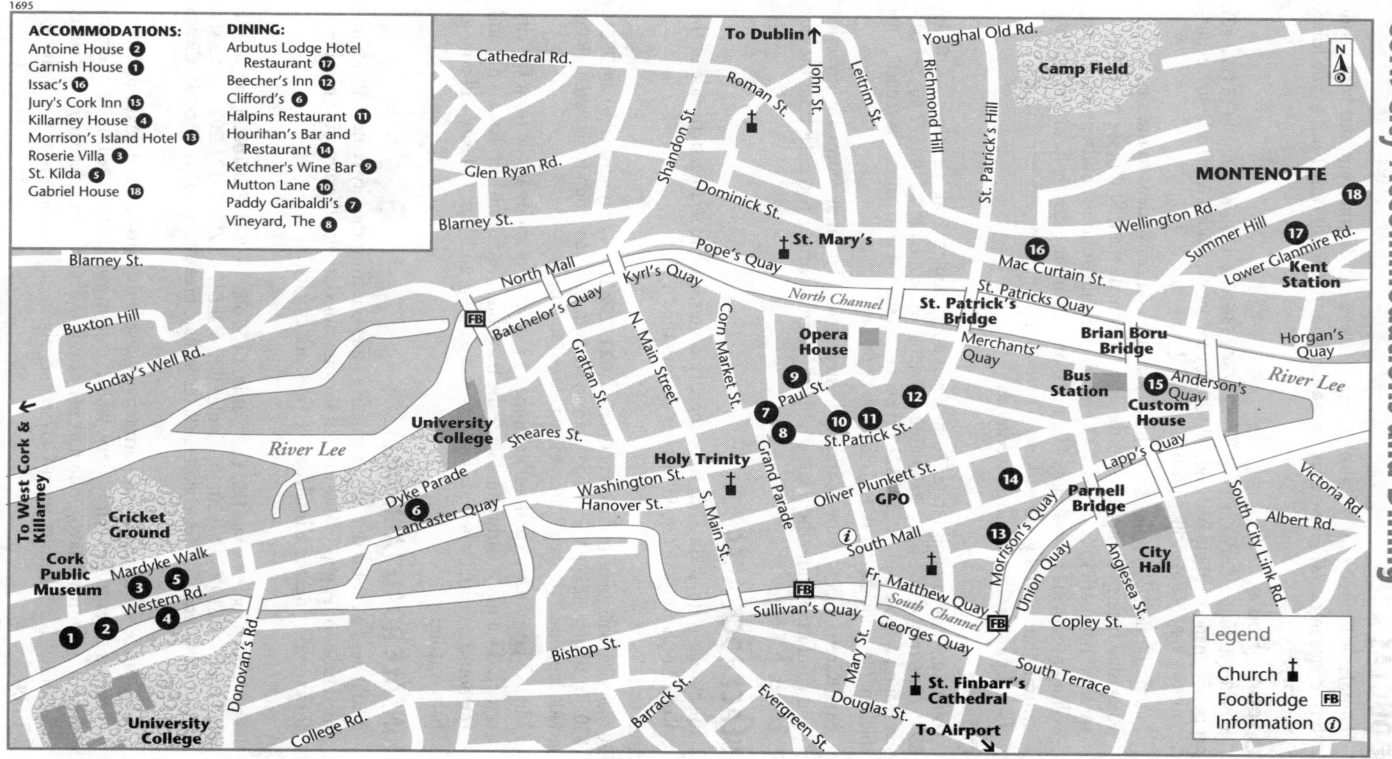

DOUGLAS AREA

Douglas is located southwest of the city center a fair distance out, but with good bus service into town. It's clearly signposted from the South Ring Road as you leave the city.

✪ Fatima House

Grange Rd., Douglas, Cork, Co. Cork. ☎ **021/362536.** 5 rms, 2 with bath. IR£14 ($22.40) per person sharing without bath; IR£16 ($25.60) per person sharing with bath. 40% reduction for children. (Rates include breakfast.) ACC, MC, V. Bus: 6 or 7.

Fatima House, 2½ miles from the city center and convenient to the airport and Ringaskiddy ferry (signposted on the Airport-Kinsale road, R600), is presided over by Mrs. Elizabeth O'Shea. Mrs. O'Shea is especially fond of children and is quite willing to provide baby-sitting. Her bedrooms all are attractively furnished; there's central heating and good parking. There are many good restaurants nearby, and a local pub has live music on weekends.

✪ Sarto

2 Lislee Rd., Mayborough Estate, Rochestown Rd., Douglas, Cork, Co. Cork. ☎ **021/895579.** 6 rms, 4 with bath. IR£19 ($30.40) single without bath; IR£14 ($22.40) per person sharing without bath; IR£17 ($27.20) per person sharing with bath. 10% reduction for children. (Rates include breakfast.) No credit cards. Bus: 7.

Mrs. Gretta Brien is the charming hostess here. Her guest rooms are attractive and comfortable, and the house is centrally heated. Sarto is two miles from the city center.

BLACKROCK AREA

Blackrock is a fair distance from the city center, on the southeastern side of the River Lee, and there's good bus service into the city.

Belrose

50 Maryville, Ballintemple, Cork, Co. Cork. ☎ **021/292219.** 3 rms, none with bath. IR£19 ($30.40) single; IR£14 ($22.40) per person sharing. 10% reduction for children. (Rates include breakfast.) No credit cards. Closed Nov–Mar. Bus: 2.

Mrs. O'Leary has a comfortable home in a quiet area about a mile from the city center. Two guest bathrooms serve the bedrooms, each of which has a sink, and the house is centrally heated. There's good parking, and Mrs. O'Leary will arrange baby-sitting.

KINSALE ROAD (AIRPORT)

You'll need a car for this area, about five miles out from the city center. All accommodations offer good value in rural surroundings close to the airport, a good base for exploring nearby Kinsale, as well as Cork city itself.

✪ Au Soleil

Lisfehill, Cork Airport–Kinsale Rd., Ballinhassig, Co. Cork. ☎ **021/888208.** 3 rms, 2 with bath. IR£15–IR£19 ($24–$30.40) single; IR£16–IR£17 ($25.60–$27.20) per person sharing. 20% reduction for children. (Rates include breakfast.) No credit cards. Closed Oct–May.

This modern bungalow with attractive guest bedrooms is the domain of Helen Deasy, a sister to Noreen Raftery, whose Shalom you'll find listed in the Western Region (County Mayo). She and her family will make you feel right at home. Au Soleil is four miles from Carrigaline, about eight miles from Cork city via R600.

✪ Fuchsia

Adamstown, Five-mile Bridge, Ballinhassig, Co. Cork. ☎ **021/888198.** 4 rms, 3 with bath. IR£18.50–IR£20.50 ($29.60–$32.80) single; IR£13.50–IR£15.50 ($21.60–$24.80) per person sharing. (Rates include breakfast.) No credit cards. Closed Nov–Feb.

Set in a terraced garden, Mrs. Kathleen O'Mahony's home overlooks hedgerows bordering green fields. It's four miles from Carrigaline, and about five miles from Cork city via N71. The house is centrally heated, and there are two twin- and two double-bedded rooms, all with feather comforters and sinks. The lounge, with a bay window affording splendid views, has tourist literature on this area. Both Mr. and Mrs. O'Mahony delight in recommending points of interest. Breakfast is served in a lovely conservatory and features homemade jam and bread, as well as the delicious local sausage. The evening meal is available with advance notice.

BLARNEY

Blarney is some four miles northwest of Cork city and makes an ideal touring base. The Cork-Blarney road (N617) is well signposted from Cork city at the Patrick Street Bridge.

Ashlee Lodge

Tower, Blarney, Co. Cork. ☎ **021/385346.** 5 rms, 4 with bath. IR£15 ($24) per person without bath. IR£16 ($25.60) per person with bath. (Rates include breakfast.) No credit cards. Closed Nov–Mar. Private car park.

Mrs. A. Callaghan runs this outstanding guesthouse. About 2½ miles from the town center on the Blarney-Killarney road (R617), it is beautifully decorated and immaculate, and every possible convenience is thoughtfully anticipated and provided. There's private parking and lovely gardens to enjoy in fine weather.

The Gables

Stoneview, Blarney, Co. Cork. ☎ **021/385330.** 3 rms, 2 with bath. IR£14 ($22.40) per person sharing without bath, IR£16 ($25.60) per person sharing with bath. 50% reduction for children. (Rates include breakfast.) No credit cards. Closed Nov–Feb.

Anne Lynch will make you feel right at home at this lovely period house set in its own grounds 1½ miles from Blarney, which was once given to the parish priest by the owners of Blarney Castle. Guest rooms are attractive as well as comfortable, and home baking is a specialty here. Anne will also help plan touring itineraries.

✪ Glenview House

Tower, Blarney, Co. Cork. ☎ **021/385370.** 3 rms, none with bath. IR£19 ($30.40) single; IR£14 ($22.40) per person sharing. 50% reduction for children. (Rates include breakfast.) High tea IR£8.50 ($13.60) extra. No credit cards. Closed Nov–Apr.

This two-story stone house has been charmingly renovated with due regard to retaining its original character. May and Finbarr O'Brien take a personal interest in all their guests, and Mr. O'Brien (this is his family home) is especially helpful to those tracing their Irish ancestors. Glenview is a short drive from the town center on the Blarney-Killarney road (R617).

Knockawn Wood

Curraleigh, Inniscarra, Blarney, Co. Cork. ☎ **021/870284.** Fax 021/870-284. 4 rms, 3 with bath. IR£13.50 ($21.60) per person sharing without bath; IR£1 ($1.60) per person additional with bath. 50% reduction for children. (Rates include breakfast.) No credit cards.

Mrs. Ita O'Donovan's lovely modern home sits at the top of well-cared-for lawns, with tranquil rural views from all guest rooms. Mrs. O'Donovan's hospitality extends to providing tea and snacks, as well as an evening meal, even without advance notice. The house is centrally heated and the four attractive bedrooms all have electric blankets. Knockawn Wood is 3½ miles from Blarney, signposted on the Blarney-Killarney road (R617).

St. Anthony's

3 Sunset Place, Killeens, Commons Rd., Blarney, Co. Cork. ☎ **021/385151.** 6 rms, 3 with bath. IR£18.50–IR£20 ($29.60–$32) single; IR£13.50–IR£15 ($21.60–$24) per person sharing. 10% reduction for children. (Rates include breakfast.) No credit cards. Closed Dec–Easter.

Mr. Pat O'Flynn is the charming host of this lovely bungalow two miles from Blarney and three miles from Cork. The house is centrally heated, and guest rooms are nicely done up. Mr. O'Flynn truly likes to make his guests feel that this is their "home away from home."

✪ Woodview House

Tweedmount, Blarney, Co. Cork. ☎ **021/385197.** 8 rms, 7 with bath. TV. IR£16 ($25.60) single without bath, IR£20 ($32) single with bath; IR£14 ($22.40) per person sharing without bath, IR£16 ($25.60) per person sharing with bath. 20% reduction for children. (Rates include breakfast.) Dinner IR£13 ($20.80) extra. ACC, MC, V. Closed Christmas.

Catherine and Billy Phelan operate this pretty guesthouse on the outskirts of Blarney on the main Cork-Blarney road (N617), and as one reader wrote, "Both are charming, intelligent, and provide the utmost of excellent company and conversation." Guest rooms are tastefully decorated, there's a bright, sunny lounge overlooking peaceful fields, and the house is centrally heated. A big bonus here is the excellent restaurant run by the Phelans in their attractive dining room (see Section 3, "Where to Eat," below), with the above special reduced dinner price for residents.

A Farmhouse

Birch Hill House

Grenagh, Blarney, Co. Cork ☎ **021/886106.** 6 rms, 1 with bath. IR£19 ($30.40) single; IR£14–IR£16 ($22.40–$25.60) per person sharing. 25% reduction for children. (Rates include breakfast.) High tea IR£8 ($11.60) extra; dinner IR£10 ($16). Closed Nov–April.

Birch Hill House is a longtime favorite with readers. The lovely century-old Victorian home sits on a wooded bluff, part of a 105-acre farm half a mile off N20, four miles from Blarney (signposted from Blarney town center). Mrs. Dawson is the interesting hostess of this plant-filled home. Some of the guest rooms are quite large. All are nicely decorated and comfortably furnished, all with sinks. There are wood fires downstairs, electric heaters in guest rooms.

COBH

Cobh (pronounced "Cove") is just 15 miles southwest of Cork city; by car it's a 20-minute drive to Cork. Regular train service (approximately every half hour) connects Cobh and Cork. (See also "What to See and Do" below in this chapter for sightseeing in Cobh.)

Tearmann

Ballynoe, Cobh, Co. Cork. ☎ **021/813182.** 3 rms, 2 with bath. IR£18 ($28.80) single; IR£13.50–IR£14.50 ($21.60–$23.20) per person sharing. 20% reduction for children. (Rates include breakfast.) No credit cards. Closed Nov–Feb.

Mrs. Bernadette Maddox presides over this lovely 19th-century home just 1.2 miles from the center of Cobh. Guest rooms are nicely appointed, and Mrs. Maddox is happy to share her knowledge of Cobh with her guests.

Watersway

E. Ferry Rd., Great Island, Cobh, Co. Cork. ☎ **021/812-451.** 3 rms, 1 with bath. IR£18 ($28.80) single; IR£13 ($20.80) per person sharing; IR£3 ($4.80) per person extra with bath. (Rates include breakfast.) No credit cards. Closed Mid-Oct to mid-Mar.

Surrounded by a large garden, facing the sea, Watersway is about 3 1/2 miles from Cobh in a beautiful country setting. Mrs. Mary Shorten is the soul of hospitality and happily recommends nearby leisure activities and sightseeing attractions. There's ample private parking.

CORK-YOUGHAL-MIDLETON ROAD

Touring East Cork is a cinch from a base along N25, the main road from Cork to Youghal, with easy access to major sightseeing attractions.

✪ Cedarville

Carrigtwohill, Co. Cork. ☎ **021/883246.** 4 rms, 2 with bath. IR£18.50 ($29.60) single without bath; IR£14 ($22.40) per person sharing without bath; IR£1.50 ($2.40) per person additional with bath. 50% reduction for children. (Rates include breakfast.) No credit cards. Closed Nov–Mar. Private car park.

Breda Hayes, the warm, bubbly hostess here, takes a keen interest in all her guests, and those lovely blooms that welcome you out front are the handiwork of husband Dennis, a high school science teacher who must have been born with a green thumb. The house itself is spotless, and the four bedrooms are nicely decorated in soft pastels, all with sinks, as well as wide windows that look out to colorful flowers in front and green pastures in back of the house. Meals here are superb, reflecting Breda's College of Catering training. Highly recommended. It's nine miles east of Cork city, two miles to Midleton, signposted on N25, with sightseeing attractions like Fota House and Midleton Heritage Centre nearby. Golf nearby.

SOUTHEAST OF THE CITY

On the southern side of Cork Harbour, the coastal villages of Crosshaven and Myrtlesville—about twelve miles from Cork city, eight miles from the airport, and seven miles from Ringaskiddy—make idyllic sightseeing bases. Follow the signs for the ferry port of Ringaskiddy, then the signs on R613 and R612.

✪ Bunnyconnelan

Myrtleville, Co. Cork. ☎ **021/831237.** 12 rms, 2 with bath. IR£19 ($30.40) per person. Dinner IR£28 ($44.80) extra. (Rates include breakfast.) No credit cards.

In the little village of Myrtleville, about 12 miles southwest of Cork city and three miles from Crosshaven (signposted on the Crosshaven road), a quite extraordinary guesthouse perches atop a high cliff overlooking the sea. Built as a holiday home for a British diplomat back in 1830, it was not given its unusual name until a Scotsman bought it soon after World War II and christened it after his four daughters—Bunny, Connie, Nellie, and Ann. Now it's in the capable hands of Pat and Sheila O'Brien. The view is spectacular, with the Roches Point lighthouse blinking in the distance and award-winning gardens sloping down the cliffside. The ground-floor bar/lounge features stone fireplaces, a beamed ceiling, and the most eclectic collection of decorations you can imagine: bagpipes, barometers, a brass hunting horn, and tartan drapes. Outside, umbrella tables dot a flag-paved patio. On weekend nights this place is mobbed with people from Cork, often bringing their own music with them. The dining room is moderately priced and excellent (see Section 3, "Where to Eat," below). Pub grub is available in the bar during the day. Upstairs, there are a dozen simply furnished rooms, most with that smashing view. Advance reservations are absolutely essential in summer months.

NORTHWEST OF THE CITY

The listing below is close to Cork city, yet in a scenic rural location. Take the Cork-Mallow road (N20) to the turnoff for the village.

Evergreen House

Rathpeacon, Co. Cork. ☎ **021/305715.** 6 rms, all with bath. IR£15 ($21.75) per person. (Rates include breakfast.) No credit cards. Closed Dec.

Noreen Curran is the very hospitable proprietor of this pleasant rural home two miles from Cork (take the Mallow road [N20] and look for the signpost for the village) near the Country Squire Restaurant on the right-hand side of the road. Guest rooms are nicely appointed, with bucolic views from each window, and Mrs. Curran greets guests with complimentary tea and scones. Out front, there is a fountain, a pond, and a small waterfall beside the patio. There are two excellent restaurants within walking distance, making a trip to town for a meal unnecessary.

A BUDGET MOTEL FOR FAMILIES

✪ Forte Travelodge

Kinsale Rd. Roundabout, Blackash, Cork, Co. Cork. ☎ **021/310722.** Fax 021/310707. 40 rms, all with bath. IR£33.50 ($53.60) per room (sleeps three adults or two adults, one child, and an infant). AE, MC, V.

This motel-type lodging between Cork city and the airport is ideal for families with an eye to the budget. Rooms are quite spacious, with a double bed, single sofa bed, and a child's bed and/or baby cot if requested. Each has its own central heating controls, as well as TV, radio/clock, and tea- and coffeemaking facilities. The adjacent Little Chef restaurant specializes in snacks, drinks, and a wide variety of moderately priced meals. Both the accommodations and the restaurant have facilities for the handicapped.

HOSTELS & DORMS

Note: In addition to the listings below, self-catering apartments are offered by University College Cork from June to mid-September. For details, telephone 021/276-871.

Cork International Youth Hostel

1/2 Redclyffe, Western Rd., Cork, Co. Cork. ☎ **021/543289.** 124 beds. IR£5.50 ($8.80) per person over 18. IR£4.50 ($7.20) per person under 18. Breakfast IR£1.50–IR£3.50 ($2.40–$5.60) extra; dinner IR£5 ($8). MC, V. Bus: 8.

These hostel facilities are rated "superior," and with good reason. In addition to the excellent sleeping accommodations and showers, there's a TV room, a bureau de change, a hostel shop, and bicycle rental. Also, unlike many hostels, both breakfast and the evening meal are served at low rates. They also run a hostel bus to the ferry port at Ringaskiddy. Although run by An Oige, prior membership in the International Youth Hostel Association is not required here. Advance booking during summer months is absolutely essential.

Issac's

48 MacCurtain St., Cork, Co. Cork. ☎ **021/500011.** Fax 021/506355. 220 beds. 14-bed dormitory (excluding breakfast) IR£7.50 ($12) per person. Including breakfast: four- to six-bed dorm IR£7.50 ($10.90) per person; double room IR£15 ($24) per person; single room IR£20

($32); family suite with private bath IR£44 ($70.40) for two adults and two children. ACC, MC, V.

Only a two-minute walk from the city center and/or the railway station, this large Victorian red-brick building has been rescued from dereliction and transformed into one of Cork's most attractive hostels. White walls, colorful curtains, and pine floors create a light and airy setting. Meals served here, too.

✪ Kinlay House

Bob and Joan Walk, Shandon, Cork, Co. Cork. ☎ **021/508966.** Fax 021/506927. 118 beds. Four-bed dorm IR£7 ($11.20) per person; two-bed unit IR£10.50 ($16.80) per person; single room IR£15 ($24) per person. (Rates include breakfast.) No credit cards.

Operated by the Irish Student Travel Service (USIT), Kinlay House is a renovated town house located in the old city neighborhood of Shandon, just behind St. Ann's Church with its famous Shandon Bells and very near the Shandon Craft Centre. All units are nicely appointed, and there are self-catering kitchens, a TV/video lounge, a launderette, and security lockers, as well as left-luggage facilities.

Worth a Splurge

✪ Fitzpatrick Silver Springs Hotel

Lower Glanmire Rd. (N25), Tivoli, Cork, Co. Cork. ☎ **021/507533,** 212/355-0100 in New York, 800/367-7701 in the U.S., 800/268-9051 in Canada. Fax 021/507641. 110 rms and suites, all with bath. TV TEL. IR£75–IR£89 ($120–$142.40) single; IR£92–IR£124 ($147.20–$198.40) double, depending on season. Special weekend and summer break rates. ACC, AE, DC, MC, V.

This tall white hotel overlooks the River Lee in a beautiful setting of some 40 acres of wooded and landscaped grounds, and has long been a Cork city landmark. Since coming under the ownership of the Fitzpatrick family (see Fitzpatrick's Castle in Killiney, County Dublin, and the Bunratty Shamrock, in Bunratty, Shannonside), it is fast taking its place as one of the city's leading hostelries.

Under a massive renovation program the 110 bedrooms have been decorated in cool pastels, with two double beds or one double and one twin bed in each. Most have lovely views of the Lee, the city, or the shady grounds from large picture windows. There are also elegant one- and two-bedroom suites.

Readers Recommend

Victoria Lodge, Victoria Cross, Cork, Co. Cork. ☎ 021/542233. Fax 021/542572. *"We were lucky to find this marvelous B&B in a former monastery. Set in its own grounds on the outskirts of Cork city, it has been renovated with 22 executive-style bedrooms, each with its own bath, orthopedic beds, telephone, TV, and tea maker. It's a lovely, unique atmosphere. There's good parking in the grounds. We could walk to the nearby Crow's Nest Pub, a good place for a pint or a light meal, which they serve all day."*

—J. O'Reardon, Long Island City, NY

Garrycloyne Lodge, Garrycloyne, Blarney, Co. Cork. ☎ 021/886-214. *"This is a working farm, complete with cows, dogs—the works. We were welcomed with hot tea and homemade scones, served in front of the dining-room fire. Our room included such extras as a fireplace, large armoire, vanity, numerous pillows and blankets, and an excellent view. An ideal place to call "home" while traveling in the south of Ireland."*

—M. McCloud, Oxford, OH

Superb meals are served in the attractive Truffles Restaurant, and there's a more informal Waterfront Grill Room for less expensive dining. You can order afternoon tea in the spacious lobby lounge, something stronger from the Lobby Bar or the cozy downstairs Thady Quill's Bar, both of which are favorite gathering places for Cork businesspeople as well as guests. After dark, repair to Thady Quills downstairs nightclub. On a Sunday afternoon go along for their jazz brunch.

In the leisure complex, there's an Olympic-size heated pool, sauna, steam room, Jacuzzi, sunbeds, snooker, indoor/outdoor tennis courts, a squash court, and a gymnasium. There's a nine-hole golf course right on the grounds.

The Silver Springs is an ideal touring base, since the attractions of Cork city are just minutes away, and Fota House only a short drive, as are Blarney, Kinsale, Cobh, and other County Cork sightseeing highlights.

3 Where to Eat

✪ Beecher's Inn

Faulkner's Lane. ☎ **021/273144.** Pub grub IR£1.50–IR£5 ($2.40–$8); hot and cold plates IR£2–IR£5 ($3.20–$8). No credit cards. Mon–Sat 12:30–2:30pm. SEAFOOD/PUB GRUB.

Pat O'Donovan is the general proprietor, Ita Magee the manager, of Beecher's, which wears the soft patina of time. Cork regulars gather at lunchtime for hot plates and cold salads. Seafood is a specialty, and a lunch of smoked salmon and brown bread washed down with a rich, dark pint is memorable. Coffee and scones are served all day. It's tucked away on a narrow old lane (enter from Emmet Place or Patrick Street).

✪ Halpins Restaurant

14/15 Cook St. ☎ **021/277853.** Main courses IR£6–IR£12 ($9.60–$19.20); breakfast IR£4 ($6.40). Tourist Menu available. ACC, MC, V. Daily 9am–midnight. TRADITIONAL/VEGETARIAN.

David Halpin has used traditional materials of wood, slate, and stone to reconstruct this 300-year-old wax works into a very good eatery, with an extensive menu and moderate prices. There are, for example, some 36 main courses, which range from chicken Kiev to 10 kinds of steak, with a wide variety in between. They also serve burgers, pizzas, pasta, and other light selections—a very good, inexpensive meal can be put together from the appetizer list alone. It's also a good place for breakfast if that meal doesn't come with your room. This is a great favorite with locals, who find it good value. It's on a small street between Patrick Street and South Mall.

✪ Paddy Garibaldi's

Carey's Lane. ☎ **021/277915.** Pizza IR£3.50–IR£6 ($5.60–$9.60); grills IR£5–IR£6 ($8–$9.60); pasta IR£6 ($9.60). ACC, AE, V. Daily 10am–midnight. PIZZA/TRADITIONAL.

This light, airy eatery has upstairs and downstairs dining rooms, and one of the friendliest staffs around. Pizzas are large (7 in.) and come with either french fries or a green salad; burgers are charcoal-grilled and served on toasted sesame-seed buns, with an accompanying salad, coleslaw, and french fries. Assorted salad platters are also available, and the garlic bread, Peggy Garibaldi's homemade apple pie, and Nora Garibaldi's homemade cheesecake are outstanding. The restaurant is on the pedestrian lane connecting Paul Street Shopping Centre with Patrick Street. Another Paddy Garibaldi's is on High Street out in the Wilton section (☎ **021/345-255**).

✪ Hourihan's Bar and Restaurant

Phoenix St. ☎ **021/273017.** Prices under IR£5 ($8). No credit cards. Mon–Fri 12:15–2:30pm. BAR FOOD.

Tucked away on a small street near the General Post Office, Hourihan's is a popular spot with locals. It's an old warehouse that has been transformed into a large bustling pub with traditional decor—lots of cozy seating nooks. You can step up to the long food counter, with hot plates, salads, sweets, and all kinds of snacks. A word of advice: try to get there early or around 2pm to avoid the crowd.

✪ Ketchner's Wine Bar

9 Paul St. ☎ **021/272868.** Main courses IR£5–IR£12 ($8–$19.20); pasta IR£4–IR£5 ($6.40–$8); set meal IR£7.50 ($12). AE, MC, V. Mon–Sat 10am–midnight, Sun 5pm–midnight. MEDITERRANEAN/GRILLS/VEGETARIAN/SALADS/PASTA.

I must confess to a special fondness for this attractive eatery, with its exposed brick walls, lace curtains, and traditional decor. Everything is based on the freshest of ingredients—my personal favorites include the seafood pancake in a cheese-and-mustard sauce and the chicken Kiev, highly flavored with garlic. Service is friendly and efficient, and there's a good wine list.

The Vineyard

Market Lane. ☎ **021/274793.** IR£2–IR£6 ($3.20–$9.60). No credit cards. Mon–Sat 12:30–2:30pm. PUB GRUB.

For the full atmosphere of this great old pub, see Section 8, "Cork After Dark," below. As for the food, they serve everything from soup and sandwiches to cold salad plates to hot dishes. It's on a tiny lane off Patrick Street leading to the English Market.

✪ The Wilton Pub & Restaurant

Wilton Shopping Centre. ☎ **021/344454,** 344456, or 344457. Bar food under IR£5 ($8); burgers, sandwiches, and salad plates IR£3–IR£5 ($4.80–$8); main courses IR£7–IR£12 ($11.20–$19.20). MC, V. Daily 12:30–10pm (bar open regular pub hours). BAR FOOD/IRISH/TRADITIONAL.

No need to drive into town for a meal if you're staying in the Wilton area—this large pub, with its traditional decor, offers an extensive menu that can meet just about any need, be it for a snack, a light lunch, or an excellent full hot meal. Portions are more than ample, and there's a friendly, convivial air about the place.

WORTH A SPLURGE/GOURMET DINING

✪ Arbutus Lodge Hotel Restaurant

Montenotte. ☎ **021/501237.** Main courses IR£14–IR£16 ($22.40–$25.60); fixed-price lunch IR£14.50 ($23.20). ACC, AE, DC, MC, V. Daily 1–2pm and 7–9:30pm. SEAFOOD/TRADITIONAL/IRISH/FRENCH.

Picnic Fare & Where to Eat It

If you fancy a picnic on a nice sunny day, there are any number of take-away and fish-and-chips shops along North Main Street, and stalls in the English Market sell sausage rolls, boiled eggs, and other picnic makings.

With your picnic fare in hand, head for Bishop Lucey Park (that's the city park between Grand Parade and South Main Street) or Fitzgeralds Park off the Mardyke. Then relax and enjoy!

Readers Recommend

The Barn Restaurant, Lotamore, Glanmire, Co. Cork. ☎ 021/866211. *"Locals told us The Barn was the best restaurant in Cork, and after a delightful meal there we went back on our last night in the city. It's in a cottage that has been extended to provide a very attractive and comfortable dining room, and it's only a short drive from the city center in a lovely country setting."*—Jane and Bob Green, Raleigh, NC

Blairs Inn, Cloghroe, Blarney, Co. Cork. ☎ 021/381470. *"We found this traditional pub in a picturesque setting by the river when we suddenly realized late in the afternoon that we had been so engrossed in our travels that we'd missed lunch. It was our good luck that Blairs Inn serves bar food right up to 8:30pm, and the long menu had so many enticing dishes that we found it hard to make a decision. We settled on Irish stew, which was the best we had on our entire trip, and we were served in a delightful outdoor beer garden. There's music at night, and we were really sorry that we had to move on."* —Denise and John Grant, New York, NY

This gourmet restaurant, over on lofty heights of Montenotte (on the eastern edge of town, uphill from the railway station, near St. Luke's Church), is known all over Ireland and the Continent for its legendary cuisine and exquisite service. The hotel was once an elegant Victorian town house, and the decor is that of subdued (not stuffy) formality. Large windows overlook the city below. Seafood, meats, and vegetables are the freshest—if your main course includes mushrooms, you may be sure they've been hand-gathered from the woods. If the restaurant prices are a bit steep for your budget, the Gallery Bar at the Arbutus serves smoked salmon and delicious soups for prices that average about IR£12 ($19.20). Best to reserve (a few days ahead for dinner) at both the Restaurant and Gallery Bar.

Clifford's

18 Dyke Parade, Cork. ☎ **021/275-333.** Reservations strongly recommended. Average lunch IR£12.50 ($20); average dinner IR£28 ($44.80); special vegetarian meal IR£19 ($30.40). ACC, DC, MC, V. Tues–Fri 12:30–2:30pm, Mon–Sat 7–10:30pm. Closed Christmas and holidays. INTERNATIONAL/IRISH.

The elegant town house, which was Cork's civic library for many years, has been transformed into one of the city's most prestigious restaurants. Chef Michael Clifford takes great pride in such creations as pan-fried sirloin of beef with herbs and assorted peppercorns in a rich Fleurie sauce. *Note:* Just beside the restaurant, **Michael's Bistro** (Tues–Fri 12–3pm, Mon–Sat 6–10:30pm) features a moderately priced blackboard as well as an à la carte menu.

✪ Phelan's Woodview House

Tweedmount, Blarney. ☎ **021/385197.** Reservations recommended. Fixed-price dinner IR£21.50 ($34.40) for nonresidents, IR£13 ($20.80) for residents. ACC, MC, V. Tues–Sat 7:30–10. Closed Christmas week. FRENCH/SEAFOOD/TRADITIONAL.

Billy and Catherine Phelan have won high praise from Cork's food critics for their restaurant in this pretty guesthouse on the outskirts of Blarney half a mile from the town center on the main Cork-Blarney road (N617) (see Section 2, "Where to Stay," above), and the consensus is that the short drive out to Blarney is well taken in order to enjoy one of chef Billy's specialties. Billy, who is Swiss-trained, turns out such delicacies as medallions of pork Normandy, Irish salmon in chive sauce, baked plaice with stuffed crab, an excellent rack of lamb, and a roast free-range duck in a honey and herb sauce.

4 What to See & Do

ATTRACTIONS IN TOWN

THE COAL QUAY, MUSEUMS, AND NEARBY ART GALLERIES

I can't really say that the **Coal Quay** (pronounced "kay" in this instance) qualifies as a sightseeing attraction, but I do know that it's a place unique to Cork and one I drop by on every visit. You won't find it listed anywhere under that name—the signs say Corn Market Street—but no one in town will know what you're asking for unless you say "Coal Kay." It's located in the heart of the city, to the right (opposite the Grand Parade which curves off to the left) at the end of Patrick Street, and it's as grand a collection of hardy Irish countrywomen as you're likely to run across. From stalls, tables, carts, or cardboard boxes on the sidewalk, these shrewd, witty ladies hawk secondhand clothes, fresh vegetables, old shoes, old pieces of china, and anything else they happen to have handy and can exchange for a "lop" or two ("lop" being, of course, a coin). It is slated for a major "urban renewal" in 1996, and I can only hope its essential character remains intact. As it now is, I won't guarantee that you'll catch every nuance of conversation carried on in a language that's peculiar to this bunch, but I will guarantee that you'll catch a glimpse of genuine Irish folk life.

Speaking of markets, do follow signposts on Patrick Street, Grand Parade, Oliver Plunkett Street, and/or Princes Street to wander through the **Old English Market,** sometimes called the **City Market.** A leftover from colonial days, the cavernous market is housed in a 1782 building, but it carries on a Cork tradition that goes back to the 1600s. The wall-to-wall foodstuff stalls peddle everything from meats to vegetables to pastries to just about anything else that shows up on Cork tables. The hubbub of housewives doing their daily shopping and the display of many uniquely Cork foods (crubeens and drisheen, for example—if you can't spot them, ask and initiate a lively discussion) draw me to at least one meander through the market whenever I'm in Cork. It's open Monday through Saturday from 9am to 6pm.

Combine a stroll in **Fitzgerald Park** (see "Parks," below) with a stop in **The Cork Museum** (☎ 021/270-679). Artifacts from the city's medieval days are a main attraction; some exhibits focus on Cork's legendary rebels whose lives were devoted to Irish freedom, such as Terence McSwiney, Michael Collins, and Thomas MacCurtain. Hours are Monday through Friday from 11am to 1pm and 2:15 to 5pm, Sunday from 3 to 5pm. A small admission fee is charged on Sunday.

Out in Sunday's Well, a little west of the city center, the historic old **Cork City Gaol** (☎ 021/542-478) housed many a patriotic rebel in its day, and life-size figures bring to grim life their prison existence. Haunting. A small admission fee is charged; open March through October daily from 9:30am to 8pm; November through February, Saturday and Sunday from 10am to 4pm.

Not far from the Coal Quay, the red-brick ✪ **Crawford Art Gallery,** on Emmet Place (☎ 021/273377), was built as the Custom House back in 1724 when ships unloaded at what is now the sidewalk on the King's Dock. There's something almost homey about the big, rambling halls and exhibition rooms, and I've never been inside without encountering at least one art student diligently studying the masters. There are paintings and sculptures by modern Irish artists and an interesting collection of classical casts from the Vatican Galleries presented to Cork in 1818. There's also an excellent restaurant, run by the prestigious

Ballymaloe House, with moderately priced breakfasts, snacks, and lunches daily from 9am to 5pm.

On nearby Lavitt's Quay, the Cork Arts Society operates the **Lavitt's Quay Gallery,** with continual exhibitions of fine art, paintings, sculpture, ceramics, and batiks Tuesday through Saturday (closed for lunch from 2 to 3pm).

Churches and City Hall

On Church Street, just off Shandon Street, ✪ **St. Ann's Church** (usually referred to simply as Shandon) is perhaps the most beloved of the city's many churches. Shandon takes its name from the Irish *sean dun,* meaning "old fort." The Protestant church is distinguished architecturally only by its red-and-white "pepper-pot" steeple which houses the bells. Its 170-foot height is crowned by an 11-foot-3-inch weathervane in the shape of a salmon (the symbol of wisdom), and the clocks set in its four sides are known affectionately as the "four-faced liar," since no two of them ever show the same time. Climb the steeple's winding stairs to see the famous bells, and for a small charge you can follow numbers on the bell strings that will send "The Bells of St. Mary's" pealing out over the city. Father Prout, incidentally, lies below in the small churchyard.

There are other interesting headstones in the churchyard cemetery, as well as a mass grave from famine times, and the narrow, winding surrounding streets hold some of Cork's oldest inhabited dwellings, most of which have seen decidedly better days. Also nearby is the old Butter Exchange, which flourished as a major source of salted butter for Britain, Europe, and the West Indies from 1770 until 1924. Today, it flourishes as the home of the **Shandon Craft Centre** (free admission), where you can visit craft workshops and enjoy a sit-down and refreshments at the coffee shop.

Across the River Lee from Shandon, Cork's birthplace is three blocks past the South Main Street Bridge, where **St. Finn Barre's Cathedral,** on Bishop's Street, marks the spot on which the venerable saint founded his monastery in 650. As it grew in stature as a seat of learning, it became a mark of honor among Gaelic chieftains and Norman knights to be buried in its grounds. At the time of the Reformation, St. Finn Barre's became the seat of the bishopric of the Church of Ireland, as it is today. The French Gothic structure you see today was opened in 1870, and its great West Window is of particular note.

Across the west arm of the River Lee, the magnificent **City Hall** on Albert Quay opened in 1936 to replace the one burned in 1920 during the War of Independence. This is where President Kennedy came to address an admiring throng during his visit in the 1960s, and it is the setting for special events during some of Cork's festivals (see below).

Monuments

The impressive **statue** you see at the junction of Grand Parade and South Mall commemorates Irish rebels in the 1798 and 1867 risings. Depicted are the Main of Erin, surrounded by patriots Thomas Davis, Michael O'Dwyer, O'Neill-Crowley, and Wolfe Tone, who represent the four provinces of Ireland. Alongside the river, there's a **War Memorial** to Irishmen who lost their lives in the two world wars, and the uncarved granite stone nearby is the **Hiroshima Memorial.**

At the foot of Patrick Bridge, right in the center of Patrick Street, the **Father Matthew statue** depicts the much-loved Corkman who lived from 1790 to 1861,

Touring Cork City

City Walking Tours. One of Cork's chief charms is that it is so much a walking city, which is, of course, the best possible way to get around any city if you are to capture its true flavor and mingle with the people who give it life. My first recommendation is to go by the Tourist Office and pick up their ✪ **Tourist Trail** guide to a signposted walking tour of Cork. It details a comprehensive route (in two 1¼-hour parts) around the significant landmarks and tells you about each one. One route focuses on the city center (built up from 1750 on), the other on the old medieval city from south to north. It makes for a lovely day's ramble, with a stop whenever your fancy dictates for a jar, lunch, or whatever.

Organized Tours. There are also free evening **guided walking tours** departing from the Tourist Office two or three days a week during July and August. Inquire when you're there to see if they're on.

For more personalized guided tours, contact Valerie Fleury, **Discover Cork,** Belmount, Douglas Road, Cork, County Cork (☎ 021/293873; fax 021/291175). She can, upon request, put together half- and full-day tours in and around Cork for groups of 10 or more. All are personalized and tailored to individual requirements. Some of the more interesting that go outside the city are those to Blarney, Cobh/Fota Park, Kinsale, West Cork, and Killarney.

A sister company to Discover Cork, **Arrangements Unlimited** (same address and telephone number), can arrange entertainment, sporting and leisure activities, and dining.

City Bus Tour. There's a marvelous open-top ✪ **Tourist Bus tour** every Tuesday, Wednesday, and Thursday at 11am, 3pm, and 7pm from late June through August, with a fare of IR£5 ($8) per person, IR£10 ($16) for a family ticket. Book through the Tourist Office.

Cork Harbour Tours. During the summer months, there are regular four-hour harbor cruises down the Lee. Hourly schedules vary, and they don't always run the same days every week, so check with the Tourist Office.

Also in summer, Cork Harbour Cruises operates a daily harbor tour from Kennedy Pier in Cobh, taking in harbor forts, Spike Island, the Naval Base, and other harbor highlights. Check with the Tourist Office for departure times and fares. There are also harbor cruises departing from Cork City docks—check with the Tourist Office for details.

who became known as the "apostle of temperance" because of his lifelong war against Irish alcoholism.

PARKS

The **Bishop Lucey Park,** across Grand Parade from the City Market, is named after a beloved bishop of Cork, and is also known as ✪ **City Park.** The archway at its entrance came from the 1850 Cornmarket. During excavation of the site, a section of the medieval city walls was unearthed and preserved in the park. Remains of medieval timber houses were also found. That sculptured fountain and its eight bronze swans represent the 800th anniversary of Cork's first charter, granted in 1185.

Running parallel to the Western Road is **The Mardyke,** a mile-long, tree-shaded walk—named after an Amsterdam walk called the Meer Dyke—bordered by **Fitzgerald Park,** where you'll find lovely landscaping, interesting sculptures, and a small museum.

TWO CORKMEN OF NOTE

One last Cork sight that is sure to bring a smile to your lips is located in front of the Cork County Council offices on the "Straight Road" (just ask anybody where it is), otherwise known as Carrigohane Road. Right in front of what is fondly called "the tallest building in Ireland" (it beats the height of Liberty Hall in Dublin by all of six inches!) stand two figures who could only be ✪ **Corkmen.** Heads upraised, hands in pockets, they gaze quizzically at this upstart of a building, trying to make sense of it. Ironically, these two, the work of the late Oisin Kelly, began life in Dublin, Cork's archrival. It was only when that city treated them shabbily (they were found lying in a Dublin scrap yard and rescued by the County Council) that they came "home" to the city by the Lee. The people of Cork have affectionately dubbed them "Chah and Mial" after two beloved radio and television characters from the city, and any mention of the sculpture brings a smile to the lips of the locals. If you're driving by, slow down for a tip of the hat to these two embodiments of the Cork spirit. Stop to snap a photo, surely one of your most unusual souvenirs of this spirited city.

ATTRACTIONS NEARBY

Blarney, four miles northwest of Cork city, has long been a favorite destination of American visitors, and to the southeast, Fota Wildlife Park is fast gaining like favor. Either of these locations makes a good base if you prefer a quiet, rural setting that is close enough to explore the city without a city base (see Section 2, "Where to Stay," above).

BLARNEY

The Cork-Blarney road (N617) is well signposted from Cork city at Patrick Street Bridge, and there's regular bus service to Blarney from Cork, departing the bus station on Parnell Place.

✪ Blarney Castle

Blarney. ☎ 021/385252 Admission IR£3 ($4.80) adults, IR£2 ($3.20) students and seniors, IR£1 ($1.60) children. Combination ticket with Blarney House IR£4.50 ($7.20), IR£3 ($4.80), and IR£2 ($3.20). Open May, Mon–Sat 9am–7pm; June–July, Mon–Sat 9am–8:30pm; Aug, Mon–Sat 9am–7:30pm; Sept, Mon–Sat 9–6:30pm, Sun 9:30pm–sundown. Closed Christmas Eve, Christmas Day. Bus: 154 from the bus station on Parnell Place.

Now, about that magical stone. Back in the 1830s, Father Prout wrote of Blarney Castle: "There is a stone there/That whoever kisses/Oh! he never misses/To grow eloquent." All that blather about the stone started, it is said, when the first Queen Elizabeth tried to elicit the fealty of one Cormac MacCarthy, an Irish chieftain who was then Lord of Blarney. The silver-tongued MacCarthy smiled and flattered and nodded his head, all the while keeping firm hold on his own sovereignty until the queen, in exasperation, is reputed to have exclaimed, "This is nothing but Blarney—what he says, he never means!" Which may be the first recorded instance of that lovely Irish talent for concealing a wily mind behind inoffensive words.

Be that as it may, if you'd like to acquire a bit of Irish eloquence, be warned that kissing the stone involves climbing 120 steep steps, having a guard hold your feet

Cork City Attractions

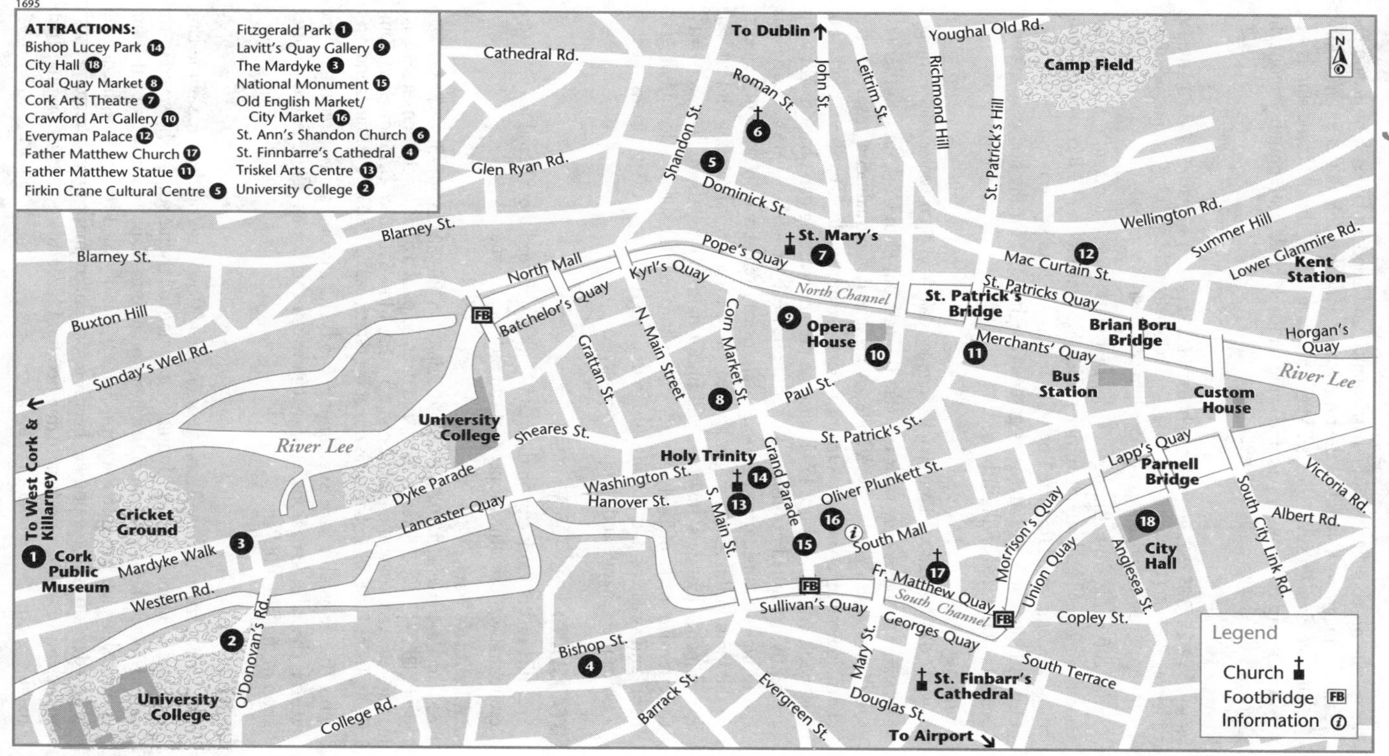

as you lie on your back on the battlements, and bending far back until you can reach the magic rock—and by the time you've gone through all those contortions, you'll have *earned* a silver tongue! Magic aside, however, the old castle ruin is well worth the trip in its own right, and there's a lovely sense of tranquillity about the grounds filled with ancient trees.

Blarney House

Blarney. ☎ **021/385252.** Admission to house IR£2.50 ($3.65) adults, IR£2 ($3.20) students and seniors, IR£1.50 ($2.40) children. House open June to mid-Sept, Mon–Sat noon–5:30pm. Gardens open year-round, daily noon–5:30pm (sundown in winter).

Some 200 yards from Blarney Castle, Blarney House is a magnificent turreted Scottish baronial building, with fine gardens designed in the 18th century. Within those gardens, you'll find the Rock Close, a spot legend says was much favored by Druids long before the advent of garden designers. As for the house, it has been beautifully restored and refurbished.

✪ Blarney Woollen Mills

Blarney. ☎ **021/385280.** Admission free. Summer, daily 9am–8pm; winter, daily 9am-6pm.

Dedicated shoppers may want to make the trek out from Cork for no other reason than to visit the Blarney Woollen Mills, but it also qualifies as a sort of Irish crafts sightseeing attraction. One of Ireland's oldest mills, it has been producing fine wools and cloths since 1741, and the present building dates back to 1824. In a recently renovated extension, a hand loom weaves tweeds. There's a marvelous traditional pub inside, and a moderately priced self-service restaurant adjacent to the main building, making it an ideal place for a bit of browsing and a bit of refreshment. Shoppers, however, will find it hard to draw themselves away from the extensive stocks of lovely Blarney Castle knitwear, the superb selection of Aran hand-knit sweaters, and literally hundreds of high-quality Irish gift items. There's a Bureau de Change and shipping service.

FOTA ISLAND

Six miles east of Cork city on the main Cork-Cobh road, Fota Island is a 790-acre estate that was once the property of the earls of Barrymore.

Fota Wildlife Park

Fota Island, Carrigtwohill ☎ **021/812-736.** Admission IR£3.50 ($5.60) adults; IR£3 ($4.80) students; IR£2 ($3.20) children, seniors, and disabled persons; free for children under 3. No dogs are allowed inside the park. Open Apr–Oct, Mon–Sat 10am–5:15pm, Sun 11am–5:15pm. Train: The Cork-Cobh train stops at the estate; call 021/503399 for times and fares.

This 70-acre wildlife park is set among woods and lagoons, a fitting setting for the zebras, cheetahs, kangaroos, etc., that now call this home. There is also a coffee shop in the Wildlife Park.

COBH

Once a tiny fishing village, Cobh (pronounce it "Cove") sits on the banks of the largest natural harbor in Europe. It quickly grew into a bustling seaport, however, in the early 1800s, when fleets assembled here to sail into Napoleonic Wars battles and convict ships left for Australia with their cargoes of exiled Irish. Once discovered, it also developed into a popular health resort, and to mark Queen Victoria's visit to Ireland in 1849, its official name became Queenstown, and its original Irish name was not restored until 1920.

It's an attractive town, with town houses rising above the waterfront on the terraced hillside that is crowned by the graceful spire of **St. Colman's Cathedral.** Begun in 1868, the Gothic Revival cathedral was not completed until 1916, and the melodious tones of its 47-bell carillon concerts are much loved by the townspeople. The interior is memorable for the main doorway and the rose window above it, polished marble columns, mosaic flooring, richly colored windows, and beautiful detail of marble reredos. Cobh's **Old Church Cemetery** is the last resting place for hundreds who died in 1915 when the *Lusitania* was sunk by a German submarine.

For visiting Americans, however, it is the tug of ancestral emigration that has the most appeal, since this was the port of embarkation for thousands of Irish families fleeing the destitution of the famine years. Sadly, many of those leaving for America never reached its shores because of the incredibly appalling conditions on over-crowded and ill-equipped "coffin ships" profiteering from Irish misery. The story is told in heartrending detail in **"The Queenstown Story,"** a dramatic multimedia exhibition in the Victorian Railway Station that now serves as Cobh's **Visitors Centre (☎ 021/811391)**. Spare a moment for the statue of 14-year-old Annie Moore, who sailed from Cobh in 1891 and became the first immigrant to land at the newly built Ellis Island station.

Only 15 miles from Cork, Cobh is an ideal base for day trips to the city and East Cork (see Chapter 12).

5 Special Events

If you doubt that Cork is a party-loving town, just take a look at the festivals they put on every year. A festival in Cork, I might add, is a truly gala affair, with the entire city involved in the activities, and if you hit town in the middle of one, you're in for a treat. As this is written, firm dates are not available for 1996, but the tourist board should be able to furnish them before you leave home.

My favorite of Cork's special events is the ✪ **Jazz International Festival,** usually in October. This is a truly international event, as some of the world's most outstanding musicians show up for concerts held all around town, as well as impromptu jam sessions that break out in pubs, B&B drawing rooms, and wherever two jazz devotees happen to meet. It's a joyous, free-spirited time.

In April or May, the **Cork International Choral and Folk Dance Festival** attracts top-ranked performers from America, Great Britain, and the Continent. In 1990, a **Summer Festival** was inaugurated in late July and has become an annual event. Come September, it's the **Cork Folk Festival.**

The **Cork Film Festival** enjoyed a worldwide reputation for years as a showcase for independent filmmakers and was the gala of galas in Cork. It was canceled for a year or two, but since 1986 it has been revived each year in late September or early October. Very good news for those of us who have always looked forward to the festival as a time of great gaiety in the city. Check with the Tourist Office to see if it stays alive—if so, it's well worth a day or two to join in the festivities.

As if all those festivals weren't enough, Cork also goes all out for the **Boat Show** in February, the **Summer Show** in June, the **Irish Assembly of Veteran/Vintage Motor Cycles** in September, and the **Cork 20 International Car Rally** in October! Pretty hard to *miss* a party, no matter when you come.

6 Sports & Outdoor Activities

The **Cork Greyhound Stadium,** out on Western Road (☎ 021/43013), is a good place to enjoy one of Ireland's favorite spectator sports. There's racing on Monday, Wednesday, and Saturday starting at 8pm. Other nights, there are trial heats which you can attend at no charge (but no betting); on race nights, admission is IR£3 ($4.80).

Golfers can rent clubs at the Cork Corporation–owned **Mahon Golf Course,** off Skehard Road, Blackrock (☎ 021/362480). Drive out, or take bus no. 7 or 10 from Patrick Street. If you have your own clubs, there are 18-hole courses at the **Douglas Golf Club,** Carr's Hill, Douglas, and **Monkstown Golf Club,** Monkstown. (☎ 021/841-376 or 021/841-686), which has recently undergone impressive upgrading.

Tennis buffs will find six indoor courts and nine floodlit courts at the **Tennis Village,** Model Farm Road (☎ 021/342727). It's open 8am to midnight and has a bar and a restaurant on the premises. Rackets and other equipment can be rented.

7 Shopping

Cork City is a major shopping center for the county. The ✪ **City Market,** sometimes called the English Market, is a block-long covered space between Patrick Street, Prince's Street, and Grand Parade. Its origins stretch back to the 1610 Charter of James I. It's a lively marketplace, with Cork housewives busily stall-hopping for the best buys on vegetables, fruits, meats, flowers, and occasionally secondhand clothes. (See "What to See & Do," above in this chapter.)

A whole collection of boutiques, specialty shops, and bookshops are waiting to be discovered along a quaintly cobbled square just off Patrick Street (on Patrick Street, turn right at a store called Moderne).

Below I've listed some of the finest shops in Cork city. Shopping hours are Monday through Saturday from 10am to 6pm; some shops observe one late-night opening each week, usually Friday, remaining open until 9pm.

Cash's of Cork

Patrick and Caroline Sts. ☎ **021/276771.** Fax 021/274792.

This is perhaps Cork's leading department store, with everything from Waterford crystal, Belleek, Royal Tara, and Aran knits to the latest fashions.

Crafts of Ireland

11 Winthrop St. ☎ **021/275-864.**

Turn left at Cash's department store to reach Cork's only "All Irish" shop, with its wide and wonderful range of Irish crafts. Opposite the GPO.

Eason & Son Ltd.

113 Patrick St. ☎ **021/270477.**

Eason's stocks books of Irish interest, as well as a full line of current and classic fiction, and carries an extensive range of stationery, greeting cards, cassettes, magazines, and toys.

✪ Fitzgeralds Menswear Shop

24 Patrick St. ☎ **021/270095.**

This is Cork's only source of Burberry raincoats (with very competitive prices). It also stocks an excellent selection of Irish woolens, tweeds, and knitwear, and there is a Bureau de Change.

Kelly's Music Shop
15 Grand Parade. ☎ **021/272355.**

There's not much in the way of Irish music that you won't find at Kelly's—records, tapes, books, and even musical instruments.

✪ **Lee Book Store**
10 Lavitt's Quay. ☎ **021/272307.**

This marvelous bookshop is browsing country par excellence, especially for out-of-print secondhand books on Irish topics. Worth a walk over to the Quay.

✪ **Mercier Press and Bookshops**
5 French Church St. ☎ **021/504022.**

A good many of the Irish books you browse through in bookshops around the country are published by this Cork publisher. Their inexpensive paperback editions are all by Irish writers on Irish subjects, fiction and nonfiction.

Roches Stores
Patrick St. ☎ **021/277727.**

This upmarket department store features giftware, travel goods, toys, sports goods, gourmet food delicacies, and clothing.

✪ **Waterstone's Booksellers**
69 Patrick St. ☎ **021/276522.** Fax 021/276-253.

This large bookshop has extensive stocks of books on every conceivable subject, and they stay open until 8pm Monday through Thursday, until 9pm on Friday, and 7pm on Saturday and Sunday.

8 Cork After Dark

THEATER

✪ **Cork Opera House**
Emmet Place. ☎ **021/270022.** Tickets IR£6–IR£12 ($9.60–$19.20).

There is always something going on in this popular entertainment venue. It could be first-rate drama, musicals, comedy, concert, dance, or an artist's recital—check with the tourist board or local newspapers for current schedules.

✪ **Everyman Palace Theatre**
MacCurtain St. ☎ **021/501673.** Tickets IR£6–IR£12 ($9.60–$19.20).

In 1990 this outstanding playhouse moved from its 12-year home on Father Matthew Street to the Old Palace Theatre, built in 1897 beside the Metropole Hotel as a music hall and used in later years as a cinema. Its gilt-and-gingerbread decor is protected by a preservation order, as well it might be, since it is so steeped in the theatrical history of the city. Resident company productions of outstanding quality are presented regularly, and leading companies from Dublin, Belfast, Derry, Galway, Limerick, Great Britain, and America play here as well, and if the past is any indication, standards will be high. A nice feature is the intermission coffee service, and you'll still be able to hobnob with the actors after each production by dropping in at the Theatre Bar.

Triskle Arts Centre

15 Tobin St. ☎ **021/272022.** Tickets under IR£5 ($8); gallery free.

Located next to City Park, just off South Main Street, Triskle is host to a wide variety of talented artists and performers, many of them in the early stages of their careers. There are contemporary film exhibitions, literary readings, theatrical productions, and music sessions. There's an intimate little cafe that serves homemade food all day.

TRADITIONAL & CONTEMPORARY MUSIC

✪ An Bodhran

42 Oliver Plunkett St. ☎ **021/274544.**

The traditional music sessions here are much more informal. The brick-walled century-and-a-half-old pub is a favorite with university students, most of whom take their traditional music quite seriously, while never losing that Irish twinkle of the eye. You'll usually find the ballads going Wednesday through Saturday nights, but you might drop in other nights to see what's doing. Open daily, regular pub hours.

An Phoenix

Union Sq. ☎ **021/964275.**

You'll find bagpipes, bodhrans, fiddles, and guitars holding forth with superb traditional Irish music four nights a week in this relaxed, friendly pub alongside City Hall. Open daily, regular pub hours.

Reardon's Mill

25 Washington St. ☎ **021/271969.** Cover charge IR£5 ($8).

A variety of musical treats are offered at Reardon's Thursday through Sunday night. The music could be anything from traditional to country/western to jazz.

THE PUB SCENE

Cork has, according to some experts, a pub for every 200 residents. In a city populated by some 129,000 souls, that's a lot of pubs! You're just not likely to be seized by a terrible thirst without rescue close at hand, that's for certain. The pubs of Cork come in all sizes, styles, and decor, and I have no doubt you'll find your own "local" during your stay. The following few are some I've found appealing, with convivial conversation usually on tap along with libations.

✪ An Bodhran

42 Oliver Plunkett St. ☎ **021/274544.**

A few years back, owner Daniel Teegan set about renovating this old pub, and wisely he gave a great deal of attention to its original character. It's a small, cozy place with brick walls, dim lights, low ceiling, lots of timbered beams, and a lively clientele. It's a student hangout, but you'll usually find a mix of older types as well. Traditional music is loved here with all the fervor of a truly Irish heart, as is stimulating conversation.

✪ The Vineyard

Market Lane. ☎ **021/274793.**

I first dropped into this old pub on the tiny lane off Patrick Street at the end of an exhausting afternoon of researching entries for this book. Things were pretty quiet except for a gaggle of Cork housewives, also exhausted from shopping, who had sensibly decided there was nothing for it but a "drop" before heading home to fix the dinner. It's an old, rambling place that dates back more than two centuries, but Liam Mackesy, the present owner, is the third generation of his family to run it. He has lightened it by installing a huge, high skylight in the center of the main bar. Rugby followers and players congregate in the Vineyard, where the "crack" (chat) leans a lot toward sports. Young, old, and in-between faces line up at the bar. It's a good pub in the evening, there's pub grub at lunch, and it can be a lifesaver in the late afternoon.

Mutton Lane Inn

Mutton Lane. ☎ **021/273471.**

Down one of the quaint little laneways leading off Patrick Street to the English Market, the Mutton Lane was established way back in 1787, when whiskey was brewed in the kitchen. Today's owners, Vincent and Maeva McLaughlin, have made some renovations to the well-preserved old pub, and its interior these days is one of dark-stained timbers, soft lighting, and a noteworthy old pewter collection. They're also renowned locally for their excellent pub-grub lunches.

An Phoenix

Union Sq. ☎ **021/964275.**

Located alongside City Hall, An Phoenix dates back to the early 1700s, when it set up shop in the premises of an old mill. With walls of old brick, pitch-pine verticals, exposed rafters, and redwood-and-pine seating, it's the perfect setting for the traditional music that holds sway four nights a week.

12 Around County Cork

Scattered throughout County Cork are quiet villages peopled with strong characters and whimsical spirits. Every Irishman knows that a Corkman is distinctive from other Irish, and a West Corkman is unique unto himself! Truly this is a region of the country to be explored as fully as time will permit and savored in memory for years to come.

SEEING COUNTY CORK

We'll start our exploration of County Cork (the largest county in Ireland, with 2,880 square miles) in Youghal, a picturesque harborside town in East Cork.

Heading west from Youghal, historic Kinsale with its boat-filled harbor lies southwest of Cork city. Here a scenic coastal drive will take you through the southern part of West Cork, meandering through small villages out a long peninsula to Mizen Head Ireland's southernmost point), and back inland to Bantry, Glengarriff, and the Beara Peninsula.

The northern part of West Cork holds the pleasant market town of Kanturk, from which easy day trips can be made to much of West Cork, as well as County Kerry.

1 Youghal & East Cork

YOUGHAL

Be sure to allow time to linger in Youghal (it means "yew wood" and is pronounced "yawl"). Youghal is 30 miles east of Cork city via N25. This picturesque fishing harbor and seaside resort has distinctive American connections. Movie buffs will be interested to know that this is where *Moby Dick* was filmed back in 1954, and there are still tales told in the town of Gregory Peck, the movie folks, and the giant white rubber whale that twice broke its moorings and drifted out to sea (local fishermen went to the rescue).

More important in the annals of history, however, is the fact that this was where Sir Walter Raleigh took his first puff on a pipe of American tobacco and it was here that he put the first spud into Irish soil. So important do the Irish consider this last event that they celebrate with a Walter Raleigh Potato Festival every year the last week of June and first week in July. If you should miss the festivities, you can still see the Elizabethan house that sheltered the Englishman (Myrtle Grove) while he lived in Youghal.

What to See & Do

Your first order of business should be to go by the **Tourist Office,** located at the harbor in Market House, Market Square (☎ 024/92390), and pick up the **"Tourist Trail"** booklet (IR£1, $1.60). It features a signposted walking tour of the town. Highlights of the tour include the historic **Clock Tower,** right in the middle of town, erected in 1776 as a jail, which soon became so overcrowded with rebellious Irish that an entire new floor had to be added. A short distance away are fragments of the **old town walls,** constructed in 1275 and added to up to 1603. **Myrtle Grove,** the Youghal home of Sir Walter Raleigh, is at the top of Nelson Place. It's open to the public during summer months—check with the Tourist Office for hours and admission. Next door is **St. Mary's Collegiate Church,** built in the 13th century on the site of an 11th-century church that was destroyed by a mighty storm. Its neighbor, the **College of Youghal,** was founded in 1464.

Quaint, narrow ✪ **Main Street** is a microcosm of an ancient Irish town successfully melding into today's lifestyle, and **Market Square,** now a pedestrian plaza, is a focal point for locals and visitors alike. Across the square from Market House the Water Gate is a reminder that this was once the shoreline of the harbor. Youghal's importance as a harbor over the centuries is best visualized from the water.

From June through September, Bernard O'Keeffe (126 N. Main St.; ☎ 024/92820) runs marvelous **harbor cruises** aboard the *Naomh Coran,* departing from Jetty Market Square in the late afternoon (about 4:30pm), for fares of IR£2.50 ($4) for adults, half fare for children. **River cruises** leave around 3pm, with fares of IR£3.50 ($5.60) for adults, half that for children. He can also arrange two-, three-, four-hour, and all-day **deep-sea fishing trips,** a great break from sightseeing. **Guided walking tours** cost IR£2 ($3.20) and leave from the Tourist Office Monday through Saturday (call for departure times). For the younger set, there's the small **Parks Amusements** out at the beach, with rides and games, open daily from 11:30am to 11:30pm from June through September.

Sightseeing aside, do stop by the ✪ **Moby Dick** pub on Market Square (☎ 024/92756), which dates back to 1798, for a pint and some conversation with the locals who frequent the place. If you're lucky, owners Paddy and Kevin Linehan will be on hand and you might prevail on them to bring out the scrapbook that chronicles their many years as publicans, as well as souvenirs of the *Moby Dick* crew, who adopted the pub as their local during filming.

Where to Stay

✪ Avonmore House

South Abbey, Youghal, Co. Cork. ☎ **024/92617.** 8 rms, all with bath. IR£14 ($22.40) per person. Dinner IR£10 ($14.50) extra. (Rates include breakfast.) MC, V.

Eileen and Jack Gaine open their Georgian home (built 1752) to guests, with nicely done-up guest rooms and superb meals. Avonmore is conveniently located at the harbor entrance, and is only a short walk from the beach and town center.

Bromley House

Killeagh, Youghal, Co. Cork. ☎ **024/95235.** 4 rms, all with bath. IR£18.50 ($29.60) single; IR£15 ($24) per person sharing. 20% reduction for children. (Rates include breakfast.) Dinner IR£12 ($19.20) extra. No credit cards. Closed Nov–Feb. Private car park.

The friendly Mrs. Eileen Fogarty gives a warm welcome to every new arrival at this modern, centrally heated bungalow 3 miles west of Youghal on N25. There's a TV lounge and open fires for cool evenings.

Where to Eat

✪ Aherne's Pub and Seafood Bar

163 N. Main St. ☎ **024/92533** or 92424. Reservations recommended, especially for dinner. Main courses IR£6–IR£12 ($9.60–$19.20); bar food IR£2–IR£6 ($3.20–$9.60). ACC, AE, DC, MC, V. Tues–Sat 12:30–2:15pm; Tues–Sat 6:30–9:30pm. Closed Good Friday and four days at Christmas. SEAFOOD/BAR FOOD/TRADITIONAL.

Aherne's serves bar food of such quality that it has won the National Bar Food award for several years. But pub grub is not its only distinction, for John and David Fitzgibbon have also installed an outstanding full restaurant and enhanced its decor with paintings, wood paneling, and soft lighting. Seafood dishes, such as mussels in garlic butter, take star billing, but beef, lamb, and chicken dishes are equally well prepared. Except for bar food, available all day, prices in this attractive eatery will run slightly above budget. Elegant luxury guest rooms available.

EAST CORK

Although you'll seldom see the term "East Cork," it's a good way to define that part of County Cork that lies east and north of Cork city.

What to See & Do

Some 10 miles east of Cork city on N25, look for signposts pointing to **Barryscourt Castle** in the small town of Carrigtwohill (☎ 021/883-864). From the 12th to the 17th centuries, this was the principal residence of the lords of Barrymore. The present castle keep houses an exhibition on the history of the Barrys and the castle, and there are guided tours for a small fee. This, incidentally, is an excellent lunch stop, since the farmhouse outside the castle wall has been transformed into a charming tea shop with delicacies such as chicken with white wine and tarragon and shrimp in garlic butter (and house wine available by the glass) on offer daily from 11am to 6pm. The craft shop that shares the premises features unique handicrafts from local artisans. The castle is open daily from 11am to 6pm from June through September, and 11am to 6pm other months. Well worth a stop.

Five miles or so farther east, still on N25, plan to stop in the bustling market town of Midleton to visit the **Jameson Heritage Centre** (☎ 021/613-594), part of the sprawling Irish Distillers' complex, where all Irish whiskies except Bushmills are produced. Set in a disused distillery, the Heritage Centre tour begins with a short, informative audiovisual presentation depicting nostalgic scenes of Irish distilleries over the centuries. You'll then be guided through the maze of old buildings of beautiful stonework, old wood, and red brick, learning as you go just as much as you could possibly want to know about the whiskey-making process. At the end of the tour, you land in the restaurant bar (with a free sample of Jameson, of course), craft shop, and a tasteful gift shop. The center is open March to November daily from 10am to 6pm (last tour at 4:30pm) and there's an admission of IR£3.50 ($5.60) for adults, IR£1.50 ($2.40) for children.

About midway between Youghal and Cork city, the little seaside fishing village of ✪ **Ballycotton** (take R632 at Castlemartyr on N25) slopes down picturesque

County Cork

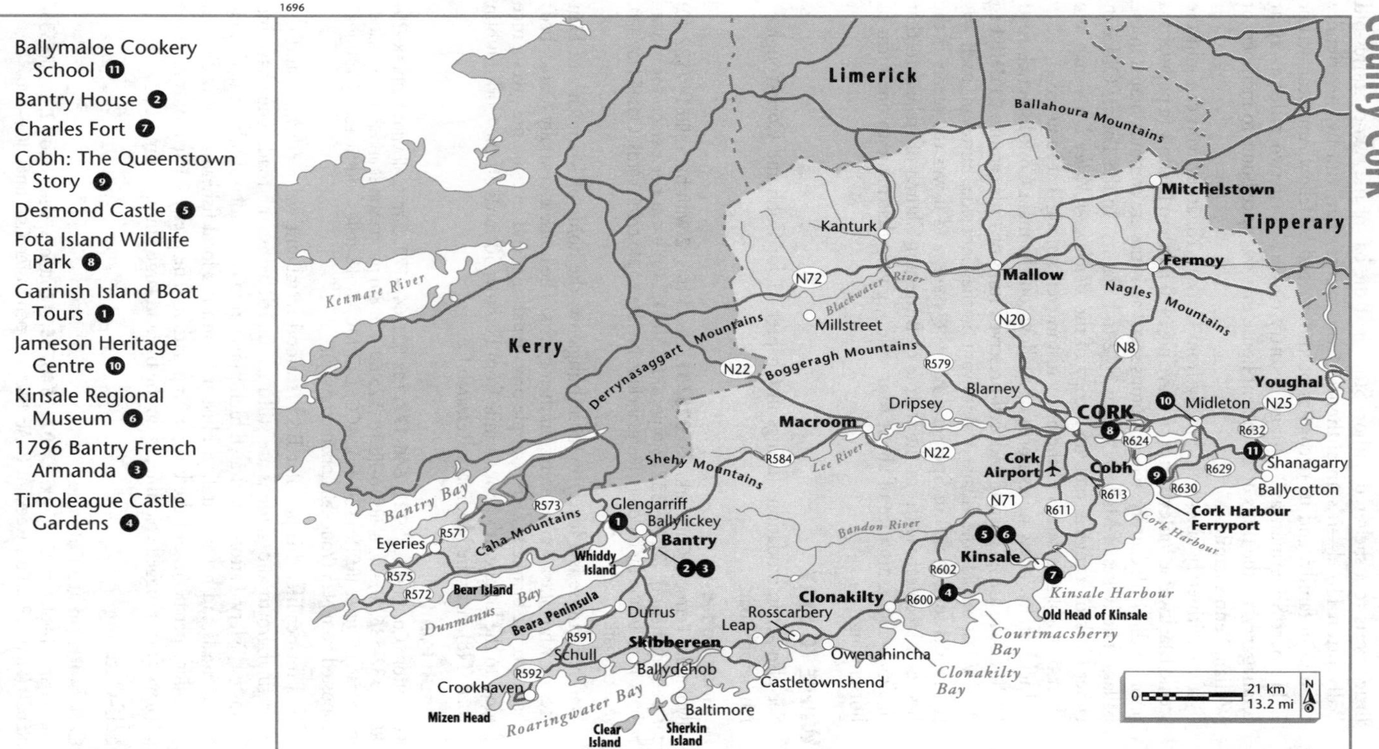

1696
Ballymaloe Cookery School 11
Bantry House 2
Charles Fort 7
Cobh: The Queenstown Story 9
Desmond Castle 5
Fota Island Wildlife Park 8
Garinish Island Boat Tours 1
Jameson Heritage Centre 10
Kinsale Regional Museum 6
1796 Bantry French Armanda 3
Timoleague Castle Gardens 4
Limerick
Ballahoura Mountains
Mitchelstown
Tipperary
Kanturk
Mallow
Fermoy
Kenmare River
N72
Blackwater River
Nagles Mountains
Millstreet
N20
Kerry
Mountains
Boggeragh Mountains
N8
Derrynasaggart
N22
R579
Youghal
Blarney
Dripsey
CORK
Midleton
N25
Macroom
R632
R624
Shehy Mountains
R584
Lee River
N22
Cork Airport
Cobh
Shanagarry
R629
R630
Ballycotton
Bantry Bay
R573
Glengarriff
N71
R611
R613
Cork Harbour Ferryport
Caha Mountains
Ballylickey
Bandon River
Cork Harbour
R571
Bantry
Eyeries
Whiddy Island
Kinsale
R575
R602
Bear Island
Bay
Kinsale Harbour
R572
Clonakilty
R600
Old Head of Kinsale
Dunmanus
Beara Peninsula
Durrus
Rosscarbery
Courtmacsherry Bay
R591
Leap
Skibbereen
Schull
Owenahincha
Clonakilty Bay
R592
Ballydehob
Castletownshend
Crookhaven
Roaringwater Bay
Baltimore
Mizen Head
Clear Island
Sherkin Island
0
21 km
13.2 mi
N

little streets to a sheltered harbor. Stop in at the bar of the two-centuries-old Ballycotton Hotel—it's an authentic Irish country bar, run by the friendly O'Sullivan family, and its decor has been described by fellow American writer J. Herbert Silverman as "vintage country classic." Just two miles away at **Shanagarry** are the ruins of an ancient house that was once home to members of William Penn's family.

If your itinerary takes you directly from Cork to Killarney, you can join the scenic **Blackwater Valley Drive** by traveling N20 north to **Mallow** (a popular spa resort in the 18th century, whose riotous social activities are commemorated in the ballad "The Rakes of Mallow"), then N72 to Killarney. In the Tourist Office in either Cork or Youghal, pick up a copy of the *Blackwater Valley Drive* map and chart that will give details of the many historic relics along that route.

Incidentally, a few miles north of Mallow, on the main Cork-Limerick road (N20), there are interesting and well-preserved ruins of 13th-century ✪ **Ballybeg Abbey** just outside the village of Buttevant on the Cork side. Buttevant itself was the model for "Mole" in Spenser's *Faerie Queene,* and it was the scene of the first-ever steeplechase (from the steeple of Buttevant Church of Ireland to that of Doneraile, a distance of about four miles), giving that name to one form of horseracing.

WHERE TO STAY

See also accommodations listings in Chapter 11 for Cobh and Cork-Youghal-Midleton Road.

Danmar House

Ballyhindon, Fermoy, Co. Cork. ☎ **025/31786.** 4 rms, 2 with bath. IR£14 ($22.40) per person sharing; IR£20 ($32) single; IR£1.50 ($2.40) extra per person for private bath. 10% reduction for children. (Rates include breakfast.) No credit cards. Closed Nov–Jan. Private car park.

Danmar House is a lovely modern bungalow, the home of Maureen and Dan Regan, who take a warm interest in their guests. The house is centrally heated, beds have electric blankets, there's ample private parking, and an open fire gives a nice glow to the lounge. It's about a mile from Fermoy, 50 yards off the Cork-Dublin road (N8), near the Moorpark Research Centre.

Spanish Point

Ballycotton, Co. Cork. ☎ **021/646-177.** Fax 021/646-179. 5 rms, all with bath. IR£20–IR£23 ($32–$36.80) single; IR£16–IR£18 ($25.60–$28.80) per person sharing. (Rates include breakfast.) Dinner IR£19 ($30.40). ACC, DC, MC, V. 18 miles southwest of Youghal, signposted from N25 (Youghal/Cork motorway).

In a former life, this popular B&B/seafood restaurant was a convent, and the original grotto and gardens are still maintained across the road. The charming hostess, Mary Tatton, has drawn high praise from our readers, both for her excellent meals and her hospitality. Husband John is a local fisherman, providing an insider's perspective of the busy fishing harbor. The pretty guest rooms have sea views of this rugged coastline, as do the bar and large dining room.

Self-Catering

✪ Kinoith House Cottages

Shanagarry, Midleton, Co. Cork. ☎ **021/646785.** 4 cottages, sleep 8 to 12. TV. IR£535–IR£620 ($856–$992) per week. ACC, AE, MC, V. Open Easter, Christmas, July–Aug.

You can relax into the peaceful Irish countryside in these very special holiday cottages, spend your days sightseeing in the area—Ballycotton and Shanagarry are both just a short drive away—and return at night armed with free-range eggs and fresh vegetables and fruits you can buy from the farm. Kinoith House Cottages, 18 miles southwest of Youghal (signposted from N25, the Youghal-Cork road), are in what were once the outbuildings of the 18th-century farmhouse known as Kinoith. Darina Allen's internationally known Ballymaloe Cookery School is held here at Kinoith House. The proximity of Ballymaloe is a bonus for cottage renters, since one of Ireland's finest restaurants is right at hand for those times you'd really rather not cook.

From the graveled courtyard, where vivid blooms are bright splashes of color, stroll through the garden and out into the apple orchard. Inside each cottage are such modern conveniences as a dishwasher and TV (and you have the use of laundry facilities). As well as central heating, there's the added, old-fashioned comfort of an open fire (the rent includes your firewood). The Pink Cottage sleeps ten to twelve; the White Cottage sleeps six to eight; the Barn sleeps twelve, with two twin- or double-bedded rooms en suite and eight single rooms; the Playroom sleeps six; and the Coach House sleeps eight. As you can see, on a per-person basis, these cottages are actually quite inexpensive. Early reservations are advised to avoid disappointment.

Worth a Splurge

Bayview Hotel

Ballycotton, Co. Cork. ☎ **021/646-746.** Fax 021/646-824. 35 rms, all with bath. IR£50 ($80) single, IR£40 ($64) per person sharing. Breakfast IR£6.50 ($10.40); dinner IR£22.50 ($36). Weekend specials available. ACC, AE, DC, MC, V. 18 miles southwest of Youghal, signposted from N25 (Youghal-Cork motorway).

Set on a low bluff overlooking Ballycotton Bay and the fishing harbor, this lovely small hotel has gardens that lead to steps down to a small beach. This is one of the most beautiful sites in these parts, and both public and guest rooms match their setting. Just a short drive from Ardmore, Youghal, Midleton, Cobh, and Cork, the hotel makes a special base for day trips.

✪ Longueville House

Longueville, Mallow, Co. Cork. ☎ **022/47156.** Fax 022/47459. 16 rms, all with bath. IR£55–IR£69 ($88–$110.40) per person. (Rates include breakfast.) Dinner IR£26 ($41.60) extra. ACC, AE, DC, MC, V. Closed Mid-Dec to Apr.

Set in a 500-acre farmland estate three miles west of Mallow on the Mallow-Killarney road (N72), Longueville House overlooks the Blackwater River valley. Off in the distance are visible the ruins of 16th-century Dromaneen Castle, ancestral home of owner Michael O'Callaghan, and on the front lawn, rows of huge oaks are planted in the same formation as French and English troops at the Battle of Waterloo. There's significance in both these views, for the castle was forfeit to Cromwell in 1641 and the family heritage was reclaimed only in 1938 when Michael's father purchased the land and castle.

The handsome 1720 Georgian mansion sports a wide entrance hall whose walls are hung with O'Callaghan portraits, and a lounge with a carved fireplace and a beautifully detailed stucco ceiling. The lounge bar is Victorian in style, with wine-red upholstery, and in the gourmet restaurant (see "Where to Eat," below), portraits of every Republic of Ireland president dub it the Presidents' Room.

There's trout and salmon fishing in the Blackwater right on the estate, and free golf three miles away. A decided bonus to those of a literary bent is the excellent library. *Note:* Children are not encouraged as guests, since Longueville House is essentially an adult retreat.

Midleton Park Hotel

Midleton, Co. Cork. ☎ **021/631-767.** Fax 021/631-605. 40 rms, all with bath. 1 room for disabled. TEL TV. Seasonal rates (excluding breakfast) IR£40–IR£45 ($64–$72) single; IR£25–IR£38 ($40–$60.80) per person sharing. 1- to 3-day golf specials available. ACC, AE, MC, V. 15 miles east of Cork city on N25.

Set on the western edge of Midleton, this modern hotel has exceptionally spacious guest rooms, each with a comfortable seating area, hairdryer, and trouser press. The bar and restaurant feature traditional decor, with lots of dark wood andbrass.

Where to Eat

✪ Ballymaloe House

Shanagarry, Midleton. ☎ **021/652531.** Fax 021/652021. Reservations required. Buffet lunch IR£16 ($25.60): fixed-price dinner IR£32 ($51.20). Service charge optional. ACC, DC, MC, V. Daily 7–9:30pm, Sun 12:30–2pm. Closed three days at Christmas. IRISH/SEAFOOD/FRENCH.

Myrtle Allen's Ballymaloe House is internationally famous, and one of the chief reasons for its excellence is the fact that the cuisine rests on strictly local products. The nightly menu is quite small, but quality looms immense. The simplest dishes have flavor you'd never expect to find outside the little auberges of rural France. There's no predicting exactly what will be on the menu the evening you dine here, but I know that every meal offers a choice of three soups, three or four fish dishes, six main courses, and at least four desserts—all prepared with the flair of traditional Irish recipes. I can only hope that Mrs. Allen's superb pâté is on the menu, followed, perhaps, by watercress soup, escalopes of stuffed baby beef, and the savarin au rhum as a topper.

✪ Longueville House

Longueville, Mallow. ☎ **022/47156** or 47306. Reservations required. Bar lunch under IR£7 ($11.20); fixed-price meal IR£18 ($28.80) at lunch, IR£26 ($41.60) at dinner. ACC, AE, DC, MC, V. Daily 12:45–2pm and 7–9pm. Closed Christmas–early Mar. TRADITIONAL/SEAFOOD.

The Presidents' Room restaurant is one of the best in the country, and even if you're only passing through this part of the southern region, you'll be in for a very special treat if you phone ahead to book a meal here. Meals are served in the stately Georgian dining room under the gaze of all of Ireland's presidents, beneath an ornate plaster ceiling. In fine weather the Victorian conservatory, with its massed greenery, white ironwork, and glorious views of the garden, is open to diners as well.

As for the food, it has won just about every award and international recognition going. Chef William O'Callaghan oversees the preparation of gourmet selections that utilize produce grown in the Longueville fields, local lamb, and fish fresh from waters that flow through the estate. Mallard and venison are featured in season, and the wine list includes wines produced from Michael's own vineyards (among the first—and only ones—in Ireland).

You'll find Longueville House three miles west of Mallow on the Mallow-Killarney road (N72).

2 Kinsale & West Cork

Between Cork and Killarney are several possible routes, each with its own special appeal. If time is all-important, you can take the Blackwater Valley Drive, or follow N22 through Macroom (the castle right off the town square belonged to the father of William Penn, founder of Pennsylvania), with a detour to Gougane Barra. My personal preference is the lengthy, meandering N71 that follows the coastline through West Cork, leading to Bantry and Glengarriff before turning northward to Killarney. You can also reach Bantry by diverting onto R586 at Bandon, which takes you through Dunmanway and Timoleague en route. An even better idea is to base yourself somewhere in this wondrous region and make day trips to explore it at your leisure.

KINSALE

A scenic 18 miles south of Cork city, the fishing and boating village of Kinsale has figured prominently in Ireland's history since it received its charter in 1333. Back in 1601 it was the scene of a decisive Irish defeat when Don Juan d'Aguila arrived from Spain with a large force to assist the Irish rebels. And for a time, it looked as though the Irish might prevail. Even though Mountjoy, the English general, threw some 12,000 soldiers into a siege of the town, his position seemed doomed when Irish chieftains O'Donnell and O'Neill massed their forces behind the English, leaving them surrounded. History might well have been dramatically changed had it not been for an Irish soldier (reportedly in his cups) who let slip vital information to Mountjoy, enabling him to successfully rout both Irish and Spanish.

WHAT TO SEE & DO

Stop by the Tourist Office on Main Street (☎ 021/772-234) to pick up copies of the information sheet "Kinsale, a Town for All Seasons" and a **Tourist Trail** guidebook that details a 1½-hour walking tour of the town's historic sites. South of town, you can visit the remains of star-shaped **James Fort** at Castlepark, which was so named for James II, who arrived here in 1689 in an attempt to regain his throne. Long before his arrival, however, the original fort was occupied in 1601 by Spanish forces who suffered such a disastrous defeat in the Battle of Kinsale.

In Summer Cove, on the east side of the bay, there's quite a lot left of **Charles Fort** (☎ 021/772263), built by the English in 1678 and in constant use as late as the 1920s. It sits high on a clifftop, and the view of Kinsale Harbour is spectacular. Open mid-April–mid-June, Tues–Sat 9am–4pm and Sun 11am–5:30pm; Mid-June–Oct, daily 10am–5pm (small admission charge). Six miles south is the **Old Head of Kinsale,** where a 12th-century castle sits in ruins atop high cliffs overlooking the spot where the *Lusitania* lies in its deep-water grave, sent there (along with some 1,500 souls) in 1915 by a German submarine.

The **Old Courthouse** in the Market Square was originally the old Market House, built in 1600 and built onto in 1706 to serve as Kinsale's municipal administration center. These days, it houses the **Kinsale Regional Museum,** and you can visit the courtroom in which an inquest was held after the *Lusitania* disaster.

Other Kinsale tag ends of history to look for include the **town stocks** in **St. Multrose Church,** erected in the 12th century. A ruined 12th-century **Carmelite friary** and 15th-century **Desmond Castle** provide interesting poking around.

One bit of Kinsale miscellany: The town's womenfolk once wore the long, black, hooded cape that's known as the **Kinsale cloak**—you'll see it copied in rich fabrics to be used as an elegant evening cloak, but these days it's rare to see it on Kinsale streets.

Pubs

If, by this time in your travels, you've become an Irish pub addict, there are several in Kinsale you won't want to miss. My personal favorite is the ✪ **Seanachie Pub** on Market Street. If time permits, I'll warrant you won't be able to go along to the Seanachie just once—it's habit-forming! It's tucked away on a picture-postcard-pretty street, uses a second, phonetic spelling of its name (Shanakee), and is more than 200 years old. In the two small front rooms are original old stone walls, open fires, and a marvelous painting of the legendary Irish storytellers for whom the pub is named. Brothers Vincent and Gerard McCarthy, both musical, are genial hosts. A larger back room has been added, opening up equally old adjacent buildings, retaining stone walls, and restoring ceiling beams and crumbling fireplaces. During summer months there's music seven nights a week—and that means traditional Irish music as well as the favorite sing-along ballads. Michael Buckley, the beloved All-Ireland accordion player, performs regularly, as do other local musicians. There's also dancing in the back room on weekends all through the summer, but absolutely nothing could draw yours truly from those front rooms where music and talk and the brown stuff flow easily until one of the McCarthys sings out "Time, gentlemen, please."

Another noteworthy pub is **The Spaniard,** an atmospheric converted stable where fishnets seem right at home in the horse-stall cubbyholes. This is where you'll find a crowd of international sportsmen, here for the world-famous shark fishing, and a fair smattering of local characters. In summer months there's frequently live music in the evenings.

Summer Cove is where you'll find the **Bullman Pub,** a popular hangout for the younger generation that gets quite lively at night.

Fishing

If you'd like to get in some fishing, arrangements can be made through the **Trident Angling Centre,** Trident Hotel, Kinsale (☎ 021/774099). Sailboat cruises varying from one day to a full week can be booked by **World's End Charters** (☎ 021/271551; fax 021/277180).

Where to Stay

Ard Cuain

Forthill, Summercove, Kinsale, Co. Cork. ☎ **021/772-451.** 4 rms, 3 with bath. IR£20 ($32) single; IR£15–IR£16 ($24–$25.60) per person sharing. 20% reduction for children. (Rates include breakfast.) No credit cards. No smoking. Open Mar–Nov. 1 mile from Kinsale.

Striking harbor views are had from this dormer bungalow in the Charles Fort area. Mrs. Mary Fitzgerald, a former nurse, is the gracious hostess, and her home gleams with beautiful French–polished woodwork and lovely furnishings that provide the utmost comfort. Central heating and plenty of parking.

✪ Blue Haven Hotel

3 Pearse St., Kinsale, Co. Cork. ☎ **021/772209.** Fax 021/774268. 18 rms, all with bath IR£35–IR£48 ($56–$76.80) per person. Special two- and three-day rates available. (Rates include breakfast.) ACC, AE, DC, MC, V.

Right in the heart of town, Ann and Brian Cronin have created a haven of quiet, relaxed comfort in this small hotel. Guest rooms are nicely done up, the staff excells in friendliness and genuine helpfulness, and the Blue Haven is known far and wide for its superb seafood bar (see "Where to Eat," below). A little above the budget in rates, but well worth it. Advance booking is strongly advised in summer months.

Danabel

Sleaveen, Kinsale, Co. Cork. ☎ **021/774-087.** 4 rms, all with bath. IR£21 ($33.60) single; IR£16 ($25.60) per person sharing. (Rates include breakfast.) No credit cards. Closed Christmas.

A short walk from the town center, Danabel is a 2-story bungalow close to beaches. Mrs. Phil Price's friendly hospitality has won many fans among our readers, who are impressed with her breakfast menu. Rooms are nicely furnished, with orthopedic beds and tea/coffeemakers. Central heat and private parking.

Hillside House

Camp Hill, Kinsale, Co. Cork. ☎ **021/772315.** 6 rms, 3 with bath. IR£18.50 ($29.60) single without bath; IR£13.50 ($21.60) per person sharing without bath; IR£2.50 ($4) per person additional with bath. 20% reduction for children. (Rates include breakfast.) Dinner IR£12 ($19.20) extra. V.

About a mile outside Kinsale, Mrs. Margaret Griffin's spacious modern bungalow has sea views and a pleasant garden. The house is centrally heated, and there's ample parking. This is an especially nice place to stay if you prefer the country but don't want to be too far from town.

Sceilig

Ard-Brack, Kinsale, Co. Cork. ☎ **021/772-832.** 3 rms, all with bath; 1 suite. IR£20 ($32) single; IR£13.50 ($21.60) per person sharing. Suite IR£25 ($40) single; IR£16.50 ($26.40) per person sharing. 35% reduction for children. (Rates include breakfast.) No credit cards. 1/2 mile from Kinsale town center.

Mrs. Mary Hurley is the warm, friendly hostess here, and her charming husband is a fount of information on County Cork, as well as the entire country. Guest rooms have magnificent sea views. The one suite comes with its own private patio, a perfect spot to sit and watch the harbor lights come on at sunset.

Walyunga

Sandycove, Kinsale, Co. Cork. ☎ **021/774-126.** 4 rms, 3 with bath. IR£19–IR£21 ($30.40–$33.60) single; IR£13.50–IR£16 ($21.60–$25.60) per person sharing. 20% reduction for children. (Rates include breakfast.) No credit cards. Open Feb–Nov. 1 mile west of Kinsale.

This strikingly designed modern home is perched on a hill with panoramic views of the Atlantic Ocean and quiet green valleys. It's surrounded by landscaped gardens, and sandy beaches and scenic coastal walks are close by. Mrs. Myrtle Levis presides over the bright, spacious house, and her breakfasts have been called "terrific" and her coffee "great" by readers. Floor-to-ceiling windows in the lounge and dining room open onto those magnificent views, and guest rooms look out to ocean, countryside, or garden views.

Where to Eat

Kinsale is internationally known as "The Gourmet Capital of Ireland," and the following are only a few of the fine restaurants that justify that claim.

✪ Blue Haven Hotel

3 Pearse St. ☎ **021/772209** or 772206. Main courses IR£6–IR£10 ($9.60–$16); bar food IR£3–IR£5 ($4.80–$8). Service charge 10%. ACC, AE, MC, V. Daily 10:30am–11:30pm. Closed Christmas Day. SEAFOOD/TRADITIONAL/BAR FOOD.

Superior light lunches are served in the cozy Blue Haven Hotel's lounge bar. The hotel has won culinary awards for the seafood here, but the menu also includes lamb, corned beef, and sometimes very good lasagna. There's also a pricier and more extensive menu in the higher ranges listed above.

Man Friday

Scilly. ☎ **021/772260.** Reservations recommended. Main courses IR£8–IR£12 ($12.80–$19.20). ACC, V. Mon–Sat 7:30–10:30pm. Closed Mon in winter, two weeks in Jan. SEAFOOD/INTERNATIONAL.

Overlooking the harbor on the outskirts of town, Man Friday is the sort of cozy eatery that invites you to relax from your first step inside. Among the outstanding dishes are baked black sole with a seafood stuffing, roast stuffed loin of lamb with mint-and-rosemary sauce, and Chinese beef, but anything you select will come to table at its very best, a fact testified to by the many awards given Man Friday over the past few years.

Max's Wine Bar

Main St., Kinsale. ☎ **021/772-443.** Reservations recommended. Main courses IR£6.50–IR£12.50 ($10.40–$20); set lunch and early-bird dinner IR£12 ($19.20). MC, V. Daily 12:30–3pm and 6:30–10:30pm. SEAFOOD/TRADITIONAL.

Wendy Tisdall's lovely little restaurant right in the heart of town has been a "must" for Kinsale visitors (and a host of regulars) for more than twenty years. It's a charming place, with a light, airy conservatory adjoining the dining room (no smoking in this part of the restaurant, which only seats 10). The menu is a delight. Seafood devotees will gravitate to the just-out-of-the-water catch of the day or sweet and sour scampi, while landlubbers are in for a treat with rack of lamb with red wine and rosemary sauce or poached chicken. I recommend the baked goat cheese as a starter, and Wendy's great bread-and-butter pudding for dessert.

Paddy Garibaldi's

The White Lady Hotel, Lower O'Connell St., Kinsale. ☎ **021/774-077.** Pizza IR£3.50–IR£6 ($5.60–$9.60); grills IR£5–IR£6 ($8–$9.60); pasta IR£6 ($9.60). ACC, AE, MC, V. Mon–Sat 5–11pm, Sun 1–11pm. PIZZA/TRADITIONAL.

A sister to the two Cork city restaurants of the same name (see Chapter 11), this pleasant eatery offers seven-inch pizzas, charcoal-grilled burgers, outstanding grills, and an extensive offering of assorted selections. Gluten-free pizzas are available on request.

The Vintage

Main St., Kinsale. ☎ **021/772-502.** Reservations advised. Main courses (including fresh vegetables and Irish potato cakes) IR£15–IR£17.50 ($24–$28). ACC, AE, MC, V. Mid-Apr–Nov, Wed–Mon 12:30–3pm and 6:45–10pm. IRISH/CONTINENTAL/VEGETARIAN.

This small restaurant is very cozy and very romantic; its fare is totally delicious. There's an open fire in the dining room, 200-year-old beams, and original masts from sailing ships that once came into Kinsale. Meals that come to table in this lovely ambience can best be described as traditional country food prepared in an international way. Under the direction of Swiss-born owner Raoul de Gendre, a crew of Irish, Swiss, and French chefs uses only fresh produce and meats, with oysters and other seafood from neighboring waters. The soupiere atlantique, a wonderful soup of fresh Atlantic fish, is superb. In addition to innovative seafood main courses, there's a marvelous oven-roast Barberry duck en maigret and confit with a seed mustard sauce, as well as rack of Bandon lamb with thyme seasoning and vegetarian paraise (vegetables in filo pastry with a spicy tomato sauce). As you might expect in a restaurant with this name, the wine list is outstanding.

WEST CORK

It has been written that "West Cork is bigger than Ireland." Well, an hour or two of gazing at its wild, unspoiled, and magnificent vistas of coastline, tiny villages, sheer cliffs, and miles and miles of emptiness will go a long way toward convincing you of the truth of that statement!

The ghosts of Ireland past who roam this ruggedly beautiful region include that of independence fighter Gen. **Michael Collins,** who was ambushed at a place called Beal na Blath in August 1922 (there's a memorial marking the spot on the Dunmanway-Crookstown road). And in Castlestownend, surely the shades of two Victorian novelists named Edith Somerville and Violet Martin Ross still haunt the hallways and grounds of their beloved Drishane House, where together they wrote gently humorous tales of their Irish neighbors. The entire English-speaking world has chuckled over the misadventures recounted in the television dramatization of their most famous work, *The Experiences of an Irish R.M.*

WHAT TO SEE & DO

En route to **Clonakilty,** birthplace of Michael Collins (about two miles west, at Woodfield), stop by the **Timoleague Castle Gardens,** which date from the 1800s. Drive on to Clonakilty, where castles dot the shores of the bay and a regional museum displays minute books of the town corporation that date back to 1675, along with Michael Collins memorabilia and many other interesting relics. Stop for lunch or dinner or overnight at **Leap** (see the Leap Inn in "Where to Stay" and "Where to Eat," below). In **Skibbereen,** visit the **West Cork Arts Centre** on North Street to see contemporary arts and crafts produced by artists and artisans from the southwest. The Maid of Erin monument you see in the town square was put there by the Young Ireland Society in 1904. About a mile west of town, 14th-century Abbeystewery Abbey shelters one of Ireland's mass famine graves. Some four miles southwest of Skibbereen, Lough Hyne is a unique marine reserve that shelters literally thousands of water plants and animals. It's best at low tide when you can walk along the shore and look at the tiny sea creatures in the water. Detour south to visit **Baltimore,** with its ruined O'Driscoll castle brooding over the town from a high cliff and its tales of horror in 1631, when Algerian pirates massacred all but 200 of the inhabitants and carried off the survivors to a life of slavery in North Africa. Lovely **Sherkin Island,** with its ancient, ruined Franciscan abbey and peaceful, lonely coves, can be visited by passenger boat from Baltimore during the summer. Pass through villages like **Ballydehob,** and linger a while at the picturesque fishing village of **Schull** and stroll its waterfront. From Schull, travel the 18 miles to **Mizen Head** at land's end, through **Goleen,** with its sandy strand, **Crookhaven,** and around **Barley Cove.**

Mizen Head is Ireland's most southerly point, and its signal station is open to the public for the first time since it was built in 1910. The Visitor Centre (☎ 028/35115 in summer months, 028/35225 or 35253 October to May) is found in the Lightkeeper's House and the engine room. A breathtaking 172-foot long suspension bridge (I *dare* you to cross it!) soars 150 feet above crashing waves at the cliff base below. Views up and down the south and west coasts are simply magnificent. The station is open daily (small admission fee) from June to September from 11am to 5pm—varying hours October to May.

Return to Schull along Dunmanus Bay on the other side of Mount Gabriel, which rises 1,339 feet.

Where to Stay

✪ Abbey Heights

Skibbereen, Co. Cork. ☎ **028/21615.** 4 rms, all with shower. IR£14 ($22.40) per person without bath; IR£2 ($3.20) per person additional with bath. 33 1/3% reduction for children. (Rates include breakfast.) Dinner IR£12 ($19.20) extra. No credit cards. Closed Oct–Easter.

The Glavin family will welcome you to their pretty bungalow, less than a mile from Skibbereen, with beautiful river views. The house is centrally heated, and dinner is available with advance notice. It's 54 miles southwest of Cork city via N71, 21 miles southeast of Bantry, signposted from R556.

Atlantic Sunset

Butlerstown, Bandon, Co. Cork. ☎ **023/40115.** 4 rms, 2 with bath. IR£17.50 ($28) single; IR£13.50–IR£15.50 ($21.60–$24.80) per person sharing. 20% reduction for children. (Rates include breakfast.) No credit cards.

Mrs. Mary Holland's modern country home has a beautiful view of the Atlantic, and there's a lovely sandy beach about half a mile from the house. Guest rooms are nicely done up, with washbasins in every room, and each has easy access to the bathroom with shower. Golf, horseback riding, and sea fishing can be arranged at nearby facilities.

Dun Mhuire

Kilbarry Rd., Dunmanway, Co. Cork. ☎ **023/45162.** 5 rms, all with bath. TEL TV. IR£20 ($32) per person. 50% reduction for children. (Rates include breakfast.) ACC, MC, V.

Mrs. Carmel Hayes presides over this lovely, modern guesthouse and restaurant, centrally heated and set in nice, peaceful surroundings. The luxury guest rooms are well worth the higher price. The restaurant has won accolades from locals and visitors alike (see "Where to Eat," below). It's 37 miles west of Cork via N72 with signposted turnoffs, and 20 miles east of Bantry via R586.

✪ Leap Inn

Leap, Co. Cork. ☎ **028/33668.** 9 rms, 5 with bath. IR£16 ($25.60) per person (no extra charge for private bath. (Rates include breakfast.) Weekly rates available. Dinner IR£27 ($43.20) extra. ACC, V.

In the little West Cork village of Leap (pronounced "Lep"), a night in this comfortable, old-fashioned hotel is like taking a giant step back to a time when friendliness and hospitality were the mark of all country inns. The same family has run this place since 1834, and today Brian and Ann Sheahan continue the traditions of innkeeping that have grown with the years. Public rooms include a bar (which serves pub grub all day and is often the venue for spontaneous musical sessions), a lounge, and a dining room (see "Where to Eat," below). Upstairs, bedrooms are simply furnished, but very comfortable. The setting is idyllic, an ideal place for a quiet, relaxing stop. It's on the main Cork-Bantry road (N71), 50 miles southwest of Cork city, 43 miles southwest of Kinsale, and 15 miles southeast of Bantry. A personal favorite.

Palm Grove

Coolnagurrane, Bantry Road, Skibbereen, Co. Cork. ☎ **028/21703.** 3 rms, 2 with bath. IR£20 ($32) single; IR£13.50–IR£15.50 ($21.60–$24.80) per person sharing. Dinner IR£12 ($19.20). 20% reduction for children. ACC, MC, V. Open Apr–Oct. 1 mile from Skibbereen.

Set in open countryside, overlooking the Llen river, Mrs. Eileen O'Driscoll's modern bungalow is nicely furnished, and guest rooms look out to peaceful rural scenes. Mrs. O'Driscoll is the soul of hospitality and always eager to help with sightseeing plans. Central heating and a private car park.

Riverview

7 Riverview Estate, Bandon, Co. Cork. ☎ **023/41080.** 4 rms, all with bath. IR£18.50 ($29.60) single; IR£13.50 ($21.60) per person sharing. 25% reduction for children. No credit cards. Open all year. 1/4 mile from town center.

In a quiet cul-de-sac just a short walk from town, Mrs. Carmel Nash's attractive two-story home has comfortable guest rooms, central heating, and private parking.

Bed-and-Breakfast in a Castle

✪ Kilbrittain Castle

Kilbrittain, Co. Cork. ☎ **023/49601.** Fax 023/49702. 5 rms, all with bath. IR£35 ($56) per person sharing; IR£30 per person sharing in triple room; IR£8 ($12.80) single supplement. 50% reduction for children ages 4–12 (no children 3 and under). (Rates include breakfast.) No credit cards. Closed Nov–mid-Mar. 6 miles from Bandon; 35 minutes from Cork Airport; 20 minutes from Kinsale.

Kilbrittain Castle is the oldest habitable castle in Ireland, built in 1035 by Brian Boru's grandson, and its history is that of Ireland itself, having been home to Irish chieftains, Norman invaders, Cromwellian troops, and English planters. In an incredibly beautiful setting close to the sea and long, sandy beaches, it's now the home of Tim and Sylvia Cahill-O'Brien, who stress that it is *not* a hotel, and their only aim is to give visitors a unique experience in a castle atmosphere. Each of the five bedrooms is different in size and decor, and all are beautifully appointed. All in all, this is an ideal base for exploring West Cork.

A Farmhouse

Findus House

Ballyvoige, Kilnamartyra, Macroom, Co. Cork. ☎ **026/40023.** 5 rms, all with bath. IR£15 ($24) per person sharing. 50% reduction for children. (Rates include breakfast.) Dinner IR£14 ($22.40) extra. ACC, AE, V. Closed Nov–Apr.

Findus House is the family-run, working farm of Mary O'Sullivan and her lively family, as well as winner of the coveted Farmhouse of the Year award. Guest rooms are pleasant, and Mary has won much praise for her dinners; salmon dishes are her specialty, with wine and Irish coffee available at a small extra charge. The O'Sullivan children not only help at table and around the farm, but in the evenings they often join guests to entertain them with music, song, and dance. A delightful base for exploring this part of West Cork, Findus Farm is 30 miles west of Cork city, 24 miles south of Killarney, 3 miles south of the main Cork-Killarney road (N22), and 19 miles northeast of Gougane Barra.

Self-Catering

Russalougha House

Dunisky, Lissarda, Co. Cork. ☎ **026/42339.** 2-bedroom apartment (sleeps 3). Weekly rates Apr–June and Sept IR£175 ($280); July–Aug IR£195 ($312); rest of year IR£150 ($240). No credit cards. Just off N22 (Cork-Killarney road). Cork 20 miles, Killarney 30 miles. Good bus service.

In a superb hillside setting overlooking the River Lee, Mrs. Sara McSweeney's two-bedroom apartment has lovely mountain views, too. Recently renovated, the

Readers Recommend

St. Anne's, *Clonakilty Road, Bandon, Co. Cork.* ☎ 023/44239. *Author's Note: Numerous readers have written to recommend St. Anne's, praising the 200-year-old house that has been restored to its original graciousness by Mrs. Anne Buckley. Bandon is 20 miles from Cork city, and an ideal base for touring West Cork. All guest rooms have private baths.*

apartment is a comfortable, relaxed base for day trips. Readers have praised the McSweeney's for help in planning sightseeing forays. Although there is a Stanley fire in the living room, she will gladly arrange a turf fire on request.

Worth a Splurge/A Gracious Country House

✪ Assolas Country House

Kanturk, Co. Cork. ☎ **029/50015.** 9 rms, all with bath. IR£40–IR£52 ($64–$83.20) per person; IR£15 ($24) single supplement. (Rates include breakfast.) ACC, AE, DC, MC, V. Closed Nov–Feb.

Set in beautifully landscaped grounds, this 17th-century Queen Anne–style house is surrounded by 100 acres of parkland, and its flower gardens have won the prestigious Ireland Garden Award. Towering old trees and green lawns lead down to the edge of the Blackwater River (where guests fish free). There are spacious public rooms and a large rumpus room with a stone fireplace. Upstairs, guest rooms come in a variety of sizes and shapes, all done up in country fabrics. There's a comfortable, relaxed air about the place that's the direct result of Eleanor and Hugh Bourke's gracious hospitality. Dining is superb (the restaurant is recognized internationally; see "Where to Eat," below). Guests have access to tennis, boating, and croquet. Assolas is 42 miles northwest of Cork city, signposted from the Cork-Killarney road (N72), approximately 3 miles from Kanturk town.

Where to Eat

✪ An Sugan

Wolfe Tone St., Clonakilty. ☎ **023/33498.** Bar food IR£2–IR£6 ($3.20–$9.60); fixed-price meal IR£6 ($12.80) at lunch, IR£14 ($22.40) at dinner; Tourist Menu available. ACC, MC, V. Daily 12:30–2:30pm and 6–10pm; bar food daily 12:30–10:30pm. Closed Good Friday, Christmas Day. BAR FOOD/SEAFOOD/VEGETARIAN/IRISH.

This old-style, homey pub and restaurant 33 miles southwest of Cork on N71 features a fascinating collection of bits and pieces of Irish life. It makes an ideal stop for bar food that's good enough and filling enough to serve as a main meal (I particularly like the Bantry Bay mussels). Upstairs, the restaurant has a lobster tank and serves lunch and dinner at the higher prices listed above.

Assolas Country House

Kanturk. ☎ **029/50015.** Reservations required. Fixed-price dinner IR£27 ($43.20). Service charge 10%. ACC, AE, DC, MC, V. Mar–Nov, daily 7–9pm. SEAFOOD/VEGETARIAN/TRADITIONAL.

The dining room at Assolas House (see "Where to Stay," above, for a full description) is a real gem, with Queen Anne period furnishings, Dresden china, mahogany tables, and a comfortable lounge for before- or after-dinner drinks. The pâté maison is homemade, and the menu always features homegrown fresh vegetables, and often offers salmon fresh from the Blackwater. The Irish coffee is excellent,

Readers Recommend

Mary Ann's Bar & Restaurant, Castletownshend, Skibbereen, Co. Cork ☎ 028/36146. *"This cozy, old-fashioned bar-cum-restaurant was one of our favorite dining experiences in Ireland. I had a superb seafood platter starter and my husband loved the hot crab toes served in a light cream garlic sauce. But we both left raving about our main course of monkfish Mary Ann médaillons in a creamy wine sauce lightly flavored with Pernod."* —Eleanor Diskin, Philadelphia, PA

Dunworley Restaurant, Butlerstown, Co. Cork. *"The point of my note is to ask that you alert readers to this charming place with good food and moderate prices."*

—Peter Crandall, New Haven, CT

and there's a good, extensive wine list. To all that, the Bourke family add friendly service that's of the same high standards as their meals. Assolas Country House is 42 miles northwest of Cork city, signposted from the Cork-Killarney road (N72), and approximately 3 miles east of Kanturk town.

Dun Mhuire

Kilbarry Rd., Dunmanway. ☎ **023/45162.** Fixed-price dinner IR£17 ($27.20). ACC, MC, V. June–Sept, daily 7–11pm; other months, Wed–Sat 7–11pm. SEAFOOD/VEGETARIAN.

This family-run restaurant specializes in freshly cooked food, with a heavy emphasis on seafood. The service is friendly and efficient, and only the freshest produce is used. Dun Mhuire is 37 miles west of Cork via N72, with signposted turnoffs, and 20 miles east of Bantry via R586.

✪ Leap Inn

Leap. ☎ **028/33307.** Main courses IR£8–IR£12 ($12.80–$19.20); bar food IR£1.50–IR£5 ($2.40–$8); fixed-price five-course dinner IR£12 ($19.20). No credit cards. Dinner daily 6:30–9:30pm; bar food daily 10am–7pm. BAR FOOD/SEAFOOD/TRADITIONAL.

Excellent bar food is served here all day, making it an ideal lunch or snack stop. At dinnertime, the homey dining room in this little country inn is a relaxing venue for a meal of the freshest local produce and seafood just out of local waters. Try their Galley Head prawns—delicious! Leap Inn is on the main Cork-Bantry road (N71), 50 miles southwest of Cork city, 43 miles southwest of Kinsale, and 15 miles southeast of Bantry.

3 Bantry, Glengarriff & the Beara Peninsula

BANTRY

The little town of Bantry (named for an ancient Celtic chieftain) sits at the head of lovely Bantry Bay, surrounded by hills. The 21-mile-long inlet of the sea apparently had great appeal to the French, who twice (in 1689 and 1796) selected it for attempted naval invasions of Ireland. One relic of the ill-fated Wolfe Tone expedition, the French frigate *La Surveilante,* lies in a remarkably good state of preservation at the bottom of Bantry Bay, and work has begun to raise it from the deep. A 1796 French Armada Intrepretive Centre has been installed at Bantry House.

WHAT TO SEE & DO

You'll see fishing boats tied up right at the foot of the town, and if you elect to stop over here, your B&B hostess will be able to arrange a trip on the water with

Ken Minehan. During the summer, 1 1/2-hour **cruises on the bay** take you past Whiddy Island and its oil terminal and castle ruins. Sea-angling trips can also be arranged. For schedules and rates, contact Ken Minehan (☎ 027/50318).

Bantry House

Bantry. ☎ **027/50047.** Admission IR£3 ($4.80) adults, IR£1.75 ($2.80) students and seniors, children under 12 free. There's no charge to visit the grounds.

Bantry House, on the southern outskirts of the town, sits in a magnificent demesne and is the ancestral home of the earls of Bantry. Beautifully landscaped lawns and gardens slope downward from the front of the Georgian mansion that looks out over the bay. Inside is an impressive collection of European antiques, paintings, sculptures, and other items that caught the fancy of globe-trotting earls over the centuries. A tearoom and a craft shop are entered through a separate building. The fascinating French Armada Interpretive Centre on the premises holds a wealth of mementos of the disastrous invasion of 1796 that bring the event to vivid life.

1796 Bantry French Armada Exhibition Centre

East Stables, Bantry House, Bantry. ☎ **027/51796.** Admission IR£3 ($4.80) adults, IR£2 ($3.20) seniors and students, IR£1 ($1.60) children under 14. Open daily 10am–6pm.

It was to have been a glorious victory—the British would at last be sent packing and Ireland would regain its freedom. That, at least, was Theobold Wolfe Tone's scenario in 1796, when he and his United Irishmen followers persuaded the French government to send some fifty warships and 15,000 foot soldiers to Ireland's southwest coast. A great plan—and like all great plans, subject to the vagaries of nature and man. Powerful Atlantic storms sank ten ships, fleet communications broke down, and the invasion simply never happened. Two centuries later, the remains of one of the sunken ships, the frigate *Surveilante,* send the imagination soaring back to that tumultuous time in Irish history.

Nearby Attractions

There are lovely ✪ **scenic drives and walks** around Bantry, one of the most spectacular being to the top of Seskin Mountain, where there's a lookout with incredible views of Bantry Bay. The antiquity of the region's settlement is attested to by many stone circles, standing stones, and cairns dating to the Bronze Age.

One of Ireland's most beautiful spots, **Gougane Barra** (which means "St. Finbar's Cleft") is a still, dark, romantic lake a little northeast of the Pass of Keimaneigh 15 miles northeast of Bantry off T64 (also well signposted on the Macroom-Glengarriff road). The River Lee rises here, and all around are deeply wooded mountains. St. Finbar founded a monastery here, supposedly on the small island connected by a causeway which now holds a tiny chapel (nothing remains of the good saint's 6th-century community) and eight small circular cells, dating to the early 1700s, as well as a modern chapel. Its isolation and connection with St. Finbar made this a natural refuge for Irish worshipers during Penal Law days when they were forbidden to hold mass and turned to the out-of-doors for their services. Today Gougane Barra is a national forest park, and there are signposted walks and drives through the wooded hills. There's a small admission charge per car to enter the park.

SHOPPING

Philip J. Dix & Co., Ltd., on New Street (☎ 027/50112), has an exceptionally good range of Waterford and Galway crystal, Belleek, Irish-made pewter, silver, and a host of other quality giftwear.

Between Bantry and Glengarriff, on the edge of the little town of Ballylickey, you'll see an unpretentious sign in a curve of the road reading ARTIST'S STUDIO, PAINTINGS OF IRISH SCENES. That modest sign, however, gives little indication of the fine paintings you'll find inside ✪ **Raymond Klee's studio** (☎ 027/50157), which adjoins his home; the Welsh-born artist has lived and worked all over the world and has won coveted awards from the French Salon and the Fine Arts Guild (in England). He and his talented wife, Florence, have settled here to devote his art to depicting the very scenes that have won your own heart. His landscape canvases are remarkable in the way they capture the elusive colors and sweeping majesty of the Irish landscape. Sunsets over a dune-rimmed strand, storm skies that set fishermen scurrying to bring curraghs to safety ashore, and graceful configurations of sun-touched clouds are there to perpetuate your memories of those same scenes. Stone-enclosed fishing harbors and mountain stretches are other subjects, and hanging on the walls of his studio are portraits of that craggy Irish farmer and fisherman you were talking to just last night over a friendly pint. Prices are surprisingly low, and there are sizes small enough to wrap securely and take back home easily, as well as larger canvases that might well become the focal point of a Stateside room. Whether or not you buy a painting, stop by to see these marvelous works and chat with an interesting and talented artist.

After Dark

If you're in Bantry in the evening, there's usually ballad singing and dancing at **Crowley's Bar,** on the Square, in the summer, and the **Bantry Bay Hotel** has entertainment every night (special Irish nights during the summer).

Where to Stay

Shangri-La

Bantry, Co. Cork. ☎ **027/50244.** 6 rms, 4 with bath. IR£22 ($35.20) single without bath; IR£16 ($25.60) per person sharing without bath; IR£2 ($3.20) per person additional with bath. 20% reduction for children. (Rates include breakfast.) Dinner IR£15 ($24) extra. ACC, MC, V. Closed Christmas. Private car park.

The Shangri-La is a modern bungalow perched on a hill on the western edge of town (signposted from N71, the Bantry-Glengarriff road) overlooking Bantry Bay. The glass-enclosed front porch affords gorgeous panoramic views of the bay, and chairs are often set out on the beautifully landscaped lawn for guests to savor spectacular sunsets. Guest rooms are comfortably furnished and each is decorated around a different color; all have tea/coffeemakers and two have lovely semi-poster beds. Angela Muckley knows the area well and loves helping her guests plan their time here. A former president of the Town & Country Homes Association, she is keenly interested in tourism and provides a helpful printed guide to attractions in the area. She is also a superior cook and her evening meals are memorable, with wine available. For breakfast, she offers guests a choice of the traditional Irish menu or pancakes or crumpets and honey (a nice change). There's central heating and a private car park. They also have bicycles for rent.

Worth a Splurge

✪ Sea View House Hotel

Ballylickey, Bantry, Co. Cork. ☎ **027/50073** or 50462. Fax 027/51555. 18 rms, all with bath. TV TEL. IR£35–IR£110 ($56–$176) per person, depending on type of room and season. Special reduction for children. (Rates include breakfast.) ACC, AE, MC, V. Closed Mid-Nov to mid-Mar.

Set back from the road in spacious grounds, Sea View House is a sparkling white three-story house built back in 1888. The deft hand of Miss Kathleen O'Sullivan, owner and manager, can be seen in every room, where antiques are placed for convenient use. Every room is different in size and shape and is furnished in traditional style and fairly shouts "gracious" (tea/coffeemakings are available upon request); all have hairdryers. There's a lovely cocktail bar and a library, and the dining room is the setting for exceptional meals (see "Where to Eat," below).

Westlodge Hotel

Bantry, Co. Cork. ☎ **027/50360.** Fax 027/50438. 90 rms, with bath. TV TEL. Rates IR£41–IR£55 ($65.60–$88) single; IR£35–IR£45 ($56–$72) per person sharing, depending on season. AE, MC, V.

Set on a hillside on the outskirts of Bantry on the eastern edge of town, this modern hotel is surrounded by extensive landscaped grounds and wooded walks. There's a leisure center with heated pool, squash courts, sauna, gym, tennis, pitch-and-putt, and children's play area (during summer months, there are organized activities for children). The Saddlers Tavern Lounge offers regular entertainment during the summer season.

Where to Eat

✪ Blairs Cove Restaurant

Blairs Cove, Durrus. ☎ **027/61127.** Reservations required. Fixed-price dinner IR£18–IR£24 ($28.80–$38.40). Service charge 10%. ACC, AE, DC, MC, V. Tues–Sat 7–9:30pm. SEAFOOD/INTERNATIONAL.

About eight miles south of Bantry on Mizen Head Peninsula, Blairs Cove is the loving creation of Phillippe and Sabine De Mey, who have converted the stone stables of a 250-year-old mansion overlooking Dunmanus Bay in West Cork into a casually elegant restaurant. In summer, meals are served on the covered terrace overlooking the courtyard. Specialties are fresh seafood, lamb, and beef grilled over a big oak-log fire in the dining room, and there's an exceptionally good wine list. Candlelight and soft piano music complete the romantic setting.

The Hungry Trout Seafood Bistro

Glengarriff Rd., Bantry. ☎ **027/51337** or 66227. Main courses IR£7–IR£14 ($11.20–$22.40). No service charge. ACC, MC, V. Easter–Sept, daily 6–10pm. Just west of town center. SEAFOOD/TRADITIONAL/VEGETARIAN.

Jane and Nigel Bevan (he's the chef) have chosen an elevated site with magnificent views over Bantry Bay and the mountains of the Beara Peninsula for this culinary gem. Utilizing only the freshest of local seafoods and produce, they bring to table dishes such as mussels provençale, scallops à la cacciatora, fillet steaks in a selection of sauces, and a choice of vegetarian dishes. Lovely ambience and good value.

✪ O'Connor's Seafood Restaurant

The Square. ☎ **027/50221.** Main courses IR£11–IR£15 ($17.60–$24); bar food IR£2–IR£9 ($3.20–$14.40). ACC, MC, V. Bar food daily noon–6pm; dinner daily 6–9:30pm. Closed Sun–Mon Nov–Mar; Sun lunch Apr–Oct. SEAFOOD/TRADITIONAL/BAR FOOD.

Matt and Ann O'Connor run this cozy pub and restaurant, and their seafood dishes are truly special (try the mussels Cordon Bleu). So keen are the O'Connors on freshness that they feature a live lobster and oyster tank. There are also good local lamb and steak for nonseafood lovers, and salads, sandwiches, shepherd's pie, and the like are on tap in the bar.

Sea View House Hotel

Ballylickey. ☎ **027/50073** or 50462. Reservations recommended. Fixed-price dinner IR£23 ($36.80). ACC, AE, MC, V. Mid-Mar to mid-Nov, daily 7–9:30pm. SEAFOOD/TRADITIONAL.

Sea View is known for its excellent dining room, which has won several food awards. Seafood, as you might expect in this location, is fresh from local waters, and lamb, beef, veal, and the like are selected from local sources. Service here is both friendly and professional. This is one of the nicest dinner spots in the Bantry-Glengarriff area.

GLENGARRIFF

Glengarriff is set in a beautiful, mountain-ringed cove on Bantry Bay, and you're not likely to get out of town without taking the boat trip out to **Garinish Island,** about a mile offshore—bold boatmen have been known to stop cars in midroad to hawk the trip. As in Killarney, however, I urge you to listen to their good-humored pitch and let yourself be hawked. The lovely little island is a riot of subtropical plants, and there's a landscaped Italian garden you shouldn't miss. George Bernard Shaw loved the place and wrote portions of *Saint Joan* here. The cost is nominal, and both time and money are well spent. It's worth a stop at some of the **craft shops** you'll see lining the streets. I've found good values here over the years.

Where to Stay

Sea Front

Glengarriff, Co. Cork. ☎ **027/63079.** 3 rms, none with bath. IR£18.50 ($29.60) single; IR£13.50 ($21.60) per person sharing. 25% reduction for children. (Rates include breakfast.) No credit cards. Closed Nov–Mar.

As its name implies, Sea Front looks out over the harbor. Mrs. Ann Guerin knows the area well and is always happy to help her guests plan sightseeing, fishing, or other activities. Her centrally heated house is comfortably furnished and has a nice decor; all guest rooms have sinks. She'll prepare an evening meal, given enough notice.

THE BEARA PENINSULA

The Beara Peninsula—a 30-mile-long, mountainous finger of land between Bantry Bay and the Kenmare River—has Glengarriff at its head. The Peninsula encompasses the Cork-Kerry county border running along the Caha mountain range, and its northwest corner falls within County Kerry. The drive around the peninsula is a pleasant day trip and can easily be a three- or four-hour detour en route from Glengarriff to Killarney. I must warn you, however, you may well find this wild, sparsely populated spot so appealing that you may have to stop and linger at least one night.

What to See & Do

From Glengarriff, the road follows the shoreline of Bantry Bay, winding along the rocky coastal strip at the foot of the Caha Mountains. At Ardrigole Bridge, the spectacular **Healy Pass** crosses the mountains and is an alternative (and shorter) route to Kenmare and Killarney. Farther south along Bantry Bay, the long **Bere Island** lies just offshore, with regular ferry service from **Castletownbere.** If time permits, you may want to drive the 15 miles farther south to the cable car that connects **Dursey Island** with the mainland. The ruins of **Dunboy Castle** (destroyed in 1602) lie two miles outside Castletownbere, and the road continues south to Black Ball Head before turning to the northwest to reach Allihies through a gap in the hills. This was once a rich copper district, and the **sea views** are absolutely magnificent. From Allihies, the road leads north along the Kenmare River through rugged scenery to the little villages of Eyeries and Lauragh, the northern end of Healy Pass, and on to Kenmare and Killarney. **Antiquities** to look for along the way are the mass rock north of Allihies, the Ogham stone in Ballycrovane, near Eyeries, that is believed to be the tallest in western Europe, and the stone circle in Canfie on the Lauragh road.

Where to Stay

Castletownbere

Realt-Na-Mara

Castletownbere, Co. Cork. ☎ **027/70101.** 5 rms, 4 with bath. IR£14 ($22.40) per person without bath, IR£16 ($25.60) with bath. (Rates include breakfast.) Dinner IR£14 ($22.40) extra. No credit cards.

This attractive modern home perches on the high side of the main road into Castletownbere, with a stone terrace overlooking Bantry Bay. Mrs. Mary Donovan opens spacious guest rooms, some of which have views of the bay, others overlooking the mountainside. There are two family rooms, central heating, and plenty of private parking space. Mrs. Donovan is a gracious hostess, her home is spotless, and when I visited, there were lambs sporting about on the front lawn.

Bere Island

Harbour View

Bere Island, Beara, Co. Cork. ☎ **027/75011.** 5 rms, 3 with bath. IR£14–IR£16 ($22.40–$25.60) per person sharing. 30% reduction for children. (Rates include breakfast.) Dinner IR£12 ($19.20) extra. No credit cards. Ferry: From Castletownbere (☎ 027/75009 for sailing times).

Mrs. Ann Sullivan's large two-story house overlooks Berehaven Harbour, near the Gleanns Sailing School. Fishing, golf, and mountain walks are other activities in the vicinity. Guest rooms are attractive and comfortably furnished, and there's central heating. Mrs. Sullivan is well known for her excellent evening meals, with the freshest of seafoods her specialty.

Adrigole

✪ Bayview Farmhouse

Faha, Adrigole, Beara (Bantry), Co. Cork. ☎ **027/60026.** 5 rms, none with bath. IR£15.50 ($24.80) single; IR£13.50 ($21.60) per person sharing. 25% reduction for children. (Rates include breakfast.) Dinner IR£12 ($19.20) extra. No credit cards. Closed Nov–Apr.

This bright, cheerful home overlooking Bantry Bay—nine miles from Glengarriff, two miles from the foot of Healy Pass—is presided over by Mrs. Sheila O'Sullivan. Rooms are spacious and well appointed, and there's a pony and a donkey and trap (riding cart) for use by guests at no charge.

Where to Eat

Castletownbere

✪ Old Cottage Restaurant

Derrymihan West, Castletownbere. ☎ **027/70430.** Main courses IR£9–IR£16 ($14.40–$25.60). ACC, MC, V. Daily 12:30–2pm and 6–9pm. Closed Tues in winter months. SEAFOOD/CONTINENTAL/VEGETARIAN.

Readers Recommend

The Lighthouse Bar, Allihies, Beara Peninsula, Co. Cork. *"Among a scattering of homes, we discovered a craft shop in Allihies. Deidre McCot is the inspiration for reviving native crafts, and she took us to the nearby Lighthouse, a gem overseen by Mary Sullivan. Mary's homemade soups are fantastic, homemade soda bread delicious, and we were served fresh salmon sandwiches. Fresh lobster is served in season, and prices are very reasonable. We highly recommend both craft shop and the Lighthouse."*

—Virginia DeArmond, Exton, PA

Vincent and Lidy van Nulck brought their young family to the Beara Peninsula from Amsterdam, and their handsome restaurant has drawn raves from a regular clientele as well as visiting tourists. Lunch usually consists of soup, sandwiches, salads, and burgers. At dinner, chef Vincent uses fish and shellfish from nearby waters, as well as salmon, lobster, steak, lamb, and pork to create his dishes (black sole pan-fried on the bone is a standout). Wine is available by the glass or bottle.

13 Killarney & Its Lakes

Its ancient Irish name is *Cill Airne* (Church of the Sloe); it was aptly described by the poet Moore as "Heaven's Reflex"; the sheer perfection of that beauty has defied the best efforts of many a writer, poet, and artist to capture its essence; and your first glimpse of the lakes in their magnificent setting is certain to leave you wonderstruck. Nor will that wonder be diminished by repeated viewings, for the mercurial nature of this splendid landscape colors its grandeur with whimsical, ever-shifting nuances of sun and cloud and mist.

As for the inhabitants of Killarney, get set for a treat—they're a marvelous combination of wit, independence, pride, and hospitality in a special blend all their own, like no other in the country.

1 Killarney

190 miles SW of Dublin, 54 miles NW of Cork, 68 miles SW of Limerick, 21 miles W of Kenmare, 42 miles SE of Dingle

And what of Killarney town? Well, it was a quiet little country market town until a visiting Englishman named Arthur Young discovered it in the 18th century and told the rest of the world about this natural beauty spot. Since then, of course, the rest of the world has arrived on Killarney's doorstep in droves, demanding accommodations, eateries, guides, entertainment, and a good deal more than a quiet little country market town could be expected to provide.

In response to all those visitors, Killarney has bred some of the best—and most entertaining—sightseeing guides in the world. As for accommodations, there are scads of high-quality, low-priced B&Bs and guesthouses as well as some pretty elegant luxury hotels whose prices are high, but not exorbitant. Meals can be in any number of inexpensive and charming restaurants, in moderately priced establishments that bring near-gourmet dishes to table, or you can be as lavish as you please in the upper-price range in one of the hotels. There's also good shopping in Killarney, with competitive prices, well-stocked shops, and a number of craft workshops. As for entertainment, there are good singing pubs and hotel cabarets, and—if your timing is right—the Killarney races. Then of course, there's all that magnificent scenery that doesn't cost a cent.

Right here, I'd like to dispel what seems to be a very popular myth about Killarney. It is, I grant you, more "commercial" than any other town in Ireland, but—and this is what I'd like to put to rest—if this is a "tourist trap," then the world could do with a few more like it! Sure, there are jarveys lined up ad infinitum, each hawking his own jaunting car ride. But no matter which car you climb aboard, you can do so in the sure knowledge that fees are carefully controlled (so you won't be ripped off) and you'll hear at least one good story (like the one about the lad who plunged into the Devil's Punchbowl and was never heard from until his poor mother got a postcard from Australia asking would she please send along a change of clothes).

What I'm trying to get across is that you'll get your money's worth in Killarney. And you'll get it from some of Ireland's friendliest, most ebullient citizens. From your landlady to your waiter or waitress to the clerk behind a shop counter to your jarvey or boatman, everyone seems delighted that you've come and can't wait to see that you have a good time. Commercial? Well, I'll grant you there's more than a touch of that, but a *tourist trap?* Not in my book!

ORIENTATION

GETTING THERE **By Bus and Train** There is bus service from most points in Ireland, and train service from Dublin, Limerick, Galway, and Cork. The bus and train station is off East Avenue (across from the Great Southern Hotel). For bus information call 064/34777. For train information call 064/31067 on the 24-hour "Talking Timetable" line 066/26555.

DEPARTING For those heading north to Limerick or Galway, there is the quick inland route via Abbeyfeale and Newcastle West (N21), the long and lovely coastal drive along the Shannon estuary (N69), or a delightful ferry alternative that shortens both of these routes. For highlights of the Shannon estuary drive along N69, see Section 3 of Chapter 15.

If, like me, you fancy a ferry ride anytime one comes along, you can take the Shannon car-ferry from Tarbert over to Killimer in County Clare, about a 30-mile drive into Limerick (see "Tralee and North Kerry" in Chapter 14). The crossing takes 20 minutes aboard the *Shannon Willow* or *Shannon Heather,* and from April through September there are 30 sailings per day, beginning at 7am and ending at 9:30pm (first sailing on Sunday at 9am); from October through March the last sailing is at 7:30pm. Departures from Tarbert, County Kerry, are on the half hour, and from Killimer, County Clare, on the hour; during peak holiday periods, there are half-hourly sailings from each side. For your car and all passengers, you'll pay IR£6 ($9.60) one way, IR£9 ($14.40) round-trip. Those on foot pay IR£1.50 ($2.40) one way, IR£2 ($3.20) round-trip.

VISITOR INFORMATION The Tourist Office is located in the Town Hall on Main Street (☎ 064/31633), open July to September, Monday through Friday from 9am to 8pm, and on Saturday from 10am to 1pm; others months, Monday through Friday from 9:15am to 5:30pm.

I highly recommend *Where Killarney,* a locally published monthly magazine with comprehensive practical information on Killarney and the entire region as well as detailed self-guided tours. Look for it in accommodations.

SPECIAL EVENTS Killarney is an ideal base from which to be a part of one of Ireland's major annual events, the ✪ **Rose of Tralee International Festival,** held in Tralee, just 20 miles to the north. For six days and nights in late August the competition is fierce to see which of the international beauties gathered in Tralee best fits the time-honored description "lovely and fair as the rose of the summer." The Rose of Tralee International Festival, however, is a far cry from other beauty pageants. This festival is one of lighthearted fun and frolic, with parades, pipe bands, street entertainment, interfestival singing competitions for the **Folk Festival of Ireland** (which takes place at the same time!), and, finally, the crowning of the Rose.

There are usually several package deals that cover transportation and accommodations; details can be obtained from the General Secretary, Festival of Kerry Office, 5 Lower Castle Street, Tralee, County Kerry. If you're making your own arrangements, be sure to do it well in advance, whether you plan to stay in Tralee or in Killarney, 20 miles to the south.

In mid-August, Killorglin lets its hair down in three days of what many Irish call sheer madness disguised under the name of the ✪ **Puck Fair.** It has been held every year since 1613, and things get off to a right rowdy start when a tremendous male (or puck) goat is hauled up to a high platform in the square and crowned as King of the Fair. What follows is a sort of carnival/country fair/free-for-all, as most pubs stay open around the clock, and there's all sorts of street entertainment, and over on the green, some pretty serious horse and cattle trading. Just how all this began is a matter of dispute: Some say a goat bleated to alert a shepherd boy of approaching enemy forces and he, in turn, alerted the town about impending attack. Traditionally it is a gathering place for the country's traveling people, who come to drive some hard bargains in the horse-swapping business, catch up with travelers' gossip, and indulge in nonstop revelry.

TOWN LAYOUT Killarney is a small town, easy to find your way around. Main Street is its chief artery, and becomes High Street at its northern end. New Street runs to the west of Main Street, and Plunkett Street (which becomes College Street) runs east.

GETTING AROUND **By Bicycle** Cycling is easy around Killarney Town. O'Neill Cycles, Plunkett St. (☎ 064/31970, fax 064/35689) has rental bikes: they cost IR£3 to IR£4 ($4.80 to $6.40) for a half day, IR£5 to IR£7 ($8 to $11.20) per day.

By Bus There's no local bus service, but Bus Eireann runs several good day trips to nearby locations, including the Ring of Kerry and the Dingle Peninsula.

By Taxi Taxi ranks are at the railway station and in College Square, and taxis are unmetered. Phone 31331 for hire.

On Foot It's easy walking in town, with many beauty spots within longish walking distance from the town center.

By Car Killarney's streets are narrow and a little nerve-wracking when traffic is heavy, but there's a good network of wide major roads outside the city center. There's a large municipal parking lot (entrance from New Street) in the center of town back of the Town Hall, another on East Avenue (across from the railway station), and a third at the intersection of High Street and New Road.

FAST FACTS: KILLARNEY

Area Code The telephone prefix for the area is 064.

Emergencies Dial 999 and ask for the service you require (police, medical, fire).

Post Office The General Post Office is on New Street, open Monday through Saturday from 9am to 5:30pm; Wednesday 9:30am–5:30pm.

Killarney

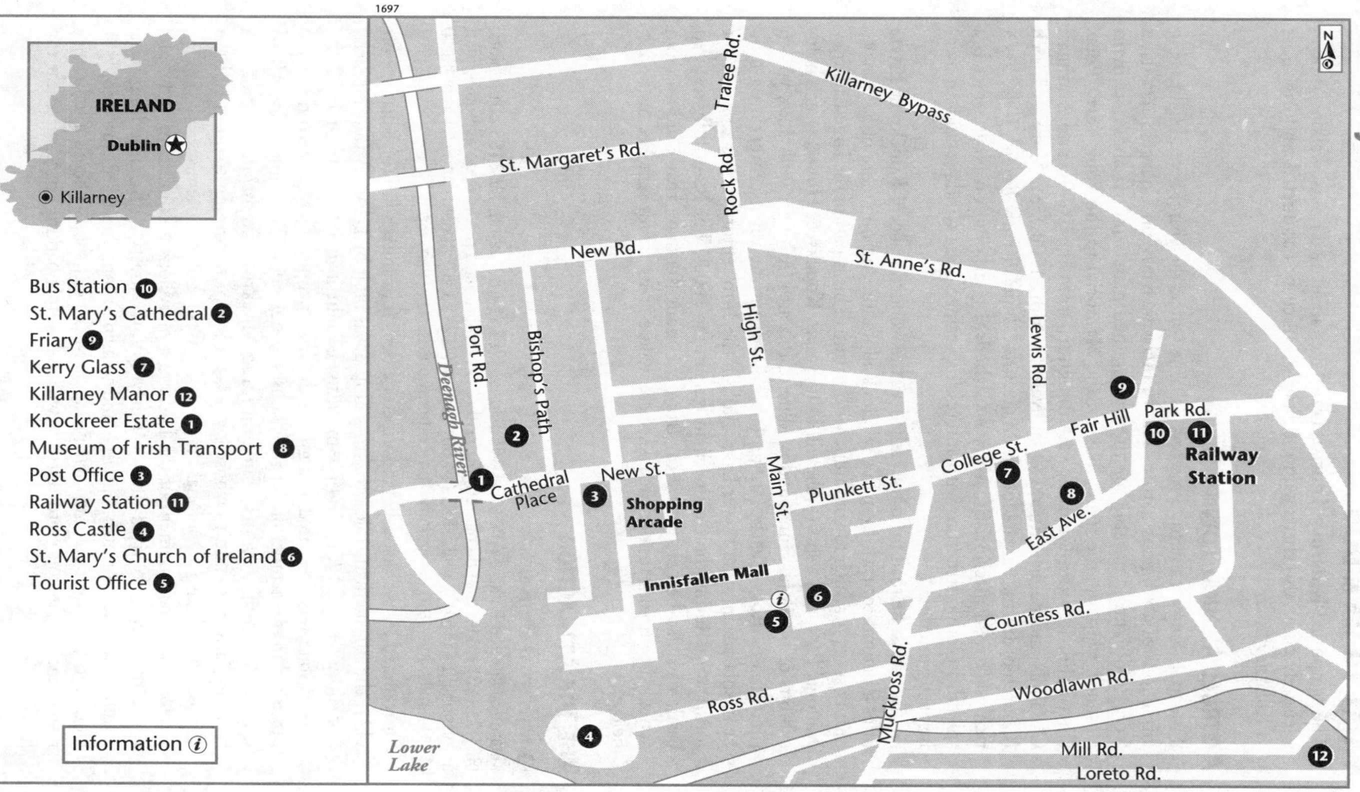

1697
IRELAND
Dublin
Killarney
Bus Station 10
St. Mary's Cathedral 2
Friary 9
Kerry Glass 7
Killarney Manor 12
Knockreer Estate 1
Museum of Irish Transport 8
Post Office 3
Railway Station 11
Ross Castle 4
St. Mary's Church of Ireland 6
Tourist Office 5
Information
Tralee Rd.
Killarney Bypass
St. Margaret's Rd.
Rock Rd.
New Rd.
St. Anne's Rd.
High St.
Lewis Rd.
Port Rd.
Bishop's Path
Deenagh River
Fair Hill
Park Rd.
Railway Station
College St.
New St.
Cathedral Place
Plunkett St.
Main St.
Shopping Arcade
East Ave.
Innisfallen Mall
Countess Rd.
Muckross Rd.
Woodlawn Rd.
Ross Rd.
Lower Lake
Mill Rd.
Loreto Rd.

WHAT TO SEE & DO

The signposted **Killarney Tourist Trail** takes about two hours' walking time at a leisurely pace. Also check with the Tourist Office for **conducted walking tours** of Killarney town.

A STROLL AROUND TOWN

True to its long ecclesiastical history, Killarney offers the visitor several sightseeing attractions of a religious nature. The **Franciscan friary** on College Street dates from 1860 and is notable for the fine stained-glass window above its main entrance. Opposite the friary, look for the **Memorial to the Four Kerry Poets** (Pierce Ferriter and Geoffrey O'Donoghue, from the 1600s, and Aodhgan O'Rahilly and Eoghán Ruadh O'Sullivan, from the 1700s). **St. Mary's Church** (Church of Ireland) at the foot of Main Street, built in Early English style, has a richly adorned interior. **St. Mary's Cathedral** (Catholic) on New Street is a splendid Gothic structure with interesting stained-glass windows and an awe-inspiring interior.

Just across the road from the cathedral, the wooded walks of **Knockreer Estate** offer a natural contrast to man's religious adoration and one more of Killarney's beauty spots in which to commune with nature. This is part of the large Killarney National Park, and a short walk will bring you to **Knockreer House,** which holds exhibits of the flora, fauna, and wildlife of this area. A longer walk takes you to the ruins of **Ross Castle** (about 1¹/₂ miles from the town center) on a long peninsula out into the Lower Lake. Built in the 14th century, it was a prominent fortification during the Cromwellian wars in the 1600s. The beautifully restored castle can also be reached by car from the main Kenmare road, and you can actually begin your tour of the lakes here, where boats are for rent (see Section 2, below).

THE TOP ATTRACTION

✪ Muckross House, Gardens, and Traditional Farms

Killarney National Park. ☎ **064/31440.** House IR£3 ($4.80) adult; IR£2 ($3.20) seniors; IR£1.25 ($2) students and children; IR£7.50 ($12) family. Farm prices same as house; joint admission IR£4 ($6.40) adult; IR£3 ($4.80) seniors; IR£2 ($3.20) students and children; IR£10 ($16) family. July–Aug, daily 9am–7pm; other months, daily 9am–6pm.

Surrounded by marvelously landscaped gardens four miles south of Killarney off N71, the Elizabethan-style Muckross House was built by Henry Arthur Herbert, a wealthy Kerry MP, in 1843. Americans bought it in 1911, and in 1932 the entire estate was presented as a gift to the Irish people. The first two floors are furnished in the manner of the great houses of Ireland, while its upper floors hold some fascinating exhibits. The adjoining Muckross Traditional Farms is a working farm community whose everyday life depicts farming traditions of the 1930s. There is also a National Park Visitors Centre on the premises.

Housed in the basement of the house is a marvelous folk museum and crafts shops that bring to vivid life the Kerry country lifestyle of a time long past. Exhibits include a printshop, dairy, and weaving shop. You'll see craftspeople at work and you can purchase their products in the gift shop. There's a light, airy restaurant off the courtyard. Drivers will find ample parking space very near the house.

More Attractions Nearby

Walkers will be able to reach the following on foot, and, of course, jaunting cars are available for nonwalkers.

Three miles outside Killarney on the main Kenmare road (N71), the ruins of **Muckross Abbey** are about a 10-minute walk from Muckross House. Dating from 1448, it occupied the site of an even earlier ecclesiastical establishment, and the ruins are in remarkably good condition. The Abbey was the last resting place for Kerry's four great Gaelic poets: Piaras Feirtéar (Pierce Ferriter, 1616–1653) is buried in the churchyard, and inside the Abbey are the remains of Geoffrey O'Donoghue (1620–1690), Aodhgan O'Rahilly (1670–1726), and Eoghán Ruadh O'Sullivan (1748–1784). The tomb of The McCarthy Mór, King of Munster, is in the chancel.

About a mile beyond Muckross House, signposted from the main Kenmare road, the 60-foot-high ✪ **Torc Waterfall** sits in a beautiful wooded area and is reached by way of a scenic footpath that continues up the top of the falls, where there are magnificent views of the lakes.

In the opposite direction, three miles from the town center, the **Prince of Peace Church** is in Fossa, on the main Ring of Kerry road (R562). It was designed and built by men and women from the four provinces of Ireland, and its back wall is glass, bringing the wondrous beauty of mountains and lakes into focus as an integral part of religious worship. Catholics will find mass in this beautiful building a very special experience.

SPORTS & OUTDOOR ACTIVITIES

Check with the Tourist Office or the free *Weekly Killarney* to see if anything is on at Fitzgerald Stadium on Lewis Road, the venue for Sunday **hurling and Gaelic football matches.** Killarney **horseracing meets** occur in May and July, and it's worth juggling your schedule to catch them—the town assumes a "country fair" air.

You may go **swimming** in any of the lakes without charge, and you'll only need a license to go **fishing** for salmon—none needed to go after all those lovely brown trout. O'Neill's Fishing Tackle Shop, 6 Plunkett St. (☎ **064/31970**), can furnish licenses, rental rods, tackle, and bait; Donie Brosnan, at the Handy Store on Kenmare Place, can also fix you up with bait and up-to-the-minute information about the best fishing spots. There are excellent championship **golf courses** in and near Killarney (the Tourist Office can furnish a complete list), and most have clubs, caddies, and caddy-cars available at the clubhouse.

SHOPPING

An Art Gallery

✪ Frank Lewis Gallery

6 Bridewell Lane. ☎ **064/31108.**

This excellent small gallery is a welcome addition to the Killarney scene. Bridewell Lane is entered from New Street near the General Post Office, and it's worth the walk just to take a look at this interesting little lane housing a variety of artisans. It's the only one in Killarney where all the more-than-a-century-old cottages are still lived in. Frank features leading and emerging Irish artists, with styles ranging from classic to abstract. Specialties are landscapes of the Killarney area, portraits,

…ptures, all of which are for sale. Hours are 9am to 6pm Monday through …y.

Boo…

Killarney Bookshop

32 Main St. ☎ **064/34108.**

Along with a good selection of Irish-interest publications, this shop also stocks books on the latest best-seller lists and a comprehensive range of general publications. Mail-order catalog available. Open daily from 9am to 10pm April through October, to 6pm other months.

Clothing & Gifts

The Kilkenny Shop

Main St. ☎ **064/31888.**

Under the same ownership as the shops in Kilkenny and Dublin, this large store carries huge stocks of Irish-made goods (over 3,000 pieces of Waterford crystal, umpteen hundred pieces of Belleek and Royal Tara, Irish porcelain character figures, and a whole host of other items) at competitive prices. They'll ship and insure any purchase, and you can write for their extensive mail-order catalog. Open in summer daily from 9am to 11pm; other months, daily from 9:30 to 6pm.

✪ Macken of Ireland

Fossa. ☎ **064/34766.** Fax 064/34761.

Although a short drive from the town center (three miles) on the main Ring of Killarney road, this shop rates top billing on my personal shopping list. The attractive building is adjacent to the modern Prince of Peace Church (see above) and follows much the same lines in its structure, even to the extent of a large rear window that frames the magnificent mountain and lake scenery beyond. Inside, its shelves are brimming with what must be Killarney's largest stock of Aran knits, as well as a wide selection from such top Irish designers as Jimmy Hourihan, Henry White, and Brian Tucker. There's also an interesting line of women's clothes called Private Collection by a collective of leading designers around the country, and a wide range of tweed, cashmere, and mohair jackets. In the extensive gift department, Belleek, Tipperary Crystal, Claddagh jewelry, and Duiske hand-cut glass from County Killkenny are just a few of the hundreds of Irish-made items. There's a bright, cheerful coffee shop with a terrace out back for fine-weather dining.

Quill's Woollen Market

Market Sq., Main St. ☎ **064/32277.**

There's an enormous selection of designer hand-knits and woollen goods in this large store, along with a good selection of other Irish-made goods and souvenirs.

Crafts

✪ Bric In

26 High St. ☎ **064/34902.**

This attractive, stone-walled shop specializes in pottery and other Irish crafts, handmade pine furniture, and Irish books. Upstairs, there's a moderately priced cafe serving traditional Irish dishes.

John J. Murphy

Weaver, Currow Rd., Farranfore. ☎ **066/64659.** Fax 066/64993.

Approximately 10 miles from Killarney on the Tralee road (N22), John Murphy produces a lovely range of woolen shawls; scarves in wool, lambswool, mohair, alpaca, and linen/cotton; and placemats in wool and linen/cotton. The small retail shop is an extension to his larger workshop and is just off the main road (clearly signposted). It's open Monday through Saturday from 9am to 6pm; other times, John (whose home is adjacent to the workshop) will be glad to open—simply go next door and ring the bell.

Kerry Glass Studio & Visitor Centre

Fossa. ☎ **064/44666.** Fax 064/44712.

Just past the village of Fossa, on route to the Ring of Kerry, you can watch the blowing of exquisite glass items at this studio. Vivid colors swirl in the heart of lovely paperweights, bowls, plates, miniature animals and birds, vases, and a host of other objects. Factory prices prevail in their shop. Upstairs, an attractive restaurant serves light snacks. Open daily 9am–4:30pm.

JEWELRY

Brian de Staic

18 High St. ☎ **064/33822.** Fax 066/51832.

Silversmith Brian de Staic, whose home base is in Dingle town, now offers his distinctive jewelry in this shop, with an attractive traditional storefront. In addition to the Ogham nameplate pendants for which he is best known, there are also gold and enamel items, all at reasonable prices.

AFTER DARK

After dark, take your pick from singing pubs, traditional music sessions, cabaret, or theater performances.

✪ Killarney Manor Banquet

Loreto Rd. ☎ **064/31551.** Fax 064/33366. IR£26 ($41.60) per person. Apr–Oct, performance 8–10:30pm.

A Killarney friend described the Killarney Manor Banquet as a "rousing good show," and I certainly echo that sentiment. The setting is a stately manor house of the 1800s, and after an 8pm welcome drink in the chapel, there's a succulent four-course dinner served during a lively program of Irish music, song, and dance. The festivities do not, of course, end with the meal, but go on until your departure.

✪ Siamsa Tire

National Folk Theatre, Godfrey Place, Tralee. ☎ **066/23055** or 066/23049 (for credit cards). Fax 066/27276. Admission: IR£9 ($14.40) adults, IR£7 ($11.20) children and seniors, IR£28 ($44.80) family ticket (two adults and up to four children). There's a special bus and theater ticket available from Deros Tours, 22 Main St., Killarney (☎ 064/31251).

At the top of my own list of favorite nighttime entertainment in the Killarney area is at least one performance of Siamsa (pronounced "*Sheem*-sa"), the National Folk Theatre troupe that performs in their own Siamsa Tire ("*Tee*-ra") Theatre in nearby Tralee. "Merrymaking" is the English translation of the Gaelic *siamsa,* and this is as merry a show as you'll come across, as it depicts through music, song, dance, and mime Irish country life of the past. In a stage setting of thatched cottage and farmyard, expert performers go about the business of thatching, churning, milking, harvesting, and other routine tasks that were the foundation of everyday life on the farm. So professional is the performance that it will no doubt surprise you—as it did me—to know that the troupe operates on a very limited budget, with just a handful of full-time performers, and that most of those skilled musicians, actors, singers, and dancers give hours and hours of their time to perfect the show and travel with it on a strictly voluntary basis.

Hotel Gleneagle

Muckross Rd., Killarney. ☎ **064/31870.** Admission varies with performance.

There's something on every night at the Gleneagle in July and August, with the program changing every two nights or so. Cabaret, jazz, ballads, folk songs, traditional music, and stories as only the Irish can tell them are on tap, with top-flight entertainers like the Wolfe Tones, Susan McCann, and Joe Dolan frequently on the bill. There's dancing after the show until 1am, or you might want to opt for the pub, where a resident pianist and guitarist hold sway (no cover charge), and they'll have you singing your heart out in a true Irish sing-along.

TRADITIONAL MUSIC

Killarney has two singing pubs to tempt your vocal cords. There's ballad singing and general hilarity (which can get pretty hokey if the likes of "Dixie" breaks out) in the backroom of ✪ **The Laurels** pub on Main Street (☎ 064/31149), from May to October, and letters pour in from readers with enthusiastic endorsement of this liveliest of Killarney pubs. Go along about 9pm, when things are just tuning up. The larger and ever-so-slightly more subdued **Danny Mann** pub, on New Street, has traditional Irish music every night right through the summer, and it's likely to be packed with Yanks rendering heartfelt versions of such stock Irish exports as "Danny Boy" and "When Irish Eyes Are Smiling." The action starts about 9:30pm on weekends during winter.

The **Crock of Gold,** 19 High St. (☎ 064/32432), features music every night of the week in summer and has proved very popular with our readers.

During summer months there's ceili dancing (you'll recognize this as the ancestor of our square dancing) Friday through Sunday at the **Ceili Club,** Scotts Hotel, East Avenue (☎ 064/31060), and traditional Irish music every night of the week in Scotts Pub.

The ✪ **Whitegates Hotel,** on Muckross Road (☎ 064/31164), has a traditional music seisiun and sing-along on Friday night and other entertainment on Saturday, as well as a sing-along session on Sunday at 12:30pm during the season.

WHERE TO STAY IN TOWN

When it comes to accommodations, Killarney has an abundance of high-quality, low-priced B&Bs and guesthouses, as well as some elegant luxury hotels whose prices are high but not exorbitant. Some of the "Out of Town" places are within reasonable walking distance of town, though not with heavy luggage.

BED-AND-BREAKFASTS

Beaufield House

Cork Road, Killarney, Co. Kerry. ☎ **064/34440.** Fax 064/34663. 15 rms, all with shower. TEL TV. IR£20–IR£25 ($32–$40) single; IR£18 ($28.80) per person sharing. (Rates include breakfast.) ACC, AE, MC, V. From N22 (Limerick-Cork road) turn right at Ryan's Hotel (on Cork road), and Beaufield House is on the left.

Danny and Moya Bowe greet guests with a welcoming cuppa in their guesthouse only 1/2 mile from the town center. The large two-story house has been built and furnished with guest comfort firmly in mind, based on Danny's years of experience as manager of the Ryan Hotel across the way. A full Irish breakfast is cooked to your order (no black pudding if you don't want it!). Central heating and a private car park. Both the Bowes enjoy sharing their extensive knowledge of this area with their guests.

The Gardens

Countess Rd., Killarney, Co. Kerry. ☎ **064/31147.** 21 rms, all with bath. IR£23 ($36.80) single; IR£19 ($30.40) per person sharing. (Rates include breakfast.) No credit cards.

This charming place, owned and run by Mary and Tom O'Reilly, is set in private grounds very convenient to the railway station and the town center. In the main two-story building, 11 nicely appointed bedrooms are on the ground floor, motel-style, and 10 are on the floor above. One measure of the O'Reillys' consideration for their guests is the installation of a TV/reading lounge designated "No Smoking" and a *separate,* similar lounge for smokers! There's central heat and good parking. I can't praise the O'Reillys highly enough. Their establishment is spotlessly clean, and their full Irish breakfast superb.

Knockcullen

New Rd., Killarney, Co. Kerry. ☎ **064/33915.** 4 rms, all with shower. IR£14 ($22.40) per person. (Rates include breakfast.) No credit cards. Closed Nov–Feb.

Knockcullen is the sparkling-clean two-story home of Marie and Sean O'Brien, on a quiet, tree-lined street. The four guest rooms are all attractively furnished, and Marie's table is laden with fresh and healthy fare—she even caters to vegetarians at breakfast. The town center is a short walk away, and both the railway station and Killarney National Park are nearby.

✪ Linden House

New Rd., Killarney, Co. Kerry. ☎ **064/31379.** Fax 064/31196. 20 rms, all with bath. IR£20–IR£26 ($32–$41.60) single; IR£20–IR£32 ($32–$51.20) per person sharing. Partial-board rates available. 25% reduction for children. (Rates include breakfast.) ACC, MC, V. Closed Dec–Jan.

Set on this quiet residential street, just one block down from Main Street, Linden House's location is ideal. The Knoblauch family have won special praise from our readers for the quality of their lodgings and the warmth of their hospitality. There's something of an old-world, small-inn air about the three-story stucco house, and bedrooms are exceptionally comfortable and attractively appointed. There's central heat and one of the best moderately priced restaurants in Killarney, with a large local following (see "Where to Eat," below). Popular with traveling Irish as well as tourists, Linden House is one place you must be certain to reserve ahead.

Mystical Rose

Woodlawn Rd., Killarney, Co. Kerry. ☎ **064/31453.** 6 rms, all with bath. IR£22 ($35.20) single; IR£16.50 ($26.40) per person sharing. 33 1/3% reduction for children. (Rates include breakfast.) No credit cards. Closed Nov–Feb.

Mrs. Noreen O'Mahony is the friendly hostess of this award-winning guesthouse with its beautiful rose garden (which guests are free to use). The house is located near the Killarney lake district and Noreen will arrange tours for guests who want it. Guest rooms are both attractive and comfortable.

St. Anthony's Villa

Cork Rd., Killarney, Co. Kerry. ☎ **064/31534.** 4 rms, all with bath. IR£16 ($25.60) per person. 50% reduction for children. (Rates include breakfast.) No credit cards. Closed Nov–Feb.

Mrs. Mary O'Connell is the friendly hostess of this attractive, modern bungalow that is convenient to town and the bus and railway station. She is very helpful and will arrange tours around Killarney for anyone who may want it.

Worth a Splurge/A Small, Characterful Hotel

✪ Arbutus Hotel

College St., Killarney, Co. Kerry. ☎ **064/31037.** 34 rms, all with bath. High season, IR£50 ($80) single; IR£40 ($64) per person sharing. Low season, IR£35 ($56) single; IR£28 ($44.80) per person sharing. Reduced weekly rates available. Ask about discounts for holders of this book. (Rates include breakfast.) ACC, DC, MC, V.

This three-story, distinctively Irish hotel has been owned and operated by the Buckley family for more than 70 years. There's an old-fashioned air about the place, enhanced by such touches as lots of etched and stained glass, a fireplace in the lounge, and an intimate lounge-bar presided over by the amiable Dennis, who has been here many years. There's marvelous traditional music in the bar nightly in summer, weekends October to April. I'm particularly fond of the cozy dining room, and connecting to the Arbutus is a low-priced coffee shop called Pat's that offers very good value. Bedrooms are comfortably furnished, and this is a good place to settle if you plan to use Killarney as a base for as long as a week. Ask about possible discounts to readers of this book.

Hostels

The Four Winds International Hostel

43 New St., Killarney, Co. Kerry. ☎ **064/33094.** 100 beds. IR£6–IR£9.50 ($9.60–$15.20) per person depending on season. Continental breakfast IR£2.50 ($4). Ask about discount for holders of this book. No credit cards.

The Four Winds is one of the nicer things to happen in Killarney in recent years. It provides comfortable, attractive, and inexpensive lodgings right in the center of town. There are sleeping accommodations for 80 in bunk-bedded dormitories, as well as four private rooms, plus a lounge, dining room, and kitchen. The building is centrally heated, and there are two open fireplaces for inner warmth. There's also a private garden for the exclusive use of guests. Guides and maps to local outdoor activities are provided, and they are agents for Raleigh Rent-a-Bike.

Neptune's Killarney Town Hostel

New St., Killarney, Co. Kerry. ☎ **064/35255.** Fax 064/32310. 100 beds, including family rooms with bath. IR£6 ($9.60) per dormitory bed; family room rates on request. Dinner IR£4–IR£6 ($6.40–$9.60). No credit cards.

Tucked away from street noises, Neptune's is right in the heart of the town, with exceptionally attractive facilities: social (games/TV) rooms, self-catering kitchen, laundry/drying room, car park, and a safe available for valuables. No membership is required. Wheelchair-bound travelers have easy access and are catered to. Neptune's will store your luggage at no cost, as well as furnish baby-sitters. Central heating and good parking.

NEARBY ACCOMMODATIONS

BED-AND-BREAKFASTS

Beauty's Home

Tralee Rd., Killarney, Co. Kerry. ☎ **064/31567** and 31836. Fax 064/34077. 3 rms, 2 w... bath. IR£19 ($30.40) single; IR£13 ($20.80) per person sharing; IR£3 ($4.80) extra per person with bath. 20% reduction for children. (Rates include breakfast.) ACC, MC, V.

Mrs. Catherine Spillane is the lively and gracious hostess in this modern bungalow about a five-minute drive from the town center. All guest rooms have TV (with satellite transmissions that include live CNN news). Mrs. Spillane will be happy to meet guests at the bus or railway station if requested. Plenty of private parking.

✪ Coffey's Loch Lein House

Fossa, Killarney, Co. Kerry. ☎ **064/31260.** 10 rms, all with bath/shower. IR£20–IR£25 ($32–$40) single; IR£18–IR£20 ($28.80–$32) per person sharing. 25% reduction for children. (Rates include breakfast.) ACC, MC, V. Closed Nov–Feb. Gravel car park.

This lovely modern one-story guesthouse is the domain of the delightful Kathleen Coffey and her daughter-in-law Eithne. Just three miles from Killarney, it's set in green lawns sloping down to the Lower Lake, and is approached via a country lane that's signposted on the main Ring of Kerry road (R562) just past the golf course (on your left as you approach from Killarney). The L-shaped guesthouse holds the exceptionally large and well-furnished guest rooms. There's a TV lounge with a fireplace and a bright, window-walled dining room, as well as central heating.

As attractive and sparkling as is the house, it is outshone by Kathleen, a small, pixielike lady who is an accomplished conversationalist and storyteller. The family has been in this area for generations, giving the Coffeys a treasure trove of local legends they're only too happy to pass on to you—very special mementos of your Irish holiday.

Marian House

Woodlawn Rd., Killarney, Co. Kerry. ☎ **064/31275.** 6 rms, 5 with shower. IR£21 ($33.60) single; IR£14–IR£16 ($22.40–$25.60) per person sharing. 25% reduction for children. (Rates include breakfast.) No credit cards.

Marian House sits just off the main Muckross road, less than half a mile from the town center, atop a small hill that looks out onto the mountains. It's a centrally heated two-story house with six prettily decorated guest rooms, all with sinks. Mrs. Eileen Lucey is the hostess, always helpful to guests in planning their Killarney stay.

Osprey

Lough Guitane Rd., Muckross, Killarney, Co. Kerry. ☎ **064/33213.** 3 rms, 2 with bath. IR£18.50 ($29.60) single; IR£14 ($22.40) per person sharing; IR£1.50 ($2.40) extra per person with bath. (Rates include breakfast.) No credit cards. Closed Mid-Oct to Apr.

Osprey's scenic location overlooks the lakes and mountains and is less than a mile from Killarney National Park. Hosts Maureen and Genie Fogarty are keen walkers and can advise on easy or difficult walks in the vicinity. And if you decide to try your luck fishing on the lakes, Genie is just the man to send you off to the best spots, not only in Kerry, but throughout the country. Guest rooms are nicely appointed, and there's a TV lounge. Maureen's home baking is a decided bonus, and if daughters Anne, Karen, Clare, and Susan happen to be at home, an Irish song or jig will be forthcoming at the drop of a request.

Shillelagh House

Knockasarnett, Aghadoe, Killarney, Co. Kerry. ☎ **064/34030.** Fax 064/35761. 6 rms, 4 with shower. IR£15 ($24) single without bath; IR£13.50 ($21.60) per person sharing without bath; IR£14 ($22.40) per person sharing with bath. 25% reduction for children. (Rates include breakfast.) ACC, MC, V. Closed Nov–Feb.

Denis and Karen Greene's modern two-story home is about 1½ miles from the town center in Aghadoe Heights, just off the main Ring of Kerry road (R562). The pretty guest rooms are comfortably furnished and have quilted headboards for the beds. There's a lounge with TV, and full Irish breakfasts are served in the bright dining room. This is a non-smoking house.

FARMHOUSES

Carriglea House

Muckross Rd., Killarney, Co. Kerry. ☎ **064/31116.** 9 rms, 6 with bath. IR£14.50 ($23.20) per person without bath. IR£16.50 ($26.40) per person with bath. (Rates include breakfast.) No credit cards. Closed Nov–Mar.

A beautiful 200-year-old country home, Carriglea sits a little over a mile from the town center on a rise overlooking the lakes. From the sweeping front lawn, approached by a tree-lined curving avenue, the view takes in the Lower Lake and Purple, Torc, and Mangerton Mountains. Marie and Michael Beasley own this working dairy farm and take great pleasure in helping guests plan their holiday time in Killarney. The lovely old centrally heated house has spacious rooms furnished with many antiques and tastefully decorated in restful colors. Particularly noteworthy is the dining room's chandelier of gold, blue, and pink porcelain. There are several additional guest rooms in the adjoining coach house. One large coach house room has a bay window overlooking the front lawn.

✪ Gap View Farm

Firies, Killarney, Co. Kerry. ☎ **066/64378.** 6 rms, 5 with bath. IR£15.50 ($24.80) per person without bath; IR£16 ($25.60) per person with bath. 33⅓% reduction for children. (Rates include breakfast.) No credit cards. Closed Nov–Apr.

Mrs. Kearney is the hostess of this large 18th-century farmhouse eight miles from Killarney, off the Farranfore road (N22), with its lovely views of the Gap of Dunloe and the Kerry mountains. The house is centrally heated as well as having turf fires, and fresh farm foods are served at every meal. There is a garden that guests can use, and five lovely bedrooms, all with good views. Killarney Golf Course is five miles away.

HOSTELS

Aghadoe House

Killarney International Youth Hostel, Killarney, Co. Kerry. ☎ **064/31240.** Fax 064/34300. 220 beds. IR£5 ($8) per person. Breakfast IR£2 ($3.20); packed lunch IR£2.50 ($4); evening meal IR£5 ($8). No credit cards.

Killarney's An Oige youth hostel is one of the best in the country. An impressive 200-year-old brick mansion set in 75 wooded acres, it's about two miles from the town center (signposted on R562, the main Ring of Kerry road), with a courtesy bus from the railway station (phone the warden when you arrive or notify the hostel in advance). There's a TV room, self-catering kitchen and dining room, free

Readers Recommend

Glencool House, Lissivigeen, Killarney, Co. Kerry. ☎ 064/31315. *"We were welcomed at this two-storied home by Mary O'Donoghue and her family, who helped in arranging a Ring of Kerry tour. Her breakfast menu included yogurt and fruit for the health-conscious and the best soda bread I encountered."*

—Wayne B. Garrett, Nashville, TN

The Purple Heather, Gap of Dunloe, Beaufort, Killarney, Co. Kerry. ☎ 064/44266. *"This is one of the most enjoyable B&Bs we stayed in on our trip to Ireland. Tim and Nora Moriarty have six lovely children, and four of them gave us a display of Irish dancing in full costume. We think they deserve full marks."*

—David MacSweeney, Vienna, VA

Muckross Lodge, Muckross Road, Killarney, Co. Kerry. ☎ 064/32660. *"Mrs. Bernadette O'Sullivan is a truly delightful person. Her home is immaculate, tastefully decorated, and each room is en suite."* —Irene Klar, North Palm Beach, Fla.

Author's Note: This is a smoke-free house.

Shraheen House, Ballycasheen, Killarney, Co. Kerry. ☎ 064/31286. *"We loved this very attractive two-story house in a quiet area and surrounded by 2½ acres of lawn. Mrs. Maureen Fleming was the ideal hostess. It's only one mile out of town on an extension of Woodlawn Road."* —Pat Higgins, Syracuse, NY

The Wren's Nest, Woodhaven, Woodlawn Road, Killarney, Co. Kerry. ☎ 064/33580. *"This lovely new home is only about a 15-minute walk from the town center. It sits in its own grounds in a peaceful setting, and our en suite room was immaculate."*

—William Anthony, Giessen, Germany

Mulberry House, Rookery Road (off Countess Road), Killarney, Co. Kerry. ☎ 064/341121. *"My wife and I were astounded by the size and beauty of this spectacular home. Every detail, from the Waterford chandelier in the entrance hallway to the fine polished woodwork throughout the house was meticulously kept."*

—Mr. and Mrs. Eamonn Cannon, North Ridgeville, OH

Marlfield House, Lissivigeen, Killarney, Co. Kerry. ☎ 064/32129. *"Eileen McAuliffe is the best hostess possible. I was sick one day and she spent all day with me, making me feel at home, making tea and scones and a fire."*

—Mr. & Mrs. Thomas Collins, Manville, NJ

Author's Note: On N72, just off N22.

Nashville, Tralee Rd., Killarney, Co. Kerry. ☎ 064/32924. *"We have stayed with David Nash and his children several times, and they never fail to make us feel instantly at home. All the rooms have been beautifully remodeled, and David and his kids serve a wonderful Irish breakfast that leaves you full until well in the afternoon. Nashville is two miles from town on N22, and it's set back from the road with spacious gardens and plenty of parking."* —Ellen Koch and Lis Boggs, Oakland, CA

Gleann Fía Guest House, Deerpark, Killarney, Co. Kerry. ☎ 064/35035. *"This beautiful home is located on three acres beside a river, only a five-minute drive to the town center. It is beautifully furnished, with some antiques"*

—Florence and Vernon Heeren, Barrington, IL

hot showers, laundry facilities, rental bikes, and a small store. It's advisable to book in advance during July and August, and because many hostelers are hikers as well, the wardens here ask that you be reminded that the mountains in the area can be quite dangerous—if you intend hiking or climbing them, you should be sure to notify them of your intended route. The wardens can arrange discount tours of the Ring of Kerry, as well as the lakes and several other areas, and there's an excellent Activities Program.

✪ Fossa Holiday Hostel

Fossa, Killarney, Co. Kerry. ☎ **064/31497.** 60 beds. IR£5 ($8) per person; IR£13 ($20.80) per person for bed, breakfast, and dinner. No credit cards.

The Brosnan family run this bright, modern hostel three miles from Killarney on the main Ring of Kerry road (R562), just beyond and across the road from the Prince of Peace Church (look for the large Texaco sign). In addition to dormitories, there are family rooms, as well as a fully equipped kitchen, well-stocked shop, TV lounge, games room, laundry facilities, tennis court, and children's play area. A good, moderately priced restaurant, which also serves take-aways, is on the premises. They have bikes for rent and can help you arrange fishing or golf nearby. The Brosnans are always on hand to provide friendly assistance.

Worth a Splurge

If you have promised yourself one "bust out" splurge in Ireland, Killarney—because of its plethora of first-class hotels with "value for money" rates—is a good spot to keep that promise. Each of the hotels listed below has a character of its own and each is distinctly Irish.

✪ The Great Southern Hotel

Town Center, Killarney, Co. Kerry. ☎ **064/31262,** or 800/444-UTELL in the U.S. Fax 064/31642. 180 rms, all with bath. Seasonal rates, IR£47–IR£54 ($75.20–$86.40) per person sharing; IR£13–IR£16 ($20.80–$25.60) single supplement. 12.5% service charge. AE, DC, MC, V.

This gracious old hotel, built in 1854, is located just across from Killarney's railroad station in a setting of mature gardens, and only a short walk from the town center. It was recently renovated to its original elegance, and from the moment you walk into the spacious lobby with its soft rose-and-green Irish-made carpet and open fires, that past era comes alive. The same ambience is reflected in its wide corridors and staircases, as well as all the public rooms—the wood-paneled bar; the pleasant conservatory off the lobby; the beautiful main dining room with its huge original Victorian marble fireplace, ornate chandeliers, and windows looking out to the garden; and the smaller, award-winning Malton Room, with its classic French cuisine. Both restaurants are very popular with locals as well as guests, as is afternoon tea, served in the lounge or conservatory.

Guest rooms, each individually decorated, all have telephones, radios, TVs, hairdryers, and trouser presses (if your tastes run to days gone by, ask for a room in the old section). Amenities include an indoor heated swimming pool, sauna and steam room, Jacuzzi, gymnasium, snooker room, beauty salons, boutique, and two tennis courts. They can also arrange baby-sitting. Perhaps the Great Southern's greatest asset is its staff—one of the most polished and professional, as well as one of the friendliest, I've encountered in my travels around the country.

✪ Killarney Park Hotel

Kenmare Place, Killarney, Co. Kerry. ☎ **064/35555.** Fax 064/35266. 55 rms, all with bath. Seasonal rates, IR£68–IR£100 ($108.80–$160) single; IR£48–IR£75 ($76.80–$120) per person sharing. (Rates include breakfast.) AE, MC, V.

Just around the corner from the Great Southern, the sparkling white Killarney Park sits back from the street, a quiet refuge from the "busy-ness" of the town. The inviting lobby features an open fire; the bar is an oasis of dark wood and soft colors; and another fire glows in the Park Restaurant. Luxuriously decorated guest rooms all have telephones and TVs, as well as hairdryers. There's a super indoor pool, a steam room, and a gym.

✪ Killeen House Hotel

Aghadoe, Killarney, Co. Kerry. ☎ **064/31711.** Fax 064/31811. 15 rms, all with bath. Seasonal rates, IR£36–IR£46 ($57.60–$73.60) single; IR£23–IR£35 ($36.80–$56) per person sharing. 10% service charge. 33% discount for children. (Rates include breakfast.) AE, DC, MC, V. Closed Jan.

A short distance from town, Killeen House sits on the heights of Aghadoe and is the epitome of the small, intimate Irish hotel. Hosts Geraldine and Michael Rosney take a personal interest in their guests, generous with advice on sightseeing, golf, fishing, and other Killarney activities, and they'll personally arrange any outing that takes your fancy. There's a warm, homey ambience to the hotel that is evident from the lobby, with its comfortable seating and open fire, the pretty restaurant, and the convivial bar. Guest rooms all have telephone and satellite TV, and there's a private car park. Chef Gillian Kelly has made the dining room a favorite of locals, and many visitors staying elsewhere book in for at least one of her superb dinners.

Readers' Recommendations in Brief

The volume of reader mail concerning Killarney accommodations confirms the exceptional hospitality in this popular spot—space does not permit full descriptions of the following, each of which has been praised by readers.

Bed-and-Breakfast Accommodations

- Kilbrogan House, Muckross Road, Killarney, Co. Kerry (☎ 064/31444), Mrs. Evelyn O'Leary.
- Alderhaven, Ballycasheen, Killarney, Co. Kerry (☎ 064/31982), Norrie O'Neil.
- Lisaden, Countess Grove, Killarney, Co. Kerry (☎ 064/32006).
- Crystal Springs, Ballycasheen Cross, Killarney, Co. Kerry (☎ 064/33272 or 31188), Mrs. Eileen Brosnan.
- Lohan's Lodge, Tralee Road, Killarney, Co. Kerry (☎ 064/33871), Cathy and Mike Lohan.
- The Silver Spruce, New Road, Killarney, Co. Kerry (☎ 064/31376).
- St. Rita's Villa, Mill Road, Killarney, Co. Kerry (☎ 064/31517), Mrs. Peggie Cronin.
- Gorman's, Tralee Road, Killarney, Co. Kerry (☎ 064/33149), Moira and Jim O'Gorman.

Farmhouses

- Mrs. Kathy Brosnan, Woodlawn Road, Killarney, Co. Kerry (☎ 064/32782).
- Lois Na Manach Farmhouse, Mill Road, Killarney, Co. Kerry (☎ 064/31283), Mrs. Noreen O'Sullivan.

Where to Eat

Pub Grub

The King's Inn Bar

Three Lakes Hotel, Main St. ☎ **064/31479.** IR£1.50–IR£6 ($2.40–$9.60). ACC, AE, MC, V. Daily 12:30–2:30pm. BAR FOOD.

The bar in this centrally located hotel (next door to the Tourist Office) is an attractive, cozy sort of place with a terrific bar-lunch menu that ranges from soup (I like the cockle-and-mussel soup) and sandwiches to piled-high hot dishes (such as homemade shepherd's pie and pan-fried rainbow trout) to smoked salmon salad. And if you want to go over budget, they'll do a sirloin steak for around IR£8.50 ($13.60). There's also a hot lunch-of-the-day special for just IR£4 ($6.40). They also offer good-value meals for dinner (see below).

✪ The Laurels Pub

Main St. ☎ **064/31149.** IR£1.50–IR£5 ($2.40–$8). ACC, MC, V. Mon–Sat 12:20–2:30pm. BAR FOOD.

There's terrific pub grub at the Laurels in old-style surroundings of low, beamed ceilings and rustic wooden tables. The food is good, the company congenial, and the *craic* (talk) stimulating. In addition to soup, sandwiches, and salad plates, there are hot specialties such as Irish lamb stew, Guinness beef stew, and stuffed roast pork. The Laurels also serves an excellent dinner menu in summer months only (see below).

Restaurants in Town

✪ Dingles Restaurant

40 New St. ☎ **064/31079.** Reservations recommended. Main courses IR£8–IR£15 ($12.80–$24). ACC, AE, DC, MC, V. Mar–Oct, daily 6–10:30pm. Closed Nov–Feb and Thurs Mar–May and Oct. IRISH/TRADITIONAL/VEGETARIAN.

Gerry and Marion Cunningham have created a traditional eatery in both decor and menu. It's a low-ceilinged, flagstoned place, with an open fire on cool evenings and a rustic look. The very freshest, most wholesome ingredients are used, and there is usually at least one vegetarian dish on the menu. Outstanding are the mussels in a sauce of garlic and herbs; smoked wild Killarney salmon; tender spring lamb chops; steak in a piquant sauce of green peppercorns, white wine, cream, and whiskey; and old-fashioned Irish stew.

✪ Foley's Steak & Seafood Restaurant

23 High St. ☎ **064/31217.** Reservations recommended in summer months. Main courses IR£8–IR£14 ($12.80–$22.40); breakfast IR£5 ($8). ACC, AE, DC, MC, V. Breakfast daily 8–10am; lunch and dinner daily noon–11pm; bar food daily noon–3pm. TRADITIONAL/SEAFOOD/VEGETARIAN/BAR FOOD.

Foley's was a coaching inn many years ago, and there's an old-style air about the front bar lounge, where a fireplace with turf fires adds to the coziness. The two pretty back dining rooms are more formal, decorated with soft shades of rose and green. Carol and Denis Hartnett are the family team responsible for turning out superb meals with the highest standards. Seafood, Kerry mountain lamb, and steaks are the specialties, and Carol (who does the cooking) uses only the freshest produce. Denis cuts all their steaks and buys only Kerry mountain lamb, using nothing but centerline cuts. Actually, this is a full-service eatery, serving all three meals, and there's a pianist on Friday, Saturday, and Sunday nights during the summer.

✪ Linden House

New Rd. ☎ **064/31379.** Fixed-price dinner IR£17.50 ($28); house special IR£12 ($19.20). ACC, MC, V. Daily 6:30–9pm. Closed Dec–Jan, and Mon in off-season. SEAFOOD/TRADITIONAL/EUROPEAN.

One of the best places in town for a delicious, home-cooked evening meal is this small hotel run by owners Ann and Peter Knoblauch, who have created a Bavarian-type dining room of exposed brick and wooden booths. It's a cozy place, very popular with locals, and the menu is good, solid family fare. Peter supervises the spotless kitchen and insists on the freshest ingredients. In July and August it's a good idea to book ahead—other months you'll usually have only a few minutes' wait at the most. There is also an à la carte menu available. Incidentally, residents are served a "House Special" menu at 6pm at the reduced price of IR£12 ($19.20).

Sheila's Restaurant

75 High St. ☎ **064/31270.** Plate lunch IR£4.50 ($7.20); four-course dinner IR£15 ($24). ACC, MC, V. June–Sept daily 11am–11pm. Oct–May daily noon–3pm and 6–10pm. SEAFOOD/TRADITIONAL/VEGETARIAN.

Sheila's has a dark-green front and lots of light-blond wood inside. Good, inexpensive lunches (sandwiches, soups, quiches, and four-course hot meals) are served from noon to 3pm, four-course dinners of seafood, steaks, pork, chicken, and vegetarian dishes are served from 6 to 10pm, and there's an à la carte menu from 3pm on through the dinner hours. Wine is always available by the glass or bottle.

Recommendations in Brief

In addition to this listing, I highly recommend dinner at the ✪ **Great Southern Hotel** and **Killeen House Hotel** (see "Where to Stay," above), which will run under IR£30 ($48). The Great Southern also serves a scrumptious **traditional afternoon tea** (from 3 to 5:30pm) for about IR£5 ($8), and a lighter **cream tea** for about IR£3 ($4.80).

✪ The Strawberry Tree

24 Plunkett St. ☎ **064/32688.** Reservations strongly recommended. Main courses IR£10–IR£18 ($16–$28.80). Service charge 10%. ACC, AE, DC, MC, V. Morning coffee daily 11am–noon; lunch daily 12:30–3:30pm; dinner daily 6:30–10:30pm. Closed Good Friday, Dec 25–26. IRISH/VEGETARIAN.

The Strawberry Tree exudes a warm, pubby feeling, and well it might, since for well over a century that's exactly what occupied these premises. The small bar up front is a perfect spot to have a before-dinner drink and study the menu. You do, in fact, place your order from this oasis of warmth before being seated in the small dining room in the back.

Owner Evan Doyle, who came to Killarney from a restaurant in Clifden, has produced an interesting menu using Irish fish, fowl, meats, and farm produce prepared with a slight French flavor. The menu changes monthly, and a typical starter is baked St. Killian (Irish farmhouse cream cheese baked in phyllo pastry accompanied by a raspberry sauce). Roast quail and chicken with pan-fried breast of wood pigeon with a sauce of strawberry vinegar and red currant is one of the more unusual main dishes, and there are several fresh fish dishes, meats, and vegetable purses (pastry filled with diced root vegetables served over three rices surrounding a mousse of three vegetables and accompanied by a sorrel sauce). A standout among desserts is the "chocolate box," a luscious creation of rich chocolate cake, ice cream, and fresh cream that comes in the form of a box of chocolates. Portions are ample but not overwhelming, and presentation is well nigh perfect. The restaurant is small (26 seats) and extremely popular, so book ahead.

In Nearby Killorglin

Some 14 miles west of Killarney is the village of Killorglin, with two restaurants worthy of mention.

✪ Nick's Restaurant

Lower Bridge St., Killorglin. ☎ **066/61219.** Main courses IR£10–IR£14 ($16–$22.40); bar food IR£2.50–IR£6 ($4–$9.60). ACC, AE, MC, V. Morning coffee daily 10am–noon; bar lunch daily noon–5pm; dinner daily 6–10pm. Closed Nov–Dec. STEAKS/SEAFOOD/BAR FOOD.

Nick and Ann Foley have converted what was once a butcher shop into a charming multilevel steak-and-seafood restaurant with exposed-stone walls, lots of dark wood, open fires, and comfortable seating. You'll be served only the best meats, since Nick is himself a master butcher. Prime beef comes in enormous steaks that actually *earn* the well-worn accolade "melt in your mouth." Lobsters, crayfish, and oysters reside in the restaurant's fish tank, and other fish dishes feature only same-day catches. The soups are thick and hearty, with the unmistakable taste of "homemade." Lunch salads of ham, beef, or seafood are featured on the special pub menu, and the dinner menu has 10 starters and a choice from more than a dozen main courses, followed by a mouthwatering dessert trolley. But if you should have a yen for a special dish not listed—and if the makings are available—the Foleys are quite happy to prepare it for you. There's an extensive wine list, with all the varieties imported directly from France. Traditional music some nights. This popular eatery can get very busy after about 7:30pm, and my best advice is to come early.

✪ The Bianconi

Lower Bridge St., Killorglin. ☎ **066/61146.** Bar food under IR£5 ($8); hot meals under IR£10 ($16). AE, MC, V. Mon–Sat, bar food 11am–9:30pm, restaurant 6:30–9:30pm; Sun, bar food only 12:30–2pm and 5:30–9pm. BAR FOOD/SEAFOOD/SALADS.

Rick and Ray Sheehan have created one of Killorglin's most popular eateries in this large bar/restaurant. Lots of dark wood, leather seats, and cozy booths create a traditional setting, and the kitchen serves up excellent home-cooked meals made from fresh local ingredients. *Note:* The Bianconi also has a B&B upstairs, with bright, cheerful rooms that have telephones and TVs, and a guest lounge. Rates run IR£35 ($56) single, IR£25 ($40) per person sharing.

2 Seeing the Lakes

A broad valley holds Killarney's three main lakes, with Lough Leane (the Lower Lake) closest to town and separated from the Middle Lake by the Muckross Peninsula. It was on one of its 30 islands that dedicated monks faithfully recorded Irish history from the 11th to the 13th century in the *Annals of Innisfallen.* The Middle Lake covers 680 acres, holds four islands, and is connected to the small, narrow Upper Lake and its eight islands by a broad river called the Long Range. Each lake has several streams flowing into it, and the River Laune connects them to the Atlantic. Their waters hold the shimmering reflections of birch and oak and mountain ash and arbutus, while hovering over all are the peaks of some of Ireland's finest mountains: Macgillycuddy's Reeks, with Carrantuohill, the country's highest mountain at 3,414 feet; the Tomies; the Mangerton range; and Torc.

Killarney's wealth of natural beauties can be a bit overwhelming, but not to worry—the jarveys and boatmen and coach-tour people have it all worked out for you. Their routes will take you to the high points. Although it's perfectly possible to wander around on your own, this is one time I highly recommend that you plan the budget around at least one or two of the guided tours, whether by jaunting car, boat, or bus. Fares are reasonable, and the guides love the scenery and know the folklore of the places through which they escort you. After you've done that, I recommend just as strongly that you go back on your own to linger and savor all that beauty. The two experiences make a soul-restoring combination.

BY JAUNTING CAR

No need to stop by the Tourist Office to make arrangements—you'll be hassled by the long line of jaunting car drivers down the street, and my advice is to look them all over and pick the Irish face and twinkling eye that tickles your fancy most. In high season it's a good idea to reserve your seat the evening before you plan to go. Uniform rates and routes are set each year for the season.

If the budget can be stretched to include the ✪ **all-day trip,** you'll go home with glorious memories worth far more than the IR£25 ($40) fare. You can book in advance through Killarney Boating Centre, 3 High St., Killarney, County Kerry (☎ 064/31068), or through the Tourist Office. The day begins about 10am, when you hop into a luxury coach and head out to Kate Kearney's Cottage (which is not the traditional thatched cottage you might expect from its name, but a gift shop, pub, restaurant, and snack bar) at the mouth of the Gap of Dunloe. Next comes a transfer to either a pony's back (for experienced riders only) or a pony trap to make the six-mile trek through wild, silent walls of granite with still, mysterious lakes on either side. The legend says that the last snake in Ireland was drowned by the good St. Patrick in Black Lough—which explains, no doubt, why no fish have ever inhabited its depths. Lunch is a picnic at the end of the Gap (everyone brings his own) before meeting your boatman at the Upper Lake. The afternoon is a water tour of all three lakes, ending when your boat docks at Ross Castle, where your coach waits to return you to town about 5:30pm. A lovely day, and unrivaled by any other in my own travel experience.

Half-day tours take you through the Killarney Estate along the lake shores to Muckross Abbey, home to Franciscan monks from 1448 until Cromwell ordered it burned in 1652. There's time to wander around Muckross House and its gardens, then on to view the lovely Torc waterfall before returning to town. In 1995, the charge was IR£18 ($28.80). For the same fare, you can choose the heights of Aghadoe Hill for a breathtaking view of mountains, lakes, and the town below. A church and round tower date back to the 7th century. The return to town is by the way of the Lower Lake and Ross Castle. Various other routes are available at fares of IR£8 to IR£14 ($12.80 to $22.40).

BY BOAT

Killarney's boatmen are legendary for their skillful navigation of the lakes and their store of wondrous tales. Their numbers are diminishing, but arrangements can be made for a day on the lakes with a party of four at fares that are set each year for the season. If you want to do the rowing yourself, rowboats are available at Ross Castle and Muckross House, and bookings can be made with or without boatmen from Ross Castle Pier (☎ 064/32252); Muckross House Boathouse, Killarney National Park, Muckross; and Sweeneys Boathire, Tomies, Beaufort (☎ 064/44207). Charges are about IR£3 ($4.80) per hour unaccompanied, IR£4 ($6.40) with a boatman/guide.

The watercoach ✪ ***Lily of Killarney*** leaves the Ross Castle slipway several times daily to cruise the Lower Lake, with shuttle-bus service from the Boating Center to the departure point. The glass-enclosed cabin is completely heated, and there's a commentary on the history and legends of the lake as you pass Innisfallen Island, O'Sullivan's Cascade, Tomies Mountain, Darby's Garden, the old copper mines, Library Point, and many other points of interest. Fares in 1995 were IR£5 ($8) for adults, half that for children, and IR£12 ($19.20) for a family with two children. To book, contact Killarney Boating Centre, 3 High St., Killarney (☎ 064/31068), or the Tourist Office.

ON YOUR OWN

A delightful day can be spent **biking** along the Lower Lake and through the national park (entrance just off Muckross Road) or along the lakeside paths in Ross Castle Western Demesne. Cars are prohibited in both, and you'll feel very close to nature as you wheel along wooded paths, with stops to contemplate the timeless waters of the lake. Bicycles may be rented from O'Callaghan's on College Street, O'Neill's on Plunkett Street, and O'Sullivan's on Pawn Officer Lane, off High Street.

One-, two-, or three-hour trekking and trail riding jaunts in Killarney National Park, which take in Ross Castle and Ross Island, with lovely views of the lakes and mountains, can be booked through **Killarney Riding Stables,** Ballydowney, Killarney (☎ 064/31585; fax 064/34119). They also organize three- and six-day Killarney Reeks Trail rides. Horses may also be rented at the Gap of Dunloe for the two-hour ride to the top of the Gap and back, but as sure-footed as are these steeds, you want to be a good rider before attempting it. Those who prefer the exhilaration of **hiking** over the Gap should allow a minimum of three hours.

14 Around County Kerry

Your entire visit could well be spent within the confines of County Kerry, and you'd still go home without seeing it all. No matter how much or how little you manage to get in, however, you will know beyond doubt that it well earns its honorary title, the Kingdom of Kerry.

An entire book could be—and many have been—written about this wonderfully varied county, with its magnificent scenery, relics of prehistory, and population of highly individualistic people. I'll hit the highlights, but do take time to explore on your own—this is "nook and cranny" country!

SEEING COUNTY KERRY

The famed scenic drive known as the Ring of Kerry circles the broad Iveragh Peninsula. A good starting point is Kenmare, ending up at Killorglin, but you can just as easily travel in the opposite direction. To cover the 112 miles properly, you should allow an entire day, with plenty of time for stops along the way. The same applies to its neighbor to the north, the Dingle Peninsula, some 132 miles long. If two full days are out of the question, my recommendation goes to Dingle, which has a unique character that in some mystical way seems to touch the soul.

Two especially helpful publications to pick up from the Tourist Office in Killarney are the "Ring of Kerry Area Guide" and the "Dingle Peninsula Area Guide," both of which have excellent maps and detailed information on points of interest.

1 The Ring of Kerry

Some of Kerry's most outstanding scenery lies along the 112 miles that are known far and wide as the Ring of Kerry. If you're coming to Killarney via West Cork and Glengarriff, you may well want to begin the Ring in Kenmare, ending in Killarney. From Killarney, the route lies through Killorglin and around the Iveragh Peninsula to Kenmare, then back over the mountains via a lovely scenic drive to complete the circle at Killarney.

SEEING THE RING OF KERRY

No matter how you approach this peninsula circle, it's a traveler's delight. The marvelous folder **"The Ring of Kerry Area Guide"** (mentioned in the introduction to this chapter and available from the Tourist Office) will make the trip even more meaningful. Again, however, from a Killarney base I strongly recommend that you stash the car and join one of the inexpensive bus tours.

By Bus

From Killarney, **Dero's Tours,** 22 Main St., Killarney, County Kerry (☎ 064/31251 or 31567), runs tours of the Ring daily from Easter to October, and you'll be picked up at your accommodations in the morning and returned there in the evening. When booking a tour, ask about possible discounts for holders of this book.

Barry O'Connor, of **O'Connor's Auto Tours,** Andross, Ross Road, Killarney, County Kerry (☎ 064/31052), operates coach tours, which run year-round. When booking a tour, ask about discounts for holders of this book.

By Car

If time permits, a leisurely drive around the Ring—with an overnight stop en route—is the ideal way to savor all the magnificent scenery you'll be passing through, and you'll find several recommended accommodations below.

With Killarney as a departure point, head for Killorglin via R562. A few miles to the north via N70 lies the little village of **Castlemaine,** home of Jack Duggan, "The Wild Colonial Boy."

At Killorglin, take N70 southwest to **Glenbeigh,** along the north coast of the peninsula through some of the Ring's most spectacular scenery, with the peaks of the Dingle Peninsula visible across the water.

If a break from driving would be welcomed here, take the short detour via R564 out to a long (three-mile) sandy beach that invites a swim in its sheltered waters—from mid-July to mid-September, there's also a lifeguard on duty.

From Glenbeigh, continue along the southern coastline of Dingle Bay to **Kells Bay,** a lovely sandy cove, where John Golden presides over ✪ **Caitin Baiter's Thatched Pub** overlooking the bay, a good stopping point for a great Irish coffee or a light lunch (if you're overnighting in the vicinity, there's traditional music here every night during the summer months).

About halfway between Glenbeigh and Caherciveen (on N70), look for **Pat's Craft Shop & Quarry Restaurant** (☎ 066/77601) in Kells, a combination craft shop, restaurant, convenience store, post office, and filling station—very much in the tradition of rural Ireland. They also maintain a fine collection of sheep breeds, some quite rare, and hold daily sheepdog competitions at 1pm and 2pm, with a sheltered viewing point for spectators.

A little farther on from Kells Bay is **Caherciveen,** where **The Barracks Interpretative Centre** explores the Fenian Rising and other historical events of the Iveragh Peninsula, and the "Man and the Landscape" exhibition features the area's archeology and natural history. **Sceilig Crystal** (☎ 066/72141) produces exquisite hand-cut gift items at reasonable prices.

Then, travel via R565 to ✪ **Valentia Island,** reached from the mainland by a causeway. Although its name would imply Spanish origin, it is from a romanticized pronunciation of the Irish *Beal Inse* ("Harbor at the Mouth of the Island") that "Valentia" evolved (its Irish name is actually *Oileán Dairbhre,* or "Island of the Oaks").

County Kerry

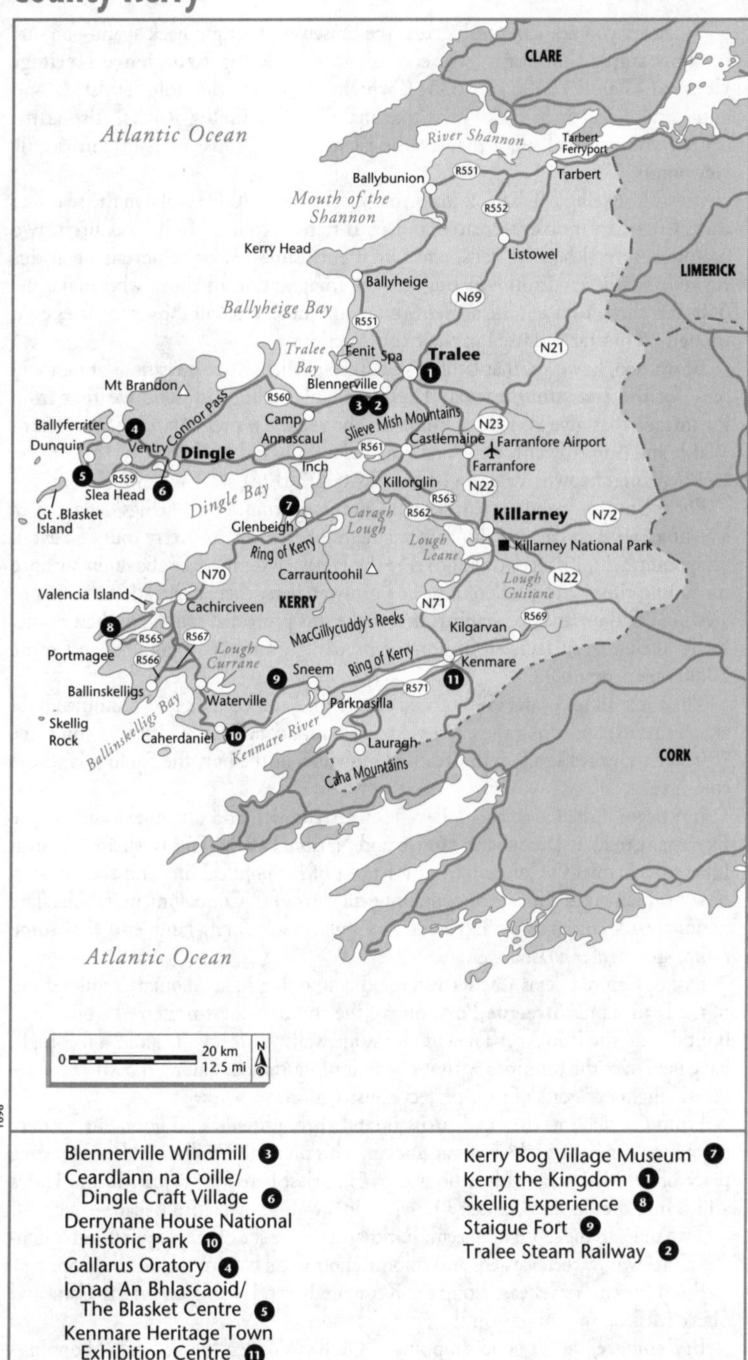

Whatever you do, *don't* rush across the causeway and right back again—be sure to allow ample time for a leisurely visit to the **Skellig Experience Heritage Centre** (☎ 066/76306 or 76351), which focuses on the unique history and antiquity of the three rocky piles that make up the **Skellig Rocks.** Also at the center, you can pick up a map of the island showing historic sites and scenic viewpoints.

It was to Skellig Michael, a massive hulk that rises 700 feet above the sea, that early Christian monks retreated and used native stone to build a church, two oratories, several beehive cells, and burial enclosures. Their achievement in this rugged, hostile environment staggers the imagination of those who make the 640-step climb to reach the ancient ruins, still intact after all those centuries even though no mortar was used in their construction.

Be warned, however, that landings on Skellig Michael are precarious at best and only for the *truly* stouthearted. There are daily sailings in good weather from Portmagee that give you three hours on the rock. To prebook, contact Dermot Walsh and Son (Owen), Knightstown, Valentia Island (☎ 066/76115), or Des Lavelle, Knightstown, Valentia Island (☎ 066/76124).

For the not-so-stouthearted, several ✪ **cruises** around the Skelligs depart from Valentia Pier each day at 2:30pm, a highlight of any Ring of Kerry tour. To avoid disappointment, it's a good idea to ring the Heritage Centre (see above) in advance for sailing times and prebooking. For birdwatchers, there's the added bonus of viewing the thousands of seabirds that make this protected sanctuary their home. Little Skellig is, in fact, an important breeding ground for gannets, and some 20,000 pairs nest here.

Then it's on to **Waterville** (noted for its fine golf courses and a multitude of ancient ruins) and along the coast via the **Coomakista Pass,** which lifts you some 700 feet above sea level, with breathtaking views of the bay, the Skelligs, and the coastline.

Just beyond the Coomakista Pass lies **Caherdaniel,** and one mile away, on the Derrynane road, is **Derrynane House and National Park.** This is where the Great Liberator, Daniel O'Connell, lived for most of his political life, and the house is now maintained as a museum containing all sorts of O'Connell memorabilia. The national park covers some 320 acres and is worth a leisurely ramble to view some rather spectacular coastal scenery.

East of Cahirdaniel is **Castlecove,** another loitering spot. About 1½ miles north of the road stands **Straigue Fort,** one of the country's best-preserved stone forts, built during the Iron Age. The circular stone walls, 13 feet wide and 18 feet high, have held over the centuries without benefit of mortar, and along their interior are several flights of stairs of near perfect construction.

From Castlecove, the road turns inland through wild and gorgeous scenery before coming back to the coast at **Sneem.** This pretty little village is the last resting place of Fr. Michael Walsh, who was parish priest here for 38 years in the 1800s and is immortalized as "Father O'Flynn" in a well-known Irish ballad.

Two miles to the south of Sneem, **Parknasilla** is the site of the elegant Great Southern Hotel, whose rock gardens and colorful subtropical blooms are worth a stop.

From Sneem, travel east along the Kenmare River, looking across the Caha and Slieve Miskish mountains on the opposite shore.

In **Kenmare,** there's good shopping at Quill's Woollen Market (see "Shopping" in the Killarney section in Chapter 13) and Cleo 2, Shelbourne Street (see Dublin "Shopping" in Chapter 6).

Stop by the **Heritage Centre** (it's just off the square in the Courthouse/Tourist Office) for an insight into the town you see today. Plan to allow two hours for a **Scenic and Wildlife Cruise** on Kenmare Bay; call 064/83171 for reservations and rates. Golfers may want to play around the 18-hole course at **Kenmare Golf Course** (☎ 064/41291).

From Kenmare, take the mountain road (N71) to Moll's Gap, Ladies' View, and back to Killarney.

Where to Stay

A Bed-and-Breakfast in Glenbeigh

✪ Ocean Wave

Ring of Kerry Rd. (N70), Glenbeigh, Co. Kerry. ☎ **066/68249.** 6 rms, all with bath. IR£21 ($33.60) single; IR£18 ($28.80) per person sharing. (Rates include breakfast.) No credit cards. Closed Oct–Mar.

This attractive modern home sits in beautifully landscaped grounds on the high side of the Ring of Kerry road, with sweeping views out over Dingle Bay. Noreen O'Toole has won much praise for her breakfast menu, as well as for her warm, friendly interest in her guests. One of the six rooms is a triple, and if you prefer a sea view, ask for a front room—the view from those in back is one of mountains and green fields. A spacious upstairs lounge has wide windows that take full advantage of the gorgeous Dingle Bay view, and there's an 18-hole golf course just across the road.

A Bed-and-Breakfast and Hostel on Valentia Island

✪ The Ring Lyne

Chapeltown, Valentia Island, Co. Kerry. ☎ **066/76103.** 10 rms, 6 with bath; 18 hostel bunk beds. IR£13 ($20.80) per person without bath; IR£15 ($24) per person with bath; IR£5 ($8) hostel bed. (Rates include breakfast.) No credit cards.

Jack O'Sullivan and his family have won a loyal following among avid fisherpeople who return year after year from other parts of Ireland and abroad for superb shore angling that yields as many as 20 species of fish during a single season. For those of us immune to the spell of casting a line, the O'Sullivans provide comfortable, inexpensive lodging in a rural Ireland ambience that is fast disappearing. Hostelers are also well looked after in bright, clean dormitories. The place holds a very real charm for me, personally, especially when the spacious bar fills up with locals and the enthusiastic, voluble fisherfolk at the end of the day. Good bar food is served all day, and meals in the Sceilig Room restaurant are centered around seafood fresh from the waters outside, along with a good smattering of beef, pork, and chicken dishes (see "Where to Eat," below).

Waterville

Klondyke House

New Line Rd., Waterville, Co. Kerry. ☎ **066/74119.** Fax 066/74666. 6 rms, all with bath. IR£19 ($30.40) single; IR£14 ($22.40) per person sharing. (Rates include breakfast.) AE, MC, V. Closed Nov–Mar.

Cirean Morris is the hospitable proprietor of this attractive home overlooking Waterville's famous championship golf course on the outskirts of the village. Decor throughout is bright and cheerful, and beds have orthopedic mattresses. There's also a spacious TV lounge and a drying room for guests.

An Inviting Alternative: An Inland Drive

Incidentally, an inviting alternative to continuing along the coastal Ring of Kerry route is the unmarked (but well-surfaced) road just before you reach Waterville that turns inland into a long valley up the center of the peninsula. After passing through Sallahig and Lissatinng Bridge, you can continue north to reach Killorglin, or turn south onto another unmarked road that goes through Ballaghbearna Gap to rejoin N70. The mountain, valley, and bog scenery presents a quite different landscape than that of the coastline.

Lake Rise

Lake Rd., Waterville, Co. Kerry. ☎ **0667/4278.** 4 rms, 2 with bath. IR£11.50 ($18.40) per person without bath, IR£13 ($20.80) per person with bath. 10% reduction for children. (Rates include breakfast.) No credit cards.

Mrs. Breda McAuliffe's country home half a mile from the village center has gorgeous views of Waterville, and she gives a warm welcome, as well as real local expertise, to guests who come to fish, golf, explore archeological sites, or simply relax.

The Smugglers Inn

Cliff Rd., Waterville, Co. Kerry. ☎ **066/74330.** Fax 066/74422. 9 rms, all with bath. Seasonal rates, IR£16.50–IR£25 ($26.40–$40) per person sharing; IR£20–IR£25 ($32–$40) single. Weekly and three-day rates available. (Rates include breakfast.) AE, MC, V. Open year-round.

This small, charming inn is owned and operated by Lucille and Harry Hunt, whose hospitality is well known throughout County Kerry. In addition to attractive, comfortable rooms overlooking the sea, they offer gourmet seafood and shellfish delicacies (see "Where to Eat," below).

Sunset House

Waterville, Co. Kerry. ☎ **0667/4258.** 8 rms, 4 with bath. IR£13.50 ($21.60) per person without bath; IR£15 ($24) with bath. Lower rates in off-season. (Rates include breakfast.) No credit cards. Closed Dec–Jan.

Mrs. Fitzgerald is the hostess of this lovely house overlooking Dingle Bay and Ballinskellig Island. Guest rooms are attractive and comfortable, and there's a homey atmosphere.

A Hostel in Waterville

Waterville Leisure Hostel

Waterville, Co. Kerry. ☎ **0667/4400.** 120 beds. IR£6–IR£8 ($9.60–$12.80) per person. 25% reduction for children. No credit cards. Open Apr–Sept, daily; Oct–Mar, weekends only.

Vincent Counihan has converted a big old stone building (that once housed the first cable station linking Ireland to the U.S. and Europe) into an outstanding privately owned hostel and outdoor adventure, sport, and leisure-training center. There are beds for 120, with bunk beds (continental quilts, pillows, and undersheet) in rooms for two, four, six, eight, ten, and twelve. Other facilities include shower rooms, washrooms, toilets, kitchen, dining room, laundry and drying room, two games rooms, a gym, and a TV lounge. Advance reservations are recommended.

Sneem

Avonlea House

Sportsfield Rd., Sneem, Co. Kerry. ☎ **064/45221.** 5 rms, all with bath. IR£18.50 ($29.60) single; IR£14 ($22.40) per person sharing. 25% reduction for children. (Rates include breakfast.) Dinner IR£10 ($14.50) extra. No credit cards. Closed Dec–Feb.

Mrs. Maura Hussey's two-story home is on the outskirts of town (signposted in town), with nicely done-up guest rooms. The food here is excellent, and there's a turf fire blazing in the residents' lounge most nights.

✪ Bank House

North Sq., Sneem, Co. Kerry. ☎ **064/45226.** 3 rms, all with bath. IR£14.50 ($23.20) per person. No credit cards. Closed Dec–Feb.

Margaret and Noel Harrington open their home—which one reader described as "clean, cute, and charming"—and welcome guests with a warmth that is exceptional, even for the Irish. Noel operates a shop of hand-knits and hand-loomed sweaters in the delightful village of Sneem, good browsing and shopping territory. Guest rooms are light and airy, and Margaret excels in home baking and delicious snacks.

Kenmare

✪ Ardmore House

Killarney Rd., Kenmare, Co. Kerry. ☎ **064/41406.** 6 rms, all with bath. IR£20 ($32) single; IR£16 ($25.60) per person sharing. 50% reduction for children. (Rates include breakfast.) V. Closed Dec–Feb.

On the outskirts of Kenmare, in a quiet cul-de-sac just off the main Kenmare–Ring of Kerry road, Ardmore House is a modern one-story bungalow framed by a colorful rose garden. Toni and Tom Connor have six rooms with shower and toilet (one is a four-bed family room). Those in the front look out to the roses, and the back view is of peaceful green pastures, with mountains in the background. Central heat and plenty of parking space, and it's only about a five-minute walk to the town center.

Marino House

Reen, Kenmare, Co. Kerry. ☎ **064/41154** or 41501. 8 rms, 1 with bath. IR£14 ($22.40) per person. (Rates include breakfast. No extra charge for private bath.) Self-catering house (sleeps 6) IR£350 ($560) per week. 20% reduction for children. Dinner IR£11 ($17.60) extra. No credit cards. Closed Oct–Apr.

Marino House occupies a scenic site two miles from the town center on a small, wooded finger of land extending out into Kenmare Bay. There's an old-fashioned air about the place, yet there's total modern comfort inside—an irresistible combination. Run by Mrs. Edna O'Sullivan and her family, centrally heated Marino House features comfortable guest rooms and excellent meals, served in a dining room overlooking the green lawn. Much patronized by regulars, this place gets booked quickly from year to year, so best reserve as far in advance as possible. The 3-bedroom self-catering house will sleep six and has a fitted kitchen, dining room, and lounge as well as central heating.

Kilgarvan

Sillerdane Lodge

Coolnoohill, Kilgarvan, Co. Kerry. ☎ **064/85359.** 6 rms, all with bath. IR£20 ($32) single; IR£15.50 ($24.80) per person sharing. 25% reduction for children. (Rates include breakfast.) Dinner IR£13.50 ($21.60) extra. No credit cards. Closed Oct–Easter.

Sillerdane Lodge offers a most unusual feature for an Irish B&B—a heated outdoor swimming pool! Set in a beautiful valley 13 miles east of Kenmare via R569, the pretty bungalow has more than just that to offer, however, and perhaps its most appealing feature is the gracious Mrs. Joan McCarthy. This lovely lady takes a personal interest in all her guests and her home reflects her concern for their comfort. The bright dining room has huge windows to take advantage of gorgeous views, and bedrooms have tea/coffeemakers and are beautifully decorated and spotless; not surprising, since Joan is a talented interior decorator. There's central heating and plenty of parking space.

WHERE TO EAT

Most of the small hotels you'll pass in your trip around the Ring of Kerry serve exceptional meals of fresh seafood and local Irish lamb, beef, or pork, and many also add vegetarian dishes to their menu. Unfortunately, space permits only the limited listing below. (See also "Where to Eat: In Nearby Killorglin" in Chapter 13.)

Portmagee/Valentia Island

✪ Fisherman's Bar and Restaurant

Seafront, Portmagee. ☎ **066/77103.** Bar food under IR£5 ($8); salad and meat platters IR£4.50–IR£8 ($7.20–$12.80); average à la carte dinner IR£15 ($24); set four-course meal IR£14 ($22.40). No credit cards. Apr–Sept, daily 7am–9pm (bar food served 10am–6pm). BAR FOOD/SALADS/SEAFOOD/STEAK/IRISH.

This atmospheric waterfront bar in Portmagee (just across the bridge from Valentia Island) features seafood even in the pub grub menu, and if fresh lobster from local waters is on offer, you're in for a real treat. And if you've been looking for an authentic Irish stew, you'll find an excellent rendition of the traditional dish in a setting made cozy by lots of wood and a glowing open fire.

✪ The Ring Lyne

Chapeltown, Valentia Island. ☎ **066/76103.** Bar food under IR£5 ($8); set dinner IR£13 ($20.80); average à la carte dinner IR£14 ($22.40). No credit cards. Daily 12:30–9pm. BAR FOOD/SEAFOOD/MEAT/POULTRY.

For a full description of the Ring Lyne, see "Where to Stay," above. The bar food here is quite good and often includes local seafood. But it is in the Sceilig Room that the food really excels—scallops, scampi, plaice, and salmon are prepared in the traditional manner, with few frills to obscure the fresh, subtle flavor of each. Steak, lamb, and chicken dishes are also excellent, as are the homemade desserts (don't miss their apple pie and thick cream).

Waterville

Lobster Bar Restaurant

Waterville. ☎ **066/74183.** Bar food under IR£5 ($8); salad plates IR£4.50–IR£5.50 ($4.70–$8.80); grills IR£7–IR£9.50 ($11.20–$15.20); seafood dinners IR£7–IR£14 ($11.20–$22.40). No credit cards. Open Mon–Sat 8am–9pm. BAR FOOD/SEAFOOD/MEAT/POULTRY.

There's a warm, friendly atmosphere in this informal bar/restaurant. It's self-service, and grill and fish dishes come with salad and vegetables. Daily specials can include fresh local lobster at very reasonable prices, and there's an extensive restaurant menu. During the high season, there's music on some weeknights, and on Friday and Saturday in other months. Good value for money.

Readers Recommend

The Final Furlong, Boherbue, Carhan, Cahirciveen, Co. Kerry. ☎ 066/72810. *"This brand new B&B is situated on the banks of a river just outside of Cahirciveen. The accommodations are lovely, and it's not far from the birthplace of liberator Daniel O'Connell."* —Mary Boyle, Broomall, PA

Rockcrest House, Gortamullen, Kenmare, Co. Kerry. ☎ 064/41248. *"Marian O'Dwyer runs this spacious, beautiful B&B that overlooks the valley below. Most rooms have a private bath, and there is more than enough drawer and closet space. She served a generous breakfast, with extra helpings of her soda bread. Kenmare is only a five-minute walk away."* —Mark Noguchi, Honolulu, HI

Dunkerron Lodge, Sneem Road, Kenmare, Co. Kerry. ☎ 064/41102. *"This beautiful 19th-century lodge is on a 70-acre parkland bordering Kenmare Bay; and the ruins of Dunkerron Castle, stronghold of the O'Sullivan Mór, are next to the lodge. Rooms are beautifully furnished and larger than any rooms we had stayed in on our trip. The glass-enclosed breakfast room overlooks the castle ruins and the parkland, and Moya Gubbins serves the most exceptional homemade brown bread I've tasted."* —Michael Harte, Reston, VA

Ard na Mara, Pier Road, Kenmare, Co. Kerry. ☎ 064/41399. *"This is a pleasant B&B with a lovely setting and views, run by Jutta and Edel Dahm. Jutta, a very friendly, knowledgeable, and helpful hostess."* —Joseph Keilin, Mendham, NJ

Fern Rock, Tinnahalla, Killorglin, Co. Kerry. ☎ 066/61848. *"Mrs. Clifford is a lovely lady and very helpful. The rooms, lounge, and dining rooms are spotless and very comfortable."* —Christine McDermott, Essex, England

Hollybough House Cappagh, Kilgobnet, Beaufort, Killarney, Co. Kerry. ☎ 064/44255. *"Mrs. Tess Donna is hostess here, and the house is equidistant from Killarney, Kilorglen, and Glencar, just within the Ring of Kerry. The loudest noises you'll hear in the morning are the cows or the braying of Bessie, the Doonas' pet donkey. The view out my window of McGillycuddy's Reeks was breathtaking. Tess serves a hearty breakfast, accompanied by the most delicious brown bread."* —Michael Haran, Vienna, VA

✪ The Smuggler's Inn

Cliff Road, Waterville. ☎ **066/74330.** Snacks IR£2–IR£8 ($3.20–$8); main courses IR£12–IR£18 ($19.20–$28.80); set lunch IR£13 ($20.80); set dinner IR£22 ($35.20). AE, MC, V. Daily 12:30–2:30pm and 6–10pm. Snacks 12:30–10pm. SNACKS/SEAFOOD/MEAT/POULTRY.

This waterside gourmet restaurant is widely known for its seafood creations, and a mark of their insistence on the freshest of ingredients is the tank from which your lobster and/or crayfish are taken alive. Although there are lovely nonfish dishes on the menu, most diners opt for seafood, and with filet of plaice provençal, monkfish sauté with garlic butter, grilled Waterville Lake salmon with béarnaise sauce, and a score of other delicacies, who could blame them. That is not to say, however, that the roast rack of Kerry lamb, filet steak and pepper sauce, and the like are any less excellent. Even the snack menu here is outstanding, and includes many of their specialties from the à la carte menu.

Readers Recommend

Rascal's Restaurant & Wine Bar, Ballinskelligs, Co. Kerry. *"At the far half-way point of the outer Ring of Kerry is this cute, quaint wine bar with an attractive wooden interior, a casual manner, and a nice selection of wines by the glass. They are very accommodating for either full meals or snacks."* —Fred Trietach, Devan, PA

Kenmare

✪ The Purple Heather Bistro

Henry St. ☎ **064/41016.** Cold and hot plates IR£4–IR£7 ($6.40–$11.20). No credit cards. Mon–Sat noon–6:30pm. SEAFOOD/TRADITIONAL/VEGETARIAN.

There's excellent bistro food here, in a setting best described as eccentric. Walls and ceiling are decorated with objects of wood and copper, with hanging wine bottles and an assortment of various other items. Lunch specialties include excellent omelets as well as salads and smoked salmon and mackerel, the latter two served with fresh brown bread, and wonderful crab or prawn open sandwiches.

2 The Dingle Peninsula & the Blasket Islands

The 30-mile-long Dingle Peninsula is the most westerly point of land in Europe; its offshore Blasket Islands are affectionately known as the "last parish before New York." Its beginnings are shrouded in the mists of prehistory, which left its marks scattered over the face of the Slieve Mish mountains, along small coves and rocky cliffs, and in the legends that persist to this day. To date, no fewer than 2,000 archeological sites have been identified on the peninsula.

The English named it "Dingle" (in Irish, *An Daingean,* "the fortress") because Dingle is the largest town on the peninsula—its ancient Irish name, however, which is still in wide use, is *Corca Dhuibhne* (approximate pronunciation "Corka Graina"—not exact, but the best I can do!), which means the "seeds" (descendants) of Duibhne, a goddess of this area.

Remains of seven earthen ring forts and two headland stone forts attest to the fortified nature of the peninsula, so perhaps "Dingle" is appropriate. Its Glenagalt Valley translates as the "Valley of the Madmen," so called because as far back as the 12th century, or even earlier, the mentally afflicted came to roam its wilds, drink the waters of Tobernagalt ("The Well of the Madmen"), and eat the watercress that grew along the stream, and return home sound in mind and body after a few months. Mystical? Oh, yes! I sometimes feel that the very essence of Celtic magic has been distilled into the soft air of the Dingle Peninsula. Or perhaps it is the lyrical accents of Gaelic, the everyday language here, that makes it seem so.

The West Kerry Gaeltacht ("*Gail*-tuckt") is one of several areas around the country officially designated as Irish-speaking by the government in an effort to assure the survival of this ancient language. In summer months those interested in learning or improving their knowledge of Irish can arrange language courses with stays in Irish-speaking homes and many social activities based on traditional music and dance. For full details, contact **Oidhreacht Chorca Dhuibhne,** Ballyferriter, County Kerry (☎ 066/56100; fax 066/56348).

DINGLE TOWN

GETTING THERE Leaving Killarney, the route is well signposted all the way to Dingle town. Take the main Killorglin road (R562), and at Killorglin turn north on to N70 to Castlemaine, where R561 turns west, passing through Inch and Anascaul to reach Dingle town.

From Tralee, take R559 through Blennerville, Derrymore, and Camp; then follow signs over the Conor Pass into Dingle.

ESSENTIALS Orientation Dingle town is a bustling little market town, with a boat-building industry right in the middle of things, ideal for walking. In the old Spanish trading days this was the chief Kerry port, and in Elizabethan times it was a walled town.

These days, fishing and tourism hold sway. There are several Irish goods shops, plenty of places to get a good meal, and enough music after dark to fill all your evenings.

Information The Tourist Office on Main Street (☎ 066/51188) is open only in summer; other months, make inquiries about Dingle and the peninsula at the Killarney or Tralee tourist office.

Area Code The telephone area code for Dingle is 066.

WHAT TO SEE & DO

You'll look at Dingle's narrow streets and tiny medieval lanes through different eyes after a one-hour historic/archeology **walking tour** led by Micheál or Padraic. There are two tours daily, leaving from outside the **Tourist Office** (check with them for exact times; ☎ 066/51937 or 51606). The cost is IR£3 ($4.80) per person—money well spent.

Dingle residents have always been known for their strong, individualistic character. In recent years they've been joined by ✪ **Fungi the dolphin,** who has moved in and promptly become the beloved pet of the entire peninsula. The friendliest, most lovable dolphin in these waters, he has become Dingle town's No. 1 tourist attraction, cavorting through the waters of Dingle Bay, following the boats that regularly ferry visitors out to his watery home, playing with scuba divers, and even, on one occasion, joyfully leaping right over a small boat. You can watch his antics from Hussey's Folly, an old Customs watchtower, or from the tiny sandy beach at Fladden. You'll find the boats down by the harbor, and the fare for an on-the-water encounter with Fungi is IR£5 ($8).

There's an interesting **historical exhibition** of Dingle photos and memorabilia from the past at the Old Presbyter, Main Street, which is open without charge in summer months, Monday through Saturday from 10am to 6pm.

It is now possible to plant a bit of Ireland in your garden back home; stop by ✪ **Irish Wildflowers Ltd.,** Cooleen, Dingle (☎ 066/51000; fax 066/51991) to see their annual, perennial, and biennial wildflower seed packets, as well as other fine floral gifts. Marianne Begley, a transplanted American, lost her heart to the wildflowers of Ireland and set up what has become a thriving business, with the packets on sale in gift and craft shops around the country. She also welcomes mail orders, and prices run all the way from IR£1 ($1.60) to IR£60 ($96). You'll find her shop down a small lane (turn left just before the roundabout at the eastern edge of town) at the end of a row of fishermen's cottages.

On the western edge of town, the ✪ **Cearolann Craft Village** is a cluster of small cottages housing shops and workshops. On the opposite side of the road, look for the workshop of silversmith Brian de Staic, who also has a shop in Green Street in town (☎ 066/51298). One very appealing item he fashions is an unusual silver necklace in the shape of an Ogham stone with your name inscribed in the strokes of that ancient language. He also has silver, gold, and enamel pendants of Fungi.

On Dykegate Lane, ✪ **An Café Liteartha** (☎ 066/51388) is a very special place that carries an impressive array of Irish-interest publications and recordings in the front shop section, with inexpensive food service in a back room. It's open year-round, Monday through Saturday from 10am to 6pm and on Sunday from 11am to 6pm. For good buys in Waterford crystal, Aran sweaters, and other Irish goods, it's hard to beat **McKena's,** on Dykegate Street (☎ 066/51198), which gives a discount for payment in cash.

There's bar food during the day and music on summer nights at the **O Gairbhi pub** and **Garvey's Pub,** both on Strand Street, and at **Benner's Hotel** on Main Street. But for a night of traditional music and song that comes from true family tradition, look for the red-and-white pub on Bridge Street with the name ✪ **UaFlaibeartaig,** which translates to O'Flaherty's. The late father of the present O'Flaherty clan was recognized as one of the country's best traditional musicians, and now son Fergus and daughter Maire raise instruments and voice each night surrounded by locals and visitors who've come to hear the best. It's a warm, informal gathering in a setting that's as traditional as the music, with the haphazard collection of pictures, posters, and other assorted items that has accumulated here as in almost any country pub in Ireland.

WHERE TO STAY

Dykegate House

8 Dykegate St., Dingle, Co. Kerry. ☎ **066/51549.** 5 rms, none with bath. IR£14 ($22.40) per person. 50% reduction for children. (Rates include breakfast.) No credit cards.

You'll get a very warm welcome from Mrs. Mary Leonard at Dykegate House. Conveniently located within walking distance of everything in town, the two-story house is rather plain but homey. Mrs. Leonard serves up one of the best breakfasts I've had in Ireland in a light and airy dining room. Guest rooms vary in size, but all have sinks and are comfortably furnished. This has been a favorite of readers for years, and after several personal stays, I heartily concur in their endorsements.

✪ Greenmount House

Gortanora, Dingle, Co. Kerry. ☎ **066/51414.** 6 rms, all with bath. TEL TV. IR£13.50–IR£20 ($21.60–$32) per person sharing, depending on season. (Rates include breakfast.) No credit cards. Parking available.

Set on a secluded site with panoramic views of Dingle town and harbor, this outstanding accommodation, with its beautifully landscaped garden, is owned by John and Mary Curran. Both of the Currans have a deep knowledge of the peninsula, coming as they do from families rooted in this area for many generations. Their interest in helping guests makes staying here much like having your own personal guide. All bedrooms have orthopedic beds with electric blankets, radios, tea/coffeemakers, and hairdryers. Their award-winning breakfasts are served in a plant-filled conservatory looking out to Dingle Bay. To find them, turn right at the roundabout on the eastern edge of town, then right again at the next junction, and drive to the top of the hill, where you'll see Greenmount on your left.

✪ Mrs. Betty Hand

Green St., Dingle, Co. Kerry. ☎ **066/51538.** 5 rms, 4 with bath. IR£14 ($22.40) per person without bath, IR£15 ($24) per person extra with bath. 50% reduction for children. (Rates include breakfast.)

Mrs. Betty Hand's large two-story home is also conveniently located in the heart of town and has nicely appointed guest rooms. The friendliness of the Hand family is legendary, and they are always delighted to have American guests. There's central heat and a garden where guests are welcome to sit on a sunny afternoon.

Marian House

Marian Park, Dingle, Co. Kerry. ☎ **066/51773.** 5 rms, all with bath. IR£22 ($35.20) single; IR£15 ($24) per person sharing. 40% reduction for children. (Rates include breakfast.) No credit cards. Closed Nov–May.

Mrs. Ann Cahillane's attractive town house is in a quiet cul-de-sac in Dingle town, with pubs and restaurants an easy walk away. Guest rooms are nicely done up, and each has a color TV. Mrs. Cahillane is the soul of Irish hospitality, always happy to help with touring plans.

The Old Stone House

Cliddaun, Dingle, Co. Kerry. ☎ and fax **066/59882.** 3 rms, none with bath. IR£21 ($33.60) single; IR£16 ($25.60) per person sharing. (Rates include breakfast.) ACC, M, V.

Becky and Michael O'Connor have lovingly transformed this 1864 farmhouse 2½ miles west of Dingle town into a haven of peace and quiet replete with comforts of the modern world. Simple country antiques furnish the house, and the cozy sitting room and dining area carries on the tradition of hospitality and friendly gatherings in what was originally the home's heart, the kitchen. The O'Connors happily share with guests their excellent collection of books on local archeology, history, early Christian Ireland, Celtic lore, and folk and fairy tales, as well as their firsthand knowledge of the peninsula's attractions.

Worth a Splurge

✪ Dingle Skellig Hotel

Dingle, Co. Kerry. ☎ **066/51144.** Fax 066/51501. 100 rms, all with bath. TV TEL. IR£44–IR£53 ($70.40–$84.80) single; IR£68–IR£96 ($108.80–$153.60) double, depending on season. Excellent Weekend Break rates available. AE, MC, V.

With one of the most dramatic locations on the Dingle Peninsula, the Skellig overlooks the harbor of Dingle Bay, and public rooms take full advantage of the view. The nicely furnished guest rooms all have private baths, satellite TVs, radios, and direct-dial telephones.

Dining: The restaurant, with its pretty conservatory, specializes in seafood from local waters and overlooks Dingle Bay.

Facilities: There's a leisure center with swimming pool, sauna, and sunbed, and other amenities include a children's playground, snooker room, jumbo chess (great fun), and tennis court. Guests are given reduced rates at the nearby golf course, and pony trekking and deep-sea fishing can be arranged.

✪ Doyle's Seafood Bar and Townhouse

John St., Dingle, Co. Kerry. ☎ **066/51174.** Fax 066/51816. 8 rms, all with bath. TV TEL. IR£39 ($62.40) single; IR£31 ($49.60) per person sharing. (Rates include breakfast.) ACC, DC, MC, V.

Settle in here and you're right in the heart of Dingle town. Over the past several years John and Stella Doyle have gained an international reputation for the quality of seafood served in their small, flagstone-paved restaurant in Dingle, a tribute to their single-mindedness in adhering to the highest standards in whatever they undertake. So it comes as no surprise that they have maintained that same high standard in renovating an adjacent 1830s house into eight attractive and comfortable bedrooms. Antique furnishings with a Victorian flavor add to their appeal, but comfort is not overlooked, with extra-large orthopedic beds. The two houses are interconnected, making access to the restaurant easy, while maintaining a high degree of privacy.

Self-Catering

Beginish Apartments

Green St., Dingle, Co. Kerry. ☎ **066/51588.** Fax 066/51591. 3 apts, 1 one-bedroom, 2 two-bedroom. Seasonal weekly rates IR£175–IR£330 ($280–$528). No credit cards. In heart of Dingle town.

In the ultimate convenient location, just two doors up from the restaurant of the same name, these apartments are decorated and furnished to an exceptionally high standard. They come complete with color satellite TV, dishwasher, microwave, washing machine and dryer, and a coffee percolator. The ground floor apartment has a patio garden, with one bedroom suitable for two people. The two first-floor apartments have two bedrooms that will accommodate three.

Nearby Accommodations

✪ Cleevaun

Lady's Cross, Miltown, Dingle, Co. Kerry. ☎ **066/51108.** 9 rms, all with bath. TV. IR£18–IR£20 ($28.80–$32) per person. 25% reduction for children. (Rates include breakfast.) No credit cards. Closed Dec–Feb.

This modern bungalow's name, *Cliabhan* in Irish, means "cradle," and it's only about a 10-minute walk from Dingle town. Sean and Charlotte Cluskey have a seemingly inexhaustible knowledge of the Dingle Peninsula and a keen desire to share it with their guests. From the pleasant lounge and dining room, there are views of green pastures dotted with grazing sheep and a panorama that takes in Dingle Bay and Mount Brandon. There's an ancient Ogham stone in the field out back and a ring fort down in the pasture. The lounge and breakfast room decor makes use of pine wood and yellow walls, and guest rooms have an old-country pine theme, as well as orthopedic beds. Charlotte is one of the few Irish hostesses to serve percolated coffee to Americans who've overdosed on tea, and on arrival you'll be offered coffee (or tea) and homemade porter cake. Some guest rooms also have tea/coffeemakers. The award-winning breakfast menu not only includes the traditional Irish breakfast, but adds choices of pancakes, cheese, and fruit.

Dúinin House

Conor Pass Rd., Dingle, Co. Kerry. ☎ **066/51335.** 5 rms, all with bath. IR£14–IR£16 ($22.40–$25.60) per person sharing. (Rates include breakfast.) No credit cards. Central heating and private parking. 1/2 mile from Dingle.

This modern bungalow, fronted by a green lawn bordered by colorful flowers, is the home of the charming Mrs. Anne Nelison. Her husband, who teaches history in the local secondary school, plays and teaches traditional music, a real bonus for guests. In addition to the attractive guest rooms, there's a lounge and TV room for guests and tea/coffee facilities in the conservatory. The breakfast menu is extensive.

Where to Eat

Armada Restaurant and Star Bar

Strand St. ☎ **066/51505.** Bar food IR£2–IR£10 ($3.20–$16); restaurant main courses IR£8–IR£15 ($12.80–$24); fixed-price dinner IR£16 ($25.60). July–Aug, daily 12:30–2:15pm and

6–9:30pm. Sept–Nov. Tues–Sun 12:30–2:15pm and 6–9:30pm. Closed Dec–Feb. BAR FOOD/SEAFOOD/TRADITIONAL/VEGETARIAN.

The Armada is a pleasant, moderately priced eatery run by Mark and Ann Kerry (Ann does the cooking), who also own the Star Bar on the ground floor, which has won several awards for its à la carte menu. Meals in the upstairs restaurant feature seafood and local meats, and there's also a good vegetarian salad on the menu. The Special Tourist Menu is also offered.

✪ Beginish Restaurant

Green St. ☎ **066/51588.** Reservations recommended. Average à la carte dinner IR£15 ($24). ACC, AE, DC, MC, V. Tues–Sun 6–9:30pm. SEAFOOD/VEGETARIAN.

Mrs. Pat Moore runs this delightful small restaurant. She has managed to achieve a light and airy—and at the same time, cozy—look, and there's a lovely conservatory overlooking the garden out back. The food, with an emphasis on fresh seafood (what else, in Dingle!), is beautifully prepared and nicely served.

Country Kitchen

Anascaul. No phone. Snacks and main courses IR£1.10–IR£7 ($1.76–$11.20). No credit cards. June–Oct daily 9am–9pm. 11miles east of Dingle, signposted on Castlemain/Dingle road. BREAKFAST/LIGHT MEALS.

This small, two-story farmhouse has been dishing up home-cooked meals for more than ten years in an unpretentious but friendly setting. A good stop for lunch of quiche, salad plates, or sandwiches; mid-afternoon tea of scones, apple pie, and/or ice cream; or dinner of fish, lamb, beef, and always a vegetarian selection.

Dingle Skellig Hotel

Dingle, Co. Kerry. ☎ **066/51638.** Bar food IR£5–IR£8 ($8–$12.80); set dinner IR£20 ($32); main courses IR£7–IR£15 ($11.20–$24). AE, MC, V. Daily, bar food 12:30–6pm, dinner 7–9:30pm. BAR FOOD/SEAFOOD/TRADITIONAL/VEGETARIAN.

Budget watchers can dine in style in the bar of this waterfront hotel (see "Where to Stay"), which has one of the best bar menus I've run across. Seafood is featured, along with the usual pub fare of sandwiches, soup, hot plates, and salads. The pricier Coastguard Restaurant is the only eatery in Dingle that overlooks Dingle Bay. While I find it almost impossible to bypass fresh seafood on offer, the menu also includes Kerry mountain lamb, beef, pork, chicken, and even duck. Vegetarian dishes are imaginative as well as healthy (try the vegetarian Stroganoff, served with a paprika and brandy sauce on a bed of pasta).

✪ Doyle's Seafood Bar

John St. ☎ **066/51174.** Reservations recommended. Main courses IR£11–IR£16 ($17.60–$25.60). Service charge 10%. ACC, AE, DC, MC, V. Mid-Mar to mid-Nov, Mon–Sat 6–9pm. SEAFOOD.

John and Stella Doyle have created one of the best restaurants in Dingle, winner of Bord Fáilté's Award of Excellence year after year. The restaurant adjoins their luxury town house accommodations (see above), and the cozy old pub has rock walls, a flagstone floor, and a blackboard menu showing a selection of seafood from local fishing boats' same-day catch. You'll find John up front at the bar, while Stella reigns in the kitchen. In addition to lobster (a specialty of the house), salmon, oysters, and other shellfish, there's good homemade soup and Stella's freshly baked scones. If you haven't booked in advance you can expect a wait in this small, popular place (but that's no problem at all if you're ensconced at the friendly bar with other waitees). Don't plan to get there much after 7pm, however, to be sure of being seated.

THE DINGLE PENINSULA

If you have made the wise decision to base yourself locally, a good touring plan is to make a leisurely drive around the southern edge of the peninsula the first day, saving the Conor Pass and the northern shoreline for the next. For nondrivers, there are bus tours departing Dingle town, and you can get details from the Tourist Office. Pick up a copy of **"The Dingle Peninsula Guide"** from the Tourist Office before you set out. Walkers can also inquire about **The Dingle Way** walking track, as well as Maurice Sheehy's excellent guide, **"The Dingle Peninsula: 16 Walks Through Its Heritage."**

A marvelous introduction to the peninsula is a 2/3-hour **Archeological Coach Tour** led by a local archeologist. Limited to eight people, the tours visit four or five monuments, dating from 3000 B.C. to A.D. 1700. The bus leaves from the top of the pier in Dingle three times daily, and advance booking is strongly recommended through **SCIUIRD,** Holy Ground, Dingle, Co. Kerry (☎ 066/51937 or 51606). Cost is IR£5 ($8).

Unfortunately, space will not permit a detailed description of the thousands of prehistoric relics around the Dingle Peninsula—that's best left to the guides named above. The peninsula also has some outstanding potteries and crafts shops, and interesting historical exhibitions.

FROM DINGLE TOWN TO SLEA HEAD

Driving west from town, **Ventry Harbour** was, according to legend, the scene of a fierce battle between the King of the World, Daire Doon, and the King of Ireland, Fionn MacCumhaill.

Stop in at **Sheehy's Pottery,** Ventry (☎ 066/59962). Penny Sheehy is the potter who specializes in unique ceramic Celtic murals and explanation plaques of old Celtic myths. She also has a nice range of unusual small kitchen utensils, ashtrays, and personalized mugs with your name in the Gaelic style, etc., that fit easily into your suitcase. The old timber-ceilinged building that was once a ballroom is almost a sightseeing attraction in itself, and light meals of home-cooked food are served.

Still farther west, ✪ **Dunbeg Fort** perches on a high promontory, its landward side surrounded by earthen trenches, and its 22-foot-thick wall riddled with an elaborate souterrain (inner passage). Farther along, at the high cliffs of ✪ **Slea Head** you get the most sweeping view of sheltered coves below and the Blasket Islands across the water.

THE BLASKET ISLANDS

The Great Blasket is the largest of these seven offshore islands. It was once inhabited, but the last of its tiny population was moved to the mainland in 1953, when the fishing industry failed to provide a living wage and the government offered land grants for small farm holdings on the peninsula. Visitors from Springfield, Massachusetts, may feel a special bond to the people of the Blaskets, since many islanders who emigrated settled in that city. Boats go out from Dunquin Harbor (☎ 066/56455 to book) during summer months, and a trip out to the island provides a break of sheer tranquility and scenic beauty that is exceptional even for Ireland.

Steps are being taken by the Irish government to acquire title to the Great Blasket and maintain it as an official national historic park, preserving the ruined village intact and developing activities that reflect the island's culture and traditions.

Between Dunquin and Ballyferriter, look for signposts to the **Blasket Island Interpretative Centre** overlooking the sea. The strikingly designed building affords spectacular views of the islands, and visual displays cover the social, literary, and economic lifestyles of islanders.

The Rest of the Peninsula

Another of the very good potteries on the peninsula is **Dunquin Pottery,** on the road between Slea Head and Dunquin. Operated by local people—Maureen, Eiblin, Helena, and Sean Daly, who worked for founder Jean Oldfield for many years—the pottery turns out hand-thrown, ovenproof stoneware in shades of sand and browns and blues. The prices are reasonable, and the small cafe at the pottery serves Rambouts coffee, Irish porter cake, and other snacks.

On beyond Dunquin, in the center of Ballyferriter, stop at the old school that houses the **Oidhreacht Chorca Dhuibhne** (the Corca Dhuibhne Regional Museum; ☎ 066-56333) for an overview of the peninsula from its geological beginnings through its rich archeological heritage right through to modern-day topics. Curator Isabel Bennett is usually on hand to answer questions and advise on how to visit the spectacular archeological sites of the region, some famous and others less well known. The exhibit contains artifacts found on excavations in the area, as well as ogham stones, cross slabs, and other ancient objects. The museum is open year-round (weekends only in winter). In summer, a small tea and coffee shop serves homemade soup, sandwiches, and snacks.

Also in Ballyferriter, the **West Kerry Co-op** has an excellent illustrated guidebook, which outlines a driving tour. The co-op can book you into local lodgings if you've fallen under Dingle's mystical spell and can't bear to leave just yet. The office is open Monday through Friday from 9am to 5:30pm. The story behind the co-op is an inspiring one, beginning in 1968 when young people were leaving in droves and there was great concern that the unique culture and heritage of the Gaelic-speaking region would wither and die. Much of the land had been untillable, but by banding together, 800 members of the farming community were able to import a special deep-plowing machine to break up the layer of iron that lay just inches beneath the surface of the land, to turn it into productive acres. The co-op has now reclaimed more than 12,000 acres. They've also taken an active part in upgrading tourist facilities, as well as expanding the summer-school program that brings students to study Gaelic.

At Ballyferriter, internationally known Louis Mulcahy (☎ 066/56229; fax 066/56366) operates a ✪ **pottery studio/workshop,** where he trains local potters in the production of many unusual items made from clay and finished with glazes developed in the workshop. There are the standard dinner sets, mugs, pitchers, and the like, but in addition, giant jugs and vases, unusual lamp bases, and beautiful wall plaques are on display in the studio. Louis's distinctive designs set his work apart from any other. Visitors are welcome to visit the workshop, and prices are quite reasonable for the unusually high quality. Open seven days a week year-round.

One of the peninsula's most astonishing relics is ✪ **Gallarus Oratory,** just off the road from Ballydavid back to Dingle town. It's a marvelous specimen of early Christian architecture. Built in an inverted boat shape, it has remained completely watertight for more than 1,500 years, its stones perfectly fitted without benefit of any kind of mortar. In the same vicinity, look, also, for the **Alphabet Stone** in the churchyard of Cill Maolkeador, an ancient ruined church. The pillar is carved with both the Roman alphabet and Ogham strokes.

At **Brandon Creek** (the legendary starting point of St. Brendan's voyage to the New World), stop in at ✪ **An Bother** (it means "The Road," and it sits right at the roadside). It's a place to relax by the fire in the lounge or sit at the bar in the small front room, with the constant flow of Gaelic conversation lulling you into a sense of the timelessness that is Dingle. You'll meet mostly locals here, and they welcome visitors warmly, breaking into English often enough to keep you from feeling excluded.

To reach the northern shores of the peninsula, take the **Conor Pass** road from Dingle town over to ✪ **Castlegregory** with its views from the pass and along the coastal road.

In the little town of **Camp,** turn off the main road and drive up to ✪ **James Ashe's Pub.** This is the Irish pub you dreamed of before you came to Ireland—smoke-darkened wood, low ceilings, a peat fire glowing on the hearth, and Irish faces in the pub their families have frequented for generations. Margaret Ashe or her son, Thomas, will likely be behind the bar. The adjoining restaurant serves excellent lunches from 12:30 to 2:30pm from mid-May to mid-September, and dinner from 6 to 9:30pm from March to January with menu emphasis on fresh local seafood.

WHERE TO STAY

Guesthouses

Aisling

Castlegregory, Tralee, Co. Kerry. ☎ **066/39134.** 5 rms, 2 with bath. IR£13 ($20.80) per person without bath. IR£15 ($24) per person with bath. 15% reduction for children. (Rates include breakfast.) No credit cards. Closed Nov–Apr.

This is one of the prettiest guesthouses on the Dingle Peninsula. The home of Mrs. Helen Healy, the two-story charmer is a mecca for visitors interested in Irish history and this unique region. Mrs. Healy is very helpful in directing her guests to good local eateries, craft workshops, etc. The house shines, with parquet floors, artistic arrangements of dried flowers, and examples of Irish pottery on display. The three upstairs bedrooms have sinks, but share two bathrooms with showers, while two downstairs rooms off a patio have private baths. At breakfast, Mrs. Healy's justly famed brown scones star. There are tennis courts next door and golf links overlooking Brandon Bay just one mile away.

An Lúivín

Ballyferriter, Dingle Peninsula, Co. Kerry. ☎ **066/56124.** 3 rms, none with bath. IR£15 ($24) single; IR£12 ($19.20) per person sharing. (Rates include breakfast.) No credit cards. Next door to the church on the main street.

Graciousness reigns supreme in this large traditional two-story house right in the center of the village. Siobhán Fahey, its lovely (and lively!) hostess, is a lifelong resident of this area, and she likes nothing better than to chat with guests (often over a cup of tea) about the nooks and crannies they might otherwise miss. Guest rooms are all quite comfortable, and the location couldn't be more convenient.

Bed-and-Breakfast

Cois Abhann

Emila, Ballyferriter, Dingle, Co. Kerry. ☎ **066/56201.** 6 rms, all with bath. IR£18.50 ($29.60) single; IR£14.50 ($23.20) per person sharing. 50% reduction for children. (Rates include breakfast.) No credit cards. Closed Oct–Feb.

In Ballyferriter, Miss Breda O'Sullivan's Cois Abhann (pronounced "Cush Owen"—it means "by the side of the river") is a pretty, modern bungalow whose floor-to-ceiling windows frame magnificent mountain views. The six guest rooms are all done in pastel colors, and there's central heat and plenty of parking space.

✪ Drom House

Coumgaugh, Dingle, Co. Kerry. ☎ **066/51134.** 3 rms, all with bath. IR£16 ($25.60) per person. 33 1/3% reduction for children. (Rates include breakfast.) No credit cards.

Rita and Gerald Brosnan, of Drom House (it means "hilly"), are both Dingle Peninsula natives. Rita was born in a house just up the road, and Gerald is manager of the West Kerry Co-op that has resurrected farming as a viable occupation hereabouts. Their hillside home sits amid sweeping mountain vistas 3 miles from Dingle town, and the modern bungalow is nicely decorated throughout. There's a nice lounge, as well as a playground for children. Guest rooms come with TV, clock radios, and hairdryers.

MacGearailt's Bungalow

Bothar Bui, Ballydavid, Dingle, Co. Kerry. ☎ **066/55142.** 4 rms, all with shower. IR£14 ($22.40) per person. 20% reduction for children. Dinner IR£14 ($22.40) extra. (Rates include breakfast.) No credit cards. Closed Oct–Easter.

There are views of lofty Mount Brandon from all four guest rooms at this bright, modern bungalow, home of Maura and Thomas MacGearailt, who delight in pointing out the splendors of the Dingle Peninsula. There's central heating and private parking.

Caife na Mara Restaurant and Accommodation

Glaise Bheag, Ballydavid, Dingle, Co. Kerry. ☎ **066/55162.** 3 rms, none with bath. IR£16 ($25.60) single; IR£13 ($20.80) per person sharing. (Rates include breakfast.) ACC, MC, V.

Sile and Vincent O'Gormin run this charming B&B/restaurant in one of the peninsula's most scenic locations near the small fishing village of Ballydavid (a *great* place to watch the glorious sunsets in this region). Rooms are both attractive and comfortable, and meals in the restaurant are outstanding (see "Where to Eat," below). The O'Gormins also have a bike-rental service and can arrange guided cycle tours.

Self-Catering

✪ Ventry Holiday Cottages

c/o John P. Moore, Green St., Dingle, Co. Kerry. ☎ **066/51588.** 8 cottages. IR£110–IR£375 ($176–$600) per week, depending on season.

Overlooking the picturesque little village of Ventry and its harbor, 4 1/2 miles from Dingle town on the coast road to Slea Head, these charming cottages are traditional in design, yet equipped with fully fitted-out kitchens and other conveniences. Each features a large lounge/dining area, and there's a fireplace for cool days and nights. The three carpeted bedrooms will sleep six adults.

Kerry Cottages

Castlegregory, Dingle Peninsula, Co. Kerry. ☎ **066/39240.** Fax 066/39392. *Book through:* Ray and Christine Marshall, Kerry Cottages, 37 Dalkey Park, Dalkey, Co. Dublin. ☎ 01/285-3851. Fax 01/285-4354. 9 cottages; 2, 3, 4, and 5 bedrooms. Weekly rates 2–3 bedrooms, Jan–May and Oct–Dec IR£199–IR£405 ($318.40–$648), June–Sept IR£199–IR£704 ($318.40–$1,126.40); 4–5 bedroom supplement IR£105–IR£395 ($168–$632); final cleaning fee IR£20 ($32). No credit cards. 1 mile from Castlegregory.

Each of these traditional-style cottages has a fireplace, as well as washing machine, dryer, and dishwasher. With advance notice, cots and high chairs are available at an additional cost. There's a playground for the children, and beaches are only a few minutes away.

Where to Eat

Caife na Mara

Ballydavid, Dingle. ☎ **066/55162.** Snacks IR£1.60–IR£7.50 ($2.56–$12); main courses IR£7–IR£13 ($11.20–$20.80). ACC, MC, V. Daily 1–3pm (snacks only) and 6–9pm. SEAFOOD/IRISH/TRADITIONAL/SNACKS.

With wide windows to take advantage of the scenery hereabouts, this charming restaurant (see "Where to Stay," above) specializes in fresh local produce and seafood just out of local waters. There's also a wide variety of beef, lamb, and chicken dishes, as well as a vegetarian dish of the day. Irish stew is especially good here.

Tig an Tobair

Ballyferriter. ☎ **066/56404.** Main courses IR$5–IR£8 ($8–$19.20); sandwiches and snacks under IR£5 ($8). MC, V. Open Mar–May daily 9am–6pm; June–Aug daily 9am–8pm; Sept–Oct daily 9am–6pm. IRISH/TRADITIONAL.

The wishing well that gives this small restaurant at the tip of the Dingle Peninsula its name ("House of the Well") is in the very center of the dining area. The chef makes good use of locally caught fish in a menu that changes daily depending on the current catch. A menu staple is the excellent fish salad platter that includes smoked salmon, smoked mackerel, and tuna. Traditional dishes such as Irish stew are also featured.

Thomasin's Bar

Stradbally, Castlegregory. Bar food under IR£10 ($16); average dinner under IR£15 ($24). ACC, MC, V. Daily, 12:30–5pm and 6–10pm. BAR FOOD/SEAFOOD/SALADS.

Readers Recommend

Cois Corrigh, Emila, Ballyferriter, Tralee, Co. Kerry. ☎ 066/56282. *"Mrs. Breda Ferris welcomed us here with tea, muffins, and porter cake. Her house is immaculate and commands a lovely view of the meadows, mountains, and the sea."*

—Marge Woodbury, Corning, NY

Mrs. M. O'Mahoney, Reask View House, Reask, Ballyferriter, Co. Kerry. ☎ 066/56126. *"These are superb modern accommodations in a truly rustic area. Outstanding amenities of golf and food nearby."* —G. W. Howard, Silver Spring, MD

Goulane, Castlegregory, Co. Kerry. ☎ 066/39147. *"Mrs. Catherine Griffin's country farmhouse overlooks the bay, with a sandy beach. Our rooms were most comfortable."*

—Tracy Shepard, Fort Lauderdale, FL

Grianan Allach, Kilcooley, Ballydavid, Co. Kerry. ☎ 066/55157. *"Mrs. Mary McHugh and her family are always happy to assist you in seeing the local sights. The meals served family style are a great example of Irish country cooking, and the rooms and facilities are modern and very comfortable."* —W. V. Steele, New York, NY

Clooneevin, Ballymore, Ventry, Dingle, Co. Kerry. ☎ 066/59916. *"We stayed with Mrs. Siobhan Kennedy and her family in this house, set in beautiful grounds just two miles from Ventry beach and three miles from Dingle town."*

—Wayne B. Garrett, Nashville, TN

You can't miss this attractive yellow and brown bar and restaurant on the edge of Stradbally village. The bar is housed in a traditional-style two-story house, and there's an adjacent craft shop that stocks a very good gift item selection, many of them made locally. In the small courtyard, umbrella tables afford outside eating. Seafood is the specialty here, and I especially liked their smoked salmon salad, which included portions ample enough to make it the main meal of the day. Homemade soups, sandwiches, and other traditional pub grub are available. Thomasin's is also well known for its frequent traditional music sessions—the perfect ending for a day on the northern side of the peninsula.

3 Tralee & North Kerry

North Kerry is a vibrant mixture of Tralee (its Irish name is *Traighli*, the "Strand of the River Lee"), the busy county capital town, sites of medieval settlements, sandy beaches quite safe for swimming, and bogs imbued with their own haunting beauty.

TRALEE

Americans probably know Tralee, some 19 miles northwest of Killarney via N22, best as the setting for the Rose of Tralee Festival held each year in late August or early September. That, however, is far from *all* it has to offer to visitors, and it is wise to plan at least one day exploring the town and vicinity. The **Tourist Office,** in Ashe Memorial Hall, Denny Street (☎ 066/21288), is open year-round and can furnish detailed information on the town as well as the entire region. They can also arrange booking for a performance of **Siamsa Tire,** the National Folk Theatre (see "Killarney After Dark" in Chapter 13), which should be done as far in advance as possible.

Make one of your first stops Ashe Hall, in Denny Street, to experience the re-created ✪ **Geraldine Street,** with lifelike models in authentic period dress. A buggy ride takes you back in time some 300 years. **St. Brendan the Navigator,** a native of this area, is portrayed in a fine statue at **St. John's Church** in Castle Street, an impressive Gothic Revival structure with beautiful cut stonework in its interior. No less than 13 earls of Desmond have been laid to rest in the grounds of the **old priory** in Abbey Street, where the church holds superb stained glass executed by Michael Healy. After dark, you'll find **traditional music** in ✪ **Bailys Corner Bar,** 52 Ashe St. (☎ 066/26230), and **The Olde Brassil Inn,** 12 Russell St. (☎ 066/21274), on varying nights of the week. **A. Caball & Sons,** 12 Bridge St. (☎ 066/21847) has one of the best stocks of Irish music, both traditional and contemporary, that I've run across outside Dublin. They also carry a comprehensive selection of toys, Irish souvenirs, and other gift items.

If you're going to or from Dingle from Tralee, the restored 200-year-old ✪ **Blennerville Windmill** (☎ 066/21064) holds an interesting Irish milling history exhibit (complete with working millstones), and a fascinating exhibition depicting 19th-century emigration from Blennerville port. It's open daily from May to November from 9:30am to 6pm (small admission), and a coffee shop and craft shop make this a comfortable break in the day's sightseeing. Train buffs won't want to miss the one-mile run of a beautifully restored **steam train** between Tralee and Blennerville (you can leave the car at one end during the round trip).

Take time out for family fun at **Aqua Dome** (☎ 066/28899 for hours and prices), with a super swimming pool, a river-rapids ride, and a wave machine.

In the little village of **Ardfert** some five miles north of Tralee (St. Brendan's part of the world), a ruined medieval cathedral sits fully excavated and partially restored. Nearby are the ruins of a 13th-century Franciscan friary.

Over the years, **Listowel,** 17 miles northeast of Tralee, has produced a host of important Irish writers (such as John B. Keane and Bryan MacMahon), and there's an interesting display of the town's literary activity in the library. Incidentally, John B. Keane's pub is in William Street. ✪ **Writer's Week,** in late June or early July, is a "don't miss" if you're in the area—a solid week of serious-minded daytime workshops and lectures and unrestrained revelry in the pubs at night. In the town square, look for the **St. John's Arts & Heritage Centre.** In September, the **Listowel Races** draw huge crowds from around the country.

A short drive northeast of Listowel brings you to **Ballybunion** (21 miles from Tralee), a popular seaside resort famous for its golf course and dramatic seascape of soaring cliffs and sandy cove beaches. There are some 14 Celtic promontory forts in this area. If time permits, walk at least a portion of the celebrated Cliff Walk (out the Doon road and turn left after the convent).

Due north of Listowel, **Tarbert** looks down from a steep slope to one of the widest and most scenic parts of the Shannon River, where a car-ferry shortens the drive north (see Chapter 13, "Killarney: Departing"). ✪ **Tarbert House** (☎ 068/36198), on the ferry road, is a fine Georgian-style house that has been the Leslie family home since it was built in 1690. Over the centuries, such notables as Daniel O'Connell, Charlotte Brontë, Dean Jonathan Swift, Winston Churchill, and Benjamin Franklin were visitors of the Leslies. Much of its original Georgian furniture is still in use, and among its historical artifacts is the original application for Catholic Emancipation. It's open daily from May to mid-August from 10am to noon and 2 to 4pm (small admission). The Leslies now in residence (Ursula and John) are renowned for their dinner parties, and if you book ahead, they'll prepare an elegant seated meal for parties of four to six, or an equally elegant buffet for 20 to 30.

Where to Stay

✪ Ashgrove House

Ballybunion Rd., Listowel, Co. Kerry. ☎ **068/21268.** 4 rms, all with bath. IR£17.50 ($28) single; IR£14 ($22.40) per person sharing. 50% reduction for children. High tea IR£9.50 ($15.20) extra. (Rates include breakfast.) No credit cards. Closed Nov–Feb.

Tim and Nancy O'Neill will welcome you here. They're a charming couple, and their two teenagers, John and Carol, are very much a part of the hospitality they extend to guests. All four pretty guest rooms are on the ground floor. The dining room overlooks the garden where there's a pleasant patio, and out front, tea and scones are often served on the glassed-in sun porch. Ashgrove House is about half a mile outside town on the Ballybunion Golf Course road.

Ballingowan House

Mile Height, Killarney Rd., Tralee, Co. Kerry. ☎/Fax **066/27150.** 4 rms, all with bath—1 on ground floor. TV. IR£20 ($32) single; IR£15 ($24) per person sharing. 30% reduction for children. No credit cards. Closed Dec–Feb. 1mile from Tralee on N21/22.

Guest rooms in Sheila Kerins' gracious two-story home are especially spacious, and all have tea/coffeemakers. The breakfast menu is excellent. The house has central heating and private parking.

Brianville

Clogherbrien, Fenit Rd., Tralee, Co. Kerry. ☎ **066/26645.** 5 rms, 4 with bath. IR£16–IR£18 ($25.60–$28.80) single; IR£14–IR£16 ($22.40–$25.60) per person sharing. 50% reduction for children. No credit cards. 1mile from Tralee.

This pretty modern bungalow is the home of Joan Smith. Fronted by green lawns, the house has wide floor-to-ceiling windows that give the interior a light, airy ambience and afford striking views of the nearby mountains. Guest rooms are attractive as well as comfortable. Central heating and private parking.

Burntwood House

Listowel, Co. Kerry. ☎ **068/21516.** 6 rms, 4 with bath. IR£14 ($22.40) per person without bath; IR£15 ($24) per person with bath; IR£2 ($3.20) per person extra for special events and holidays. 20% reduction for children. Dinner IR£13 ($18.85). (Rates include breakfast.) No credit cards. Closed Nov–Mar.

Mrs. Josephine Groarke is the pleasant hostess of this beautiful Georgian-style house set in very scenic countryside half a mile from town. The centrally heated house is comfortable and modernized, and the food is delicious. All six guest rooms are attractive, with country views.

✪ Ceol Na H'Abhann

Tralee Rd., Ballygrennan, Listowel, Co. Kerry. ☎ **068/21345.** 4 rms, 3 with bath. IR£14 ($22.40) per person sharing without bath; IR£16 ($25.60) per person with bath; slight increase during events and holidays. (Rates include breakfast.) No credit cards. Closed Nov–Mar. Private car park.

Our readers have been profuse in their praise of this beautiful two-story, thatch-roofed home on a riverbank near a lovely wooded area about half a mile outside Listowel. Mrs. Kathleen Stack takes great pride in her beautifully furnished home, one of the very few thatch-roofed homes open to guests in Ireland. She offers tea and scones upon arrival, and breakfasts are served in the Georgian dining room, with fine linen, china, and silver. The house is centrally heated, and there's private parking. The famous Ballybunion golf course and beach are only nine miles away. Mrs. Stack has won several awards, including one from the Department of Environment.

✪ Curraheen House

Curraheen, Tralee, Co. Kerry. ☎ **066/21717.** 5 rms, 4 with bath. IR£18.50 ($29.60) single; IR£13.50 ($21.60) per person sharing. 25% reduction for children. Dinner IR£12 ($17.40) extra. (Rates include breakfast.) No credit cards. Closed Dec–Feb.

Mrs. Bridget Keane's traditional farmhouse is on the Tralee-Dingle road (R559), four miles from Tralee, overlooking Tralee Bay, with mountain views in the distance. The very embodiment of Irish hospitality, Mrs. Keane is known for her delicious high tea and dinner, often featuring salmon and fish fresh from local waters, as well as a lovely mixed grill. She has, in fact, opened a restaurant and bar adjacent to the house. Those fantastic Dingle Peninsula sandy beaches are only two miles away, and golfing, pony trekking, and sea fishing are all available locally.

Mountain View

Ballinorig West, Tralee, Co. Kerry. ☎ **066/22226.** 6 rms, 4 with bath. IR£18.50–IR£20 ($29.60–$32) single; IR£13.50–IR£15 ($21.60–$24) per person sharing. 25% reduction for children. No credit cards. Closed Christmas. Approaching Tralee on N21, turn right just before roundabout.

Eileen Curley is a gracious hostess and her lovely home is set in its own landscaped grounds just outside Tralee. Her lively interest in guests' welfare adds

Readers Recommend

The Spinning Wheel, Listowel, Co. Kerry. ☎ 068/21128. *"A spotlessly clean, friendly restaurant with excellent food and reasonable prices."*
—Al and Eileen O'Sullivan, Long Beach, NY

The Three Mermaids, William Street, Listowel, Co. Kerry. ☎ 068/21454 or 21784. *"This is an excellent bar/restaurant, where we had a superb meal, one of us opting for fresh fish, the other for steak."* —Josephine Dailey, Lynchburg, VA

Manor Inn, Coast Road, Doon East, Ballybunion, Co. Kerry. ☎ 068/27757 or 27577. *"This solid, two-story brick house, in its unique site at the mouth of the Shannon, is the finest B&B we came across in Ireland—we felt that we were in a mansion. Thomas Boyle, a master carpenter, designed and built the place himself. Each room has an individual architectural style and decor. Furnishings would compare favorably with the best suites in a four-star hotel. After an excellent breakfast in the cheerful dining room, my wife and I walked across a couple of nearby fields to reach a rock promontory, Doon Point, overlooking the broad Shannon. The view rivaled the Cliffs of Moher, and we had it all to ourselves."* —Martin Sokolinsky, Brooklyn, NY

immeasurably to their stay, since she knows the area well. Guest rooms are exceptionally well done up. Central heating and private parking.

Oak Haven

Sallowglen, Ballylongford Rd., Tarbert, Co. Kerry. ☎ **068/43208.** 3 rms, 2 with bath. IR£19 ($30.40) single; IR£14 ($22.40) per person sharing; IR£2 ($3.20) per person extra with bath. (Rates include breakfast.) No credit cards. Closed Christmas.

Philomena Walsh is the gracious hostess of this modern bungalow set in spacious gardens some 3½ miles from Tarbert. Decor is attractive and guest rooms are tastefully furnished. *Note:* A good place to overnight if you plan to dine at Tarbert House (see page 344).

Where to Eat

✪ Larkins Restaurant

Princes St., Tralee. ☎ **066/21300.** Main courses: lunch under IR£5 ($8); dinner IR£9–IR£13 ($14.40–$20.80); early-bird menu (6–7pm) IR£13.50 ($21.60). ACC, AE, MC, V. Mon–Sat 12:30–2pm and 6–9pm (Sunday hours in July and August). IRISH/SEAFOOD/TRADITIONAL/VEGETARIAN.

Conveniently situated beside the Brandon Hotel, this spacious culinary gem is superby decorated in the Irish country style, with antique pine furnishings and fine contemporary works of art creating a light, cheerful ambience. There's a small bar, and the larger dining room features an open fire and a balcony. Service, supervised by owner Michael Fitzgibbon, also harks back to traditional Irish style—friendly, helpful, and efficient. A la carte menu selections might include fillet of plaice encased with smoked salmon and fresh spinach with sorrel sauce, a marvelous rack of lamb with potato rostis, and Gaelic sirloin steak flamed in Irish whiskey, garnished with onion and watercress. Seafood specialties, which change daily to reflect the latest catch from local sea fisheries, typically include lobsters, oysters, monkfish, brill, or wild salmon with appropriate sauces. Superb food and good value for money.

✪ The Skillet

Barrack Lane, Tralee. ☎ **066/24561.** Bar food under IR£5 ($8); main courses IR£4–IR£12 ($6.40–$19.20). ACC, MC, V. Mon–Sat 9am–5:45pm. MORNING COFFEE/BAR FOOD/SEAFOOD/STEAK/VEGETARIAN.

Located in one of Tralee's historic narrow laneways, the Skillet has earned a local reputation for good food at "value for money" prices. Seafood here is outstanding, but its old-world ambience also makes it a pleasant place just to drop in for a morning or afternoon cup of tea or coffee. In addition to succulent steaks, there are curries, pizzas, and salads.

Keanes Bar and Restaurant

Curraheen, Tralee. ☎ **066/28054.** Bar food under IR£6 ($9.60); main courses IR£10–IR£12 ($16–$19.20); tourist menu IR£9.95 ($15.92); children's menu IR£2 ($3.20); four-course Sun lunch IR£10 ($16) MC, V. Bar Mon–Sat 10:30–11:30pm, Sun 12:30–2:30pm and 4–11pm; restaurant Mon–Sat 12:30–2:30pm and 6–10pm, Sun 12:30–3pm. BAR FOOD/SEAFOOD/MEAT/POULTRY.

Located four miles from Tralee on the main Tralee-Dingle road, Keanes serves bar food right through the day. Its restaurant menu features fresh local ingredients, with specialties like pork filet with mushrooms and brandy cream or trout papillote. Desserts are noteworthy, especially the brandy, honey, and almond trifle.

A Reminder

If you're traveling north to counties Clare and/or Limerick, see Chapter 13 for details of the **Tarbert/Killimer ferry** that can save you hours of driving.

15 Shannonside: Counties Clare, Limerick & Northern Tipperary

All too often, visitors rush through the Shannonside region, perhaps because so many deplane at Shannon and they're off and away without realizing that so many of Ireland's treasures lie right at their point of entry. Yet it is quite possible, as I once did, to spend two full, happy weeks in Ireland and not go far beyond the boundaries of the area that has been dubbed Shannonside. Incidentally, Ireland's longest river, whose Irish name of An tSionnainn ("on chunnan") means something like "old one," was probably named in honor of some ancient river god personified by the flowing water.

In County Clare you can span Ireland's history from Stone Age relics around Lough Gur, to Craggaunowen's Bronze Age lake dwelling and 15th-century castle, to mementos of the 1800s in the Clare Heritage Centre. Nature has turned up such wonders as the Aillwee Cave, the Cliffs of Moher, and the rocky expanse of Burren.

There's much, much more in Shannonside, like the traditional music that lives so vigorously in generation after generation of County Clare fiddlers, whistle players, and pipers. And the days of medieval Ireland that live on in the nightly banquets and musical entertainment at both Bunratty and Knappogue castles. And the crafts that flourish with such a flair in this part of the country. And the mighty River Shannon, with waters ideal for fishing, boating, or just plain loafing.

With so many riches in such a small region, it would be a pity to make Shannonside simply an overnight for the first-day-in and the last-day-out. Limerick city is full of history, with fascinating sightseeing in and around town, and theater and good pubs after dark. Northern Tipperary's Holy Cross Abbey is an enduring tribute to the dedication and devotion of early Christians, and in Roscrea there's a beautiful home built within ancient castle walls.

Any one of the accommodations listed in the three sections of this chapter will be convenient as a base for leisurely day trips to cover the entire region. On arrival at Shannon, my best advice is to book into your B&B and catch a few hours' sleep, then you'll be refreshed and ready for one of the medieval banquets that night (be sure to book ahead)—or you might want to while away the evening at Durty Nelly's or one of Limerick's other great pubs—either choice is a great way to begin your Irish holiday. The next day, you can be off to explore Shannonside's outstanding attractions and the rest of the country.

One more bit of advice: It's a good idea to return to Shannonside at least one day *before* your departure date so you'll arrive back home fresh instead of frazzled.

1 County Clare

SHANNON AIRPORT

Chances are your first and last glimpses of Ireland will be from a plane arriving in or parting from Shannon Airport. For information on flight arrivals and departures, phone 061/471666 or 471444.

Shannon is, however, much more than a passing-through sort of airport. There's a **Tourist Information Desk** in the Arrivals Hall to help you book accommodations if you've arrived without them (I *implore* you not to in July or August!), to assist you with itineraries, and to be as generally helpful as Tourist Offices all around the country.

Here, too, you can book the medieval banquet you'd decided to forgo but which grew irresistible on the flight over (look for the Castle Tours desk).

Bus Eireann has a tour desk from April to October (a free phone other months) where you can find out about tours around the country and book, if you choose.

There's a VAT-refund desk and scads of car-rental desks (again, please don't arrive in high season without having reserved a car in advance).

The bank in the Arrivals Hall is open from the first flight in the morning until 5:30pm, with full banking services, including currency conversion.

Budgeteers will find good, inexpensive food in the bright and attractive Shannon Airport Grill. It's self-service and offers a wide variety, from snacks to full meals, hot and cold. For a special meal, there's the buffet restaurant, the Lindbergh Room, named for our American aviator who had a hand in selecting Shannon as the site of this international airport. For bar snacks, drop in at the ground-floor Burren Lounge and Bar. All have hours coinciding with flight arrivals and departures.

Getting to and from the Airport Local buses will drop you off at Ennis road guesthouses (ask the driver when you get on); the buses also stop at the bus terminal and along O'Connell Street.

If you're going to the airport from Limerick, you can catch the bus at the main bus terminal on Parnell Street, at the Henry Street stop, or flag the bus down on Ennis Road; the one-way fare to the airport is IR£3.50 ($5.60).

The taxi fare to and from Limerick will run about IR£14 ($22.40).

WHAT TO SEE & DO IN COUNTY CLARE

THE TOP ATTRACTIONS

✪ Bunratty Castle and Folk Park

Shannon Airport Rd. (N18), Bunratty. ☎ **061/361511.** Admission IR£5 ($8) adults, IR£2.50 ($4) children. Daily 9:30am–5:30pm. Bus: Limerick-Shannon Airport bus.

You can drive or take a bus (the Shannon Airport bus makes a stop here) out to **Bunratty Castle.** Allow a full morning or afternoon for the excursion. The marvelously restored 15th-century castle was built for the O'Briens, earls of Thomond, and its restoration has included heavy carved-wood chests, woven tapestries, ornate wooden chairs, and pieces that look as though they have been here forever—furnishings so complete that the O'Briens who first lived here would feel right at home should their shades come back today. (That brings up a little aside: Officially, Bunratty has no ghosts, but if you should chance to encounter a sad lady dressed in pink, or a soldier wearing a torn tunic and holding an empty scabbard, look quickly before they vanish—the lady threw herself into the courtyard upon learning that her lover had been killed the night before their wedding day, and from time to time they're spotted wandering the castle, though never together. As I said, officially the story is not true, but unofficially, it is widely told.) Enter across a drawbridge into the vast, vaulted Great Hall, the center of castle life where the tradition of elaborate feasts is re-created these days with nightly medieval banquets (see "After Dark," below). Narrow, winding stone steps lead to upper floors where family life went on.

The authentic cluster of homes, shops, and workshops from early Irish life that make up the **Folk Park** on the castle grounds came about almost by accident. When a centuries-old farmhouse was moved from the Shannon Airport to make way for a longer runway, it became the nucleus of a collection of traditional buildings that include a blacksmith shop, a fisherman's cottage, a coastal cottage with thatch firmly tied against Atlantic gales, and several craft shops. Each is a "working" exhibit: A costumed "housewife" bakes brown bread in a covered iron pot on the hearth, weavers are at their looms, and the blacksmith is hard at work. At one end of the park, a typical village street has been reconstructed, complete with post office, draper, tearoom, a tiny pub, and a reconstruction of Kearney's Hotel, a typical rural 19th-century hotel (its fully licensed bar is a great place to rest weary feet). This is a good place to pick up gifts, crafts, and souvenirs.

A nice end to a Bunratty visit is a stop at the nearby **Winery** (☎ 061/362222), which produces the honey-based Bunratty Mead.

✪ Durty Nelly's

Bunratty. ☎ **061/364861.** Daily 10:30am–11:30pm.

While at Bunratty, day or night, you won't want to miss Durty Nelly's pub, even if you sip a nonalcoholic white lemonade. It's on a stone arched bridge right at the entrance to Bunratty Castle grounds, and it served the soldiers of the garrison for centuries after it was built in 1620. Like the earls of Thomond in the castle, those soldiers would feel perfectly at home in today's Durty Nelly's. The wooden chairs and benches are the same, peat still burns in the fireplaces, and some of the hodgepodge hanging on the walls and from the rafters looks as though it was put there by one of the earl's protectors and hasn't been moved since. Even the pigeon cote has survived in one room of the loft. Durty Nelly's draws huge crowds: Tourists you'd surely expect, but amazingly, large numbers of locals come to the place. There's good pub grub (I never go past without stopping for a toasted corned beef and cheese sandwich or soup and brown bread), as well as two good eateries (see "Where to Eat," below). After about 9pm things get pretty lively with music and singing, and even those drinking in the outside patio join in.

✪ The Craggaunowen Project

Quin. ☎ **061/367178.** Admission IR£3.25 ($5.20) adults, IR£2 ($3.20) children. Mid-Mar to Oct, daily 10am–6pm; Oct–Apr, Fri–Sun 9:30am–4:30pm.

One of County Clare's most interesting sightseeing stops is the Craggaunowen (pronounced "*Crag*-an-owen") Project near Quin, 14 miles from Shannon Airport (signposted from Quin, north on R469). Craggaunowen Castle has an interesting display of medieval art objects, and in the lake a short walk away is a fascinating re-creation of a crannog, a Bronze Age lake dwelling. A cooking site of the Iron Age and a bowl dated to 148 B.C. can also be seen. The earthen ring fort on the

Shannonside

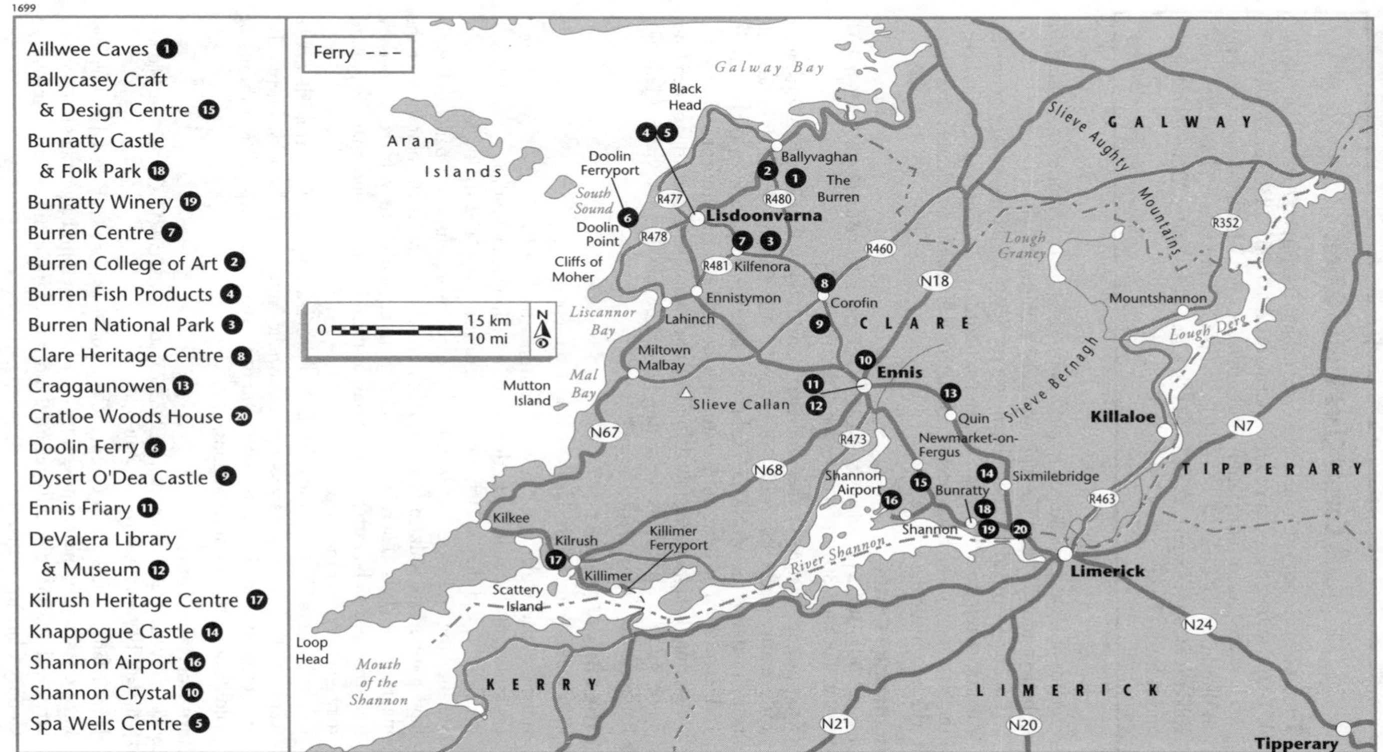

1699

County Clare Visitor Offices

Tourist offices open year-round are located at Shannon Airport Arrivals Hall (061/471-664) and in the town of Ennis (Clare Road, ☎ 065/28366 or 28308).

There are tourist information offices that are open March through October at: Bunratty Folk Park (☎ 061/360133); the Cliffs of Moher (☎ 065/81171); Kilkee (O'Connell Street, ☎ 065/56112); Killaloe (the Bridge, ☎ 061/376866); and Kilrush (Town Hall, ☎ 065/51577).

grounds holds a reconstructed farmer's home of some 15 centuries ago, with fields of barleys and wheats of the types grown by prehistoric Celts.

For me—thrilled as I have been at Tim Severin's daring voyage across the Atlantic to retrace St. Brendan's legendary route of A.D. 700—a highlight here is the glass shelter which has been constructed to house the tiny leather *Brendan* in which he made the voyage.

Knappogue Castle

Quin. ☎ **061/361-511.** Admission IR£2.50 ($4) adults, IR£1.50 ($2.40) children. Daily May–Oct, 9:30am–5:30pm (last admission 4:30pm).

Knappogue Castle (of the medieval banquets) is furnished in authentic 15th-century pieces, somewhat more formally than Bunratty Castle. It's one of the many castles of the McNamara tribe, who held great power from the 5th to the 15th century. The beautifully restored courtyard has an excellent souvenir and crafts shop. Knappogue, about 12 miles from Shannon Airport (signposted from Quin, south on R469), is the setting for one of the Shannon Castle Mediaeval Banquets (see "After Dark," below).

✪ The Cliffs of Moher

Admission free. Visitor Centre, Mar–Oct, daily 10am–6pm.

Ireland's spectacular coastline really outdoes itself at the Cliffs of Moher near Liscannor on R478. In Irish, they're named Ailltreacha Mothair ("The Cliffs of the Ruin"), and they stretch for five miles, rising at places to 700 feet. They're breathtaking and shouldn't be missed. There's an extensive car park, and you'll have a moderate walk to O'Brien's Tower, which affords the best view of the magnificent cliffs. There are also cliff-walking trails, but you are warned by frequent signs to be extremely cautious, as there is some danger that the ground may give way near the edge.

The Visitors Centre at the Cliffs of Moher has a bright and cheerful self-service tearoom offering inexpensive soups, sandwiches, and assorted snacks. There's also an excellent gift, literature, music, and souvenir shop, as well as exhibits of wildlife and other local attractions.

Clare Heritage Centre

Corofin. ☎ **065/37955.** Admission IR£2 ($3.20) adults, IR£1.50 ($2.40) children. Mid-Mar to Oct, daily 10am–6pm; Nov–Feb, 9am–5pm.

If your family roots are in County Clare, you'll want to visit the Clare Heritage Centre at Corofin, near Ennis on R476, where you'll find a genealogical research service, thousands of family records, and interesting exhibits portraying life in County Clare in ages past.

More Attractions

The northwestern hump of County Clare is a strange, barren moonscape with no apparent signs of life. This is **The Burren** (An Bhoireann, "The Stony District"—the Irish call it "The Berne"). Those who walk its rocky hills, however, find that far from being sterile, it holds a wealth of tiny wildflowers, some of which are unique to this area—at their best in late spring or early summer. It was also inhabited in prehistoric times, and there are many dolmens, cairns, and ring forts. In Kilfenora, stop by the **Burren Centre** (☎ 065/88030) to see an enlightening audiovisual presentation; a tea shop and craft shop are also on the premises. Hours are mid-March to October, from 10am to 6pm. Small admission charge.

One of the best ways to see the Burren is to join one of the **Burren Walking Tours** run by the Burren Education Centre (☎ 065/78066) and by Christy Brown Tours (☎ 065/81168).

In the midst of the Burren, you'll find **Aillwee Cave** (☎ 065/77036), a fascinating underground wonderland of magnificent stalactites. There's a tearoom as well as craft shops on the premises. Admission is IR£4 ($6.40) for adults, IR£2.50 ($4) for children.

✪ **Doolin** is a tiny coastal village that has gained international fame as a center for traditional Irish music. You'll find it in full sway most nights in **O'Connor's Pub,** a large, rustic place filled with musicians, singers, tellers of tales, students who may have hitchhiked across Europe to get here, and Yanks like us here to take it all in. There's also excellent bar food, featuring fresh seafood, for IR£5 ($8) to IR£8 ($12.80). There's regular **boat service to the Aran Islands** from here, only a 25-minute run, since Doolin is the closest point to the islands on the mainland. In fact, you'll sometimes meet Aran Islanders in O'Connor's of a Sunday night if the seas are calm. Boats leave from Doolin Pier daily, beginning at 10am during the summer, and the fare is IR£15 ($24) round trip to Inishneer, IR£20 ($32) to Inishmore, with reduced rates for students and families.

The bustling market town of **Ennis** has many interesting historical buildings, and the Tourist Office (see above) can give you a walking-tour guide through the more historic sections. Of special note is the 13th-century Franciscan friary. Headquarters for traditional music, song, and dance is **Cois No hAbhna** (pronounced "*Cush* Na *How*-na"), on Gort Road. The shop has a large selection of records, tapes, and books on Irish traditional music, and they maintain a good schedule of happenings during summer months.

The **Loop Head Peninsula** is a much-overlooked County Clare attraction. A delightful day is one spent driving to seaside ✪ **Kilkee,** with its curved bay and strand, then down the long finger of land that is the West Clare Peninsula to its end, where the Loop Head lighthouse holds solitary vigil. The coastline is one of clifftops, inlets and coves, sandy beaches, and a softly wild, unspoiled landscape. Along the way there are the ruins of forts, castles, and churches, and should you stop for a pint in a country pub, there are legends to be heard, like that of Kisstiffin Bank, a shoal that lies beneath the Shannon's waters. It was once, so it is said hereabouts, a part of the mainland, but was swept into the Shannon during a fierce storm in the 9th century, carrying people and their homes to a watery grave. (According to the older residents of this area, when sailing ships used to drop anchor off the Kisstiffin Bank, they'd be visited during the night by a small man from beneath the water who would climb the anchor cable and ask them to take up the anchor, for it had gone down his chimney.)

In the little Shannonside village of **Kilbaha** (Cill Bheathach, or "Birch Church"), the Church of Moheen holds a small wooden structure that is one of Ireland's most unusual testaments to the devotion of the people to their faith. It's a tiny three-sided chapel on wheels known as the ✪ **Little Ark of Kilbaha** which, during the years when English-imposed law forbade any landlord to permit a Catholic mass to be held on his land, was hidden away during the week, but pulled down to the shore of Kilbaha Bay on Sunday and placed below the high-tide mark on land that belonged to no man. There mass was said in safety, reverence, and peace.

While you're in Kilbaha, look for sculptor **Jim Connolly's studio,** Kilkee, Kilrush (☎ 065/58034). Jim lives and works in a thatched cottage, and his bronze sculptures are brilliant (the most noted is that of Eamon De Valera in Ennis). He's an interesting man to talk to, and while the bronzes may be too pricey and heavy to purchase, he does have a ceramics shop with creative, inexpensive souvenirs. You might phone before going, since he's often away.

The 13-mile drive north of Limerick city via R463 to the charming little Lough Derg harbor village of **Killaloe** is delightful, and **St. Flannan's Cathedral** (12th century) is worth visiting to see the ornately carved Irish Romanesque doorway and **ogham stone** (which also has runic writings and a crude crucifix believed to be formed by a Viking who had converted to Christianity). Drive along the western shore of the lake to view magnificent scenery and ancient ruins on offshore islands. You're very welcome to fish or swim at no charge; coarse fishing is best at Plassy, and the Electricity Supply Board on O'Connell Street issues free fishing permits.

Ireland's largest inland marina is located at Killaloe, on **Lough Derg.** From May to September, the ✪ ***Derg Princess,*** a 48-seat enclosed river boat, has daily 1½-hour cruises past such historic spots as the site of Brian Boru's fort. Fares are IR£5 ($8) for adults, IR£3 ($4.80) for children, and IR£14 ($22.40) for a family ticket. For exact sailing times, contact Derg Line, Killaloe, County Clare (☎ 061/376364).

SHOPPING

CRAFTS

Ballycasey Craft Courtyard

Shannon.

This group of craft workshops is signposted on the Limerick-Shannon road, and it's a "don't miss" for crafts hunters. Clustered around the farmyard of the 18th-century Ballycaseymore House, individual workshops are home to artisans, from weaver to potter to fashion designer to silversmith to a host of other arts and crafts. The Barn Restaurant serves fresh, appetizing light lunches, with wine available, at modest prices.

Crafts Gallery/Workshop

Doolin. ☎ **065/74309.**

Matthew O'Connell and Mary Gray own and operate this terrific crafts shop beside the church and cemetery in Doolin. Every item is Irish made: sweaters (both wool and mohair), classic fashions, ceramics, crystal, linens, lace, sculpture, leather bags, and even Christmas ornaments. Mary is a designer of contemporary and traditional gold and silver jewelry, much of it with themes drawn from the Burren. They are happy to mail goods anywhere in the world at cost. There is also a restaurant/coffee shop on the premises. Open Monday through Saturday from 8:30am to 8pm and on Sunday from 8:30am to 6pm.

✪ Manus Walsh's Craft Workshop

Ballyvaughan. ☎ **065/77029.**

In Ballyvaughan, stop by this intriguing workshop and gallery on the main Galway road. Manus's fascination with the Burren landscape is reflected in many of his paintings, and he also has a wide selection of enamelware of Celtic design, rings, necklaces, and wall hangings. Open Monday through Saturday from 10am to 5pm.

O'Brien Studio

Bunratty Folk Park, Bunratty. ☎ **061/364-577.**

If your roots are Irish, do stop in this studio and perhaps take home an actual photograph of your ancestors' home town. Made from 1890s originals, the prints (approximately 12 × 10 inches) are hand-printed, sepia-toned, and mounted on a rich brown board with gold inlaid border, and frames are available. Unframed prints are $25, framed $45. Open daily 9:30am–5:30pm.

FASHIONS

✪ Bunratty Cottage International Fashion Shop

Bunratty. ☎ **061/364321** or 364188.

Bunratty Cottage, across from the castle, is where Irish designer Vonnie Reynolds displays her own designs as well as an exceptional stock of Irish woolens, tweeds, and gifts. Open March to December, daily from 9am to 6pm; January and February, Monday through Saturday from 10am to 5pm.

AFTER DARK

MEDIEVAL BANQUETS

Right here, I have to confess that for years I resisted the lure of the medieval banquets in County Clare, convinced of two things: that I'd spend the evening in the company of other tourists when I had come to Ireland to enjoy the company of the Irish; and that the whole show would be too "cute" to be wholesome. My second confession is that I was wrong, and that I've seldom missed attending one each trip since friends dragged me along a few years back. True, your fellow diners will almost surely be other tourists (unless, that is, you come in the off-season, when the Irish come in droves), but the great thing is that it's that mischievous Irish sense of fun that prevails, no matter *who* is in attendance.

These banquets are among Ireland's most popular attractions, and if at all possible you should book before leaving home, either through a travel agent or by writing the Reservations Manager, Shannon Castle Tours, Shannon Town Centre, Shannon, County Clare, Ireland (☎ 061/360788; 800/243-8687 in the U.S.; 800/668-2958 in Canada). Should you arrive without a reservation, any tourist office will try to get you a seat, or you can give the Reservations Manager a call to ask about an opening (sometimes there are cancellations)—just don't miss it!

✪ Bunratty Castle Medieval Banquet

Bunratty. ☎ **061/360-788.** Admission IR£30 ($48). Reservations recommended. You should reserve before leaving home if at all possible, either through a travel agent or by writing the Reservations Manager, Shannon Castle Tours, Shannon Town Centre, Shannon, County Clare, Ireland. Should you arrive without a reservation, any tourist office will try to get you a seat, or you can give the reservations manager a call to ask about an opening (sometimes there are cancellations). Two banquets nightly, at 5:45 and 9pm.

When you walk across the drawbridge into Bunratty Castle's Great Hall and are handed your first mug of mead (in off-season; it's hot mulled wine), the great good spirit of Irish fun takes over and Americans, French, German, Australians, Italians, and every other nationality represented lose their tourist trappings and become fellow conspirators in the evening's fantasy plot.

As for the show, of course it's hokey—it's meant to be! Blarney may have originated down there in County Cork, but there's lots of it afoot in Bunratty, as story follows story and song follows song, and the stuffiest, most "touristy" type turns mellow in the sometimes-hilarious struggle to get through a meal without benefit of cutlery. The talent on stage is first-rate, and I defy you to keep a dry eye as the golden notes of an Irish harp wash over you in a massive room brought suddenly to a complete hush.

A typical banquet menu will begin with a cup of broth, followed by spareribs, half a roast chicken (sometimes a hunk of well-done beef), salad, vegetables, homemade bread torn into ragged chunks, and a dessert just dripping with calories. To top it all off, you quaff a mug of mead (the traditional honey-based drink). You'll be given a knife, and after that it's you and your fingers, just as in the old days. Between each course, one little bit of stage business or another goes on, the most popular of which is the appointment of the evening's "Earl of Thomond" from among the guests, who reigns at the top of the long banquet table. His "duties" include banishing another one of the guests to the dungeon and addressing his assembled guests with as flowery a bit of oratory as he can manage. It's a memorable night—the earls of Thomond should have such a good time under their own roof!

Knappogue Castle

Quin. ☎ **061/360788.** Admission IR£30 ($48). Reservations recommended. You should reserve before leaving home if at all possible, either through a travel agent or by writing the Reservations Manager, Shannon Castle Mediaeval Banquets, Shannon Airport, County Clare, Ireland. Should you arrive without a reservation, any tourist office will try to get you a seat, or you can give the reservations manager a call to ask about an opening (sometimes there are cancellations). May–Oct, two banquets nightly, at 5:45 and 9pm.

This massive 1467 stronghold is some 19 miles from Limerick city, which means you must have a car, since it is not served by local buses. The banquet here differs from that at Bunratty in that the group is smaller and more intimate, and the entertainment tends to be somewhat less ribald, with sketches to bring to life myths and legends of Old Ireland and lots of song and dance. Many of my Irish friends prefer this to Bunratty (and there are usually a fair few Irish faces at the table), and in the best of all possible Irish holidays, you'd get to both.

Shannon Ceili

Bunratty. ☎ **061/360788.** Admission IR£30 ($48). Daily May–Sept.

While the banquets offer fun on a "lord and lady of the castle" level, over in the Bunratty Folk Park the merriment is more akin to that of the "downstairs" crew in those castles. There's traditional song and dance, as audience and performers engage in lively back-and-forth joshing. And the dishes that come to table are likely to include Irish stew, apple pie, and soda bread.

TRADITIONAL MUSIC

If there's one thing County Clare has plenty of, it's traditional music and good fiddlers, tin-whistle players, bodhran players, and pipers to play it. And their favorite venue by far is the local pub. Out at Bunratty, ✪ **Durty Neily's** (☎ 061/364861; see "The Top Attractions," above) rings with music, some professional, some spontaneous, every night. The **Merriman Tavern,** in Scarriff (☎ 0619/21011), is an ancient place with a big ballad room that frequently hosts many of Ireland's top traditional musicians and folk groups, with a small admission charge. The crowd in attendance is likely to include those cruising the Shannon who have pulled into Scarriff for the night, fishermen, and lots of locals. Seafood is also available.

On Friday nights, **Pat Donnlans** in Kilkishen (☎ 065/72204) features music most nights. Other watering holes that regularly attract musicians are: **John Lynch's pub, Doonaha,** in Kilkee (☎ 065/57004); **Hassets,** in Quin (☎ 065/25683); **John Minogues,** in Tulla (☎ 065/25106); **Lena Hanrahan,** in Feakle (☎ 0619/24090); the **Smyth Village Hotel,** in Feakle (☎ 0619/24002); and **Kennedy's Pub,** in Puckane (☎ 067/24171). The ancient **Crabtree Tavern,** Ballycar, Sixmilebridge (☎ 061/71235), has ceili dancing and traditional music several nights a week during the summer. **Morrisey's Pub,** in Doonbeg (☎ 065/55012), has traditional music and sing-alongs on Saturday nights during the summer.

WHERE TO STAY

NEAR LIMERICK & SHANNON AIRPORT

✪ Gallows View

Bunratty East, Co. Clare. ☎ **061/369125.** 5 rms, all with bath. IR£20 ($32) single; IR£15.50 ($24.80) per person sharing. 20% reduction for children. (Rates include breakfast.) No credit cards. Private car park. Closed Nov–Mar.

Donal and Mary McKenna offer a rather special brand of hospitality at this pretty two-story bungalow that's reached by a scenic country road that runs between Bunratty Castle and Durty Nelly's 1¼ miles from the castle. One nicely done up family room and a double are on the ground floor, a blessing for those who have trouble with stairs. Several of Mary's interesting antique pieces are scattered throughout the house, and there's an inviting air to the lounge and dining room. There's central heating. Highly recommended.

✪ Shannonside Country Home

Newmarket-on-Fergus, Co. Clare. ☎ **061/364191.** 8 rms, all with bath. IR£18 ($28.80) single; IR£14 ($22.40) per person sharing. 50% reduction for children. Dinner, IR£12 ($19.20). (Rates include breakfast.) No credit cards.

Mary and Noel Tobin's two-story home is a favorite not only of our readers, but of airline personnel flying into and out of Shannon. The large lounge sports a snooker table and chess board, as well as several musical instruments, which often leads to impromptu singing sessions—Noel plays the accordion, daughter Dee Dee plays the mandolin, and daughter Geraldine is an artist. Mary will provide breakfast for those with early airline departures.

To get here from Limerick, turn right at the first traffic lights after the roundabout approaching Shannon Airport, left at the next junction, and follow signposts to the top of the hill; the house is on the right. From Ennis, turn right after the Shell service station in Newmarket-on-Fergus and drive three miles—the house is on the left.

Bunratty Lodge

Bunratty, Co. Clare. ☎ **061/369402.** 6 rms, all with bath. IR£23 ($36.80) single; IR£16.50 ($26.40) per person sharing. 20% reduction for children. (Rates include breakfast.) No credit cards. Closed Dec–Jan.

Three miles along the road between Bunratty Castle and Durty Nelly's, you'll come to Mary Browne's lovely modern two-story home (it's just three miles from Shannon Airport, 1½ miles along the road between Bunratty Castle and Durty Nelly's). The house is beautifully decorated and furnished, and all guest rooms have orthopedic mattresses, TVs with satellite channels, and heated towel racks. Mary's breakfast won her the regional Galtee Irish Breakfast Award in 1993.

Grange

Wood Road, Cratloe, Co. Clare. ☎ **061/357-389.** 3 rms, 1 with bath. IR£18–IR£20 ($28.80–$32) single; IR£14–IR£15 ($22.40–$24) per person sharing. (Rates include breakfast.) Dinner IR£11 ($17.60). 25% reduction for children. No credit cards. 1 mile off N18 (at Limerick Inn Hotel), 4 miles from Limerick.

You won't find a warmer welcome in these parts than the one Mrs. Mary Corcoran extends to all her guests. Her comfortable home is quite conveniently located, and she is most helpful to guests in planning their Shannonside sightseeing.

Worth a Splurge

✪ Fitzpatrick's Bunratty Shamrock Hotel

Bunratty, Co. Clare. ☎ **061/361177.** Fax 061/471252. Telex 72114. 115 rms, all with bath. TV TEL. Rates IR£75–IR£80 ($120–$128) single; IR£45–IR£55 ($72–$88) per person sharing. Service charge 12.5%. ACC, AE, DC, MC, V.

Its location alone would justify the pricey rates at the Bunratty Shamrock—five miles from Shannon Airport, nine miles from Limerick, and just next door to Bunratty Castle. The Folk Park, the medieval banquet, and Durty Nelly's are all just a short walk away, and there's courtesy bus service to the airport upon request, as well as to Limerick twice daily.

There's much more than location, however, to recommend this lovely hotel. It's a sister to Fitzpatrick's Castle Hotel in Killiney near Dublin and the Silver Springs in Cork, and while the three bear no outward resemblance, they are all looked over with the same personal care and attention by the Fitzpatrick family. The exceptionally efficient and friendly staffs reflect that same sort of personal concern.

The Bunratty Shamrock, a low, rambling stone building, exudes low-key informality in a setting of pure luxury. The stone-floor lobby leads into a large lounge whose focal point is a huge stone fireplace (ablaze on cool evenings). Comfortable seating arranged for intimate groupings make this an inviting place to have morning coffee, afternoon tea, or late-night drinks. The pretty cocktail bar, which has picked up the medieval decor of the castle next door, with dark wood embellishments, has music Wednesday through Sunday during summer months. Shades of soft peach and brown dominate the dining room. There's an indoor heated swimming pool and a sauna on the premises and plenty of parking space. Decor and furnishings are outstanding in all guest rooms, but for a sumptuous break from the rigors of travel, treat yourself to a stay in one of the

Readers Recommend

Shannon View, Bunratty West, Co. Clare. ☎ 061/364056. *"Mrs. E. Woulfe is a wonderful, hospitable hostess, with beautifully appointed and comfortable rooms. A perfect beginning or end for Shannon Airport travelers."*

—Mr. and Mrs. W. Eich, Palo Alto, CA

Innisfree, Bunratty Co. Clare. ☎ 061/369-773. *"We stayed at Imelda McCarthy's Innisfree B&B in Bunratty for five days as a base for our short sightseeing trips. Her home was very clean and cozy, and her help with information was excellent."*

—Robert Kirwan and Monica Boyes, Clarkston, MI

beautiful and spacious River Suites—velvet chair and sofa coverings, king-size beds, and windows with a view are featured in bed/sitting rooms for two and separate bedroom and bed/sitting room for four.

Ennis & Vicinity

Ennis is a busy market town some 16 miles from Shannon Airport, 23 miles from Limerick on N18.

Avonlea

Francis Street, Ennis, Co. Clare. ☎ **065/21632.** 4 rms, all with bath. IR£15 ($24) per person sharing; IR£19 ($30.40) single. 20% reduction for children. No credit cards. April–Oct.

Teresa and Tom McGrath have been welcoming guests to their modern, two-story home near the town center for several years, and they've won accolades from our readers. Guest rooms are both comfortable and attractive, with electric blankets and tea/coffeemakers. Teresa's award-winning breakfasts are served in a bright room that looks out to the garden, with the River Fergus just beyond. Avonlea is nothing if not convenient, with the town center only a five-minute walk away.

Cloneen

Clonroad, Ennis, Co. Clare. ☎ **065/29681.** 3 rms, 1 with bath. IR£14 ($22.40) per person sharing without bath; IR£16 ($25.60) per person sharing with bath. IR£18.50–IR£20 ($29.60–$32) single, 33 1/3% reduction for children. No credit cards. Private car park and bicycle shed. April–Oct.

Set back from the road on an elevated site, this pretty two-story home is only a short walk from the town center. Martina Brennan is the gracious, lively hostess, and her intimate knowledge of Ennis and its surroundings is a guarantee that you'll get the most from your stay. Guest rooms are quite comfortable, and the breakfast room overlooks colorful flower beds and a spacious lawn.

✪ Massabielle

Off Quin Rd., Ennis, Co. Clare. ☎ **065/29363.** 5 rms, 4 with bath. IR£19 ($30.40) single without bath; IR£14 ($22.40) per person sharing without bath; IR£2 ($3.20) per person additional with bath. 25% reduction for children. (Rates include breakfast.) High tea IR£10 ($14.50) extra; dinner, IR£14 ($20.30). No credit cards. Closed Nov–Mar.

Monica O'Loughlin, mother of seven engaging children, has one of the prettiest homes in this scenic area. The small lawn bordered by colorful flower beds gives some indication of the attractive interior. Monica has made extensive use of antiques and authentic reproductions in her furnishings, and her musical brood (among other instruments, they play the piano, viola, and tin whistle) echo their

Readers Recommend

Carberry, Kilrush Road, Ennis, Co. Clare. ☎ 065/24046. *"I highly recommend Mrs. Pauline Roberts, who provides a breakfast that can't be beat, and the rooms are immaculately clean and tastefully decorated."*

—Kate and Stan Katz, Albany, NY

Author's Note: Another reader wrote to praise the good, firm mattresses at Carberry

Laurel Lodge, Clare Road, Ennis, Co. Clare. ☎ 065/21560. *"We liked this home of Mr. and Mrs. Cahil so much that we stayed for eight nights. We had a lovely and spacious room with a private bath and a pretty view of the garden. Breakfasts included fresh fruit as well as scones, muffins, and the usual bacon and eggs—good cooking."*

—Gene and Marylee Natkin, Seattle, WA

Sanborn House, Edenvale, Kilrush Road, Ennis, Co. Clare. ☎ 065/24959. *"This good-looking Georgian home, set well back from the Kilrush ferry road, was an excellent choice for my last night in Ireland—convenient for my departure from Shannon Airport the next morning. Terry O'Donohue couldn't have been friendlier, and my room was attractive and comfortable. Hearty breakfast, bathroom down the hall, and pettable family cat."* —Carol Fredlund, Port Hueneme, CA

mother's warm hospitality. Among the five bedrooms, one family room will sleep three. Outside, there's a well-maintained tennis court. Massabielle is two miles from Ennis off the Quin road (from Shannon Airport and Limerick, turn right at the first traffic lights, then right at the next traffic light; it's signposted on the Quin road).

NEAR KILLALOE

Killaloe is a lovely village on the shores of Lough Derg, some 13 miles north of Limerick city via R463.

Lantern House

Ogonnelloe, Tuamgraney, Co. Clare. ☎ **061/923-034.** Fax 061/923-139. 9 rms, all with bath. TEL TV. IR£20–IR£24 ($32–$38.40) single; IR£16–IR£18 ($25.60–$28.80) per person sharing. ACC, AE, MC, V. Mid-Feb to Nov. Six miles north of Killaloe.

Liz and Phil Hogan preside over this modern guesthouse on a hilltop overlooking Lough Derg. There's a "home-from-home" ambience to the place, and some of the comfortable guest rooms look out to the Shannon. Residents can relax in the small bar or in the lounge, made cozy by an open fire. The Hogans also have an excellent restaurant on the premises (see "Where to Eat," below).

KILRUSH

Kilrush, on the Loop Head Peninsula drive, is only five minutes from the Killimer/Tarbert car ferry.

Bruach-na-Coille

Killimer Road, Kilrush, Co. Clare. ☎ **065/52250.** 3 rms, 2 with bath. TV. IR£15–IR£18 ($24–$28.80) single; IR£12–IR£15 ($19.20–$24) per person sharing. Dinner IR£12 ($19.20). No credit cards. 1 mile from Kilrush, 8 miles from Kilkee.

Michael and Mary Clarke's two-story home is a good landing place if you're coming from North Kerry over to County Clare via the car ferry, or for an overnight before going the other way. The nicely furnished guest rooms come with tea/coffeemakers and hairdryers. Mary's home-cooked meals feature superb baking. The Clarkes will also arrange baby-sitting if you fancy a night out.

KILKEE

Kilkee is a popular family seaside resort set on the shores of a beautiful horseshoe-shaped bay surrounded by high cliffs. It's some 35 miles southwest of Ennis, and the perfect base for exploring West Clare and getting in some safe swimming or other water sports.

✪ Halpin's Hotel

2 Erin St., Kilkee, Co. Clare. ☎ **065/56032.** Fax 065/56032. 12 rms, all with bath. IR£24–IR£32 ($38.40–$51.20) per person, depending on season. ACC, AE, DC, MC, V.

Halpin's is a small, family-run hotel in this charming seaside resort. Rooms all have telephones, TVs, and hairdryers; the dining room serves good food at moderate prices; and there's entertainment in the bar during the summer season.

DOONBEG

Doonbeg is a small village on the coast road 6 miles north of Kilkee and 18 miles south of the Cliffs of Moher.

An Tinteán (The Doonbeg Inn)

Doonbeg, Co. Clare. ☎ **065/55036.** 5 rms, all with bath. IR£18 ($28.80) single; IR£15 ($24) per person sharing. (Rates include breakfast.) No credit cards.

Francie and Connie Killeen are hosts at this gracious home, and they are happy to share with guests their extensive knowledge of the area. Guest rooms are all tastefully decorated and comfortably furnished, and there's private parking.

✪ Aran Country Home

Kilkee Rd., Doonbeg, Co. Clare. ☎ **065/55014.** 3 rms, none with bath. IR£18 ($28.80) single; IR£14 ($22.40) per person sharing. (Rates include breakfast.) No credit cards. Mar–Oct.

Mrs. Della Walshe is one of the warmest Irish hostesses I've met, and her modern bungalow is in spacious grounds, with a garden for use by her visitors. Guest rooms are nicely done up, there's private parking, and Dora is always happy to accept single bookings (sometimes so hard to find).

MILTOWN MALBAY

Miltown Malbay is about halfway between Lahinch and Kilkee on a scenic coastal road, N67. Its greatest claim to fame is the large number of traditional Irish musicians and singing pubs in the area.

Leagard House

Miltown Malbay, Co. Clare. ☎ **065/84324.** 6 rms, 2 with bath. IR£14 ($22.40) per person sharing without bath, IR£16 ($25.60) per person sharing with bath; IR£16 ($25.60)

Readers Recommend

Duggerna House, West End, Kilkee, Co. Clare. ☎ 065/56152. *"Mrs. Maureen Haugh's Duggerna House is everything one might dream of for accommodation—recently renovated rooms decorated with exquisite taste, with complete bathrooms discreetly hiding behind the doors of cupboards; a hugh Irish breakfast, with special fare for children."* —Christine Minette-Pagnoulle, Liege, Belgium

---

single without bath, IR£20 ($32) single with bath; 33 1/3% reduction for children. (Rates include breakfast.) Dinner IR£13 ($20.80). No credit cards. Closed Nov–Mar.

Leagard House is set in quiet, rural surroundings and is an interesting, rambling, one-story house that once was run as a nursing home by Ireland's President Hillary before he went into politics. Suzanne and John Hannon, the present owners, take a personal interest in all their guests, and John is happy to give advice on such important matters as getting to the right pub at the right time to hear some of County Clare's fine traditional musicians. Suzanne excels in the kitchen, and her meals have won such praise that they now accept dinner reservations for nonguests; there's also a wine license. The six guest rooms are all light and airy, and I especially was drawn to the two up front which open onto a small glass-enclosed room. All look out on peaceful country scenes, and the dining room opens to a windowed porch.

Ennistymon and Vicinity

Some 16 miles northwest of Ennis on N85, Ennistymon ("Enn-iss-*teye*-mon") is a holiday center on the main Ennis-Lisdoonvarna road, just 2 1/2 miles from Lahinch, with its beautiful sandy strand and excellent golf course. Many pubs in the town feature Irish music.

✪ Harbour Sunset Farmhouse

Cliffs of Moher Rd., Rannagh, Liscannor, Co. Clare. ☎/Fax 065/81039. 4 rms, 2 with bath. IR£18.50–IR£19.50 ($29.60–$31.20) single; IR£13.50–IR£14.50 ($21.60–$23.20) per person sharing. (Rates include breakfast.) High tea IR£8 ($12.80); dinner IR£12 ($19.20). 25% reduction for children. No credit cards.

In a setting of green fields on an 86-acre dairy farm, Harbour Sunset is loaded with charm. Panoramic views of the nearby golf course and beach add to the beauty of the site. The 200-year-old farmhouse has been beautifully modernized, while still retaining its unique traditional aura. But it's Mrs. Bridget O'Gorman and her talented and gracious family who make it very special. Not only do the O'Gormans extend a warm welcome, but at day's end, they gather around the living room's peat fire for a lively evening of traditional Irish music. Guest rooms are attractive as well as comfortable; hairdryers are provided. Out front are colorful gardens. The "pet corner" is filled with a variety of pet farm animals for hands-on visits by guests. The family also does beautiful Irish crochet work, hard to come by these days, some of which is for sale. A great base for Shannonside sightseeing.

MacMahon's Pub

Church St., Ennistymon, Co. Clare. ☎ **065/71078.** 5 rms, none with bath. IR£14 ($22.40) per person. (Rates include breakfast.) Dinner IR£12 ($19.20) extra. No credit cards.

In Ennistymon, Tom and Mary McMahon have five homey guest rooms above this popular country-style pub. Mary is a cousin of a former Rhode Island governor, and Americans are given an especially warm welcome. Guest rooms are scattered about on several upstairs levels, and each has an individual size, shape, and character. Pub grub is available in the pub (along with good conversation with the locals who favor this place) at lunchtime.

Tullamore Farmhouse

Kilshanny, Ennistymon, Co. Clare. ☎ **065/71187.** 4 rms, 3 with bath. IR£18 ($28.80) single without bath; IR£14 ($22.40) per person sharing without bath; IR£2 ($3.20) per person additional with bath. 20% reduction for children. (Rates include breakfast.) High tea IR£8 ($12.80) extra; dinner IR£12 ($19.20). No credit cards. Closed Nov–Feb.

Mrs. Eileen Carroll is the charming hostess of this large house which is set in lovely countryside six miles from the Cliffs of Moher (signposted on the main Lahinch-Cliffs road). The house is centrally heated and there is a beautiful TV lounge with a view overlooking the hills. The food is excellent and there is a very relaxed atmosphere about the place.

LISDOONVARNA

One of Ireland's most popular holiday spots, Lisdoonvarna is eight miles north of Ennistymon on N85, with a spa, therapeutic springs, and the sea just five miles away. Single readers may also want to look into the very active matchmaking program here.

✪ Tessie's Fernhill Farmhouse

Doolin Rd., Lisdoonvarna, Co. Clare. ☎ **065/74040.** 6 rms, all with bath. IR£19 ($30.40) single; IR£17 ($27.20) per person sharing. 15% reduction for children. (Rates include breakfast.) High tea IR£9 ($14.40); dinner IR£13 ($20.80) extra. No credit cards. Paved car park. Closed Dec–Feb.

This marvelous old (200 years at least, according to its owner, Tess Linnane) farmhouse, set on a hill overlooking fields and distant hills, two miles from Lisdoonvarna and two miles from Doolin, has twice won Best Farmhouse awards. There's a large front lounge with picture windows looking out to the fields, and one guest room on the ground floor is ideal for the handicapped. Upstairs bedrooms have kept the character of the house, some with wooden peaked or slanted ceilings. All are nicely furnished, and there's central heat. Tess's lively personality is a bonus.

Sunville

Off Doolin (coast) Rd., Lisdoonvarna, Co. Clare. ☎ **065/74065.** 5 rms, all with bath. IR£19 ($30.40) single; IR£15 ($24) per person sharing. 20% reduction for children. (Rates include breakfast.) ACC, MC, V.

Sunville is a short walk from the town center on N67 (turn off at the Burren Tourist Hostel). Teresa and John Petty are the friendly owners, and their attractive guest rooms are all comfortably furnished, with electric blankets and tea/coffeemakers. There's a TV lounge for guests, as well as private parking.

Readers Recommend

Rozel, Station Road, Lahinch, Co. Clare. ☎ 065/81203. *"Lahinch is a gem of a town, a beautiful base if you're driving on to Galway and points north. It's on the sea, and we actually saw kids surfing! Rozel is run by Margaret O'Dwyer and her husband, and it is one of the nicest B&Bs we've ever stayed in, with the most comfortable beds in all of Ireland."* —Bill Hinchey, Bethlehem, PA

Author's Note: This is a "No Smoking" guesthouse.

Edenlandia, School Road, Lahinch, Co. Clare. ☎ 065/81361. *"My wife and I had the good fortune of being referred to Martin and Joanne Barrett in Lahinch. I am an avid golfer and was pleasantly surprised to learn that we were staying with one of the oldest families associated with the Lahinch Golf Club. Martin and Joanne and their lovely daughters, Aileen and Annmarie, made our stay most enjoyable and memorable."* —John A. Patton, Lynbrook, NY

DOOLIN

Doolin is a small, vibrant coastal village some 27 miles northwest of Ennis, and 5 miles southwest of Lisdoonvarna. Traditional Irish music reigns supreme throughout the year.

✪ Aran View House Hotel and Restaurant

Doolin, Co. Clare. ☎ **065/74061.** Fax 065/74540. 15 rms, all with bath. IR£25–IR£30 ($40–$48) per person. 25% reduction for children. (Rates include breakfast.) AE, V. Closed Dec–Apr.

A longtime favorite of our readers when it operated as a bed-and-breakfast accommodation, this large country home, built about 1736 high on a hill, is notable for its breathtaking sea views of the Aran Islands and the Cliffs of Moher. Owners Chris, Theresa, and John Linnane extend an especially warm Irish welcome to guests. The window-walled lounge takes advantage of the magnificent views, and the cozy drawing room bar, with its crackling log fire, adds to the loveliness of this charming place. The rustic-style dining room, with its big bay window, is the perfect setting for an excellent Irish meal. Activities available to guests include fishing, golfing, horseback riding, walks on the Burren, boat rides to the Aran Islands, and, of course, musical nights in local pubs.

✪ Churchfield

Doolin, Co. Clare. ☎ **065/74209.** Fax 065/74622. 6 rms, 5 with bath. IR£20 ($32) single; IR£13.50 ($21.60) per person sharing; IR£1 ($1.60) per person extra with bath. 33.5% reduction for children. (Rates include breakfast.) V. Closed Dec 20–28.

Maeve Fitzgerald's modern two-story home is right in the middle of Doolin village at the post office. Guest rooms are spacious and attractively furnished, with a lovely view of the sea, mountains, and the Cliffs of Moher. The dining room is bright and cheerful, and one reader wrote that in six tours of Ireland he has never found a finer Irish breakfast than Maeve's. Her extensive knowledge of the area is matched only by her boundless enthusiasm and good humor.

BALLYVAUGHAN

About 10 miles northeast of Lisdoonvarna via N67, Ballyvaughan is on an inlet of Galway Bay at the edge of the Burren.

✪ Hyland's Hotel

Ballyvaughan, Co. Clare. ☎ **065/77037.** Fax 065/77131. 19 rms (all with bath). IR£25–IR£35 ($40–$56) single; IR£20–IR£30 ($32–$48) per person sharing, depending on season. ACC, AE, MC, V. Closed Jan.

Readers Recommend

Ballinalacken Castle, Hotel Lisdoonvarna, Co. Clare. ☎ 065/74025. *"This is a 19th-century three-Star hotel (bed and breakfast) with the castle right next door. We enjoyed the luxury of the huge double rooms. There is a bar and dining room downstairs and the owners even offer to bring drinks to your room. We enjoyed free babysitting services there as well. The bar manager will give you the key to the castle next door so you may explore on your own."* —K. O'Brien, Tujunga, CA

Lynch's Hotel, The Square, Lisdoonvarna, Co. Clare. ☎ 065/74010. *"We loved this small, family-run hotel. It's very modern in outward appearance, but inside there's a very warm, homey atmosphere. Maureen Lynch and her family made us feel very much at home, and an added bonus was their family rate that saved us money."*

—Sarah Caliri, Bogota, NJ

Readers Recommend

Harbour View, Doolin, Co. Clare. ☎ 065/74154. *"This is a first-rate accommodation. Mrs. Kathleen Cullinan's home is set on a hillside, with a magnificent view of the surrounding countryside. Mrs. Cullinan was very friendly and was helpful in recommending things to see and do in Doolin."*

—G. Wazeter and S. Strazzella, Bayonne, NJ

This small hotel is a real charmer. Dating back to the early 18th century, the two-story hotel is now in the hands of the eighth generation of the Hyland family, and the personal atmosphere is evident the minute you walk through the front door. The comfortable, attractive residents' lounge has a fireplace glowing with a turf fire, as does the public lounge on the premises, where local musicians gather nightly and in impromptu sessions uphold the County Clare tradition of good music and good spirits. Dunguaire Castle is just 15 miles away, and the hotel will arrange for you to attend the medieval banquet there if you wish. Bedrooms differ in size, but are quite nicely decorated.

Feakle

About 17 miles northwest of Killaloe via R461, Feakle is one of the Rent-A-Cottage holiday villages, a good spot for exploring the Lough Derg area.

✪ Smyth Village Hotel

Feakle, Co. Clare. ☎ **061/924002.** Fax 061/924244. 12 rms, all with bath. TEL. IR£20 ($32) single; IR£17 ($27.20) per person sharing. 33$^1/_3$% discount for children. (Rates include breakfast.) Dinner IR£12 ($19.20) extra. MC, V. Closed Dec–Mar.

The Smyth Village is unique among Irish hotels. Located in the Rent-a-Cottage village of Feakle, the hotel is a sort of hotel/guesthouse, owned and operated by natives of the region, the Smyth family. The hotel consists of three connected two-story cottage-type buildings, and its bluff-top site overlooks the traditional cottages of the rental scheme. Hotel amenities include a full liquor license, tennis courts, a games room, and a restaurant that is open to nonresidents as well as guests. Meals are served family-style, with "the very best quality done in the simplest way" and Mrs. Smyth's home-baked bread. There's an old-fashioned pub that draws local musicians as well as visitors from the rental cottages below. All 12 bedrooms have private bath and are nicely decorated.

Where to Eat

Pub Grub in Bunratty

✪ Durty Nelly's

Bunratty. ☎ **061/364861.** IR£3–IR£6 ($4.80-$9.60). ACC, AE, DC, MC. Daily 12:30–2:30pm. BAR FOOD.

Soup, sandwiches, salads, and hot dishes featuring roasts, seafood, or chicken are excellent value at this memorable pub next to Bunratty Castle (see "What to See and Do," above). It also houses the moderately priced Oyster Restaurant and pricier Loft Restaurant (see below).

Pub Grub and a Restaurant in Ennis

Brogans Restaurant and Bar

24 O'Connell St., Ennis. ☎ **065/29480.** Fixed-price bar lunch and restaurant grills IR£4.50 ($7.20). ACC, AE, MC, V. Mon–Sat 10:30am–4pm and 5–10:30pm. BAR FOOD/GRILLS.

Brogans serves bar food, as well as salads and hot or cold lunch plates and grills in the evening in the same price ranges. Soup and sandwiches are available in the bar continuously, beginning at 10:30am.

Cruises Restaurant

Abbey St., Ennis, Co. Clare. ☎ **065/41800.** Average lunch IR£8 ($12.80); average 3-course dinner IR£10 ($16). ACC, AE, MC, V. Mon–Sat 12–10:30pm. IRISH.

This 200-year-old restaurant, with its beamed ceiling and glowing open fires, is the perfect setting for Irish dishes, such as the excellent Gaelic steak cooked in Paddy whiskey and the heaping Harvest of the Sea plate, with fish and shellfish served in a light mushroom sauce. Traditional music breaks out several nights a week, to make the setting even more perfect.

A Restaurant in Doolin

✪ Bruach Na Haille

Doolin. ☎ **065/74120.** Main courses IR£6.50–IR£13.50 ($10.40–$21.60); fixed-price dinner IR£16 ($25.60). No credit cards. May–Oct, Mon–Sat 6–9:30pm. SEAFOOD/CONTINENTAL/VEGETARIAN.

In Doolin alongside the Aille River you'll find this terrific little restaurant whose name means "Bank of the River." Helen and John Browne serve marvelous seafood and local dishes in a restored country house with flagstone floors and whitewashed walls. The menu features everything from soup and salads to fresh mackerel, salmon, and local shellfish, and a limited range of foreign specialties, with the emphasis on local seafood. Soups, desserts, and bread are all homemade. Wine is available by the glass as well as by the bottle.

Gourmet Dining in Bunratty

✪ MacCloskey's at Bunratty House

Bunratty. ☎ **061/74082.** Reservations required. Fixed-price dinner IR£26 ($41.60), plus 10% service charge. AE, DC, V. Tues–Sat 6:30–10pm. Closed Christmas–Feb. TRADITIONAL/CONTINENTAL.

Bunratty House (just back of the castle) is an elegant mansion that dates back more than a century and a half. Its living quarters have seen comings and goings that would probably fill a book, but it's a sure bet that its arched-ceiling cellar has never before seen the likes of MacCloskey's gourmet restaurant. Gerry and Marie MacCloskey left West Cork and their award-winning Courtyard restaurant in Schull to bring their expertise to Shannonside, and the result is one of Ireland's most beautiful restaurants. The low ceilings and 1½-foot-thick walls have been whitewashed to a pristine white as a background for delicate shades of pink and rose, which are punctuated by the deep blue of tall candles at each table. The mansion's original wine cellar has been retained, and behind its ironwork gates rests an excellent selection of good wines.

Main courses of the fixed-price dinner change often to be sure that only the freshest produce, meats, and seafood are served. A typical five-course offering might include such starters as snails in garlic butter, a selection of melon with kiwi fruit, or smoked salmon; cream of lettuce soup or salad with Stilton cheese dressing; main courses of sea trout with hollandaise sauce, rod-caught salmon baked with herbs, leeks, and mushrooms, or black sole on the bone; fresh garden vegetables; and dessert of iced lemon-and-lime soufflé, rhubarb tart, or stuffed chocolate-covered pears.

A Restaurant Near Killaloo

Lantern House

Ogonnelloe, Co. Clare. ☎ **061/923-034.** Reservations recommended. Main courses IR£9–IR£15 ($14.40–$24). ACC, AE, MC, V. Mid-Feb–May and Sept–Oct, Tues–Sat 6–9:30pm, Sun 7–8:30pm; June–Aug Mon–Sat 7–9:30pm, Sun 7–8:30pm. SEAFOOD/IRISH.

Beamed ceilings, candlelight, and wall lanterns set the warm, intimate tone of this hilltop restaurant overlooking Lough Derg. A speciality is salmon fresh from local waters, and if your taste is less finny, you can opt for pork steak with white wine or duck à l'orange.

A Restaurant on the Loop Head Peninsula

The Long Dock Bar & Seafood Restaurant

West St., Carrigaholt, Co. Clare. ☎ **065/58106.** Dinner reservations recommended. Bar food under IR£5 ($8); main courses IR£8–IR£12 ($12.80–$19.20). No credit cards. Daily bar food 12:30–6pm; dinner 7–10pm. SEAFOOD/BAR FOOD/VEGETARIAN.

This cozy establishment is a happy blend of open fires in the bar and gracious informality in the dining room. Daniele (on a first-name basis with all and sundry) is the Ballymaloe-trained chef, and her innovative use of freshly caught seafood from local waters (as well as her meat and poultry dishes) makes this a good place to stop for a mouthwatering snack or to indulge in one of the superb evening meals. Vegetarian dishes are also available.

Restaurants in Kilkee

✪ Halpins Hotel

Erin St., Kilkee. ☎ **065/56032.** Bar food under IR£5 ($8); main courses IR£8–IR£12 ($12.80–$19.20). AE, MC, V. Daily 12:30–2:30pm and 6–9pm. BAR FOOD/SEAFOOD/TRADITIONAL.

The cozy bar has an old-fashioned air, with lots of dark wood, and there's an open-hearth fireplace in the lounge. Meals in the dining room feature seafood fresh from local waters, as well as lamb, pork, steak, and chicken main courses. Halpins well deserves its fine reputation for good food at reasonable prices.

2 Limerick City

15 miles E of Shannon Airport, 123 miles SW of Dublin, 23 miles SE of Ennis, 68 miles NE of Killarney

Limerick gets its name from the Irish *Luimneach,* meaning "Bare Spot," and centuries ago, that's just what was here—a barren, hilly bit of land on an island. Today you'll find a well-laid-out city with row after row of Georgian-style houses. In the intervening years, the site has been changed and molded by just about every group that has shaped the country's history. Because the island sat at the lowest ford of the Shannon, it is believed early Celts built an earthen fort at the island's highest point. Then came the Danes, in A.D. 831, to build a base from which to go aplundering. More than a century later Brian Boru sent them packing and installed the O'Briens as rulers. Next it was the Normans, with their stout city walls and castles. Portions of their walls remain to this day, as does King John's Castle. They were the first to bridge the Shannon (at the spot now crossed by the 1838 Thomond Bridge). Native Irish, of course, had no place in that Anglo-Norman stronghold, but were exiled to the south side of the river, where they eventually built their own walls and called their area Irish Town.

It was in 1691 that William III's siege of Limerick (which had once been abandoned as the city's stubbornly brave defenders prevented any breach of their walls) ended with the signing of a treaty of honorable and reasonable terms. You can see the stone on which it was signed at one end of Thomond Bridge, where it is enshrined as a memorial to a treaty whose terms were never carried out by the British. Even now Limerick is known as the "City of the Violated Treaty." During the 18th century Limerick took on its present-day form, with stylish town houses going up along broad avenues extending far beyond the old boundaries of Irish Town and English Town.

In the last few decades of this century, Limerick had declined into a dingy, somewhat gray city, with few outward charms. In the 1980s, however, the city began a restoration program that has put a bright new face on things, with even more improvements in the planning stage.

GETTING THERE There is direct train service to Limerick City from Cork, Dublin, and Killarney, with good bus connections from almost any destination in the country. By car, Limerick City can be reached via N7 from the east, N24 and N20 from the south, N18 from the north.

ORIENTATION **City Layout** Limerick's main street is the ¾-mile-long O'Connell Street, which becomes Patrick Street at its northern end. The west-to-east road that leads to Shannon Airport is called Ennis Road west of the Shannon, Sarsfield Street at its western end in the city, and William Street at its eastern end. The major intersection of O'Connell and Sarsfield is the center of most of the city's business and shopping, and all city bus lines pass this junction.

ESSENTIALS **Information** You'll find the Tourist Office on Arthur's Quay (☎ 061/317522). Behind the Tourist Office is a lovely riverside park, with a pathway joining the historic medieval quarter with the city center. The office is open Monday through Saturday from 9am to 7pm, with limited Sunday hours during the summer months. The Limerick Junior Chamber of Commerce publishes a Shannonside entertainment guide weekly during summer months, which is available at most hotels as well as at the Tourist Office.

Telephone Area Code The telephone area code for Limerick is 061. *Note:* At press time, Limerick telephone numbers were being changed; dial 1190 if you have difficulty reaching listed numbers.

GETTING AROUND **By Bus and Train** The bus and railway station is in Parnell Street on the southeast side of town, and the number to call for all bus and rail information is 061/313333 (bus) or 315555 (rail).

By Taxi Taxi ranks are at the railway station and at the corner of Thomas Street and Cecil Street, just off O'Connell Street. Call 332266 for a taxi.

WHAT TO SEE & DO

The very first thing to do is to go by the **Tourist Office.** This is one of the best in the country, and they're prepared to book accommodations for you; steer you to eateries; help plan sightseeing excursions; tell you about craft shops in the area; alert you to any special events, festivals, or evening entertainment currently on; and send you away loaded down with maps and brochures to make your time in Shannonside a joy. There's also a very good selection of Irish publications for sale in the office.

Limerick City

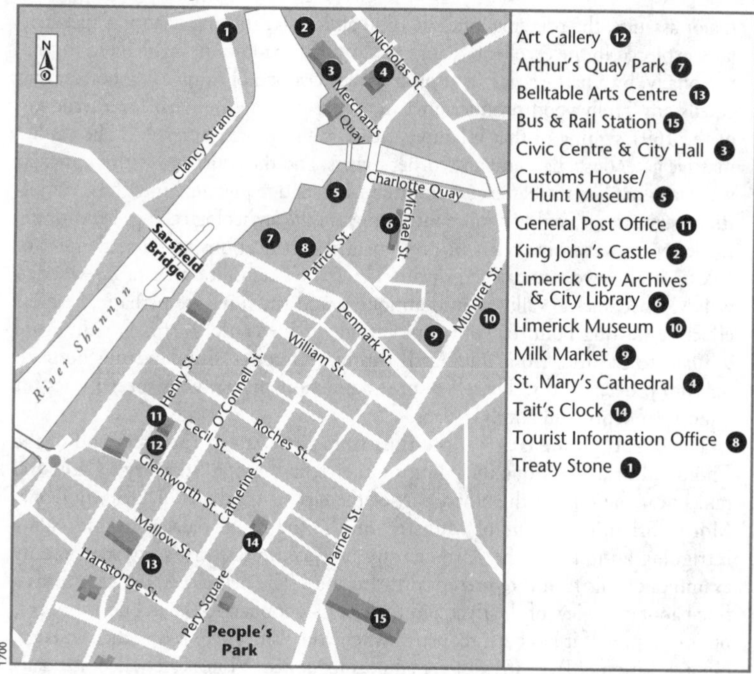

Monday through Saturday they conduct **walking tours** of Old Limerick. Ask about the **Shannon Heritage Trail Explorer Ticket** that saves you money on sightseeing admissions.

If you're not a walker, Paddy O'Toole (☎ 061/455521) is the perfect guide for personally ✪ **conducted driving tours.** In addition to his extensive knowledge of Limerick and the Shannonside area, Paddy is well up on local folklore and is an entertaining as well as informative guide. He will also tailor tours to focus on any special interests you may have. Or contact Mr. Tom Jordan, **Fáilte Chauffeur-Drive Tours,** Elsinore, Castletroy, Limerick, Co. Limerick (☎ 061/332-266), for very special escorted tours of up to four persons per car. Rates are quite reasonable on a per-person basis, and Tom can give you an insider's tour of Limerick, as well as more far-flung trips like the Cliffs of Moher/Galway Bay/Allwee Cave, Galway/Connemara, or Killarney/Blarney.

For sightseeing out of town, pick up the Bus Eireann **day trips** folder from the Tourist Office. There are some 17 tours during the summer months, and they go as far afield as Connemara to the north and the Ring of Kerry to the south.

Gray Line Sightseeing Tours (☎ 061/413088 or 416099) also operates day tours, overnight tours, and nighttime excursions to local medieval banquets.

The Top Attractions

Restored ✪ **King John's Castle** (☎ 061/411201) rises from the riverbank at one end of Thomond Bridge, and without doubt it is the jewel in the crown of Limerick's Heritage Precinct. Built in the early 1200s as a royal authority administrative and military fortress, the castle's 10-foot-thick walls have endured several major assaults, the principal ones in 1690 and 1691. Its long history is spectacularly explored in the excellent "Kings in Conflict" exhibition, highlighted for me, personally, by a battle scene (complete with the sound of thundering horses) that equals any Hollywood production I've ever seen. The life-sized reconstruction of the 1691 signing of that infamous treaty is also quite impressive. The castle's massive gatehouse, battlements, corner towers, and the courtyard with its ancient war machines like the battering ram, trebuchet, and mangonel bring those tumultuous centuries alive. Even more intriguing are the archeological digs beneath the castle, where extensive relics of pre-Norman fortifications and a settlement of Viking houses were unearthed during the castle's restoration. A raised wooden walkway becomes a walkway into antiquity, and the ruins are perhaps the most effective starting point of your explorations of the castle. It's open daily from 9:30am to 5:30pm from mid-April through October, Sunday from noon to 5:30pm other months. There's a small admission charge, with special rates for seniors, students, and family groups.

The **Treaty Stone** is across the river from the castle at the other end of the Thomond Bridge. Among the points of interest in the city, **St. Mary's Cathedral** ranks near the top. In the oldest part of the city, it was built in 1168 by Donal Mor O'Brien, then King of Munster, on the site of his palace. It holds some intriguing antiquities (the 13th-century bog oak misericord seats are the only examples of this furniture preserved in Ireland). The bell tower, which affords a fine panoramic view of the river and the city, is not open to the public at present, but do inquire if it has been reopened when you visit. There is no official charge, but a donation of IR£1 ($1.60) per adult is requested. Visitors are welcomed daily mid-June to September from 9am to 5pm, 9am to 1pm other months. From mid-June to mid-September there's an excellent *son-et-lumière* (sound-and-light show) nightly at 9:15pm inside the cathedral.

The award-winning **Limerick Museum,** 1 St. John's Square (☎ 061/417826), exhibits artifacts from the Lough Gur area, as well as city charters, chains of office, the "nail" from the City Exchange on which merchants once struck their deals, currencies from periods in the city's history as far back as the Vikings, and a good deal more. It's free, and open Tuesday through Saturday from 10am to 1pm and 2:15 to 5pm. Another interesting collection of ancient Irish metalwork, medieval bronzes, and enamels is in the **Hunt Museum,** University of Limerick, Plassey (☎ 061/333644).

Irish art from the 18th, 19th, and 20th centuries is featured in temporary and permanent exhibitions at the **Limerick City Gallery of Art,** Pery Square (☎ 061/310633); hours vary, so check locally.

Items ranging from lace handkerchiefs to bridal veils of the exquisite ✪ **Limerick lace** are painstakingly created on a base of fine Belgian net under the supervision of the sisters of the Good Shepherd Convent. In today's world, fewer and fewer women are willing to undertake the demanding work, which means that your purchases of today will be your family's heirlooms of tomorrow. Visits to the workroom are by appointment only—call 061/415-183.

The Pub Scene

Sadly, a good many of the city's finest pubs have been modernized right out of their character, but ✪ **W. J. South's,** also known as the **Crescent Bar** (☎ 061/318850), on the Crescent (that's where Daniel O'Connell's statue commands the center of O'Connell Street), holds on to the trappings of age with a firm grip. There's a long white marble bar up front, divided by wood and etched-glass partitions. Faded tapestries hang on the wall, and behind the bar is an elaborate mahogany structure, its arched niches framing old bottles and backed by mirrors speckled with age. Just back of the small front bar, a larger room has walls devoted to a display of rugby photos (the Garyowen rugby team consider South's their "local"). The best pint in Limerick is said to be pulled here, and you'll hear a lot about sports. An attractive lounge bar has been added to the old pub; morning coffee is served, as well as good, traditional Irish food at pub-grub prices (see "Where to Eat," below).

The "aged" look at **Flannery's,** 20 Catherine Street, at the corner of Cecil Street (☎ 061/414450), comes from woodwork that once graced an old distillery, and according to Jerry Flannery, "there's still plenty of whiskey salted in it." The pub itself is only a little more than 50 years old, but it has the comfortable atmosphere of a country pub, with a small snug at one end, and in the evening a core of regulars ever ready to converse with the visiting Yank. Flannery's also serves good pub grub at lunch.

My personal favorite of all Limerick pubs is neither aged nor particularly atmospheric, but it's very, very Irish. ✪ **Matt Fennessy's Pub,** New Street, Punches Cross (☎ 061/229-038), is the epitome of a neighborhood local, filled with convivial souls, a good pint pulled, and in general just the sort of place to pass a pleasant evening. A bit out from the city center, but easily reached via either a longish walk or a short bus ride, New Street turns off O'Connell (it's the intersection with Dan Ryan's Garage on one corner, Punches Pub on the opposite). Inside, there's an old-fashioned bar, a lounge, and a snug affectionately dubbed "The Senate" by regulars, who often debate the affairs of the country. While there's no *scheduled* sing-along at Fennessy's, spontaneous sing-alongs often break out on weekend nights. The clientele is nearly all local, and they make Americans very welcome. Look for Mick Feerick behind the bar, one of Ireland's charmers. Incidentally, bar food is served from 12:30 to 2pm, should you find yourself in the neighborhood.

✪ **Nancy Blake's (Mulcahy's Pub),** 19 Denmark Street (☎ 061/416443), is a cozy, old-style pub popular for pub lunches and traditional music (see below) and for its summer barbecues in the courtyard out back.

AFTER DARK

From the Tourist Office, pick up the "What's On" booklet, which lists current goings-on in Limerick and its environs, as well as a Calendar of Events. Check with Jurys Hotel (☎ 061/327777) to see if their cabaret is currently on.

THE PERFORMING ARTS/DANCING

✪ Belltable Arts Centre

69 O'Connell St. ☎ **061/319866.** Tickets IR£3–IR£8 ($4.80–$12.80).

The Belltable puts on very good concerts and plays at low to moderate prices. They have a very strong program of theater, visual arts, music, opera, and dance. In summer months, Irish theater is presented by Limerick's professional company, Island Theater Company. The center also has a full bar and restaurant on the premises.

TRADITIONAL MUSIC

Limerick has many atmospheric pubs that provide traditional music evenings. The problem is that those evenings vary during the week and by season. As well as that, several pubs are now bringing in other types of music, including blues, jazz, country/western, and even some rock. Those listed below are likely to have music of one genre or another during your visit—a telephone call before you go should land you in the venue you prefer. And do ask your B&B hostess—locals are often the best possible source of information on the best traditional music currently on offer.

A personal favorite, ✪ **Nancy Blake's (Mulcahy's Pub),** 19 Denmark Street (☎ 061/416443), has traditional music most summer nights in the old-style front rooms, made cozy with glowing fireplaces, as well as blues and jazz in the large, stone-walled lounge and bar out back. Other music pubs are: **Foley's Bar,** Lower Shannon Street (☎ 061/48783); ✪ **The Locke Bar,** George's Quay (☎ 061/413-733); **Doc's Bar,** The Granary, Michael Street (☎ 061/417-266); **Costello's Tavern,** 4 Dominic Street (☎ 061/47266); and **Taits Tavern,** 54 Parnell Street (☎ 061/48133).

SHOPPING

You'll find Limerick's leading concentration of shops in **Arthurs Quay Shopping Centre,** which, in addition to shops and boutiques, also holds a coffee shop and pâtisserie, a restaurant, a bank, a post office branch, and a beauty salon. The charming, old-style **Cruises Street Shopping Promenade** holds upmarket boutiques, craft shops, and Bewley's Café.

Elsewhere in the city, look for antiquarian and secondhand publications at **O'Brien Books & Photo Gallery,** Bedford Row (☎ 061/412833). An interesting drop-in, even if you're a nonsmoker, is ✪ **M. Cahill & Son Tobacconists,** 47 Wickham Street (☎ 061/441821). It's the oldest tobacco shop in Ireland, and owner Eleanor Purcell is the country's only woman tobacconist. As a pipe smoker myself (no comments, please!), I am drawn to the quaintly old-fashioned shop, with its wooden benches and expanse of pipes, cigars, snuff, and all sorts of accessories for the smoker. Eleanor, whose father bought the place in 1950 after working there half a century, knows the business from A to Z and is usually available for a friendly chat with customers.

WHERE TO STAY

✪ Annesville

Ennis Rd., Limerick, Co. Limerick. ☎ **061/452703.** 4 rms, 3 with bath. IR£13.50 ($21.60) per person sharing without bath; IR£15 ($24) per person sharing with bath. (Rates include breakfast.) No credit cards.

Opposite Dunne's Store on Ennis Road, this is the modern home of Carmel Beresford, and has been one of my most popular recommendations with readers. Airport and city buses stop just outside the door. The five guest rooms are spacious, the house is centrally heated, and there's good off-street parking. Carmel will gladly book banquets and help you arrange transport to them. She can also provide chauffeur-driven minibus packages for small touring or golfing groups of 8 to 10 people for three, four, or seven days.

✪ Cloneen House

Ennis Rd., Limerick, Co. Limerick. ☎ **061/454-461.** 6 rms, all with bath. TV. IR£18 ($26.10) single without bath; IR£14 ($20.30) per person sharing without bath; IR£4 ($5.80) per person additional with bath. (Rates include breakfast.) ACC, AE, MC, V. Private car park.

Mary Cusack has made extensive renovations in this red-brick Edwardian home, only a five-minute walk from the city center. The airport bus and city buses stop just outside the front gate, and there's ample parking in the rear. Guest rooms are most attractive, and the bay-windowed dining room overlooks a lovely rose garden.

✪ Curraghgower

Ennis Rd., Limerick, Co. Limerick. ☎ **061/54716.** 4 rms, 2 with bath. IR£18–IR£20 ($28.80–$32) ($24.65) single; IR£15–IR£17 ($24–$27.20) per person sharing. 20% reduction for children. (Rates include breakfast.) No credit cards.

Friendly Mrs. Power makes visitors feel right at home in her three-story brick home. There are four guest rooms, all with sinks, nicely decorated, and comfortably furnished, and you'll breakfast with a view of the pretty back garden. There's central heat and off-street parking.

✪ Glen Eagles

12 Vereker Gardens, Ennis Rd., Limerick, Co. Limerick. ☎ **061/455521.** 4 rms, all with bath. IR£20 ($32) single; IR£15.50 ($24.80) per person sharing. (Rates include breakfast.) MC, V. Closed Dec–Feb.

Vivacious Carole O'Toole is the sort of caring hostess who will pack a lunch for you to take along on a day trip. She's active in all kinds of city activities (ask about her two award-winning rowing-club sons) and an invaluable source of information about local goings-on. Husband Paddy is retired from many years in the tour business and puts together personally conducted driving tours for visitors (see "What to See and Do," above). The two-story house is in a quiet cul-de-sac signposted on Ennis Road (just before you reach Jurys Hotel if you're coming from the airport) and is centrally heated. The attractive guest rooms all have tea/coffeemakings and hairdryers. There's a TV lounge, a pretty garden, and off-street parking.

✪ St. Anthony's

8 Coolraine Terrace, Limerick, Co. Limerick. ☎ **061/452607.** 3 rms, 1 with bath. IR£13.50 ($21.60) per person; IR£1 ($1.60) per person additional with bath. (Rates include breakfast.) No credit cards.

The Misses Mary and Kathleen Collins are delightful sisters first brought to my attention by a reader who wrote that "they really put themselves out to make a tourist's stay pleasant." The two-story house is their family home. It's neat as a pin and has a warm, homey atmosphere. Meals are served in a dining room overlooking a garden, and breakfast comes with homemade apricot and other fruit jams. They also serve a lovely afternoon tea with home baking. The guest rooms are comfortably furnished and have sinks and built-in wardrobes.

St. Martin's

4 Clanmorris Gardens, Limerick, Co. Limerick. ☎ **061/455-013.** 3 rms, none with bath. IR£14 ($22.40) single; IR£10 ($16) per person sharing. 10% reduction for children. (Rates include breakfast.) No credit cards. Closed Nov–Feb.

Mrs. Roche is a warm, friendly woman and her home is situated off the Ennis road, in a quiet area close to the city center. Her three bedrooms are nicely done up, and her breakfasts are delicious.

A Hostel

An Oige Hostel

1 Pery Sq., Limerick, Co. Limerick. ☎ and fax **061/314672.** 66 beds. IR£3.50–IR£6 ($5.60–$9.60) per person, depending on season; some reduction for under-18s. Breakfast IR£1.50 ($2.40). No credit cards.

The An Oige hostel in Limerick is a large old Georgian house. Right in the heart of the city center, it is located on a public park and has a fully equipped kitchen, dining room, common room, and showers. There are bicycles for rent, and meals can be provided on request. Advance booking is advisable during the summer months.

Worth a Splurge

✪ Hotel Greenhills

Ennis Rd., Limerick, Co. Limerick. ☎ **061/453033.** Fax 061/453307. 66 rms, all with bath. IR£60–IR£70 ($96–$112) single; IR£46–IR£53 ($73.60–$84.80) per person sharing. (Rates include breakfast.) AE, MC, V.

Set back off Ennis Road in beautifully landscaped gardens, the Greenhills location is one of the most convenient in Limerick. The city center is no more than five minutes away, and Shannon Airport is about a 10-minute drive. Owner Brian Green built the hotel almost a quarter of a century ago and has run it ever since on the theory that "our personal attention and supervision are the hallmark of our success." That same caring attitude is evident in every member of the staff, as well as in all facilities of the recently refurbished hotel. The tastefully decorated guest rooms have satellite TV, direct-dial telephones, tea/coffeemakers, and hairdryers; the more spacious deluxe rooms also have a pleasant seating area and a trouser press. There's a leisure center with an indoor heated swimming pool, separate childrens' pool (and a varying activities program for children), sauna, steam room, Jacuzzi, gymnasium, and tennis court. Guests also enjoy privileges at the Limerick County Golf and Country Club. There's often live music in the traditional-style Jockey Club bar, and the Grill Room offers good food service at moderate prices (see "Where to Eat," below), while there's gourmet fare at the small, intimate Bay Leaf Restaurant.

Self-Catering

Kilmurry Village

General Manager, Plassey Campus Centre Limited, University of Limerick, Plassy Technological Park, Limerick. ☎ **061/330-316.** 48 units (4 single and 2 double bedrooms in each house). IR£10 ($16) per person self-catering; IR£14–IR£16 ($22.40–$25.60) per person with continental breakfast and maid service. No credit cards.

In an attractive village-style setting overlooking the Shannon, these charming lodge-style houses feature bright, cheerful, tastefully furnished bedrooms; fully equipped kitchen/living room; cable TV; and card telephone. There are self-service restaurants on campus for moderately priced meals, as well as a laundry, bars, concert hall, sports complex, shopping mall, banks, and art galleries. Regular taxi and bus service into Limerick city (3 miles).

Where to Eat

Pub Grub

Outstanding pub grub, with Irish specialties, salad plates, hot dishes, sandwiches, and soup is served at the following Limerick pubs between the hours of 12:30 and 2:30pm at a cost of IR£3 to IR£4 ($4.80–$6.40).

Flannery's, 20 Catherine Street, Limerick (☎ 061/444450), at the corner of Cecil Street; ✪ **W. J. South's,** also known as the **Crescent Bar,** on the Crescent (☎ 061/318850), which specializes in traditional Irish food; **Matt Fennessy's Pub,** New Street, Punches Cross (☎ 061/29038); and **Nancy Blake's (Mulcahy's**

Pub), 19 Denmark Street (☎ 061/416443); and the **Jockey Club** in Hotel Greenhills (☎ 061/453033).

RESTAURANTS

De La Fontaine

12 Upper Gerald Griffin St., Limerick. ☎ **061/414-461.** Reservations recommended. Main courses IR£11–IR£16 ($17.60–$25.60); set dinner IR£22 ($35.20). 10% service charge. ACC, DC, MC, V. Mon–Sat 7–10pm. FRENCH.

One of Limerick's finest, this pretty upstairs restaurant is the domain of French chef Alain Bras-White and his Irish wife, Gerardine. Using all local produce whenever possible, Alain recreates the "Grand Mère" cuisine of France in such dishes as filet of beef flambéed with peppercorns and foie gras and medallions of pork with ginger and exotic fruits.

✪ Greenhills Brasserie & Grill Room and Bay Leaf Restaurant

In the Hotel Greenhills, Ennis Rd. ☎ **061/453033.** Brasserie & Grill Room, main courses IR£7–IR£12 ($11.20–$19.20); Bay Leaf Restaurant, set dinners IR£16–IR£18 ($25.60–$28.80). AE, MC, V. Brasserie & Grill Room, daily 7:30am–11pm; Bay Leaf Restaurant, Tues–Sat 7:30–11:30pm. TRADITIONAL/GRILLS/SEAFOOD.

The light, airy Brasserie & Grill Room is a pleasant setting for continuous food service all day, and prices are more than reasonable. I especially enjoyed the grilled spring lamb cutlets with mint sauce and the grilled Shannon salmon steak, but lighter fare such as burgers, omelets, and salads are also excellent. The kitchen of the elegant Bay Leaf Restaurant prides itself on their roast rack of lamb coated in mustard and herb crust and glazed with a honey dressing. There's game in season, as well as superb seafood main courses. In both eateries, you can count on being served the freshest of ingredients; both have extensive wine lists; and the service is as friendly in both as it is throughout the hotel.

✪ Bridges Restaurant

In Jurys Hotel, Ennis Rd. ☎ **061/327777.** Average lunch under IR£10 ($16); set lunch IR£10 ($16); average à la carte dinner about IR£13 ($20.80); set dinner IR£13 ($20.80). 10% service charge. AE, MC, V. Daily 8am–10pm. TRADITIONAL/SALADS/SANDWICHES.

This bright, cheerful two-level eatery provides excellent fare ranging from omelets, salads, sandwiches, and light meals to hot meals that include dishes as varied as roast stuffed loin of pork with herb stuffing, venison pie served on a bed of wild rice, roast prime rib of beef with Yorkshire pudding and red wine sauce, and pan-fried filet of cod with a Noilly Prat sauce.

Molly Darby's Pizzeria & Bistro

8 George's Quay. ☎ **061/417270.** Pizza IR£4–IR£6 ($6.40–$9.60); main courses IR£8–IR£10 ($12.80–$16). No credit cards. Daily 6–10:45pm. PIZZA/EUROPEAN.

Tree-lined George's Quay is the setting for this cozy old-style eatery. Loaded with charm, and blessed with a friendly and efficient staff, it has also gained wide

Readers Recommend

Boylans, 22 Davis Street, Limerick, Co. Limerick. ☎ 061/418-916. *"I spent 13 days in this bed and breakfast, which is less than three minutes from the rail and bus terminal. Mrs. Teresa Boylan and family are the happiest and most accommodating people I have yet to meet, the rooms are immaculate, and the breakfast without comparison."*

—Evelyn Chorlton, Cambridge, MA

popularity with locals for its extensive menu of moderately priced meals. The pizza is special, and other fish, meat, and poultry dishes are prepared with meticulous care.

Worth a Splurge

✪ The Copper Room

In Jurys Hotel, Ennis Rd. ☎ **061/327777.** Set dinner IR£23 ($36.80). 10% service charge. AE, MC, V. Mon–Sat 7–10pm. CLASSICAL.

This elegant restaurant, with its polished, professional service and innovative menu, has long been a favorite with Limerick residents and visiting notables. Even appetizers on the fixed menu are creative and very special, as exemplified by the avocado baked with crab in a rich cream and brandy sauce with thin slices of chicken sausage that appeared on a recent menu. Fish dishes might include scampi tempura in a beer batter served with a julienne of leek and carrot in a soya sauce, or jumbo prawns pan-fried at table and served with a rich Noilly Prat sauce. A personal favorite is the roast magret duck breast served with a traditional orange sauce, although I must admit to being tempted to try the more exotic wild boar with a calvados and diced red applesauce.

3 County Limerick

Some 10 miles southeast of Limerick city via N20, with a turnoff on to the Kilmallock road (R518), ✪ **Lough Gur** is one of Ireland's most important archeological sites, and thousands of Stone Age relics have been found in and around it. The lifestyle of those long-ago Irishmen comes vividly alive in the **Stone Age Centre** at Lough Gur (☎ 061/85186). It's designed in the style of Neolithic period dwellings, and inside there are replicas of many of the artifacts discovered in this area, as well as models of burial chambers, stone circles, and dolmens. An audiovisual show tells you what we know of Stone and Bronze Age people and their habits, and, periodically, walking tours are conducted to some of the more important archeological sites. The centre is open mid-May through September, daily from 10am to 5:30pm, and there's a small admission charge.

The little town of **Dromcollogher,** 25 miles southwest of Limerick city (turn off N21 at Newcastle West onto R522), is where you can visit the **Irish Dresden Ltd.** plant and shop (☎ 063/83236), open Monday through Friday from 9am to 1pm and 2 to 5pm. Watch exquisite Dresden figurines being made; then browse through their showroom.

Virtually the entire little village of **Adare,** 10 miles southwest of Limerick city on N21, is a sightseeing attraction, with its pretty thatched cottages, monastic ruins, and a ruined Desmond castle. If your route between Limerick city and points southwest passes through this lovely place, I urge you to stop and ramble a bit. Focal point of the village, **Adare Manor,** is now a luxury hotel, but even if you aren't a guest, you can drive through the demesne or stop in for lunch or afternoon tea in the manor. Look for the ruined **Franciscan friary** on a slope overlooking the River Maigue, which was founded by the earl of Kildare in 1464 and added to over the centuries. Stop in **Black Abbey Crafts** in the Heritage Centre for items such as hand-crafted ceramics, glass, wood, and a wide range of Irish linens.

Look for **traditional music** in Collins Bar, Main Street, Adare (☎ 061/396400); the Magpie Bar, Main Street, Glin (☎ 068/34146); and Charlies, Sarsfield Street, Kilmallock (☎ 063/98615).

Visitor Information

Whether you're driving or making use of Bus Eireann's excellent day trips by bus, there are several worthwhile attractions in County Limerick. The Limerick Tourist Office will send you off armed with loads of information about this interesting region.

Tourist offices in County Limerick are located at **Lough Gur Stone Age Centre,** Bruff (☎ 061/85186), open May through September; and the **Thatched Cottage and Craft Shop,** Main Street, Adare (☎ 061/396-255), open June to early September.

In **Rathkeale,** some eight miles southwest of Adare, **Castle Matrix** (☎ 069/64284) is open to the public. Built in 1440, it is named for the ancient Celtic Mother Goddess Matrix, whose sanctuary once occupied this site. It was here that Sir Walter Raleigh and Edmund Spenser first met, and the 12,000-volume library contains rare first editions of Spenser's works, and those of other leading Elizabethan poets. There are also authentic furnishings, historic documents, and art objects.

Some of County Limerick's most scenic and historic attractions lie southwest of the city on the N69 ✪ **Shannon Estuary Drive,** a pleasant day's outing from the city. At **Askeaton** (16 miles west of Limerick), you'll pass virtually in the shadow of the ruined 15th-century Desmond Castle on a rocky islet in the River Deel just beside the road. There are also extensive remains of a **Franciscan friary** on the river bank. Farther west, plan to stop in **Foynes** to visit the fascinating **Flying Boat Museum** (☎ 069/65416), open daily from 10am to 6pm from April through October for a small admission charge. This important Shannon River port was the focal point for planes flying between Europe and America from 1939 to 1945, and you can visit the original terminal building (a far cry from modern-day airports), see the original radio and weather equipment, and browse through a whole range of graphic illustrations and other exhibits, as well as take in the audiovisual presentation. Before moving on, stop in the 1940s-style tearoom for a bit of refreshment. From Foynes, the roadway runs right along the river, with beautiful vistas of the opposite shore. Eight miles farther west is the village of **Glin,** with its ruined Fitzgerald (Knights of Glin) **castle,** destroyed in 1600, and lofty 19th-century castellated **Hamilton's Tower** overlooking the pier. The present **Glin Castle** sits in a beautiful demesne out of sight of the road. You can, however, stop in for an exceptionally good lunch or snack at **Glin Castle Gate Shop,** which also has a good craft shop and Irish-interest publications. Check to see if the Glin Castle **walled gardens** are open during your visit—this serene demesne overlooking the Shannon estuary is open to the public periodically for a small admission charge. The roadway follows the Shannon on west to **Tarbert,** in County Kerry.

WHERE TO STAY

ADARE

Abbey Villa

Kildimo Rd., Adare, Co. Limerick. ☎ **061/396-113.** Fax 061/396-969. 6 rms, all with bath. TV. IR£25 ($40) single; IR£17 ($27.20) per person sharing. 33¹/₃% reduction for children. (Rates include breakfast.) ACC, MC, V.

Readers Recommend

Kilmallock is about 21 miles south of Limerick city on T50A, with several interesting ecclesiastical ruins in the vicinity.

Flemingstown House, Kilmallock, Co. Limerick. ☎ 063/98093. Fax 063/98546. *"We found a wonderful farmhouse located just south of the town of Kilmallock. Each bed had a down bedspread, and the rooms were exceptionally clean. Breakfast was excellent, and the hospitality shown by Mrs. Imelda Sheedy-King was outstanding."*

—James and Dorothy Riley, San Jose, CA

Mrs. May Haskett's home is a modern bungalow in a scenic setting, and she greets each guest warmly. Like the best of hostesses, she invites guests to sit and chat while working out the best travel routes, and she also recognizes the need at times to retire to the warmth, comfort, and privacy of their own rooms. All guest rooms are tastefully decorated, and all have satellite TV, electric blankets, and hairdryers. There are laundry facilities, central heating, and private parking.

Hillcrest

Ballinvera, Croagh, Co. Limerick. ☎ **061/396534.** Fax 061/396-534. 4 rms, 3 with bath. IR£18.50 ($29.60) single without bath; IR£13.50 ($21.60) per person sharing without bath; IR£1.50 ($2.40) per person additional with bath. 25% reduction for children. Dinner IR£12.50 ($20) extra. (Rates include breakfast.) MC, V. Closed Nov–Mar.

Some three miles outside the picture-pretty village of Adare off the main Limerick-Killarney road (N21), Jennie and Michael Power's home sits amid peaceful, bucolic beauty. The Powers are warm, hospitable hosts who take a keen interest in their visitors. With advance notice, Jennie will prepare an excellent dinner.

Worth a Splurge

✪ Dunraven Arms Hotel

Adare, Co. Limerick. ☎ **061/396633.** Fax 061/396541. 66 rms, all with bath. TV TEL. IR£55–IR£70 ($88–$112) single; IR£40–IR£50 ($64–$80) per person sharing. 50% discount for children. Service charge 12½%. Special weekend rates available. ACC, AE, DC, MC, V.

On the edge of what has been called Ireland's prettiest village, the Dunraven Arms is a traditional-style, two-story, yellow-colored hotel that has the look of an old-time inn. Indeed, that small inn–type hospitality greets you at the door and never diminishes throughout your stay. The spacious lounge bar overlooks the gardens and offers excellent bar lunches at budget rates, and the dining room features French cuisine, using fresh ingredients from local farms. Comfortable, traditional furnishings add a homey touch. Public rooms, guest rooms, and executive bedrooms are attractively done up in country prints. This is where Princess Grace and Prince Rainier stayed during their 1963 visit. Not only is this a great sightseeing base—only 10 miles from Limerick, 16 from Bunratty Castle, 25 from Shannon Airport, and about 60 from Killarney and Cork—but fishing, horseback riding, and golf are all close at hand.

Castleconnell

Castleconnell is a pleasant village some eight miles north of Limerick city on the east bank of the Shannon River, via an unmarked road off R464 from Limerick city.

Spa House

Castleconnell, Co. Limerick. ☎ **061/377171.** 4 rms, 2 with bath. IR£17 ($27.20) per person without bath; IR£18 ($28.80) per person with bath. 20% reduction for children. (Rates include breakfast.) No credit cards. Closed Oct–Mar.

This lovely renovated 18th-century house is half a mile from the village of Castleconnell, about seven miles from Limerick, on the banks of the Shannon, with its own historic spa well in the gardens. Mrs. Helen Wilson's four bedrooms are attractive and comfortable. There's central heat, plenty of parking, fishing, and marvelous scenic surroundings.

BRUREE

Cooleen House

Bruree, Co. Limerick. ☎ **063/90584.** 4 rms, none with bath. IR£19 ($30.40) single; IR£15 ($24) per person sharing. 10% reduction for children. (Rates include breakfast.) Dinner IR£12 ($19.20) extra. No credit cards. Closed Nov–Apr.

This 300-year-old Georgian-style home is the happy domain of Mrs. Eileen McDonogh. Set on a working dairy farm overlooking the Maigue River half a mile off the main Limerick-Cork road (N20) and four miles west of Kilmallock, the house is beautifully furnished. There's private fishing on the grounds for salmon and trout, and in the village of Bruree the De Valera museum was the late president's first shrine in the country. Guest rooms are attractive, there's central heat, and guests are welcome to relax in the garden.

WHERE TO EAT

✪ Dunraven Arms Hotel

Adare. ☎ **061/396-633.** Main courses IR£9–IR£12 ($14.40–$19.20); bar food IR£3–IR£5 ($4.80–$8). ACC, AE, DC, MC, V. Daily 12:30–2:15pm and 7:30–9:30pm. Closed Good Friday, Christmas Day. BAR FOOD/TRADITIONAL/CONTINENTAL.

You will find the Dunraven Arms bar lunches more than ample to serve as your main meal of the day, and the setting overlooks gardens to the side and back of the hotel. In the dining room, prices are higher and menu choices include such dishes as roast beef, eels in white wine sauce, duckling, and poached salmon.

Readers Recommend

Mrs. Mary Harnett, Duneeven Croagh, Rathkeale, Co. Limerick. ☎ 069/64049. *"Only a few miles outside Adare, we rented this self-catering farmhouse, which has four bedrooms and two baths, dining room, living room, lounge, and kitchen. It came complete with Mr. Harnett's cows and chickens. He was great with the children."*

—Barbara Groogan, Milford, NJ

Ardkeen, Castlematrix, Rathkeale, Co. Limerick. ☎ 069/64168. *"Ardkeen is outstanding in every way. The welcome was warm; the rooms clean, neat, and tidy; the beds comfortable (fitted with electric mattress pads); the sanitary facilities fine. Breakfast was properly cooked and served in a friendly fashion. We were so impressed that we returned for another night a week later."* —Charles D. Fitzgerald, Hallstead, PA

Shemond House, Killaloe Road, Clonlara, Limerick, Co. Limerick. ☎ 061/343767. *"Ray and Sheila Devine have the cleanest house I have ever been in. We were greeted with an invitation for tea, and after three days we hated to leave."*

—Mrs. H. Kemp, Ottawa, Ontario, Canada

St. Andrew's Villa, Main Street, Kilfinane, Co. Limerick. ☎ 063/91008. Fax 063/91330. *"St. Andrew's was formerly a boys' school, and as a result has four or five guest rooms with several baths. There's a large dining room and lounge, the rooms were blessedly quiet, and the air was like wine. Patricia and Eamon Nunan were most hospitable and responded to our every wish."* —Fred Lisker, Berkeley, CA

✪ Chaser O'Brien Restaurant & Lounge Bar

Pallasgreen. ☎ **061/84203** or 84550. A la carte bar menu IR£1.50–IR£10.50 ($2.40–$16.80); four-course lunch special IR£7 ($11.20); à la carte dinner menu IR£9–IR£15 ($14.40–$24). AE, DC, MC, V. Daily 10am–11pm. BAR FOOD/CONTINENTAL.

About halfway between Limerick city and Tipperary town, on N24, Chaser O'Brien's is chock-full of character and practically oozes country charm. The beamed ceiling, glowing turf fire, and walls covered with horse prints (it is extremely popular with fans who frequent the nearby Tipperary racecourse) create a cozy ambience in the bar/lounge, and the same atmosphere extends into the adjoining restaurant area. The impressive bar menu features such dishes as crab claws in garlic butter, steak, and homemade chicken curry in addition to standard salads, sandwiches, and burgers. The more sophisticated restaurant menu leans to dishes such as filet steak coated with brandy pâté and smothered in red wine sauce.

4 North County Tipperary

Tipperary town, some 25 miles from Limerick city via N24, is an important dairy farming center, and this area figured prominently in the Land League campaign of the late 1800s. **St. Michael's Church** is an impressive limestone Gothic-style structure, with interesting architectural features (notice especially the beautiful west door and fine lancet windows in the east and west gables). Only the chancel arch of the Augustinian abbey of the 13th century remains (on the grounds of the Christian Brothers school). Just north of town, you can see the ruins of a 17th-century motte-and-bailey castle from the Norman era.

Four miles south of Thurles (25 miles northeast of Tipperary town via R661), **Holy Cross Abbey** (☎ 0504/43241) was founded in 1180, and before it was restored in 1976, had lain roofless for more than two centuries. It is so named because a relic of the True Cross was enshrined there in 1180. Notice particularly the beautiful window tracery, especially in the east and west windows and those of the south transept. It's open to visitors daily from 9am to 6pm and there is no admission charge.

In Roscrea (21 miles north of Thurles via N62), a large Georgian residence, **Damer House,** was actually built within the curtain walls of Roscrea Castle. In the castle yard, the ✪ **Roscrea Heritage Centre** (☎ 0505/21605) displays local artifacts. It's open Monday through Friday from 10am to 5pm, and from mid-May through September, also on Saturday and Sunday from 10am to 5pm. Small admission charge.

The historic town of Nenagh, 25 miles northeast of Limerick city via N7, is the home of the **Nenagh District Heritage Centre** (☎ 067/32633). It's located in the former county gaol, and the governor's house, built in octagonal shape, houses a museum of rural life and a re-created shop, forge, schoolroom, and dairy. In the gatehouse, you can visit cells in which condemned persons awaited execution, as well as the execution room itself. There's a good pictoral exhibit on the history of the gaol and 19th-century crime and punishment. The centre also operates a genealogical service for those with North Tipperary family connections. It's open to the public Monday through Friday from 10am to 5pm, and Sunday from 2:30pm to 5pm, with a small admission charge.

Visitor Information

You'll find a tourist information office in Nenagh (Silverline Building, Connolly Street; ☎ 067/31610).

Traditional music holds forth in Callanan's Bar, Keynon Street (☎ 067/32494), and the Derg Inn, Terryglass (☎ 067/22037), in Nenagh; and Central House, Market Square (☎ 0505/21127), and Market House, Main Street (☎ 0505/21505), in Roscrea.

WHERE TO STAY

NENAGH

Nenagh is 25 miles northeast of Limerick city via N7.

✪ The Country House

Thurles Rd., Kilkeary, Nenagh, Co. Tipperary. ☎ **067/31193.** 4 rms, all with bath. IR£18 ($28.80) single; IR£15 ($24) per person sharing. 33¹/₃% reduction for children. Dinner IR£12 ($19.20) extra. (Rates include breakfast.) No credit cards.

This modern bungalow is the home of Joan and Matt Kennedy. The family lounge, which guests are invited to share for TV or just visiting, has a peat-burning fireplace, and the house is set in scenic rural surroundings four miles out from Nenagh on R498. Lough Derg is only about 20 minutes away. Guest rooms come with tea/coffeemakers and hairdryers, and there's steam heat and good parking. An ideal location for exploring North Tipperary.

ROSCREA

Roscrea is 21 miles north of Thurles via N62.

Cregganbell

Birr Rd., Roscrea, Co. Tipperary. ☎ **0505/21421.** 4 rms, all with shower. IR£18 ($28.80) single; IR£14.50 ($23.20) per person sharing. 25% reduction for children. (Rates include breakfast.) No credit cards.

Mrs. Mae Fallon has four guest rooms with sinks and private showers; all beds have electric blankets. This is a lovely modern bungalow on the outskirts of town via N62, with river fishing nearby. Centrally heated, and plenty of parking.

WHERE TO EAT

Gurthalougha House

Ballinderry, Nenagh, Co. Tipperary. ☎ **067/22080.** Reservations essential. Average 3-course dinner IR£25 ($40). AE, DC, MC, V. One sitting only, daily, 8pm. Closed Christmas week.

Reach this lovely mid-19-century country home set in 150 wooded acres on the shores of Lough Derg by land or by water; its own quay provides docking for cruiser drop-ins. The candlelit dining room overlooks the lake. The small menu features produce grown on the estate. A good wine list complements such specialties as pike with fennel sauce and leg of lamb baked with herbs and served with red currant, mint, and orange jelly.

16 Galway Town

Galway owes its existence to a tragedy: Breasail, an ancient Celtic chieftain, was so overwhelmed by grief when his daughter drowned in the River Corrib that he established a permanent camp on the riverbank. Located at the only point at which the river could be forded, the camp had become a tiny fishing village by the time the Normans arrived. The newcomers set about building a trading town utilizing the fine harbor, and in time a medieval town with fine houses and shops grew up, around which were built stout stone walls. Trade soon flourished between Galway, Spain, and France. Fourteen of the most prosperous merchant families became known early on as the "Tribes of Galway," and in 1984 when the city celebrated the 500th anniversary of its charter there was a great "Gathering of the Tribes," with their descendants arriving from around the globe. During the mid-1800s, at the height of the Great Famine, the city was filled with starving men, women, and children who fought to board the infamous "coffin ships" to go to America and a new life.

Today Galway is a prosperous commercial center, proud of its university and welcoming visitors with open arms. Traces of its history abound: the Spanish Arch, a gateway of the old city walls; Lynch's Castle, a 14th-century town house that is now a bank; tiny cobblestone streets and lanes; and along the banks of the Corrib, the Long Walk, a much-loved waterside promenade for centuries.

1 Orientation

Galway is 135 miles west of Dublin via N6, 65 miles northwest of Limerick via N18, and 86 miles southwest of Sligo via N17.

ARRIVING **By Train** There is train service between Galway and Dublin.

By Bus There is direct bus service to Galway from Dublin, Cork, and Limerick, with connecting service from virtually anywhere in the country.

By Car Major highways and dual carriageways lead into Galway from every direction except due west. See above for routes.

VISITOR INFORMATION The Tourist Office is in a modern building called Aras Failte, just off the Great Southern Hotel side of

Eyre Square (☎ 091/63081; fax 091/65201). It's open from 9am to 6pm; and in July and August, hours are 9am to 6:45pm daily. During summer months an office is open on the Promenade in Salthill from 9am to 8:30pm.

The staff at the Tourist Office can book accommodations, excursions, and ferry services, and arrange bicycle and car rentals. It's a busy office in July and August, so allow plenty of time if you need their help. You can, however, pick up helpful literature on Galway and the surrounding area, as well as a free "Tourist Guide to Galway, Gateway to Connemara" without a long wait.

The Junior Chamber of Commerce publishes an annual guide to the city. It's available from the Tourist Office and most hotels. Look also for the newspaper-type publication *Western Tourism News,* distributed free in the Tourist Office and many hotels.

TOWN LAYOUT The River Corrib flows through the heart of Galway, with the main shopping and business districts centered between the river and Eyre Square (where John F. Kennedy once addressed the citizens of Galway). To the west, along the shores of Galway Bay, the popular seaside resort of Salthill holds a concentration of the best inexpensive accommodations in the area. There's good bus service between Eyre Square and Salthill, with stops along the main Galway-Salthill road. The Claddagh (An Cladach, "the seashore") district is just across the river from the Spanish Arch, although its jumble of thatched cottages and narrow lanes has long since been replaced by neat Corporation houses laid out in neat rows. Only the lovely Claddagh ring (two hands clasping a heart surmounted by a crown) remains as the legacy of a people who once had their own manner of dress, dialect, customs—and even their own king—in this fishing village outside the walls of Old Galway.

ORGANIZED TOURS Bus Eireann runs several excellent day tours from Galway and Salthill: Clew Bay and Killary Harbor, the Maam Valley and Cong, Knock shrine, Carraroe, the Burren, Connemara, etc. Some are half-day trips; others last the entire day. All are moderately priced, and you can book at the Tourist Office in Galway or Salthill, or at the railway station.

Check with the Tourist board about several private coach companies offering day trips.

A Cruise A pleasant way to see Galway and its environs is the 90-minute cruise on the River Corrib aboard the 72-passenger Corrib Princess. There are daily sailings from Wood Quay, and its full-length sunroof lets you enjoy the scenery no matter what the weather. You'll cruise along a traditional trade route, past historical points of interest, castles, and scenes of great natural beauty, with an interesting commentary all the way. There's full bar service, and tea and coffee. There are morning and afternoon sailings from Wood Quay daily, and the fare is IR£5 ($8). For exact times and to book, call 568903.

A Walking Tour For an interesting walking tour of Old Galway, just show up outside the Tourist Office Monday through Friday at 11am and a guide will lead you through two hours of Galway history and legend. The charge is IR£3.50 ($5.60), and be warned—wear comfortable walking shoes.

GETTING AROUND **By Bus and Train** The bus and railway station is at the rear of the Great Southern Hotel on Eyre Square. For bus information, call 563-555; call 564-222 for rail information.

By Taxi Taxis can be found at ranks around Eyre Square and the railway station. Also call Eyre Square Cabs (☎ 569-444) or Claddagh Cabs (☎ 588-434).

By Car Galway's streets are a mixture of narrow lanes and wide avenues. A network of clearly marked one-way streets makes driving in town relatively easy, and there are several well-placed car parks that charge very small fees—a blessing for motorists, since on-the-street parking can be difficult to impossible.

FAST FACTS: GALWAY

Area Code The telephone prefix for Galway is 091.

Currency Exchange In addition to banks, Bureau de Change services are offered at the Tourist Office (Eyre Square and Salthill); the Imperial Hotel, Eyre Square; and the Great Southern Hotel, Eyre Square.

Post Office The General Post Office is on Eglinton Street, with hours Monday through Friday from 9am to 5:30pm.

2 Where to Stay

There are very few inexpensive lodgings in Galway proper, so my best recommendation is to choose from the many superior accommodations listed in nearby Salthill.

IN TOWN

Adare Guest House

Fr. Griffin Place, Galway, Co. Galway. ☎ **091/582-638** or 586-21. Fax 091/583-963. 10 rms, all with bath. Seasonal rates, IR£16–IR£18 ($25.60–$28.80) per person sharing. Special golf holiday rates available. 25% reduction for children. (Rates include breakfast.) No credit cards.

Padraic and Grainne Conroy have taken over for his parents, Kay and Pat Conroy, who were for many years the hosts of Adare Guest House, halfway between the city center and Salthill. There's private parking out front, and in the lovely dining room you'll eat from Royal Tara china. The three-story centrally heated house has guest rooms with built-in sinks. Padraic continues his family's tradition of warm hospitality, and Kay and Pat have moved to a smaller bed and breakfast in Lower Salthill (see below). Several superior golf courses are nearby.

HOSTELS

Galway City Hostel

25–27 Dominick St., Galway, Co. Galway. ☎ **091/66367.** Fax 091/64581. 60 beds. IR£5.50–IR£7 ($8.80–$11.20) per person. ACC, MC, V. Open year-round.

Readers Recommend

De Soto, 54 New Castle Rd., Galway, Co. Galway. ☎ 091/585-064. *"Dermot and Margaret Walsh own this new and very superior modern family home. There are six comfortable and sparkling bedrooms, TV in the lounge, central heat, and small favors over and above the usual, to say nothing of the marvelous Irish breakfast and private off-street parking. Located right in the city center."*

—Bill and Mary Treacy, Fort Walton Beach, FL

Galway Town

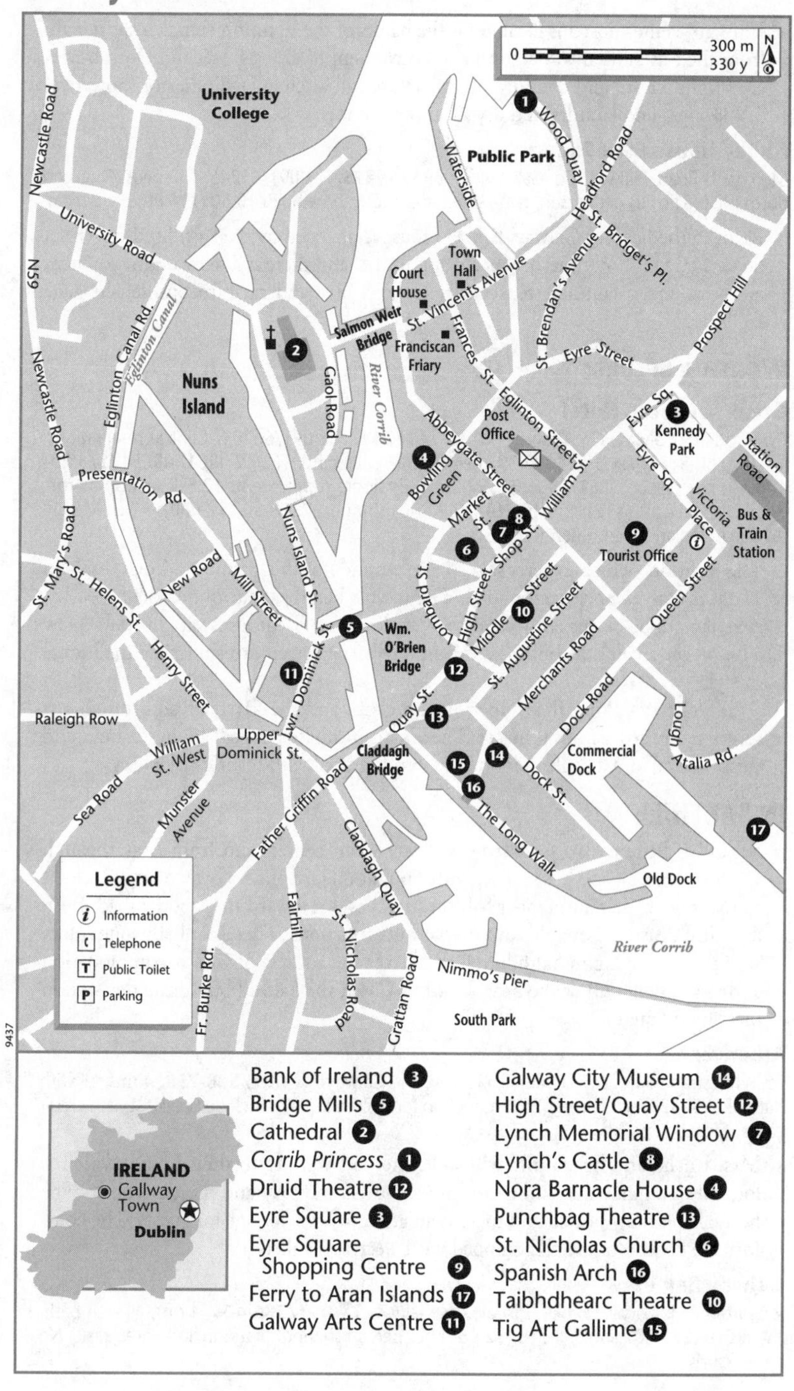
0
300 m
330 y
N
University College
Public Park
Wood Quay
Waterside
Headford Road
St. Bridget's Pl.
St. Brendan's Avenue
Town Hall
Court House
St. Vincents Avenue
Salmon Weir Bridge
Franciscan Friary
Frances St.
Eyre Street
Prospect Hill
Newcastle Road
University Road
N59
Eglinton Canal Rd.
Eglinton Canal
Nuns Island
Gaol Road
River Corrib
Post Office
Eglinton Street
Eyre Sq.
Kennedy Park
Station Road
Abbeygate Street
Bowling Green
Market St.
William St.
Victoria Place
Bus & Train Station
Presentation Rd.
Tourist Office
Shop St.
High Street
Lombard St.
Middle Street
St. Augustine Street
Queen Street
St. Mary's Road
St. Helens St.
New Road
Mill Street
Nuns Island St.
Wm. O'Brien Bridge
Lwr. Dominick St.
Henry Street
Merchants Road
Dock Road
Quay St.
Lough Atalia Rd.
Raleigh Row
Upper Dominick St.
William St. West
Claddagh Bridge
Commercial Dock
Dock St.
Sea Road
Munster Avenue
Father Griffin Road
The Long Walk
Claddagh Quay
Old Dock
Legend
Information
Telephone
Public Toilet
Parking
River Corrib
Fairhill
St. Nicholas Road
Grattan Road
Nimmo's Pier
Fr. Burke Rd.
South Park
9437
IRELAND
Gallway Town
Dublin
Bank of Ireland 3
Bridge Mills 5
Cathedral 2
Corrib Princess 1
Druid Theatre 12
Eyre Square 3
Eyre Square Shopping Centre 9
Ferry to Aran Islands 17
Galway Arts Centre 11
Galway City Museum 14
High Street/Quay Street 12
Lynch Memorial Window 7
Lynch's Castle 8
Nora Barnacle House 4
Punchbag Theatre 13
St. Nicholas Church 6
Spanish Arch 16
Taibhdhearc Theatre 10
Tig Art Gallime 15

This city-center hostel is located on the banks of the Eglinton Canal, a short walk from the bus and railway station and convenient to city sightseeing. Dormitories are bright, clean, and comfortable; there are full kitchen facilities, hot showers, a TV lounge, and laundry and dry-cleaning services.

Kinlay House Eyre Square

Merchants Road, Galway, Co. Galway. ☎ **091/65245.** Fax 091/65245. 150 beds. Four-bed dorm IR£7 ($11.20) per person; two-bed unit, some with bath, IR£10.50 ($16.80) per person.

Right in the heart of Galway, Kinlay House is operated by the Irish Student Travel Service (USIT). All units are nicely appointed, and there is a self-catering kitchen, a TV lounge, a launderette, security lockers, bike and car hire, and left-luggage facilities.

Worth a Splurge

Great Southern Hotel

Eyre Square, Galway, Co. Galway. ☎ **091/64041.** Fax 091/66704. Central reservations: ☎ 01/280-8031; fax 01/280-8039. 116 rms, all with bath. TEL TV. IR£47–IR£54 ($75.20–$86.40) per person; IR£17–IR£20 ($27.20–$32) single supplement. 12.5% service charge. Breakfast IR£7.50 ($12); lunch IR£14 ($22.40); dinner IR£18.50 ($29.60). ACC, MC, V. Advance booking recommended.

The location (which experts say is "everything") of this grand old hotel, built in 1845, is convenience exemplified. The town's heartbeat surrounds the hotel. Inside, the public rooms fairly exude old-world charm. Bedrooms vary in size—a few a bit on the small side, but most exceptionally spacious. Furnishings are traditional in style.

O'Flaherty's Pub offers superior pub grub, and the Oyster Room restaurant serves up award-winning meals. There's an intimate cocktail lounge; sauna and steam room; and a rooftop indoor swimming pool with terrific city views.

IN SALTHILL

Salthill is little over a mile from Galway town center, and from May through October there's good bus service, with stops at major points. Lower Salthill is closer to the town center and Upper Salthill stretches out toward the Spiddal road. Both are within easy walking distance to Salthill attractions. There's only the one route, so if you're staying in Salthill, tell the driver the address of your accommodation and you'll be let off at the nearest point. Catch the Salthill bus at the bus station or at Eyre Square.

Alkenver

39 Whitestrand Park, Lower Salthill, Galway, Co. Galway. ☎ **091/588-758.** 4 rms, all with bath. IR£15 ($24) per person. 25% reduction for children. (Rates include breakfast.) No credit cards. Closed Sept–May.

Mrs. Rushe and her family will welcome you warmly to their home, which is located in a quiet area and is convenient to Galway Bay and the city center. The house is centrally heated and there is an attractive TV lounge for guests. The comfortable bedrooms are all equipped with electric blankets.

Galway Bay View

2 Grattan Park, Lower Salthill, Galway, Co. Galway. ☎ **091/586-466.** 4 rms, all with bath. TV. IR£18 ($28.80) single; IR£16 ($25.60) per person sharing. (Rates include breakfast.) No credit cards.

Kay and Pat Conroy are the hosts in this delightful small bed-and-breakfast overlooking Galway Bay. Guest rooms are attractive in decor and very comfortable, and come complete with color TV.

High Tide

9 Grattan Park, Lower Salthill, Galway, Co. Galway. ☎ **091/584-324.** Fax 091/584-324. 4 rms, all with bath. IR£15 ($24) per person sharing. 20% reduction for children. (Rates include breakfast.) No credit cards. Closed Nov–Mar.

Grattan Park is a short, quiet road that turns off the coastal road known as Grattan Road before it joins the Promenade. High Tide looks out to Galway Bay, with the hills of Clare in the distance across the water, and Mrs. Patricia Greaney is the hostess who makes her guests feel right at home. The guest rooms are all nicely decorated, and there's central heat and good parking.

Inishmore House

109 Fr. Griffin Rd., Lower Salthill, Galway, Co. Galway. ☎ **091/582-639.** 8 rms, 5 with bath. TV. IR£18 ($28.80) single without bath; IR£13 ($20.80) per person sharing without bath; IR£2 ($3.20) per person additional with bath. 25% reduction for children. (Rates include breakfast.) ACC, MC, V. Closed Jan.

Marie and Peter Power are the friendly hosts of this large, attractive house. Each bedroom is nicely done up, and the house is centrally heated. Meals are delicious.

Knockrea

Lower Salthill, Galway, Co. Galway. ☎ **091/21794.** 9 rms, none with bath. IR£14 ($22.40) per person. 10% reduction for children. (Rates include breakfast.) No credit cards. Closed Nov–Apr.

Knockrea sits in its own grounds and garden on a quiet street in northeastern Salthill. The attractive guest rooms all have sinks, and Eileen and Padraic Storan are the gracious hosts.

Lawndale

5 Beach Court, Salthill, Galway, Co. Galway. ☎ **091/66676.** 5 rms, all with bath. TV. IR£20 ($32) single; IR£16 ($25.60) per person sharing. (Rates include breakfast.) No credit cards.

Set back on a quiet street just off Grattan Road, overlooking Galway Bay, Lawndale is the bright, welcoming home of Margaret Walsh. All of the attractive bedrooms have tea/coffeemakers, and can sleep three people; Margaret is glad to add a bed to make it four, if necessary.

✪ Marless House

8 Seamount, Threadneedle Rd., Salthill, Galway, Co. Galway. ☎ **091/523-9311.** 6 rms, all with bath. TV. IR£20 ($34) single; IR£16 ($25.60) per person sharing. 25% reduction for children. (Rates include breakfast.) ACC, MC, V. Closed Christmas.

Mary and Tom Geraghty's lovely, large two-story Georgian-style house sits on Threadneedle Road, just steps from the promenade along Galway Bay. This is one of Galway's prettiest accommodations, with the friendliest of hosts. Central heating, electric blankets, and good parking. Highly recommended.

Osterly Lodge

142 Lower Salthill, Galway, Co. Galway. ☎ **091/23794.** Fax 091/23565. 12 rms, all with bath. Rates IR£25 ($40) single; IR£18–IR£20 ($28.80–$32) per person sharing. No credit cards.

Pat and Barbara Guider's attractive guesthouse has won praises from readers for its cheerful, bright accommodations and for the graciousness of the owners, who go out of their way to accommodate any special interests of their guests. There's a private car park, and good bus transportation into the city center. When booking, ask about possible off-season discounts to holders of this book.

✪ Roncalli House

24 Whitestrand Ave., Lower Salthill, Galway, Co. Galway. ☎ **091/64159.** 6 rms, all with bath. TV. IR£20 ($32) single; IR£15 ($24) per person sharing. 20% reduction for children. (Rates include breakfast.) No credit cards.

A glowing fireplace takes the chill off cool evenings at Carmel and Tim O'Halloran's two-story house overlooking Galway Bay. There's a sunny front lounge and two outdoor patios for guest use. There are two ground-floor bedrooms and four others upstairs, all with sinks and built-in wardrobes, hairdryers, and tea/coffeemakers. There is central heat and good parking.

Ross House

14 Whitestrand Ave., Lower Salthill, Galway, Co. Galway. ☎ **091/587-431.** 4 rms, all with shower. TV. IR£15 ($24) per person. 20% reduction for children. (Rates include breakfast.) No credit cards.

Mrs. Sara Davy's attractive home is located beside Galway Bay in a quiet cul-de-sac. Guest rooms are nicely appointed, and the house is centrally heated.

✪ Sailin

Gentian Hill, Upper Salthill, Galway, Co. Galway. ☎ **091/521-676.** 4 rms, all with bath. IR£20 ($32) single; IR£16 ($25.60) per person sharing. 50% reduction for children under 10. (Rates include breakfast.) No credit cards. Closed Mid-Oct to Apr. Enclosed car park.

Sailin ("*Saw*-leen") is next door to a bird sanctuary on the shores of Galway Bay. The modern two-story house is home to Mary and Noel McLoughlin and they extend an enthusiastic welcome to visitors, often joining them for bedtime cups of tea and conversation about Galway and the area. The upstairs bedrooms are bright, airy, and attractive, with built-in wardrobes. Two of the bedrooms are adjoining, making an ideal suite for families or friends traveling together. This is a non-smoking home; there is central heating and an enclosed car park. A personal favorite, and highly recommended by readers.

Villa Maria

94 Fr. Griffin Rd., Lower Salthill, Galway. ☎ **091/589-033.** 4 rms, all with bath. TV. IR£16 ($25.60) per person sharing; IR£5 ($8) single supplement. (Rates include breakfast.) No credit cards. Private parking.

Long-time readers may remember the charming Frances Tiernan from her years as a B&B hostess in Clifden. Now a resident of Galway town, she extends the same warm, friendly hospitality in this attractive two-story home, located less than a ten-minute walk from both the town center and Salthill. Guest rooms are spacious and nicely furnished, with tea/coffeemakers. Choose between a full Irish breakfast or lighter fare such as fruit, cheese, and yogurt. A native of Roundstone, Frances happily shares her Connemara sightseeing tips with her guests.

KNOCKNACARRA

Loch Lurgan

Barna Rd., Knocknacarra, Galway, Co. Galway. ☎ **091/522-450.** 4 rms, 3 with bath. IR£14 ($22.40) per person sharing without bath. IR£16 ($23.20) per person sharing with bath. 25% reduction for children. (Rates include breakfast.) No credit cards. Closed Oct–Mar.

Mrs. Christina Maloney is the hostess of this bungalow overlooking Galway Bay and the Clare hills across the bay. The house is centrally heated, and there's

Readers Recommend

Ard Mhuire, Knocknacarra Road, Salthill, Galway, Co. Galway. ☎ 091/522-344. *"The proprietors of Ard Mhuire, Pat and Teresa McDonagh, are extremely friendly and hospitable, and this establishment is charming and first-rate."*

—Judith Metcalf, Atlanta, GA

Bay View, Gentian Hill, Salthill, Galway, Co. Galway. ☎ 091/522-116 or 526-140. *"Mrs. N. Guilfoyle presides over this delightful, clean, hospitable, and picturesque bed-and-breakfast home located on a hill overlooking Galway Bay."*

—James and Gwen McColm, Venice, FL

Ivernia, 31 Maunsells Park, Taylors Hill, Galway, Co. Galway. ☎ 091/523-307. *"As a single traveler, I was most appreciative of the gracious and warm hospitality extended to me by the Hassell family. I was flattered to be temporarily a part of the family and enjoy their delightful conversation and insights regarding things to do and see in the Galway area. The house was immaculate, and tasty and filling meals were served."*

—Joseph Siren, Allendale, SC

a garden for guests' use. To quote one reader, "Christina Maloney must be one of the most outstanding hostesses in Ireland. In this lovely house, she provides an immaculately clean home, decorated in lovely pastels with sparkling collections of Irish china displayed in many rooms. Vases of flowers and hand-embroidered pillows are beautifully arranged. Both comfortable and welcoming." Don't think I can improve on that!

3 Where to Eat

As one of Ireland's most popular holiday spots (with natives as well as visitors), Galway is blessed with numerous exceptionally good places to eat. Pub grub is plentiful and the best budget buy, of course, but there are many moderately priced restaurants as well. In addition, the surrounding area has eateries that draw Galway residents and have gained nationwide kudos for the quality of the food, service, and ambience.

PUB GRUB

In all the pubs listed below, heaping plates of roast beef or pork or lamb plus at least two vegetables seldom cost more than IR£5 ($8), and all offer soup, sandwiches, and salad plates at well under that price. Unless otherwise noted below, food service is offered between the hours of 12:30 and 2:30pm.

Donnelly's of Barna

Coast Rd., Barna. ☎ 091/92487.

About five miles west of Galway town on R336, this popular spot has won praise from locals, who quickly spread the word to visitors. The bar menu features lots of seafood (no surprise when Galway Bay is only steps away), such as a crab bake, crab claws, salmon, and mussels. There's also a vegetarian platter and an avocado-pear dish served with smoked salmon, crab, or prawns. Back of the bar, which faces the road, is an excellent seafood restaurant (see below).

✪ McSwiggans Pub and Restaurant

3 Eyre St., Wood Quay. ☎ **091/568-917.**

Walk into this corner pub and you'd swear it's at least 400 years old rather than its actual age of four years! So fantastic has the renovation of this old building been that it won an award for interior design. And no wonder—after gutting the entire insides of the building, the owners filled it with lots of dark wood, old pews from local churches, old bar objects, and antiques. Upstairs, there's an excellent restaurant (see below).

Rabbitt's

23 Forster St. ☎ **091/566-490.**

Just off Eyre Square, this is Galway's oldest family-run pub. More locals than tourists, and a place for good conversation and conviviality as well as moderately priced food. There is an off-license shop open during bar hours—convenient shopping for that drink back in your room.

RESTAURANTS

IN THE CITY CENTER

✪ G. B. C. Restaurant and Coffee Shop

7 Williamsgate St. ☎ **091/563-087.** Fixed-price lunch IR£4 ($6.40); fixed-price dinner IR£9 ($14.40); coffee shop à la carte under IR£5 ($8). ACC, AE, DC, MC, V. Coffee shop daily 8am–10pm; restaurant daily noon–10pm. TRADITIONAL/SEAFOOD/VEGETARIAN.

The restaurant is upstairs from the self-service coffee shop and is bright and pleasant, with booths along the walls, tables in the center of the large room. The extensive à la carte menu features good, solid traditional dishes of beef, pork, turkey, chicken, and seafood. Salad plates are less than the prices shown above, and wine is available by the glass, carafe, or bottle at moderate prices.

✪ Galleon Restaurant

Salthill. ☎ **091/22963** or 21266. Main courses IR£4.50–IR£10 ($7.20–$16); evening special from IR£5 ($8); children's menu under IR£3 ($4.80). ACC, AE, MC, V. Daily noon–midnight. SEAFOOD/GRILLS/TRADITIONAL/VEGETARIAN.

This small, cozy restaurant, beside the church on the main street in Salthill, is a popular spot with locals, and is one of the few late-night eating spots in Galway. There is a widely varied menu.

✪ Lavelle's Delicatessen & Restaurant

Middle St. ☎ **091/568-522.** Snacks IR£1.50 ($2.40); sandwiches IR£2.50 ($4); salad plates IR£2.50–IR£3.50 ($4–$5.60); picnic hampers IR£2–IR£7 ($3.20–$11.20). MC, V. Mon–Sat 9am–7pm. SNACKS/SANDWICHES/SALADS/SEAFOOD/PASTRIES/PICNIC HAMPERS.

Owners Ray and Ethnea Lavelle dish up some of the best food in Galway in this small, bright, cheerful eatery. At street level, there's a delicatessen counter for take-aways, and downstairs is a small cafe. Seafood lover that I am, I was drawn to their garlic mussels and seafood chowder (a meal in itself, and one of the best I've found anywhere). Lasagna, quiche (including a vegetarian quiche), homemade soups, pâté, and homemade brown bread are also on the menu, and no one should leave without having tried their luscious chocolate fudge cake.

McSwiggans

3 Eyre St. ☎ **091/568-917.** Main courses IR£6–IR£9 ($9.60–$14.40). ACC, AE, DC, MC, V. Daily 12–10:30pm. STEAK/TRADITIONAL/SEAFOOD/LIGHT MEALS.

This attractive, pleasant upstairs restaurant is famed for fast, friendly service and geared to budgeteers, with a touch of "Old Galway" ambience. The decor harks back to the days of Galway's thriving sea trade with Spain.

See McSwiggans Pub and Restaurant in "Pub Grub," above, for a complete description of this renovated building. The restaurant features a conservatory skylight and carries on the "Old Galway" decor of the downstairs bar. As for the menu, it varies widely, from seafood to sirloin steak to escalope of pork to grills. All main dishes come with a vegetable and potato.

Maxwell McNamara's Restaurant

Williamsgate St. ☎ **091/565-727.** Lunch under IR£7 ($11.20); fixed-price dinner IR£11 ($17.60). ACC, AE, DC, MC, V. Daily 9am–10pm. SEAFOOD/STEAK/IRISH/VEGETARIAN.

There's a delightful old-fashioned look about this centrally located place just off Eyre Square that was known for many years as the Cellar Restaurant. Renovations have brought dark-wood booths, lots of brass, and old prints on the walls. The extensive menu offers light selections (hamburgers, salads, etc.), and it's fully licensed, with wine by the glass. Service is continuous, making it handy if hunger pangs strike outside regular meal hours.

Nora Crub's

8 Quay St. ☎ **091/568-376.** Main courses IR£5–IR£10 ($8–$16). No credit cards. Summer, Mon–Sat 9am–10pm; winter, Mon–Sat 9am–6pm. TRADITIONAL/VEGETARIAN.

It's a pleasure just to go inside this old 16th-century stone building down in Old Galway in the docks area. There really *was* a Nora Crub who lived here, and the stone walls, arches, and cozy alcoves are just about the same as she would have known them. Wholesomeness and good home cooking are stressed here, and the menu extends from soup (try the seafood chowder) to chicken Kiev, to beef and pork, to lasagna and salads. Service is friendly and efficient.

✪ Rabbitt's Bar and Restaurant

23 Forster St. ☎ **091/566-490.** Main courses IR£5–IR£11.50 ($8–$18.40); bar food IR£5 ($8) and under. ACC, MC, V. Daily 12:30–2:30pm and 6:30–9:30pm. TRADITIONAL/IRISH/VEGETARIAN.

Very popular with Galway locals, this is a congenial, family-run bar and restaurant, where the conversation is often quite as good as the food, which says a lot, indeed. See above for pub food. The regular lunch and dinner menu includes fresh seafood, Irish stew, oysters, lamb, and chicken.

✪ The Round Table Restaurant

6 High St. ☎ **091/564-542.** Snacks and à la carte IR£2–IR£7 ($3.20–$11.20). No credit cards. Mon–Sat 9am–6pm. TRADITIONAL/IRISH/SNACKS.

Located in a building that dates back at least to 1586, with a 17-foot stone fireplace, stuccoed walls, and exposed ceiling beams in the back dining room, the Round Table is a great place to drop in virtually any hour of the day. Breakfast is served all day; there's a wide variety of snacks, sweet pastries, and the like; and the menu includes roasts of beef or pork or lamb, chicken, and fish. Everything's homemade and quite tasty.

COFFEEHOUSES

Bewley's of Galway

The Cornstore, Middle St. ☎ **091/565-789.** IR£2–IR£8 ($3.20–$12.80). ACC, MC. Mon–Sat 9am–6pm. LIGHT MEALS/SNACKS/VEGETARIAN.

This is the local branch of this famous old Dublin confectionery and coffee shop. There's a huge range of hot and cold dishes, as well as pastries that will keep your sweet tooth happy.

deBurgos

15/17 Augustine St. ☎ **091/62188.** Reservations recommended. Bar food under IR£6 ($9.60); main courses IR£11–IR£15 ($17.60–$24); set lunch IR£10 ($16). ACC, AE, MC, V. Mon–Sat 12:30–3pm and 6–10pm. BAR FOOD/CONTINENTAL.

Atmospheric is the only word for deBurgos, which inhabits what was, back in the 16th century, a wealthy merchant's wine cellar. Its whitewashed walls, medieval wall hangings, and candlelight befit its history, while the cuisine reflects the very best of today's world in innovative dishes such as chicken Nicole stuffed with farci of chicken, shrimp, and chervil cream sauce, as well as the delicious, straightforward rack of Connemara lamb. If you can't make it for dinner, do try the pub lunch—a step back in time in the middle of a busy day.

Eyre House and Park House Restaurants and Lounges

Forster St. ☎ **091/562-396** or 563-766. Lunch IR£4–IR£9 ($6.40–$14.40); early-bird dinner IR£14 ($22.40); fixed-price dinner IR£20 ($32). ACC, MC, V. Mon–Sat noon–3pm and 6–10pm (early-bird dinner served 5:30–7pm). CONTINENTAL/IRISH.

This is a combination of two lovely restaurants, with a decor both sophisticated and warmly inviting. Lunchtime brings hordes of locals to settle in for specialties like chicken and mushroom vol-au-vent, osso buco (braised veal on the bone with garlic, white wine, onions, celery, carrots, and tomatoes), freshly caught fish, and roast rib of beef. Menus feature such dishes as roast stuffed duckling normande or escalope of veal Cordon Bleu. It is fully licensed, and on weekends there's entertainment and dancing (no charge).

Hooker Jimmy's Steak and Seafood Bar

The Fishmarket, Spanish Arch, Galway, Co. Galway. ☎ **091/68-351.** Fax 091/68-352. Main courses IR£4–IR£16 ($6.40–$25.60). ACC, AE, MC, V. Daily 11am–11pm. Reservations recommended for dinner. SEAFOOD.

This pleasant family-run eatery is located in an old stone building beside the Spanish Arch, one of Galway town's most historic sites. In fine weather, meals are served outside on a terrace overlooking the River Corrib and Claddagh Village. Shellfish come directly from the restaurant's own boat, and Galway Bay salmon is a star among fish dishes. A long list of chicken and meat listings often appear in unusual combinations.

NEARBY RESTAURANTS

KILCOLGAN

✪ Moran's Oyster Cottage

Kilcolgan. ☎ **091/96113** or 96083. Oysters IR£9 ($14.40) per dozen; smoked salmon or crabmeat IR£7.50–IR£9.25 ($12–$14.80). ACC, AE, MC, V. Daily 10:30am–11pm. SEAFOOD.

About 10 miles south of Galway town on the main Galway-Limerick road (N18), keep a keen eye out for the signpost on the edge of the village that directs you down a side road to this 200-year-old thatched pub. The fifth generation of Morans are running this place, and at least a part of their success stems from the fact that oysters come straight from their own oyster beds. They're served with home-baked brown bread, as are smoked salmon, mussel soup, and other seafood items. There's food service all through normal pub hours.

Clarenbridge

Paddy Burkes Oyster Inn

Clarenbridge. ☎ **091/96226.** Main courses IR£7–IR£12 ($11.20–$19.20). ACC, AE, DC, MC, V. Daily 11am–10:30pm. SEAFOOD/STEAK.

Paddy Burkes, eight miles south of Galway town via N18, the Galway-Limerick road, is a local institution. The old pub dates back three centuries, and beamed ceilings, wooden benches, copper, and brass give the place a settled, comfortable feeling. It has been the hangout of such celebrities as John Huston, Paul Newman, and Burl Ives. Needless to say, oysters get star billing, and in fact, Paddy Burkes is headquarters for Galway's annual Oyster Festival. The menu also includes smoked salmon, prawn cocktail, fish chowder, and fresh cockles and mussels in garlic sauce. For nonseafood lovers, there are cold and hot platters of chicken, ham, beef, steak, and hot homemade apple pie with fresh cream.

Barna

Barna is about five miles from Salthill on the coast road to Spiddal, R336.

Donnelly's of Barna

Coast Rd., Barna. ☎ **091/92487.** Fixed-price dinner IR£19 ($30.40). ACC, MC, V. Mon–Sat 7–10pm, Sun noon–3pm. SEAFOOD/TRADITIONAL/VEGETARIAN.

In an old stone building that was once a stable, Donnelly's has created an attractive, light and airy eatery, with stone wall, vaulted ceiling, and an open loft overlooking the main dining room. Although steak au poivre, guinea fowl, pheasant, and vegetarian platters appear on the dinner menu, it's in the seafood department that Donnelly's really shines. Try the grilled scallops with lemon, or the Aran seafood medley Mornay, or prawns in garlic cream. But before you make your choice, inquire about the "catch of the day," which is bound to be the best of that day's haul from the sea. For lunches, see "Pub Grub," above.

4 What to See & Do

To catch the full flavor of Galway's rich and colorful history, go by the tourist board and pick up their booklet **"Tourist Trail of Old Galway"** (small charge), which will lead you along a signposted route through medieval streets with an informative and entertaining narrative filled with legends and anecdotes associated with places along your way.

ATTRACTIONS IN TOWN

You can't really miss **Eyre Square** (pronounce it "Air")—in the center of town, it's the site of impromptu street entertainment during the summer. That statue of the old Irish storyteller, hat perched back and pipe in hand, is of Padraic O'Conaire, who traveled the countryside telling stories to children and committing them to paper, having begun life in New Docks in what is now the Anchor Bar. The other statue (of a standing figure) represents patriot Liam Mellows, a prominent Galway leader during the 1916 military engagements outside Dublin. John F. Kennedy addressed the people of Galway here on his presidential visit in 1963.

Other things to look for include the Civic Sword and Great Mace on display in the **Bank of Ireland** on Eyre Square. You'll want to see the **Spanish Arch** and the somewhat cramped **Galway City Museum** just beside it. Not only is the museum filled with interesting artifacts, but its spiral staircase leads to a gallery that, in turn, leads to an open terrace with great views of the city and harbor.

On Market Street, look for two interesting **"marriage stones"** set into the walls of houses there. The stones are carved with the coats-of-arms of two families united in marriage, and these two date from the early 1600s.

Of even more interest on Market Street is the **Lynch Memorial Window.** The window claims that it was on this site that Mayor James Lynch FitzStephen carried out a harsh sentence against his own son in 1493. The story goes that the Lord Mayor's 19-year-old son, Walter, was much enamored of a lovely girl named Agnes. He was also very good friends with a young Spanish lad—good friends, that is, until Walter developed an acute case of jealousy when he thought the young Spaniard was courting Agnes. In a fit of rage he murdered his friend; then, filled with remorse, turned himself in. It was his own father who sat as magistrate and condemned the boy to death when he entered a plea of guilty. The town executioner, however, refused to perform his grisly duty, a tribute to the boy's local popularity, and the sorrowing father gave his son a last embrace and did the deed himself. From this tragic hanging—so the legend says—came the term "Lynch Law."

At the corner of Abbeygate Street and Shop Street, **Lynch's Castle** is a superb example of a medieval town house, dating back to around 1490. It's now home to a branch of the Allied Irish Bank, but look above for carved gargoyles and a lion biting off the head of an animal clutched in its claws.

At O'Brien's Bridge on Bridge Street, the **Bridge Mills** sit where milling has been going on since 1558. The mill buildings had fallen into terrible disrepair, but were rescued by one Frank Heneghan in 1988, when he began a renovation that brought back to life the old stonework and mill wheel. Today the building flourishes as home to the Millwheel Café and Coffee Shop, where you can sit outside in fine weather to watch swans on the river below. This is good browsing country—craft shops, clothing boutiques, jewelry shops, art galleries, and gift shops now inhabit much of the building's interior.

Take a stroll down one of Galway's last remaining late medieval laneways, **Kirwans Lane,** and drop in to **Design Concourse Ireland** (☎ 091/66016, fax 091/66927). This is where two enterprising Galway women, Hannah Kiely and Judy Greene, took a long look at a 17th-century merchant's home that had deteriorated into a near ruin, saw that many of the building's fine original features were still intact, and set about transforming it into a unique showcase for the very best of Irish design and manufacture in interior furnishings. In this now beautifully restored old building, ever-changing exhibits show each product in real-life settings, which makes for interesting viewing.

St. Nicholas Collegiate Church, in Market Street, dates from 1320 and is the largest medieval church in the country, with many relics of that era. It is the burial place of the Mayor Lynch mentioned above, and tradition says that Christopher Columbus prayed here before setting off across the Atlantic. The impressive **Galway Cathedral** faces one branch of the River Corrib and was built in the 1960s of native limestone, with local marble flooring.

Walk through Galway's version of the "Left Bank," the ✪ **High Street/Quay Street** quarter of old buildings that retain the old fireplaces, cut stones, and arches from centuries past. Craft shops, smart boutiques, excellent restaurants, and convivial pubs are located there.

For the Literary Enthusiast If you're a James Joyce fan, you'll find the girlhood home of his lady love, Nora Barnacle, at **8 Bowling Green.** It's the second house on the left as you enter the lane from Market Street.

ATTRACTIONS NEARBY

Salthill, a Galway suburb, is only a longish walk from the town center, with good bus service between the two from May to October. One of Ireland's most popular seaside resorts, it has good beaches and a broad promenade, an 18-hole golf course (see Section 6, "Sports and Outdoor Activities," below), lawn tennis, loads of restaurants, shops, pubs, discos, and some of the best accommodations in this area. Three-wheel bicycle carriages are for rent and form a traffic flow all their own along the promenade. Give the young set and yourself a break by dropping them off at the **Leisureland Amusement Park.** There's a heated indoor pool, a super waterslide, and lots of rides.

5 Special Events

✪ **RACE WEEK** The Irish can come up with an instant party on an occasion no more auspicious than two friends' happening to be in the same place at the same time. And if there's a race meet, the party often turns into a gala! The folks in Galway have, in fact, perfected their party-throwing skills to such an extent that it sometimes seems the entire country shuts down to travel up this way for the six-day Race Week in late July or early August. There's music everywhere, food stalls, private parties (to which strangers are often warmly welcomed), honest-to-goodness horse trading, and lots of activity at the track. Because so many Irish descend on the town during that week, best book way ahead if you'll be arriving during the festivities.

✪ **SEPTEMBER OYSTER FESTIVAL** This is the other big event in Galway, an international affair. In a colorful ceremony, the Lord Mayor of Galway gets things under way by opening and eating the first oyster of the season. After that, it's two solid days (usually a weekend) of eating and drinking: Oysters, salmon, prawns, and almost anything else that comes from the sea are washed down with buckets of champagne or Guinness. Oyster-openers from around the world enter competitions for opening the most oysters in the shortest period of time. The action centers around Moran's of the Weir and the Great Southern Hotel, and a ticket to all the scheduled partying is costly—around IR£100 ($160) for the two days—but since the entire town becomes a party, the general gaiety spills over into the streets and pubs at no cost at all. Again, advance booking is an absolute must. It's usually the third or fourth weekend in September, but you should check the tourist board's calendar of events.

BLESSING OF THE SEA To open the herring season in mid-August, there's a lovely ceremony on the waters of Galway Bay. Fishing boats form a procession to sail out of the harbor, led by an entire boatload of priests who petition heaven for a good and profitable season.

6 Sports & Outdoor Activities

The most popular spectator sport in Galway is undoubtedly **horseracing,** especially during Race Week, but with other meets scheduled during the year. There's also

greyhound racing at the track at College Road off Eyre Square. For information on dates and times for both, contact the Tourist Office (☎ 563-081).

There's an excellent **golf course** at Salthill, and to arrange tee-off times, you should contact the club secretary at 091/21827 or 22169 as far in advance as possible.

Fishing has been the very life's blood of Galway for centuries. To arrange angling (the season runs from February to September) at the Salmon Weir Bridge or other nearby waters, contact the tourist board (☎ 563-081) or the Fishery Office, Nun's Island (☎ 562-388), for information on license and booking, since rods are limited in number in some spots. The Tourist Office can also help in booking **sea angling.**

For information about **tennis, badminton,** or **squash,** contact the Galway Lawn Tennis Club, Threadneedle Road, Salthill (☎ 091/53435 or 51400).

7 Shopping

IN TOWN

The strikingly designed **Eyre Square Centre,** right in the heart of the town center, with entrances in Williamsgate Street and Eyre Square, holds more than 50 shops, as well as a multilevel car park.

BOOKS

✪ Kenny's Bookshop and Art Galleries

High St. ☎ **091/562-739,** 561-014, or 561-021. Fax 091/568-544.

Kenny's is widely recognized as being just about the best bookshop and art gallery in the country. First opened in the 1930s, the small bookshop has grown into a fascinating multilevel maze of rooms in ancient buildings lovingly restored by the Kenny family. There are works of Irish art, antiquarian maps and prints, old magazine issues, and rare books on Irish subjects. You'll nearly always find Mrs. Kenny behind the front counter, and at least one of her sons on hand. They'll search for a specific book, and if necessary, mail it to you in the U.S. Ask for details of their "book club" plan that keeps you in touch with current Irish writing, with the right of refusal for books you don't want to keep. Their own bindery will wrap a prized edition in fine, hand-tooled covers. Periodically, they issue catalogs of Irish-interest publications. Go by to browse, and look for that special Irish book to carry home, but be warned—this is not an easy shop to leave! Open Monday through Saturday from 10am to 6pm. A newly opened branch on Merchants Road (near the docks) also carries a large stock.

CLOTHING AND TWEEDS

Faller's Sweater Shop

35 Eyre Square. ☎ **091/61255.** Also, 25 High Street (☎ 091/64833).

An outstanding selection of sweaters, including wool, cotton, and linen in a variety of styles. With a wide range of stylish accessories—linen, wool, and mohair scarves; tweed caps; and lovely cashmere capes. Open Monday through Saturday 9am–6pm, late opening Friday.

✪ Padraic O'Maille's

Dominick St. ☎ **091/562-696.**

In 1938 the late Mr. Padraic O'Maille opened his shop, and today his nephew, Gerry, and his widow, Ann, carry on the tradition. John Ford, John Wayne,

Maureen O'Hara, and Peter Ustinov have been patrons, and the business gained international recognition when O'Maille's made the costumes for *The Quiet Man.* There's a vast stock of gorgeous handwoven tweeds by the yard, as well as ready-made jackets, men's and ladies' suits, ladies' cashmere knits and tweed coats, ties, scarves, Irish "paddy" hats, and much more. This is also a good place to shop for Aran hand-knit sweaters (O'Maille's was the first place ever to market them commercially). There's a good mail-order catalog, and major credit cards are accepted. The store is open Monday through Saturday from 9am to 6:30pm.

GIFT/SPECIALTY STORES

Fallers

Williamsgate St. ☎ **091/561-226.**

Fallers began as a jewelry shop back in 1879 and today is still run by the fourth generation of Fallers. They carry a huge stock of crystal, silver, china, porcelain, linen, jewelry (including a wide range of in-house-made Claddagh rings), and quality souvenirs. They do an international mail-order business, and you can write for their color catalog (with prices in U.S. dollars). Open Monday through Saturday from 9am to 6pm. Open Sunday in summer.

✪ Galway Irish Crystal

Merlin Park. ☎ **091/57311.**

On the outskirts of town, this factory sells beautiful crystal at one-third off prices you'd pay in shops. In the showroom it's a joy to watch master cutter John Wynne at work, Monday through Friday, creating pieces like those displayed on the shelves. Open daily from 9am to 5pm.

Royal Tara China

Dublin Rd. ☎ **091/51301.** Fax 091/57574. Telex 50027.

You can tour the factory and watch master craftspeople creating this fine bone china. There are also considerable savings on purchases here. It's located off the Dublin road at Flannery's Motel, and there's a full-service restaurant on the premises. It is open September through June, daily from 9am to 6pm; in July and August, daily from 9am to 9pm. Free tours are offered Monday through Friday at 11am and 3pm, and on Saturday and Sunday by video.

Curiosity Corner

Cross St.

This tiny corner shop holds a wealth of Irish-made crafts, gift items, and basketwear. Open Monday through Saturday from 10am to 6pm.

Archway Craft Centre

Victoria Place, Eyre Sq. ☎ **091/563-693.**

Just opposite the Tourist Office, Bernadette Doyle runs this lovely two-story shop, which is chockablock with Irish craft items, including woolens and knitwear, as well as a pretty good selection of souvenirs and gifts.

SHOPPING NEARBY

Abbey Craft Centre

The Weir, Kilcolgan. ☎ **091/96104.** At turnoff for Moran's Oyster Cottage.

This attractive shop carries a great selection of Irish crafts, specializing in hand-knit Aran sweaters, made by local women in their own homes. Sweater prices are considerably lower than you'll find elsewhere. Styles from leading Irish designers are featured upstairs, and they carry the entire line of Irish prints by Cork artist Phillip Gray. Pottery, Celtic jewelry, china, Irish linen, and heraldic gifts are among other craft items. Good value for money here. Open Monday through Saturday 9:30am to 6pm year-round.

Mairtin Standun

Galway-Spiddal Rd., Spiddal. ☎ **091/83108.**

There are very good bargains to be found in this shop, 12 miles from Galway town on R336. It's very much a family business, and the selection of Aran sweaters, tweed coats and jackets, glassware, china, souvenirs, and gifts is incredibly large. There's also a currency-exchange service. In the rear of the shop there's a pleasant tearoom with a traditional fireplace; fresh bread and scones baked over an open turf fire are served here—a welcome refuge for weary shoppers. The shop is open March through November, Monday through Saturday from 9:30am to 6:30pm.

Spiddal Craft Centre

Spiddal.

On the outskirts of this picturesque little village, this cluster of craft shops and workshops includes pottery, weaving, knitwear, jewelry, an art gallery, and a coffee shop for light snacks and lunch. Hours during the summer season are 9am to 6:30pm daily, but may vary during the off-season.

8 Galway After Dark

THE PERFORMING ARTS

✪ Taibhdhearc Theatre

Middle St. ☎ **091/562-024.** Tickets, IR£7 ($11.20).

Since 1928, the Taibhdhearc ("*Thive*-yark") Theatre has existed for the sole purpose of preserving Gaelic drama. It also plays host to many touring theater companies. From Monday to Friday in July and August it presents *Siamsa,* an evening of top-quality Irish music, singing, dancing, and folk drama. Following the action is no problem, and the musical program is simply spectacular, with step dancing that will leave you breathless. This is where Siobhán McKenna began her career, and you'll see talent of much the same caliber on the stage. It's very "Irish" entertainment, and good value for money as well. This is a small, intimate theater, and you should book as far in advance as possible through the Tourist Office or at the theater.

✪ The Druid Theatre

Chapel Lane. ☎ **091/568-617.** Tickets, IR£5–IR£7 ($8–$11.20).

There is exceptionally good drama here. The resident professional company features productions of avant-garde plays, new Irish plays, and Anglo-Irish classics nightly year-round. There are frequent lunchtime and late-night shows, and local newspapers usually publish the schedule. Tickets can be booked by telephone or at the theater, and they should be booked as far in advance as you can manage, since the Druid has earned itself a worldwide reputation in a very short space of time, and it's extremely popular with locals as well as visitors.

✪ A Medieval Banquet & Literary Evening at Dunguaire Castle

Much more intimate than the medieval banquets at Bunratty and Knappogue, this is certainly not a budget item, but it is special enough to warrant a splurge from the most devoted budgeteer. The castle is a small 16th-century keep, with banquet seating limited to 62. You'll learn its legend when you enter the reception hall and quaff a cup of mead as a young woman in medieval dress relates the story. In the upstairs banquet hall you'll dine by candlelight on such delicacies as smoked salmon, "chekyn supreme," and sumptuous desserts, accompanied by a plentiful supply of wine. When dinner is over, your costumed waiters and waitresses repair to the stage and bring to vivid life Ireland's literary heroes and heroines through their stories, plays, and poems.

Because attendance is so limited, this is one banquet you must reserve well in advance—through a travel agent before you leave home if possible, through the Galway Tourist Office, or the Tours Manager at Shannon Airport (☎ 061/360788).

The cost is IR£30 ($48), and the banquet is presented mid-May to September, daily at 5:45 and 9pm.

Punchbag Theatre

Quay Lane, Galway, Co. Galway. ☎ **091/65422.** Tickets IR£7 ($11.20). Box office open Mon–Sat noon–6pm, Tues–Sun 9pm.

In a renovated Victorian town house opposite the Spanish Arch, the emphasis is on the development and advancement of original theatrical works by up-and-coming theatrical writers, as well as new interpretations of Irish classics.

TRADITIONAL MUSIC

An Pucáin

11 Forster St. ☎ **091/561-528.**

There's always traditional music going in this atmospheric pub, which is one of Galway's most popular gathering spots, both for locals and for visitors.

✪ Crane Bar

Sea Rd. ☎ **091/567-419.**

The upstairs ballad room in this old-style pub is often packed, and the music here is very good.

Flanagan's Corner Bar and Lounge

Henry St. and William St. W. ☎ **091/563-220.**

This popular pub has traditional and folk music from Wednesday through Sunday nights, and they invite musicians to bring along their instruments and join in.

The King's Head

High St. ☎ **091/566-630.**

Traditional music is only one of the musical forms presented at this popular pub, which has live music seven nights a week. It's best to call ahead if you fancy a particular kind of music, since you're likely to encounter country and western on some nights; on Sunday morning, jazz usually takes over. Depending on the group performing, there may be a small cover charge.

O'Connor's

Salthill. ☎ **091/46223.**

O'Connor's is Galway's leading sing-along pub, with a session every night of the week.

17 Counties Galway & Mayo

The west of Ireland. A simple phrase, yet one that conjures up an immediate and vivid image—brooding mountains, stony fields, wind-swept cliffs along a rugged coastline dotted with offshore islands, and air so heady that to breathe it is akin to drinking champagne. Oliver St. John Gogarty put it this way:

There's something sleeping in my breast
That wakens only in the West;
There's something in the core of me
That needs the West to set it free.

The distinctive delights of Connemara, the Aran Islands, and Achill Island are among the scenic stars in counties Galway and Mayo.

1 County Galway

Galway's landscape in the east is made up of flat, fertile plains that reach from Lough Derg and the Shannon Valley north to County Roscommon, while to the northwest, lumpy mountains push the mainland into a great elbow bent against the Atlantic. Lough Corrib stretches its 27 miles along an invisible line that marks the change.

GORT & CRAUGHWELL

If you're a dedicated fan of the poet William Butler Yeats (and most Yeats fans *are* dedicated), you won't want to miss a visit to Thoor Ballylee, his County Galway home for many summers. Lady Gregory lived and entertained her literary friends at her home in Coole Desmene nearby.

To reach the picturesque little village of Craughwell, take the R347 off N18 at Ardrahan. This is the burial place of the famous 19th-century poet Anthony Raftery, but in these parts, it's better known locally as the location of the colorful Galway Blazers Hunt. It is also the home of one of the country's leading makers of Irish harps, Paddy Cafferky, Lisduff, Craughwell (☎ 091/846-265).

WHAT TO SEE & DO

✪ Thoor Ballylee

Gort. ☎ **091/31436** or 63081. Admission IR£2.50 ($4) adults, 75p ($1.20) children, IR£5 ($8) families (parents and two children). May–Sept daily 10am–6pm.

From 1917 to 1929 Yeats spent his summers in this square 16th-century castle keep, having bought it as a ruin for a paltry £35 and restored it to living condition. Among its chief advantages was its proximity to his dear friend Lady Gregory at Coole Desmene. On one wall is inscribed this poignant poem:

I, the Poet William Yeats
With old millboards and seagreen slates
And smith work from the Gort forge
Restored this tower for my wife George,
And may these characters remain
When all is ruin once again.

Fortunately, the tower has not reverted to ruins, and from Easter to September there's a resident staff to assist visitors, as well as sound guides that lead you through the tower. It's four miles northeast of Gort on the Loughrea road (N66) or the Galway road (N18).

✪ Coole Desmene

Gort. Admission free. Open daily during daylight hours.

Now a national forest and wildlife park, Coole Desmene was once the setting for Coole House, the stately home of Lady Gregory, one of Ireland's most influential patrons of the arts and a founder of the Abbey Theatre. Here, she entertained and encouraged illustrious literary figures such as W. B. Yeats, George Bernard Shaw, and Sean O'Casey, as well as Douglas Hyde, the first president of Ireland. The house no longer stands, its site marked only by ruined walls and stables. However, you can still see the famous "Autograph Tree," on which many of Lady Gregory's guests carved their initials. There's a great atmosphere about the place that sets the imagination to work. It's two miles north of Gort and due west of N18.

WHERE TO EAT

✪ The Blazers Bar

Main St., Craughwell. ☎ **091/46004.** Reservations not accepted. Hot lunches under IR£5 ($8); bar snacks under IR£4 ($6.40). No credit cards. Lunch Mon–Fri noon–3pm (bar and lounge daily, normal bar hours). BAR FOOD.

The Galway Blazers Hunt members have their headquarters and kennels just behind this attractive pub, and in winter this is the meeting place before and after hunts. Run by Teresa and Donal Raftery, the pub has a glorious mixture of rural personalities, gentlemen farmers, and visitors like yourself. If you get there at teatime, you'll be served on beautiful china from a menu of seafood, soup, and sandwiches.

THE ARAN ISLANDS

Some 30 miles offshore, where Galway Bay empties into the sea, the Aran Islands are an outpost of rugged fishermen and their families who perpetuate a heritage of self-sufficiency and culture passed from generation to generation through the centuries. The walls of pre-Christian stone forts have endured the ravages of time to remind islanders of their "Celtic Twilight" origin. Round towers, oratories, and tiny churches tell of early Christians who spoke the musical Gaelic language, as do their descendants, today's islanders. Menfolk still put out to sea in lightweight, tough little wood-and-canvas curraghs, as they have done over the ages, while their womenfolk spin and weave and knit the clothing that is so distinctly theirs.

Life has been made easier on the islands with the introduction of electricity, modern plumbing, and regular sea and air service to the mainland. Still, much of the culture and old customs remain, and the hardy islanders are a breed apart, conditioned by generations who have braved the seas in their frail curraghs and laboriously built up the rocky soil with seaweed and sand in which to grow their meager crops. On Inishmore alone, there are said to be some 7,000 miles of stone walls, a testament to the industry of a persevering people.

ORIENTATION

Lying almost directly across the mouth of Galway Bay, the Aran Islands consist of a group of three islands: **Inishere** (pronounced Inis Oirr, meaning "eastern island"), the smallest and nearest to the mainland (Doolin, County Clare, is six miles away); **Inishmaan** (pronounced Inis Meain, meaning "middle island"), three miles distant from each of the other two and three miles long by two miles wide; and **Inishmore** (pronounced Inis Mor, meaning "big island"), seven sea miles from the Connemara coast, eight miles long and 2½ miles wide, with the only safe harbor suitable for steamer docking at **Kilronan,** its main village.

GETTING THERE **By Ferry** Doolin Ferries and Aran Ferries operate regular service to the Aran Islands from the Galway docks in July and August, and you can book the day before at the tourist office, or pay at the dockside kiosk. The round-trip fare at time of press was IR£15 ($24), half that for children under 16. Inquire about their special family fares.

It takes just over 2½ hours for the trip, and the water can be choppy; so if you're not a good sailor, take a motion-sickness remedy. Ferries dock only at Inishmore, but are met by curraghs at the other two islands to take off cargo.

A shorter boat trip from Rossaveal (on the coastal road past Spiddal) takes only 45 minutes and is run by Aran Ferries and Island Ferries. The round-trip fare at time of press was IR£13 ($20.80), half fare for children, with special family and student fares. Book at the Galway Tourist Office or call 091/93031 or 93034.

By Plane You can fly to Inishmore with Aer Arann (☎ 091/93034 or 93054), in a nine-seat, twin-engined aircraft from Connemara Airport. The round-trip fare is about IR£35 ($56), and you can also book through the tourist office. Ask about their special packages that include an overnight stay on the islands. They can also arrange package deals with rail or bus connections to Galway from Dublin and almost any other part of the country.

TOURIST INFORMATION Detailed information on the Aran Islands is available in the tourist office in Galway (see Chapter 16), which can also book accommodations on the islands.

A wonderful introduction to these special islanders is the film *Man of Aran,* which is shown three times daily (at 3, 5:30, and 8pm) at the Village Hall in Kilronan, with a small admission charge.

WHAT TO SEE & DO

You'll debark at Kilronan pier on Inishmore, to be greeted by lines of jaunting cars and minibuses to take you around the island, with delightful and informative narratives by your driver/guide and a terrific vantage point from which to view the network of small fields marked off by meandering stone walls. You'll ride through the village and down the one main road that runs the length of the island past an

Counties Galway & Mayo

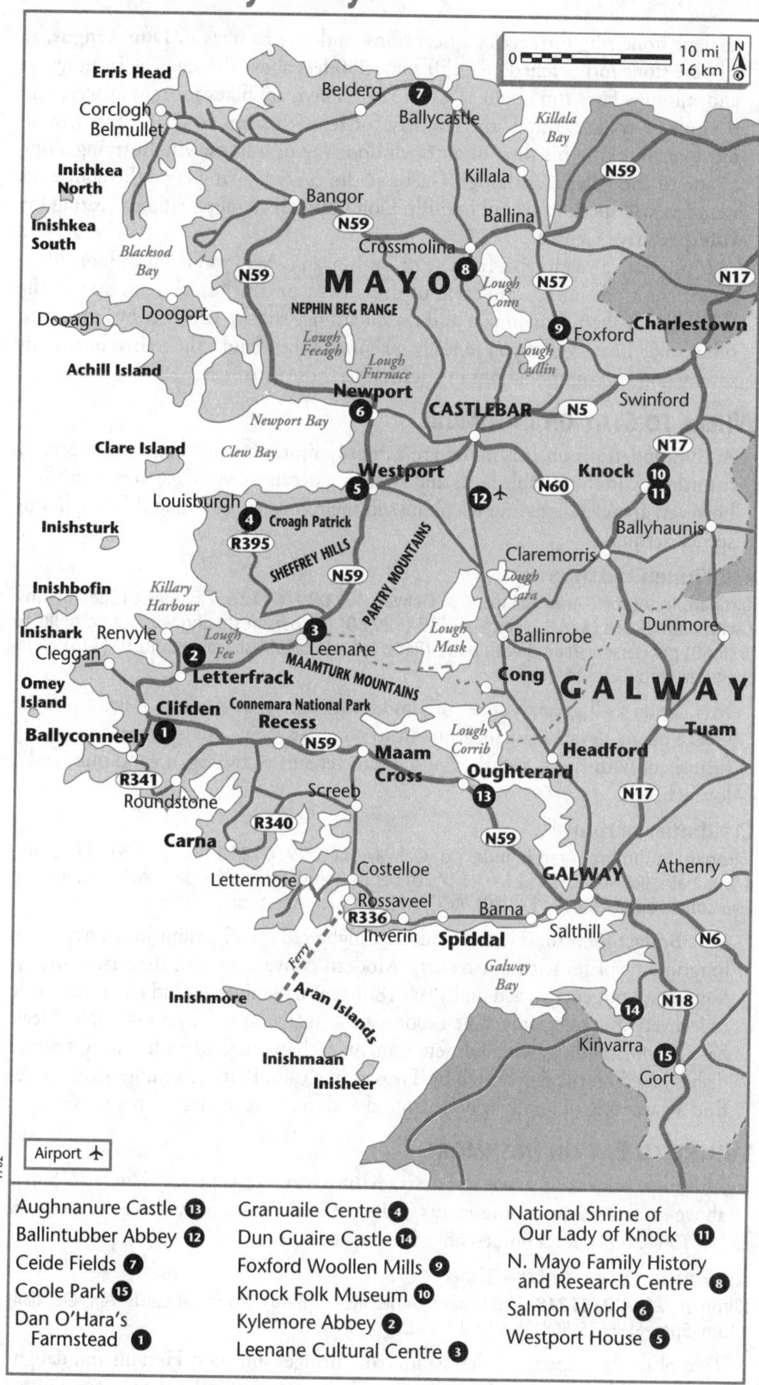

ancient stone ring fort, ecclesiastical ruins, and tiny hamlets to **Dun Aengus,** an 11-acre stone fort perched on a cliff some 300 feet above the sea. The jaunting car and minibus fares run about IR£15 ($24). There are bikes for rent as well, and if you're a walker, this is the country for it, with stops to chat a bit with an old man smoking his pipe in an open doorway or a housewife hurrying along a lane to the village. Although Gaelic is the everyday language, the courteous islanders will speak to you in English. Don't leave Inishmore without visiting the **Interpretative Centre.**

If you have a yen to visit Inishere or Inishmaan (where you're much more likely to see the traditional Aran style of dress than on Inishmore), ask any of the fishermen at the Kilronan pier and they'll arrange to take you over by curragh or other small boat. And if you're really taken with the islands, the tourist board lists several good accommodations in addition to those listed here.

Where to Stay on Inishmore

Accommodations on Inishmore are certainly more than adequate: comfortably furnished, with hospitable hosts and sweeping ocean views. What you *won't* find, however, are televisions and telephones in the rooms, as is right and fitting in this special setting.

Ard Einne Guesthouse

Kilronan, Inishmore, Aran Islands, Co. Galway. ☎ **099/61126.** Fax 099/61388. 11 rms, 7 with bath. IR£18 ($28.80) single; IR£13 ($20.80) per person sharing without bath; IR£16 ($25.60) per person sharing with bath. (Rates include breakfast.) Dinner IR£10 ($16) extra. No credit cards. Closed Dec–Feb.

Mrs. Enda Gill greets you at this modern home that sits 1¼ miles from the village on an elevated site looking out to gorgeous views. All bedrooms are nicely furnished, with sinks, and the house is convenient to fishing, a good pub, and a lovely beach.

✪ Kilmurvey House

Kilronan, Inishmore, Aran Islands, Co. Galway. ☎ **099/61218.** Fax 099/61397. 8 rms, 4 with bath. IR£14–IR£17 ($22.40–$27.20) per person sharing. IR£5 ($8) single supplement. Five-course dinner IR£13 ($20.80). ACC, MC, V. Open Apr–Sept.

Mrs. Bridget Johnston-Hernon and her daughter, Treasa Hernon-Joyce, have been longtime favorites with our readers. Modern conveniences in their large manor house have not encroached on its late 18th-century ambience, and guests are made to feel very much at home. Guest rooms are attractive as well as comfortable. Meals here are outstanding, with a different menu each evening, often featuring seafood dishes based on the day's catch by Treasa's husband, Bertie. Evenings many times find a gathering of family friends around a roaring fire to chat with guests.

Where to Eat on Inishmore

Although priority is given to guests, **Kilmurvey House** (see "Where to Stay," above) will welcome nonresidents if dining room space is available, at a cost of IR£13 ($20.80) for a home-cooked five-course meal.

An Sunda Caoch Coffee Shop

Kilronan. ☎ **099/61218.** Light meals under IR£4 ($6.40). No credit cards. Apr–Oct daily 11am–5pm. SWEETS/SOUPS/LIGHT MEALS.

Two of the best cooks on the island, Mrs. Bridget Johnston-Hernon and daughter, Treasa Hernon-Joyce (see Kilmurvey House, above), offer the perfect spot for a break in sightseeing or a light repast. Everything is homemade, and their cakes are great local favorities. Hearty soups and brown bread are a meal in themselves, and there are a few light meals to satisfy larger appetites.

✪ Dun Aonghusa Restaurant

Kilronan. ☎ **099/61104.** Reservations recommended. Lunch IR£7 ($11.20); dinner IR£12–IR£21 ($19.20–$33.60); lower prices for groups of 10 or more. MC, V. June–Aug daily 10am–10pm; Apr–May and Sept–Oct daily noon–9pm. Closed Nov–Mar. SEAFOOD/TRADITIONAL.

If you gravitate toward traditional settings, you'll love this wood-and-stone restaurant with its cozy open fire. Overlooking Galway Bay, it specializes in the freshest of local seafoods, as well as mouthwatering home baking.

CONNEMARA

This westernmost point of County Galway is a wild, thinly populated, yet enchanting stretch of land between Lough Corrib and the Atlantic. In Connemara the serried Twelve Bens (sometimes called the Twelve Pins) look across a lake-filled valley at the misty peaks of the Maamturk range, and the jagged coastline is a solitary place of rocks and tiny hamlets and stark, silent beauty.

As you drive the winding little roads past blue-washed cottages, you encounter a landscape made beautiful by incredibly shifting light and shade and the starkness of rock-strewn fields and hills. Glimpses of sandy strands at the sea's edge and the tiny villages dot your route and add another dimension.

This is Gaeltacht area, where government grants make possible the survival of a language and the people who speak it. Among its rocky, untillable fields wander the spirits of Irishmen banished by Cromwell "to Hell or Connaught."

Farther north, the long, narrow finger of Killary Harbour marks the County Mayo border. All in all, Connemara is an *experience* more than a place.

ESSENTIALS Information The tourist office in Galway (see Chapter 16) has extensive information on Connemara, as well as several helpful publications on the region.

GETTING AROUND By Bus There's regular bus service from Galway to Clifden, as well as narrated day trips by coach. The tourist office in Galway can furnish details.

SUGGESTED ROUTES By Car Although Clifden, at the extreme western edge of Connemara, is only 49 miles from Galway by the most direct route, those are slow *Irish* miles.

If your time is really limited you may want to drive through the heart of Connemara via N59, which takes you through Moycullen, Oughterard, and Recess to reach Clifden, returning via N59 through Letterfrack and Kylemore to Leenane, where N59 is the direct route to Westport, County Mayo, and R336 takes you back through Maam, Maam Cross, Oughterard, and Moycullen to Galway. With more time, you might follow this route through Moycullen and Oughterard as far as Maam Cross, then cut south to Screeb and west along the coast.

A much more memorable drive is the coastal road from Galway to Clifden, which will add perhaps as much as three hours to your travel time, but will leave photographs upon your heart to be examined and reexamined for years to come. This route runs along the coast from Galway via R336 to Spiddal, Inverin, Costelloe, Carraroe, Screeb, Derryrush, Kilkieran, Carna, Glinsk, and Ballynahinch. At Ballynahinch you can join the main Galway-Clifden road for a quick run into Clifden or continue around the coastline through Roundstone, Ballyconneely, and

Ballinaboy, to Clifden, returning to Galway via Letterfrack, Kylemore, Leenane Maam, Maam Cross, Oughterard, and Moycullen.

One final word: If you don't plan to return to Galway from Leenane, you can continue northward to Westport via N59, or turn east at Maam for a drive along the shores of Lough Corrib via R345 to Cong and Castlebar in County Mayo.

SPECIAL EVENTS The ✪ **Connemara Pony Show** in Clifden is held in August and buyers come from around the world to bid on the sturdy little animals; the town takes on a country-fair look, with much revelry, handcraft demonstrations, etc. Sometimes spontaneous, there are "flapper races," in which children race Connemara ponies while families gather for a great day of eating and drinking in the out-of-doors.

Clifden is also the setting for weeklong sessions of the **Irish School of Landscape Painting,** founded and conducted by master painter Kenneth Webb, now assisted by his daughter, Susan. Individual instruction is given, with emphasis on techniques to catch the shimmering Connemara light shadings. You attend for the week, with accommodations and two meals a day an optional extra. For details, contact Miss C. Cryan, Blue Door Studio, 16 Prince of Wales Terrace, Ballsbridge, Dublin 4 (☎ 01/668-5548).

What to See & Do

Pleasures are simple in Connemara, most often associated with the natural rhythms of country life. Turf is cut and dried in the boglands from April through June, and especially along the coastal road you may see donkeys with loaded creels transporting the dried turf to be stacked against the winter's cold. Sheepshearing is done by hand, often within the roofless walls of ruined cottages, and if you come across sheep being herded through the fields in June and July, they're probably on their way to be shorn.

If you're driving out to Clifden via N59, between Maam Cross and Recess, look for the ✪ **small stone pillar** on the left-hand side of the road at the edge of a young forest plantation. Bostonians may want to stop and read the brass plaque, dated 1985, which dedicates the trees to "the memory of Irish immigrants who contributed so greatly to America in general and Boston in particular."

At Ballynahinch Castle near Recess (see "Where to Stay," below) the ruined castle on a small island in Ballynahinch Lake is said to be the keep in which the O'Flaherty clan once imprisoned their captured enemies.

The picturesque village of ✪ **Roundstone** is beautifully situated on Bertraghboy Bay, overlooking the Atlantic from the foot of Errisbeg Hill. Small trawlers from the village fish year-round, and in summer months there's fishing from open lobster boats and curraghs. It's worth a stop just to walk at least one of the two fine white-sand beaches nearby, Goirtin and Dog's Bay. If there's time, make the easy climb up Errisbeg Hill, where your reward at the top will be spectacular views of the Aran Islands and, on a clear day, parts of Kerry. It's in Roundstone, too, that you'll find one of the finest makers of the traditional bodhrán in Ireland (see "Shopping," below).

Thatchers are usually at work in September and October, and the greatest concentration of **thatched cottages** is between Roundstone and Ballyconneely. Between Ballyconneely and Kilkieran, you can sometimes watch **seaweed being harvested** (done at the full and new moons for four hours only in the middle of the day). Little villages all along the coast hold frequent ✪ **curragh races.** Finding out the when and where of the races is a matter of keeping your eyes and ears open—and of a well-placed inquiry over a pint at the local pub.

At **Ballynaboy,** a little south of Clifden, look for the signposted memorial to **Alcock and Brown,** who landed near here on the first transatlantic flight in 1919—it's on a high hill between Ballynaboy and Clifden, with magnificent panoramic views.

One thing you won't want to miss in **Clifden** is the spectacular ✪ **Sky Drive,** a cliff road that forms a nine-mile circle around a peninsula and opens up vast seascapes. It's well signposted from town. Boats are also available (through most accommodations) for **deep-sea fishing** for mackerel, blue shark, conger, cod, ling, and many other varieties. Summer evenings bring traditional music in many of Clifden's hotel bars and pubs; check with the tourist office or your accommodation hostess. In August, join in the fun at the **Connemara Pony Show** in Clifden (see "Special Events," above).

North of Clifden, the road to **Cleggan** via Claddaghduff has several traditional **thatched cottages,** and the village is the home port for small fishing trawlers and, in summer, open lobster boats and curraghs. This is an area of remarkable cliff scenery and good beaches. Cleggan is also the gateway to the offshore ✪ **Inishbofin Island,** with its wide, sandy beaches and extraordinary seascapes. You can reach the island year-round via the mailboat (for details, contact P. C. O'Halloran, St. Joseph's, Inishbofin; ☎ 095/45866); from Easter to September, there are other sailings from Cleggan (details from the Pier Bar, Cleggan; ☎ 095/44663). If you are beguiled into lingering in this nature lover's dream place for a day or two, budget-priced accommodations are available at **Day's Bofin House** (☎ 095/45829 or 45809) and **Doonmore** (☎ 095/45804).

The entrance to ✪ **Connemara National Park** is near Letterfrack, and within its 3,800 acres are short- and long-distance walks, a paddock of Connemara ponies, and a Visitor Centre with interesting exhibitions of the park's main features. Well worth a stop.

At **Letterfrack** sits ✪ **Kylemore Abbey** in a picture-postcard setting of woodlands on the banks of Pollacappal Lough, its impressive facade reflected by the lake's mirror surface. The stone mansion dates from the 19th century, and is home to an order of teaching nuns who have established a thriving pottery industry and welcome visitors to the shop. There's a tearoom for refreshment, and you can stroll the lovely grounds.

At **Derryinver,** 1½ miles from Letterfrack, John Mongan, Connemara Sea Leisure Ltd. (095/43473), runs three-hour **fishing and sightseeing cruises** on his 31-foot *MV Lorraine-Marie* year-round, weather permitting. The fare is IR£60 ($96) for up to six people, IR£10 ($16) per person for 7 to 12 people. Call to check on departure times and to book.

A little farther along, look for the **Leenane Cultural Centre** (☎ 095/42323 or 42231), where a small wool museum has demonstrations of the ancient arts of carding, spinning, and weaving wool. A short video in several languages highlights local places of interest.

At **Maam Cross,** lovers of *The Quiet Man* will want to stop for a look at Peacocks Restaurant's replica of the traditional Irish thatched cottage featured in that film. Its half-door, open fire, and period furnishings are reminders of rural Ireland in years gone by. Owner Theresa Keogh is an authority on that film and is delighted to chat with visitors. For more about the making of the film, see below.

SHOPPING

In Spiddal, look for the **Spiddal Craft Centre** at the western edge of the village, a delightful complex of workshops for weavers, potters, silversmiths, etc.

Malachy Kearns, of ✪ **Roundstone Musical Instruments** (☎ and fax 095/35808), works in the ancient Franciscan monastery IDA Craft Centre in Roundstone. The bell tower and outer walls of this 16th-century monks' home and local school are still there, and in summer seals and dolphins gather at its outer walls near the workshop. Malachy is a master craftsman, and the only full-time bodhrán maker in the world. The bodhrán is an ancient Irish one-sided frame drum, and for the best results, it is vital to have the quality goatskin Malachy uses. While you wait, his wife, Anne, a Celtic artist, can decorate the skin with Celtic designs, initials, family crests, or any design you request in old Gaelic script. Malachy's workshop also makes wooden flutes (ebony), tin whistles, and Irish harps, and he has an excellent mail-order service. The workshop/craftshop and Folk Instrument Museum is open daily from May through October from 8:30am to 6:30pm, Monday through Friday other months. This is one of my personal favorite stops in Connemara. The Kearns also have a shop on Main Street in Clifden (☎ 095/21516), open daily from 9am to 7pm from April through October, Monday through Saturday in winter.

In the same complex, look for **Roundstone Ceramics** (☎ 095/35874), where you'll find high-fired stoneware and porcelain, hand-thrown by Séamus Laffan and decorated by Rose O'Toole. Each original decorative design is a reflection of the local environment, a lasting bit of the feel of Ireland to take home or give as gifts.

✪ **Millar's Connemara Tweeds** (☎ 095/21038) has long been a Clifden landmark, with shop shelves filled with beautifully colored pure-wool lengths produced by weavers in the locality. Their mill, one of the oldest in Ireland, uses only local mountain wool. Irish linens, glass, pottery, books of Irish interest, native food specialties, and other items complete the downstairs displays. Up the iron spiral stairs is a display of Connemara scenes depicted by Irish painters. In a stone-walled wing of the shop, you can browse through Irish fashions in a setting that includes a turf fire on the stone hearth and furnishings such as an old spinning wheel. Patchwork quilts are beautifully executed and much sought after, thus not always available. In short, this is a happy hunting ground for almost anything Irish-made. Open Monday through Saturday from 9am to 6pm.

On the Leenane–Maam Bridge road, look for the ✪ **Maam Country Knitwear Sweater Shop and Art Gallery,** Maam Valley (☎ 091/71109). The well-stocked shop features hand-loomed ties, hats, scarves, wool knitwear, and a host of other items—most locally produced. There are year-round exhibitions of paintings and photographs, and Dublin escapees Ann and Dennis Kendrick, the helpful owner/operators, welcome visitors all year. Teas and snacks are served on the premises.

East of Maam Bridge, less than a mile from the village of Cornamona, ✪ **Connemara Socks** (☎ 092/48254) is a small local business run by the Brennan family, who welcome visitors for tours of their plant. As well as spinning sock yarns for other sock knitters, they knit some 3,000 pairs of heavy socks per week on the premises. If you're a skier, fisherperson, hiker, hunter, or any other outdoor type, you'll surely want to take away several pairs of these moderately priced, heavy-duty socks. Air trapped between fibers gives wool its insulating quality, and the surface of the wool is water resistant, its interior highly absorbent, which means that the socks absorb perspiration and then slowly release it through evaporation, keeping you warm in winter and cool in summer. *Note:* On the same small industrial estate, visitors are also welcomed by a salmon smokery.

✪ **Fuchsia Craft,** Main Street, Oughterard (☎ 091/82644), is a small shop presided over by Margaret Donnellan, who stocks a wide range of Irish crafts. You'll find Royal Tara china, Galway crystal, an interesting selection of Irish-made jewelry, Irish linen, quality knitwear, pottery, decorated bodhráns, and prints and watercolors of local scenes. Prices are quite reasonable, and Margaret is a delight.

Also in Moycullen, the **Connemara Marble Products** (☎ 091/85102) factory offers a tremendous stock of items made from polished marble, ranging from inexpensive souvenirs to moderately expensive items like jewelry, bookends, clocks, etc. Prices are better here than in shops, and they're open during the summer months daily from 9am to 5:30pm; the rest of the year, Monday through Friday from 9am to 5:30pm. Across the road there's a tearoom serving tea, coffee, and cookies.

Take a look, while you're in town, at the good buys at **Moycullen Crafts and Antiques.**

Where to Stay

Spiddal

Some 12 miles west of Galway town along the coast road (R336), Spiddal is a charming little village with a good beach, an excellent craft center (see "Shopping Nearby" in "Shopping" in Chapter 16), and an excellent restaurant, The Boluisce Seafood Bar (see "Where to Eat: Spiddal," below).

✪ Ardmore Country House

Greenhill, Spiddal, Co. Galway. ☎ **091/83145.** 8 rms, all with bath. IR£21 ($33.60) single; IR£16 ($25.60) per person sharing. 20% reduction for children. Discounts for stays of three days or more. (Rates include breakfast.) No credit cards. Closed Jan–Feb.

On the Galway Bay coastal road, just half a mile from Spiddal, Mrs. Vera Feeney's Ardmore is a modern bungalow overlooking the bay and the Aran Islands. The Cliffs of Moher are clearly visible on clear days and the panoramic view is framed by large windows in the lounge, or you can relax in the sun outside on the terrace to enjoy the landscaped gardens. The guest rooms are spacious and attractively decorated. The gracious Mrs. Feeney has thoughtfully provided washing and drying facilities. You're offered a menu that has three times won the coveted Breakfast Award. There's central heating and parking.

Roundstone

✪ St. Joseph's

Roundstone, Co. Galway. ☎ **095/35865.** 6 rms, 3 with bath. IR£18–IR£20 ($28.20–$32) single; IR£14–IR£15 ($22.40–$24) per person sharing. (Rates include breakfast.) Dinner IR£12 ($18.20) extra. 25% reduction for children. V.

Christine and Séamus Lowry's town house sits on the high side of Roundstone's main street, and its glass-enclosed sun porch looks out over the colorful harbor. Christine's mother, often in residence, ran the guesthouse for over 20 years, and her tradition of providing a "home from home" for guests still prevails. Guest rooms are spacious, and those in front overlook the bay. Evening meals consist of four courses, with a choice of fish, meat, or vegetarian dishes, and high tea is available. Christine is an accomplished Irish set dancer and lover of traditional music and knows where it may be found locally. The Lowrys can also arrange sea angling, as well as golf at nearby Ballyconneely.

Clifden

Ard Aoibhinn

Ballyconneely Rd., Clifden, Co. Galway. ☎ **095/21339.** 3 rms, all with bath. IR£18 ($28.20) single; IR£15 ($24) per person sharing. (Rates include breakfast.) Dinner IR£12 ($18.20) extra. No credit cards. Closed Nov–Feb.

In a scenic setting about half a mile from Clifden, Mrs. Carmel Gaughan's modern bungalow has three nicely done up bedrooms and a pretty, picture-window lounge. There's central heat and parking; safe beaches and a golf course are close at hand.

Ben View House

Bridge St., Clifden, Co. Galway. ☎ **095/21256.** 6 rms, all with bath. IR£15–IR£26 ($24–$41.60) single; IR£13–IR£17 ($20.80–$27.20) per person sharing. 10% reduction for children. (Rates include breakfast.) No credit cards.

This is the comfortable two-story home of Mrs. Morris, a hospitable hostess, and is now run by the third generation of the same family. The house is centrally heated and guest rooms are attractively decorated and comfortably furnished. Its location puts you within easy walking distance of pubs, restaurants, and shops.

Failte

Ardbear (off Ballyconneely Rd.), Clifden, Co. Galway. ☎ **095/21159.** 5 rms, 2 with bath. IR£13.50–IR£18.50 ($21.60–$29.60) single; IR£13.50 ($21.60) per person sharing; IR£2 ($3.20) per person extra with bath. 33½% reduction for children. (Rates include breakfast.) No credit cards. Closed Oct–Mar.

A little over one mile from town and a short drive off the main road, Mrs. Maureen Kelly's home perches on an elevation affording lovely views of the town and the bay. Her guest rooms are immaculate, and there is one large family room with four beds. Her breakfasts were among the regional Galtee Irish Breakfast Awards winners in 1991. There's central heat and private parking.

Readers Recommend

Col-Mar, Salanoona, Spiddal, Co. Galway. ☎ 091/83211. *"Maurine and Máirín Keady are the warm and gracious hosts at this lovely home just one block from Galway Bay. Their home is on property that has belonged to their family for a dozen generations. The gardens are varied and among the finest I've seen in Ireland, and the house is tastefully decorated and immaculately clean. Both reflect Maureen's artistic gifts. Breakfasts are 'to order,' generous, and delicious, and Maureen serves an evening meal with a little advance notice."* —Constance M. Kerwin, Washington, DC

Tuar Beag, Spiddal, Co. Galway ☎ 091/83422 *"We spent a couple of days at Tuar Beag with the Feeneys, a young couple who have turned Eammon's family home into a beautiful bed-and-breakfast, totally remodeling it, yet retaining a portion of the old home, which now serves as the entry and dining room. It retains the original stone floor, warm wood, and lovely fireplace and is furnished with typical Irish dining furniture. The location is excellent; and the breakfast menu offered several selections, all delicious. The American in me was thrilled to find face cloths and large bath sheets in the bathrooms."* —Jeanne and Ron Merkhofer, Cincinnati, OH

Author's Note: The Feeneys also have self-catering two-bedroom apartments for rent.

✪ Hyland's Bay View House

Westport Rd., Clifden, Co. Galway. ☎ **095/21286.** 4 rms, all with bath. IR£18 ($28.80) single; IR£15 ($24) per person sharing. 50% reduction for children. (Rates include breakfast.) MC, V. Closed Dec–Jan.

With one of the best views in this area, Mrs. Bridie Hyland's modern bungalow overlooks Streamstown Bay. Guest rooms are both attractive and comfortable, and you're likely to find a peat fire glowing in the picture-window lounge, which also has a TV. Bridie knows the area well, is always helpful in planning sightseeing for her guests, and can arrange a day's deep-sea fishing.

Sunny Bank (Ard Mhuire) Guesthouse

Church Hill, Clifden, Co. Galway. ☎ **095/21437.** 10 rms, all with bath. IR£20 ($32) per person; IR£7 ($11.20) single supplement. (Rates include breakfast.) AE, MC, V. Closed Nov–Apr. Private car park.

This large, two-story Georgian house is set in attractive gardens on an elevated site overlooking the town. It's run by Jackie and Marion O'Grady (members of the family who are known for their seafood restaurant in Clifden—see below), and there's a heated swimming pool and a tennis court on the grounds.

Cleggan

Cois Na Mara

Cleggan, Co. Galway. ☎ **095/44647.** 6 rms, 3 with bath. IR£18.50 ($29.60) single; IR£13.50 ($21.60) per person sharing; IR£1.50 ($2.40) per person extra with bath. 25% reduction for children. (Rates include breakfast.) No credit cards. Closed Oct–Apr.

Bernie Hughes is well known for her warm hospitality. Her modern home is set in a scenic area, with safe beaches a short walk away. Guest rooms are quite comfortable, and there's central heating. Bernie can help you book the boat trip out to Inisboffin Island. There's plenty of private parking.

Maam

✪ Leckavrea View Farmhouse

Maam-Cong Rd. (L101), Maam, Co. Galway. ☎ **092/48040.** 6 rms, all with bath. IR£18 ($28.80) single; IR£15 ($24) per person sharing. 25% reduction for children. Weekend rates available. (Rates include breakfast.) Dinner IR£11 ($17.60). No credit cards. Closed Christmas.

This large old farmhouse on the shores of Lough Corrib, 2½ miles from Maam Bridge and 32 miles from Galway town, is the comfortable home of John and Breege Gavin. Marvelous views of Lough Corrib include the little island just offshore crowned by Castle Kirk ("Hen's Castle"), once a stronghold of pirate queen Grace O'Malley. Fishing on the lough is free (the Gavins have boats for rent), and if Castle Kirk intrigues you, John will (for a small fee) row you over to the island for a bit of exploring. In consideration for her guests who've come for peace and quiet, Breege keeps the TV in a separate lounge and usually keeps a fire glowing in the main lounge. She will also pack picnic lunches, provide dinner with advance notice, and arrange baby-sitting.

Oughterard

Lakeland Country Home

Portacarron, Oughterard, Co. Galway. ☎ **091/82121** or 82146. 9 rms, 5 with bath. IR£15 ($24) per person sharing without bath; IR£2.50 ($4) per person additional with bath; IR£6 ($9.60) single supplement; IR£2 ($3.20) per person additional during special events. (Rates include breakfast.) No credit cards. Closed Christmas.

This lovely lakeside home of Lal and Mary Faherty is a great place for relaxing, and there are nice scenic walks nearby. They also have boats for hire if you fancy a day on the lake. The house is centrally heated as well as having turf fires, and electric blankets are supplied in the attractive bedrooms. The Fahertys have also kept families in mind by providing triple bedrooms. It's two miles from Oughterard.

Knockferry

✪ Knockferry Lodge

Knockferry, Roscahill, Co. Galway. ☎ **091/80122.** Fax 091/80328. 10 rms, all with bath. IR£21 ($33.60) per person. Reductions for three- and seven-day stays; 33% reduction for children. (Rates include breakfast.) Dinner IR£16 ($25.60) extra. AE, DC, MC, V.

Set in a secluded spot on the Connemara shores of Lough Corrib, just 14 miles northwest of Galway town, the lodge is run by Des and Mary Moran. It was originally occupied by the author of *Galway Bay,* Dr. Arthur Colohan. It was also Des's family home, to which he returned after several years in the hotel business in Europe to establish a first-class accommodation with a superior cuisine. It is his own irrepressible personality that also added an element of fun that has attracted a loyal following of fishermen and relaxation-seekers. There are turf fires in both of the large lounges, and there's a spacious dining room for outstanding meals (with such specialties as Corrib salmon, trout, and pike; Viennese goulash; Connemara lamb; and spiced beef, among others). A games room provides table tennis and bar billiards. Fishing boats are available for rent (no charge for fishing, except for salmon).

Guest rooms are lovely, most with lake views; one large room has a double and two single beds, sink, bidet, toilet, shower, and bath. There's central heating and plenty of parking.

Knockferry Lodge is 13 miles from Oughterard; take N59 to Moycullen and turn left onto a small, unclassified road (the lodge is signposted) and drive six miles.

Self-Catering

Two comfortably furnished traditional cottages, ideal for family holidays, may be rented by contacting. Mrs. Olivia Walker, 5 Elgin Road, Dublin 4 (☎ 01/660-6832; fax 01/493-4538). One is adjacent to a safe, sandy beach, with spectacular sea and mountain views, and the other is on the edge of a small picturesque lake near the Connemara golf course. Each cottage sleeps eight in three bedrooms. Electricity is extra. Rates are IR£410 ($656) per week June, July, and August; IR£325 ($520) per week other months.

Worth a Splurge

✪ Ballynahinch Castle

Ballinfad, Recess, Connemara, Co. Galway. ☎ **095/31006.** Fax 095/31085. 28 rms, all with bath. June–Sept IR£75–IR£84 ($120–$134.40) single; IR£58–IR£68 ($92.80–$108.80) per person sharing. Lower rates other months. (Rates include breakfast.) Dinner IR£25 ($40) extra. Winter break, Christmas, and fly-casting tutorial packages available. Deposit required when booking. AE, DC, MC, V. Seven miles from Clifden, signposted from N59.

If there is such a thing as casual elegance, this lovely small hotel certainly has it. Set in lush woodlands at the base of Ben Lettry in the Twelve Bens mountain range seven miles from Clifden (signposted from N59), the impressive manor house overlooks the Owenmore River. This was the ancestral territory of the O'Flaherty chieftains, and in more recent years Ballynahinch was built as the sporting home of an Indian maharajah. There's excellent fishing on the grounds, with boats available for rent, and miles of walking or biking paths, with bicycles for hire. Guest rooms are individually named and decorated. Log fires, oil paintings, and wall tapestries give a warm, comfortable air to the two beautifully furnished lounges, and the dining room overlooks the river and gardens. The Castle Pub is a favorite gathering place for residents of the locality, with traditional music on tap often during summer months.

Cashel House Hotel

Cashel, Connemara, Co. Galway. ☎ **095/31001.** Fax 095/31077. 32 rms, all with bath. Seasonal rates, IR£49–IR£106 ($78.40–$169.60) per person. (Rates include breakfast.) Dinner IR£27 ($43.20) extra. AE, MC, V.

Set in 50 acres of gardens and woodland walks at the head of Cashel Bay among the jagged peaks and rocky headlands of Connemara, the Cashel House Hotel has a delightful country-house atmosphere. Among the notables who have chosen to come here for holidays were Gen. and Mme Charles de Gaulle in 1969, who turned out to be enthusiastic boosters of the warm Irish hospitality shown them by owners Kay and Dermot McEvilly. The stylish 19th-century house blends antique pieces with comfortable modern furnishings, and the cozy bar is the setting for many a friendly gathering at the end of a day of sightseeing. The pretty dining room overlooks the gardens—crackling peat and log fires add to the hominess—and enjoys a country-wide reputation for its fine food. The McEvillys are happy to arrange trout and salmon fishing for their guests, and they provide horseback riding and picnic itineraries. Nine rooms have sitting areas that transform them into small suites, and all rooms have superb views as does the conservatory.

✪ Rock Glen Manor House

Clifden, Connemara, Co. Galway. ☎ **095/21035** or 21393. Fax 095/21737. 29 rms, all with bath. Seasonal rates, IR£51–IR£57 ($81.60–$91.20) single; IR£36–IR£42 ($57.60–$67.20) per person sharing. (Rates include breakfast.) Dinner IR£21 ($33.60) extra. 12.5% service charge. 33% reduction for children. AE, MC, V. Closed Nov–Feb.

This former shooting lodge is beautifully situated about 1½ miles out the Roundstone-Ballyconneely road from Clifden. Its low, rambling profile belies the spaciousness inside, where a large, lovely drawing room sets a gracious and informal tone. There's also a cozy bar and a dining room that features excellent meals prepared by the friendly owner/manager, John Roche. Fifteen guest rooms are on the ground floor (a boon to the handicapped and those of us who tote around tons of luggage!).

Readers Recommend

Trá Mór, Kilroe West, Inverin, Co. Galway. ☎ 091/83450. *"Kieran and Pat Moss, along with their son and daughter and two grandmas, run this B & B, which overlooks the ocean. They are the most delightful people, and Mrs. Moss cooks wonderful breakfasts, as well as a first-rate evening meal on request. Mr. Moss works seasonally as a tour guide, so he is quite knowledgeable as to scenic day-trips and excursions."*

—Christopher Dwyer, San Diego, CA

Connemara Country Lodge, Westport Road, Clifden, Co. Galway. ☎ 095/21122. *"Not only do proprietors Gerard and Mary Corbett-Joyce have beautiful, clean rooms, but the breakfasts are sumptuous and delicious. More important was the hospitality provided by this delightful couple."*

—Dr. and Mrs. Richard Slawsky, Palo Alto, CA

Where to Eat

Spiddal

✪ The Boluisce Seafood Bar

Spiddal. ☎ **091/83286.** Reservations recommended. Lunch IR£6 ($9.60); dinner IR£16 ($25.60). MC, V. Mon–Sat noon–10pm, Sun 4–10pm. Closed Good Friday, Christmas Eve and Day. SEAFOOD/TRADITIONAL.

This is a true "Irish" restaurant, piling your plate high with generous portions at moderate prices. You can choose anything from soup to lobster and other delicacies. Seafood dishes are often innovative, with fish from local waters, and nonseafood lovers, as well as vegetarians, can choose from several selections.

Clifden

✪ Central Restaurant and Lounge

Main St., Clifden. ☎ **095/21430.** Bar food under IR£5 ($8); hot plates IR£6 ($9.60). AE, DC, MC, V. Mon–Sat 12:30–9:30pm, Sun 12:30–3pm and 6–9pm. BAR FOOD/TRADITIONAL.

This large bar/lounge/restaurant is made cozy by lots of dark wood and a cheerful open fire (especially welcome on cool, dull days). The seafood chowder here is superb, and hot meals include bacon and cabbage, lasagna, and chicken curry.

✪ O'Grady's Seafood Restaurant

Market St. ☎ **095/21450.** Reservations recommended. Lunch IR£11 ($17.60); dinner IR£20 ($32). AE, DC, MC, V. Daily 12:30–2:30pm and 6–10pm. Closed Nov–Mar. SEAFOOD/TRADITIONAL/VEGETARIAN.

This attractive family-run restaurant has been around a long time, earning an international reputation for their excellent seafood dishes. They have their own fishing boats, so you may be sure the fish you eat is not long out of Atlantic waters. On Saturday night there are candlelight dinners, and from Halloween to Easter they feature game as well as seafood. Business lunches are served at moderate prices every day, and the Tourist Menu is offered up to 2:30pm.

Maam Cross

Peacockes

Maam Cross. ☎ **091/82306,** 82375, 82412, or 82501. Reservations not required. Breakfast IR£4 ($6.40); lunch IR£6 ($9.60); dinner IR£13 ($20.80). AE, MC, V. Daily 9am–11pm. SEAFOOD/TRADITIONAL/VEGETARIAN.

Located at this important crossroad, Peacockes is a virtual mini-conglomerate, with a host of services for travelers. To begin with, they have built an enviable reputation for outstanding seafood at moderate prices. Depending on availability, you'll find lobster, salmon, prawns, oysters from the west of Ireland, and Lough Corrib trout on the menu, and they also feature prime steaks and a selection of vegetarian dishes. There's a well-stocked craft shop, and evenings are enlivened with traditional music, as well as a disco.

Moycullen

Drimcong House

Moycullen. ☎ **091/85115** or 85585. Set 5-course dinner IR£20 ($32); set 3-course dinner IR£17 ($27.20); 5-course vegetarian dinner IR£18 ($28.20). ACC, DC, MC, V. Tues–Sat 7–10:30pm. Closed Jan, Feb, and holidays. One mile west of Galway. IRISH/VEGETARIAN.

Gerry and Marie Galvin are the owners of this lakeside 17th-century country house, one of Ireland's top award-winning restaurants. It's only a short drive from Galway town. Unpretentious elegance is the keynote, with gleaming oak tables and glowing turf fires. Gerry is the chef, and his menu changes weekly—baked chicken breast accompanied by smoked salmon and avocado is typical of the cuisine, which, though based on classical dishes, is quite often adventurous. Vegetarians will love the five-course set menu.

A Country Inn Along the Connemara Coast Drive

Picnic spots abound in the wilds of Connemara, and country pubs often serve delicious, hearty bar food. On the coastal drive from Galway to Clifden, **Carna Bay Hotel,** Carna, Connemara, County Galway (☎ 095/32255), is a small hotel on the Clifden side of this little village. It offers quite adequate and comfortable bed-and-breakfast accommodations for about IR£20 ($32) and serves good bar food at inexpensive prices, as well as the evening meal for IR£15 ($24). There's also periodic entertainment in the evenings. A good overnight stop or meal break.

EN ROUTE TO COUNTY MAYO

After touring Connemara and returning to Galway, there are two routes north. N17 will take you through **Tuam,** a small market town whose importance as an ecclesiastical center in years gone by is marked by the **Cross of Tuam** in the market square, and by **St. Mary's Cathedral,** rebuilt in the 1800s, but incorporating the magnificent chancel arch of its 12th-century ancestor.

The alternative route via N84 brings you to **Headford** and historic **Ross Abbey,** some two miles northwest of town. The abbey was founded in 1357 and fell victim to Cromwell's forces in 1656. Just north of Headford, you'll cross the County Mayo border, and at Cross, **Cong** is only a short detour west en route from Headford to Castlebar.

WHERE TO STAY

Balrichard Farm

Galway Rd., Headford, Co. Galway. ☎ **093/35421.** 3 rms, none with bath. IR£15 ($24) per person. (Rates include breakfast.) Dinner IR£12 ($19.20) extra. 50% reduction for children. No credit cards. Closed Dec–Feb.

Mrs. Margaret McDonagh is hostess of this lovely farmhouse less than a mile south of town on the Galway road. It is set in beautiful countryside and there's a golf course opposite the farm. The house is centrally heated as well as having open turf fires.

Kilmore House

Galway Rd. (N17), Tuam, Co. Galway. ☎ **093/28118.** 7 rms, all with bath. TV. IR£16 ($25.60) single; IR£15 ($24) per person sharing. 20% reduction for children; discounts for stays of more than one night. (Rates include breakfast.) High tea IR£8 ($12.80) extra; dinner IR£13 ($20.80). No credit cards.

Josephine ("Jo") O'Connor is hostess in this lovely modern home half a mile south of Tuam. Her warm hospitality first surfaces as she brings tea and scones to guests when they arrive. She has two family rooms, and has provided a playground for children out back. Guest rooms are bright and cheerful, and Jo's substantial Irish breakfast is served in a window-walled dining room overlooking the farm and bogs beyond. The house is centrally heated, and there's good parking.

A Special Adventure Center, Not Only for the Adventurous

✪ Delphi Adventure Holidays

Leenane, Co. Galway. ☎ **095/42208,** 42307, or 42223. Fax 095/42303. Single, double, and dormitory rms; self-catering cottage. IR£195–IR£305 ($312–$488) per week; weekend, midweek, and public holiday special rates available. (Rates include breakfast and dinner.) MC, V. Closed Mid-Dec to Jan.

Set in one of the most scenic portions of the road from Ashleagh to Louisburgh (R335), the low-slung, native stone buildings seem to have grown from the landscape itself. Interiors of natural woods, open fires, and flagstone floors create a warm, welcoming environment that invites lingering, even if you shun the excellent activities programs and only drink in the scenic grandeur and tranquility that surround you. You're quite welcome to do just that, but be warned—so congenial are the staff and so well planned are the programs that many a dedicated "do-nothing" guest has wound up happily involved in each day's activities. There are classes in surfing, canoeing, boardsailing, waterskiing, sailing, horseback riding, hill walking, rock climbing, and archery, as well as special activity programs for children. Needless to say, I am personally hooked on this place and plan to return many times in the future—and I'm *not* an outdoor type! Write for their excellent brochure that outlines facilities and programs in detail.

2 County Mayo

Like County Galway, eastern County Mayo is also flat, and it was near Cong, on the Plain of Southern Moytura, that a prehistoric battle raged between Tuatha De Danann and the Firbolgs, ending in the first defeat of the latter, who declined in power afterward until they were crushed forever seven years later in Sligo.

Northeast of Cong is the small village of Knock, a shrine to the many visions reported here and a place of pilgrimage for thousands of Christians. Pilgrims gather on the last Sunday in July each year to walk barefoot in the steps of St. Patrick to the summit of Croagh Patrick on Clew Bay's southern shore.

Connected to the mainland by a causeway, Achill Island presents a mountainous face to the sea, its foot ringed by golden sandy strands.

CONG

There are several good reasons to turn toward Cong—the magnificent ruins of an Augustinian abbey, Ashrod Castle, and the fact that it was in this locale that most of the film classic *The Quiet Man* was filmed.

Cong is a picturesque little village where, in a phenomenon known as "The Rising of the Waters," the waters of Lough Mask, which go underground three miles to the north, come rushing to the surface to surge through the center of town before they dissipate into several streams that empty into Lough Corrib. At the edge of town, the **Royal Abbey Cong** was built by Turlough Mor O'Connor, High King of Ireland, in 1120 on the site of an earlier 7th-century St. Fechin community. Considered to be one of the finest early-Christian architectural relics in the country, it is also the final resting place of Rory O'Connor, the last High King, who was buried here in 1198.

ASHFORD CASTLE AND THE QUIET MAN

You'll find **Ashford Castle** just outside Cong on the shores of Lough Corrib. The oldest part of the castle was built by the de Burgoes, an Anglo-Norman family, in 1228, and its keep is now a part of the impressive, slightly eccentric Ashford Castle Hotel, which also incorporates a French-château-style mansion of the Oranmore and Browne families built in the early 1700s and the additions made by Sir Benjamin Guinness in the mid-1800s (undertaken as much to provide employment for famine-starved natives as to improve the property). It's a marvelous, fairyland sort of concoction that makes a superb luxury hotel favored by international celebrities (President and Mrs. Reagan stayed here during their 1984 visit). No less marvelous are its grounds, with beautifully landscaped lawns sloping down to the island-dotted lake. While its rates are definitely out of reach for budgeteers, not so for a stroll through its elegant public rooms with massive fireplaces and wall-high oil paintings, or a drink in the **Dungeon Bar.** Not a penny charged to soak in all that luxurious beauty!

Now, about *The Quiet Man:* Successive generations of Americans have loved Ireland as a direct result of the antics of John Wayne, Maureen O'Hara, and Barry Fitzgerald as they romped through this film, which has become a classic. So I've done a little research, and if you want to track down some of the locales, look for these. (Also, if you can get a good crack going in one of Cong's pubs, there's bound to be a local there who remembers the filming and has tales to tell, like how some scenes had to be reshot many times because the inquisitive head of a local "extra" would be seen peering out from a hedge in the background.) Many of the exterior shots were taken on the grounds of Ashford Castle—the woodlands, the church, Squire Danaher's house, and the salmon river with its arched bridge. The main village street scenes took place near the cross in the market square of Cong, and the nearby general store was transformed into Cohan's Bar for the picture. Over in front of the abbey, that pretty house you see at the side of the bridge was the Reverend Playfair's house. Many other locales, such as John Wayne's ancestral cottage (now a ruin near Maam Bridge) were shot on the hillsides of the Maam Valley in County Galway, and the village of Inishfree as seen from a distance at the very beginning of the film is actually a shot of Clifden, taken from the Sky Road. There, that should get you started—and one simple comment in a Cong pub will carry you a long way in the footsteps of *The Quiet Man.*

The Prehistoric Plain of Moytura

Immediately east of Cong toward Cross lies the Plain of Moytura, where you'll find the **Ballymagibbon Cairn.** Dating from about 3,000 B.C., the 60-foot-high, 129-yard-circumference cairn was erected to commemorate a fierce prehistoric battle between the Firbolg and de Danann tribes. It seems that the Firbolgs carried the day during the early fighting, and that first evening each presented a stone and the head of a Danann to his king, who used the stones to build the cairn in honor of the grisly tribute.

On a happier note, nearby Moytura House (privately owned and not open to the public) was once the home of Sir William Wilde and his wife, Speranza, parents of Oscar Wilde.

Ballintubber Abbey

North of Cong lies the little town of Partry, four miles north of which you will find Ballintubber Abbey. It is the only church in the English-speaking world with a 7½-century history of uninterrupted services. What makes this all the more remarkable is that mass has been said within its walls since 1216 despite years of religious suppression, two burnings, and the assault of Cromwellian troops. At times during those centuries it was necessary for supplicants to kneel before the altar in secret and under open skies when there was no roof. That it has now been completely restored is due almost solely to the devoted efforts of its pastor, Father Egan, who labored from 1963 to 1966 to push the project forward. The abbey's doors are open every day and visitors are welcomed.

WHERE TO STAY

Hazel Grove

Drumsheel, Cong, Co. Mayo. ☎ **092/46060.** 5 rms, 4 with bath. IR£15 ($24) single without bath; IR£13 ($20.80) per person sharing without bath; IR£3 ($4.80) per person additional with bath. 20% reduction for children. (Rates include breakfast.) Dinner IR£11 ($17.60) extra. No credit cards. Closed Dec–Mar.

Mrs. Ann Coakley will welcome you warmly to her luxurious, modern bungalow with its pretty garden about half a mile from the village. The house is centrally heated, and guest rooms are nicely done up.

Lydon Lodge

Cong, Co. Mayo. ☎ **092/46053.** 6 rms, all with bath. IR£17 ($27.20) per person. (Rates include breakfast.) Dinner IR£15 ($24) extra. ACC, MC, V. Closed Oct–Mar.

Mrs. Carmel Lydon's large, modern house in the village is built in the Georgian style. Set on Lough Corrib (boats available for rent) and near Ashford Castle, the house is nicely decorated throughout, with comfortable guest rooms, central heating, and parking.

Robins Roost

Drumsheel, Cong, Co. Mayo. ☎ **092/46051.** 5 rms, none with bath. IR£15 ($24) single; IR£13 ($20.80) per person sharing. Dinner IR£12 ($19.20). No credit cards. Open June–Oct.

Among other things, Mrs. Christine Lydon has been praised by readers for her beautiful garden and charming breakfast room. Her breakfasts and evening meals are pretty special, the latter often featuring local salmon and trout. Cong village is a short (about one mile) walk away, down a quiet road.

EN ROUTE TO WESTPORT

If your northward route from Connemara heads directly for Westport, I suggest you leave the main road (N59) at Aasleagh and turn northwest on R335, which passes through stony, barren hillsides to Louisburgh, where Clew Bay opens before you.

At Louisburgh, visit the ✪ **Granuaile Interpretive Centre,** Chapel Street (☎ 098/66195), to see mementoes of the fascinating pirate Grace O'Malley ("Granuaile"), who roamed the waters of Clew Bay.

Offshore, at the mouth of Clew Bay, ✪ **Clare Island** was a Granuaile stronghold; and a day trip to the island, with its 15th-century abbey and spectacular views of Clew Bay and the mountains of Connemara and Mayo, explains her deep love of the place. The mailboat has regular sailings, and for details about signing on as a passenger, contact Chris O'Grady, Bay View Hotel, Clare Island, County Mayo (☎ 098/26307 or 25380).

Between Louisburgh and Westport, the drive (R335) touches the bay at several points, and on the other side of the road rises 2,510-foot high **Croagh Patrick,** where St. Patrick is believed to have fasted for 40 days, and modern-day pilgrims climb the stony paths in their bare feet in July for a 4am mass at its top.

WHERE TO STAY

Self-Catering

Lakeshore Holiday Home

Cahir, Ballinrobe, Co. Mayo. ☎ **092/41389** or 63081. Fax 091/65201. 1 bungalow (sleeps six). Apr–June and Sept IR£100 ($160) per week; July–Aug IR£250 ($400) per week; lower rates other months. No credit cards.

With spectacular views of Lough Mask and the mountains, this modern bungalow has three bedrooms (one double bed, four single beds, and two cots). The kitchen has a microwave oven, and there's a barbecue in the garden. Great for quiet walks in the surrounding countryside or as a base for touring Connemara and County Mayo.

WESTPORT

Dating back to 1731, ✪ **Westport House** (☎ 098/25141 or 25430) sits on the grounds of an earlier O'Malley castle, the dungeons of which are now visited by children who are happily "terrified" by the terrors that have been installed for their entertainment. The lovely old Georgian mansion house is a virtual museum of Irish memorabilia and craftsmanship, with a magnificent drawing room, two dining rooms (one large, one small), a long gallery, and a grand entrance hall. Up the marble staircase, four bedrooms hold such treasures as state robes and coronets and 200-year-old Chinese wallpaper.

Lord and Lady Altamont and their five daughters are in residence here, and over the years they have turned their estate into a stylish visitor attraction as a means of maintaining such an expensive operation. There is an antique shop and a gift shop; two giant slides (the Slippery Dip and a Hill Slide); a miniature half-mile-long railway through the grounds; a children's zoo; and boating on the lake. A good family outing.

Note: There are cottages and apartments for rent on the Westport House Country Estate grounds, as well as a beautiful caravan and camping park with a food store, laundry room, recreation rooms, pitch-and-putt, tennis, and a bar with regular live music. On request, the Altamonts will send an informative brochure.

Admission IR£6 ($9.60) adults, IR£3 ($4.80) children, IR£17 ($27.20) family ticket for house and zoo.

Open mid-May to mid-Sept, daily 2–5pm; longer hours July–Aug and Sat–Sun.

A Drop-In at a Pub

A nice end of a Westport day is a drop-in to **Matt Malloy's Pub.** Matt's claim to fame is as the flute player with the Chieftains, and you may just catch him in residence.

WHERE TO STAY

Cedar Lodge

Kings Hill, Newport Rd., Westport, Co. Mayo. ☎ **098/25417.** 4 rms, 3 with shower. IR£20 ($32) single; IR£14 ($22.40) per person sharing; IR£2 ($3.20) per person extra with bath. (Rates include breakfast.) No credit cards.

You'll be greeted with a welcome cuppa on arrival at Maureen Flynn's split-level bungalow on route N59. The house sits on beautifully landscaped grounds, and is only a short walk from the seafront and the town center. The tastefully furnished guest rooms are a refuge in this quiet location, and there's private parking.

Rath-A-Rosa

Rosbeg, Westport, Co. Mayo. ☎ **098/25348.** 5 rms, 4 with bath. IR£16 ($25.60) single without bath; IR£14 ($22.40) per person sharing without bath; IR£2 ($3.20) per person additional with bath. (Rates include breakfast.) Dinner IR£15 ($24) extra. ACC, MC, V. Closed Nov–mid-Mar.

This modern farmhouse 1½ miles from Westport on the Louisburgh road (R335) has magnificent views across Clew Bay to the mountains of Achill Island. Mary

O'Brien, the lady of the house, is known far and wide for her cooking, using the freshest of ingredients and locally grown meats, as well as fish straight from local waters. Dinners must be booked before noon. The breakfast menu often features just-caught mackerel along with Mary's special mustard sauce. Husband John, a fluent Gaelic speaker, is a witty and informative conversationalist. There's central heating and never a problem with parking. With advance notice, the O'Briens are happy to arrange golfing, freshwater or deep-sea fishing, cycling, hill climbing, or horseback riding.

A Nearby Fishing Lodge

Traenlaur Lodge

Louch Feeagh, Newport, Co. Mayo. ☎ **098/41358.** 32 beds; self-catering facilities. IR£6 ($9.60) for adults, IR£4.50 ($7.20) for under 18s. No credit cards.

Located 13 miles from Westport and five miles from Newport, in a 250-year-old fishing lodge on a famed salmon lake, this is a superior hostel for outdoors enthusiasts. Activities at the hostel or nearby include hill walking, fishing, and swimming, and there are bicycles for rent. Letterkeen Forest, nature walks, and a salmon research center are nearby points of interest, as well as the 9th-century Burrishule Abbey and Rockfleet Castle. There's also traditional music nearby at least one evening a week. Home-cooked meals are available by reservation.

Where to Eat

✪ The Asgard Tavern and Restaurant

The Quay, Westport. ☎ **098/25319.** Reservations not required. Bar food less than IR£5 ($8); lunch IR£7–IR£9 ($11.20–$14.40); dinner IR£15–IR£17 ($24–$27.20). AE, DC, MC, V. BAR FOOD/SEAFOOD/IRISH/VEGETARIAN.

This is a delightful nautical pub where owners Mary and Michael Cadden serve award-winning seafood dishes as well as bar snacks. In the evening, you'll usually find traditional or folk music here. It's a bright, cozy place, and among the menu items not to be missed are the seafood chowder, quiche Lorraine, smoked salmon, garlic steak, and barbecued spareribs.

ACHILL ISLAND

Achill is Ireland's largest island, and its 57 square miles are connected to the mainland by a causeway that takes you into breathtakingly beautiful, unspoiled, and varied scenery. High cliffs overlook tiny villages of whitewashed cottages, golden

Readers Recommend

Coral Reef, Lecanvey, Westport, Co. Mayo. ☎ 098/64814. *"Mrs. Anne Colgan is a knowledgeable and gracious hostess. Coral Reef is several cuts above the usual B&B in appearance and facilities and sits at the foot of Croagh Patrick. Dinners are superlative, and breakfasts include cheese, yogurt, and fruit."*

—Kathleen Horoszewski, Whippany, NJ

Moher House, Liscarney, Westport, Co. Mayo. ☎ 098/21360. *"Marian and Tommy O'Malley are charming hosts. On our arrival, we had hot scones and coffee. Marian served an evening meal, which was just superb. After dinner we were treated to an Irish coffee. The guest book is full of glowing tributes."*

—Patrick and Brigid Talty, Rocky River, OH

beaches, and heathery boglands. The signposted **Atlantic Drive** is spectacular, and will whet your appetite to explore more of the island's well-surfaced roadways. This is a wild and at the same time profoundly peaceful place, peopled by friendly, hardy natives who welcome visitors warmly. In late May the entire island is covered by such a profusion of rhododendrons that my bed-and-breakfast landlady smilingly told me, "every car that leaves will be loaded with those blooms, and we won't even miss them!" Achill has long been a favorite holiday spot for the Irish from other parts of the country, and there are good accommodations available in most of the beach villages. If time permits, I highly recommend an overnight stay on Achill (in summer there's traditional music in many of the pubs), but if you can only spare a part of a day, this is one off-the-beaten-track place you really shouldn't miss.

Where to Stay

✪ Rockmount

Achill Island, Co. Mayo. ☎ **098/45272.** 4 rms, 3 with bath. IR£18 ($28.80) single without bath; IR£13 ($20.80) per person sharing without bath; IR£2 ($3.20) per person additional with bath. 25% reduction for children. (Rates include breakfast.) High tea IR£8 ($12.80); dinner, IR£11 ($17.60). No credit cards.

This modern bungalow, set at the eastern edge of the village and convenient to a bus stop, is the home of Mrs. Frances Masterson, who happily shares her knowledge of the island with guests. Guest rooms are all comfortably furnished, and during my last stay, other guests included natives who had come from other parts of the country to holiday here, making for lively Irish conversation. Central heating and off-street parking.

Teach Mwewillin

Currane, Achill Island, Co. Mayo. ☎ **098/45134.** 4 rms, 3 with bath. IR£18.50–IR£19.50 ($29.60–$31.20) single; IR£13.50–IR£14.50 ($21.60–$23.20) per person sharing. 50% reduction for children. (Rates include breakfast.) Dinner IR£11 ($17.60) extra. Closed Nov–Mar.

Across the sound and 5½ miles from Achill Island, this modern bungalow sits on a hill overlooking sound and island. Mrs. Margo Cannon keeps a pony for children to ride, and gladly helps guests arrange fishing, sailing, or golf. Guest rooms are attractive and nicely furnished. Central heating and good parking.

West Coast House

School Road, Dooagh, Achill Island, Co. Mayo. ☎ **098/43317.** Fax 098/43317. 3 rms, 2 with bath. IR£18.50–IR£20 ($29.60–$32) single; IR£13.50–IR£14.50 ($21.60–$23.20) per person sharing. Dinner IR£11 ($17.60). 20% reduction for children. No credit cards. 1 mile from Keel.

Mrs. Teresa McNamara's modern bungalow sits in a quiet location, just off the main road, surrounded by some of Achill's most spectacular scenery. Even the bedrooms have gorgeous views, and each comes with orthopedic beds and electric blankets. Evening meals feature the freshest of seafoods. Mrs. O'Gorman also has bicycles (a great way to get around the island) for hire. Central heating and private parking. This is a no-smoking house.

Where to Eat

Most of the hotels on Achill Island serve excellent meals, and pubs offer good bar food.

The Boley House Restaurant

Keel. ☎ **098/43147.** Set dinner IR£18.50 ($29.60). ACC, MC, V. Daily 6–10pm.

Boley House owner Tom McNamara is committed to using only the freshest ingredients. Straight from local or nearby waters, fish and other seafoods come to table in specialties like the popular monkfish Provençale. If fish is not to your taste, opt for the roasted free-range duckling.

CASTLEBAR

Only 11 miles northeast of Westport via N60, Castlebar is the county town. If you have read *The Year of the French,* you will remember that this is where Humbert's French forces won a complete rout over the English in 1798. In modern times, it is the birthplace of one of Ireland's top politicians, Charles Haughey, and it's a good base for touring County Mayo.

If you're touring Ireland in October, check for dates of the **Castlebar International Song Festival,** which annually draws big crowds from around the world for a week of singing, dancing, and general revelry.

WHERE TO STAY

Lakeview House

Westport Rd., Castlebar, Co. Mayo. ☎ **094/22374.** 4 rms, all with bath. IR£8.50 ($29.60) single; IR£14 ($22.40) per person sharing. 20% reduction for children. (Rates include breakfast.) No credit cards. Closed Christmas. Paved car park.

Mary and Joe Moran's bungalow sits on spacious grounds with a large, sloping lawn out front, 2 1/2 miles from Castlebar on the Westport road. This was Mary's family home area, and both lounge (with fireplace) and dining room look out to green fields and rolling hills. Mary bakes her own brown bread and scones and is always happy to share the recipe with guests (a frequent request). The four pretty guest rooms include one family-size room (two double beds) with private bath. Central heating.

✪ Shalom

Westport Rd., Castlebar, Co. Mayo. ☎ **094/21471**. 3 rms, none with bath. IR£18.50 ($29.60) single; IR£14 ($22.40) per person sharing. 50% reduction for children. (Rates include breakfast.) No credit cards. Closed mid-Oct to mid-Mar.

Noreen Raftery and her husband Liam, who is a Garda, take a personal interest in their guests, and conversations around the turf fire in their lounge have elicited glowing letters from readers. The three nice guest rooms have sinks and built-in wardrobes, and there's one family-size room with a double and a twin bed. Central heating and good parking. Shalom is 1 1/4 miles from Castlebar on N60.

WHERE TO EAT

✪ Davitt Restaurant and Lounge Bar

Rush St. ☎ **094/22233.** Reservations recommended for dinner. Lunch IR£5–IR£6 ($8–$9.60); dinner IR£15 ($24). AE, MC, V. Daily 12:30–11:30pm. Closed Good Friday, Christmas Day. INTERNATIONAL/IRISH/SEAFOOD/VEGETARIAN.

This is an attractive bar/restaurant, with traditional leaded windows and a warm, friendly staff. Owner Raymond Kenny has a devoted local following, a testament to his fine continental creations and wonderful traditional Irish dishes. Garlic-filled chicken Kiev is terrific, and other specialties are carpetbagger steak, Mexican beef kebabs, and sole garnished with prawns and lobster sauce. Good service.

KNOCK

Twenty-five miles southeast of Castlebar, the little church in the village of Knock has become a shrine to which thousands of pilgrims come each year, for it was here, on August 17, 1879, that an apparition of Our Lady was seen at the **Church of St. John the Baptist.** After a Commission of Enquiry ruled that the apparition was genuine, Knock was officially designated a Marian Shrine. When mass pilgrimages became too much for the little church, a magnificent basilica was built on the grounds, and a highlight of the shrine's history was the visit of Pope John Paul II in 1979. Those huge crowds of pilgrims also prompted a long and eventually successful campaign for an airport to serve Knock.

On the south side of the basilica, the **Knock Folk Museum** (☎ 094/88100) portrays life in the west of Ireland around the time of the apparition through exhibits that illustrate folk life, history, archeology, and religion. It's open July and August, from 10am to 7pm daily; May, June, September, and October, from 10am to 6pm daily; other months by appointment.

WHERE TO STAY

Ashfort

Galway-Knock road, Charlestown, Co. Mayo. ☎ **094/54706.** 5 rms, 1 with bath. IR£18.50–IR£19.50 ($29.60–$31.20) single; IR£13.50–IR£14.50 ($21.60–$23.20) per person sharing. 20% reduction for children. No credit cards. Open March–Nov.

Philip and Carol O'Gorman's striking two-story Tudor-style home is the perfect base for exploring this part of the West, from Connemara to Castlebar and Ballina to Knock to Sligo. Guest rooms are exceptionally well appointed, and the O'Gormans are the epitome of Irish hospitality.

Riverside

Charlestown, Co. Mayo. ☎ **094/54200.** 7 rms, 6 with shower. IR£14.50 ($23.20) per person sharing. IR£4 ($6.40) single supplement. 33 1/3% reduction for children. (Rates include breakfast.) Dinner IR£10–IR£17.50 ($16–$20). ACC, MC, V.

Mrs. Evelyn O'Hara is the delightful hostess of this attractive, century-old, family home, northeast of Knock in Charlestown at the intersection of N5 and N17. Guest rooms are quite comfortable. There is also a family-run, award-winning restaurant with good food at moderate prices, open from February to December, and an enclosed car park.

FOXFORD

About 20 miles north of Castlebar en route to Ballina, stop in the little village of Foxford and spend an hour or so at ✪ **Foxford Woollen Mills** (☎ 094/56104 or 56756; fax 094/56415). The industry was set up by a nun, Sister Arsenius, in 1892, as a means of providing work for the many unemployed in the area. Since then, it has grown into one of the country's leading plants, producing world-renowned blankets, tweeds, and rugs. Be sure to allow enough time to go through the Visitors Centre to see the multimedia presentation of the mill's history, after which you might go along on the Industrial Tour of the mill. There's a good restaurant on the premises, and, of course, a mill shop. It's open Monday through Saturday from 10am to 6pm and on Sunday from 2 to 6pm, with a small admission fee to the exhibitions and tour.

BALLINA

Set on the banks of the River Moy, 31 miles northeast of Westport, Ballina is the largest town in County Mayo, as well as the cathedral town for the Catholic diocese of Killala. There are pleasant river walks in the town, and if fishing is your cup of tea, this is one of Ireland's best angling centers, especially noted for salmon fishing.

Pipe smokers should look for ✪ **Gaughan's Pub** in O'Rahilly Street, a pub that has changed little in the last half century. Along with a popular public house trade, Edward Gaughan carries on a well-loved tobacco counter started by his father, Michael, and is adept at matching smokers with the appropriate pipe. The pub also serves an excellent lunch special Monday through Friday.

A short drive farther northwest on R314 will bring you to one of the world's best preserved relics of Stone Age rural life. The ✪ **Ceide Fields,** 22 miles northwest of Ballina and 5 miles northwest of Ballycastle, is the oldest enclosed farm system in the world, a rural landscape of more than 5,000 years ago that was revealed virtually intact underneath the bogs of north County Mayo. In the 12-square-mile site, the remarkably preserved remains include stone walls that surrounded the ancient community and magnificent tombs. There's a Visitors Centre (☎ 096/43325), open daily from 9:30am to 6:30pm from May to mid-September (shorter hours other months), and there's a small admission charge.

Eight miles north of Ballina via R314, Killala's small harbor was the landing place for French forces under the command of General Humbert in 1798. There's a fine round tower, and nearby well-preserved ruins of 15th-century Moyne Abbey include a six-story square tower.

WHERE TO STAY

Cnoc Breandain

Quay Rd., Ballina, Co. Mayo. ☎ **096/22145.** 4 rms, all with bath. IR£18.50 ($29.60) single; IR£14.50 ($23.20) per person sharing. (Rates include breakfast.) Dinner IR£12 ($19.20) extra. 25% reduction for children. No credit cards. Closed Oct–Apr.

Some 3 miles from Ballina on the Enniscrone road (1.2 miles past the Riverboat Inn), this country home overlooks the Moy estuary. Mary O'Dowd is especially known for her warm hospitality, and her home is a haven of graciousness and comfort. Central heating and plenty of private parking.

San Remo

Bunree, Sligo Rd., Ballina, Co. Mayo. ☎ **096/70162.** 4 rms, all with bath. IR£20 ($32) single; IR£15 ($24) per person sharing. (Rates include breakfast.) No credit cards. Closed Christmas.

Mrs. Patricia Murphy Curham is the gracious hostess here. The house is a little over a mile from the town center, and guest rooms are tastefully furnished.

Readers Recommend

Bayview, Knockmore, Ballina, Co. Mayo. ☎ 094/58240. *"Set on Lough Conn, Bayview is owned and operated by Mr. and Mrs. Bernie Canavan. Mrs. Canavan not only prevailed on a family friend to take me fishing, but also cooked my catch of trout and refused payment for the meal! Though of tender age, the Canavan boys provided room service with distinction."* —J. G. Cummings, Silver Spring, MD

Where to Eat

Murphy Bros. Pub and Restaurant

Clare St. ☎ **096/22702.** Bar food under IR£6 ($9.60); main courses IR£7–IR£16 ($11.20–$25.60). No credit cards. Mon–Sat, bar food 12:30–2:30pm and 5–8pm; restaurant dinners 5–10pm. BAR FOOD/SEAFOOD/STEAK/PASTA.

Paul and Allen Murphy's beautifully appointed 19th-century style pub, winner of the Black-and-White Provincial Super Pub Award, should rightly be called (in *this* female's opinion) "Brothers and Sister," since it is their sister Gina who supervises the upstairs verandah overlooking the River Moy. Seafood creations like Monkfish and Prawn Aioli (monkfish cubes sautéed with tiger prawns in a garlic, wine, and cream sauce) set your mouth watering, and non-fishy dishes are equally appealing. Lighter offerings include salads, burgers, and a good selection of pastas.

BELMULLET

Belmullet, 39 miles west of Ballina, is the gateway to the ✪ **Mullet Peninsula,** where the soaring Cliffs of Erris open up breathtaking seascapes.

Where to Stay

Drom Caoin

Belmullet, Co. Mayo. ☎ **097/81195.** Fax 097/82292. 4 rms, none with bath. IR£18 ($28.80) single; IR£13.50 ($21.60) per person sharing. (Rates include breakfast.) Dinner IR£12 ($19.20) extra. 33 1/3% reduction for children. No credit cards. Closed Christmas.

Mrs. Mairin Maguire-Murphy is the accommodating hostess in this modern home just a short walk from the village center. The view of Blacksod Bay is terrific, and guest rooms are quite comfortable. Mairin will prepare vegetarian or other alternative evening meals if requested. There's central heat and private parking.

18 Counties Sligo & Leitrim

The Northwest is not so much a place that offers things to "do" as it is a region to be experienced and absorbed. There are special places you won't want to miss, but mostly you'll remember the sense of tuning in to a part of your inner self that all too often has been lost in the frenetic pace at which most of us gallop through modern life.

It was this region, with some of Ireland's most wondrous landscapes of sea and mountains and far-flung vistas, that shaped the poet Yeats's life and work. His words about this part of Ireland cannot, of course, be bested, and you will find yourself recalling them again and again as you travel the Northwest.

All through the county are countless cairns, dolmens, passage graves, and other prehistoric relics, bearing silent witness to the lives that so engaged the poet. Along the western part of the county are the Ox Mountains; the north holds high, flat-topped limestone hills like Benbulben; and for the pleasure-bent traveler, there's a fine beach at Strandhill, a golf course at Rosses Point, and good fishing in any number of rivers and lakes.

1 Sligo Town

Sligo (Sligeach, "Shelly Place") grew up around a ford of the River Garavogue, which rises in Lough Gill and tumbles over swift rapids as it approaches its estuary. The town's strategic position gave it early prominence as a seaport; as a religious center, it's the cathedral town of both a Catholic and a Protestant diocese. For Yeats devotees and scholars, it offers a wealth of information and memorabilia, and all visitors will find a friendly welcome and accommodations that are friendly to the budget.

ORIENTATION

GETTING THERE **By Plane** Aer Lingus has daily flights between Sligo and Dublin. For schedules, fares, and booking, phone Sligo Airport at Strandhill (☎ 071/68280).

By Train/Bus There's train service from Dublin to Sligo, with stops in Longford and Carrick-on-Shannon. Good bus connections are available from around the country. The bus and railway station is just above Lord Edward Street on the western edge of town. For schedule information, call 071/60066.

ESSENTIALS

Sligo's telephone area code is 071. The General Post Office is on Wine Street, west of the bridge, open Monday through Saturday from 9am to 5:30pm.

VISITOR INFORMATION

You'll find the tourist office on Temple Street (☎ 071/61201), open daily from 9am to 6pm, and until 8pm in July and August.

TOWN LAYOUT

Sligo sits astride the River Garavogue. The Hyde Bridge at Stephen Street (named for Ireland's first president, Dr. Douglas Hyde) is a central point of reference. O'Connell Street runs south of the bridge and holds the major shopping and business district of the town. The Sligo Regional Airport is located at the beach resort of Strandhill, five miles to the west. Rosses Point is five miles to the north. Several buses a day run to Strandhill and Rosses Point from the main bus station.

Yeats is buried in Drumcliffe Churchyard, five miles north of town.

GETTING AROUND **By Taxi** For taxi service, call 071/43000 or 45577; there's a taxi rank at the train station and one at Quay Street. Fares are preset to most points of interest, and cabs are not metered, so be sure to ask the fare.

On Foot Sligo town is well laid out and compact, and the best possible way to appreciate its interesting narrow streets is on foot. There are guided and self-guided walking tours available (see below), but simply rambling around the town is a real delight.

ORGANIZED TOURS **Walking Tours** The Tourist Office has an excellent booklet that outlines a signposted **Tourist Trail** do-it-yourself walking tour (a nice souvenir, even if you go along with the guided tour described below).

To get the most out of your stay in Sligo town, join one of the walking tours conducted during July and August by young **student guides** who love the town and are intimately acquainted with all major points of interest. Tours leave the Tourist Office at 11am and last one hour and 15 minutes. It's perfectly in order to tip your enthusiastic young guide a minimum of IR£2 ($3.20).

Bus Tours Bus Eireann's day tours from Sligo include the Hills of Donegal and Glenveagh National Park, with adult fares of IR£10 ($16), half that for children.

SPECIAL EVENTS For two weeks every August there's a glut of activity in Sligo centered around the works of William Butler Yeats. That's when the **Yeats International Summer School** presents seminars, lectures, workshops, poetry readings, and dramas for dedicated Yeats scholars. Afternoon tours are conducted, and evenings are filled with social and theatrical events. Tuition is in the IR£250 to IR£300 ($410 to $480) range, and the staff will help you find inexpensive accommodations. For full details, exact dates, a brochure, and an application, contact the Secretary, Yeats English Language Institute, Hyde Bridge, Sligo, County Sligo (☎ 071/44741; fax 071/42780). If you should happen into Sligo while the summer school is in session, you can attend many of the events by buying individual tickets.

FESTIVALS The week following Easter is dedicated to the ✪ **Feiseanna,** with competitions in traditional music, dancing, singing, plays, and all sorts of other activities. It draws the Irish from all over the country, and the town is alive with festivities day and night.

The **Sligo Arts Festival** is a joyous street fair, when the town comes alive with music that ranges from the classics to rock and roll, a feast of visual arts, and spectacular fireworks. For specific dates and accommodations information, contact Sligo Arts Festival, Business Centre, Market Yard, Sligo, Country Sligo (☎ 071/69802).

WHAT TO SEE & DO

While many visitors come to Sligo and head straight out to those spots associated with Yeats, it would be a mistake not to see the highlights of the old town itself.

THE TOP ATTRACTIONS

✪ County Sligo Museum and Yeats Art Gallery

Stephen St. ☎ **071/42212.** Admission free. Museum, daily 10:30am–12:30pm and 2:30–4:30pm. Gallery, June–Sept, Tues–Sat 10:30am–12:30pm and 2:30–4:30pm. Both are open other months by arrangement with the tourist board.

Located in a pretty 1851 chapel, this museum holds many interesting exhibits relating to the poet W. B. Yeats, including a complete collection of his poetry written from 1889 to 1936 and an extensive collection of his prose and plays. The gallery, housed in former schoolrooms, is dedicated to his artist brother, Jack Yeats. The gallery, in fact, contains Ireland's largest collection of his drawings and paintings, as well as works by his contemporaries.

Yeats Memorial Building

Hyde Bridge. ☎ **071/42693.** Admission free. June–Aug, Mon–Fri 2–5pm.

This 1895 red-brick building beside Hyde Bridge is headquarters for the Sligo Yeats Society, the ultimate source of information on the poet. It also houses the **Sligo Art Gallery,** the setting for changing art exhibitions.

ARCHITECTURAL HIGHLIGHTS

Sligo's streets are literally filled with quaint old shopfronts and 19th-century buildings of architectural interest. The following are outstanding:

Town Hall, on Quay Street, which dates from 1865, is a graceful, Italian Renaissance building that legend says stands on the site of a 17th-century Cromwellian fort. At Teeling Street and Chapel Street, the **Courthouse** incorporates part of the earlier courthouse. In 1832, when cholera swept over Sligo, the building housed coffin builders. You can't miss the impressive **Pollexfen Ships** building at the corner of Adelaide Street and Wine Street. The large stone building originally belonged to the largest ship owners in Sligo, who provided the sail power to transport thousands of emigrants to Canada and America in the 1860s. When Yeats's grandfather owned the building, he added the tower as a lookout point for his ships returning to port.

On Adelaide Street, the **Cathedral of the Immaculate Conception** is a massive limestone structure of Renaissance Romanesque style. ✪ **Sligo Dominican Abbey,** on Abbey Street, is the town's only surviving medieval building, built in the mid-1400s to replace a 1250s structure destroyed by fire. **St. John's Church,** on John Street, dates from the mid-1700s and was designed by the same architect as Leinster House, the seat of the Irish government in Dublin. Its churchyard makes for interesting rambles among headstones that go as far back as the mid-1600s.

Sligo Town

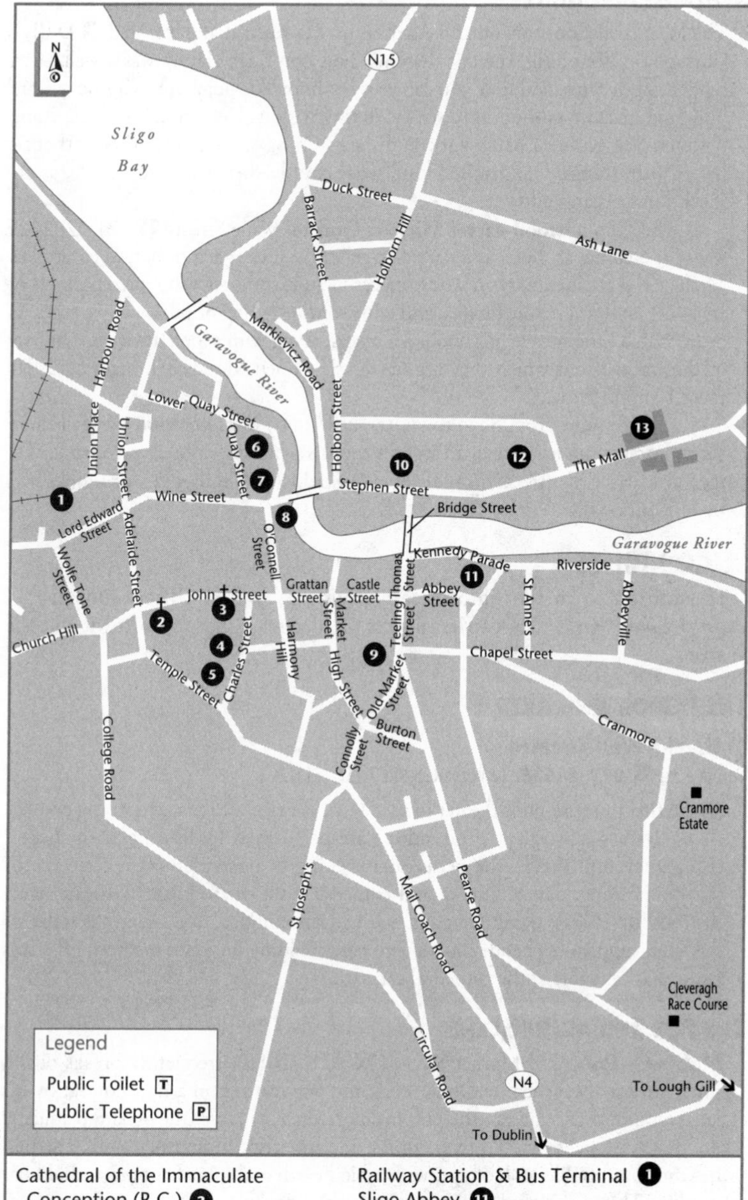

Cathedral of the Immaculate Conception (R.C.) 2
Town Hall 6
Courthouse 9
General Hospital 13
Hawks Well Theatre 4
Model Arts Centre 12
Post Office 7
Railway Station & Bus Terminal 1
Sligo Abbey 11
Sligo Art Gallery 8
Sligo County Museum & Art Gallery 10
St. John's Cathedral (C. of I.) 3
Tourist Information Office 5
Yeats Memorial Building 8

Other Attractions

The local Irish Countrywoman's Association has rescued and restored ✪ **Dolly's Cottage,** in Strandhill, the last thatched house in Sligo. Dolly was a well-loved resident of the area, and now you can visit her home Monday through Friday from 3 to 5pm in summer months to see the dresser with its Delft-chinawear collection, a pouch bed with its patchwork quilt, a spinning wheel, and other authentic period furnishings. Handcrafted knit, wool, and leather items are on sale, as are sheepskin rugs and pottery.

✪ The shop of **wood-carver Michael Quirke,** Wine Street (☎ 071/42624 or 45800), qualifies as much as a sculpture gallery as it does a commercial enterprise. Michael is a fascinating artist whose pieces include some superb representations of Ireland's mythical heroic figures, and with your browsing or purchase, he supplies more than a little storytelling about his pieces, along with expert advice on the care of the woods from which they are made. He's open Monday through Saturday from 10am to 5pm.

Just three miles from Sligo town, the little town of Hazelwood on Halfmoon Bay is home to no fewer than 13 wood sculptors whose workshops are open to visitors. Ask at the Tourist Office for their ✪ **Sculpture Trail** guide, or simply stop by on your own.

SLIGO NIGHTS

In addition to current information from the Tourist Office, consult *The Sligo Champion,* which carries notices of current goings-on in town and the area.

The Performing Arts

✪ Hawks Well Theatre

Temple St. ☎ **071/61526.** Tickets IR£5–IR£7 ($8–$11.20).

As the first purpose-built theater in the West, Hawks Well places a strong emphasis on Irish playwrights, productions are performed by leading Irish theater companies, and there's the occasional evening of poetry, musical concerts, or traditional song, dance, drama, and comedy. It's a small, intimate theater with the most up-to-date equipment and, with advance notice, facilities in the stalls for the handicapped. It's beside the tourist board building on Temple Street; off-street parking is available at the cathedral car park.

The Pub and Music Scene

McLynn's Pub, Old Market Street (☎ 071/42088), frequently breaks out in song, almost always led by Donal McLynn, who carries on a tradition set by his late grandmother, who ran the pub for more than 30 years (the ogham plaque by the doorway spells out "Granny" in the ancient script in her memory). The pub has the comfortable look of age, with a big hearth and lots of copper and old bar mirrors. The crowd tends to be on the young side, and you can usually count on ballads on Thursday.

Another gathering place is in Ballisodare, a few miles south of Sligo town via N4. **The Thatch,** Ballisodare (☎ 071/67288), is a small cottage pub with a huge fireplace and church-pew seats in one of its two rooms, and kitchen furnishings in the other. There's usually music on Thursday.

On the bridge at Drumcliffe, the **Yeats Tavern,** Drumcliffe (☎ 071/63117), has nightly musical goings-on all year in a very popular, modern setting. It's out the Donegal road, about five miles from town.

Not for music, but for a uniquely traditional Irish "local," where the crack is good and your company welcome, is ✪ **Hargedon's,** O'Connell Street (☎ 071/70933). It's more than two centuries old and is as authentic as they come (see also "Where to Eat," below).

WHERE TO STAY

IN AND AROUND TOWN

✪ Aisling

Cairns Hill, Sligo, Co. Sligo. ☎ **071/60704.** 5 rms, 3 with bath. TV. IR£18.50 ($29.60) single; IR£14 ($22.40) per person sharing. IR£1.50 ($2.40) per person extra with bath. (Rates include breakfast.) No credit cards.

Nan and Des Faul's modern, centrally heated bungalow is set in landscaped grounds, with good views from the side garden of Sligo town and Rosses Point across Sligo Bay. The lounge, dining room, and bedrooms are tastefully furnished, but it is Nan and Des who give Aisling its special warmth and charm.

Glebe House

Collooney, Co. Sligo. ☎ **071/67787.** 4 rms, all with bath. IR£20–IR£25 ($32–$40) single; IR£17.50 ($28) per person sharing. (Rates include breakfast.) MC, V. Closed Nov–Apr.

Brid and Marc Torrades have rescued this fine old Georgian house from years of neglect and transformed it into lovely accommodations for guests, with an outstanding restaurant on the ground floor (see "Where to Eat," below). The beautiful setting overlooks Collooney Village and the Owenmore River, and guest rooms are furnished with period pieces and authentic reproductions. The house is signposted from N4 on the Sligo-side outskirts of the village.

✪ Rathnashee

Teesan, Donegal Rd. (N15), Sligo, Co. Sligo. ☎ **071/43376.** 4 rms, 3 with bath. IR£18 ($28.80) single; IR£15 ($24) per person sharing; IR£1 ($1.60) per person extra with bath. (Rates include breakfast.) Dinner IR£12 ($19.20). AE. Closed Christmas.

Rathnashee (it means "Fort of the Fairies") is the home of Tess and Sean Haughey, and it's the kind of place where guests often wind up sitting around the table for long conversations in which the Haugheys share their extensive knowledge of what to see in Sligo. They also have one of the best private libraries in Sligo, and they can arrange sightseeing tours with archeologists. Tess serves traditional Irish food and homemade preserves. The centrally heated modern bungalow has beautiful antique furnishings in the lounge and dining room, nicely appointed guest rooms, and there's good parking off the road. It's two miles from the town center. When booking, ask about possible discounts for holders of this book.

✪ Renate Central House

9 Upper John St., Sligo, Co. Sligo. ☎ **071/62014.** 5 rms, 2 with bath. IR£18.50 ($29.60) single without bath; IR£13.50 ($21.60) per person sharing without bath; IR£1.50 ($2.40) per person additional with bath. (Rates include breakfast.) No credit cards.

This small gabled house is surely one of the most convenient in Sligo town. Annie and Leo Hunt (he's a former mayor of Sligo) have five attractive guest rooms, plus a pretty dining room and a color TV in the drawing room. Central heating, off-the-street parking, and within easy walking distance of the town center.

St. Martin's

Cummeen, Strandhill Rd., Sligo, Co. Sligo. ☎ **071/60614.** 4 rms, all with bath. TV. IR£18.50 ($29.60) single; IR£14.50 ($23.20) per person sharing. 25% reduction for children. (Rates include breakfast.) No credit cards.

Mrs. Carmel Carr will welcome you to her attractive modern bungalow 2½ miles past the Southern Hotel on the main Strandhill road. The house is centrally heated and there is a garden for guests to use. All guest rooms are nicely appointed, and Mrs. Carr is always happy to help guests with sightseeing advice. Good parking.

Seisnaun

Kintogher, Sligo, Co. Sligo. ☎ **071/43948.** 4 rms, 2 with bath. IR£18.50 ($29.60) single; IR£13.50 ($21.60) per person sharing without bath; IR£1.50 ($2.40) per person additional with bath. 25% reduction for children. (Rates include breakfast.) No credit cards. Closed Nov–May.

Mrs. Phil Clancy is hostess of this modern luxury bungalow, which is convenient to Rosses Point, Yeats Country, and Drumcliffe. Situated in a peaceful area in town, off the Donegal road, it has beautiful views of Benbulben mountain and Yeats Country. The house is centrally heated and the food is delicious, complete with home baking. All four attractive bedrooms are comfortably furnished, and there's central heating as well as good parking.

Tree Tops

Cleveragh Rd., Sligo, Co. Sligo. ☎ **071/60160.** Fax 071/62301. 6 rms, 4 with bath. TEL. IR£20 ($32) single without bath; IR£14.50 ($23.20) per person sharing without bath; IR£1.50 ($2.40) per person additional with bath. 20% reduction for children. (Rates include breakfast.) MC, V.

Mrs. Doreen MacEvilly is hostess of this attractive home about a five-minute walk from the town center. About 100 yards off N4, the road to Lough Gill, Inisfree, and Holy Well, it's an ideal base for touring. The house is centrally heated and all six comfortable bedrooms are fitted with orthopedic beds; come with hairdryers, tea/coffeemakers, and telephones; and are attractively decorated. This is a no-smoking house.

Nearby Accommodations

Cillard

Carrowmore, Sligo, Co. Sligo. ☎ **071/68201.** 3 rms (all with bath). IR£14–IR£15 ($22.40–$24) per person sharing; IR£5 ($8) single supplement. 20% discount for children. (Rates include breakfast.) No credit cards. Closed Nov–Mar.

Mrs. Brid Dillon's modern farmhouse is in a scenic area just 2½ miles from Sligo, close to the airport, sandy beaches, golf, a horseback-riding center, and megalithic tombs. There's a garden for guests, and meat, vegetables, and fruit fresh from the farm turn up at table. Mrs. Dillon is a warm, welcoming hostess, always eager to help with touring plans.

WHERE TO EAT

In Town

✪ Beezies

45 O'Connell St. ☎ **071/45030.** Reservations not required. Lunch IR£5.50 ($8.80); dinner IR£12 ($19.20). AE, MC, V. Mon–Sat 10:30am–11pm, Sun 4–11pm. Closed Good Friday, Christmas Day. BAR FOOD/TRADITIONAL/VEGETARIAN.

In addition to the good food dished up at Beezies, it's worth a visit, if only for a drink or a look around. The turn-of-the-century marble counters, bar partitions of Tiffany glass, and lamps with tulip-shaped shades give a real 19th-century look to the place. Bar food stars up front, and in back there's a full restaurant serving lunches and five-course dinners featuring traditional Irish ingredients.

✪ Gulliver's

24 Grattan St. ☎ **071/42030.** Reservations not required. Burgers, pizza, salads IR£4–IR£6 ($6.40–$9.60); hot lunch IR£3–IR£5 ($4.80–$8); dinner IR£9–IR£14 ($14.40–$22.40); children's menu IR£2–IR£3 ($3.20–$4.80). MC, V. Daily 12:30pm–midnight. BURGERS/SALADS/FISH/STEAKS.

This old-style pub/restaurant has an appealing wooden front, and there's something of the nautical about the interior, with false portholes around the walls and fish nets draped from the ceiling. The menu is huge, and I particularly like the chicken Hibernia (with a whiskey sauce). Other standouts include trout and chicken Maryland. Service is friendly and efficient, and of course it's fully licensed.

✪ Hargedon's

O'Connell St. ☎ **071/70933.** IR£4–IR£7 ($6.40–$11.20). No credit cards. Mon–Fri 10am–5:30pm (bar open regular bar hours). BAR FOOD.

For years, Hargedon's has been a personal favorite simply because, as the Irish say, they pull a good pint and the *craic* is mighty. Well, now they've extended the atmospheric old pub to accommodate large crowds who show up for excellent pub grub. The amazing thing about it is that the expansion has been so skillfully done that you'd swear the new rooms had been there as long as the original front pub—it's a lovely conglomeration of snugs, flagstone floors, and wooden counters. As for the food, it outshines other bar food by far, with specialties like smoked salmon, country baked mushrooms, ratatouille, and pork Stroganoff—and be sure to sample their whiskey cake.

Truffles Restaurant

11 The Mall. Sligo, Co. Sligo. ☎ **071/44226.** Reservations recommended. Main courses IR£6.25–IR£7.10 ($10–$11.20). No credit cards. Tues–Sat 7–10:30pm, Sun 7–10pm. Closed Christmas and Easter. NEW AGE/MEDITERRANEAN/PIZZA.

"Pizza parlor," takes on new meaning at Bernadette O'Shea's Truffles. The menu has a decidedly Mediterranean flavor, with an occasional Californian and Mexican influence. Careful and imaginative handling of natural and organically-grown ingredients means a slightly longer than usual waiting time, but well worth it when the end result is the likes of a seafood pizza with three cheeses and homemade sauce. It's a small place (seating 38) and very popular, so book ahead if possible.

Nearby Restaurants

✪ Glebe House

Collooney. ☎ **071/67787.** Reservations required. Set dinner IR£18 ($28.80). MC, V. May–Sept, daily 6:30–9:30pm; other months, days vary. CONTINENTAL/VEGETARIAN.

Readers Recommend

Standford Village Inn, Dromahair, Co. Leitrim. ☎ 071/64140. *"Dromahair is a picturesque village near the beautiful Isle of Inisfree and the restored Parke's Castle, as yet largely undiscovered by most tourists. The inn was lovely, with a very helpful staff. Excellent value for both meals and accommodations, with the added benefit of a historic pub on the premises."* —Hugh and Kay Martin, Novato, CA

Author's Note: See "Where to Eat," below.

Brid and Marc Torrades, the attractive young couple who have brought new life into this Georgian country home, offer a gourmet menu in this small, intimate restaurant. Fresh herbs, vegetables, and fruit come from their own garden and from farms in the locality. Meats and seafood are also from local sources, and from such fresh ingredients Brid creates specialties like baked brill with mushrooms and brandy, sautéed filet of beef with garlic and wild mushrooms, and braised duck breast Grand Marnier, as well as at least one vegetarian dish. Desserts feature her mouthwatering home baking. The restaurant is some seven miles from Sligo town, signposted on N4 on the Sligo outskirts of the village. (See "Where to Stay," above, for more details on Glebe House.)

✪ Stanford's Inn Pub and Restaurant

Dromahair. ☎ **071/64140.** Reservations recommended for restaurant in winter months. Bar food IR£4–IR£7 ($6.40–$11.20); main courses IR£7–IR£12 ($11.20–$19.20). MC, V. Bar daily 11am–10pm; restaurant daily 6–9pm. BAR FOOD/TRADITIONAL.

Set in the pretty little village of Dromahair, just 10 miles southeast of Sligo, Stanford's is a fourth-generation family-run inn, pub, and restaurant. The atmospheric old pub has a warm, cozy feel, with an open turf fire, flagstone flooring, and lots of dark wood. The pub food is exceptional, and the restaurant, whose windows look out to the lovely River Bonet, specializes in sea trout and other seafood from local waters as well as traditional meat and poultry dishes based on local produce.

Picnic Fare and Where to Eat It

Picnic grounds are close at hand, with picnic tables scattered throughout lovely **Dooney Wood,** some four miles outside Sligo. Beside the car park, flat-topped Dooney Rock is where Yeats wrote of the fiddler playing. There are also parking areas and picnic tables at **Carns,** setting of many cairns and giants' graves, $1^1/_2$ miles from Sligo out the Holywell road, as well as at **Deerpark,** on the old road to Manorhamilton.

Sligo boasts two excellent delicatessens, both specializing in take-aways for meals in the open or, if your fancy so dictates, in your room.

✪ Kate's Kitchen Delicatessen & Gourmet Take-Away

24 Market St. ☎ **071/43022.**

Deli and take-away take on new meaning in this bright, busy shop. There are wines, cheeses, salami, pâtés, Irish smoked salmon, cooked meats, handmade Irish chocolates, French bread baked on the premises, gourmet dishes cooked to order, and a large range of fresh breads, sandwiches, salads, quiche, and cakes. They will also prepare a picnic hamper, using your choice of the large selection of pretty baskets, with a minimum of advance notice.

2 Yeats Country

It was County Sligo that nurtured Yeats all his life, from boyhood stays in Magheraboy with his grandparents to the end of his life, when he was laid to rest in Drumcliffe churchyard. His imagination was fired by local legends of ancient heroes and heroines who lived out their sagas in this part of Ireland and left the countryside strewn with mementos of their passing. Beautiful Lough Gill is where you'll find his Isle of Inisfree, and at Knocknarea's summit is the cairn where, according to legend (and Yeats), "passionate Maeve is stony-still."

Counties Sligo and Leitrim

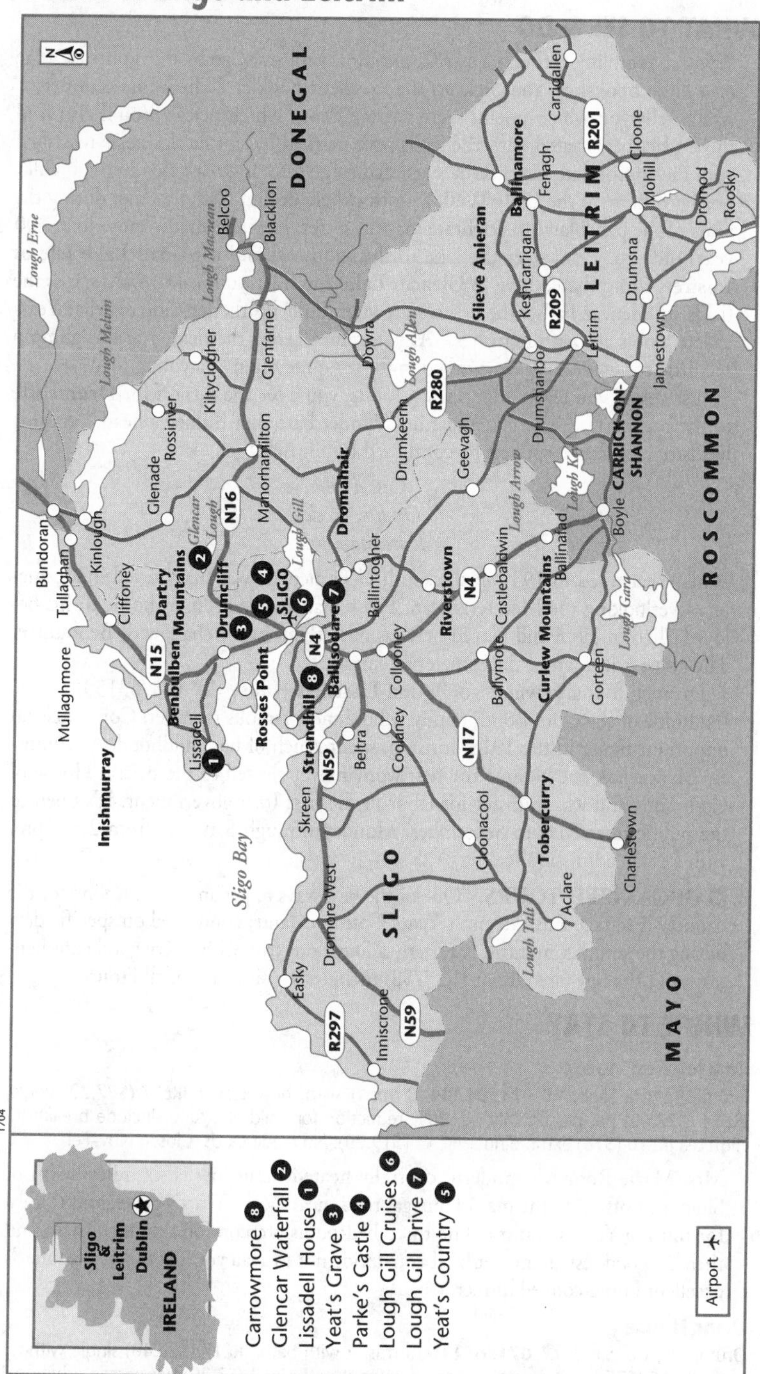

WHAT TO SEE & DO

If you're rambling through Yeats Country on your own, go by the Tourist Office or a Sligo bookshop and pick up the excellent booklet **"The Yeats Country,"** which tells you which poems were written about which places. You'll also find those places associated with the great poet marked by simple signposts inscribed with the appropriate verses. One suggested route is to drive east along Lough Gill's northern shore to the **Holy Well,** a grotto where devout Catholics met during the years of the penal laws to celebrate mass in secret. Its stone altar is more than 300 years old. Look out over the lake to the southeast and the small **Lake Isle of Inisfree.** From there, drive to **Glencar Lake** and leave your car to walk across the fields to Glencar Falls, where there are steps built up the left side of what Yeats called "pools among the rushes." As you return across the field, you can glimpse the little cottage where Yeats called in for tea quite often as a young man.

Just before you reach Sligo's town limits, you'll see the turnoff for **Drumcliffe** to the north. This is where Yeats lies "Under bare Ben Bulben's head," and his headstone bears the epitaph he composed for himself:

Cast a cold eye
On life, on death.
Horseman, pass by!

When Yeats died in 1939 in the south of France, he was first buried in a cemetery overlooking the Mediterranean. His remains were brought home to his beloved Sligo in 1948 and placed here, as he wished, in the shadow of Benbulben. The grave is just left of the cemetery's entrance.

Drumcliffe is also where you'll find **Lissadell House** (☎ 071/63150), ancestral home of the Gore-Booth family, whose most famous member, Constance, an important figure in the 1916 uprising, spent much of her childhood. As Countess Markievicz, she became the first woman ever elected to the British House of Commons and was minister for labor in the first Irish government. It's open to the public from May to September, Monday through Saturday from 2 to 5pm, with a small admission fee.

✪ **ORGANIZED TOURS** One of the best ways to get an overall feeling for the country is to take Bus Eireann's **Yeats Country Tour,** conducted on specific days during the summer months. It's nearly a four-hour trip, with a very good commentary, and the low fare (about IR£5/$8) includes a visit to Lissadell House.

WHERE TO STAY

Castletown House

Drumcliffe, Co. Sligo. ☎ **071/63204.** 3 rms, 1 with shower only. IR£17 ($27.20) single; IR£14 ($22.40) per person sharing. 20% reduction for children. (Rates include breakfast.) High tea IR£10 ($16) extra; dinner IR£12 ($19.20). No credit cards. Closed Nov–Feb.

Mrs. Mazie Rooney's modern, centrally heated bungalow is six miles north of Sligo, just off N15, the main Donegal road, near W. B. Yeats's grave, and is ideal for touring Yeats Country. The three bedrooms are comfortably furnished, and there's a good restaurant nearby if you decide not to avail yourself of Mrs. Rooney's excellent home-cooked dinner.

Urlar House

Drumcliffe, Co. Sligo. ☎ **071/63110.** 5 rms, 2 with bath. IR£17 ($22.40) single without bath; IR£16 ($25.60) per person sharing without bath; IR£2 ($3.20) per person additional with bath. 25% reduction for children. (Rates include breakfast.) High tea IR£8 ($12.80) extra, dinner IR£13 ($20.80). No credit cards. Closed Oct–Mar.

Just a mile outside Drumcliffe on N15, the main Sligo-Bundoran road, Mrs. Healy's large, centrally heated farmhouse sits right next to Benbulben mountain. There is beautiful scenery all around the house, and the period residence is registered in Country Inns and Historical Houses of Ireland. There are five nice bedrooms, and dinner is available with advance notice.

Westway Farmhouse

Drumcliffe, Co. Sligo. ☎ **071/63178.** 3 rms, 1 with bath. IR£17 ($22.40) single; IR£14 ($22.40) per person sharing. 20% reduction for children. (Rates include breakfast.) Dinner IR£11 ($17.60) extra. No credit cards. Closed Oct–Apr.

The McDonagh family's modern farm bungalow is six miles north of Sligo (signposted off N15) overlooking Drumcliffe Bay at the foot of Benbulben mountain. The house is centrally heated and electric blankets are supplied. You'll be greeted with complimentary tea or coffee in the lovely sitting room with a log and peat fire, and the pretty bedrooms are comfortably furnished.

3 Around County Sligo

Although Sligo is a relatively small county, it encompasses an amazing variety of landscape, with mountains, lakes, and a coastline fringed with sandy beaches and low cliffs.

WHAT TO SEE & DO

Scattered over the face of the county are traces of the prehistoric races who lived here during three main periods: the Late Stone Age (Neolithic, 2500–2000 B.C.), the Bronze Age (2000–500 B.C.), and the Early Iron Age (500 B.C. to A.D. 500). The Tourist Office has a marvelously detailed leaflet, **"Prehistoric Sligo,"** that tells you where to find the most important of these court cairns, portal dolmens, passage graves, ring forts, and gallery graves. In the immediate vicinity of Sligo town, you'll find **Carrowmore** (south of town near Ballisodare), a cemetery of about 65 megalithic tombs—one of the largest concentrations in Europe—in a one-mile-long, half-mile-wide area. And at the top of **Knocknarea,** there's the great Misgaun Maeve, an unopened cairn some 200 feet in diameter and about 80 feet high that archeologists believe covers a vast passage grave, but that legend insists is the burial monument to Queen Maeve.

Along the western part of the county are the **Ox Mountains;** the north holds high, flat-topped limestone hills like **Benbulben;** and for the pleasure-bent traveler, there's a fine **beach** at Strandhill, a **golf course** at Rosses Point, and good **fishing** in any number of rivers and lakes.

WHERE TO STAY

✪ Cruckawn House

Ballymote-Boyle Rd., Tubbercurry, Co. Sligo. ☎ **071/85188.** 5 rms, 4 with bath. IR£18.50 ($29.60) single; IR£13.50 ($21.60) per person sharing; IR£1.50 ($2.40) per person additional with bath. 33 1/3% reduction for children. (Rates include breakfast.) Dinner IR£12 ($19.20) extra. No credit cards. Paved car park.

My mail has been full of praise for Mrs. Maeve Walsh and her modern, centrally heated two-story house just outside town. Guest rooms are nicely decorated, fitted with built-in bookshelf/headboards, and most have good views of the Ox

Mountains. There's a sun lounge, games room, and laundry facilities for guest use. Cruckawn sits on its own grounds (with a large garden) overlooking a golf course that visitors may use. Meals are superb, and there's a wine license.

Rossli House

Doocastle, Tubbercurry, Co. Sligo. ☎ **071/85099** or 85672. 4 rms, none with bath. IR£18.50 ($29.60) single; IR£13.50 ($21.60) per person sharing. Dinner IR£11 ($17.60). 33 1/3% reduction for children. No credit cards. 4 1/2 miles from Tubbercurry.

Mrs. Noreen Donoghue's pleasant bungalow is in a peaceful location, yet convenient to golf, fishing, and pubs that feature Irish music. One of the four tastefully decorated bedrooms is a single. Central heating and plenty of parking.

WHERE TO EAT

✪ Killoran's Traditional Restaurant/Lounge

Teeling St., Tubbercurry. ☎ **071/85111** or 85679. Reservations not required. Bar food less than IR£5 ($8); lunch IR£6 ($9.60); dinner IR£8–IR£10 (12.80–$16). AE, MC, V. Daily 10am–11:30pm. BAR FOOD/TRADITIONAL.

Service by owners Anne and Tommie Killoran is pleasant and personal in this restaurant and bar/lounge. Antiques carry out the traditional theme, and the menu features such traditional Irish dishes as boxty, colcannon, crubeens, and potato cakes. There are quick snacks as well as full meals, and prices are moderate to inexpensive. From June to September, Thursday night is Irish-music night.

✪ Cromleach Lodge Country House

Castlebaldwin. ☎ **071/65155.** Fax 071/65455. Set lunch IR£17 ($27.20); set dinner IR£29.50 ($47.20). ACC, AE, MC, V. Lunch by reservation only, year-round. Dinner Apr–Sept, daily 6–9pm; Oct–Mar, Mon–Sat (except for residents) 6–9pm. TRADITIONAL.

Moira Tighe is chef in this luxurious lodge in scenic surroundings off the Dublin road (N4) near Boyle (see "Where to Stay," above). She insists on only organic vegetables, locally grown herbs and meats, farmhouse cheeses, and the freshest of fish and seafood in the creation of gourmet dishes. Moira also offers superior accommodations.

4 Around County Leitrim

Long and narrow, County Leitrim is split down the middle by Lough Allen, an extension of the Shannon. North of the lake, tall mountains stretch to the borders of County Sligo, while to the south the countryside is dotted with lovely lakes. In Lough Scur there are remnants of prehistoric lake dwellings, called crannogs. The harbor at Carrick-on-Shannon is alive with cruisers, and there's good fishing both here and in nearby lakes.

WHAT TO SEE & DO

Dromahair (Druim Dha Eithiar, "The Ridge of the Two Air-Demons"), 12 miles east of Sligo town, is where a royal lady inadvertently set in motion the first Norman invasion of Ireland. It seems that back in the 12th century, Dervogilla, wife of Tiernan O'Rourke, eloped with the King of Leinster, who was promptly outlawed by his fellow chieftains. He went to England's Henry II for assistance, and Henry gave his permission to any of his vassals who so chose to join up with the Irish king to win back his lost lands. A group of Anglo-Normans threw in with the Irish chieftain and landed near Wexford in 1169. The ruins of the lady's residence, **Breffni Castle,** are found on the riverbank adjacent to the 1626 Old Hall, built by Sir William Villiers.

There's an excellent Interpretive Centre for National Monuments of the Northwest at ✪ **Parke's Castle,** Dromahair (☎ 071/64149), a splendid example of a fortified manor house of the Cromwellian era. From June to September the Office of Public Works has daily guided tours of period rooms, as well as an audiovisual presentation on national monuments in this region. Hours are 10am to 6:30pm, and there's a tea shop for refreshment. Small admission charge.

On the other side of the river are the ruins of the 1508 **Creevelea Abbey,** and the remains of an even-older church nearby are thought to be those of one founded by St. Patrick when he spent some time here.

If your Irish roots are in Leitrim soil, the **Leitrim Genealogy Centre,** County Library, Ballinamore (☎ 078/44012), stands ready to help you trace your ancestry. The center maintains a full-time professional genealogical service for the county, and if your ancestors came from this area, you can write ahead with all the details you can furnish, or call in when you come to Ireland. Fees are based on the amount of work involved, and the knowledgeable staff will let you know before any charge is made whether or not there is a high probability of success in your search. The centre is open Monday through Friday from 10am to 1pm and 2 to 5pm.

Carrick-on-Shannon (Cara Droma Ruisg, "The Weir of the Marshy Ridge") is a center for **fishing and boating** on the River Shannon. Carrick Craft (☎ 078/20236) is based here and can arrange a few days of boating on the Shannon. (See "Outdoor and Special-Interest Vacations," Chapter 4 for details.)

The 100-acre ✪ **Lough Rynn House and Gardens,** Mohill (☎ 078/31427), was the seat of the earls of Leitrim for more than two centuries. From May to mid-September, the estate is open to the public for a small fee from 10am to 7pm, with guided tours to the principal historic buildings, and there are miles and miles of ornamental gardens and nature trails, as well as a picnic site and playground.

WHERE TO STAY

BED-AND-BREAKFAST ACCOMMODATIONS

Corbally Lodge

Dublin Rd. (N4), Carrick-on-Shannon, Co. Leitrim. ☎ **078/20228.** 4 rms, 3 with bath. IR£18 ($28.80) single without bath; IR£14 ($22.40) per person sharing without bath; IR£2 ($3.20) per person additional with bath. 25% reduction for children. (Rates include breakfast.) Dinner IR£12 ($19.20) extra. MC, V.

Set on spacious grounds 1½ miles south of town, this pretty modern bungalow is the Rowley family home. Open turf fires are the cozy centerpiece for evening gatherings. Antiques are scattered among the tasteful furnishings, and guest rooms are both attractive and comfortable. Central heat and good parking.

Glenview

Aughoo, Ballinamore, Co. Leitrim. ☎ **078/44157.** 6 rms, 4 with bath. IR£14.50 ($23.20) per person sharing without bath; IR£2 ($3.20) per person additional with bath; IR£5.50 ($8.80) single supplement. 20% reduction for children. (Rates include breakfast.) Dinner IR£13 ($20.80) extra. No credit cards. Closed Dec–Mar.

Mrs. Teresa Kennedy is the warm and hospitable hostess of this lovely modern farmhouse in peaceful rural surroundings 1¼ miles south of town. There are pony, donkey, and cart that are free for children. The house is centrally heated and there is an attractive TV lounge with turf and log fires. There is a good restaurant on the premises, as well as self-catering bungalows.

✪ Gortmor House

Lismakeegan, Carrick-on-Shannon, Co. Leitrim. ☎ **078/20489.** 4 rms, 2 with bath. IR£19 ($30.40) single; IR£14 ($22.40) per person sharing; IR£2 ($3.20) per person extra with bath. 20% reduction for children. (Rates include breakfast.) Dinner IR£12 ($19.20) extra. ACC, AE, MC, V. Closed Dec–Jan.

This modern farmhouse, set in quiet, scenic countryside, is the home of Imelda and Kevin McMahon, who welcome each guest as a new friend. Imelda is the Farmhouse Association representative for Counties Leitrim, Cavan, and Monaghan. This is angling country, with no less than 41 free fishing lakes, as well as the Shannon River, within a 10-mile radius, and the McMahons can help you try your luck. Rooms are quite comfortable, there's a TV lounge for guests, and the house has central heating. Gortmor House is three miles from Carrick-on-Shannon, two miles off the Dublin-Sligo road (N4), and one mile off R280 road, well signposted along the way.

Riversdale Farmhouse

Ballinamore, Co. Leitrim. ☎ **078/44122.** Fax 078/44813. 9 rms, all with bath. IR£25 ($40) single; IR£21 ($33.60) per person sharing. 25% reduction for children. (Rates include breakfast.) ACC, MC, V. Advance reservations required Nov–Feb. Closed Christmas.

Violet and Raymond Thomas are hosts at Riversdale. The large farmhouse sits a mile south of town in beautiful countryside on 85 acres of sheep farm. There are open fires on cool evenings to supplement central heating, and fishing right on the property, as well as an indoor swimming pool, squash court, and sauna.

19

County Donegal

County Donegal sits at the very top of Ireland, its jagged coastline ringed by wide strands backed by steep cliffs. Its inland mountains are cut by deep valleys, and its countryside filled with antiquities and legends. This is a county of vast uninhabited stretches, natives as rugged as the landscape in which they live, and an ancient culture kept alive in the Gaelic language. In the rhythmic patterns of Donegal speech can be heard the distinctive cadence of Ulster. From Donegal cottages come some of the world's most beautiful hand-woven woolens. Donegal tweeds are characterized by nubby textures peppered with the colors of traditional vegetable dyes, and while much is still handwoven, the style and colors are also reproduced in machine-woven woolens.

County Donegal's jagged, cliff-filled coastline, rocky mountain pastures, and breathtaking mountain passes that open a view that seems to go on to eternity can lead to an overload of the senses, and it's when you've reached the saturation point that you'll welcome the company of the warm and friendly inhabitants of County Donegal.

1 Donegal Town

Where other Irish towns have a square right in the middle of town, Donegal (Dun na nGall, "the Fort of the Foreigners") has a wide triangular space they call the Diamond. It's the meeting place of three major roadways—from Derry, west Donegal, and Sligo—and it points up Donegal town's strategic location at the head of Donegal Bay and the mouth of the River Eske; a position of such importance that in ancient times the princes of Tir Chonaill (the O'Donnells) made this their chief seat. Red Hugh O'Donnell founded a Franciscan friary here in 1474, and when it was ransacked in the 1600s and the monks were sent scurrying in fear of their lives, four went to Bundrowes for safety and set about compiling the scholarly *Annals of the Four Masters,* one of Ireland's most valuable sources of early church history. In the Diamond look for a 25-foot-high obelisk, inscribed with the names of the four monks at its base. Today Donegal town, 154 miles from Dublin and 41 miles north of Sligo, is a friendly, thriving market town, famed for its woolens and as a touring base for the rest of this wildly beautiful county.

ORIENTATION **Essentials** Donegal's telephone area code is 073. The post office is on Tir Conaill Street.

Tourist Information The Tourist Office is on Quay Street (☎ 073/21148), open May through September with hours of 10am to 6pm. Check with the Tourist Office for what's going on when you're in Donegal. Be sure and ask for a copy of their excellent, minutely detailed **"Touring Donegal"** booklet, published by Northwest Tourism.

Town Layout Small and compact, Donegal town is centered around the Diamond, with side streets radiating from this focal point.

GETTING AROUND **By Bus** There's a bus pickup station on the Diamond for Bus Eireann buses with regular service to Derry, Dublin, Galway, Killybegs, Portnoo, and Belfast. There's no in-town bus service.

By Car My best advice for drivers is to park the car and leave it during your stay in Donegal town. Streets are narrow, and parking can be a real problem.

On Foot Every point of interest in town and on its fringes is within easy walking distance.

By Bicycle With a bike, you can ramble even farther than on foot, and Doherty's, on Main Street, has bicycles for rent.

WHAT TO SEE & DO

Once the chief stronghold of the O'Donnells, **Donegal Castle** is just north of the Diamond, and the west tower dates from 1505, built by Red Hugh O'Donnell on the site of an earlier castle. The handsome house was built around the old tower by Sir Basil Brooke in 1607 and features a mammoth Jacobean fireplace, windows, and gables. As we go to press, renovations are in progress, so check to see if it is open.

Tip your hat to the **Four Masters Memorial** in the Diamond, then examine the large mounted anchor by the bay—it's from a French ship, perhaps one of those bringing troops to fight with Wolfe Tone in 1798, and was salvaged from the sea by fishermen in the mid-1800s.

South of town at the river's estuary, there are the interesting, but slight, ruins of **Donegal Abbey,** founded in 1474. **Lough Eske** is roughly five miles northeast of Donegal town, with wooded shores and a backing of mountains.

There are pleasant **river walks** along the east and west banks of the River Eske, with marvelous views of the town and surrounding area.

SHOPPING

Although Donegal is not a spectacular shopping town, it is ideal for acquiring at competitive prices woolens, Donegal Parian China, and other products made in the county. Some shops close early on Wednesday, although this practice is disappearing.

✪ Donegal Craft Village

Ballyshannon-Sligo Rd.

Just outside Donegal town on the Ballyshannon-Sligo road is a group of cottagelike buildings around a courtyard. Each is the workshop of a true artisan, and you'll find pottery, hand weaving, batik, jewelry, ceramics, and crystal. The coffee shop is a pleasant spot for a shopping or browsing break. Open Monday through Saturday from 10am to 6pm and on Sunday from 1 to 5pm (but check with the Tourist Office, as hours may vary).

Donegal Town

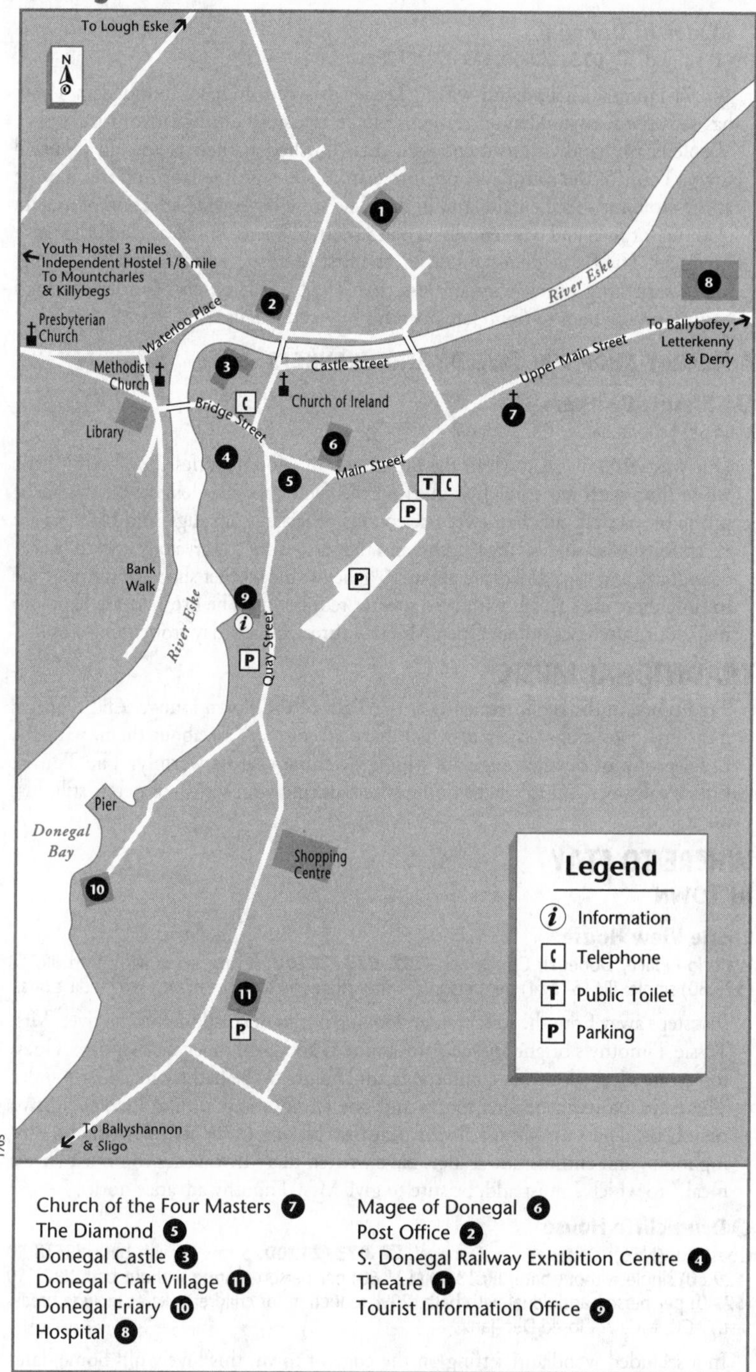

✪ Magee of Donegal

The Diamond. ☎ **073/22660.** Fax 073/21283.

World-famous for its hand-woven Donegal tweed, Magee, founded in 1866, has set up a weaving demonstration right in the store during the tourist season. Woolens are handwoven in cottages, then finished at their factory in Donegal town. Tours of the factory are organized from time to time, and you can inquire at the store for specific dates and hours. The store has a wide selection of quality clothing for men and women and a good variety of linens, knitwear, and other Irish products. The Belshade restaurant on the first floor specializes in home cooking, and a satisfying lunch will run less than IR£5 ($8). Open Monday through Saturday from 9am to 6pm, late opening July and August.

A Nearby Shop for Tweeds and Blankets

✪ Gillespie Brothers

Main St., Mountcharles, Co. Donegal.

Due west of Donegal town in the little town of Mountcharles, stop by this little white shop with red trim. Just meeting the Gillespies is a delight, but it can be profitable as well, for their tweed selections of jackets, lap rugs, and blankets are exceptional (also sold by the length), and they also carry a marvelous stock of waistcoats, hats, and caps. Prices are about 10% below most other shops, and from time to time there are specials with even greater reductions. The brothers are happy to mail your purchases home. Open Monday through Saturday from 9am to 6pm.

TRADITIONAL MUSIC

Traditional music is on frequently at the **Talk of the Town** lounge. And Donegal has some good pubs, many of which have a "country" air about them, with the usual group of devoted regulars who'll welcome visitors warmly. The Tourist Office can steer you to what's doing where during your visit—or better still, just ask a local.

WHERE TO STAY

In Town

Castle View House

Waterloo Place, Donegal, Co. Donegal. ☎ **073/22100.** 3 rms, none with bath. IR£18 ($28.80) single; IR£15 ($24) per person sharing. (Rates include breakfast.) No credit cards.

Just steps away from the town center, looking out to the castle across the river, Mrs. Tessie Timothy's bright and cheerful home is an ideal Donegal town base. Guest rooms are nicely done up, comfortable, and handy to the bathroom; all have sinks. There are two twin-bedded rooms and one family room with a double and two twin beds. There are almost always peat fires blazing in the living room and dining room, and enthusiastic readers have written that "If you stay you must have a meal," to which I must add, be sure to give Mrs. Timothy advance notice.

✪ Drumcliffe House

Coast Rd. (N56), Donegal, Co. Donegal. ☎ **073/21200.** 5 rms, 2 with bath. IR£18.50 ($29.60) single without bath; IR£13.50 ($21.60) per person sharing without bath; IR£1.50 ($2.40) per person additional with bath. 20% reduction for children. (Rates include breakfast.) ACC, MC, V. Closed Dec–Jan.

In a secluded woodland setting on the edge of town, this lovely old home dates back some 300 years. Both the house and its antique furnishings are interesting, and meals feature Mrs. Pearl Timony's home baking. The attractive guest rooms all have nice views, there's good parking, and the house is centrally heated.

Lyndale

Doonan, Donegal Town, Co. Donegal. ☎ **073/21873.** 4 rms, 3 with bath. IR£18 ($28.80) single; IR£13 ($20.80) per person sharing; IR£1.50 ($2.40) per person extra for bath. 20% reduction for children. No credit cards. Open Easter–November.

Lyndale is a split-level bungalow, just off the Coast Road (N56). Mrs. Marie Campbell is the hostess, and has drawn high praise from our readers for her friendly hospitality, as well as for her home cooking, especially the breakfast menu. Guests are also served tea and/or coffee each evening. Guest rooms all have electric blankets; there's central heating and plenty of private parking.

Riverside House

Waterloo Place, Donegal, Co. Donegal. ☎ **073/21083.** 3 rms, none with bath. IR£16 ($25.60) single; IR£13.50 ($21.60) per person sharing. 20% reduction for children. (Rates include breakfast.) No credit cards.

This attractive home is just across the River Eske from Donegal Castle on a quiet residential terrace only a short walk from the center of town. Mrs. Kathleen Curristan welcomes guests here, and her comfortable guest rooms are decorated in cheerful colors. All have sinks, and there's one large family room with a double and two twin beds. Even the bathroom is bright, with matching floral wallpaper and shower curtains. The lounge frames the river and castle view through wide front windows, and its piano is often in use by guests as well as the Curristans.

Nearby Accommodations

Ardeevin

Lough Eske, Barnesmore, Co. Donegal. ☎ **073/21790.** Fax 073/21790. 5 rms, 4 with bath. IR£18.50 ($29.60) single without bath; IR£14 ($22.40) per person sharing without bath; IR£1.50 ($2.40) per person additional with bath. 20% reduction for children. (Rates include breakfast.) No credit cards. Closed Nov–Mar.

Five miles outside Donegal town, this dormer bungalow sits on a rise overlooking Lough Eske and the Bluestack Mountains. The guest rooms are nicely furnished, and four have private bath with shower, all have tea/coffeemakers. Mrs. Mary McGinty is the charming hostess, and the house is centrally heated.

Atlantic Guest House

Main St., Donegal, Co. Donegal. ☎ **073/21187.** 12 rms, 7 with bath. TV. IR£15–IR£17.50 ($24–$28) per person. ACC, MC, V. Private car park.

Located right in the center of town, the Atlantic is presided over by Edith and Victor Browne. It's a pleasant, rambling building with comfortable guest rooms and an inviting lounge. Color TV in all rooms is a plus, and just one of the reasons this place is good value for the money. Another bonus is the adjoining restaurant (see "Where to Eat," below). The Brownes can arrange baby-sitting and the house is centrally heated.

Worth a Splurge

✪ Harvey's Point County Hotel

Lough Eske, Donegal, Co. Donegal. ☎ **073/22208.** Fax 073/22352. 20 rms, all with bath. TV TEL MINIBAR. IR£48–IR£55 ($76.80–$88) single; IR£38–IR£45 ($60.80–$72) per person sharing. AE, MC, V. Closed Oct–May.

Readers Recommend

Eske View, Lough Eske, Barnesmore, Donegal, Co. Donegal. ☎ 073/22087. *"This lovely, immaculately kept modern bungalow (with bathrooms en suite) overlooks Lough Eske, about five miles from Donegal town. Our comfortable, beautifully decorated room had a stunning view of the lake, with the Bluestack Mountains as a dramatic backdrop."* —Richard and Beverly Smith, Medford, NJ

Author's Note: Take N15 from Donegal town for about three miles and look for the Lough Eske signpost.

The Arches Country House, Lough Eske, Barnesmore, Donegal, Co. Donegal. *"Mrs. Noreen McGinty's home is a luxurious and peaceful one overlooking Lough Eske and the Bluestack Mountains. The rooms were beautifully decorated and very well appointed. Although we didn't have time to use them, the boating facilities on the lake looked very appealing."* —Jeanne Bodin, Tarrytown, NY

This lovely period house sits four miles from Donegal town, on the very edge of Lough Eske at the foot of the Bluestack Mountains. Its modern, elegant decor complements this idyllic setting, and guest rooms are as nicely appointed as public rooms with satellite TV, tea/coffeemakers, minibars, and hairdryers. There's boating on the lake, a marina, and two tennis courts. As for the restaurant, see "Where to Eat," below.

✪ Hyland Central Hotel

The Diamond, Donegal, Co. Donegal. ☎ **073/21027.** Fax 073/22295. 75 rms, all with bath. TV TEL. IR£40–IR£50 ($64–$80) single; IR£30–IR£40 ($48–$64) per person sharing. (Rates include breakfast.) AE, MC, V. Private car park.

This sparkling-clean family-run hotel is that rare combination of modern facilities with an old-fashioned, homey atmosphere and a helpful, friendly staff. The dining room, overlooking the river, is lovely and serves moderately priced meals (see "Where to Eat," below). Rooms here are spacious and have a light, airy look and comfortable modern furnishings. For a gorgeous view of Donegal Bay, ask for one in the back (the view in front is of the Diamond). The recently added Leisure Complex includes a fully equipped gym, a steam room, Jacuzzi and plunge pool, indoor swimming pool, and children's pool.

WHERE TO EAT

In addition to the listings below, there are many coffee shops around the Diamond, and most are good value.

The Atlantic Restaurant

Main St. ☎ **073/21080.** Reservations not required. Lunch or dinner IR£2.50–IR£5 ($4–$8); children's menu IR£1–IR£2 ($1.60–$3.20). MC, V. Daily 10am–10:30pm. TRADITIONAL.

In the Atlantic Guest House (see "Where to Stay," above), this busy restaurant offers exceptionally good value. Chicken curry, plaice, salmon steaks, and lasagna are featured on the extensive menu, and all plates come with two vegetables and potato.

Harvey's Point Restaurant and Bar

Lough Eske. ☎ **073/22208.** Reservations recommended for dinner. Lunch IR£12 ($19.20); dinner IR£20 ($32). AE, MC, V. Apr–Dec, daily 12:30–2:30pm and 6–9:30pm. Four miles from Donegal town. FRENCH/TRADITIONAL.

This elegant dining room and lounge bar in the hotel on the shores of Lough Eske (see "Where to Stay," above) is the perfect setting for a romantic dinner. Local fish and beef accompanied by the freshest of Irish produce arrive at the table prepared in tempting French-style creations, and service is both friendly and efficient.

Hyland Central Hotel

The Diamond. ☎ **073/21027.** Fax 073/22295. Main courses IR£5–IR£10 ($8–$16); set lunch IR£9.50 ($15.20); set dinner IR£19 ($30.40). AE, MC, V. Daily 12:30–2:30pm and 6–9:30pm. TRADITIONAL.

The best inexpensive meals are found in this superb small hotel (see "Where to Stay," above). There's an excellent lunch special (hot meat and vegetables, and ample portions) for less than IR£5 ($7.25) served in the comfortable lounge. Evening meals are in the cream-colored dining room, which has wide windows along one wall, lots of dark-wood trim, and softly lighted, gold-framed oil paintings hung about.

EASY EXCURSIONS

About 19 miles south of Donegal town, right on the Donegal-Sligo border, is the popular seaside resort of **Bundoran,** and **Ballyshannon,** home of Donegal Parian China, lies between the two towns. See Section 2, below, for details on both towns.

The spectacular, three-mile-long **Barnesmore Gap** is seven miles to the northeast, through wild, mountainous country that once harbored highwaymen. Keep an eye out for **Biddy O'Barnes Pub,** which has survived unchanged for over two centuries, and even though Biddy has been gone lo these many years, she'd still feel right at home, and so will you.

North of town, **English Glen** cuts between the Bluestack Mountains and Banagher Hill, and farther along you'll find the **Grey Mare's Tail waterfall** in Sruell Glen. The good St. Patrick knew Donegal well, and he once fasted for 40 days on an island in isolated **Lough Derg,** where pilgrims still come faithfully to observe a three-day fast.

2 Around County Donegal

Base yourself in Donegal town or Ardara to explore the splendors of southern Donegal. Heading north, the most direct route is N15 from Donegal town to **Ballybofey,** and N56 to the cathedral town of **Letterkenny,** a good base for exploring northern County Donegal. However, although this is a lovely drive, passing through **Barnesmore Gap** (known locally as Barnes Gap), you will miss a real scenic treat by passing up the longer drive around the county's coastline. If time permits, I strongly recommend that from Ardara you take the main roadway that circles the northern part of the county, N56. The route takes you to **Dungloe, Burtonport, Gweedore,** around the **Bloody Foreland** (so named for the blood-red sunsets on this part of the coast), **Dunfanaghy,** and on to **Letterkenny.**

In Dungloe, you can hear terrific Irish traditional music at **Delaney's Hotel** (☎ 075/21033), especially handy if you plan an overnight stop in this small town (see "Where to Stay Along the Coastal Route" below). Incidentally, this was Sweeney's Hotel for many years, and most locals still call it by that name (just in case you have to ask for it!).

About halfway between Rann na Feirste and Gaoth Dobhair, look for **Leo's Tavern** (☎ 075/48143) in the little village of Meenaleck. Leo, a talented musician, is father of the internationally famed **Clannad** group, and if any of his famous offspring happen to be there when you come along, music of top quality won't be long breaking out. The **Dunfanaghy Workhouse** (☎ 074/36540), on the outskirts of town, was built in 1845 and was the only refuge that many Irish could find during the Great Famine.

WHERE TO STAY ALONG THE COASTAL ROUTE

Delaney's Hotel (Sweeneys)

Dungloe, Co. Donegal. ☎ **075/21033.** 16 rms, all with bath. IR£22 ($35.20) single; IR£20 ($32) per person sharing. No credit cards. Open mid-Apr–Dec.

This small, family-run hotel has been a Donegal institution, run by the Sweeney family for many years, and now under the direction of a Sweeney daughter whose name it now carries. Guestrooms are quite comfortable and the food quite good—but its very *best* features are the traditional music and warm hospitality of the place. One reader informed me that he has returned year after year for more than twenty years—that's a testimonial worth heeding.

A Word About Accommodations In County Donegal For budget travelers, County Donegal is especially rich in hostel accommodations, ranging from simple to superior facilities: Consult the An Oige handbook for details on hostels at Killybegs and Ardara. Basic facilities are at the Red House, Carrick, and five miles from Dungloe there's a good hostel at Crohy Head, and good facilities at the Youth Hostel, Aranmore Island, Burtonport, with regular ferry service between Burtonport and the island. Near Glenveagh National Park, you'll find good hostels at Erigal, Dunlewy, Gweedore, and four miles from Downings at Tra na Rosann, Downings. On the shores of Lough Swilly, there are good facilities at the Youth Hostel, Bunnaton, Glenvar; and on Tory Island (with irregular ferry service from Magheraroarty), basic facilities at the Youth Hostel.

BUNDORAN

Located on the southern shore of Donegal Bay only 22 miles north of Sligo via N15, Bundoran is $17^1/_2$ miles south of Donegal town (on N15) and is one of the county's finest seaside resorts. There's a long strand for **swimming,** and an inviting promenade for invigorating seaside walks. **Sea angling** in the bay is excellent, and the nearby Rivers Bunduff and Bundrowes are also rewarding venues for salmon and trout **fishing.** Youngsters will love **Water World** (☎ 072/41172), a wonderland of watery amusements. Horseback riding can be arranged through the **Stracomer Riding School,** Bundoran (☎ 072/41787 or 41685). **Bundoran Golf Club** welcomes visitors, there are three outdoor municipal swimming pools, and during summer months there are **live music** and amateur **drama productions** in this lively town.

If time limits will prevent your driving farther north in County Donegal, Bus Eireann has excellent, inexpensive **day tours** from Bundoran to Glenveagh National Park and the Hills of Donegal; book through the bus office (☎ 072/51101) or Meehan's Travel agency, Main Street, Bundoran (☎ 072/41351).

WHERE TO STAY

✪ Holyrood Motel

Bundoran, Co. Donegal. ☎ **072/41232.** Fax 072/41100. 61 rms, all with bath. TV TEL. IR£37–IR£42 ($59.20–$67.20) single; IR£26–IR£30 ($41.60–$48) per person sharing. Breakfast IR£8 ($12.80) extra; dinner IR£17 ($27.20). AE, DC, MC, V.

Around County Donegal

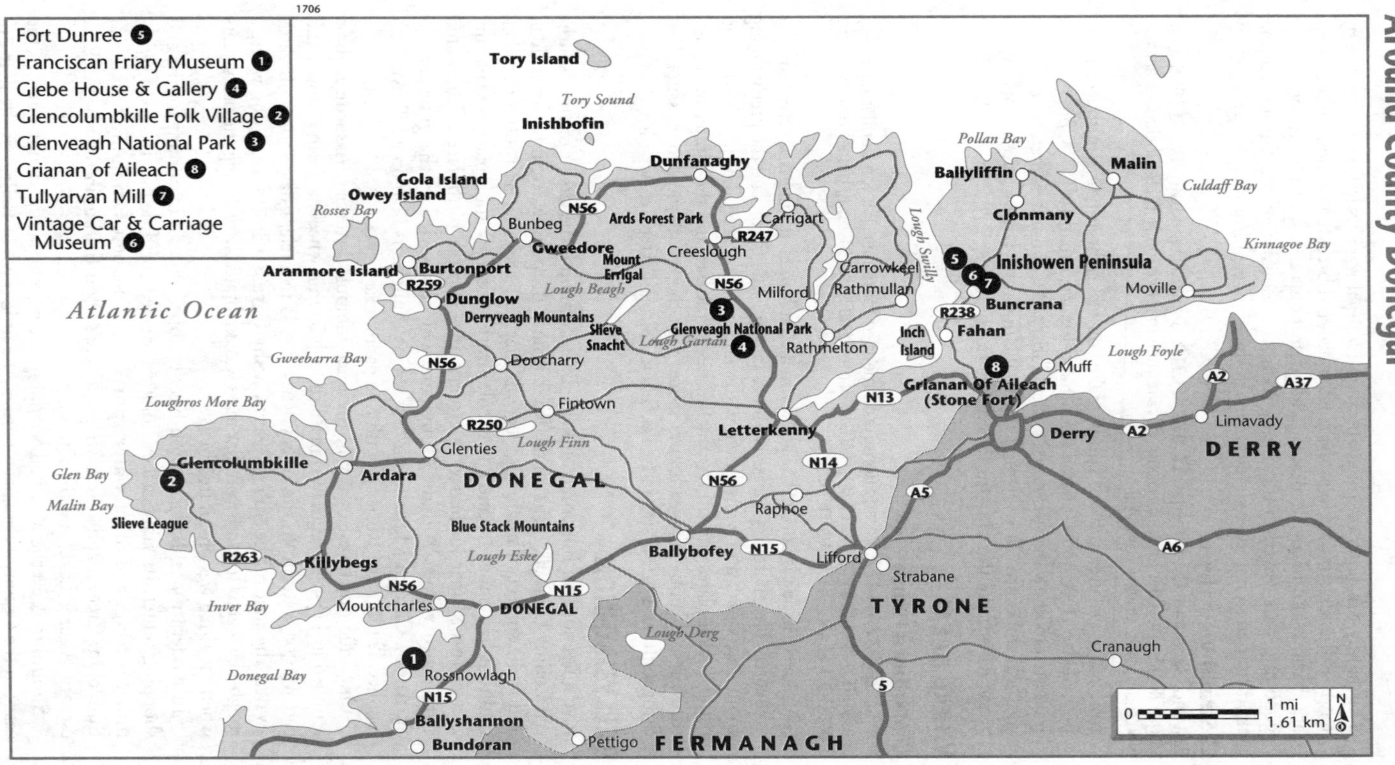

This family-run hotel on the main Sligo-Donegal road (N15), in the town center, is as friendly and warm as the smaller bed-and-breakfast homes. Public rooms are spacious and nicely decorated, and guest rooms are especially attractive. Very good meals are served in the dining room at reasonable prices. During summer months, there's nightly entertainment in the lounge and/or bar.

✪ Strand View House

East End, Bundoran, Co. Donegal. ☎ **072/41519.** 6 rms, all with bath. TV. IR£19 ($30.40) single; IR£15 ($24) per person sharing. 20% reduction for children. (Rates include breakfast.) No credit cards. Private car park.

Mrs. Mary Delaney and her family make you feel right at home in this centrally located two-story house on the main Sligo-Donegal road (N15). Golfers will be interested to know that the noted golfer Christy O'Connor lived here when he was the local club's pro. The six guest rooms include three large family rooms. All are attractive and comfortably furnished. Central heating.

WHERE TO EAT

✪ Marlboro House

Sea Rd. ☎ **072/41471.** Reservations recommended for dinner. Bar food under IR£5 ($8); dinner IR£7–IR£11 ($11.20–$17.60). MC, V. Bar food daily 12:30–6pm; dinner daily 6–10pm. BAR FOOD/SEAFOOD/TRADITIONAL.

This lovely little restaurant/bar gives you an "at home" feeling from the moment you enter. The charming bar is very like a family living room, and the pretty dining room sports pink and white linen, with tables nicely spaced. During the day you can get salad plates and other casual dishes in the bar, and the dinner menu features dressed lamb chops with mint sauce, pork chops with mushroom sauce, beef Stroganoff, and prime sirloin steaks. There's also an extensive wine list.

BALLYSHANNON

Five miles north of Bundoran on N15, Ballyshannon is the largest town in southern County Donegal. It sits on the River Erne at the point where it becomes tidal, and is the subject of myths and legends that go back as far as 1500 B.C., when tradition has it that Ireland's first colonization actually took place on the tiny islet of Inis Saimer in the river's estuary. It is also the birthplace of the noted 19th-century poet William Allingham, who lies buried in the graveyard of **St. Anne's Church** a little north of town. St. Anne's sits high on a hill (Mullach na Shee, "Hill of the Fairies"), with fine panoramic views.

One mile northwest of town, the once-famous Cistercian **Assaroe Abbey,** founded in 1184, now lies in ruins, although its mill wheel has been restored and is driven by water from the Abbey River just as in ancient days. Some 50 yards away at the edge of the Abbey River, **Catsby Cave** is a grottolike setting where a rough-hewn altar reminds you that mass was celebrated here during the penal years when the ritual was prohibited by law.

In modern times, Ballyshannon has developed into an important tourist and shopping center. Its safe beaches along the rugged coastline provide good swimming, surfing, and other **water sports,** with the best swimming beaches at Bundoran, Creevy, and Rossnowlagh. There's good **fishing** in the sea, the Erne estuary, Assaroe Lake, and the Drowse River.

Shopping is excellent in Ballyshannon (see below), and just four miles to the east (on the County Fermanagh border) the little town of **Belleek** is the home of lovely handmade Belleek Parian China (see Section 2 in Chapter 25).

Evening entertainment comes in the form of traditional music in some of the town's 21 lively pubs (inquire locally about current venues, and check Sweeney's Pub; see "Where to Eat," below). In late July or early August there's the famous **Ballyshannon Folk Festival,** when music rings through the streets day and night.

Shopping

Celtic Weave China

Cloghore. ☎ **072/51844.**

Owner Tommy Daly and his family learned the art of making cobweb-light woven Parian China baskets in Belleek, then opened their own factory and showroom in this little village. Each piece is individually crafted in unique designs by Tommy and his son, Adrian; and Tommy's wife, Patricia, then hand-paints each one in delicate floral shades. This is the only place in Ireland you can buy these exquisite pieces, and in the U.S., Tiffany & Co. is the only outlet. The shop is three miles east of Ballyshannon on Belleek Road, one mile west of Belleek. It's open Monday through Saturday from 9am to 6pm.

✪ Donegal Irish Parian China

Ballyshannon. ☎ **073/51826.**

A relative newcomer to Irish handcrafts is the delicately beautiful Donegal Irish Parian China (much like porcelain) made in Ballyshannon. It has already made an enormous impact on the homefront as well as the export scene. The Exhibition Centre in their large, modern complex is really something of an art gallery; free tours of the factory are conducted every half hour. Look for the graceful shapes and soft green shamrock or pastel floral designs. Prices run the gamut from *very* expensive to moderate, and your purchases can be mailed home. The factory is a quarter mile from the town center on the main Ballyshannon-Bundoran road (N15). It's open Monday through Saturday from 9am to 5pm.

Where to Stay

Ardeelan Manor

Rossnowlagh, Co. Donegal. ☎ **072/51578.** 5 rms, none with bath. IR£20 ($32) single; IR£15 ($24) per person sharing. 20% reduction for children. (Rates include breakfast.) No credit cards. Closed Sept–June.

This beautifully restored 1800 stone house is the home of Borneo-born Mrs. Fun Britton, who met her husband, Conor, when both were working in Scotland. They and their three charming young children extend warm hospitality to guests. The house is done in country style with many antique furnishings, reflecting its peaceful setting. Two of the guest rooms have sea views, while others face the garden. The Brittons can arrange baby-sitting, the house is centrally heated, and there's plenty of parking. They're located five miles northwest of Ballyshannon on R231.

Ardpatton Farm House

Cavangarden, Ballyshannon, Co. Donegal. ☎ **072/51546.** 6 rms, all with bath. IR£18.50 ($29.60) single; IR£15 ($24) per person sharing. 50% reduction for children. (Rates include breakfast.) Dinner IR£12 ($19.20) extra. No credit cards. Closed Jan.

Mrs. Rose McCaffrey presides over this 200-year-old farmhouse three miles north of town on the Donegal road (N15), and she and those of her 10 children still living at home extend a traditional warm Irish farmhouse welcome to visitors. The house sits on 380 rural acres, and the large lounge and dining room overlook peaceful fields. The nicely furnished guest rooms are more spacious than most—one family room will, in fact, accommodate up to six people. On cool evenings there are open fires, although the house has central heating.

✪ Bri-Ter-An

Bundoran Rd., Ballyshannon, Co. Donegal. ☎ **072/51490.** 3 rms, 1 with bath. IR£18 ($28.80) single; IR£14 ($22.40) per person sharing; IR£1.50 ($2.40) per person additional with bath. 20% reduction for children. (Rates include breakfast.) No credit cards. Closed Jan.

Mrs. Margaret Barrett is the gracious hostess at this modern bungalow half a mile from the town center. The house is set on the shores of Donegal Bay, and as one reader wrote, "The view across the bay from the lounge is worth the price of the room." Leaving aside the view, however, the lounge is a bright, cheerful gathering point for guests, and there's a separate TV lounge. Guest rooms have built-in wardrobes, and all are close to the bath.

✪ Cavangarden House

Cavangarden, Ballyshannon, Co. Donegal. ☎ **072/51365.** 6 rms, 5 with bath. IR£18 ($28.80) single; IR£13.50 ($21.60) per person sharing without bath; IR£1.50 ($2.40) per person additional with bath. 50% reduction for children. Dinner IR£12 ($19.20) extra. (Rates include breakfast.) AE, V. Closed Nov–Apr.

This lovely old Georgian home set in spacious grounds three miles north of town on the main Donegal road (N15) dates back to 1750 and is the home of Mrs. Agnes McCaffrey. Furnishings in the large three-story house feature antiques, and there are turf and log fires on cool evenings, when impromptu singsongs sometimes break out around the piano in the dining room. Guest rooms here are exceptionally spacious, and two family rooms will accommodate up to four people each.

Smugglers Creek Inn

Rossnowlagh, Co. Donegal. ☎ **072/52366.** 5 rms, all with bath. Seasonal rates IR£25–IR£30 ($40–$48) single; IR£19.50–IR£24 ($31.20– $38.40) per person sharing. (Rates include breakfast.) ACC, MC, V.

In one of the most spectacularly beautiful settings in these parts, this atmospheric inn is delightful, either as an overnight stop or as a base for exploring this part of the county. Guest rooms, all with good sea views, are a little on the small side, and each one is different in decor and comfortably furnished. The pub/restaurant (see "Where to Eat," below) is a center of conviviality as well as good food.

Worth a Splurge

✪ Sand House Hotel

Rossnowlagh, Co. Donegal. ☎ **072/51777.** Fax 072/52100. 39 rms, all with bath. TV TEL. IR£40–IR£50 ($64–$80) single; IR£35–IR£45 ($56–$72) per person sharing; additional charge for sea-view rooms. 50% reduction for children. (Rates include breakfast.) $40-per-person deposit required on booking. Weekend rates available. AE, DC, MC, V. Closed Nov–Feb.

With one of the most beautiful settings in the Northwest, five miles northwest of Ballyshannon on R231, the Sand House is a modern, first-class hotel perched among the dunes that line a two-mile crescent beach. The entrance lounge, with its large black Kilkenny slate fireplace, is more akin to a gracious country house than a hotel lobby. Owner Mary Britton and her sons have put in chintz-covered couches and armchairs that invite friendly chats before the fire, and Georgian credenzas are filled with Belleek china and other treasures. Lovely antique pieces are sprinkled all through the hotel. As for guest rooms, deluxe sea-view rooms have a small sitting area, and many of the superior sea-view rooms have antique furnishings, some with four-poster beds. Those without a sea view are also beautifully decorated and overlook a nine-hole golf course.

The Surfers Bar decor has a nautical feel, with walls done in wood in the shape of a wave breaking, while another small residents' snug bar features cases of stuffed birds. The dining room specializes in fresh seafood, as well as a nice selection of continental and Irish dishes and a good wine list. Golf is free to guests, canoes can be rented, and pony trekking is available.

WHERE TO EAT

Smugglers Creek Inn

Rossnowlagh, Co. Donegal. ☎ **072/52366.** Bar food under IR£7 ($11.20); average dinner under IR£20 ($32). ACC, MC, V. Daily, bar food 1–6pm, dinner 6–9:30pm. BAR FOOD/SEAFOOD/VEGETARIAN.

Conor Britton, who learned his trade in the family-run Sand House Hotel (see above), has created an outstanding pub/restaurant on this spectacular clifftop site. Bar food, in the comfortable bar with its open fires, is superb and comes from the same kitchen as the restaurant. Homemade soups (try one of the fish soups) and nutty brown bread make a hearty lunch, and if your capacity can cope, you might add the lovely garlic mussels or smoked salmon. Dinners in the restaurant, with its stone floors and smashing sea views, might consist of a delicious warm salad of smoked bacon, blue cheese, and croutons as starter; followed by a seafood main course; with Irish farmhouse cheeses to finish. Vegetarians will find a stir-fry or tagliatelle on offer, and children are well catered to.

✪ Sweeney's Pub and White Horse Bar

Assaroe Rd. (N15). Reservations not required. IR£5–IR£10 ($8–$16). No credit cards. Mon–Sat 10:30am–11:30pm; Sun 12–2pm and 4–11:30pm. BAR FOOD.

Sweeney's is a delight to visit—partly because of its congenial hosts, John and Pat Sweeney, and partly because of its warm, inviting, and atmospheric interior. The first recorded sale of the premises is dated 1793, and the Sweeneys have managed to create a comfortable, semimodern environment that still retains much of the character of the old building. If you happen by on a Friday, drop in for traditional Irish music in the stone-arched Cellar Bar. Other times, excellent snacks, soup, and salads provide nourishment and a well-pulled pint provides refreshment in the bar and lounge upstairs.

KILLYBEGS

If you can manage to get to the picturesque little harbor town of Killybegs (17 miles west of Donegal town via N56) in the late afternoon, go down to the pier to watch the ✪ **fishing fleet** come in—it's a memorable experience, with sea gulls screeching overhead and half the town gathered to greet the fishermen.

Should you arrive in August, the **Killybegs International Sea Angling Festival** is great fun, with European fishing enthusiasts converging on the little town and festivities from morning to night.

Three miles south of town, **Drumanoo Head** affords splendid coastal views.

There's **traditional music** in several pubs, including the Harbour Bar, the Lone Star, the Sail Inn, and Fawlty Towers.

SHOPPING

Eight miles west of Killybegs on the Glencolumbkille road (T72A), the village of **Kilcar** is a center of the Donegal handwoven tweed industry, as well as for hand-embroidery and knits. Monday through Saturday from 10am to 5pm, you can stop by ✪ **Studio Donegal** (☎ 075/38194) in the village center, where the misty tones of Donegal tweed come in jacket, skirt, or pants lengths, as well as ready-made garments.

You'll also be welcomed at the **Gaeltarra Eireann Factory, Connemara Fabrics,** and **Gaeltarra Snath,** all in the village center and open Monday through Friday from 10am to 5pm.

One mile west of Kilcar on the coast road, **Annmarie's Handknits** is the happy hunting ground for a good selection of knits at reasonable prices.

WHERE TO STAY

✪ Bannagh House

Finta Rd., Killybegs, Co. Donegal. ☎ **073/31108.** 4 rms, all with bath. IR£20 ($32) single; IR£15 ($24) per person sharing. (Rates include breakfast.) No credit cards. Closed Dec–Feb. Private car park.

This lovely hilltop bungalow on the outskirts of town on the coast road has sweeping views of Killybegs harbor and fishing fleet. The home of Phyllis and Fergus (he's an ambulance driver) Melly and their five children, the centrally heated house is beautifully decorated and guest rooms are well appointed (some with harbor views). Best of all, the Melly family are as attractive and welcoming as their home.

Castlereagh House

Castlereagh, Bruckless, Co. Donegal. ☎ **073/37202.** 3 rms, 2 with bath. IR£20 ($32) single; IR£16 ($25.60) per person sharing. 20% reduction for children. (Rates include breakfast.) ACC, MC, V. Closed Oct–Mar. Located 2.5 miles east of Killybegs, 11 miles west of Donegal town on the N56 coast road.

Castlereagh House is an early-20th-century two-story farmhouse, the family home of Elizabeth and Ernest Henry and their son, Howard. Although there is good central heating, turf and log fires are usually aglow in the dining room. The spacious lounge has splendid views overlooking Bruckless Bay and the surrounding countryside. Guest rooms are attractive and comfortably furnished. There's a private car park.

Conkay House

Roshine Rd., Killybegs, Co. Donegal. ☎ **073/31273.** 3 rms, 1 with shower. IR£17 ($27.20) single; IR£13 ($20.80) per person sharing. 25% reduction for children. (Rates include breakfast.) No credit cards. Closed Oct–Mar.

Mrs. McGuinness will welcome you warmly to her modern bungalow, which overlooks Killybegs Bay, a short walk from the town center. The house is centrally heated and there is a garden that guests may use. The three pretty bedrooms are comfortably furnished.

Lismolin Country Home

Fintra Rd., Killybegs, Co. Donegal. ☎ **073/31035.** 5 rms, all with bath. IR£19 ($30.40) single; IR£15 ($24) per person sharing. 33 1/3% reduction for children. (Rates include breakfast.) Dinner IR£12.50 ($20) extra. MC, V.

This is the home of Mrs. Bernie Cahill, which sits half a mile from the town center right at the edge of a beautiful forest area. The modern, centrally heated bungalow is tastefully decorated, with five spacious guest rooms. Guests are greeted with tea, scones, and homemade jams, and tasty meals feature Mrs. Cahill's home baking. Turf and log fires are aglow every day in the lounge, even though the house has good central heating.

Where to Eat

✪ Sail Inn Restaurant and Bar

Main St., Killybegs, Co. Donegal. ☎ **073/31130.** Reservations recommended for dinner. Bar food IR£2–IR£5 ($3.20–$8); dinner IR£10–IR£14 ($16–$22.40). MC, V. Bar menu daily noon–2:30pm; dinner daily 5:30–10pm. BAR FOOD/TRADITIONAL.

This popular bar and restaurant at the western end of Main Street has loads of character in the downstairs bar, where soup, sandwiches, salads, and hot plates are all well prepared. Upstairs, the cozy restaurant seats only 26, and dinner is served by candlelight. The extensive menu includes such specialties as beef Stroganoff, steak au poivre, roast duckling, and chicken Madras. There's also a good wine list at moderate prices. *Note:* They also have accommodations for about IR£15 ($24) per person.

GLENCOLUMBKILLE

Glencolumbkille sits at the very end of T72A, some 35 miles west of Donegal town. The drive from Killybegs to Glencolumbkille ("St. Colmcille's Glen"), through lonely mountain country with occasional glimpses of the sea, is a journey through history and a culture that has changed little since the days when (or so local legend insists) Bonnie Prince Charlie hid out in the glen. The stony hills are dotted with more than 40 cairns, dolmens, souterrains, and other relics of a past that goes back as far as 5,000 years.

The Top Attraction

✪ Glencolumbkille Folk Village Museum

Glencolumbkille. ☎ **073/30017** or 30035. Admission IR£2 ($3.20). Easter Sat–Oct, Mon–Sat 10am–6pm, Sun noon–6pm.

This is one of the most authentic folk villages in the country, with three cottages built and furnished to bring to life three different eras stretching from 1700 to 1900. There are guided tours every hour that explain the workings of each cottage. The home of a 1720 cotter is earthen-floored, and its open hearth has no chimney; by the 1820s the cotter's home has a flagstone floor, chimney, and oil-lamp lighting (as well as, sad to relate, a tin trunk that would carry the immigrating family's treasures to "Amerikay"); and the 1920 cottage is very like many you'll have seen in your travels around today's Irish countryside. The courtyard around which the cottages are grouped holds such everyday items as a peat cart and fishing boat, with the large "famine pot," a somber reminder of famine days, when starving peasants lined up to be served a meager ration. A schoolhouse from a century ago and a country pub, or "sheebeen" (where more often than not the drink sold was illegal poteen!), complete the village. There's a cottage craft shop and tearoom, where hot tea and scones are sold from June through September.

Where to Stay

Corner House

Cashel, Glencolumbkille, Co. Donegal. ☎ **073/30021.** 5 rms, 4 with bath. IR£20 ($32) single; IR£13.50 ($21.60) per person sharing; IR£1.50 ($2.40) per person additional with bath. 20% reduction for children. (Rates include breakfast.) No credit cards. Closed Oct–Mar.

Mrs. John Byrne presides over this nice two-story home set in the peaceful valley of Glencolumbkille five miles east of town on the Ardara road, and this location allows you to sink into the very special character of this remote part of Ireland. Guest rooms are quite comfortable, and sandy beaches are within easy reach, as is good fishing. The folk museum is less than five minutes away.

ARDARA

Ardara has long been a center of the home-weaving industry, and its few streets are lined with shops selling tweeds at good prices. Shoppers will have a field day, and they shouldn't miss the following factory shops, the first two of which have tearooms on the premises: **John Molloy & Co.** (☎ 075/41133), **Kennedy's of Ardara** (☎ 075/41106), and **Cornelius Bonner & Son Ltd.** (☎ 075/41196). All are open Monday through Saturday from 10am to 6pm and all accept most credit cards. No matter where you end up buying, however, prices hereabouts are likely to be the best you'll find anywhere in the country. For a better understanding of how Donegal tweed is made—from the shearing of the sheep to the finished product—spend some time in the **Ardara Heritage Centre** (☎ 075/41262). An audio-visual production explores some of the scenic highlights of the area.

I'm told that **Woodhill House,** on the Portnoo road in Ardara (owned by Nancy Yates's family—see below) is "very large in local character." **Peter Oliver's** is another character-laden pub, where you'll find traditional music most nights during the summer months.

WHERE TO STAY

Bay View Country House

Portnoo Rd., Ardara, Co. Donegal. ☎ **075/41145.** 7 rms, all with bath. IR£18.50 ($29.60) single; IR£15 ($24) per person sharing. Reduction for children. (Rates include breakfast.) Dinner IR£14 ($22.40) extra. AE, MC, V. Closed Mid-Nov to Feb.

With magnificent views of Loughros Bay and the Owenea River, this centrally heated country home on the northern edge of town on the coast road has a spacious lounge with picture windows and turf fires, and a large dining room, where dinners include traditional Irish dishes as well as fresh local fish. The comfortable bedrooms all have tea-making equipment. Marian and Charles Bennett are helpful hosts, and Charles (who plays traditional music in pubs with a local group) is an active member of the Ardara Tourism Committee.

✪ Greenhaven

Portnoo Rd., Ardara, Co. Donegal. ☎ **075/41129.** 6 rms, all with bath. IR£15 ($24) per person. (Rates include breakfast.) V. Closed Christmas.

Eileen and Ray Molloy are the delightful hosts at Greenhaven, at the northern edge of town on the coast road, which overlooks Loughross Bay and Slieve Tooey on the other side of the bay. There's a window-walled breakfast room open to the gorgeous view, and a large back garden. A modern extension holds the comfortable guest rooms, with lovely, puffy eiderdown quilts on all beds. The Molloys are especially helpful in pointing their guests to the things to see and do in the area (this is Ray's family territory, and he knows it well).

✪ Pinewood

Straboy, Glenties, Co. Donegal. ☎ **075/51223.** 4 rms, 3 with bath. IR£18 ($28.80) single; IR£13.50 ($21.60) per person sharing without bath; IR£1 ($1.60) per person additional with bath. 33 1/3% reduction for children. (Rates include breakfast.) Dinner IR£12 ($19.20). No credit cards. Closed Dec–Mar.

Mrs. Mary Ward is the friendly hostess of this modern bungalow located on the main Glenties-Letterkenny road two miles northwest of Glenties and five miles northwest of Ardara. It is set in lovely surroundings and the house is centrally heated, with electric blankets supplied. Mary is an excellent cook and serves wonderful meals. Her husband, Michael, is a schoolteacher and familiar with historic and scenic sites all over Ireland. The four attractive bedrooms are all nicely furnished and comfortable.

Worth a Splurge

✪ Woodhill House

Ardara, Co. Donegal. ☎ **075/41112.** 5 rms, all with bath. IR£18 ($28.80) single; IR£22–IR£26 ($35.20–$41.60) per person sharing. (Rates include breakfast.) AE, DC, MC, V.

This beautiful old country house sits on four acres at the edge of the village, with magnificent views of the Donegal hills. John and Nancy Yates (he's an Englishman, she's local) are the owners, and it was Nancy's great-grandmother for whom Nancy's Pub was named. The Yateses have installed a cozy bar with peat fires, and guest rooms in the house, as well as those in the renovated coach house, are beautifully done up. Both are keenly interested in their guests and are enthusiastic about this area's charms. There's central heating and good parking.

WHERE TO EAT

Nesbit Arms Hotel

Ardara. ☎ **075/41103.** Reservations not required. Breakfast IR£6 ($9.60); lunch IR£8 ($12.80); dinner IR£12 ($19.20). MC, V. Daily 8:30–10am; 12:30–2:30pm; and 6–9pm. Closed Dec 24–25. TRADITIONAL/VEGETARIAN.

The dining room in this family-owned and -operated hotel serves meals featuring local produce, meat, and fish cooked in the traditional Irish manner. It's a friendly place, serving all three meals, and service is quite good.

✪ Woodhill House

Ardara. ☎ **075/41112.** Reservations recommended. Breakfast IR£5 ($8); lunch under IR£10 ($16); dinner IR£13–IR£22 ($20.80–$35.20). AE, DC, MC, V. Easter–Oct. TRADITIONAL.

This country house, in a scenic setting on the edge of the village (see "Where to Stay," above), specializes in dishes that feature local produce and seafood served in a beautiful dining room.

ARDARA TO LETTERKENNY

Heading north via N56, the cliff and coastal scenery is hauntingly beautiful and lonely. Drive through towns and villages with sonorous names like Glenties (Na Gleannta, "The Valleys"); Dungloe, home of the famous "Mary of Dungloe" Festival; Burtonport; Gweedore, where there's always good traditional music; Bunbeg, on the alternative loop around County Donegal's fabulous Bloody Foreland where the setting sun infuses the rocks with color, turning the landscape blood-red; at Magheroarty Pier near Gortnahork, there's mailboat service out to remote **Tory Island** (in summer months there's a ferry service—inquire locally), with a population of only 200, but with magnificent cliff and sea views; and Dunfanaghy, where you'll find **Alan Harley's Art Gallery,** which features Irish painter Tom Egginton's glowing landscape canvases and a huge stock of local crafts. This is also the takeoff point for the dramatic clifftop **Horn Head Drive.**

Between Dunfanaghy and Creeslough, take time to visit ✪ **Ards Forest Park,** on the shores of Sheep Haven Bay. It's Ireland's most northerly forest park, and its 1,200 acres hold beautiful woodlands, salt marsh, sand dunes, seashore, freshwater lakes, fenland, and rock faces. Legend has it that back when time began this was the domain of Bioróg, the *bean si* (Banshee), the fairy woman who thwarted Balor of the evil eye, god of drought and plague. Be that as it may, the park's Fairy Glen is, to this day, said to be the haunt of Bioróg. There are traces of Ireland's earliest inhabitants in the four ring forts within the park, and nature paths are well marked. Informative literature is available at the park entrance.

At Creeslough, turn north again on R245 for a gorgeous drive to Carrigart. En route, some three miles from Creeslough, look for **Doe Castle,** the 16th-century home of the MacSweeny clan that was in residential use until 1843. At Carrigart, turn south to Milford. At Milford, R246 takes you north through beautiful scenery to Kerrykeel, where you join R247 southeast to the shores of ✪ **Lough Swilly** at historic Rathmullan. The little harbor here was the debarkation point of the tragic Flight of the Earls in 1607, and in 1798, this is where Wolfe Tone was taken prisoner. The **Flight of the Earls Heritage Centre** (☎ 074/51178) tells the story of the earls (the O'Neill and the O'Donnell) through interesting artworks, artifacts, and wax-model exhibits. On the outskirts of town, there are interesting 15th-century **Carmelite friary ruins.** The coast road south takes you to Ramelton and on to the cathedral town of Letterkenny via N56.

Where to Stay En Route

Ardeen

Ramelton, Co. Donegal. ☎ **074/51243.** 4 rms, 2 with bath. IR£19 ($30.40) single without bath; IR£16 ($25.60) per person sharing without bath; IR£1.50 ($2.40) per person additional with bath. 25% reduction for children. (Rates include breakfast.) AE. Closed Nov–Easter.

Mrs. Anne Campbell is the delightful hostess of this beautiful country home furnished with antiques, on the outskirts of town overlooking Lough Swilly. Mrs. Campbell and her family are all helpful and friendly. The house is centrally heated and the four pretty bedrooms are nicely furnished. There's a hard-surface tennis court for guests to use.

Self-Catering

✪ Donegal Thatched Cottages

On Cruit Island, c/o Conor and Mary Ward, Rosses Point, Co. Sligo. ☎ **071/77197.** Fax 071/77500. 10 cottages. IR£170–IR£550 ($272–$880) per cottage per week; weekends Oct–May. IR£95–IR£180 ($152–$288) per cottage. Rates depend on season. No credit cards.

Ireland has many good self-catering cottages for visitors, but few in as breathtakingly beautiful a location—just offshore on an island connected to the mainland by a bridge (signposted on N56 between Burtonport and Annagry). The cottages are traditional in design (with thatch roofs and turf-burning fireplaces as well as central heat), and are set on a sheltered clifftop with spectacular seascapes of Donegal's rugged coastline, with Aranmore and Owey islands clearly visible. At the foot of the cliff is a lovely little half moon of a beach, and at the other side of the cliff, a golden strand safe for swimming goes on for miles. The fishing, boating, and swimming around here are all superb. Nearby are good local pubs and one very good restaurant. The cottages have been built and furnished with all Irish-made products, and while there's all the charm of bygone days in the decor, there are modern conveniences such as the automatic washer and dryer that are kept out of sight behind cabinet doors so as not to interfere with the traditional decor. Some cottages also have dishwashers. Turf is furnished in generous quantities so you can indulge any penchant for the open hearth. Each cottage can sleep as many as seven adults comfortably, which makes the weekly rates fall easily within budget limits if you bring a full party. You can book into this very special place by contacting the owners, who will be glad to send you a brochure with full details.

✪ Rathmullan Country House

Rathmullan, Co. Donegal. ☎ **074/58188.** Fax 074/58200. 23 rms, all with bath. Per person IR£25–IR£30 ($40–$48) for budget rooms; IR£35 ($56) for standard rooms; IR£48–IR£58 ($76.80–$92.80) for superior rooms. IR£10–IR£20 ($16-$32) single supplement. 10% service charge. 50% reduction for children. Daily and weekly half-board rates available. (Rates include breakfast.) AE, DC, MC, V. Closed Nov to mid-Mar.

This lovely old house sits at the edge of town amid spacious, landscaped grounds that slope down to Lough Swilly, and in the more than 30 years that Robin and Bob Wheeler have been in residence, it has become a beloved favorite with the Irish from all over the Republic, as well as nearby Northern Ireland. The house dates back to the early 1800s, and the Wheelers have brought back a graciousness and charm that disappeared during the years of its rather checkered career. The soft glow of turf or log fires in the drawing room and library lights furnishings that combine a tasteful mixture of period and comfortably overstuffed modern pieces. The glass-enclosed Pavilion Dining Room looks out to award-winning gardens, and the cellar bar is a cozy spot for relaxed conviviality. Accommodations come in a wide range, from large, luxuriously furnished guest rooms that look out to the lough to plainer, somewhat smaller and less expensive rooms. The Egyptian Baths Leisure Centre includes a swimming pool, sauna, and steam room. Sumptuous dinners, for which chef Bob has earned an international reputation, are quite moderately priced and feature local seafood and other products (see "Where to Eat En Route," below). Advance reservations for both accommodations and meals in this very popular place are absolutely essential.

Where to Eat En Route

Pub grub will be your mainstay for lunches en route, and you'll find some very good cooking going under that name. As for the evening meal, it's possible to find yourself far from a large, populated town when hunger strikes, but there are hotel dining rooms in most of the main towns (like **Arnold's Hotel,** Main Street, Dunfanaghy) that dish up quite good dinners at prices well below those in other parts of the country.

Danny Minnie's Restaurant

Annagry, The Rosses. ☎ **075/48201.** Reservations not required. Lunch IR£5 ($8); average dinner IR£16 ($25.60). MC, V. Mar–Dec, daily 10am–10pm. Closed Jan–Feb, Good Friday, Christmas Day. SEAFOOD/TRADITIONAL/VEGETARIAN.

This charming traditional-style, family-run restaurant is a delight to the eye as well as to the palate. There's a warm, welcoming atmosphere very much in keeping with Irish traditions of hospitality, and the menu offers a nice selection of local seafood and fresh produce.

✪ Pavilion Dining Room

Rathmullan Country House, Rathmullan. ☎ **074/58188.** Reservations required. Dinner IR£23 ($36.80) plus 10% service charge. Sun lunch IR£13 ($20.80). AE, DC, MC, V. Mid-Mar to Nov daily 7:30–8:30pm; Sun 1–2pm. SEAFOOD/TRADITIONAL/VEGETARIAN.

This elegant glass-walled dining room looks out over well-kept lawns that slope down to the shores of Lough Swilly. The domain of chef Eamon O'Reilly, its menu includes locally caught salmon hollandaise; roasts from Irish beef, pork, and lamb; and vegetables from their own garden. Fresh fruits from trees right on the premises go into luscious homemade pies, and if you've ever been curious about the seaweed-based Carrageen dessert, this is the place to try it. There's a very good wine list, and service is both friendly and professional. In 1987, the Pavilion won the Best Breakfast Award.

SHOPPING IN RAMELTON

You'll pass through Ramelton en route from Rathmullan to Letterkenny, and thanks to a reader, I can pass along this shopping tip. Just outside Ramelton on the road to Milford, there's a wonderful **craft shop** owned by Mrs. S. Browne, Black's Glen. The Aran sweaters on display were knit by Mrs. Browne and her neighbors, and she sells them at substantial savings. They're as beautiful and well crafted as you'll find anywhere. Do take time to browse through the host of other interesting handcrafts in her shop.

LETTERKENNY

Letterkenny is the chief town of County Donegal and an important ecclesiastical city. If you chose the short route from Donegal town north via N15 and N56, this is an ideal base from which to make day trips to explore northern Donegal's Fanad and Rosguill peninsulas or the coastline drives outlined above. The town sits at the point where the River Swilly empties into Lough Swilly, and its main street is one of the longest in Ireland.

Visitor Information For information, contact the **Letterkenny Tourist Office,** Derry Road, Letterkenny, County Donegal (☎ 074/21173). It's open June through September, daily from 10am to 5pm; other months, Monday through Friday with shorter hours.

WHAT TO SEE & DO

You can't miss Letterkenny's most outstanding attraction—**St. Eunan's Cathedral,** near Sentry Hill on Cathedral Street, dominates the skyline and is floodlit at night. Completed in 1901, it is Gothic in style, with much Celtic carving, richly decorated ceilings, and beautiful stained-glass windows.

The **County Donegal Museum** on High Road is in the only surviving portion of an old workhouse which has only recently been converted to a museum—consult the Tourist Office for hours.

Golfers are welcomed at the 18-hole **golf course** on the outskirts of town off the Ramelton road (☎ 074/21150). There's excellent **fishing** in Lough Swilly as well as other lakes and rivers nearby. For fishing information, phone Mr. Gerry McNulty (☎ 074/24476). The **Letterkenny Leisure Centre** (☎ 074/21793) has excellent facilities, including a swimming pool, kiddies' pool, spa pool, sauna, and steam room.

Attractions Nearby

✪ Glenveagh National Park

Churchill. ☎ **074/37090.** Admission IR£2 ($3.20) adults, IR£1 ($1.60) children, IR£1.50 ($2.40) seniors. Easter–Oct, 10:30am–6.30pm. Closed Fri Oct–Nov.

This is one of County Donegal's premier visitor attractions. Set aside at least half a day to take in the deeply wooded reaches of the park and its impressive castle. Set in the very heart of the Donegal highlands, between the Derryveagh and Glendowan mountain ranges, the park covers almost 25,000 acres of wilderness, with the castle and its magnificent gardens set like a jewel on the edge of Lough Veagh. There's a very good audiovisual show at the Visitors Centre, and tea and scones with homemade jam are available in the castle kitchen.

The park is 18 miles northwest of Letterkenny on the Churchill road (R251); access also from N56 north to Kilmacreanan, turning left onto the Gweedore road.

Glebe Gallery and St. Columb's

Churchill. ☎ **074/37071.** Admission IR£2 ($3.20) adults, IR£1 ($1.60) children, 1.50 ($2.40) seniors. June–Sept, Mon–Sat 11am–6:30pm, Sun 1–6pm (last tour at 5:30pm).

Some 11 miles northwest of Letterkenny on the Churchill road (R251) near Churchill Village, St. Columb's sits amid informal gardens and was the home of noted landscape and portrait painter Derek Hill, who has given the property and the paintings to the nation. The adjacent Glebe Gallery houses his extensive art collection, and the house itself contains a wide range of antique artworks, Victoriana, and prints from China and Japan.

Lurgyvale Thatched Cottage

Kilmacrennan. ☎ 074/39024. Admission IR£2 ($3.20). May–Oct, Mon–Wed and Fri–Sat 10am–7pm, Thurs 10am–12:30am, Sun 11am–7pm.

This 150-year-old cottage has been carefully restored so faithfully that it won a European Heritage Conservation Award. Visitors are welcomed with homemade scones in the kitchen, with its flagstone floor and open hearth, then given a guided tour of the homey interior. Periodic craft demonstrations include spinning, flailing, churning, and straw-rope making, and on Thursday at 8:30pm, there are traditional music and dancing sessions. Outside, there's a landscaped picnic area and a nature walk through lovely wooded areas down to the Lurgy River.

Where to Stay

An Crossog

Downings, Letterkenny, Co. Donegal. ☎ **074/55498.** 4 rms, 1 with bath. IR£13.50 ($21.60) per person sharing; IR£1 ($1.60) per person extra for bath; IR£5 ($8) single supplement. High tea IR£8 ($12.80); dinner IR£11 ($17.60). No credit cards. Open May–Sept. 18½ miles from Letterkenny on R245, 6 miles off N56.

Mrs. Marrietta Herraghty makes guests very welcome in this large old farmhouse, just off the Atlantic Drive scenic route. Guest rooms are spacious and comfortably furnished. Her meals feature fresh local produce and seafood from nearby waters.

Ardglas

Lurgybrack, Letterkenny, Co. Donegal. ☎ **074/22516.** 6 rms, 5 with bath. TV. IR£18 ($28.80) single; IR£14.50 ($23.20) per person sharing; IR£1.50 ($2.40) per person extra with bath. 30% reduction for children. (Rates include breakfast.) No credit cards. Closed Nov–Mar.

Breid and Paddy Kelly's spacious country home sits on extensive grounds overlooking Letterkenny and the Muckish Mountains. It's one mile out the Derry road, then a mile on N56 (take the Sligo road at the roundabout). The entire Kelly family welcomes guests and helps with local and regional sightseeing plans. There's a large garden, much used by guests in fine weather, and the attractive bedrooms all have tea/coffeemakers, TVs, and hairdryers. Guests also have a TV lounge, and there's plenty of private parking.

Readers Recommend

Bella Vista, *Old Derry-Letterkenny Road, Letterkenny, Co. Donegal.* ☎ 074/22529. *"Mrs. Mary Lee is a friendly, welcoming person who has attractive rooms, all en suite, and offers yogurt and fresh fruit for breakfast in addition to the usual cooked fare."*
—Mary Vail, Dublin, Ireland

✪ Hill Crest House

Lurgybrack, Letterkenny, Co. Donegal. ☎ **074/22300** or 25137. 6 rms, 5 with bath. IR£20 ($32) single; IR£13.50 ($21.60) per person sharing; IR£1.50 ($2.40) per person extra with bath. 35% reduction for children. (Rates include breakfast.) MC, V. Closed Christmas.

Two miles from Letterkenny (on the main Ballybofey-Sligo road), this modern dormer bungalow sits on a slight elevation that opens up splendid views of the River Swilly, Letterkenny, and the mountains. Margaret and Larry Maguire welcome guests with complimentary tea and buns, and since they are both locals, they enjoy helping guests plan itineraries. Four bedrooms are on the ground floor; some rooms have TV; and there are orthopedic mattresses and electric blankets. In addition to the spacious no-smoking dining room, there's a TV and video lounge, as well as a large private car park.

Radharc Na Giuise

Kilmacrennan Rd., Letterkenny, Co. Donegal. ☎ **074/22090.** 6 rms, all with bath. TV. IR£20 ($32) single; IR£15 ($24) per person sharing. 35% reduction for children. (Rates include breakfast.) MC, V. Closed Christmas.

Mrs. Jennie Bradley is the gracious hostess at this pretty dormer bungalow overlooking the town. Situated on the main Glenveagh National Park road (N56), it is only about a 15-minute walk to the town center. Bedrooms are tastefully furnished. There's a large garden for visitors' use. Private car park.

✪ Town View

Leck Rd., Letterkenny, Co. Donegal. ☎ **074/21570** or 25138. 4 rms, all with bath. TV. IR£20 ($32) single; IR£16 ($25.60) per person sharing. 20% reduction for children. (Rates include breakfast.) No credit cards.

Vivacious May Herrity is hostess at this pretty two-story house perched on a hilltop on the outskirts of town. Panoramic views of Letterkenny are stunning, especially at night when the cathedral is spotlighted. Guest rooms, each with its own color TV, are unusually attractive, decorated, according to May, "the way I like to live myself." Those in the back of the house face peaceful green fields that resemble 18th-century landscape paintings. The pretty lounge, where breakfast is served, has a huge fireplace and picture windows overlooking the town. Breakfast often features a selection of fresh fruits and other items, as well as the traditional full Irish menu. May is active in tourism in this area and a delightful assistant in planning your sightseeing and recreation.

To get to Town View, take the Ballybofey road (N56), cross the stone bridge at Dunnes Stores in Letterkenny, and keep left for half a mile.

Where to Eat

Carolina House Restaurant

Milford Rd. ☎ **074/22480.** Main courses IR£9–IR£14 ($14.40–$22.40). AE, DC, MC, V. Tues–Sat 6–9pm.

Vegetables and herbs come straight from the large kitchen garden of this homey, family-run restaurant set in landscaped grounds overlooking Lough Swilly, about a mile outside town. Chef Mary Prendergast holds to the theory that fish must swim three times: in water, in butter, and in wine, and her seafood dishes are outstanding. For non–seafood lovers, there are traditional Irish specialties such as spiced beef and Donegal lamb.

Gleneany House Restaurant and Guest House

Port Rd. ☎ **074/26088.** Fax 074/26090. Lunch under IR£5 ($8); average dinner 14.50 ($23.20). ACC, MC, V. Daily 12:30–2:30pm, 2:30–7pm (early-bird dinner), and 6–9pm. TRADITIONAL.

This attractive restaurant is made bright and cheerful by lots of blond wood. They specialize in dishes created only from locally produced ingredients. Good, moderately priced wine list.

CARRIGANS

The town of Carrigans is strategically placed for exploring most of northern Donegal, with the Inishowen Peninsula and the Grianian of Aileach fort (see below) nearby; Glenveagh National Park an easy drive; and Northern Ireland highlights such as Derry City (only five miles), the Ulster Folk Park, and the Giant's Causeway (an hour's drive) easy day trips.

WHERE TO STAY

Mount Royd Country Home

Carrigans, Co. Donegal. ☎ **074/40163.** 4 rms, 3 with bath. TV. IR£18.50 ($29.60) single; IR£13.50 ($21.60) per person sharing; IR£1.50 ($2.40) per person extra for bath. 50% reduction for children. High tea IR£6.50 ($10.40); dinner IR£11 ($17.60). No credit cards.

Not only does Mrs. Josephine Martin greet arriving guests with tea and scones, but she provides tea/coffee and biscuits in each bedroom. Her large, creeper-clad home is furnished with antiques. Some of the spacious guest rooms have lovely views of the River Foyle. Her breakfasts have won awards.

3 The Inishowen Peninsula

This long, broad finger of land stretching north to the Atlantic between Lough Swilly to the west and Lough Foyle to the east is Ireland's northernmost point. The Inishowen Peninsula was the home territory of King Niall of the Nine Hostages, a contemporary of St. Patrick in the 5th century. Along the shores of both loughs and the Atlantic Ocean, long stretches of sandy beaches are backed by sheer cliffs. Inland are some of Ireland's most impressive mountains, with 2,019-foot Slieve Snacht dominating the center of the peninsula. Its heritage reaches back beyond recorded history, with relics of those distant days scattered across its face.

Relatively undiscovered by far too many visitors to Ireland, Inishowen is a world apart, where present-day residents revere their ancient heritage and treasure the legends and antiquities of this remote region and still observe many traditions of their ancestors. Turf is cut in the time-honored fashion and in summer months it's not unusual to see it piled beside the roads waiting to be transported to Inishowen cottages to be stacked and dried to ensure a warm winter. Traditional music and dance thrive here, and it is unlikely you will face an evening when there's not a session in a nearby pub.

Despite its completely unspoiled character, however, the peninsula provides comfortable accommodations and recreational facilities for those visitors who come for the scenic splendor and "get away from it all" peacefulness.

GETTING THERE & GETTING AROUND

By Bus There is regular bus service to Buncrana from Derry and from Letterkenny; however, service farther north is sparse to nonexistent.

By Car This is really the only way to see Inishowen properly, although stops for mountain or beach walks should figure prominently in your time schedule. The drive from Letterkenny around the peninsula to Derry is approximately 150 miles. Leaving Letterkenny, take N13 north to the turnoff onto R238 into Burnfoot, where the **Inishowen 100 Scenic Drive** is signposted. If your Irish itinerary will take you on into the six counties of Northern Ireland, the signposts will lead you around the peninsula through its most spectacular points (with my strong recommendation for an overnight stop en route) into the province's second city, Derry (Londonderry). If you're coming from Derry, take A2 west and join R238 at Muff.

VISITOR INFORMATION

The **Tourist Office** in Letterkenny can furnish Inishowen information, as can the office in Sligo, which covers the entire Northwest. If at all possible, however, write or call ahead for more detailed brochures from **Inishowen Tourism,** Chapel Street, Carndonagh, County Donegal (☎ 077/74933 or 74934, fax 077/74935).

WHAT TO SEE & DO

At the little township of Burt, three miles south of Bridgend (10 miles south of Buncrana), look for signposts to the unclassified road that leads to a great circular stone cashel known as **Grianan of Aileach** ("Sun Palace of Aileach"), once the royal seat of the O'Neills and a sacred meeting place for High Kings of Ireland. From its 800-foot-high perch atop Greenan Mountain, there are vast panoramic views of Lough Swilly, Lough Foyle, and the distant sea. The dry-stone fort was built, as far as archeologists can determine, in about 1700 B.C., and its 76-foot diameter is enclosed by walls 13 feet thick and 17 feet high. During the Iron Age the earthen enclosures served as a temple of the sun. Virtually dismantled stone by stone in 1101 by Murtagh O'Brien, King of Munster, it was restored in the 1870s. As you descend from this lofty antiquity, look again at **Burt Church,** which sits at the foot of the access road—its circular design follows that of the fort itself, and it is being developed as a Visitor Centre, focusing on the history, legends, and folklore of the Grianan of Aileach. There's a traditional tearoom, as well as a craft shop.

A few miles farther north, **Inch Island** (reached by a bridge from the mainland) is home to the **Inishowen Heritage Centre** (☎ 077/60152). At the little resort town of **Fahan,** the old graveyard holds a flat, two-faced cross from the 7th century and two rather curious carved stones.

Buncrana, the principal town of Inishowen, is a pleasant seaside resort with three miles of sand beach. Along a pleasant walk and overlooking the Crana River are the ruins of **Buncrana Castle,** dating back to the late 16th century, with extensive rebuilding in 1718. This is where Wolfe Tone was taken after his capture in 1798. Close by are the ruins of **O'Doherty's Castle.** Reflecting more modern times, the **Vintage Car & Carriage Museum,** Buncrana (☎ 077/61130), has an

Inishowen Peninsula

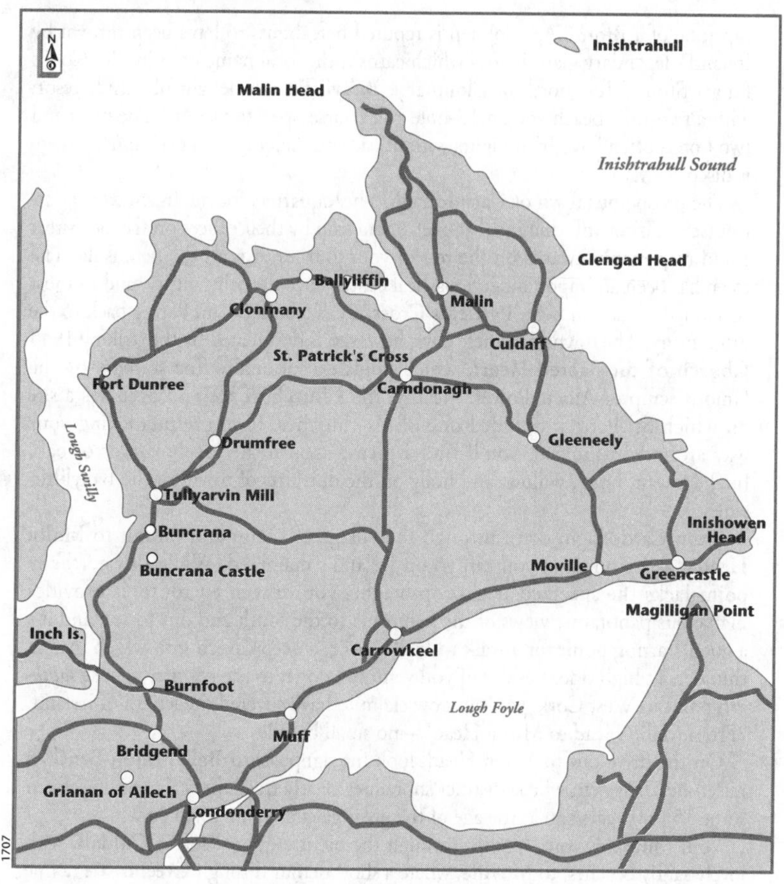

impressive collection of classic cars, horse-drawn carriages, Victorian bicycles, motorcycles, and model cars. During summer months, it's open daily from 10am to 8pm, with a small admission charge. Half a mile north of town, **Tullyarvin Mill** (☎ 074/21160, Letterkenny Tourist Office, for details) is an imposing old restored mill being developed as a cultural and exhibition center. Buncrana has an 18-hole seaside **golf course** (☎ 074/61027) that welcomes visiting golfers. There's also good **fishing** for sea trout, salmon, and brown trout in the Crana River.

From Buncrana, signposts will lead you north to Dunree Head and **Fort Dunree,** a restored coastal defense battery stretching from the Napoleonic era to the departure of the British militia in 1938 that commands superb views of Lough Swilly. Now a museum, it also provides an audiovisual demonstration on the history of the fort and this region. There's also a good cafeteria, making this a good lunch break.

From here, your route takes you on north through the **Gap of Mamore,** some 800 feet above sea level, with spectacular views. For dedicated hill walkers, this is a good starting point for exploring the Urris Hills to the west or Mamore Hill and Raghtin to the east. Some 10 miles north of Buncrana, you encounter the village of **Clonmany;** and two miles east, on the face of Magheramore Hill, the huge capstone of a Bronze Age dolmen is reputed hereabouts to have been thrown by Ireland's legendary giant hero—which earns it the local name of "Finn McCool's Finger Stone." Just north of Clonmany, **Ballyliffin** is a delightful seaside resort with a two-mile beach and an 18-hole golf course open to visitors. The pubs and two hotels often have Irish nights with music and dancing, and occasionally there is disco.

The prosperous town of **Carndonagh** is headquarters for the Inishowen Tourism (see "Visitor Information," above), and a stop by their offices on Chapel Street could reap many rewards on the rest of your journey around the peninsula. The town has been an important ecclesiastical center since the 5th century, and its most acclaimed attraction is **St. Patrick's Cross,** 11½ feet high and dating back to the 7th century. The townscape these days, however, is dominated by the striking 1945 **Church of the Sacred Heart,** which holds exceptionally fine statuary by the famous sculptor Albert Power. Nearby, the **Church of Ireland** occupies a site on which St. Patrick founded one of his churches. If you're picnicking your way around Inishowen, you'll find a picnic area in the lovely woods of oak, birch, rowan, hazel, willow, and holly on the outskirts of town on the Ballyliffin side.

From Cardonagh, drive through the village of Malin and on out to **Malin Head**—as far north as you can go on Ireland's mainland. While this northerly point lacks the spectacular clifftop heights you've seen en route, it provides marvelous panoramic views of the peninsula to the south and out to sea, and it's a good starting point for a walk to Hell's Hole, a deep cavern into which the sea thunders at high tide. Besides, if you ventured down to the country's most *southerly* point in West Cork, you can now claim to have covered the length of Ireland, "From Malin Head to Mizen Head"—no small boast!

On the drive out to Malin Head, look for signposts to **Ballyhillion Beach,** a raised-beach system whose distinct shorelines clearly trace the sea's activities from some 15,000 years ago as the age of the great glaciers came to an end.

Your route now turns south, through the picturesque village of **Culdaff,** with lovely sandy beaches, to **Moville,** where a short detour through **Greencastle** (a fine beach resort named for the castle of Richard de Burgo, the Red Earl of Ulster) leads to **Inishowen Head,** site of a maritime disaster in 1588 when a number of Spanish Armada galleons sank in Kinnagoe Bay. One such vessel was located in near-perfect condition some years back, and artifacts recovered by the Derry Sub-Aqua Club are on display in Derry. With your arrival a bit farther south in **Muff,** your **Inishowen 100** Scenic Drive comes to an end.

WHERE TO STAY

BUNCRANA

Kincora

Cahir O'Doherty Ave., Buncrana, Co. Donegal. ☎ **077/61774.** 3 rms, 2 with bath. IR£15 ($24) single; IR£13 ($20.80) per person sharing; IR£2 ($3.20) per person extra with bath. (Rates include breakfast.) No credit cards.

Mrs. McEleney is the hostess in this modern bungalow set in a flower-bordered lawn in a quiet location in town facing Lough Swilly. The three nice bedrooms are all twin-bedded, with sinks and built-in wardrobes. Breakfast is served in a bright, cheerful dining room.

Clonmany

✪ Four Arches

Letter, Urris, Clonmany, Co. Donegal. ☎ **077/76109** or 76561. 5 rms, all with bath. IR£14 ($22.40) per person sharing; IR£3 ($4.80) single supplement. (Rates include breakfast.) No credit cards. Closed Oct–Mar.

This modern Spanish-style bungalow 4 1/2 miles east of Clonmany is the perfect place to experience the splendor and spirit of the Inishowen countryside. There are panoramic views on all sides, and its 10 acres hold 40 sheep and three goats. This is the home of Fidelma and Michael McLaughlin and their five children, all the very essence of Irish hospitality. Fidelma's breakfasts add fruit and scrambled eggs to the traditional Irish breakfast, and guest rooms are nicely appointed, one with two double beds.

✪ Keg O'Poteen

Clonmany, Co. Donegal. ☎ **077/76415.** 4 rms, none with bath. IR£12 ($19.20) per person. (Rates include breakfast.) No credit cards.

It must be said right up front that these accommodations would not suit everyone, since they're above a popular, typical village bar and lounge on the main street of the village. However, I must also tell you that I found the rooms, although somewhat plain, very comfortable, with a full bath and separate toilet within easy reach. The availability of very good bar food right downstairs was a decided plus (see "Where to Eat," below). Danny and Geraldine McCarron are the owners, and they extend a cordial welcome to guests both upstairs and down in the bar, where there's traditional music on weekends. Something a little different from the usual bed and breakfast, but the hospitality is the same.

Ballyliffin

Worth a Splurge

✪ Strand Hotel

Ballyliffin, Co. Donegal. ☎ **077/76107.** 12 rms, all with bath. TV TEL. IR£20–IR£25 ($32–$40) single; IR£19–IR£23 ($30.40–$36.80) per person sharing. Weekend rates available. (Rates include breakfast.) AE, MC, V.

This small, family hotel is a delightful stop on your tour of Inishowen. Its location in the village is ideal, and the sandy strand just outside the door has a playground for children. All public rooms are bright and cheerful, with plenty of windows to enjoy the marvelous views. Guest rooms also take advantage of the views, and furnishings are attractive and very comfortable. During the summer months there's regular live music and other entertainment.

Malin Head

✪ Barraicin

Malin Head, Co. Donegal. ☎ **077/70184.** 3 rms, 1 with bath. IR£16.50 ($26.40) single; IR£13 ($20.80) per person sharing; IR£1 ($1.60) per person extra for bath. (Rates include breakfast.) No credit cards. Closed Nov–Mar.

Mrs. Maire Doyle will welcome you to her modern bungalow overlooking the sea some 6 1/2 miles north of Malin village and 3 1/2 miles from Malin Head. There are three nice guest rooms, all with sinks, and hairdryers and a tea kettle are available on request. Mrs. Doyle, who has been a moving force in Inishowen tourism development, has won much praise from our readers for her warmth and graciousness, as well as for her tremendous help in steering them to highlights of the peninsula.

WHERE TO EAT

FAHAN

✪ Restaurant Saint John

Fahan. ☎ **077/60289.** Reservations recommended. Dinner IR£16 ($25.60) and IR£20 ($32) plus 10% service. ACC, DC, MC, V. Wed–Sat 7–9:30pm. Closed Good Friday, Christmas Day. CONTINENTAL/TRADITIONAL/VEGETARIAN.

Set back off the road on the southern outskirts of the village (signposted on R328) and surrounded by lovely old trees, this restored Georgian house has sweeping views of Lough Swilly. Two menus are offered each night, and both are extensive, making full use of locally produced meats, seafood, and vegetables in sophisticated as well as traditional dishes.

BUNCRANA

White Strand Motor Inn

Buncrana. ☎ **077/61059** or 61144. Reservations not required. Bar food IR£3–IR£5 ($4.80–$8); fixed-price meal IR£6 ($9.60) at lunch, IR£14 ($22.40) at dinner. MC, V. Daily 12:30–3pm and 6:30–9:30pm. BAR FOOD/SEAFOOD/TRADITIONAL.

This attractive, modern motel at the southern edge of town on Lough Swilly is a good lunch or dinner stop, even if you're not staying here (see "Where to Stay," above). While the menu is not overly adventurous, all ingredients are fresh and nicely prepared in rather traditional styles. Good value for the dollar.

CLONMANY

✪ Keg O'Poteen

Clonmany. ☎ **077/76415.** IR£1.50–IR£5 ($2.40–$8). No credit cards. Daily noon–11pm. BAR FOOD.

It's good to know that if you're wandering the vast reaches of Inishowen mountains or coastlines, you can stop in this village bar and lounge for exceptionally good bar food at minuscule prices from noon until closing. In addition to the usual soup, sandwiches, and salads, they offer hot dishes such as stuffed roast chicken. On the main street of the village, it's a good place to meet locals, and on weekends there are traditional music sessions.

MALIN HEAD

✪ Bree Inn

Malin Head. ☎ **077/70161.** IR£2–IR£6 ($3.20–$9.60); Sun dinner IR£10 ($16). No credit cards. Daily 11am–11:30pm; Sun dinner 4–6pm. BAR FOOD/TRADITIONAL/VEGETARIAN.

This lively country pub about six miles north of Malin village serves delicious bar food, offering fish-and-chips, salads, and hot dishes all through the day and evening. Sunday dinners feature roast beef, pork, lamb, ham, or chicken as well as vegetarian dishes—with advance notice, they will even prepare vegan meals. Behind the small bar, there's a spacious lounge, and to one side, pool and darts star in a larger room. Owners Andrew and Sarah McLaughlin have also built a large recreational center just next door (easy access for wheelchairs), where there's traditional music and other entertainment during the season.

The Midlands Region

20

Ireland's Midland counties are often called Lakeland, and indeed the landscape is dotted with lakes. The Rivers Shannon and Erne glide between broad banks, spreading here and there into Lough Ree and Lough Sheelin.

This is the land of fishing, boating, and hunting; hikers and walkers can tramp forest parks and lakeshores; there's golf in County Westmeath's Mullingar and Athlone; and picnics are a joy in the Midlands region's idyllic woodland and lakeshore settings. In ancient days this was the land of the lake dwellers, who built artificial islands called *crannogs* on which to raise their round huts, protected from enemy attack by the surrounding waters. At the geographical heart of the country, the great monastic community of Clonmacnois was settled near Athlone, withstood assaults by Vikings, Normans, and Cromwell, and has left us a rich heritage of Celtic crosses and round towers.

The great Irish poet Patrick Kavanagh was born in the Midlands, but "escaped" to live out most of his life in Dublin. Although Kavanagh wrote of his birthplace, "O stoney grey soil of Monaghan,/ You burgled my bank of youth," there must be something in the nearly flat, faintly rolling land of Ireland's innards that nurtures literary talent. Oliver Goldsmith spent much of his life here, and you can trace his footsteps, guided by the "Goldsmith Country" booklet published by the tourist board. The blind harper O'Carolan lies buried in County Roscommon. William Percy French was born in County Roscommon. Country Longford was home to Maria Edgeworth, an 18th-century writer and angel of mercy during the famine years. Padraic Colum—poet, playwright, novelist, and essayist—was a product of County Longford, and chronicled the lives of its peasantry with an honest eye. And Americans may be surprised to learn that Edgar Allan Poe's ancestors lived in the village of Kildallon, near Cavan town.

The **Lakeland Regional Tourist Office** is just off the Dublin road in Mullingar (☎ 044/48761; fax 044/40413), and the good folk there can furnish an amazing amount of literature to steer you to the treasures of most Midland counties. There are, however, two exceptions—for information on **County Roscommon,** check with the Galway Tourist Office (see Chapter 16), and the Shannonside Tourist Office in Limerick (see Chapter 15) is the source of **South**

County Offaly information. There are also **Tourist Information Offices** in the Market House in Monaghan town (☎ 047/81122), Rosse Row, Birr, County Offaly (☎ 0509/20110), and in Farnham Street in Cavan town.

1 County Cavan

County Cavan's gently undulating landscape of water-splashed rolling hills rises to some 2,188 feet at its highest point at the summit of Cuilcagh Mountain right at the Northern Ireland border south of Enniskillen. Ireland's longest river, the Shannon, rises on the southern slopes of this mountain, and the River Erne flows northward from Lough Gowna through the center of the county, past Cavan town and on up into the Upper Erne, spreading its waters into myriad lakes along the way.

WHAT TO SEE & DO

The country's chief town, **Cavan,** sits among low green hills on the eastern edge of the Lough Oughter lake system. **Percy French,** composer of some of Ireland's best-loved ballads, including "Come Back Paddy Reilly to Ballyjamesduff" and "The Mountains of Mourne," lived at 16 Farnham St. This is also the home of **Cavan Crystal** (☎ 049/31800 for shop and guided factory-tour hours). There's traditional music periodically at the **Well Bar & Singing Lounge** on Bridge Street, Cavan town (☎ 049/32022), which also serves bar food all day, and at the **Hillside Tavern** in Killeshandra.

Plan to spend some time in the 600 acres of ✪ **Killykeen Forest Park,** located between Killeshandra and Cavan town (signposted on L15). There's plenty to enjoy: fishing, swimming, boating, shady nature trails, and picnic sites, as well as a self-catering holiday village. Within its grounds you'll also find crannogs, ring forts, and the ruined **Lough Oughter Castle,** where in 1649 the great chieftain Owen Roe O'Neil died (to this day some say he was poisoned by a treacherous hand).

Four miles north of Cavan town via N3, **Butlersbridge** sits on the banks of the Annalee River, with excellent fishing. The **Derragarra Inn** pub and restaurant in Butlersbridge (see "Where to Eat," below) is a sightseeing attraction. Butlersbridge is an ideal fishing center, as it's situated midway between Upper Lough Erne and Lough Oughter.

Some 16 miles northeast of Cavan town on R188, the little town of **Cootehill** has good fishing on Dromlona Lake, and three miles southeast on the Shercock road, near Cohaw village, there's a prehistoric **court cairn tomb.** It was near Shercock, at Lough Sillan, that the largest horns of the extinct giant Irish elk were found.

WHERE TO STAY

BELTURBET

Hilltop Farm

Belturbet, Co. Cavan. ☎ **049/22114.** 10 rms (8 with bath). IR£18.50 ($29.60) single; IR£13.50 ($21.60) per person sharing; IR£2 ($3.20) per person extra for private bath. Dinner IR£13 ($20.80) extra. 50% reduction for children. (Rates include breakfast.) MC, V.

Just off the Cavan-Belturbet road, this large modern farmhouse is about halfway between Butlersbridge and Belturbet. Rooms are both attractive and comfortable, and Mrs. Elizabeth Dunne enjoys helping guests take advantage of local fishing.

She provides a tackle room, bait stocklist, and has a boat for hire. Horseback riding and cruising on the Erne can also be arranged.

COOTEHILL

Ker Maria

Station Rd., Cootehill, Co. Cavan. ☎ **049/52293.** 4 rms, none with bath. IR£15 ($24) per person. 20% reduction for children. (Rates include breakfast.) No credit cards. Closed Oct–June.

Gardens surround this pretty Georgian-style home midway between Donegal and Dublin, half a mile from Cootehill town. Mrs. Teresa Colhoun is a helpful, informative hostess, and the four nice guest rooms are comfortably furnished. This house has central heating and good parking.

LOG CABINS IN KILLYKEEN FOREST PARK

✪ Killykeen Forest Chalets

Killykeen Forest Park, Co. Cavan. ☎ **049/32541.** Fax 049/61044. 20 chalets. IR£180-IR£320 ($288–$512) per chalet per week, depending on season. Electricity extra. No credit cards.

This is one of the prettiest sites for getting away from it all in Ireland, and the owners, *Coillte,* have worked hand-in-glove with tourism people to develop a group of log-cabin units for holidaymakers. Between Killeshandra and Cavan town (signposted on L15), the beautifully wooded park also contains good fishing and a host of recreational facilities.

WHERE TO EAT

BUTLERSBRIDGE

Derragarra Inn

Butlersbridge ☎ **049/31003.** Bar food under IR£6 ($9.60); main courses IR£10–IR£12 ($16–$19.20). MC, V. Daily, bar food 12:30–6pm; restaurant meals 12:30–2:30pm and 6–9pm. Four miles north of Cavan town. BAR FOOD/IRISH.

This old thatched cottage inn sits on the banks of the River Annalea, and relics of rural Ireland dominate the atmospheric decor. Freshwater fish, smoked salmon, and steak are among the best choices.

2 County Monaghan

County Monaghan is the ancient territory of the powerful MacMahon clan, and today it draws hordes of fishing enthusiasts. The great Irish poet Patrick Kavanagh was born in County Monaghan, and although he considered Dublin to be the place that transformed him from a "happily unhappy, ordinary countryman" into the "abnormally normal" poet, much of his poetry had to do with the place of his birth.

WHAT TO SEE & DO

Monaghan town holds the award-winning **Monaghan County Museum** (☎ 047/82928) with the medieval processional Cross of Clogher, which dates from the 14th century, as well as other artifacts from this county's rich past. They also arrange walking tours of Monaghan town. Twelve miles southwest of Monaghan on N54 is a 75-foot-high **Celtic cross** in Clones and a round tower in the graveyard near the Cavan road. Two miles east of Clones, the little village of **Aughnakillagh** is the birthplace of James Connolly, hero of the 1916 rising.

Near the village of **Inishkeen** Patrick Kavanagh first saw the light of day. In the end, he was brought back to his native county, and his grave is just opposite a small stone church and the remains of an ancient round tower. **The Patrick Kavanagh Rural and Literary Resource Centre** (☎ 042/78560) in Inniskeen commemorates the poet's early life in rural Monaghan and explores the lay of the land in this region, which had such an impact on his later life and much of his work, even when he lived in Dublin. It's open Monday through Friday from 11am to 5pm, Saturday, Sunday, and holidays from 2–7pm.

In **Castleblaney,** on the shores of Lough Muckno, **Hope Castle** (once the home of the "Hope Diamond" family) is a restaurant and leisure center, featuring a full range of water sports, with an adjacent nine-hole golf course—a nice break from sightseeing.

Stop by the ✪ **Carrickmacross Lace Co-op,** on Main Street (☎ 042/62506 or 62088), in the charming little town of Carrickmacross. The lace makers sketch out original designs to be worked in the sheerest lawn, appliquéed to even sheerer net. The tiny, invisible hand-stitching is done in some 20 cottages by skillful and patient women, whose numbers are dwindling every year, with few young girls willing to learn the ancient art. The world-famous Carrickmacross lace, introduced to the Monaghan area in the 1800s, has continued as a cottage industry from 1846 to this day. A Miss Reid built the first schoolhouse for the lace. Then the founding of the St. Louis Convent ensured the development of the lace and it has remained the center for the lace for many years. The Lace Gallery at the end of town is the display center run by the Carrickmacross Lace Co-op. It is to this historic little building that the lace makers, after many patient hours of sewing their elegant lace, bring the fruits of their labor.

WHERE TO STAY

CARRICKMACROSS

✪ Arradale House

Kingscourt Rd., Carrickmacross, Co. Monaghan. ☎ **042/61941.** 8 rms, 2 with bath. IR£15–IR£16 ($24–$25.60); IR£5 ($8) single supplement; 10% reduction for children. High tea IR£6 ($9.60); dinner IR£11 ($17.60). (Rates include breakfast.) No credit cards. Open Mar–Nov. Just off N2, 2 1/2 miles south of Carrickmacross.

Peace and serenity begin to descend as you turn into the lane leading to Arradale House. Mrs. Christine McMahon and her family welcome guests to the rambling farmhouse on a working dairy farm set in green fields. This has been a favorite with fisherfolk for many years, but if you're not after fish, there's plenty to do right in the vicinity: **Dun-A-Ri Forest Park,** with its nature trails and wishing well, is a mere three miles away; nearby pubs have live music; and just up the road is the Oasis, a moderately priced restaurant, which also houses one of Ireland's largest nightclubs, with disco every weekend. Guest rooms vary in size, but all are quite comfortable and have tea/coffeemakers. Some rooms also have TV. There's a games room, and a friendly pony has great appeal for youngsters. Mrs. McMahon's home-cooked meals are based on farm-fresh produce and home baking.

Castle Leslie

Glaslough, Co. Monaghan. ☎ **047/88109.** Fax 047/88256. 5 rms, all with bath. IR£38–IR£45 ($60.80–$72). (Rates include breakfast.) ACC, MC, V. Open mid-Feb–Dec.

Samantha (Sammy Leslie), whose family has lived here for generations, is the vivacious young hostess in this legendary country home (see "Where to Eat," below). Bedrooms vary in size and decor, but all are done in period style.

The Midlands

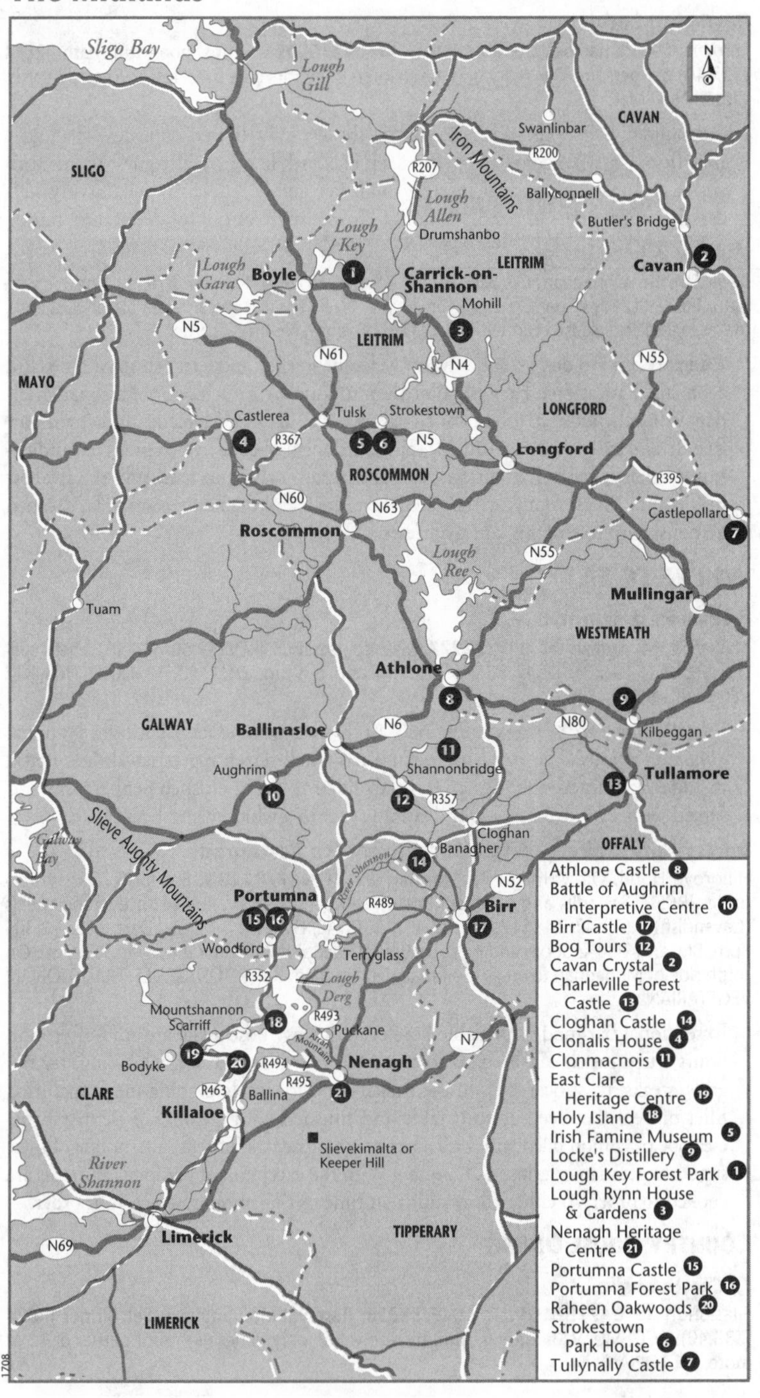

Rose-Linn-Lodge

Lurgans, Carrickmacross, Co. Monaghan. ☎ **042/61035.** 3 rms, none with bath. IR£14 ($22.40) per person. 20% reduction for children. (Rates include breakfast.) No credit cards. Closed Nov–Mar.

Surrounded by woods and nearby lakes, this centrally heated bungalow is about a mile from Carrickmacross. Mrs. Rosaleen Haworth has three nice guest rooms with sinks, and takes a personal interest in all her guests. She also owns luxury self-catering apartments in nearby Lisahisk House (write or call for details and rates).

Willow Bridge Lodge

Silver Stream, Monaghan, Co. Monaghan. ☎ **047/81054.** Fax 047/81054. 4 rms, 1 with bath. IR£15 ($24) per person, single or double; IR£5 ($8) per person extra for private bath. (Rates include breakfast.) Dinner IR£12 ($19.20) extra. No credit cards.

Ann and Bill Holden extend a warm welcome in their modern country home, and for a small additional fee will tailor their unique "A Touch More Personal" holiday, using the lodge as a base. Such extras as the use of a Mercedes and chauffeur, free drinks and wine at mealtime, and outdoor barbecue evenings are an indication of their personal attention. Ann is a superb cook and uses only the freshest ingredients. Guest rooms are tastefully furnished, and the house is set in landscaped gardens, with marvelous country views.

WHERE TO EAT

Andy's Restaurant

Market St., Monaghan ☎ **047/82277.** Main courses IR£6–IR£9 ($9.60–$14.40); chef's special IR£12 ($19.20). Daily 12:30–2:30pm and 6–9pm. DC, MC, V. TRADITIONAL/VEGETARIAN.

Located above an award-winning pub, Andy's has won no less than eight National Hygiene Awards. The extensive menu offers a half-dozen vegetarian dishes; it also includes such interesting dishes as turkey fillets rolled in crushed peppercorns and served with a Madeira sauce, and sirloin steak in a whiskey and beer sauce.

Dartry Bar, Braken Restaurant, Cavendish Restaurant

Hillgrove Hotel, Old Armagh Rd., Monaghan ☎ **047/81288.** Bar food (Dartry Bar) under IR£5 ($8); grills and lunches (Braken) IR£8–IR£10 ($12.80–$16); evening meals (Cavendish) IR£11–IR£14 ($17.60–$22.40). ACC, AE, DC, MC, V. Daily, Dartry Bar 12:30–8pm; Braken 12:30–2:30pm and 6:30–9:30pm; Cavendish 7–10pm (Sunday to 9:30pm). On south side of Monaghan town, just off main Dublin road. BAR FOOD/GRILLS/TRADITIONAL/VEGETARIAN.

Exceptional bar food is available here even during those awkward mid-afternoon hours when lunch can be hard to come by. For more substantial dining, try the grills, steaks, roast beef, etc., in the Braken, and for lovely evening meals (panfried fillet of beef flambéed at your table and finished with cream and peppercorns; escalope of salmon filled with brill and chive mousse in a butter sauce; or one of their superb vegetarian offerings). *A caution:* With the exception of bar food, all meals are cooked to order, so either allow sufficient time or ring ahead to place your order.

COUNTRY HOUSE DINING

✪ Castle Leslie

Glaslough ☎ **047/88109.** Fax 047/88256. Reservations required. Set dinner IR£24 ($38.40). ACC, MC, V. Saturdays 7pm, by reservation only; other nights for parties of 12 or more. VICTORIAN.

Samantha (Sammy) Leslie's Country House Dinners are a unique experience, as well as a culinary delight. Both setting and cuisine hark back to the days when the castle (see "Where to Stay") was fully staffed and weekend house guests dined on the same fare Sammy serves these days. Pre-dinner drinks are served in the drawing room in front of a roaring log fire. When the dinner gong sounds, guests are brought into the family dining room, which hasn't changed in over a century. A sumptuous six-course dinner is served by waitresses in Victorian dress.

3 County Offaly

Centrally located County Offaly's attractions cover a wide spectrum, appealing to saints and sinners alike, with the monastic ruins at Clonmacnois, one of Ireland's most impressive ecclesiastical sites; a unique raised bog tour near Shannon bridge; and the Tullamore Dew distillery carrying on a revered brewing tradition.

WHAT TO SEE & DO

On the banks of the Shannon, four miles north of Shannonbridge (on R357 near the County Galway border) ✪ **Clonmacnois** (Cluain Mic Nois, "Meadow of the Son of Nos") is where St. Ciaran founded a monastery in 548. It was plundered by Irish chieftains, Vikings, and Anglo-Normans, and finally gave up the ghost when Cromwell's forces desecrated it beyond restoration. Today you'll find among its ruins a cathedral, eight churches, two round towers, the remains of a castle, more than 200 monumental slabs, and three sculptured high crosses. There are guided tours during the summer months from the Information Centre (☎ 0905/4134) at the site entrance.

The country's bogs have always played a vital role in the lives of the Irish people, and the ✪ **Bog of Allen train tour** will give you a marvelous insight into the fascinating history of this internationally important raised bog that has developed over a period of 12,000 years. Before boarding the luxury railway coach, take time to view the 35-minute video "The Heritage of the Midland Bogs" that is shown continuously at the Visitors Centre (☎ 0905/74114 or 74172) located at the train's starting point, Bord na Mona Blackwater Works (signposted from Shannonbridge). There is a nice tearoom, as well as a picnic area, and the tours operate daily on the hour from 10am to 5pm from March through October.

The gardens at **Birr Castle** in the town of Birr (Biorra, "Spring Wells"), 23 miles southwest of Tullamore via N52, are open to the public. The castle was a much-besieged stronghold during the 16th and 17th centuries, and was later the seat of the earls of Rosse. The third earl had an observatory in the castle, where he designed a telescope that was, for some 80 years, the largest in the world.

The ✪ **Slieve Bloom Mountains** have been described as one vast environment park, and although the centuries (some 15,000 of them!) have rounded the peaks into hills (the highest is just over 1,700 feet), there remain 17 major valleys, forest walks of incredible beauty and accessibility, and a blanket bog that has been named a National Nature Reserve. There are several excellent viewing points and car parks, and if time permits, a day stolen from your cross-country travels to wander this peaceful park will do wonders for your soul. Before starting out, stop by the **Slieve Bloom Display Centre,** Outdoor Education Centre, Roscrea Road, Birr (☎ 0509/20028), for a wealth of information and directions (open April through September).

Seven miles north of Birr via R439, you can visit the workshop, showroom, and tearoom of **Crannog Pottery,** Banagher (☎ 0902/51324). There's traditional music most nights at **J. J. Hough's Bar,** Main Street, Banagher (☎ 0902/51499).

WHERE TO STAY

TULLAMORE

✪ Padraig Villa

Glaskill, Screggan, Tullamore, Co. Offaly. ☎ **0506/55962.** 6 rms, 2 with bath. IR£14 ($22.40) per person without bath; IR£17 ($27.20) with bath. 20% reduction for children. (Rates include breakfast.) Dinner IR£15 ($24) extra. AE, MC, V. Private car park.

Mrs. Bridie Casey is a charming, hospitable hostess and her modern country home, one mile off the Tullamore-Birr road, is surrounded by pretty gardens. You will be welcomed here with tea or coffee and home-baked cakes. Mrs. Casey also serves a lovely dinner. There's an interesting collection of vintage bikes, and bikes for hire. The house is centrally heated.

✪ Sea Dew Guest House

Clonminch Rd., Tullamore, Co. Offaly. ☎/fax **0506/52054.** 10 rms, all with bath. IR£27 ($43.20) single; IR£25 ($40) per person sharing. (Rates include breakfast.) ACC, MC, V. Closed Christmas.

Olive Williams brings years of top-class hotel experience to this lovely, purpose-built guesthouse, and she is the very epitome of graciousness. Her house is the ultimate in comfort, and beautifully decorated, with facilities and every consideration for the disabled. Bedrooms all have TV and telephone, and some are wheelchair-accessible. Sea Dew is on the signposted road to Port Laoise, just a short walk from the village center, and is a personal favorite.

BIRR

✪ The Maltings Hotel/Leisure Centre

Castle St., Birr, Co. Offaly. ☎/fax **0509/21345.** 10 rms, all with bath. TEL TV. IR£18–IR£20 ($28.80–$32) per person sharing; IR£4 ($6.40) single supplement; IR£49 ($78.40) per person sharing for two nights B&B and one dinner. 50% reduction for children under 16; under 4 free. (Rates include breakfast.) ACC, MC, V. Beside Birr Castle.

Maeve and Brendan Garry have worked wonders in these buildings, which date back to 1820, when they were used to store malt for Guinness stout. Set on picturesque grounds on the banks of the River Camcor, the hotel has all modern conveniences for guests' comfort, with terrific views of wildlife and the relaxing sound of water gushing over the wier outside the windows. The River Room Restaurant is set under the arch of the water wheel, and its menu features generous portions of fresh fish and/or traditional Irish meals.

A FARMHOUSE

Beechlawn Farmhouse

Clyduff, Daingean, Co. Offaly. ☎ **0506/53099.** 5 rms, all with bath. IR£14.50 ($23.20) per person sharing; IR£5 ($8) single supplement. (Rates include breakfast.) High tea IR£9 ($14.40); dinner IR£11 ($17.60). 25% reduction for children. No credit cards. Open mid-Mar–mid-Dec. 7 miles from Tullamore.

Mary Margaret and Sylvester Smyth's Georgian farmhouse is surrounded by landscaped lawns and colorful flower beds. There's a gracious air about the lounge, dining room, and all guest rooms. Mrs. Smyth's candlelight dinners are a real treat, and pubs in the nearby village offer conviviality with locals in the evening. Fishing, golf, and a host of sightseeing attractions close at hand make this an ideal, relaxing base for exploring the heart of Ireland.

WHERE TO EAT

The Bridge House

Bridge St., Tullamore, Co. Offaly. ☎ **0506/21704.** Snacks under IR£4 ($6.40); carvery lunch under IR£8 ($12.80); main courses IR£8–IR£12 ($12.80–$19.20). ACC, MC, V. Daily, bar food and coffee shop 9:15am–7pm; 12:30–2:30pm and 5:30–10pm. TRADITIONAL.

The Bridge is a local institution, with something for every appetite, from its coffee shop and carvery lunch fare to full evening meals in the large, busy restaurant. Look for traditional Irish specialties (Irish stew, etc.).

Moorhill Country Inn

Moorehill, Clara Rd., Tullamore, Co. Offaly. ☎ **0506/21395.** Set dinner IR£18 ($28.80). Service charge 10%. AE, MC, V. Tues–Sun 7–9pm. IRISH/TRADITIONAL.

This award-winning dining room is located in the converted stables of a lovely old country estate with beautifully landscaped grounds on the outskirts of town. Inside, stone walls, oak beams, and open fires add to the charm of the period country house setting. Traditional cooking is the order of the day here, utilizing locally grown produce and meats from nearby farms. Among the specialties is the imaginative Tullamore black pudding in puff pastry served with a port wine sauce.

4 County Laois

Except for the Slieve Bloom Mountains in the northwest, the landscape of County Laois is that of Ireland's central plain. Its borders enclose one of Ireland's most perfectly preserved round towers and other significant relics of Irish history.

WHAT TO SEE & DO

There's a perfectly preserved 96-foot-high, 12th-century **round tower** at Timahoe, a few miles southeast of Port Laoise via R426, as well as the ruins of a castle and an abbey.

Port Laoise is the principal county town, and four miles to the east atop the 150-foot-high **Rock of Dunamase,** on the site of an ancient Celtic fortress, are ruins of the Norman castle that was a part of the dowry given to the King of Leinster's daughter when she married Strongbow as part of the power struggle that first brought English forces to Irish soil.

Nine miles south of Port Laoise, a **Cistercian abbey** was founded by Conor O'More in 1183 at Abbeyleix. The **de Vesci demesne,** adjoining the town, holds the tomb of Malachi O'More, a Laois chieftain.

A delightful **scenic drive** is that through the deep glen of O Regan in the Slieve Bloom Mountains (see "County Offaly," above). At Mountmellick, north of Port Laoise via N80, take the Clonaslee road and follow signposts for "The Cut." Some seven miles south of Clonaslee, **Monicknew Woods,** with its nature trail, forest walks, viewing points, and picnic site, are an ideal spot to stop for a little spirit renewal or for a picnic lunch.

WHERE TO STAY

NEAR PORT LAOISE

Aspen

Rock of Dunamase, Port Laoise, Co. Laois. ☎ **0502/25405.** 4 rms, all with bath. IR£17.50 ($28) per person. 20% reduction for children. (Rates include breakfast.) No credit cards. Closed Nov–Mar.

In a pretty, wooded setting on the Port Laoise–Carlow road 3 1/2 miles from town, Mrs. Noreen Llewellyn is the gracious hostess in this spacious, centrally heated bungalow. Her breakfasts are outstanding, and have won The Galtee Breakfast Award. The house is tastefully furnished with a blend of modern and antique pieces. There are lovely woodland walks just outside the door.

✪ Castletown House

Donaghmore, Co. Laois. ☎ **0505/46415.** Fax 0505/46788. 4 rms, all with bath. IR£14 ($22) per person. (Rates including breakfast.) Dinner IR£12 ($19.20) extra. ACC, MC, V. Closed Dec–Feb.

There's a lot to commend in this early-19th-century farmhouse that is the center of a 200-acre beef and sheep farm. The house itself is lovely, with nicely furnished guest rooms, but perhaps its greatest asset is the gracious Moira Phelan, whose enthusiasm for rural tourism and keen personal interest in her guests led to a prestigious regional award in 1990. Guests are treated to tea and cake every night (no charge), and Moira is known for her home baking, as well as meals based on the farm's own meat, poultry, vegetables, eggs, etc. The area is liberally sprinkled with historic sites, and there are the remains of an 11th-century Norman castle on the farm, so it is not surprising that Moira has compiled a local history book that adds much to every visitor's stay.

✪ Chez Nous

Kilminchy, Port Laoise, Co. Laois. ☎ **0502/21251.** 3 rms, all with bath. IR£21 ($33.60) single; IR£17.50 ($28) per person sharing. (Rates include breakfast.) No credit cards.

Ms. Audrey Canavan has won raves for her warm hospitality, exceptionally good (and varied) breakfasts, and attention to detail in the decor of her home, two miles from town, just off the main Dublin road. Antique furnishings are displayed throughout the house, and the attractive TV lounge has oak beams and adjoins a plant-filled sunroom that opens to the patio outside. Guest rooms have canopied beds, and all are beautifully furnished. As for breakfast, Audrey offers the traditional Irish grill or an alternative that sometimes includes fish with a side salad, both served on a nicely appointed table.

A COUNTRY HOUSE

Roundwood House

Mountrath, Co. Laois. ☎ **0502/32120.** Fax 0502/32711. 6 rms, all with bath. IR£41 ($65.60) single; IR£35 ($56) per person sharing. (Rates include breakfast.) Dinner IR£20 ($32); Sunday lunch IR£12 ($19.20). ACC, AE, DC, MC, V. Closed Christmas.

This marvelous old Georgian-period Palladian villa, parts of which date from 1680, might well have finished its life as a ruin had not the Irish Georgian Society restored it in the 1970s. Its 18-acre setting includes open pasture, woodland, and gardens, and its present owners, Rosemarie and Frank Kennan, have set out to offer their guests "the opportunity to go back in time to an era when leisure, grace, and beauty symbolised the good life." Their success in achieving just that is reflected in the relaxed, informal country-house character that pervades the old-fashioned bedrooms (with shutters instead of curtains), the cozy drawing room, dining room, study, and overflowing library. Just one of the Kennan's "back in time" touches is the hot water bottle furnished each night, even though the house has perfectly good central heating. For walkers, the Slieve Bloom Way is just four miles away.

WHERE TO EAT

MOUNTRATH

✪ Roundwood House

☎ **0502/32120.** Reservations recommended. Set dinner IR£20 ($32); Sun lunch IR£12 ($19.20). AE, DC, MC, V. Dinner daily (Sun–Mon for residents only) one seating, 8:30pm; lunch Sun 1:30pm. TRADITIONAL/COUNTRY-STYLE.

Not far southwest of Port Laoise on N7, this restored Palladian villa from the early Georgian period sits in wooded grounds. Rosemarie and Frank Kennan have transformed it into a small country house hotel and restaurant whose reputation regularly draws dinner guests from as far away as Dublin. It's a small, intimate dining room (seats only 26), and there's a set menu (no choice) specializing in good, solid country-style cooking that is positively mouthwatering. You're in luck if their local roast lamb comes to table accompanied by homemade Cumberland sauce instead of the usual mint sauce.

PORT LAOISE

✪ Treacey's Pub and Restaurant

The Heath, Dublin Rd. ☎ **0502/46539.** Average meal under IR£7 ($11.20). Daily 12:30–2:30pm and 6–9pm. DC, MC, V. PUB GRUB/TRADITIONAL.

This charming thatched-cottage pub/restaurant is some three miles outside the town, but is well worth the drive. It is the oldest family-run pub in these parts, and there is a good range of pub grub (roasts, fish, salads) as well as prime steak at amazingly reasonable prices.

5 County Longford

County Longford, in addition to its hunting and fishing facilities, is noteworthy for its association with such literary figures as Oliver Goldsmith, Maria Edgeworth, John Keegan Casey, and Padraic Colum.

WHAT TO SEE & DO

In **Longford town,** look for the works of leading Irish artists at the **Carroll Art Gallery,** 6 Keon's Terrace, opposite St. Mel's Cathedral (☎ 043/41148). Of a more recreational (convivial?) nature, ✪ **Peter Clarke's Pub,** Dublin Street, is reliably reported to pull the "best pint in Ireland." The **Longford Arms Hotel** (☎ 043/46478) has live entertainment and dancing during the summer months. Visiting golfers are welcome at the **County Longford Golf Club,** Longford (☎ 043/46310).

Five miles from Longford on the main Granard road (N55), you can visit the splendid Victorian **Carrigglas Manor** (☎ 043/45165), which dates from 1857 and displays the original contents and furniture, as well as a costume collection.

Poet **Oliver Goldsmith** was born in Pallas, near Abbeyshrule (southeast of Longford town via R393), in 1728 and spent much of his life in this county. You can trace his footsteps by following the "Goldsmith Country" booklet published by the tourist board.

County Longford was also home to **Maria Edgeworth,** the 18th-century author (*Castle Rackrent*) who was an angel of mercy during the famine years. In Edgeworthstown, east of Longford town via N4, there's a small **museum** dedicated to the Edgeworth family, of whom the most notable members were Maria, English-born novelist and essayist who spent most of her life in Ireland and did much to relieve suffering during the worst famine years, and her father, an inventor and author. Both are interred in the family vault in the churchyard of St. John's Church (which also is the last resting place of Oscar Wilde's sister, Isolda). The town's **historical museum** is open during the summer months.

Padraic Colum—poet, playwright, novelist, and essayist—was a product of County Longford. Born in 1881 in the Longford Workhouse, where his father was a master, he chronicled the lives of its peasantry.

Ballymahon, south of Longford town via R392, and its environs are central to the works of poet **John Keegan "Leo" Casey.**

WHERE TO STAY

LONGFORD TOWN

Tivoli

Dublin Rd., Longford, Co. Longford. ☎ **043/46898.** 14 rms, 5 with bath. IR£13.50 ($21.60) per person. IR£2 ($3.20) per person extra for private bath. (Rates include breakfast.) No credit cards.

Mrs. Breege O'Donnell is a longtime favorite hostess with readers. Her large two-story home is immaculate and well appointed, and her warm friendliness makes guests feel like members of her family. The house is centrally heated.

✪ Carrigglas Manor

Longford, Co. Longford. ☎ **043/45165.** Fax 043/45875. 4 rms, all with adjoining bath, 3 luxury apartments. IR£55 ($88) per person single or double; IR£200 ($320) per week luxury apartments. (Rates include breakfast.) Dinner IR£20 ($32). ACC, AE, MC, V. Bookings any day except Sun and Thurs.

This magnificent Tudor Gothic mansion three miles from Longford town is the home of Jeffry and Tessa Lefroy. The house itself has a romantic history—its builder was Lord Chief Justice of Ireland in 1837, who counted Jane Austen among his close friends (some think he was the model for Darcy in *Pride and Prejudice*). Reception rooms are the epitome of elegance, filled with heirloom furniture, artifacts, and family portraits. As for the five guest bedrooms, the two doubles come with canopied beds, a bit more luxurious than the one twin-bedded and two single rooms. The luxury self-catering apartments are in renovated stables. The Lefroys ask that guests not plan to arrive before 6pm the first evening.

6 County Roscommon

Much of County Roscommon is level plain, bogland, and river meadow, broken with low hills and island-dotted lakes. Songwriter Percy French was born near the town of Elphin, north of Roscommon town via N61.

WHAT TO SEE & DO

Roscommon town sports the ruins of **Roscommon Castle** on a hillside overlooking the town, still intact enough to set your imagination flying back to its birth era in the 13th century. A wide variety of Irish crafts are available at the **Slieve**

Bawn co-op handcrafts market (☎ 078/33058) in Strokestown, north of Roscommon town via N61 and R368.

The 45-room Palladian **Strokestown Park House** (☎ 078/33013) is one of Ireland's finest great houses. It's on the main Dublin-Castlebar road (N5); from June to mid-September, it's open to the public Tuesday through Sunday from noon to 5pm. In the stableyards of the house, the **Irish Famine Museum** honors those who fled from death by starvation during the 1840s. The moving tribute can be seen from May through October, Tuesday to Sunday, 11am to 5pm, with a small admission fee.

Just west of Castlerea, 19 miles northwest of Roscommon town on N60, **Clonalis House** (☎ 0907/20014) dates from the 19th century and is the home of the O'Conor Don, chieftain of the Clan O'Conor, onetime High Kings of Ireland, traditional Kings of Connaught, and Europe's oldest family, whose descent can be traced back through 60 generations to 75 B.C. It is furnished with Sheraton pieces and a collection of artifacts that includes O'Carolan's harp, rare glass and china, paintings, and Gaelic manuscripts. There's an exhibition of horse-drawn farm machinery and carriages, plus antique lace. Afternoon tea is available, as well as a craft shop. Call ahead for opening hours.

In Boyle, 27 miles northwest of Roscommon town via N61, look for the **Una Bhan Tourism Centre** on Main Street (☎ 079/63033). This small community cooperative not only books accommodations in the area, but its helpful staff can also provide information on local historical houses, heritage sites, scenic routes, craft centers, and outdoor activities.

Also in Boyle, the ruins of a **12th-century Cistercian abbey** are impressive, and if you'd like to see the interior, look up the caretaker, whose home is just next door.

Two miles east of Boyle on N4, don't miss **Lough Key Forest Park** (☎ 079/62214). It's one of the country's loveliest, and especially interesting are the **Bog Gardens,** with heathers and other small plants that grow well in peat. During the summer months there's a good, moderately priced restaurant and a shop, but this is good picnic country any time of the year, with tables provided.

Lovers of traditional Irish music may want to make a pilgrimage to Keadue village (four miles northeast of Lough Key) where the blind harpist **Turlough O'Carolan** lies in Kilronan Abbey cemetery (just west of the village), above whose arched gateway is inscribed: WITHIN THIS CHURCHYARD LIE THE REMAINS OF CAROLAN, THE LAST OF THE IRISH BARDS WHO DEPARTED THIS LIFE 25 MARCH, 1738. R.I.P.

WHERE TO STAY

ROSCOMMON

Roscommon is a short detour off the main Dublin-Galway road, and rewarding not only for its own sightseeing attractions, but because the 50 miles from Roscommon to Galway go through lovely rural scenery too often missed by visitors who stick to the highways.

✪ Abbey Hotel

Abbeytown, Galway Rd., Roscommon, Co. Roscommon. ☎ **0903/26240.** Fax 0903/26021. 25 rms, all with bath. TV TEL. IR£45 ($72) single; IR£37.50 ($60) per person sharing. Special discounts available. (Rates include breakfast.) AE, DC, MC, V.

Within the lovely lawns and gardens that surround this marvelous 18th-century turreted mansion, ruins of a medieval monastery bear mute witness to the history of this part of Roscommon. The Abbey is a perfect base for a stopover to explore these and other monastic ruins and Norman castles en route cross-country.

Owners Tommy and Anya Grealy carry on a family tradition of gracious hospitality that began back in 1878 when the Grealy family opened a coaching inn. The hotel today provides all modern comforts, but retains such mementos of the past as the curved twin staircase with its stained-glass window at the landing, whose pattern the Grealys are having duplicated in panels for the front entry and lounge. Bedrooms are of good size, with attractive decor and comfortable furnishings. The bright, window-walled dining room overlooks the back lawn and specializes in fresh Irish produce and a good wine list.

Note: If you're traveling with a party of four or more, or if you plan a stay of several days, be sure to ask about special discounts.

Near Boyle

✪ Hillside House

Doon, Corrigeenroe, Boyle, Co. Roscommon. ☎ **079/66075.** 5 rms, 2 with bath. IR£18 ($28.80) single; IR£4 ($22.40) per person sharing. 25% reduction for children. Dinner IR£12 ($19.20) extra. (Rates include breakfast.) No credit cards.

This comfortable, slightly old-fashioned home is the domain of Mrs. Amy Taylor. It's in a beautiful, scenic location 3½ miles from town with views of Lough Key and handy to the Forest Park. The homey bedrooms, all with sinks, are comfortably furnished, there's central heating, and the evening meal is quite good.

WHERE TO EAT

Boyle

✪ Lakeshore Restaurant

Lough Key Forest Park. ☎ 079/62214. Reservations not required. Less than IR£5 ($8). No credit cards. May–Sept, daily noon– 6pm. SANDWICHES/SALADS/GRILLS.

Combine sightseeing with lunching in Lough Key Forest Park, two miles east of Boyle via N4. Picture windows overlook the boat basin, and you can choose from light meals (salads and sandwiches) or more substantial grills. Take-aways are available, and there's a wine license.

✪ Royal Hotel

Bridge St. ☎ 079/62016. Reservations not required. Lunch IR£8 ($12.80); dinner IR£14 ($22.40). AE, DC, MC, V. Daily 12:30–3pm and 6–9pm. IRISH/TRADITIONAL.

This is a comfortable, family-run hotel dining room that serves a variety of good Irish-style meals, with a wide choice of standard fish, beef, pork, lamb, and chicken dishes.

7 County Westmeath

County Westmeath is an ideal base from which to explore the entire Midlands region, as most major attractions in nearby counties are easy day trips.

WHAT TO SEE & DO

The county town of **Mullingar** is the center of one of the country's leading beef-producing areas. It's also the home of ✪ **Canten Casey's,** an intriguing 200-year-old pub, whose interior is much the same as it was in its infancy.

Mullingar was an important barracks town for the British military, and there's an interesting collection of memorabilia of those years as well as Irish Army participation in U.N. activities in Lebanon, Cyprus, and the Congo in the **Military and Historical Museum,** Columb Barracks (☎ 044/8391).

In **Athlone** (Ath Luain, "The Ford of Luan"), 29 miles southwest of Mullingar via R390, ✪ **King John's Castle,** which dates from the 13th century and figured prominently in the famous siege of 1691, is fascinating. There's a museum within its walls, as is the Visitors Centre (no phone).

Athlone is where **John McCormack,** the famous Irish tenor, was born, and his birthplace is marked by a bronze plaque in the Bawn, off Mardyke Street. You'll know this is still a musical town if you drop into **Seans Bar,** Main Street (☎ 0902/92358), one of Ireland's oldest pubs (1630), where Irish music breaks out nightly. Shoppers will want to go by the showroom and workshop of **Athlone Crystal,** 28 Pearse St. (☎ 0902/92867).

From an Athlone base, no fewer than five **stately homes** and gardens are less than an hour's drive: Birr Castle is 28 miles away; Clonalis House, Castlerea, is 40 miles; Tullynally Castle, Castlepollard, is 43 miles; Emo Court is 48 miles; and Abbeyleix, Woodland Gardens, 55 miles.

Plan to stop on the outskirts of **Kilbeggan,** east of Athlone via N6, to browse around ✪ **Locke's Distillery,** once one of the largest in Europe. Residents of the town rescued the fine old stone buildings after they fell into disrepair and then installed an interesting small museum, an antique shop, and a very good tearoom.

WHERE TO STAY

IN AND AROUND MULLINGAR

✪ Crookedwood House

Crookedwood, Mullingar, Co. Westmeath. ☎ **044/72165.** Fax 044/72166. 6 rms, all with bath. TEL TV. IR£35–IR£40 ($56–$64) per person sharing. (Rates include breakfast.) Dinner from IR£18.50 ($29.60). ACC, AE, MC, V.

Julie and Noel Kenny, whose marvelous country-house restaurant (see "Where to Eat," below) has won them acclaim for both food and hospitality, have now opened six beautiful guestrooms in the old house. This is one of the most convenient—and relaxing—spots in the county, a good Midlands base.

✪ Hilltop

Delvin Rd. (N52 off N4) Rathconnell, Mullingar, Co. Westmeath. ☎ **044/48958.** Fax 044/48013. 5 rms, all with bath. IR£20 ($32) single; IR£16 ($25.60) per person sharing. (Rates include breakfast.) No credit cards.

Dympna and Sean Casey's modern split-level home is two miles from town in a beautiful setting overlooking Lough Sheever. Dympna is an official of the Town and Country Homes Association and is warmly interested in seeing that all her guests are comfortable and get the most from their holidays. All five guest rooms are nicely furnished, and all have private toilets and showers.

✪ Woodlands Farm

Streamstown (near Horseleap), Co. Westmeath. ☎ **044/26414.** 6 rms, 2 with bath. IR£18 ($28.80) single; IR£14 ($22.40) per person sharing; IR£2 ($3.20) per person extra for bath. 50% reduction for children. (Rates include breakfast.) Dinner IR£12 ($17.40) extra. No credit cards. Closed Nov–Feb.

One of my favorite accommodations in Ireland is this farmhouse some 10 miles from Mullingar and quite convenient to Clonmachoise. Maybe it's because serenity sets in the moment you approach the rambling two-story home by way of an avenue of aged trees that often shade grazing horses. More likely it's the warm, friendly hospitality of Mary and Willy Maxwell and their attractive children that draws me back.

The house itself is charming, with a 200-year-old section to which a wing was added about a century ago that is still called the "new" addition. Parlor windows look out onto wooded grounds, and a fire is lit most evenings when a tea tray is rolled into the gracious room, which is furnished with antiques. Breakfasts are truly special, featuring fresh milk from their own cows and Mary's home-baked bread. The house has central heating, and the six bedrooms include one cozy single. Donkeys and pet sheep are an added attraction, and guests are given the run of the farmyard and grounds.

To get here, from Mullingar take the Galway road, then the road to Athlone; at Streamstown, look for the sign near the school. If you get hopelessly lost, just stop and ask—the Maxwells are well known in the Streamstown area.

WHERE TO EAT

✪ Crookedwood House

Crookedwood, Mullingar. ☎ **044/72165.** Set dinner IR£20 ($32); set Sun lunch IR£12 ($19.20). AE, DC, MC, V. Sun 12:30–2pm; Tues–Sat 7–10pm. MEAT/POULTRY/GAME.

Noel Kenny is the chef in this country house restaurant, and his talented cooking provides such superb dishes as grilled breast of wood pigeon with juniper berry and gin sauce, and roast leg or rack of lamb that regular patrons swear by. In fact, virtually every dish on the menu reflects Noel's imaginative and respectful treatment of homegrown fruit and vegetables and local meats and game. The house exudes a sort of "country house elegance," with open fires, whitewashed walls, and small, atmospheric rooms linked by arches. It's a relaxed, comfortable environment for the outstanding meals that come to table here.

L'Escale Restaurant

The Hodson Bay Hotel, Hodson Bay, Athlone ☎ **0902/92666.** Main courses IR£10–IR£18 ($16–$28.80). AE, DC, MC, V. Daily 6–9:30pm. IRISH/FRENCH.

Some five miles from Athlone, this stylish restaurant looks out to stunning views of Lough Ree. The cuisine is a happy blend of French and Irish specialties. Typical offerings are fillets of lemon sole rolled with sweet peppers, steamed and served on saffron sauce; and the delicious roast best end of lamb with a tagliatelle of leeks with red wine jus.

21

Getting to Know Northern Ireland

Yet another face of Ireland lies across the border that marks the six-county province of Northern Ireland. Its green fields, cliff-studded and cove-indented coastline, forest-clad mountains, and above all its hospitable inhabitants are reasons enough to cross that border. Beyond those, there are elements found *only* in the North that will add an extra, very special dimension to your Irish experience.

This is where you'll find the famed Giant's Causeway—mighty Fionn MacCumhaill's rocky pathway across to Scotland—along with a curving stretch of green glens; secluded inlets; towering cliffs (two of which are connected in summer months by the ingenious Carrick-a-Rede rope bridge high above a chasm between a salmon fishery island and the mainland); pleasant resort towns with safe beaches; and quiet, quaint little villages. So spectacular is the Antrim Coast that many of the 40,000 American visitors each year settle into this part of the province for their entire stay.

But what a pity to miss the gentler shoreline of County Down with its romantic Mountains of Mourne that sweep down to a sea replete with wide, curving strands fronted by charming holiday towns, and its firm claim on a good part of St. Patrick's Irish sojourn, from his first footsteps on Irish soil to his last. Quiet little villages on the Ards Peninsula look across to Scotland (clearly visible in many places), and the countryside is dotted with Norman castles, forest parks beckoning the hiker, and even a windmill still whirling away at harvest time, plus Strangford Lough and palm-tree-bordered Carlingford Lough.

And who would want to miss County Fermanagh's Lough Erne and its 300 square miles of boating and fishing amid exquisite scenery? Or the fabulous Marble Arch Caves? Or Devenish Island with its ancient abbey and tower and White Island's mysterious Celtic stone figures, just two of the lough's 154 islands? Or Armagh's two cathedrals—one Protestant, one Catholic, and both named for St. Patrick? Or the Sperrin Mountains of County Tyrone, as well as the unique folk park that so vividly depicts the rural lives of Irish immigrants on both sides of the Atlantic? Or Derry's massive old city walls? Or—well, read on and you'll find a wealth of other scenic splendors spread throughout all six counties.

THE LAY OF THE LAND

Northern Ireland occupies the northeast section of the Irish mainland, comprising the counties of Antrim, Armagh, Down, Fermanagh, Londonderry, and Tyrone, with a coast bordered by the North Channel and the Irish Sea. Its geographical features are outstanding: a coastline marked with towering cliffs, secluded inlets, and wide curving strands; the mountains of Mourne and of Sperrin; the Marble Arch Caves, the most spectacular in Europe; and the extraordinary rock formation known as the Giant's Causeway. Lough Neagh is the largest lake in the British Isles.

A LOOK AT THE PAST

In the 17th century, after the defeat of the Irish rebellion and the "Flight of the Earls," much of the land in Ulster was confiscated by the British Crown and "planted" with Protestant settlers from Scotland. Ulster gradually took on a more industrial and Protestant character than the rest of Ireland, with industry concentrated around Belfast.

The division between the two parts of Ireland began with the idea of Home Rule, first proposed in the 19th century, but finally established by the provisions of the 1920 Government of Ireland Act, which offered Home Rule to both parts of Ireland. While the 26 counties of southern Ireland became a Free State, and later an independent Republic, Protestant Northern Ireland, fearing to be overwhelmed by a Catholic majority, elected to remain part of the United Kingdom, to which it had close industrial and commercial ties.

In 1968 the Civil Rights movement began, only to bog down as violence escalated and the British army was called in to keep a peace that still eludes them. In 1973 hopes were raised when a Northern Ireland Assembly held out the promise of active participation in government by the minority, only to be dashed when it was violently opposed by extreme factions of both sides. In 1974 there was an effort made to set up a power-sharing Executive, but it was too short-lived to make any headway. Today a Secretary of State for Northern Ireland is the chief administrator and reports directly to Parliament in London.

In May 1984 a report was issued by the All Ireland Forum that seemed to hold out more real hope of an eventual solution than any other development thus far. The Forum consisted of leaders from political sectors both north and south of the border, and it met nearly 100 times over the course of a full year. Its final report contained detailed, well-thought-out discussions of several acceptable compromises. In 1986 a highly controversial Anglo-Irish Agreement was signed, giving the Republic limited participation in Northern Ireland affairs. In the intervening years, it has remained in force and, with a few deviations, has seemed to walk a fairly steady path toward an eventual permanent political solution. In conjunction with the Agreement, the two governments have held a series of joint meetings with leaders of leading political parties in the North. Only time will tell if these measures will prove to be but another step along the long road to a free and peaceful Ireland.

WHAT ABOUT THE "TROUBLES"?

The tangled threads of political events in Northern Ireland weave a pattern almost too complex to follow. It's always a temptation to oversimplify the underlying reasons for the tensions that have troubled the area since the 1921 treaty that set it apart from the rest of the country.

Injustices of the past live on in the memories of the Catholic minority who view themselves as victims of inequities of the present. The Catholic minority holds a deep yearning for a united Ireland that would improve their status. Protestants, with centuries of family history firmly rooted in Ireland, must contend with a privileged status quo not of their making, yet one they are fearful of changing. In such an atmosphere, violence reared its ugly head as an easy option to political discussions.

Nonetheless, most of the people in the two population segments live side by side, somewhat warily, but more interested in making a living and raising decent law-abiding families than professing loyalty to extremists on either side.

1 Northern Ireland Today

Over the years, visitors to Northern Ireland have been understandably concerned about the political situation and the "troubles" that made many people hesitate to plan a trip there. On August 31, 1994, however, to great rejoicing on both sides of the border, the IRA announced an end to military operations, followed some three months later by a similar declaration from Loyalist paramilitaries. As this is written, that ceasefire has held, and the terrible violence that infected Northern Ireland since 1969, sometimes with long no-incident intervals, other times with headline-grabbing frequency, has disappeared from city streets and rural villages.

In early 1995, on the heels of the ceasefire, the British and Irish governments issued a joint Framework Document of guiding principles for talks between all parties to work out a fair, just, and lasting political solution to the Northern Ireland situation. While progress towards those talks seems painstakingly slow to the peace-hungry population of the province, daily life has taken on a much more "normal" complexion. Although only time will tell if the present peace process will prove to be a final step along the long road to a free and peaceful Ireland, there is general optimism that the talks will be underway by the time you read this.

2 About the North

All that gorgeous scenery is not only a delight to the eye, but serves as well as a mighty spur to the imagination, for it has spawned a good many of Ireland's legends. It was in this part of Ireland that the brave Cuchulainn roamed and, singlehanded, guarded the border against the onslaught of Queen Maeve when she set out to capture the Brown Bull of Cooley. This was home territory for Fionn MacCumhaill (whom you may know as Finn MacCoul) and his faithful Fianna warriors. And the beautiful Deirdre o' the Sorrows played out her life's tragedy within the borders of Ulster.

If the above mention of these heroes has set your mind soaring, let me recommend a marvelous little paperback on sale in most bookstores in Ireland: it's titled *Heroic Tales from the Ulster Cycle* and is published by O'Brien Educational Press (with offices at 20 Victoria Rd., Dublin 6).

And if the landscape and legends of Northern Ireland are magical, its people are no less so. Because of all that history related back in an early chapter of this book, the accents of the North will fall on your ears with the soft burr of Scotland,

The North

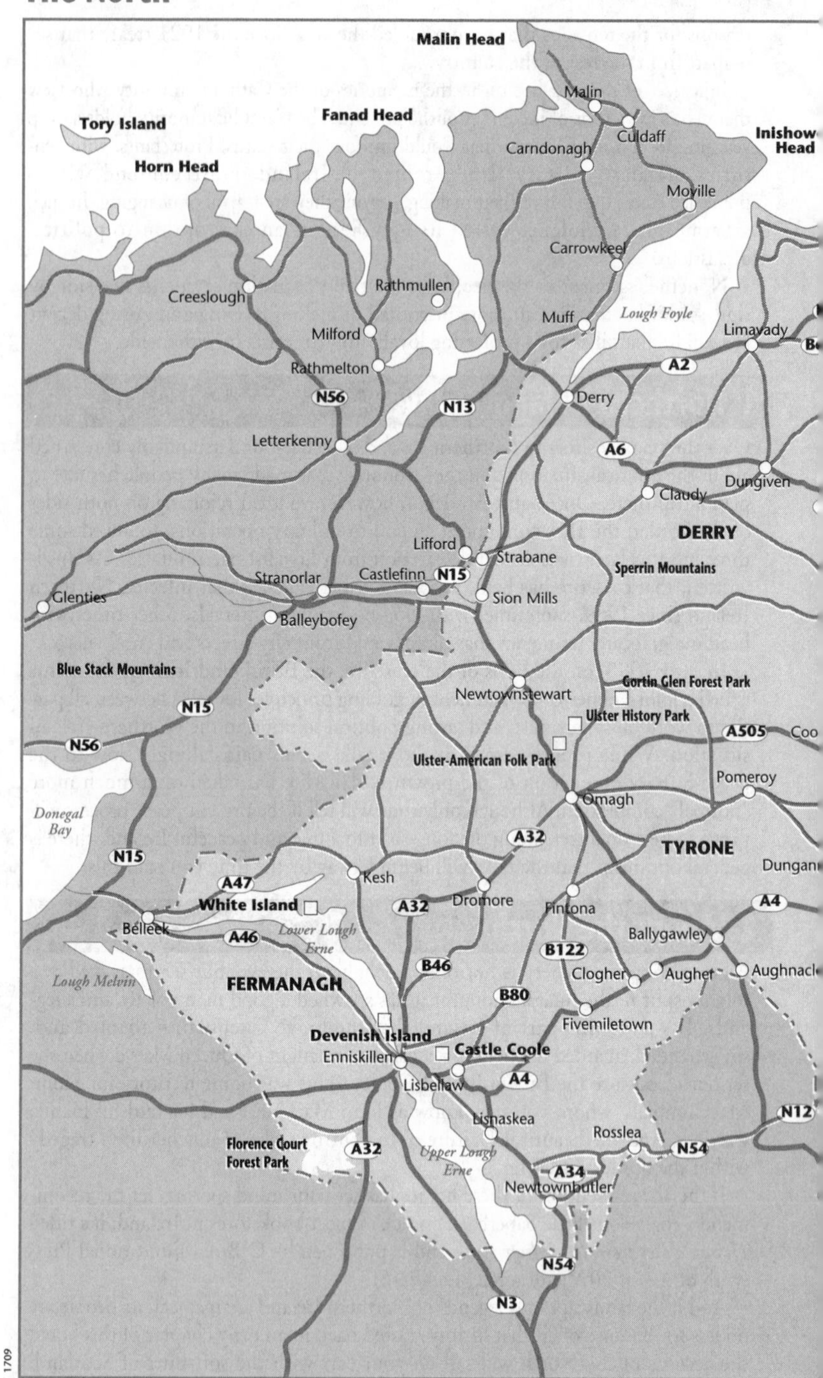

1709

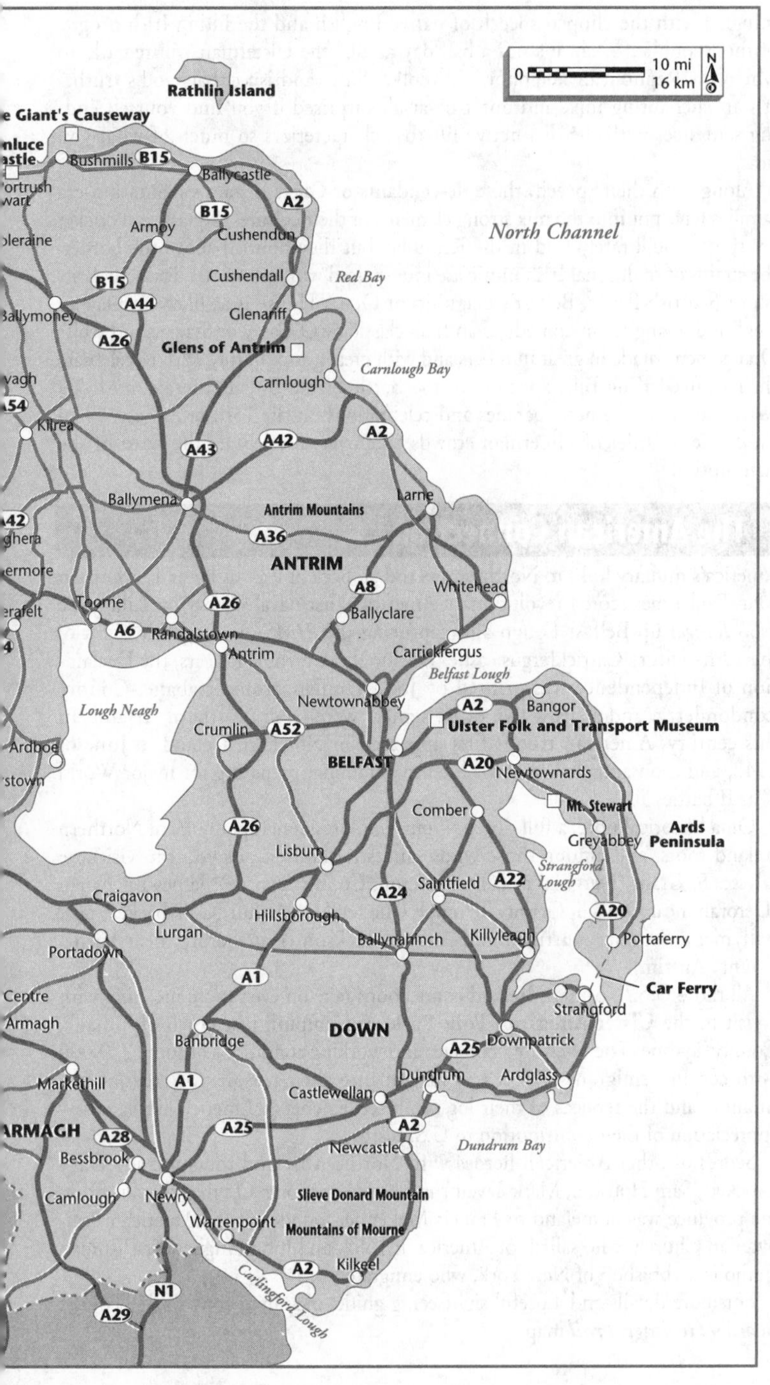

0
10 mi
16 km
N
Rathlin Island
Giant's Causeway
Bushmills
B15
Ballycastle
A2
B15
Armoy
Cushendun
North Channel
Cushendall
Red Bay
B15
A44
Ballymoney
Glenariff
A26
Glens of Antrim
Carnlough
Carnlough Bay
Kilrea
A2
A43
A42
Ballymena
Larne
Antrim Mountains
A36
ANTRIM
A8
Whitehead
Toome
A26
Ballyclare
A6
Randalstown
Antrim
Carrickfergus
Belfast Lough
Lough Neagh
Newtownabbey
A2
Bangor
Ulster Folk and Transport Museum
Crumlin
A52
Ardboe
BELFAST
A20
Newtownards
Mt. Stewart
Comber
A26
Ards
Greyabbey
Peninsula
Lisburn
Strangford
Lough
Saintfield
A22
A24
Craigavon
Hillsborough
A20
Lurgan
Portaferry
Portadown
Ballynahinch
Killyleagh
A1
Car Ferry
Strangford
Armagh
Banbridge
DOWN
Downpatrick
A25
Markethill
Dundrum
Ardglass
A1
Castlewellan
A25
A2
ARMAGH
A28
Newcastle
Dundrum Bay
Bessbrook
Camlough
Newry
Slieve Donard Mountain
Warrenpoint
Mountains of Mourne
A2
Kilkeel
N1
A29
Carlingford Lough

mingled with the clipped speech of native English and the lilting Irish brogue of the Republic. "Och, it's not a bad day at all," the Ulsterman will remark; to which his Republican neighbor will reply, "Sure, and isn't that God's truth." It's an enchanting mix, and don't be at all surprised if you find yourself ending sentences with the distinctive lift that characterizes so much of what you hear.

Along with their speech, these descendants of Great Britain's plantation-era families have put into the mix strong elements of their cultures. Squash and cricket are sports you'll rarely find in the Republic, but they flourish above the border; the strains of traditional Irish music are interspersed with music of a distinctly British or Scottish flavor; Belfast's magnificent Opera House is as likely to play an English drawing-room comedy as an Irish classic by O'Casey or Synge. And while Orangemen parade in great numbers and with great gusto on July 12th to celebrate their beloved King Billy's victory at the Battle of the Boyne, there is no less a festive air about Catholic parades and celebrations on the 15th of August, when the Ancient Order of Hibernian crowds take over to celebrate the Feast of the Assumption.

3 The American Connection

America's military links to Northern Ireland go back at least as far as 1778, when John Paul Jones scored revolutionary America's first naval victory by sailing the *USS Ranger* up Belfast Lough and capturing the *HMS Drake* within sight of the 12th-century Carrickfergus castle. During those turbulent years, the Declaration of Independence was printed by John Dunlap, from Strabane, County Londonderry, and at least five of its signers were from Northern Ireland. In this century, American troops first appeared in Northern Ireland in June of 1942, and thousands followed for intensive training, preparing for major World War II battles.

On a historical note, a full dozen of our U.S. presidents sprang from Northern Ireland roots, and among those whose ancestral homesteads you can visit are: Ulysses S. Grant (Dergina, near Dungannon, County Tyrone); James Buchanan (Deroran, near Omagh, County Tyrone); Chester Alan Arthur (Cullybackey, near Ballymena, County Antrim); and Andrew Jackson (Bonebefore, near Larne, County Antrim).

All those U.S./Northern Ireland connections take on even more meaning with a visit to the **Ulster-American Folk Park,** at Camphill just north of Omagh, County Tyrone. The re-created cottages and working conditions of some 250,000 18th-century emigrants give a real insight into their reasons for crossing the Atlantic, and the replicas of their log cabin settlements in America kindle a new appreciation of their contribution to U.S. history.

Scores of other American heroes with Northern Ireland roots include Davy Crockett, Sam Houston, Mark Twain, and Neil Armstrong. On the religious front, the province was homeland to Francis Makemie, founder of the American Presbyterian Church, who sailed for America in 1682, and John Hughes, first Roman Catholic archbishop of New York, who emigrated in 1817.

For more details and a useful sightseeing guide, pick up a copy of the Tourist Board's ***Heritage Trail*** map.

4 Visitor Information & Entry Requirements

VISITOR INFORMATION

There are about 30 Tourist Information offices around the province with helpful, friendly personnel eager to help with any problem and make sure you see the highlights of their area.

The Northern Ireland Tourist Board headquarters is at 59 North St., Belfast BT1 INB (☎ 01232/246609, fax 01232/240-960), open Monday through Friday from 9am to 5:15pm, and from Easter to September and on public holidays, also on Saturday, from 9am to 2pm. There is also an office in Dublin at 16 Nassau St., Dublin 2 (☎ 01/679-1977; fax 01/679-1863).

ENTRY REQUIREMENTS

U.S. citizens need only a valid passport to enter Northern Ireland. British citizens need no passport for Northern Ireland (except as a form of identification).

5 Money

Northern Ireland uses the currency of Great Britain. As we go to press, the exchange rate against the American dollar is £1 = $1.71, and all prices quoted in these pages are based on that rate. In these uncertain days, exchange rates fluctuate with amazing frequency, so be sure to check the current situation when you travel.

Americans will be well advised to buy pounds sterling with dollars rather than Irish punts, since the dollar exchange rate is much more favorable—you can change your money at banks in the Republic before you cross the border if it's more convenient. *One caution:* If you're arriving in the North on a weekend or bank holiday, be sure to buy pounds sterling *before you come.* And, of course, it's always best to change your currency at a bank rather than in department stores or hotels.

The Pound Sterling & the Dollar

£	U.S.	£	U.S.
.50	.86	22.50	38.48
1	1.71	25	42.75
2	3.42	27.50	47.03
2.50	4.28	30	51.30
3	5.13	35	59.85
5	8.55	40	68.40
8	13.68	50	85.50
10	17.10	75	128.25
15	25.65	100	171.00
20	34.20		

In Belfast, the Thomas Cook office, 11 Donegall Place, Belfast 1, can also convert currency at the official rate. See the appendix for an exchange rate table.

NORTHERN IRELAND CALENDAR OF EVENTS

February

- **The Ulster Harp National Steeplechase,** Downpatrick, Country Down. The only place to see horseracing in Northern Ireland. Late February to early March.

March

- **Northern Ireland Spring Opera Season.** Begins in early March.
- **St. Patrick's Day.** Celebrated most colorfully in Downpatrick, Newry, and Cultra. March 17.
- **Belfast Musical Festival,** Balmoral, Belfast. Youth speech, drama, and music competitions. Early March.
- **Horse Plowing Match,** in Fair Head, Ballycastle. A century-old competition for farmers who plow the fields in a traditional way—no tractors.

April

- **Belfast Civic Festival.** 15 days of concerts, competitions, and exhibitions culminating in a colorful parade for the Lord Mayor's Show. Late April or early May.
- **City of Belfast Spring Flower Festival,** Maysfield Leisure Centre, Belfast. Flowers and crafts star. Late April.

May

- **Belfast Marathon.** Traditional 26-mile dash. Early May.
- **Ballyclare Horse Fair,** in Ballyclare. You don't have to buy a horse to get a kick from the trading. Late May.
- **Royal Ulster Agricultural Society Show,**Balmoral, Belfast. Continuing a tradition begun in 1855, with international showjumping, sheep-shearing, goat and foxhound parades, bands, and fashion shows. Late May.

June

- **Belfast Midsummer Jazz and Blues Festival.** Gathering of jazz musicians from around the globe. First week in June.
- **Black Bush Amateur Golf Tournament,** Causeway Coast. Special awards for visitors in this four-day, four-course golf competition. Early June.
- **Fiddle Stone Festival,** Belleek. Fiddlers from all over Ireland gather during the 10-day Belleek Festival to play in honor of a famous 18th-century fiddle player. Late June or early July.

July

- **Enniskillen Festival,** Enniskillen. Music-making in pubs and street buskers make this town ring. Early July.
- **Ulster Senior Hurling Championship Final,** Casement Park, Belfast. Early July.
- **Battle of the Boyne Tercentenary Celebrations,** in Belfast, Londonderry, and 16 other town centers. Protestants (Orangemen) celebrate this important victory to the boom of gigantic drums and marching feet while bracing themselves for the flood of political and religious speeches that follow. July 12.

- **Sham Fight,** Scarva. Colorful reenactment of the Battle of the Boyne, with a joust between two horsemen garbed as William of Orange and James II. July 13.

August

- **Ancient Order of Hibernians Parades,** at various venues throughout the province. Feast of the Assumption celebrations with Gaelic pipers leading Hibernian processions and supplying the background music for open-air meetings. August 15.

September

- **Belfast Folk Festival,** Belfast. A weekend of Irish folk music, dancing, and singing. Mid-September.
- **Dromore Horse Fair,** in Dromore, County Down. Clydesdales, Shires, and other big horse breeds star in this cavalcade of horse-drawn vehicles.

6 Getting There

BY PLANE Aer Lingus flies from the U.S to Belfast International Airport via Shannon and Dublin airports, and major U.S. airlines have connections through London's Heathrow and Gatwick airports.

From Great Britain, Aer Lingus, British Airways, British Midland, and several smaller lines operate between Belfast and London, Birmingham, Blackpool, Bristol, Cardiff, Edinburgh, Glasgow, the Isle of Man, Jersey, Leeds, Manchester, and Southampton. From Europe, KLM has regular service from Amsterdam.

BY FERRY There is quite good car-ferry service between Great Britain and Northern Ireland. From England, Norse Irish Ferries (☎ 01232/779-090) sails between Liverpool and Belfast (11 hours), and the Isle of Man Steam Packet Co. (☎ 01624/661-661) has service between Douglas and Belfast. From Wales, ferry service is to the Republic (see Chapter 3). From Scotland, Seacat (☎ 01232/310-910) sails to Belfast and Larne from Stranraer.

BY RAIL/BUS The Dublin-Belfast nonstop express train runs six times a day Monday through Saturday, and three times on Sunday. Phone the Belfast Central Station at (☎ 01232/899-411) for times and booking.

Ulsterbus (☎ 01232/333-000) operates coach service between Dublin and Belfast three times daily.

BY CAR If you're driving a rental car from the Republic, you should check to see that the insurance covers your stay above the border—and the same, of course, applies if you're going the other way. When coming from the Republic, it's always advisable to enter through one of the approved checkpoints, which are clearly marked on tourist maps. You won't have to show your passport or produce a visa.

7 Getting Around

BY RAIL & BUS You can travel around the North quite easily and inexpensively using the rail and bus services. Day trips are also available to almost all sightseeing highlights. Northern Ireland Railways (NIR) has a seven-day, unlimited-travel Rail Runabout pass good April through October at a cost of £25 ($42.75) for adults, £12.50 ($21.38) for children. It's available at most railway stations. Primary rail service is from Belfast to Londonderry via Ballymena and Coleraine and Belfast to Bangor. Information on all NIR services is available at the Information Centre in Belfast's Central Station, or by calling 01232/399-411 or 230671. Ask about special student and senior discounts.

Ulsterbus service will get you almost anywhere there's no train, with departures from their stations on Glengall Street in Belfast, in the city center near the Europa Hotel (☎ 01232/320-011), and Oxford Street, near the central train station (232-356). During the summer, the Antrim Coaster follows the majestic coast road between Belfast and Coleraine, and the Sperrin Sprinter travels through the Sperrin Mountains between Belfast and Omagh. For schedule and fare information, call 01232/333000. The budget-stretching Freedom of Northern Ireland ticket costs £28 ($47.88) and covers seven days' unlimited travel in Northern Ireland (available only from Ulsterbus offices).

BY CAR As in the Republic, driving is on the left. Northern Ireland has an excellent network of highways—with speed limits of 30 m.p.h. in town (unless a slower speed is posted); 60 m.p.h. on highways and country roads; and 70 m.p.h. on Northern Ireland dual carriageways (divided highways). Traffic circles are called "roundabouts," and exits are well marked.

The Automobile Association office is at 108–110 Great Victoria St., Belfast (☎ 01345/500-600; 24-hour breakdown service 01800/887766).

Rental Cars The leading car rental firms are Avis (☎ 800/331-1084 in the U.S.) and Europcar/National (☎ 800/227-7368 in the U.S.). Cars can be booked in the United States before your arrival or from their offices in Belfast (check the yellow pages of the Belfast telephone directory) or at Belfast International Airport.

Driving Rules and Regulations There aren't that many, but you should know them in advance. The most important regulation concerns parking. When you see an area signposted CONTROL ZONE, it means that cars must not be left parked and unattended, even for a short time. In those areas, it is felt that cars left empty (even if locked) are a security risk, and the regulation is strictly enforced. There will usually be a parking lot close at hand with an attendant on duty.

BY TAXI There are taxi ranks at main rail and bus stations, ports, and airports. For other taxi service, check local telephone directories. Some of the black, London-style cabs are not metered, and you should agree on a fare to your destination when you start out. It's a rather common practice to ask passengers to share a cab with other travelers if there is a long line (a money-saver, since your fare will be lower).

BY BICYCLE Northern Ireland is good cycling country, with even minor roads well surfaced to make the going easy and plenty of overnight accommodations along your route. Tourist offices can furnish a "Cycling" information bulletin detailing several scenic bike tours. Bike rental will run about £7 ($11.97) per day, £28 ($47.88) per week, and you'll be asked for a deposit. Rental bikes are available in most major cities and are listed in the yellow pages of the telephone directory.

8 A Suggested Itinerary

The six counties of Northern Ireland are all good rambling country, and the following is by no means intended to be a rigid, not-to-be-deviated-from itinerary. It is, however, a convenient circular tour of the province that will get you to most of the highlights. My best advice is to allow at least one full week, two if time permits. As in the Republic, you're sure to discover some places not included in the outstanding sightseeing points listed in the county-by-county chapters that follow.

If you're coming from Donegal, the following route is recommended (and, of course, it can be reversed should your departure point be Belfast). From Londonderry, head east through Limavady and the Roe Valley to Coleraine and the Bann Valley. Then go on to Portrush and the Giant's Causeway. Bushmills Distillery is a short detour south from this point. Drive on through Ballycastle and enter the Antrim Coast Road, which takes you through the Nine Glens of Antrim, Larne, and Carrickfergus to Belfast. Then it's south to Downpatrick (if time permits, cut east around the Ards Peninsula) and west to Armagh, Enniskillen, and Belleek.

9 Sports & Outdoor Activities

GOLF Some eighty golf courses around the province offer golfers, be they duffers or pros, a wide choice wherever they find themselves. There are, for instance, no fewer than a dozen courses within five miles of Belfast City Hall. Greens fees are moderate (£7–£15, $12–$25.65), and many courses have clubs for hire. If an exhilarating game is high on your holiday priority list, be sure and arm yourself with the Tourist Board's ***Information Guide to Golf,*** which gives detailed information on golf courses in each of the six counties. There are also about a dozen **pitch-and-putt** courses scattered around the province, a relaxing end of the day for the entire family.

FISHING Blessed as it is with so many lakes and rivers, Northern Ireland is a fisherperson's dream territory. The River Foyle system, for example, is one of the best salmon fisheries in all of Europe. Lough Erne is brimming with brown trout, and Lough Melvin and Lough Neath breed several species of fighting trout. Pick up the Tourist Board's ***Information Guide to Game Fishing*** for details on license requirements, as well as descriptions of some of the province's prime fishing waters.

WALKING Even if you're not a dedicated walker, Northern Ireland's overflowing treasure chest of scenic beauty may well lure you from behind the wheel of your car. You won't travel far without finding tranquil, well-signposted forest trails, exciting clifftop walks, or more demanding mountain hikes. The famous **Ulster Way** trail meanders along a 560-mile-long circular path, and the Tourist Board's ***Information Guide to The Ulster Way: Accommodation for Walkers*** helps you plan reasonable walks for each day with good accommodations at night. If all those miles are a little too daunting, however, the ***Information Guide to Walking*** breaks it down for you, with details of some 14 segments. If shank's mare is your preferred mode of transport around this lovely part of Ireland, all-inclusive walking holidays are available through **Enjoy Ireland,** Ainsworth Street, Blackburn BB1 6AZ (☎ 01232/692-899). **Walk Ulster,** Wright Lines, Old Mill, Banbridge BT32 4JB (☎ 018306/62126), offers walks and accommodations along the north Antrim coast, the Mourne Mountains, and Lough Erne. Shorter breaks, with hill walking in the Antrim Glens led by qualified guides, are available from **Ardelinis Activity Centre,** Cushendall, County Antrim (☎ 012667/71340).

10 Shopping

Prices are generally lower in Northern Ireland than in the Republic for such items as Belleek, hand-woven tweeds, crystal, and many other fine products, although the price differential is fast narrowing.

In larger towns, shops are usually open from 9am to 5:30pm, while many other towns have half-day closing one day a week, and smaller shops everywhere close for lunch. If you happen on a Market Day (many towns hold a street market once a week), it's great fun to stop and wander among the stalls.

Northern Ireland is the home of Irish linen, and fascinating **Linen Trail** guided tours (choose the half-day, one-day, or two-day tour) is available from **The Linen Homelands Tours,** 200 Newry Road, Banbridge, County Down BT32 3NB (☎ 018206/23322).

Two shopping expeditions that can be enjoyable and profitable are those to **Belleek Pottery,** Belleek (☎ 0136/565501), and **Tyrone Crystal,** Dungannon (☎ 018687/25335)—but you should telephone ahead to make arrangements for your visit.

FAST FACTS: Northern Ireland

American Express In Belfast, the American Express representative is Hamilton Travel, 10 College St., Belfast BT1 6BT (☎ 01232/322455, fax 0123/322-455).

Business Hours Banks are open Monday through Friday from 10am to 12:30pm and 1:30 to 3pm; closed Saturday, Sunday, and bank holidays. Shops are usually open Monday through Saturday from 9am to 5:30pm; closed Sunday and holidays. Most shops have one early-closing day a week, usually on Thursday.

Currency See Section 5, "Money," above.

Customs Citizens of non-EC countries may bring in the following, if over the age of 17: 200 cigarettes, 50 cigars, and 1 liter of distilled beverages and spirits exceeding 38.5 proof, or 2 liters of other dutiable goods. Upon reentering the United States, you may bring back purchases valued up to $400 without paying Customs duties; anything in excess of that amount is assessed 10% on the next $1,000, and an average of 12% for anything above that. Antiques more than 100 years old are free with an authentication of age from the dealer. (Also see "Customs" in "Fast Facts: Ireland" in Chapter 3.)

Drug and Firearm Laws There are strictly enforced laws prohibiting the importation of handguns or other illegal firearms, with stiff prison sentences as penalty. The importation of illegal drugs is also strictly forbidden.

Electricity Northern Ireland's electricity is 220 volts AC, so if you bring small appliances (such as hairdryers), pack a voltage transformer and a variety of plug adapters. Electric shavers using 110 volts should be no problem, as there will be shaver points in every accommodation.

Embassies and Consulates The U.S. consulate general is at Queen's House, 14 Queen's St., Belfast BT1 (☎ 01232/228239).

Emergencies Dial 999 for fire, police, and ambulance.

Mail United Kingdom postal rates apply, and mailboxes are painted red.

Newspapers and Magazines The morning national newspapers are the *News Letter* and the *Irish News;* the *Belfast Telegraph* is the evening newspaper. All are published Monday through Saturday, and on Sunday most Northern Irish depend on U.K. papers, which are readily available.

Police The police are known as the Royal Ulster Constabulary. Except for special detachments, they are unarmed.

Safety It is important to follow all rules (such as parking rules in Section 7, "Getting Around," above), and to cooperate with security personnel if such an occasion should arise. Whenever you are traveling in an unfamiliar city or country, stay alert. Be aware of your immediate surroundings.

Taxes You will pay a VAT (Value-Added Tax) on almost every one of your expenses, with the exception of B&B accommodations. The percentages vary with the category of the services and purchases. See pg.11 for details of recovering VAT on goods you take out of the country.

Tracing Your Roots Contact the Ulster Historical Foundation, Balmoral Buildings, 12 College Square East, Belfast BTI 6DD (☎ 01232/332-288; fax 01232/239-885), for help in tracking down Irish ancestors. They'll furnish a list of helpful publications and help you get to the appropriate genealogical source. See also "Tracing Your Irish Roots" in Chapter 4.

Two private organizations to contact are: **Irish Genealogical Services,** 2 Lower Crescent, Belfast B17 1NR (☎ 01232/241-412; fax 01232/239-972; contact David McElroy); and **Historical Research Associates,** Glen Cottage, Glenmachan Rd., Belfast BT4 2NP (☎ 01232/761-490; contact Joan Phillipson or Jennifer Irwin).

22 Belfast

In ancient times, Belfast was a fort set at a ford of the River Lagan (its name in Irish is Beal Feirste, "Mouth of the Sandy Ford"). Around it a small village developed, and in the 17th century Protestant settlers from Scotland and parts of England moved in (and native villagers were moved out) by order of English rulers, thus establishing the character of the city; it grew at a steady pace until the end of the 1700s, thanks in large part to a thriving linen industry. In 1791 Wolfe Tone founded the United Irish Society in Belfast to bring together Protestants and Catholics who chafed under the repressive Penal Laws, and in 1798 their efforts led to an uprising, one which was quickly squelched by English forces. The shipyard that was to contribute so much to the city's growth was opened in 1791. By the time the Industrial Revolution was in full bloom during the 19th century, both shipbuilding and the linen trade welcomed newer, more modern operating methods. Both prospered, and Belfast's population grew by leaps and bounds.

The city today is a bustling, energetic center of industry, yet for the visitor it is easy to get around and holds many points of interest—most prominent of which has to be the good Queen Victoria, whose statue adorns Donegall Square and whose architectural style is in evidence all around the city.

1 Orientation

ARRIVING

By Air The Belfast International Airport (☎ 018494/422-888) is in Crumlin, 19 miles northwest of the city center. There is minibus service into the city center. The Belfast City Airport (☎ 01232/457745) is four miles to the northeast (for U.K. flights only).

By Train The Central Rail Station (☎ 01232/230310) is on East Bridge Street.

By Bus The Ulsterbus stations are on Glengall Street (☎ 01232/320-011) and Oxford Street (☎ 01232/232356). The Glengall Street terminal is in the city center near the Europa Hotel.

VISITOR INFORMATION

The Northern Ireland Tourist Board Information Office is at 59 North St. (☎ 01232/246609). The Irish Tourist Board maintains a Belfast office at 53 Castle St. (☎ 01232/327888) for information on the Republic.

GETTING AROUND

By Bus Tickets for bus service within Belfast are available at the Citybus kiosk in Donegall Square West, Monday through Saturday from 9am to 5:30pm, and at newsagents displaying the Citybus sign. Fares vary according to destination, and departures are from City Hall, Donegall Square, Wellington Place, Chichester Street, Upper Arthur Street, and Castle Street.

By Car Arm yourself with a good city map from the Tourist Board, then be very sure to observe parking restrictions (see Section 7, "Getting Around," in Chapter 21). Your best bet is to drive to the city center and leave the car in an attended lot or garage.

By Taxi There are taxi ranks at the Belfast International Airport, harbor ports, principal rail and bus stations, major hotels, and shopping centers, or you can call V.I.P. Taxis (☎ 666111) or Telecabs (☎ 230333 or 232523). Some of the black, London-style cabs are not metered, and you should agree on a fare to your destination when you start out.

On Foot To explore Belfast on foot, take it neighborhood by neighborhood—the city center, the university area, etc. There's good bus service to move you from one to another.

Town Layout The city center is fairly compact and easy to walk around. To the northwest is the Shankill Road area; to the west, the Falls Road area; south are the Malone and Ballynafeigh areas; while to the east are the Ballymacarrett, Sydenham, Bloomfield, and Belmont areas.

2 Where to Stay

The Queen's University area is a happy hunting ground for bed-and-breakfast accommodations, and those listed outside the city are close enough to serve as a good base for exploring Belfast while enjoying the scenic countryside. The practice of charging more for rooms with private facilities varies from accommodation to accommodation, so be sure to check when you book.

IN THE CITY

✪ Ashberry Cottage

19 Rosepark Central, Belfast BT5 7RN. ☎ **01232/482441.** 3 rms, none with bath. £16 ($27.36) single; £30 ($51.30) double. (Rates include breakfast.) Dinner £12 ($20.52) extra. No credit cards.

Cozy is the word for Hilary and Sam Mitchell's modern bungalow, and you'll be completely spoiled from the moment they greet you with a welcome tray of tea and goodies. Not only do they both know the Belfast area well, but Hilary works for the Northern Ireland Tourist Board and is well qualified to help you plan your travels throughout the province. The attractive bedrooms all have TV and tea/coffee facilities. Sam is the morning cook, and his breakfast has been described as "the best breakfast in Europe"—evening meals also draw raves from guests. Sam will meet you at the airport or railway station with advance notice, but if you're making your own way, to reach Ashberry Cottage take A20 to Rosepark, which is the second turn on the right past the Stormont Hotel.

Botanic Lodge

87 Botanic Ave., Belfast BT7 1JN. ☎ **01232/327-682** or 247-439. 15 rms, all with bath. TV. £18 ($30.78) single; £40 ($68.40) double. (Rates include breakfast.) High tea £10 ($17.10); dinner £10 ($17.10). No credit cards.

Established in 1957, Botanic Lodge is the domain of its friendly hostess, Mrs. Moore. Located in a fashionable residential area, it is convenient to Queen's University, the Botanic Gardens, and several very good restaurants. Public rooms, as well as guest rooms, are nicely decorated and comfortably furnished. Central heating. Private parking is available.

Helga Lodge

7 Cromwell Road, Belfast BT7 1JW. ☎ **01232/324-820.** Fax 01232/320-653. 29 rms, 12 with bath. TEL TV. £15–£17 ($25.65–$29.07) single; £30–£32 ($51.30–$54.72) double. (Rates include breakfast.) No credit cards.

There's lots of character in this red-brick, Victorian-style town house located in the Queen's University area. It's only a short walk to the city center, and the Botanic Gardens are also quite near. Bedrooms vary in size, but all are comfortably furnished.

Liserin Guest House

17 Eglantine Ave., Belfast BT9 6DW. ☎ **01232/660769.** 7 rms, none with bath. £17 ($29.07) single; £32 ($54.72) double. Reduction for children. (Rates include breakfast.) No credit cards.

Set on a quiet street shaded by lime trees, Liserin is about a 15-minute walk into the city center, and there's good bus service at the end of the block. The brick Victorian-style town house dates back to 1892, and original woodwork, high ceilings, and spacious rooms add to its charm. Mrs. Ina Smith is the hostess, and she takes a personal interest in guests, serving evening tea and, upon request, a simple evening meal at a modest price. Guest rooms have sinks and are attractive and well furnished, and those in the back catch more sun than the ones in front, but all are light and cheerful.

Worth a Splurge

✪ Ash-Rowan Guest House

12 Windsor Ave., Belfast BT9 6EE. ☎ **01232/661758.** Fax 01232/663227. 4 rms, all with bath. TV. £42 ($71.82) single; £66 ($112.86) double. (Rates include breakfast.) Dinner £18 ($30.78) extra. MC, V. Private car park.

After a career in award-winning restaurants, Evelyn and Sam Hazlett acquired this lovely late-Victorian residence and have turned it into a Grade A town house serving superb evening meals. Set back from the street in a quiet residential area between Lisburn Road and Malone Road, Ash-Rowan is only 10 minutes from the center of the city and provides private parking on the grounds. Each bedroom is beautifully decorated in individual style, and has a vanity unit, color TV, and razor points. An added feature is the dressing gown provided each guest—color-keyed to the room, no less! There's also a paperback library for the use of guests. The Hazletts offer a choice of either a full traditional or continental breakfast, and both the cuisine and service of evening meals rival those in a first-class restaurant.

Camera House

44 Wellington Park, Belfast BT9 6DP. ☎ **01232/660026** or 667856. 11 rms, all with bath. TV. £30 ($51.30) single; £45 ($76.95) double. (Rates include breakfast.) No credit cards.

Belfast

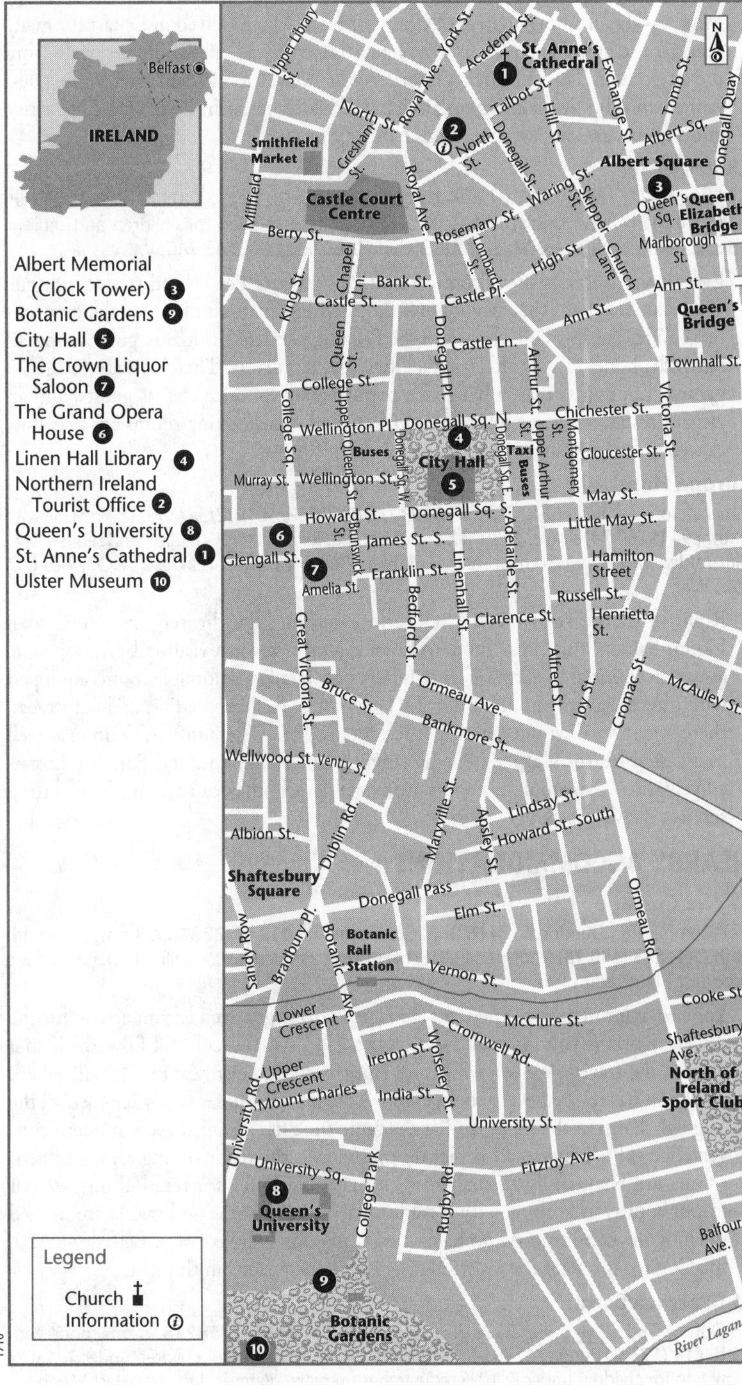
Belfast
IRELAND
Albert Memorial (Clock Tower) 3
Botanic Gardens 9
City Hall 5
The Crown Liquor Saloon 7
The Grand Opera House 6
Linen Hall Library 4
Northern Ireland Tourist Office 2
Queen's University 8
St. Anne's Cathedral 1
Ulster Museum 10
Legend
Church
Information
St. Anne's Cathedral
Smithfield Market
Castle Court Centre
Albert Square
Queen Elizabeth Bridge
Queen's Bridge
City Hall
Buses
Taxi Buses
Shaftesbury Square
Botanic Rail Station
North of Ireland Sport Club
Queen's University
Botanic Gardens
River Lagan
Upper Library St.
York St.
Academy St.
Exchange St.
Tomb St.
Donegall Quay
North St.
Royal Ave.
Talbot St.
Gresham St.
North St.
Donegall St.
Hill St.
Albert Sq.
Millfield
Waring St.
Skipper St.
Queen's Sq.
Berry St.
Rosemary St.
Lombard St.
Church Lane
Marlborough St.
Chapel Ln.
Bank St.
High St.
Ann St.
King St.
Castle St.
Castle Pl.
Queen St.
Donegall Pl.
Castle Ln.
Townhall St.
College St.
Arthur St.
Chichester St.
Victoria St.
College Sq.
Wellington Pl.
Donegall Sq. N.
Upper Queen St.
Donegall Sq. E.
Upper Arthur St.
Montgomery St.
Gloucester St.
Murray St.
Wellington St.
Donegall Sq. W.
May St.
Howard St.
Donegall Sq. S.
Adelaide St.
Little May St.
Brunswick St.
James St. S.
Glengall St.
Franklin St.
Hamilton Street
Amelia St.
Linenhall St.
Russell St.
Bedford St.
Clarence St.
Henrietta St.
Great Victoria St.
Alfred St.
Joy St.
Cromac St.
McAuley St.
Bruce St.
Ormeau Ave.
Bankmore St.
Wellwood St.
Ventry St.
Dublin Rd.
Maryville St.
Lindsay St.
Apsley St.
Howard St. South
Albion St.
Donegall Pass
Ormeau Rd.
Elm St.
Sandy Row
Bradbury Pl.
Botanic Ave.
Vernon St.
Cooke St.
Lower Crescent
McClure St.
Cromwell Rd.
Wolseley St.
Shaftesbury Ave.
Ireton St.
Upper Crescent
Mount Charles
India St.
University Rd.
University St.
University Sq.
Fitzroy Ave.
College Park
Rugby Rd.
Balfour Ave.
1710

Miss Angela Drumm, a native of County Meath who has lived in Belfast for many years, is the hostess here. This lovely guesthouse is just a few minutes' walk from the city center. The red-brick Victorian-style house has bay windows in the guest lounge and dining room, giving a light, airy look to both. Four of the attractive guest rooms are singles, sometimes hard to find.

Dukes Hotel

65 University St., Belfast BT7 1HL. ☎ **01232/236666.** Fax 01232/237177. 21 rms, all with bath. £82 ($140.22) single; £98 ($167.58) double. Reduction for children and seniors. Special midweek rates available. (Rates include breakfast.) ACC, AE, MC, V.

Every conceivable modern comfort and convenience lies behind the picturesque Victorian facade of this lovely hotel. Located less than a mile from the city center, beside Queen's University and the Botanic Gardens, its luxury guest rooms all have telephones, TVs, coffee/tea facilities, and hairdryers. There's a state-of-the-art gymnasium and saunas, a bar that's popular with locals as well as guests, and an elegant restaurant serving international cuisine. No-smoking rooms are available, as well as baby-sitting services.

Europa Hotel

Great Victoria St., Belfast BT2 7AP. ☎ **01232/327000.** Fax 01232/327800. 184 rms, all with bath. £94 ($160.74) single; £130 ($222.30) double. Reduction for children and seniors; special midweek and weekend rates available. (Rates include breakfast.) ACC, AE, DC, MC, V.

Right in the heart of the city, close to shopping, the theater, and the Crown Liquor Saloon, this classy modern hotel is a favorite with visiting businesspeople as well as tourists. In addition to tastefully decorated, comfortable rooms equipped with direct-dial telephones, color TVs, tea/coffee facilities, radios, and hairdryers, there is an award-winning gourmet restaurant (see "Where to Eat," below) as well as a casual bistro. Harper's Bar has nightly entertainment, and Paradise Lost is a lively disco. No-smoking rooms are available, and they can arrange baby-sitting services. Private parking.

NEARBY ACCOMMODATIONS

✪ The Cottage

377 Comber Rd., Dundonald BT16 0XB, Co. Down. ☎ **01247/878189.** 3 rms, none with bath. TEL. £18 ($30.78) single; £34 ($58.14) double. Reductions for children. (Rates include breakfast.) No credit cards.

Your enchantment with the Cottage is likely to begin even as you arrive, for the driveway brings you into full view of a lovely lawn and colorful flowerbeds that beckon the traveler to sit a while and enjoy such outdoor beauty. Mrs. Elizabeth Muldoon has realized every cottage-lover's dream—she has lovingly retained all the original charm of the house and at the same time has installed every modern convenience. The living room is picture-pretty, as is the rustic dining area, and bedrooms are beautifully furnished with many antiques scattered about. Decor throughout is in keeping with a traditional country home and guests are invited to enjoy the conservatory out back. Just a three-mile drive east of Belfast via A20, the Cottage is one of the most inviting accommodations in the area.

✪ Greenlea Farm

48 Dunover Rd., Ballywalter BT22 2LE, Co. Down. ☎ **01247/758218.** 5 rms, none with bath. £14 ($23.94) single; £24 ($41.04) double. 25% reduction for children under 12; 50% reduction for children under 8; 10% reduction for seniors. (Rates include breakfast.) High tea £6 ($10.26) extra; dinner, £8 ($13.68). No credit cards.

A comfortable old farmhouse that has been thoroughly modernized, Greenlea looks out from its hilltop to the Ards Peninsula and across to the misty coast of Scotland and the Isle of Man. Mrs. Evelyn McIvor is its warm, friendly hostess who teaches crafts and enjoys sharing her considerable knowledge of the area with guests. Both the lounge and dining room have picture windows that frame the spectacular view, and the dining room holds lovely antique pieces, with lots of silver and crystal on display. Recreational amenities include tennis and bowling. Mrs. McIvor has one large family room with bunk beds for two children and a double for parents, as well as accommodations for singles and doubles. Greenlea Farm is half a mile from Ballywalter, the first farm on the left on the Dunover road (about 23 miles southeast of Belfast via A2, at the top of the Ards Peninsula).

3 Where to Eat

From pub grub to elegant restaurants, you'll find meals to suit your mood and your pocketbook in Belfast. Pick up a copy of "Where to Eat" to supplement the selections below. Consult the index for restaurant listings by cuisine.

MEALS FOR LESS THAN £5 ($8.55)

You'll find good pub grub for about £5 ($8.55) from noon to 2:30pm at the following: **Crown Liquor Saloon,** 46 Great Victoria St. (☎ 249476); **Robinson's,** 36 Great Victoria St. (☎ 329812); **Beaten Docket,** 48 Great Victoria St. (☎ 242986); **The Front Page,** 106 Donegall St. (☎ 324269); **Linenhall Bar,** 9 Clarence St. (☎ 248458); **Rumpoles,** 81 Chichester St. (☎ 232840); **Botanic Inn,** 23 Malone Rd., in the University area (☎ 660460); and on the outskirts of town, **The King's Head,** Lisburn Road, Balmoral, opposite King's Hall (☎ 660455).

✪ Bewley's

Donegall Arcade. ☎ **01232/234955.** £5–£10 ($8.55–$17.10). MC, V. Mon–Sat 8:30am–5pm (until 8pm Thurs). SPECIALTY COFFEES/BREAKFAST/SALADS/HOT PLATES/PASTRIES.

Bewley's has been a Dublin fixture for a century and a half, and in recent years has opened branches in leading cities around the country. This Belfast branch is in the same traditional Irish café style, and offers their special blends of roasted coffees, blended teas, home-cooked pastries, and a wide variety of salad plates and hot lunch selections.

✪ Bittles Vittles

70 Upper Church Lane. ☎ **01232/311088.** £1.50–£4 ($2.56–$6.84). No credit cards. Mon–Sat 11:30am–3pm. TRADITIONAL/IRISH.

John Bittle is a great believer in the Irish dishes he grew up with, and this is one place you'll find a really *good* Irish stew, as well as champ, an old Irish recipe not often encountered in restaurants. The menu is likely to include at least one vegetarian selection; plaice in garlic butter; a pasta dish; filled rolls and sandwiches; and steak, ham, and chicken dishes, all served with potatoes and a fresh vegetable. Incidentally, John's cream of leek soup is terrific.

The Deer's Head

76 North St. ☎ **01232/239163.** £1.50–£4.50 ($2.56–$7.69). No credit cards. Mon–Sat 11:30am–7pm. PUB GRUB.

Just across from the tourist office, this large, busy pub has a surprisingly wide range of inexpensive dishes. The menu includes soup and sandwiches, burgers, baked potatoes with a variety of toppings, pasta, chicken, steak, fish, and vegetarian selections.

MEALS FOR LESS THAN £15 ($25.65)

Ashoka

363/365 Lisburn Rd. ☎ **01232/660-362.** Lunch specials £4.50–$6.95 ($7.59–$11.88); average dinner £15 ($25.65). No credit cards. INDIAN/EUROPEAN.

Lovers of Indian cuisine won't want to miss a meal at this outstanding restaurant in the University area, and their non-Indian-food-eating companions (if there are any) will find a nice selection of beef, pork, etc., continental dishes. The Businessman's Lunch Specials are especially good value.

✪ Nick's Warehouse

35/39 Hill St. ☎ **01232/439690.** Salads and hot plates £5–£10 ($8.55–$17.10). MC, V. Mon–Fri 12–2:30pm; Tues–Sat 6–9pm. TRADITIONAL/SALADS.

This casual restaurant and wine bar in the city center (near the tourist office, behind the cathedral) dishes up terrific meals for a pittance. Salads might include summer chicken and melon with yogurt-and-chive dressing and marinated herring with dill sauce, while lamb with red-currant sauce, filet of salmon with sorrel sauce, and sirloin steak with paprika and sour-cream sauce star on the main-dish menu, and vegetarians will go for the delicious nut roast. Between meal hours, this is a good place to drop in for a glass of wine and a nibble of their tomato-and-basil cheesecake.

Saints and Scholars

3 University St. ☎ **01232/325137.** Average meal £10 ($17.10). No credit cards. Mon–Sat noon–11pm, Sun 12–2:30pm and 5:30–9:30pm. TRADITIONAL/VEGETARIAN.

This popular eatery in the university area caters to the "scholars" in its name with a library decor downstairs, although the lively ambience does not lend itself to study. For quieter meals, opt for the upstairs dining room. In both, you'll have a choice of specialties like a cassoulet of duck, sausages, and beans; a selection of fresh fish with or without special sauces; and several vegetarian dishes.

Skandia

50 Howard St. ☎ **01232/240-239.** Main courses £3–£11 ($5.13–$18.81). ACC, AE, MC, V. Mon–Sat 9:30am–11pm. GRILLS/SANDWICHES/SALADS.

Just a block west of Donegall Square, Skandia is a cozy all-day eatery, with exceptionally good grills (cooked over charcoal—do try the grilled salmon) and marvelous salads. There are also burgers, omelets, and vegetarian dishes. No liquor license.

✪ The Washington Pub & Restaurant

15 Howard St. ☎ **01232/241891.** Average meal £3–£10 ($5.13–$17.10). No credit cards. Daily 11:30am–11pm. MEXICAN/TRADITIONAL/BARBECUE/STEAKS.

There's a touch of America in this large, very popular pub, whose walls are covered with murals depicting scenes from George Washington's life. The decor, however, is strictly traditional Irish, with lots of dark wood. The menu displays a wide diversity, with Mexico represented by specialties like a crêpe stuffed with hot chillied beef and peppers and a "gringo" burger topped with hot chili; chicken wings, as well as a burger, served with smokey barbecue sauce; several cuts and preparations of select steaks; and a fair number of seafood and chicken selections. There's also a quite good wine list reasonably priced.

MEALS FOR LESS THAN £20 ($34.20)

✪ La Belle Epoque

61–63 Dublin Rd. ☎ **01232/323244.** Reservations recommended. Set lunch £5.50 ($9.41) or £10.95 ($18.72); set dinner £20 ($34.20). AE, MC, V. Daily noon–11pm. FRENCH.

This is considered by many to be the best restaurant in Belfast. Cuisine here is of the French persuasion, with steak, pheasant, and lobster among the specialties. Reservations are recommended.

✪ The Strand

12 Stranmillis Rd. ☎ **01232/682266.** Reservations recommended. Lunch £5–£10 ($8.55–$17); dinner £10–£15 ($17.10–$25.65). AE, DC, MC, V. Mon–Sat noon–3pm, Sun 7–10pm. TRADITIONAL.

Over in the university area, near the Ulster Museum and Botanic Gardens, this restaurant is popular with academics and local residents. It has won several awards for its outstanding food with dishes such as crabmeat-stuffed courgettes and chicken roulade with tomato sauce.

✪ Roscoff

Lesley House, Shaftesbury Sq. ☎ **01232/331532.** Reservations recommended. Set lunch £14.50 ($24.79); set dinner £21.50 ($36.76). AE, DC, MC, V. Lunch Mon–Fri 12:15–2:15pm; dinner Mon–Sat 6:30–10:15pm. SEAFOOD/TRADITIONAL.

The 1930s are alive and well preserved in this sparkling, cosmopolitan restaurant at the foot of Great Victoria Street. Celebrities and public officials are often among its clientele, who come for such delicacies as roast monkfish, duck confit, and French pastry desserts. Considered one of best eateries in the province.

4 What to See & Do

Make your first stop the **Northern Ireland Tourist Board Information Office,** 59 North Street, and pick up their excellent, free street map of Belfast and brochures on sightseeing highlights, city bus tours, day trips, and sports such as fishing, golf, and cruising for Belfast and for all of Northern Ireland. They also publish a great series of "Belfast Civic Festival Trail" self-guided walking tours.

IN THE CITY

City Hall

Donegall Sq. ☎ **01232/320202,** ext. 2618. Admission free. Guided tours with advance booking, Wed at 10:30am.

You can't miss this massive Portland stone building crowned with a copper dome. It was 10 years abuilding and its interior is elegant with Greek and Italian marble. The city's industrial history is traced in a large mural. If you don't recognize it otherwise, you'll know it by the bust of Queen Victoria out front (she was a guest of the city in 1846 and is much revered). A Great War Memorial sits on the west side, with a memorial sculpture to the *Titanic,* which was built in Belfast and went to the bottom in 1912.

Albert Memorial

High St.

Look toward the river for the memorial—it pays tribute to Queen Victoria's consort and is affectionately known as Belfast's "leaning tower" because it is slightly less than straight.

St. Anne's Cathedral

Lower Donegall St. Admission free. Mon–Sat 9am–4:30pm, Sun at 11am and 3:30pm services.

Known locally simply as the Belfast Cathedral, St. Anne's was built between 1899 and 1904. It has a fine mosaic showing St. Patrick landing at Saul in A.D. 432, which you will find over the entrance to the Chapel of the Holy Spirit.

✪ The Crown Liquor Saloon

Great Victoria St. ☎ **01232/325368.** Mon–Sat 11:30am–11pm, Sun 12:30–2:30pm and 7–10pm.

This marvelous old Victorian pub across from the Europa Hotel is the ultimate in casual elegance with its carved woodwork, snugs lining one wall, flickering gaslights, and painted ceramic tiles. Some "chrome and mirror" addicts got their hands on it a few years back and nearly modernized the character out of it, but the National Trust came to the rescue and it's now back to its original state.

✪ The Grand Opera House

Great Victoria St. ☎ **01232/241-919.**

Try to catch a performance here. It's a marvel of rich, rococo eccentricity, with 24 gilt elephant heads separating boxes sporting canopies, Buddhas scattered about the draperies, and lots of gold and maroon. Closed from 1972 to 1981, it has been beautifully restored. It is centrally located, near the Europa Hotel and Crown Liquor Saloon, but suffered severe bomb damage in 1993, so check to see if it has reopened.

✪ Botanic Gardens

Stranmillis Rd. ☎ **01232/324902.** Admission free. Gardens, daily dawn–dusk; Palm House and Fernery, Mon–Fri 10am–5pm, Sat–Sun 2–5pm; Ulster Museum, Mon–Fri 10am–5pm, Sat 1–5pm, Sun 2–5pm.

Cotton, banana, and coffee plants flourish in the Palm House conservatory that dates from the mid-1800s, and the Fernery is a splendid ravine in a sunken glen that you view from a balcony. The rose garden is simply spectacular. The **Ulster Museum,** with a fine collection of Irish antiquities, art, natural sciences, and local history, as well as treasures from the Spanish Armada shipwreck *Girona,* is located within the garden. Facilities include a shop and a cafe. The entrance to the gardens is at the junction of Malone Road and University Road, adjacent to the Queen's University grounds.

NEARBY

✪ Ulster Folk and Transport Museum

Cultra Manor, Holywood, Co. Down. ☎ **01232/428428.** Admission £4 ($6.84) adults, £2 ($3.42) children (under 5 years old free). Apr–June and Sept, Mon–Fri 9:30am–5pm, Sat 10:30am–6pm, Sun 12:30–4:30pm; July–Aug, Mon–Sat 10:30am–6pm, Sun noon–6pm. Bus: Ulsterbus no. 1 from Oxford Street station; it's eight miles from Belfast on the road to Bangor.

This unique museum of folklife and transport is set on some 176 acres. The manor house holds a tearoom and conference facilities, and there is a wide range of interesting permanent and temporary exhibitions in the **Folk Gallery** and the **Transport Gallery.** The open-air museum is composed of a fascinating collection of buildings of all types, rural and urban, from the 18th to the 19th century, all furnished in the style of about 1900—a microcosm of Ulster life of that period.

Farms, an old church, a flax-scutching mill, schools, a print shop, a bank, and many other buildings make this place well worth a visit of half a day or more.

Belfast Zoo

Antrim Rd. ☎ **01232/776277.** Admission Apr–Sept, £4.20 ($7.18) adults, £3.10 ($5.30) ages 4–16; free for under 4, seniors, and disabled. Oct–Mar, prices reduced. Apr–Sept, daily 10am–5pm; Oct–Mar, daily 10am–3:30pm. Last admission is one hour before closing. Bus: 2, 3, 4, 5, 6, or 45; it's five miles north of the city off Antrim Road.

The Belfast Zoo, with its dramatic mountain site and good views of the city and the lough, is a delight. Its gorilla and chimp houses have won animal welfare awards, and some species roam free. Don't miss the penguin and sea lion enclosures with underwater viewing. Of note, too, are the spectacled bears—this is the only zoo in the U.K. in which you'll see them.

ORGANIZED TOURS

Belfast City Tours (☎ 01232/246485) operates multilingual coach tours of the city and its environs. Call for days and times of operation, as well as fares.

Maggie Shannon, 14 The Earls Court, Belfast BT4 3FA (☎ 01232/658-337), conducts several fascinating guided tours. Two-hour **Belfast City Breaks** and **Belfast Pub Walking Tours** explore the city on foot, while the three-hour **Belfast and Environs** tour is via coach and includes morning coffee or afternoon tea. Fees are modest: £5 ($8.55) for the walking tours, £10 ($17.10) for the coach tour. Call for departure times and to book.

5 Shopping

Belfast city-center shops are open Monday through Saturday from 9am to 5:30pm, with late-night opening (until 8pm) on Thursday.

The pedestrian shopping area around **Donegall Square** and nearby covered arcades (Belfast's "Golden Mile") will satisfy the most avid shopper, with scores of boutiques selling everything from fine giftware to handcrafts to Irish linen and hand-woven woolens.

Leading department stores in this area are **Marks & Spencer** and **Debenhams,** branches of the famed London chains.

There's also good shopping in the **Botanic Avenue** and **University area.** On Friday mornings, the **Variety Market** on May Street is a lively shopping experience.

6 Belfast After Dark

Belfast offers a wide variety of things to do after dark, whether you fancy an elegant evening at the theater or a rousing good time on a casual basis in a singing pub. Check with the tourist office and in local newspapers to see what's on during your visit.

THE PERFORMING ARTS Leading venues for opera, concerts, and musical variety shows are the **Grand Opera House,** Great Victoria Street (☎ 01232/241-919), which presents everything from opera to pantomime (check to see if it has reopened after bomb damage), the **Arts Theatre,** Botanic Avenue (☎ 01232/324-936), for popular and classic stage productions; the **Lyric Theatre,** Ridgeway Street (☎ 01232/381081), for Irish plays, and experimental and international theater; and **Ulster Hall,** Bedford Street (☎ 01232/323900), site of all things musical, from rock to the Ulster Orchestra (owned and operated by Belfast City Council).

THE PUB SCENE Belfast's musical pubs are anything *but* hidebound traditionalists, although you'll hear some of the finest Irish music in the country here. It is, however, just one selection on a musical menu that includes folk, jazz, blues, and rock.

In the city center, clustered around Royal Avenue, look for: **The Front Page,** Donegall Street (☎ 01232/324924); **Duke of York,** off Lower Donegall Street (☎ 01232/241062); and **Kelly's Cellars,** Bank Street (☎ 01232/324835). On Ormeau Road you'll find the **Errigle Inn** (☎ 01232/641410) and the **Parador Hotel** (☎ 02132/491883).

7 Easy Excursions

You can visit many of Northern Ireland's outstanding attractions with easy day trips from a Belfast base. See Chapter 23 for Carrickfergus Castle, the Giant's Causeway, and other Antrim Coast attractions within an easy drive to the north of the city. Chapter 24 highlights the top attractions of County Down to the south, most of which are a pleasant, relaxing day away from the city.

ORGANIZED TOURS Contact the **Ulsterbus Tours & Travel Centre,** 10 Glengall St., Belfast BT12 5AH (☎ 01232/320011), for a plethora of marvelous half- and full-day excursions from Belfast listed in their "Ulsterbus Day Tours" booklet, available also from the tourist office. Highlights are tours to the Antrim Coast and Giant's Causeway, Nine Glens of Antrim, Bushmills Distillery and Giant's Causeway, and the Mountains of Mourne, but there are many, many more, including some into the Republic. Half-day tours cost about £8 ($13.68), and full-day tours run about £10 ($17.10) for adults (half fare for children). Every tour does not run every day, so be sure to check for current days of the week and departure times.

23

Counties Antrim & Londonderry

These two counties hold some of Northern Ireland's true scenic wonders, a wealth of sightseeing attractions, and the province's second largest city.

1 County Antrim

County Antrim has perhaps the largest concentration of sightseeing attractions of any of the six counties. Americans will be interested to know that several **American presidents** had County Antrim roots: Andrew Jackson's parents came from Carrickfergus; Andrew Johnson's grandfather was from Larne; Chester A. Arthur's father was born near Ballymena; Grover Cleveland's grandfather was a County Antrim merchant; William McKinley's great-great-grandfather emigrated from Conagher, near Ballymoney; and Theodore Roosevelt's maternal ancestors were from Larne. Quite an impressive score for one county!

WHAT TO SEE & DO

Perhaps the best way to explore County Antrim is to drive north from Belfast on A2 through Carrickfergus to Larne, where the **Antrim Coast Drive** takes you along the edge of the Glens of Antrim and on to the Giant's Causeway and Bushmills. While it's quite possible to cover the approximately 70 miles in one day and return to Belfast, a better plan is to take day trips into the countryside, as far north as Larne, and then to strike out on the Coast Road and plan an overnight stop. Such are the wonders of this spectacular coastline that you will want time to stop and savor each and every one.

Return to Belfast on the inland route via A26 southeast through Ballymena and Antrim town, turning east onto A52 at Nutt's Corner.

Northern Ireland's largest and best-preserved medieval castle dominates the waterfront in Carrickfergus. Massive **Carrickfergus Castle** (☎ 01960/351-273) dates from the late 12th and early 13th centuries.

As you wander through the castle and its grounds, look for the more than 20 very lifelike models, each depicting a particular period from the castle's history. Inside the keep, a scale model of the castle, together with an audiovisual presentation, provides another entertaining insight into its past. Farther up in the keep, a banquet hall is laid out as if ready for a medieval banquet. On the Events floor, you can try your hand at chess on the giant set, or dress up in medieval costume and travel back to that era in fancy. At any rate, that's what is going on as this is written—"events" keep changing, so you may find something quite different when you stop by. Refreshments are available in the Visitors Centre. Visiting hours April through September are Monday to Saturday from 10am to 6pm, on Sunday from 2 to 6pm (last admission 5:30pm); other months, closing time is 4pm (last admission 3:30pm).

The ✪ **ancestral home of Andrew ("Old Hickory") Jackson,** U.S. president from 1829 to 1837, was just beyond the north end of Carrickfergus's seafront promenade at Boneybefore, a site now marked by a plaque. Just a few yards away, the **Andrew Jackson Centre** (☎ 01960/364-972) gives an insight into the life of his forebears. Open Monday to Friday from 10am to 1pm and 2 to 6pm, Saturday and Sunday 2 to 6pm, May to October.

Driving north from Carrickfergus, you'll pass through the nine ✪ **Glens of Antrim,** which open to the sea. You may want to call ahead and plan a stop to visit with **Jim McKillop,** 55 Ballymena Rd., Carnlough (☎ Carnlough 01574/885424). He was the Irish fiddle champion in 1976 and these days he makes, repairs, and sells all kinds of stringed instruments. He welcomes visitors unless, of course, there's a hooley, *fleadh,* or concert anywhere in the vicinity, when he's sure to be fiddling away.

Ten miles west of Cushendall (13 miles northeast of the Giant's Causeway) look for the signposted **Watertop Open Farm,** Ballyvoy, Ballycastle (☎ 012657/62576). This is a commercial hill farm in a beautiful setting beside Ballybrick Forrest Park that offers farm tours during July and August and, if you book in advance, pony trekking. It's a great experience for the younger set, and an eye-opener for parents who have never seen a working farm up close. There's also a farm trail, as well as a sheep-shearing demonstration, a museum, and a tearoom. Open daily from 10am to 5:30pm in July and August.

If you're an island lover, you'll want to reserve an overnight to spend on ✪ **Rathlin Island,** a rugged outpost off the Antrim coast that is Ireland's largest inhabited island. It has a fascinating history, and can be reached by boat daily, weather permitting, with departures from Ballycastle (☎ 012657/63917, 63934, or 63977 to book). The mail boat makes trips on Monday, Wednesday, and Friday year-round, leaving Ballycastle Harbour about 10:30am and departing Rathlin Island about 4pm. There are marvelous cliff walks, magnificent views of Ireland's northern coast, and the fun of topping off the day at the one pub in the company of some of the 100 inhabitants. The island's only accommodation is the **Rathlin Guest House,** The Quay, Rathlin, County Antrim (☎ 012657/63917), run by Mrs. Kay McCurdy. Bed-and-breakfast rate is £13 ($22.23) single, £22 ($37.62) double, with the evening meal costing £8.50 ($14.54).

If you're driving on the Antrim Coast Drive between May and September, stop about five miles northwest of Ballycastle to take a look at the **Carrick-a-Rede Rope Bridge.** The bridge has a wooden-plank walkway with rope handrails, and is strung across a 25-yard chasm to connect two clifftops separated by seas too treacherous to be crossed any other way. If you're not faint-hearted, you'll not be charged to walk over the bridge. There's a signposted roadside car park.

The ✪ **Giant's Causeway,** eight miles east of Portrush (two miles north of Bushmills on B146), is much more impressive when you walk its basalt columns (there are some 37,000!) than any photograph can possibly convey. How they came to be packed so tightly together that they form a sort of bridge from the shoreline out into the sea, submerge, and then surface on the Hebrides island of Staffa is a matter of conjecture. Scientists will tell you unequivocally that they're the result of a massive volcanic eruption about 60 million years ago, when molten lava cooled and formed into geometric shapes. But as far as the Irish are concerned, the causeway would still be above water all the way across had it not been for a ferocious tiff between the Ulster giant, Finn MacCoul, and his Scottish counterpart, Finn Gall. You see, it was the Ulsterman who built the causeway in the first place, and when he went home to rest up a bit from his labors, the wily Scotsman tripped across, club in hand, to catch his foe unawares. Now, Mrs. MacCoul was busy at the hearth with the dinner, and when Finn Gall burst into her kitchen and demanded to know if the sleeping giant were her husband, she—in a master stroke of quick thinking—assured him, "Ooh, no, sor, 'tis only ma wee babe." Well, the very thought of what the father of such a gigantic babe must be like put such a fright into the Scotsman that he hightailed it back across the water, destroying the causeway behind him to keep Finn MacCoul in Ireland where he belonged. Choose your own version, but don't miss a stop by this curiosity. It's free, and there's even a minibus (with a very small fare) down to the bottom of the cliff for those who don't care to make the short walk. You'll want time also to visit the Information Centre (☎ 012657/31855) and craft shop, and there's a cafe for refreshment. The interesting audiovisual show is well worth the small admission.

Three miles east of Portrush on A2, look for a rocky headland crowned by the great lump of ruined **Dunluce Castle.** You can pick up a guidebook from the Dunluce Centre, Sandhill Drive, Portrush, Co. Antrim (☎ 01265/823-333). Some say its name means "mermaid's fort," and they may well be right—there's a deep cave that penetrates the rock on which the castle sits at the sea's edge. It's so close to the cliff's edge, in fact, that back in 1639 a part of the castle fell away into the sea below, taking the kitchen staff with it. There are many other tales and legends surrounding Dunluce which you can read about in the official guide available at the entrance. From April through September you can visit the castle Tuesday through Saturday between the hours of 10am and 7pm and on Sunday from 2 to 7pm (also open Mondays in July and August). During other months, closing time is 4pm, and it's closed all day Monday.

A short detour off the coast road will take you to the village of Bushmills and the oldest licensed whiskey distillery in the world. Stop by the Information Centre, 44 Causeway Road, Bushmills, Co. Antrim (☎ 012657/31855). The ✪ **Old Bushmills Distillery** is a fascinating place, and still turning out "the wine of the country" after all these centuries. People in Northern Ireland will urge you to try Black Bush—do! To see an exhibition about its history and to see the distilling process, book for a guided tour Monday through Thursday or Friday morning. There are sometimes schedule changes, however, so it's best to phone ahead (☎ 012657/31521).

If you're driving on to Londonderry, continue along the coast to the pleasant little seaside resort of **Portrush.** Here, **Waterworld,** The Harbour, Portrush (☎ 01265/822001), is a terrific place to relax with or without the kids. There's a seawater aquarium, giant water slides, Jacuzzis, water cannon, kiddies' pool, and for the less energetic, a sauna, steam room, and two sunbeds. Also on the premises, the Mermaid Restaurant serves snacks, hot and cold meals, and nonalcoholic beverages. It's open in July and August Monday through Saturday from 10am to

9pm and on Sunday from noon to 9pm. Opening days vary in May, June, and September, and fees are moderate.

WHERE TO STAY

CARNLOUGH

Bethany House

5 Bay Rd., Carnlough, BT44 0HQ, Co. Antrim. ☎ **01574/85667.** 6 rms, all with bath. £14 ($23.94) single, £28 ($47.88) double. Reductions for children and seniors. (Rates include breakfast.) No credit cards.

Mrs. Mary Aiken's home on the seafront in the town center is a pleasant, homey place. Religious paintings throughout the house attest to her deep Christian faith, and as a practical measure of concern for her fellow human beings, she has provided on the ground floor one room especially suited to those who are wheelchair-bound, with a ground-level entrance from the outside and wide doors to both the bedroom and bath. There's a no-smoking rule in the lounge, dining room, and some bedrooms.

CUSHENDUN

✪ The Villa Farmhouse

185 Torr Rd., Cushendun BT44 0PU, Co. Antrim. ☎ **012667/61252.** 3 rms, 2 with bath. £15 ($25.65) per person. Reduction for children. (Rates include breakfast.) No credit cards. Closed Nov–Mar.

Mrs. Catharine Scally's Tudor farmhouse is within easy reach of the Glens of Antrim, and has an inviting, old-fashioned air, with stained-glass windows and antiques. The house has very comfortably furnished bedrooms with tea/coffeemakers and beautiful views overlooking Cushendun. It's signposted from the Coast Drive.

PORTBALLINTRAE

White Gables

83 Dunluce Rd., Portballintrae, Bushmills BT57 8SJ, Co. Antrim. ☎ **012657/31611.** 4 rms, all with bath. £25 ($42.75) single; £40 ($68.40) double. Reduction for children. Discounts for more than two-day stays. (Rates include breakfast.) No credit cards. Closed Oct–Mar.

Mrs. Ria Johnston is hostess of this attractive country house set in pretty countryside four miles from the Giant's Causeway. The house is centrally heated; there's a large guests' lounge. Guest rooms are all very comfortable and homey, many with panoramic views of the nearby coast and all with tea/coffeemakers. Mrs. Johnston is the proud winner of the 1989 Galtee All-Ireland Breakfast Award, which speaks for itself.

PORTRUSH

A word about Portrush: Facing the sea on the eastern edge of Portrush, **Lansdowne Crescent** is a Victorian terrace with great views and value-for-dollar accommodations in a quiet resort area. Space does not permit full writeups on these exceptional guesthouses, but the following have all been inspected and have my recommendations, with rates averaging about £15 ($25.65) single, £30 ($51.30) double, with discounts for families, off-season discounts for seniors, and baby-sitting services: **Alexandra,** 11 Lansdowne Crescent, Portrush BT56 8AY, County Antrim (☎ 01265/822284); **Belvedere,** 15 Lansdowne Crescent, Portrush BT56 8AY, County Antrim (☎ 01265/822771); **Clarmont,** 10 Lansdowne Crescent,

Portrush BT56 8AY, County Antrim (☎ 01265/822397); and **Prospect Guest House,** 20 Lansdowne Crescent, Portrush BT56 8AY, County Antrim (☎ 01265/822299).

✪ Ardnaree

105 Dunluce Rd., White Rocks, Portrush BT56 8ND, Co. Antrim. ☎ **01265/823407.** 5 rms, 2 with bath. £17.50–£20 ($29.93–$34.20) per person. Reduction for children. (Rates include breakfast.) No credit cards.

This chalet bungalow is on the coast road one mile from Portrush and five miles from the Giant's Causeway, overlooking the sea with the hills of Donegal in the distance. A beautiful beach is just a few minutes' walk away, and famous Royal Portrush Golf Course is in the vicinity. The centrally heated modern bungalow is the home of Mrs. Elsie Rankin, who takes a personal interest in her guests. The attractive guest rooms include two on the ground floor and one large family room, all with tea/coffeemakers.

Atlantis

10 Ramore Ave., Portrush BT56 8BB, Co. Antrim. ☎ **01265/824583.** 14 rms, 2 with bath. £14 ($23.94) single; £24 ($41.04) double. Reduction for children and seniors. (Rates include breakfast.) No credit cards.

Just off the seafront in the eastern part of town, overlooking recreation grounds and a children's venture park, this Victorian-style town house has a large residents' lounge and five of the attractive guest rooms are family-size. Some rooms on higher floors have terrific sea views. Margaret and Norman Torrens are the gracious hosts, who provide a visitor's kitchen for light snacks. (They furnish tea and coffee).

Worth a Splurge

✪ The Bushmills Inn

25 Main St., Bushmills BT57 8QA, Co. Antrim. ☎ **012657/32339.** Fax 012657/32048. 11 rms, all with bath. TV TEL. £48 ($82.08) single; £78 ($133.38) double. Reduction for children. (Rates include breakfast.) AE, MC, V.

This lovely little inn has been rescued from almost total deterioration by owners Roy Bolton and Richard Wilson, who have brought it back far beyond its beginnings as a coaching inn during the early 1800s. Its style these days is one that might be called "country elegant," with a small lobby that perfectly emulates a private drawing room. Upstairs there's a good library in the old round tower, with a whimsical concealed door. The luxury bedrooms all have pretty appointments, and two family rooms have intriguing "balcony beds" for the children—kids love them!

Dining/Entertainment: The Brasserie, a Victorian-style bar/restaurant complete with flickering gas lights, serves bar food, meals, and traditional afternoon tea daily from noon to 10pm, priced at £5 to £10 ($8.55–$17.10). The Barony Restaurant is fitted out with intimate snugs and dishes up first-class traditional meals daily from 12:30 to 2:30pm and 7 to 9:30pm; lunch runs about £8 ($13.68), and dinner costs about £15 ($25.65).

✪ Causeway Hotel

40 Causeway Rd., Bushmills BT57 8SU, Co. Antrim. ☎ **012657/31210** or 31226. 16 rms, all with bath. TEL TV. £35 ($59.85) single; £55 ($94.05) double. Reduction for children. Mini-weekend special (two nights' dinner, bed, and breakfast). (Rates include breakfast.) MC, V.

This old-fashioned, country-Victorian-style hotel is the perfect place for an overnight stop to see the Giant's Causeway—it's just next door, a very short walk to the Visitors Centre. It was built in 1836 to accommodate visitors who arrived back then by jaunting car. In recent years it operated only as a bar and restaurant until Stanley Armstrong and his wife, Doreen, set about to restore it as a functioning hotel. Doreen has done most of the decorating and made exhaustive searches to find Victorian furniture in keeping with the hotel's history. An especially appealing room is the upstairs Resident Lounge, with its sweeping views of the sea and the causeway. Its 16 bedrooms, equipped with tea/coffeemakers, vary in size and decor, but all are comfortable and nicely done up.

Dining: There's a large public bar and a dining room overlooking the sea. Bar lunches daily from noon to 2:30pm are under £5 ($8.55); dining room meals, served from noon to 2:30pm and 7 to 9:30pm, run from £6 to £14 ($10.26–$23.94).

✪ Dobbins Inn Hotel

6–8 High St., Carrickfergus BT38 9HE, Co. Antrim. ☎ **01960/351-905.** 13 rms, all with bath. TV TEL. £42 ($71.82) single; £64 ($109.44) double. Reduction for children. Weekend rates available. (Rates include breakfast.) AE, MC, V.

If you have a secret picture of the perfect little Irish country inn, you'll be certain you've found it when you see the Dobbins Inn Hotel, with its pretty window boxes flanking the simple entrance. Inside, you're met with warm, friendly hospitality in a setting that reveals something of the history of this old building. The street on which it stands was once part of the grounds of the 16th-century Dobbins Castle, and during renovations, a great stone fireplace was uncovered in the present-day Coffee Room, as well as a short, walled-up escape passage and another passageway that connected Carrickfergus Castle to St. Nicholas Church by way of this building. Be sure to ask about "Maud," a ghostly presence said to haunt the castle/church passage. In an upstairs conference room there are framed documents also discovered during renovations.

Dining/Entertainment: The lounge bar serves snacks and light lunches from noon to 2:30pm for under £5 ($8.25), and the De Courcy restaurant serves high tea from 5:30 to 7pm and a moderately priced dinner menu from 7 to 9pm.

✪ Londonderry Arms Hotel

20 Harbour Rd., Carnlough BT44 0EU, Co. Antrim. ☎ **01574/885255** or 885458. 21 rms, all with bath. TV TEL. June–Dec £45 ($76.95) single; £65 ($111.15) double. Jan–May rates are lower. Reduction for children. (Rates include breakfast.) AE, MC, V.

This lovely old ivy-covered hotel in the town center, facing the harbor on the Coast Drive, began life back in 1854 as a coaching inn. Since 1947 the O'Neill family have been owners, and Frank (the present O'Neill manager) continues the tradition of gracious hospitality. There are beautiful antique furnishings; the tavern has a traditional decor, and the spacious lounge is warmed by a copper-hooded fireplace. Both the tavern and the lounge draw lots of locals. Guest rooms are beautifully done up, and handwoven Avoca bedspreads are a nice touch. Highly recommended, both for the high standards and for the O'Neills.

Dining/Entertainment: Meals are served in a dining room replete with period pieces, and if you can get a table in the front dining room, you'll have a view of the harbor as you dine. Lunch will run about £10.95 ($18.72), and dinner is about £15 ($25.65).

WHERE TO EAT

Besides the pubs and restaurants listed here, the hotels listed above in "Where to Stay" offer excellent places to dine or stop for lunch, especially the Dobbins Inn Hotel in Carrickfergus, Ballygally Castle Hotel in Ballygally, Drumnagreach Hotel near Glenarm, the Londonderry Arms Hotel in Carnlough, the Causeway Hotel at the Giant's Causeway, and the Bushmills Inn in Bushmills.

Carrickfergus

✪ Courtyard Coffee House

Scotch Quarter, ☎ **01960/351-881.** £5 ($8.55). No credit cards. Mon–Sat 10am–4:30pm. SNACKS/SALADS/LIGHT MEALS/PASTRIES.

This is a good, inexpensive lunch stop as you set out on the County Antrim coastal drive. The self-service menu features light lunches such as soup, sandwiches, salad plates, quiche, lasagna, and pastries, and you can eat in the light, bright indoor room or outside in the inner courtyard. It's across from the seafront on the northern end of town, just north of the town hall and library.

Portballintrae

For pub grub under £5 ($8.55), stop at the **Bayview Hotel,** Portballintrae, Bushmills (☎ 012657/31453), served Monday through Saturday from 12:30 to 2:30pm. **Sweeney's Public House & Wine Bar** (☎ 012657/32404) has good food and great atmosphere (open daily).

Portrush

The **Harbour Bar** (☎ 01265/825-047) is a good place for a before- or after-dinner libation. It sits on the wharf overlooking the boat-filled harbor, and it's mostly locals you'll find in the plain, old-style bar. Very Irish.

✪ Ramore Wine Bar and Restaurant

The Harbour. ☎ **01265/824-313.** Reservations recommended for dinner. Salads, sandwiches, and burgers £4–£6 ($6.84–$10.26); full lunch £8 ($13.68); dinner £19 ($32.49). MC, V. Wine bar, Mon–Sat noon–2pm and 5–9pm; restaurant, Tues–Sat 7–10pm. SEAFOOD/ TRADITIONAL/SALADS/BURGERS.

This award-winning restaurant in the town center on the waterfront offers excellent value, with full lunches of seafood, lamb cutlets with tarragon, duck breast with honey, filet or sirloin steak, and suprême of chicken, as well as less expensive burgers, sandwiches, etc. Needless to say, there's an extensive wine list, and you can order by the glass or the bottle. Downstairs, the wine bar rings with the conviviality of contented diners, while upstairs things are more restrained and elegant.

The Inland Route

What to See & Do

Heading southeast on A26, look for signposts just north of Ballymoney for **Leslie Hill Heritage Farm Park,** Ballymoney (☎ 012656/63109). This old-time working farm gives you an authentic look into the past of rural Northern Ireland. In addition to farm animals, there's a blacksmith's forge, pets corner, carriage display, horse and trap rides, and nature trails. There is also a picnic area (terrific idea) and a tea and craft shop. It's open in July and August Monday to Saturday from 11am to 6pm; from Easter through June and all of September, on Sunday, and bank holidays from 2 to 6pm (closed October to Easter).

The farmhouse (☎ 01266/44111) from which **U.S. President Chester A. Arthur's father** left for America in 1816 is at Dreen, near Cullybackey, Ballymena, and the whitewashed thatched cottage is worth a drive through beautiful countryside to meet the delightful people who maintain it for visitors like you and me. They'll greet you June through September, Monday through Saturday from 2 to 5pm. There's a small admission charge, but none for seniors and the handicapped.

In the town of **Antrim,** look for the perfectly preserved **round tower** that is 49 feet around and more than 90 feet tall.

WHERE TO STAY

Ben Neagh House

11 Crumlin Rd., Crumlin BT29 4AD, Co. Antrim. ☎ **01849/422-271.** 6 rms, none with bath. £13 ($22.23) per person. Reduction for children. (Rates include breakfast.) No credit cards.

This Georgian-style farmhouse in its parklike setting on the outskirts of town is the home of Mr. and Mrs. Peel, who make their guests feel right at home. Guest rooms are attractive and comfortable, and among the amenities are a grass tennis court and an indoor games room.

2 Londonderry City

There's the aura of the ages about Londonderry—in ancient times, it was known as Doire Calgach ("Calgach's Oak Wood"), later simply as Doire ("Oak Grove"); then came St. Columba in A.D. 546 to found a monastic settlement that became Cholomcille Doire ("St. Columba's Oak Grove"). Some 10 centuries later, after years of seesaw battles to conquer it, King James I succeeded in 1613 and promptly transferred it by charter to the City of London to be administered by the Honourable Irish Society, and its name became Londonderry. After all that, it is still affectionately called simply Derry by most of the Irish on both sides of the border.

Strong city walls 20 to 25 feet wide and 14 to 37 feet high with seven gates went up soon after the society took over things, and despite siege after siege, those walls are largely intact today.

ORIENTATION **Tourist Information** You'll find the Tourist Information Centre at 8 Bishop St. (☎ 01504/267284), open Oct–June, Monday through Friday from 9am to 5pm; daily July–Sept. The helpful staff will arrange accommodations and walking tours, and provide sightseeing information for the city and its immediate vicinity as well as all 32 counties of Ireland.

The Irish Tourist Board is at the same address (☎ 01504/369501) providing assistance with matters south of the border.

TOWN LAYOUT The old, walled section of modern-day Londonderry is west of the River Foyle, as are the main business and shopping districts, with ancient winding lanes and rows of charming Georgian and Victorian buildings. In the northeastern portion of the walls, Shipquay Gate is only two blocks from the river, and the historic old Guildhall with its turrets and tower clock is midway between river quays and this gate. Four streets converge on the Diamond, more or less the center of the city. Most of what you'll want to see will be within a short walk of these two points, including the bus station, tourist office, and inexpensive places to eat.

Surrounding the original, walled city and across Craigavon Bridge (south of the Guildhall), modern Londonderry has sprouted along the river and hillsides, covering almost 10 times the area that spawned it.

GETTING AROUND **By Bus** For route and schedule information on intercity bus transportation, call 262-261.

By Taxi Reliable taxi companies are Central Taxi (☎ 261911) and Foyle Taxi (☎ 263905).

By Car Unless you're exploring the outlying areas, park the car and leave it—Londonderry is a great walking city, with major attractions in a compact area.

FAST FACTS: LONDONDERRY CITY

Essentials The telephone area code is 01504. The Ulsterbus station is on Foyle Street (☎ 01504/262261). The railway station is on Duke Street, Waterside (☎ 01504/42228).

Mail The main post office is at 3 Custom House St., open Monday through Friday from 9am to 5:30pm and on Saturday from 9am to 12:30pm.

WHAT TO SEE & DO

IN THE CITY

One thing you shouldn't miss in Londonderry is a walk along the ✪ **old city walls.** They are the only unbroken city walls in the British Isles, and Londonderry was the last city in Europe to build protective wall fortifications. Check with the tourist office about days and times of their guided walking tours along the walls (see below), and go along if you can—the narrative adds a lot to the city scene below and the landscape beyond. If you go on your own, enter at the Shipquay Gate.

✪ Guildhall

Guildhall Sq., Foyle St. ☎ **365151.** Tours: Call to book in advance. Year-round Mon–Fri 9am–4:30pm.

The Guildhall is a handsome building in neo-Gothic style, with a nicely decorated front having mullioned and transomed windows. The impressive rock-faced sandstone building has a somewhat troubled history: Built in 1890, it had to be almost completely reconstructed after a devastating fire in 1908, and again in 1972, when its interior was virtually gutted by a bomb. The lovely stained-glass windows you see in the building today are the work of Ulster craftsmen—look for one in the marble vestibule that depicts *The Relief of Derry.*

St. Columb's Cathedral

London St. ☎ **262746.** Mon–Sat 9am–1pm and 2–5pm.

Built in 1633, the cathedral's basic style might be labeled "Planter's Gothic," but much of what you'll see today has been added since. One of its most important features is the memorial window showing the relief of the siege in 1689, and there's an interesting audiovisual presentation of the cathedral's role in Londonderry's history.

✪ Tower Museum

Union Hall Place. ☎ **372411.** Admission £2.75 ($4.70) adults, £1 ($1.71) children. Tues–Sat 10am–4:30pm; Sun (June–Aug) 2–4:30pm.

Climb to the roof platform of this ancient tower for spectacular views of the city and its environs. It faces across to the Guildhall on the other side of the city walls, and the museum within is often the venue for temporary cultural exhibitions.

Walking Tours

Two-hour morning and afternoon guided walking tours within the city walls depart from the tourist office on Bishop Street, Mon–Fri during July and August, with a £1.50 ($2.57) charge for adults, 75p ($1.28) for children.

Attractions Nearby

Amelia Earhart Centre

Ballyarnett/Shantallow Park. ☎ **0504/353379.** Admission free. You must book three days in advance; June–Sept, Mon–Fri 9am–4:30pm, Sat–Sun 9am–6pm.

A small cottage has been dedicated to the memory of the first woman to fly solo across the Atlantic, who landed in an adjacent field in May 1932. There's a commemorative sculpture at the landing site, and the cottage holds exhibitions centered around the famous aviatrix. It's three miles north of Foyle Bridge via A2.

SPORTS AND OUTDOOR ACTIVITIES

Foyle Golf Centre, 12 Alder Road, Londonderry BT48 8DB (☎ 01504/352-222; fax 01504/353-967) welcomes guests. In addition to their 18-hole, par 72 course, there's a 9-hole course, a driving range, clubhouse, pro shop, and licensed restaurant.

SHOPPING

Shopping is concentrated around the Diamond and pedestrian streets radiating from it. **Austins,** on the Diamond (☎ 261817), is the leading department store, with an excellent, moderately priced, rooftop self-service restaurant (open late on Friday to 9pm).

The **Bookworm Community Bookshop,** 16 Bishop Street (☎ 261616), has a good selection of books of Irish interest. In an inner-city setting of 16th- to 19th-century structures, the **Derry Craft Village** (☎ 260-329) in Shipquay Street, houses a delightful mix of shops, workshops, a thatched-cottage pub, and some residential units.

CONCERTS AND DRAMA

The **Guildhall** (see above) is the venue for concerts by the Ulster Orchestra and visiting orchestras, and for dramatic productions (including premiere performances of new plays by the Derry playwright Brian Friel). **The Playhouse,** Antillery Street, and **The Foyle Arts Centre,** Laurence Hill, are settings for several amateur drama productions, and the **Rialto Entertainment Centre,** Market Street (☎ 260516), presents variety concerts and plays.

The Pub Scene

Londonderry is rich in traditional Irish music, with musicians from neighboring County Donegal often coming over to join in. Check with the Tourist Office, or go by the following pubs to see when there will be music: **Phoenix Bar,** 10 Park Avenue (☎ 268978); **Gweedore Bar,** 61 Waterloo Street (☎ 263513); **Castle Bar,** 26 Waterloo Street (☎ 263118); and **Dungloe Bar,** Waterloo Street (☎ 267716).

To join in that most favored of all Irish pastimes—good conversation spiced with wit—in a convivial setting, it's **The Linenhall,** 3 Market Street (☎ 371665), which also serves superb pub grub (see "Where to Eat," below).

WHERE TO STAY IN TOWN

Most city accommodations are well beyond the reach of budgeteers, but the tourist office can direct you to a few bed-and-breakfast homes in addition to those listed here.

Abode

21 Dunnwood Park, Victoria Rd., Londonderry BT47 2NN, Co. Londonderry. ☎ **01504/44564.** 5 rms, none with bath. £11 ($18.81) single; £20 ($34.20) double. Reduction for children and seniors. (Rates include breakfast.) No credit cards.

Mr. and Mrs. Dunn preside over this pretty bed-and-breakfast accommodation east of the River Foyle, south on Victoria Road, about one mile from the city center. Guest rooms are centrally heated and nicely furnished, and some are reserved for nonsmokers. There's private parking, a garden for guests to enjoy in fine weather, and washing and ironing facilities.

✪ Clarence House

15 Northland Rd., Londonderry BT48 7HY, Co. Londonderry. ☎ **01504/265342.** 7 rms, 4 with bath. £15 ($25.65) per person. £10 ($17.10) per person extra for bath. Reduction for children. (Rates include breakfast.) Dinner £10 ($17.10) extra. No credit cards.

Mrs. Eleonora Slevin has singles, doubles, twin rooms, and family rooms available in this well-kept brick town house. Guest rooms are quite comfortable, and the house and its hostess have become favorites of BBC and RTE television crews, who come back again and again. A bonus here are the facilities for washing and ironing those travel-weary duds. Baby-sitting can be arranged, and there are restaurants within easy walking distance.

Florence House

16 Northland Rd., Londonderry BT48 7JD, Co. Londonderry. ☎ **01504/268093.** 4 rms, none with bath. TV. £14 ($23.94) per person. Reduction for children. (Rates include breakfast.) No credit cards.

Mrs. McGinley is the helpful hostess in this city-center home. She knows the city well and has a keen interest in directing guests to points of interest, good restaurants, etc. Guest rooms vary in size, but all are nicely furnished. Central heating. Mrs. McGinley can arrange off-street parking.

✪ Ms. Joan Pyne

36 Great James St., Londonderry BT48 7DB, Co. Londonderry. ☎ **01504/269691.** 5 rms, 1 with bath. £15 ($25.65) per person. Reduction for children and seniors. (Rates include breakfast.) No credit cards.

Nonsmokers are welcomed at this Victorian town house. All guest rooms are centrally heated, and Joan provides washing and ironing facilities. She can also arrange baby-sitting as well as helpful sightseeing and restaurant information. City center is within walking distance of this convenient location.

✪ Robin Hill

103 Chapel Rd., Londonderry BT47 2BC, Co. Londonderry. ☎ **01504/42776.** 10 rms, 6 with bath. £14.50–£16.50 ($24.79–$28.22) per person. Reduction for children. (Rates include breakfast.) High tea £4 ($6.60) extra; dinner £7 ($11.97). No credit cards.

You'll know that this is a special place as soon as you turn into the leafy drive around a lawn through which wild rabbits scamper. The house was built as a Presbyterian manse back in the late 1800s, and that era is mirrored in the large, bay-windowed parlor and spacious guest rooms. Malcolm Muir, father of two charming small boys, is host here and has done much of the decorating himself. Throughout, the furnishings reflect the character of the house, and front bedrooms look out to city views, while others overlook the garden, and the original stable block has been converted to six lovely guest rooms, all with private bath. Mr. Muir cheerfully supplies a cot for children and arranges baby-sitting.

Robin Hill is east of the River Foyle. Take Spencer Road to Fountain Hill; Chapel Road is at the top of Fountain Hill, and Robin Hill is the first big house on the right (signposted).

WORTH A SPLURGE

✪ Beech Hill Country House Hotel

32 Ardmore Road, Londonderry BT47 3QP. ☎ **01504/49279.** Fax 01504/45366. 17 rms, all with bath. TEL TV. £52.50 ($89.78) single; £70 ($118.70) double. (Rates include breakfast.) Dinner £19 ($32.49). ACC, MC, V.

On an elevated, wooded site some two miles southeast of the city center, this 1729 country home exudes a relaxed elegance. Public rooms are replete with marble fireplaces, crystal chandeliers, and antique furnishings, yet they manage to create a cozy ambience. Guest rooms are beautifully furnished, some with four-poster beds. The elegant Ardmore Restaurant is a favorite with Derry businesspeople for lunch, while candlelight dining draws a local, as well as visitor, clientele.

✪ Waterfoot Hotel

Caw Roundabout, 14 Clooney Rd., Londonderry BT47 1TB, Co. Londonderry. ☎ **01504/45500.** Fax 01504/311006. 33 rms, all with bath. TV TEL. £52 ($88.92) single; £65 ($111.15) double. Reduction for children. (Rates include breakfast.) AE, MC, V.

Set back from the highway in landscaped lawns, the restful setting of this hotel makes it hard to believe you're just a stone's throw from the city center at the eastern edge of Foyle Bridge. Its decor is softly modern, and guest rooms are spacious, attractive, and comfortably furnished, all with trouser press, hairdryer, and tea/coffeemaker.

Dining/Entertainment: Tea, coffee, sandwiches, and scones are served in the lounge or foyer until 5:30pm daily at under £3 ($5.13). The nicely appointed dining room (a favorite with locals as well as guests) serves lunch daily from 12:15 to 2:30pm and dinner from 6:30 to 10:15pm Monday through Saturday, until 9:15pm on Sunday. The extensive menu is surprisingly moderate in price and includes such specialties as grilled trout in oatmeal, sirloin steak au poivre, lamb kebab, and lemon-whiskey chicken, all at prices ranging from £7 to £15 ($11.97–$25.65). A nice feature is their selection of sauces (peppered, piquant, and chasseur) that can be ordered separately to dress up any dish you fancy. Specialty coffees include Irish, calypso, and royale.

NEARBY ACCOMMODATIONS

✪ Ballycarton Farm

Bellarena, Limavady BT49 0HZ, Co. Londonderry. ☎ **015047/50216.** 5 rms, none with bath. £14 ($23.94) per person. Reduction for children. No credit cards.

Mrs. Emma Craig presides over this farmhouse which is beautifully situated on the Coast Road about 17 miles outside Londonderry, and five miles from Limavady, in 50 acres of mountain and coastal scenery. The comfortably furnished guest rooms have sinks and are all of ample size, many with good views. Mrs. Craig can arrange baby-sitting, and she doesn't mind travelers with dogs. The evening meal costs £7 ($11.97), and with advance booking, Mrs. Craig will prepare dinner for nonresidents.

✪ White Horse Hotel

68 Clooney Rd., Campsie BT47 3PA, Co. Londonderry. ☎ **01504/860606.** 44 rms, all with bath. TV TEL. £47.50 ($81.23) single; £53 ($90.63) double. (Rates include breakfast.) High tea £7.95 ($13.59); dinner £10.50 ($17.96). Special full-week and weekend rates available. ACC, MC, V.

This is one of the nicest moderately priced hotels I've run across in Ireland. Its countryside setting four miles northeast of the city, on the Limavady road, is restful, and there's good, frequent bus service into Londonderry. The owners have transformed an old inn into a modern, comfortable, and attractive hostelry. Guest rooms are spacious and well appointed, with tea/coffeemakers, and there are washing and ironing facilities.

Dining/Entertainment: The tasteful dining room serves all three meals daily, with a lunch and dinner carvery, as well as à la carte menus. There is live music in the sophisticated bar and lounge on Friday and Saturday night.

WHERE TO EAT

PUB GRUB

Within the walls of the old city, ✪ **The Linenhall,** 3 Market Street (☎ 371665), is a warm, convivial setting, very popular with local businessmen, for excellent pub lunches priced from £3 to £4 ($5.13 to $6.84). Affable owner Brian McCafferty has expanded the usual pub menu to include vegetarian dishes. Hours are noon to 2:30pm.

Other recommended pubs with similar hours and prices are: **The Venue,** Northland Road (☎ 266080); **The Metro Pub and Wine Bar,** 3 Bank Place (☎ 267401); and **New Monico,** 4 Custom House Street (☎ 263121).

RESTAURANTS

In addition to the restaurants listed here, see the hotel recommendations in "Where to Stay," above.

✪ Ann's Hot Food Shop

8 William St. ☎ **01504/269-236.** Main courses under £5 ($8.55). No credit cards. Mon–Sat 10am–6pm. LIGHT MEALS/PASTRIES/SALADS.

A great drop-in eatery right in the heart of the city, Ann's dishes up heaping plates of hot meals, fresh salads, and a variety of bakery items. It's self-service and very busy at almost any hour.

Ardmore Room Restaurant

Beech Hill Country House Hotel, 32 Ardmore Rd. ☎ **01504/49279.** Reservations strongly recommended. Set lunch £10.95 ($18.72); set dinner £16.95 ($28.98). ACC, MC, V. 12:30–2:30pm and 6:30–9:30pm. CONTINENTAL/TRADITIONAL.

Lunch in this pretty dining room has drawn a plethora of Derry businessmen, who can relax in what was once a billiard room overlooking established gardens while enjoying a superb meal. In the evening, there's a soft, romantic ambience, and among the outstanding specialties is the monkfish accompanied by vegetables with a ginger and balsamic vinaigrette.

Austins Department Store

The Diamond and Ferryquay St. ☎ **01504/261-817.** Average lunch £4 ($6.84); average dinner £5 ($8.55). MC, V. Mon–Sat 9am–5pm (Fri to 8pm). TRADITIONAL.

One of the least expensive eateries in the city, Austins features dishes like chicken and ham pie with garlic potatoes, bacon or vegetable quiche with tossed salad, lasagna, fish, burgers, and a nice salad bar. Evening hours sometimes vary, so check before you go after 5pm.

✪ Reggie's Seafood Restaurant

165 Strand Rd. ☎ **01504/262-050.** Main courses under £10 ($17.10). Mon–Fri 12–2:30pm, Mon–Sun 5:30–10:30pm. No credit cards. SEAFOOD.

The freshest of fish go into tasty seafood dishes in this bright, cheerful eatery. Very good value for money, with an excellent assorted seafood in a pasta nest with creamy white wine sauce going for a mere £6.50 ($11.12); and fillet of turbot with hazelnut mousseline sauce at £9.50 ($16.25) the priciest item on the menu. There's a good cheese board, a selection of teas, and Bewley's freshly ground coffee.

✪ Schooner's

59 Victoria Rd. ☎ **01504/311-500.** Lunch main courses under £7 ($11.97); dinner main courses £9 ($15.39). Sunday lunch £7.95 ($13.59). ACC, AE, MC, V. Daily 12:30–2pm and 5:30–10pm. SEAFOOD/STEAKS.

A huge, thirty-foot schooner (sea cargo vessel) is the magnificent centerpiece of this nautically themed restaurant. Just a half-mile from the city, it overlooks woodlands, rural cottages, and the River Foyle. In addition to finny choices such as marinated seafood on a fish paella and paupiettes of plaice (plaice fillets filled with smoked salmon and prawns coated in a smoked salmon sauce), steaks come with an assortment of sauces (peppercorn, Diane, or barbeque). Starters include tandoori taco (chicken served in a taco shell with salad) and barbeque ribs. Good value for the money.

3 Around County Londonderry

LIMAVADY

Limavady was founded back in Elizabethan times, and it gave Ireland one of its best-loved ballads, **"Londonderry Air,"** more familiarly known as **"Annie Laurie."** The tune was an ancient traditional one passed from musician to musician until one Jane Ross committed it to paper after hearing it from a passing fiddler.

The town's major attraction is the nearby ✪ **Roe Valley Country Park,** two miles south of town via B192 (☎ 015047/62074), a terrific setting for that picnic lunch. The River Roe once turned water mills for linen production and powered Ulster's first hydroelectric plant in 1896. The old mills and the power station have been restored, and there's a museum in the old weaving shed. Activities inside the park include canoeing, rock climbing, and fishing, and there's a craft shop and cafe in the Visitors Centre. The park is open daily from 9am to 5pm, to 9pm June to mid–September.

COLERAINE

Some 31 miles northeast of Londonderry via A37, Coleraine is the seat of the **University of Ulster.** There are concerts, theatricals, and other cultural events in its Diamond Hall and Octagon all through the year. Check for the current schedule by phoning the Cashier's Office (☎ 01265/52655).

About eight miles northwest of Coleraine via B67, just west of Castlerock, **Magilligan Strand** stretches for six miles, Ireland's longest beach. The charming little seaside resort of **Portstewart** is just west of the County Antrim line on the coast road, only about five miles north of Coleraine. The western end of the **Antrim Coast Drive** is less than 10 miles north of town, with easy access to Bushmills, the Giant's Causeway, and Dunluce Castle. The Coleraine area is an ideal base for touring eastern County Londonderry.

WHERE TO STAY

✪ Camus House

27 Curragh Rd., Coleraine BT51 3RY, Co. Londonderry. ☎ **01265/2982.** 3 rms, none with bath. £22 ($37.62) single; £40 ($68.40) double. (Rates include breakfast.) No credit cards.

It's hard to say which is the more attractive, this 1685 country home three miles south of Coleraine (via A54) overlooking the River Bann or its owner, vivacious Mrs. Josephine King (known to all and sundry as "Joey"), who welcomes guests with tea and scones in a cozy sitting room in front of a fieldstone fireplace. The room's warmth is enhanced by lots of wood and the 125 handmade horse brasses that line the walls. Bedrooms are beautifully furnished and have sinks, spacious closets, and lamps placed strategically to give good light for reading. One family room sleeps four, one has three single beds, and one has a double bed as well as a single. In the sunny dining room, guests can tuck into a hearty Ulster breakfast fry of eggs and ham or bacon and wheaten bread accompanied by fresh fruit and juices. Joey will direct her guests to the best fishing spots on the river. It's no wonder at all that Camus House has won numerous country-house awards and gained a widespread reputation for hospitality.

Killeague House

Blackhill, Coleraine BT51 4HJ, Co. Londonderry. ☎ **01265/868229.** 3 rms, all with bath. £16 ($27.36) single; £32 ($54.72) double. Reduction for children and seniors. (Rates include breakfast.) No credit cards.

Mrs. Margaret Moore is the gracious hostess in this 1873 Georgian home on a 130-acre dairy farm five miles from Coleraine on A29. Guest rooms are nicely furnished. Mrs. Moore can arrange horseback riding instruction in the riding arena on the farm, as well as fishing on the river that runs through the premises.

24 Counties Down & Armagh

Counties Down and Armagh are not only filled with scenic beauty, but both have ecclesiastical roots that extend far back over the ages.

1 County Down

County Down is a study in scenic contrasts, from the beautiful strands that edge its coastline to the granite mass of the Mourne Mountains in the south to the Ards Peninsula in the east that juts into the sea to all but close the entrance to Strangford Lough. Aside from the attractions listed below, the county has great appeal for walkers and hill climbers. Movie buffs may be surprised to learn that actress Greer Garson was born in Castlelarne, County Down.

SEEING THE COUNTY

Leaving Belfast, the most rewarding ramble through County Down is to follow A2 through Bangor and along the Ards Peninsula to Portarerry, where a short car-ferry ride across the mouth of Stranford Lough connects to A25 into Downpatrick. From Downpatrick, a short drive southeast on B1 brings you back to A2, which carries on to Newcastle, then south around the coastline to Kilkeel. The road turns west along the shores of Carlingford Lough to Warrenport, then northwest into Newry, a major border-crossing point for the Republic. Along the coast, Bangor, Donaghadee, Newcastle, Kilkeel, and Warrenpoint are among the more important seaside resorts of County Down, and any one of them would make a good base from which to combine sightseeing with beach activities.

The ✪ **Ards Peninsula** is 23 miles of unspoiled countryside, dotted with picture-postcard villages, windmills, and ancient ring forts. Drive out to the little 19th-century village of **Kearney** and you go back through the centuries. The car-ferry that crosses from Portaferry to Strangford gives you a look straight out to sea (if, that is, you look quick enough—the crossing takes only four minutes). It is here, at Strangford Lough, that St. Patrick made his final entry onto Irish soil.

Near Strangford Village, **Castle Ward** is a fascinating house that's a sort of architectural hodgepodge, part pseudo-Gothic and part classical. The estate, administered by the National Trust, sits on the shores of Strangford Lough and includes formal gardens, a Victorian laundry and theater in the stableyard, and a sawmill. A tearoom is open in the stableyard from April through October. The house is also open April through October from 10am to 5pm for a small admission charge; the grounds are open to the public without charge daily from dawn to sunset year-round.

St. Patrick's first stone church is thought to have been erected on the site of the present-day **Down Cathedral** in Downpatrick, and a stone in the churchyard purports to be his gravestone (it's the one under a gigantic weeping willow tree), as well as that of St. Brigid and of St. Columba. The fact that those assertions are a matter of much dispute does little to dispel the sense of the continuity of the centuries when you stand on the peaceful hillside site—certainly it would take a heart of stone not to believe that they *could* be true! To dispel doubts, stop by the **St. Patrick Heritage Centre,** in the Down County Museum, The Mall, Downpatrick (☎ 01396/615218), open Tuesday through Friday from 11am to 5pm, on Saturday from 2 to 5pm, and Sun 2 to 5pm; extended hours July to September.

Horse fanciers can check with the **Downpatrick Racecourse** (☎ 01396/5218), where there are about six race meets each year.

County Down has been immortalized by William Percy French for its **Mountains of Mourne** that "sweep down to the sea." One of the places you can best see that sweep is the resort town of **Newcastle,** which curves around a gorgeous bay with a wide, golden strand. For information on walking in the Mourne Mountains, contact the **Mourne Countryside Centre,** 91 Central Promenade, Newcastle, Co. Down (☎ 013967/24059).

Nearby ✪ **Tollymore Forest Park,** Tullybrannigan Road, Newcastle (☎ 013967/22428), is just off B180 northwest of town. It's a delightful wildlife and forestry reserve, with some magnificent Himalayan cedars and a 100-foot-tall sequoia tree in the arboretum. This is where you can walk in the foothills of the Mournes or go pony trekking or fishing. The park is open daily from 10am to dusk, and there's a small charge per car.

Drive on to the **Caslewellan Forest Park** (☎ 013967/78664), which was begun as an arboretum back in 1740 and has now grown to ten times its original size. The largest of its three greenhouses feature aquatic plants and a collection of free-flying tropical birds. A spring garden brings early color, and a woodland patch is aflame with autumn shades. Look for the sculpture trail, and rest your feet by sitting in a chair-shaped piece fondly known as the "Arboreal Throne." Open daily.

Farther south of Newcastle, **Kilkeel** still has the ambience of an old-time seaside resort.

Four miles outside Newry, on the shores of Carlingford Lough, the ✪ **Narrow Water Castle Art Gallery,** Narrow Water Castle, Warrenport (☎ 016937/53940), is the enthusiastic project of Maeve Hall, a former Dubliner. Devoting the ground floor of the imposing castle to art came naturally, since she has always had a deep devotion to art. The gallery is run as a nonprofit venture, with all proceeds going to a fund that will eventually create a place for an artist-in-residence. The gallery is usually open Tuesday through Saturday from 2 to 6pm, but it's best to call before you make a special trip.

The **Newry Arts Centre and Museum,** 1a Bank Parade (☎ 016937/61244), features exhibitions of ancient archeological items, folk art, and pottery, as well as touring exhibitions of interest. There's no admission charge, and it's open Monday through Friday from 11am to 4:30pm.

Bang in the middle of County Down (south of Belfast via A24), **Ballynahinch** might have been the setting for a dramatic change in the course of Irish history had not the 7,000 United Irishmen (led by a linen draper from Lisburn named Henry Munroe) been roundly defeated in their battle to take the town. The bloody battle raged the length of Ballynahinch's broad main street until, in the end, the royal forces were the victors. Munroe was executed, as was a young Presbyterian girl named Betsy Gray who had seized an old, rusty sword, mounted a horse, and joined in the fray. It was a last, desperate stand for the United Irishmen, and you might give a tip of the hat to their memory as you pass through.

WHERE TO STAY

NEWTOWNARDS

This thriving town sits at the top of Strangford Lough six miles south of Bangor on A21 and makes a good base for exploring the Ards Peninsula.

✪ Ballycastle House

20 Mountstewart Rd., Newtownards BT22 2AL, Co. Down. ☎ **01247/788-357.** 3 rms, all with bath. £18 ($30.78) per person. Reduction for children and seniors. (Rates include breakfast.) No credit cards.

Mrs. Margaret Deering's home, five miles southeast of town on A20, is a beautiful 300-year-old farmhouse that has been elegantly refurbished. The house is centrally heated, and washing and ironing facilities are available for guests to use. Guest rooms are nicely appointed and have restful rural views.

Beechhill

Loughries Rd., Newtownards BT23 3RN, Co. Down. ☎ **01247/818-404.** Fax 01247/812-820. 4 rms, none with bath. £14.50 ($24.80) per person. Reduction for children. (Rates include breakfast.) Dinner £10 ($17.10) extra. No credit cards.

Mrs. Joan McKee is the hospitable hostess of this country guesthouse located in a pretty country setting four miles south of town on A20 (left at the Millisle signpost and left at Loughries school). An evening meal is available with advance notice. One of the attractive guest bedrooms is a family room; all have sinks and central heating.

NEWCASTLE

The Briers Country House

39 Middle Tollymore Rd., Newcastle, Co. Down. ☎/Fax **013967/24347.** 9 rms, all with bath. £25 ($42.75) single; £35 ($59.85) double. (Rates include breakfast.) High tea £8 ($13.68); dinner £15 ($25.68). 3-day and weekly rates available. No credit cards. Situated at the foot of the Mountains of Mourne, beside the Tollymore Forest Park, 1½ miles from the beach at Newcastle.

Mary and David Bowater have lovingly converted this lovely 200-year-old house, keeping its Old World charm in the process. There are some two acres of gardens, with a trout pond, and the Bowaters grow most of their own fruit and vegetables, as well as make their own breads and preserves. The dining room overlooks the pond and gardens, and the nicely appointed guest rooms have good views.

✪ Grasmere

16 Marguerite Park, Bryansford Rd., Newcastle BT33 0PE, Co. Down. ☎ **013967/26801.** 3 rms, none with bath. £14 ($23.94) single; £28 ($47.88) double. (Rates include breakfast.) No credit cards. Closed Sept–Mar.

This modern bungalow on the edge of Newcastle, off the Bryansford-Newcastle road (B180), is presided over by Mrs. McCormick. The two double rooms and one single all have sinks and views of the Mournes. Surrounded by green fields, Grasmere is only a 10-minute walk from the beach, and there's a golf course close by, as well as forest walks.

WORTH A SPLURGE

✪ The Slieve Donard Hotel

Downs Rd., Newcastle BT33 0AH, Co. Down. ☎ **013967/23681.** Fax 013967/24830. 120 rms, all with bath. £75 ($128.25) single; £110 ($188.10) double. Reduction for children and seniors. (Rates include breakfast.) AE, MC, V.

At this turreted, red-brick Victorian hotel on the seafront, you look across Dundrum Bay to where the Mountains of Mourne sweep down to the sea, and then you can walk along the four-mile curving sandy strand to their very feet. When the hotel was built, back in 1897, there were coal fires in every bathroom. These days every modern convenience is incorporated into public and guest rooms. Front rooms overlooking the sea are especially nice. Other rooms look out to the mountains or County Down Golf Course.

KILKEEL

✪ Kilmorey Arms Hotel

Greencastle St., Kilkeel BT34 4BH, Co. Down. ☎ **016937/62220.** Fax 016937/65399. 28 rms, all with bath. £27 ($46.17) single; £44 ($75.24) double. Reduction for children and seniors. (Rates include breakfast.) MC, V.

In this pleasant seaside resort, the Kilmorey Arms is a delightful small inn that dates back 200 years, with the sort of homey atmosphere that draws Irish families back year after year. Its attractive public rooms are much favored by people in the town. There's a nice (no-smoking) cocktail lounge, and the flagstone-floored public bar is full of character, both from its relic-hung walls and from the faces passing the time of day at the bar (if you're just passing through Kilkeel, stop by this interesting bar for a pint).

WHERE TO EAT

NEWTOWNARDS

The **Tudor Tavern,** 6 Georges Street (☎ 01247/815453), serves pub grub for around £3 ($5.13) Monday through Saturday from 11:30am to 11pm and on Sunday from 12:30 to 2:30pm and 7 to 10pm. For fish-and-chips at £3 ($5.13) and less, stop by **Scrabo Cafe,** 187 Mill Street (☎ 01247/810963), Monday through Saturday from 12:30 to 2:30pm and 8 to 11pm.

DOWNPATRICK

✪ Rea's

78 Market St. ☎ **01396/612017.** Reservations not required. Lunch £3–£5 ($5.13–$8.55); dinner £10–£15 ($17.10–$25.65). No credit cards. Mon–Sat 12–3pm and 7–9:30pm. SEAFOOD/TRADITIONAL.

Readers Recommend

Wyncrest Guest House. 30 Main Rd., Ballymartin, Kilkeel, Co. Down. ☎ 06937/63012. *"Irene and Robert Adair work hard to make Americans feel welcome. The days we have spent in Northern Ireland have been delightful and very safe. Too bad more Americans don't visit and enjoy as we have."* —G. and P. Curten, Austin, TX

This charmer is an old-style place, with two small front rooms crammed full of an eclectic collection of old objects (like the pottery bottle that was once used to hold Guinness, a marble for its stopper). Second, it always has the contented hum of a good crowd—many of them obviously regulars—enjoying good company and good food. There's a more modern dining room in back of those character-filled front rooms, and an almost-formal dining room upstairs (fireplace, gilt mirrors, etc.). Fresh seafood is the specialty here, but the menu includes beef, lamb, and other main dishes for non-fish lovers.

BALLYNAHINCH

Primrose Bar

30 Main St. ☎ **01238/563177.** Reservations not required. Main courses £4–£12 ($6.84–$20.52). No credit cards. Mon–Sat 12:30–9:30pm. TRADITIONAL/SEAFOOD/SALADS.

The Primrose is known locally for its steak casseroles and open-face prawn sandwiches. Other offerings include chicken dishes, pizza, and a variety of salads. There's always a nice fire blazing, and as a Northern Ireland friend assured me, "The crack (talk) is always good."

Their adjacent **Primrose Pop-In** serves afternoon tea, quiche, and pies Monday through Saturday from 9am to 4:30pm.

2 County Armagh

Armagh, Northern Ireland's smallest county, is a land of gentle hills and fertile fields, and its principal city of Armagh, in prehistoric times the seat of Ulster kings, has been Ireland's ecclesiastical capital for some 1,500 years.

SEEING THE COUNTY

There are an amazing number of places you won't want to miss in this county, and a stop by the **Tourist Information Centre,** Old Bank Building, 40 English Street (☎ 01861/527-808), will send you off well prepared to get the most from each one.

Nearby, **St. Patrick's Trian** (☎ 01861/527-808), also on English Street, is a tourist complex incorporating several interpretive elements to depict Armagh from pre-Christian times to the present. There's also a craft shop and a restaurant. The complex is open from April through September, Monday through Saturday from 10am to 6pm, Sunday from 1 to 7pm; other months the closing hour is 5pm. There's a small admission fee.

Set in the magnificent parkland of the Palace Demesne, the **Palace Stables Heritage Centre** (☎ 01861/529-629) is a picturesque Georgian building enclosing a cobbled courtyard. Lifelike exhibits illustrate the lifestyle of the archbishop once in residence here and the living and working conditions in and around the stable yard. Hours from May to August are Monday through Saturday 10am to 7pm, Sunday 1 to 7pm; in other months closing time is 5pm. There's a small admission fee.

With imposing edifices of both the Catholic and Protestant faiths facing each other from their respective hilltops, Armagh is Northern Ireland's most interesting cathedral town. According to a tablet on the north side of the ✪ **Church of Ireland cathedral** (restored in the 18th and 19th centuries), this is the final resting place of Brian Boru. In the Gothic-style ✪ **Roman Catholic cathedral,** which dates from the mid-1800s, you'll find the red hat of every cardinal archbishop of Armagh and medallions for each of Ireland's saints.

On the Mall in Armagh town, there's a fine small **County Museum** that holds an exceptionally good collection of prehistoric relics, historical costumes, and natural-history exhibits as well as an art gallery. It's free, and open Monday through Friday from 10am to 5pm, Saturday 10am to 1pm and 1 to 2pm. Also on the Mall is the **Royal Irish Fusiliers Regimental Museum,** housed in the Sovereign's House which depicts the history of the regiment from 1783 to 1968 and is open Monday through Friday from 10am to 12:30pm and 2 to 4:30pm.

Just off A2 on Killylea Road 1.8 miles west of Armagh city, the huge mound that is ✪ **Navan Fort** was once capital of the Kings of Ulster, and the Iron Age hill fort has connections with such Irish heroes as Cuchulainn, the Hound of Ulster, and King Conor and his Red Branch Knights. Visit the Visitors Centre (☎ 01861/525550) before climbing to the top for spectacular views of the surrounding countryside.

WHERE TO STAY

ARMAGH TOWN

Altavallen House

Desart, Cathedral Rd., Armagh BT61 8AE, Co. Armagh. ☎ **01861/522387.** 6 rms, none with bath. £15 ($25.65) single; £30 ($51.30) double. Reduction for children. (Rates include breakfast.) No credit cards.

Mrs. McRoberts' pleasant home has nicely appointed and comfortably furnished guest rooms, all with sinks. She is happy to arrange baby-sitting.

NEAR PORTADOWN

Redbrick Country House

Corbrackey Lane, Portadown BT62 1PQ, Co. Down. ☎ **01762/335268.** 9 rms, 5 with bath. £15 ($25.65) single; £30 ($51.30) double. Reduction for children. (Rates include breakfast.) No credit cards.

With enough advance notice, Mrs. Moreen Stephenson, the accommodating hostess here, will arrange to meet first-time visitors. At this country house three miles from town, guests will enjoy traditional home cooking. The centrally heated modern bungalow counts one large family room among its nice guest rooms, all of which are on the ground floor, and four rooms are in an annex.

WHERE TO EAT

ARMAGH TOWN

The **Cellar Lounge,** 55 Thomas Street (☎ 01861/525147), serves good pub grub for about £3 ($5.13) Monday through Saturday from 12 to 3pm.

PORTADOWN

There's good pub grub at **Parkside Inn,** Garvaghy Road (☎ 01762/330-260), served Monday through Saturday from 11:30am to 11pm at prices of around £3 ($5.13).

25 Counties Tyrone & Fermanagh

Counties Tyrone and Fermanagh offer a veritable cornucopia of scenic beauty, from County Tyrone's mountains, gentle hills, glens, river valleys, and moorlands to County Fermanagh's fantastic lake-and-river system.

1 County Tyrone

The majestic Sperrin Mountains in the northern region near the County Derry border are County Tyrone's crowning glory. Farther south and east, the land levels out to rolling hills and level plains.

SEEING THE COUNTY

The ✪ **Sperrin Mountains** are terrific walking territory, bringing you face to face with such native inhabitants as golden plover, red grouse, and thousands of sheep, as well as friendly turf cutters getting ready for winter cold.

If you can spare half a day for this special part of Northern Ireland, take B47 from Draperstown and drive 10 miles west to the village of Sperrin, leave the car by the pub, and walk north along the road into the hills toward Sawel. After two miles, leave the road and make for the summit (about an hour's walk) and views of Lough Neagh, the Foyle estuary, and the Mournes. Continue west on the ridge to Dart Mountain, about half an hour away, then turn south for the 45-minute walk to the village of Cranagh, where you'll surely want to spend time in the **Sperrin Heritage Centre,** 274 Glenelly Road, Cranagh, Gortin (☎ 016626/48142). There are natural-history and gold-mining exhibits (you may want to hire a Klondike-style gold pan and try your luck), a craft shop, and a café. Another 45 minutes will bring you back to your car (with a stop at the pub if you've worked up a terrible thirst).

Three miles north of Omagh, on A5, the ✪ **Ulster-American Folk Park** (☎ 01662/243292) is an outdoor museum that has as its main theme the history of 18th- and 19th-century emigration from Ulster to North America. Life in rural Ulster and in the New World is re-created through exhibits that include the ancestral home of the Mellon family of Pittsburgh, whose forefathers were from Ulster and who endowed the folk park. There's a pioneer farm and gallery exhibitions and a Dockside section with a full-scale replica of a 19th-century emigration ship. In summer, it's open Monday to Saturday from 11am to 6:30pm, Sunday from 11:30am to 7pm; in other months, Monday through Friday from 10:30am to 5pm. There's a small admission charge.

Note: A new 38-bed residential center has recently been opened. For room availability, prices, and booking call 01662/240-918).

Two **American presidents** who hailed from Northern Ireland are remembered in the County Tyrone settings that nurtured their ancestors. **Ulysses S. Grant,** the 18th U.S. president, once visited the Dergina, Ballygawley farmhouse that was home to his maternal ancestors. The restored mud-floor cottage holds authentic period pieces, and the Visitors Centre (☎ 0166252/7133) has an interesting audiovisual presentation. To reach the cottage, take A4 to Dungannon from Ballygawley, and after three miles turn right, where the homestead is signposted. It's open from April through September, Tuesday through Saturday from 10am to 6pm, on Sunday from 2 to 6pm, and there's a small admission fee. The ✪ **Woodrow Wilson** ancestral home is in Dergait, Strabane (☎ 01662/243292). The 28th U.S. president's grandfather, Judge James Wilson, left for America in 1807, and members of the Wilson family still live next door in a modern farmhouse. The thatched, whitewashed cottage holds some of the original furniture, and there's wheelchair access to the ground floor. Visiting hours are the same as for the Grant homestead, above.

One of County Tyrone's most outstanding attractions is the ✪ **Ulster History Park** (☎ 016626/48188) on B48, seven miles north of Omagh. Reconstructions of Stone Age houses, round towers, and other habitations tell the story of Ulster's settlers from the first arrivals in 7000 B.C. to the end of the 17th century. It's open April through September, Monday through Saturday from 10:30am to 6:30pm, Sunday and holidays to 7pm. Other months, the closing hour is 5pm. There's wheelchair access, and a small admission charge.

WHERE TO STAY & EAT

CRANAGH

✪ Mr. & Mrs. Bennie Conway

254 Glenelly Rd., Cranagh, Plumbridge BT79 8LS, Co. Tyrone. ☎ Gortin **06626/48334.** 3 rms, none with bath. £12 ($19.80) per person. Reduction for children. (Rates include breakfast.) No credit cards.

The Conways' chalet-type farmhouse sits on a 22-acre farm on B47 east of Plumbridge, 13 miles west of Draperstown, overlooking the Glenelly River and the Sperrin Mountains. Guest rooms are quite attractive and comfortable, and all have sinks and are on the ground floor. Washing and ironing facilities are available for guests, and baby-sitting can be arranged.

OMAGH

✪ Greenmount Lodge

58 Greenmount Rd., Gortaclare, Omagh BT79 0YE, Co. Tyrone. ☎ Fintona **01662/841-325.** Fax 01662/840-019. 8 rms, all with bath. £18 ($30.78) single; £34 ($58.14) double. Reduction for children. (Rates include breakfast.) Dinner £12 ($20.52). No credit cards.

Set on a 150-acre farm eight miles southeast of Omagh on A5, this is a large country house with nicely appointed guest rooms, four of which are family rooms. Mrs. Frances Reid, the friendly hostess, is a superb cook and both breakfasts and evening meals are a delight.

✪ Royal Arms Hotel

Main St., Omagh BT78 1BA, Co. Tyrone. ☎ **01662/243262.** Fax 01662/245011. 21 rms, all with bath. TV TEL. £35 ($59.85) single; £65 ($111.15) double. Reduction for children and seniors. (Rates include breakfast.) MC, V.

Convenience, comfort, and a friendly, accommodating staff make this an ideal base. Family owned and operated, it exudes a homey warmth, and there's also an attractive lounge, a coffee shop, a hairdressing salon, and a travel agency. All 21 bedrooms are nicely appointed and comfortably furnished.

Dining/Entertainment: There's an old-world charm about the Tavern Lounge and the adjoining dining room, and the menu in both specializes in traditional Irish dishes (beef, lamb, chicken) and seafood. Lunch is served daily from 12:30 to 2:30pm, with pub grub in the Tavern Lounge at about £3 ($5.13) and a more extensive offering in the restaurant for £6 to £8 ($10.26 to $13.68). Dinner hours are 5:30 to 9:30pm Monday through Saturday, until 8:30pm on Sunday, with a choice of pub grub at £3 ($5.13) or à la carte selections at £10 to £15 ($17.10 to $24.).

BALLYGAWLEY

✪ The Grange

15 Grange Rd., Ballygawley BT70 2HD, Co. Tyrone. ☎ **016625/68053.** 3 rms, all with bath. £15 ($25.65) per person. Reduction for children. (Rates include breakfast.) No credit cards. Closed Nov– Mar.

There's loads of character in this charming little cottage near the Ballygawley roundabout and the Folk Park. It dates back to 1720, but has been thoroughly modernized, even to central heating. Mrs. Lyttle is hostess here, and her guest rooms (two doubles and one single) all are nicely done up. Washing and ironing facilities are on hand, and Mrs. Lyttle welcomes small children.

DUNGANNON

✪ Grange Lodge

7 Grange Rd., Moy, Dungannon BT71 7EJ. ☎ **018687/84212.** Fax 018687/23891. 5 rms, all with bath. £35 ($59.85) single; £55 ($94.05) double. (Rates include breakfast.) Dinner £18 ($30.78). No credit cards. Signposted 1 mile south of M1, Junction 15.

Norah and Ralph Brown are the gracious hosts of this lovely guesthouse, which began life as a 17th-century settler's hall. Set on a 20-acre estate, it's a tranquil retreat from which to launch day trips to explore all of County Tyrone. Guest rooms are attractive and comfortable, and the dining room looks out over green lawns backed by wooded parklands. Norah excels in the kitchen (she's won all sorts of culinary awards), and a breakfast specialty is porridge flavored with Bushmills Whiskey and cream.

2 County Fermanagh

County Fermanagh might well be called Northern Ireland's Lake Country, although by rights it's the River Erne from which that name would derive. It winds through the center of the county, expanding into the large Upper and Lower Lough Erne, both studded with islands. In the northwest, County Fermanagh touches the shore of Lough Melvin, and in the hills to the west are nestled Upper and Lower Lough Macnean.

SEEING THE COUNTY

The **River Erne and its Upper and Lower Loughs** are tourist centers for County Fermanagh. The river and the loughs are dotted with interesting and historical islands, and a holiday cruising their waters is a very special experience.

The **Shannon Erne Waterway** encompasses the Erne's myriad lakes and islands and the majestic River Shannon in the Republic, creating a continuous navigation of 470 miles, making this one of the longest pleasure waterways in Europe. There are 16 locks along the network of three rivers and six lakes that take cruisers through counties Fermanagh, Leitrim, and Cavan. You can book a variety of watery accommodations in Enniskillen, and the **Fermanagh Information Centre,** Wellington Road, Enniskillen (☎ Enniskillen 01365/323110), publishes a detailed "Cruising" leaflet with illustrations of many of the cruisers available. To learn more about this fascinating part of Northern Ireland (some of the mountainy country around the loughs is quite mysterious and wild, and there are historic monastic ruins on many of the islands), go by the Information Centre and browse through the literature; the staff can help plan an itinerary.

An experience not to be missed in this part of the province is the ✪ **waterbus cruise** that departs from the Round O pier in Enniskillen for two-hour cruises, some of which stop at Devenish Island in Lower Lough Erne, where there's a perfect 12th-century round tower, ruined Augustinian abbey, and intricately carved 15th-century high cross. Fares are £3 ($5.13) for adults, £1.50 ($2.57) for ages under 14. Contact **Erne Tours,** 42 Meadow Lane, Sligo Road, Enniskillen. (☎ 01365/322-882).

In Enniskillen, the **Royal Inniskilling Fusiliers Regimental Museum and the County Museum** are in the Castle Keep, Castle Barracks (☎ Enniskillen 01365/325050). The castle keep dates from the 16th century, was built by the Maguires, and was remodeled in the 18th century. The Regimental Museum features battle trophies of the Dragoons and Fusiliers from the Napoleonic Wars, arms, and a host of colorful uniforms. In the Heritage Centre, history is traced through archeological relics from the Middle Stone Age to the end of the early Christian period. It's open daily from 10am to 12:30pm and 2 to 5pm (weekends only in winter), and there's a small admission charge. Hours are subject to change, so call ahead.

On the shores of Lough Coole, 1½ miles southeast of Enniskillen via A4, **Castle Coole** (☎ 01365/322690) is a splendid neoclassical mansion set in its own parkland. The house was completed in 1798 and has a Palladian front, fine furnishings, and exquisite plasterwork. It's open daily from 2 to 6pm June through August.

Another stately home worth a visit is ✪ **Florence Court** (☎ 01365/82249), about eight miles southwest of Enniskillen via A4 and A32. The three-story 18th-century mansion has pavilions on each side, robust and eccentric architecture, flamboyant interior plasterwork, and fine Irish furniture. The woodland setting is as romantic as the house, with a landscaped "pleasure garden" and walled garden. Open weekends in April, May, and September.

Don't miss a guided tour of the ✪ **Belleek chinaware factory** (☎ 013656/58501; fax 013656/58625) in the little village of Belleek right on the County Donegal border on B52. It's not only interesting, but fun—the skilled workers always welcome a bit of a chat with visitors. There are a Tourist Centre, museum, restaurant, and factory tours, offered Monday through Friday from 9am to 6pm, on Saturday from 10am to 6pm, and on Sunday from 2 to 6pm.

One of the most awesome sights in all of Europe is the **Marble Arch Caves,** Marbank Scenic Loop Road, Florencecourt (☎ 01365/348-855), signposted eight miles southwest of Enniskillen (A4 and A32). Your underground boat travels through this vast cave system, a spectacular underground world of rivers, waterfalls, lakes, lofty chambers, and winding passages. It's chilly down there, if not downright cold, so bring along a sweater, plus good walking shoes with low heels for dealing with uneven surfaces. The caves open daily at 11am (depending on the weather) from Easter to October, and closing times vary. Indeed, all these hours can vary—best call ahead to be sure the caves are open. Adults pay £4 ($6.84); children, £3.50 ($5.98); students £3 ($5.13). A family ticket is £10 ($17.10).

WHERE TO STAY & EAT

NEAR ENNISKILLEN

Manville House

Aughnablaney, Letter, Co. Fermanagh. ☎ Kesh **013656/31668.** 5 rms, 3 with bath. £15 ($25.65) per person. (Rates include breakfast.) No credit cards.

About 12 miles from good beaches, this is the centrally heated, lakeside home of Mrs. Pearl Graham. All the well-appointed guest rooms have marvelous views of Lough Erne and the Sligo Mountains, and there's good fishing right at hand. Mrs. Graham very much enjoys visitors from America.

Manville House is 20 miles from Enniskillen and nine miles west of Kesh; take A47 from Kesh and turn right at the signpost for Letter.

A LAKESIDE HOTEL

✪ Killyhevlin Hotel

Dublin Rd., Enniskillen BT74 4AU, Co. Fermanagh. ☎ **01365/323481.** Fax 01365/324726. 24 rms, all with bath. 13 self-catering chalets. TV TEL. £55 ($94.05) single; £80 ($136.80) double. Reduction for children and seniors. Weekend rates available. Self-catering chalets £250 ($427.50) and up per week, depending on season. (Rates include breakfast.) MC, V.

This lovely hotel sits one mile from the town center on the shores of Lough Erne, with marvelous views of the gardens and lake. Guest rooms, which are spacious and attractively furnished, all have a window wall that opens onto a balcony. An especially good bargain is the weekend rate, which includes two nights' bed and breakfast, dinner, lounge entertainment on Saturday, and lunch on Sunday. Early booking is essential for the two-bedroom chalets.

Dining/Entertainment: The glass-walled lounge overlooks the lake, with food service from the adjoining dining room. Fresh fish and seafood are featured on the menu, as well as locally produced beef, pork, and lamb, and salad plates both hot and cold. Lunch, which is served from 12:30 to 2:30pm, will run around £5 ($8.55); dinner, from 6:30 to 10pm, £10 to £15 ($17.10 to $25.65). There's live entertainment on weekends.

SELF-CATERING IN BELLEEK

✪ The Carlton Cottages

Belleek, Co. Fermanagh. ☎ **01365/658181.** 14 cottages. £215–£395 ($367.65–$675.45) per week, depending on season. Weekend rates sometimes available. No credit cards.

These well-planned three-bedroom cottages are set in wooded grounds at the edge of the village on the banks of the River Erne. It's hard to imagine a more beautiful setting, and each cottage is fitted with twin beds, bath and shower, fully equipped kitchen, and a large lounge with an open-hearth fireplace. Patio doors open to the outside.

Index

Terms and Conditions:

1. Offer is available at participating locations in Europe.
2. Minimum rental period is three days.
3. Reservations must be made in the U.S. prior to departure on an Affordable Europe rate plan, using **PC #77276**. Advance reservation requirement is 8 hours before departure, or 14 days prior to departure for mailed vouchers.
4. Certificate may only be used as an allowance toward rental charges, including optional service charges, such as collision damage waiver, insurance services, refueling, luggage racks, baby seats, etc. paid at time of rental. Offer cannot be applied to charges prepaid before departure.
5. Certificate must be presented and surrendered at time of rental. It is valid one time for a value up to $10. U.S. dollar amount will be calculated in local currency at the exchange rate applicable at time of rental.
6. Certificate can neither be exchanged for cash nor negotiated.
7. Certificate may not be combined with any other offer, discount or promotion. Offer is not available on rentals reserved through tour operators, or on corporate/contract rates.
8. Standard Affordable Europe, intercity rules and restrictions apply.
9. Minimum rental age is 25. All renters must present a valid driver's license held for at least one year prior to rental.

Hertz rents Fords and other fine cars.

* Internationally Acclaimed For A Quarter Century
* Well Appointed
* Comfortably Furnished
* Heated Covered Saloons
* Large Windows
* Adequate Open Deck Seating
* Fully Licensed
* Friendly Service
* Reliability
* Good Value
* Ireland's Most Scenic Smooth River Cruise
* Delicious Home Cooking
* Convenient To Tourist Resorts
* April To October (inclusive)

The following Frommer's guides are available from your favorite bookstore, or you can use the order form on the preceding page to request them as part of your membership in Frommer's Travel Book Club.

FROMMER'S COMPLETE TRAVEL GUIDES

(Comprehensive guides to sightseeing, dining and accommodations, with selections in all price ranges—from deluxe to budget)

Acapulco/Ixtapa/Taxco, 2nd Ed.	C157	Jamaica/Barbados, 2nd Ed.	C149
Alaska '94-'95	C131	Japan '94-'95	C144
Arizona '95	C166	Maui, 1st Ed.	C153
Australia '94-'95	C147	Nepal, 3rd Ed. (avail. 11/95)	C184
Austria, 6th Ed.	C162	New England '95	C165
Bahamas '96 (avail. 8/95)	C172	New Mexico, 3rd Ed.	C167
Belgium/Holland/Luxembourg, 4th Ed.	C170	New York State, 4th Ed.	C133
Bermuda '96 (avail. 8/95)	C174	Northwest, 5th Ed.	C140
California '95	C164	Portugal '94-'95	C141
Canada '94-'95	C145	Puerto Rico '95-'96	C151
Caribbean '96 (avail. 9/95)	C173	Puerto Vallarta/Manzanillo/ Guadalajara, 2nd Ed.	C135
Carolinas/Georgia, 2nd Ed.	C128	Scandinavia, 16th Ed.	C169
Colorado '96 (avail. 11/95)	C179	Scotland '94-'95	C146
Costa Rica, 1st Ed.	C161	South Pacific '94-'95	C138
Cruises '95-'96	C150	Spain, 16th Ed.	C163
Delaware/Maryland '94-'95	C136	Switzerland, 7th Ed. (avail. 9/95)	C177
England '96 (avail. 10/95)	C180	Thailand, 2nd Ed.	C154
Florida '96 (avail. 9/95)	C181	U.S.A., 4th Ed.	C156
France '96 (avail. 11/95)	C182	Virgin Islands, 3rd Ed. (avail. 8/95)	C175
Germany '96 (avail. 9/95)	C176	Virginia '94-'95	C142
Honolulu/Waikiki/Oahu, 4th Ed. (avail. 10/95)	C178	Yucatán '95-'96	C155
Ireland, 1st Ed.	C168		
Italy '96 (avail. 11/95)	C183		

FROMMER'S $-A-DAY GUIDES

(Dream Vacations at Down-to-Earth Prices)

Australia on $45 '95-'96	D122	Ireland on $45 '94-'95	D118
Berlin from $50, 3rd Ed. (avail. 10/95)	D137	Israel on $45, 15th Ed.	D130
Caribbean from $60, 1st Ed. (avail. 9/95)	D133	London from $55 '96 (avail. 11/95)	D136
Costa Rica/Guatemala/Belize on $35, 3rd Ed.	D126	Madrid on $50 '94-'95	D119
Eastern Europe on $30, 5th Ed.	D129	Mexico from $35 '96 (avail. 10/95)	D135
England from $50 '96 (avail. 11/95)	D138	New York on $70 '94-'95	D121
Europe from $50 '96 (avail. 10/95)	D139	New Zealand from $45, 6th Ed.	D132
Greece from $45, 6th Ed.	D131	Paris on $45 '94-'95	D117
Hawaii from $60 '96 (avail. 9/95)	D134	South America on $40, 16th Ed.	D123
		Washington, D.C. on $50 '94-'95	D120

FROMMER'S COMPLETE CITY GUIDES

(Comprehensive guides to sightseeing, dining, and accommodations in all price ranges)

Amsterdam, 8th Ed.	S176
Athens, 10th Ed.	S174
Atlanta & the Summer Olympic Games '96 (avail. 11/95)	S181
Atlantic City/Cape May, 5th Ed.	S130
Bangkok, 2nd Ed.	S147
Barcelona '93-'94	S115
Berlin, 3rd Ed.	S162
Boston '95	S160
Budapest, 1st Ed.	S139
Chicago '95	S169
Denver/Boulder/Colorado Springs, 3rd Ed.	S154
Disney World/Orlando '96 (avail. 9/95)	S178
Dublin, 2nd Ed.	S157
Hong Kong '94-'95	S140
Las Vegas '95	S163
London '96 (avail. 9/95)	S179
Los Angeles '95	S164
Madrid/Costa del Sol, 2nd Ed.	S165
Mexico City, 1st Ed.	S175
Miami '95-'96	S149
Minneapolis/St. Paul, 4th Ed.	S159
Montréal/Québec City '95	S166
Nashville/Memphis, 1st Ed.	S141
New Orleans '96 (avail. 10/95)	S182
New York City '96 (avail. 11/95)	S183
Paris '96 (avail. 9/95)	S180
Philadelphia, 8th Ed.	S167
Prague, 1st Ed.	S143
Rome, 10th Ed.	S168
St. Louis/Kansas City, 2nd Ed.	S127
San Antonio/Austin, 1st Ed.	S177
San Diego '95	S158
San Francisco '96 (avail. 10/95)	S184
Santa Fe/Taos/Albuquerque '95	S172
Seattle/Portland '94-'95	S137
Sydney, 4th Ed.	S171
Tampa/St. Petersburg, 3rd Ed.	S146
Tokyo '94-'95	S144
Toronto, 3rd Ed.	S173
Vancouver/Victoria '94-'95	S142
Washington, D.C. '95	S153

FROMMER'S FAMILY GUIDES

(Guides to family-friendly hotels, restaurants, activities, and attractions)

California with Kids	F105
Los Angeles with Kids	F103
New York City with Kids	F101
San Francisco with Kids	F104
Washington, D.C. with Kids	F102

FROMMER'S WALKING TOURS

(Memorable strolls through colorful and historic neighborhoods, accompanied by detailed directions and maps)

Berlin	W100
Chicago	W107
England's Favorite Cities	W108
London, 2nd Ed.	W111
Montréal/Québec City	W106
New York, 2nd Ed.	W113
Paris, 2nd Ed.	W112
San Francisco, 2nd Ed.	W115
Spain's Favorite Cities (avail. 9/95)	W116
Tokyo	W109
Venice	W110
Washington, D.C., 2nd Ed.	W114

FROMMER'S AMERICA ON WHEELS

(Guides for travelers who are exploring the U.S.A. by car, featuring a brand-new rating system for accommodations and full-color road maps)

Arizona/New Mexico	A100
California/Nevada	A101
Florida	A102
Mid-Atlantic	A103

FROMMER'S SPECIAL-INTEREST TITLES

Arthur Frommer's Branson!	P107	Frommer's Where to Stay U.S.A., 11th Ed.	P102
Arthur Frommer's New World of Travel (avail. 11/95)	P112	National Park Guide, 29th Ed.	P106
Frommer's Caribbean Hideaways (avail. 9/95)	P110	USA Today Golf Tournament Guide	P113
Frommer's America's 100 Best-Loved State Parks	P109	USA Today Minor League Baseball Book	P111

FROMMER'S BEST BEACH VACATIONS

(The top places to sun, stroll, shop, stay, play, party, and swim—with each beach rated for beauty, swimming, sand, and amenities)

California (avail. 10/95)	G100	Hawaii (avail. 10/95)	G102
Florida (avail. 10/95)	G101		

FROMMER'S BED & BREAKFAST GUIDES

(Selective guides with four-color photos and full descriptions of the best inns in each region)

California	B100	Hawaii	B105
Caribbean	B101	Pacific Northwest	B106
East Coast	B102	Rockies	B107
Eastern United States	B103	Southwest	B108
Great American Cities	B104		

FROMMER'S IRREVERENT GUIDES

(Wickedly honest guides for sophisticated travelers and those who want to be)

Chicago (avail. 11/95)	I100	New Orleans (avail. 11/95)	I103
London (avail. 11/95)	I101	San Francisco (avail. 11/95)	I104
Manhattan (avail. 11/95)	I102	Virgin Islands (avail. 11/95)	I105

FROMMER'S DRIVING TOURS

(Four-color photos and detailed maps outlining spectacular scenic driving routes)

Australia	Y100	Italy	Y108
Austria	Y101	Mexico	Y109
Britain	Y102	Scandinavia	Y110
Canada	Y103	Scotland	Y111
Florida	Y104	Spain	Y112
France	Y105	Switzerland	Y113
Germany	Y106	U.S.A.	Y114
Ireland	Y107		

FROMMER'S BORN TO SHOP

(The ultimate travel guides for discriminating shoppers—from cut-rate to couture)

Hong Kong (avail. 11/95)	Z100	London (avail. 11/95)	Z101